Praise for *Lobbying for Zionism on Both Sides of the Atlantic*

'All the renowned qualities of Ilan Pappe's scholarship and craft as a historian are in evidence here: his comprehensiveness, his utter dedication, his command of the range of sources and material, his integrity and his humanism. Above all, this latest work on lobbying demonstrates Ilan's lifelong commitment to establishing the truths necessary to enlighten citizens across the world – so that they can change it to a more just one.'

Professor Karma Nabulsi

'Ilan Pappe is a magnificent historian and storyteller. He narrates a chilling yet illuminating saga of the systematic denial of Palestinian history and humanity. *Lobbying for Zionism on Both Sides of the Atlantic* is a haunting and powerfully instructive tale of deliberate investment in injustice and obfuscation. Essential reading.'

Professor Ussama Makdisi

'A tour de force, comprehensive, authoritative and fair-minded, unveiling the lobby's politically and ethically dubious methods that have ensured unparalleled amounts of Western military aid and a shield of diplomatic immunity for the Israeli state's apartheid-like policies for seventy-five years, as well as Zionist control of the global narrative about Palestine.'

Peter Shambrook, author of *Policy of Deceit*

LOBBYING FOR ZIONISM ON BOTH SIDES OF THE ATLANTIC

ILAN PAPPE

ONEWORLD

A Oneworld Book

First published by Oneworld Publications Ltd, 2024

Copyright © Ilan Pappe, 2024

ISBN 978-0-86154-402-8
eISBN 978-0-86154-403-5

Typeset by Geethik Technologies
Printed and bound in Great Britain by Clays Ltd, Elcograf S.p.A.

Oneworld Publications Ltd
10 Bloomsbury Street
London WC1B 3SR
England

Stay up to date with the latest books,
special offers, and exclusive content from
Oneworld with our newsletter

Sign up on our website
oneworld-publications.com

MIX
Paper | Supporting
responsible forestry
FSC® C018072

Contents

Preface   vii

1 The Christian Harbingers of Zionism   1
2 Lobbying for the Balfour Declaration   19
3 The Road to the Balfour Declaration   31
4 Lobbying in Britain During the Mandate   55
5 Early Zionist Lobbying in the USA   94
6 American Zionists and the Holocaust   128
7 Lobbying for Israel in Postwar Britain   156
8 Lobbying for Israel in Twentieth-Century America   218
9 Lobbying for Israel in Twenty-First-Century America   338
10 The War Against American Civil Society   405
11 Lobbying for Israel in Twenty-First-Century Britain   431

Conclusion   503
Afterword: 7 October and the Future   517

Acknowledgements   522
Select Bibliography   523
Notes   527
Index   575

Preface

In 2015, some of my graduate students and younger colleagues organised a conference under the title 'Settler Colonialism in Palestine' at the University of Exeter. This was not widely publicised – presenters were personally invited to deliver papers. Only a small announcement on the university's website broadcast the upcoming event.

In no time, the pro-Israel lobby exerted pressure on the university to cancel the event, branding it an anti-Semitic conference and condemning Exeter's complicity. The criticism was led by the main body of the Anglo-Jewish community, the Board of Deputies.[1] The Board and other outfits, which we will encounter later in this book, began lengthy negotiations with the university that ended with a 'compromise', allowing two pro-Israel lobbyists to take part in the conference. These two unwanted guests did not appear to have any relevant scholarly work on settler colonialism – a recognised global phenomenon and field of study that enquires about the origins and legacy of the settler movements that established the USA, Canada, many countries in Latin America, Australia, New Zealand and South Africa. All the other invitees were either known scholars in the field or postgraduates working on the topic.

The *Jewish Chronicle*'s report on the forthcoming conference expressed alarm not only about the use of the term of 'colonialism' in conjunction with Israel but about the reference to the 'land of Israel' as 'Palestine'; namely an entity the newspaper apparently believed did not exist. Bizarrely, it stated that even the campus's pro-Palestinian groups were happy with the university's concessions – a claim it did not substantiate.

At the time, I was the director of the European Centre for Palestine Studies which helped to convene the conference and conceded to the compromise the university reached with the lobby. In hindsight, I think I was wrong. I believed that the conference was important enough to be worth tolerating the pathetic presence of two lobbyists at it. Moreover, I wanted to stay on good terms with Exeter's university management who had protected Palestine Studies since we launched the programme in 2009 (which today is a recognised pathway in postgraduate studies in the university and in many other academic institutes throughout the world). A short time before this controversy arose, the University of Southampton caved to similar pressure and cancelled a conference on the potential for a one-state solution for the Palestine issue. Our conference's papers appeared in a special issue of the leading journal in post-colonial studies, *Interventions*, which went some way to compensate for the bitter taste that lingered after our temporary defeat under pressure from the pro-Israel lobby.[2]

Aside from the drama of the Exeter riot police being unnecessarily on stand-by for potential disorder after many years of calm in the city, the conference was tranquil and without incident. It was not the first time the University of Exeter disappointed the local police – a year earlier the English Defence League mistook our Institute of Arab and Islamic Studies for a mosque and wanted to come and demonstrate. But the small number of right-wing activists were too drunk and lazy to climb the steep hill from St David's Station to the campus.

The lobby's two representatives had no intention of participating in the battle of ideas: we have to remember that they had no idea what the conference would entail (these were early days in settler-colonial studies). They were there to monitor us. They didn't want to win the argument – they seemed to want to silence it. This action was part of a wider campaign by the pro-Israel lobby, on both sides of the Atlantic, to suppress the debate on Palestine and curtail the expansion of the field of Palestine Studies, preventing it from shaping the public debate. The academic study of Palestine in recent years has provided a solid scholarly basis for the main arguments supporting the legitimacy of the Palestinian nation. At times this pro-Israel lobbying succeeded:

lecturers lost their jobs for speaking out for Palestine in their research or in political activism, and institutions were asked to cancel courses, modules, workshops or conferences that were deemed 'anti-Israeli'. We'll see this in action later in the book.

Academics, for all their sins, are wordsmiths and in rare cases manage even to be educators, although the Western system of academia ceased to believe in this part of the vocation long ago, guided by the doctrine of 'publish or perish'. Words, just words alone, some of them appearing in academic journals with more authors than readers, are met with all the might of the pro-Israel lobbies in Britain and the USA as if they constitute an existential threat to Israel. As we shall see, there is a special ministerial team in Israel dealing with these dangerous wordsmiths in academia's ivory towers. The Israelis call it the battle against the 'delegitimisation of Israel'.

Israel and its lobby could have ignored the conference in Exeter. This gathering did not have the power to change the reality in Israel and Palestine; it couldn't contribute to alleviating the plight of Palestinians. But the Israeli lobby insists on being present, in town halls, schools, churches, synagogues, community centres and campuses on both sides of the Atlantic. In 2024, Israel will not allow any show of solidarity with the Palestinians in Britain and the US, even by one person, to escape its radar, and will do all it can to push for the dismissal of every person who condemns its ethical violations and the proscription of every organisation calling for boycotts, divestment and sanctions. It will brand these activities as anti-Semitic and tantamount to Holocaust denial. In essence, this is the work of an aggressive lobby that began its political advocacy for Israel in the mid-nineteenth century and still continues today. There are not many states, if there are any others at all, frenetically trying to convince the world and their own citizens that their existence is legitimate.

Being an Israeli Jew I know first-hand the toxic effect of such a propaganda effort – and the inertia that accompanies it. After a formative period in which the foundations of institutions are laid, be it a state or a lobby, there comes a time when indoctrination bears fruit: they can rely on their citizens or members to remain loyal to the founding ideology, with no coercion necessary. You cease to ask about the damage done in your name: you no longer think about whether it is moral, justifiable or even legal.

This is a book that goes back to the formative period, before inertia and self-censorship of the loyal foot soldiers of the lobbying effort ensured its longevity. This takes us back to the mid-nineteenth century when we find Zionism first as an evangelical Christian eschatological vision and as a genuine attempt to rescue Europe's Jews from anti-Semitism. Towards the end of that century Zionism became a different project, and it has transformed into a settler-colonial operation in Palestine, targeting its indigenous population as alien and as a major obstruction to building a modern and, ironically, 'democratic' European Jewish state at the heart of the Arab world.

The Holocaust provided new reasons for Zionists to insist on a homeland in Palestine. The expulsions and genocide in Nazi and Fascist Europe pushed Jews to flee, but they had nowhere to go. Few Western countries were willing to offer sanctuary; the European countries free from Nazi occupation and the USA closed their gates and imposed extremely restrictive quotas, turning away the vast majority of Jewish refugees knocking at their doors. Lobbying for Palestine as a safe haven became more logical. But the Zionist movement did not act from pure humanitarian motives – they hoped the fleeing Jews of Europe would help them gain a demographic advantage in Palestine, meaning they could claim as much of Palestine as possible with as few native Palestinians as possible.

In the twentieth century, the primary driver of lobbying was to ensure support and legitimacy for the colonisation of Palestine throughout the British Mandatory period (1918–1948). This required tremendous amounts of advocacy and lobbying statesmen of all political persuasions. In the first year of Israeli statehood, as the new United Nations confronted the mass displacement of Palestinians, this lobbying took on particular significance. The ethnic cleansing of Palestine became a precondition for the establishment of a Jewish state: Israel needed to compel the international community to accept this.

But the logic of lobbying turned into a conundrum in the twenty-first century: why does Israel still lobby for its legitimacy more than seventy-five years after its establishment, especially given its objective political and economic power? Israel is now a highly technologically developed state, with the strongest army in the Middle Eastern region, and enjoys the unconditional support of the Western world. In practice, many Arab governments recognise it, officially or informally, and even the Palestinian national movement can't be said to pose a military or political threat to Israel's existence. Yet the resources thrown into courting world powers and silencing dissent have only increased since Israel first appeared on the map.

Here's the riddle I want to solve in this book: why does Israel invest vast amounts in two major lobbies, Christian and Jewish, on both sides of the Atlantic? Why does this Jewish state still crave recognition of its legitimacy in the West? Put differently, why do Israel's elites still think its legitimacy is up for debate in Britain and the United States – despite the arms deals, the economic aid, the unconditional diplomatic support?

I offer one assumption, three hypotheses and an obvious observation, all of which I would like to test in this book. The assumption is that the key to this riddle can be found by looking at what's hidden in the human consciousness. Those who led the Zionist movement and later Israel were intuitively aware of the inherent injustice of the project, or at least the immoral dimensions of the seemingly 'noble' solution to the problem of anti-Semitism in Europe. If this assumption strikes you as far-fetched reaching back into history, it's nonetheless indisputable that key policy makers in Israel are aware today that many people globally see the Zionist project as oppressive and colonialist. As a historian, I know that there's no smoking gun document that unveils these subconscious motivations – I am not going to try to produce one. But I hope a detailed historical analysis of the lobby from its inception until today will show this assumption is correct. What I can prove is my first hypothesis: lobbying for Israel represented a Zionist obsession with demonstrating moral uniqueness or even superiority. It was a convoluted and indeed ambivalent obsession because Zionist leaders, and later the Israeli state, firstly needed to convince themselves that how

Zionism developed in historical Palestine constituted a morally unique situation – not comparable to other colonising projects – and in fact was a noble endeavour. They needed to believe this, even though some of them were aware of the questionable foundations of the project.

My second hypothesis is that from very early on, because of its self-doubt, the Zionist movement dispensed with moral arguments and with engaging with societies at large and invested all its efforts in elites; an enterprise that required money, connections and efficient advocacy. When perfected and deployed by the state of Israel, these lobbying forces enjoyed unparalleled success compared to other lobbies in Britain and the United States.

My third hypothesis is that the political clout accumulated for galvanising elites created very powerful lobbies on both sides of the Atlantic, which represented institutions in their own right, with their own vested interests. Occasionally they acted primarily to preserve their own power, and not necessarily for the sake of the Israeli cause.

There are other factors that helped Israel and aided the lobbying on its behalf. These are the military-industrial complexes in various countries and some multinational corporations which participated over the years in lobbying for Israel. Israel is a huge exporter of securitisation and arms to the world – operating on the principle of 'you scratch my back and I'll scratch yours'. This book does not cover this kind of sordid tit-for-tat trade. In the future it may be the main method employed by Israel to fortify its international legitimacy. However, historically, and from Israel's perspective, the lobbies that mattered were not to be found among the foreign industrial complexes or financial giants. The Christian and Jewish lobbies for Israel, at least until now, were deemed the most important ones by Israel. And extraordinarily, it seeks their help in gaining legitimacy in this century as well.

This is the conundrum that led me to write this book. In 1948, when Israel had just appeared on the map, its frenzied courting of existing powers was entirely understandable. But now, as a military and economic superpower, it's surprising that Israel still feels threatened by what its leaders call 'international delegitimisation'.

And now for the obvious observation: Israel's consciousness of its illegitimacy and the consequent necessity of constant advocacy are a result of Zionism's failure to complete the settler-colonial project it began in 1882, when the first Jewish settlers arrived in Palestine. Unlike other settler-colonial movements, such as those colonising north America and Australia who demonstrated inhuman efficiency, it could not eliminate the native inhabitants of historical Palestine. In places like the United States, surviving indigenous people did question the legitimacy of those who dispossessed and committed genocide on their territory, but their physical defeat was so total that the colonisers never faced any serious challenge to their legitimacy on the international stage.

Some of my friends who remain sympathetic to Zionism like to say that genocide did not occur in the colonisation of Palestine due to the high moral standards of Zionists. They think this even though people in Israel are now aware of the many massacres committed against Palestinians in 1948 and ever since. But the reality is grimmer: moral qualms or a lack of will did not pose a significant obstacle to ethnic cleansing. It failed because of resilience of the Palestinian resistance.

Palestinians are not just victims of Israel; they are also agents of their own destiny. Their survival and insistence on their rights mean that Zionists need to actively erase and deny the past in order to brush over the ethical and moral problems associated with the founding of the state of Israel. Against all odds, faced with powerful religious, economic, military and strategic Western alliances at various historical junctures, enabling their dispossession and disregarding their rights, the Palestinians are still there, fighting, surviving and challenging the moral foundations of the state that was established at their expense and on the ruins of their homeland. It took time for Palestinian demands to begin to sway global public opinion, but this is now an indispensable part of the struggle for liberation, and as we shall see in the book, forced the lobby to resort to more ruthless ways of repressing the global conversation on Palestine.

In order to test these assumptions and solve the conundrum I've posed, I will examine the lobby's origins more closely in Britain and the United States, the two key players for most of Israel's history, and follow its evolution to the present.

I could be accused of being biased; I accept this charge freely. I am aware that many aspiring professional historians are told early in their careers not to write a polemical history as it would undermine the scholarly validity of their work. This is probably a wise warning for historians who are on the cusp of being initiated into the academic community as fellow scholars. But with time, they will discover for themselves the cogency of Bertrand Russell's words in his autobiography:

> I was sometimes accused by reviewers of writing not a true history but a biased account of the events that I arbitrarily chose to write of. But to my mind, a man without a bias cannot write interesting history – if, indeed, such a man exists.[3]

I would have liked the facts to speak for themselves. But the facts are consistently whitewashed by a mammoth project of fabrication, manipulation and erasure. We need to offer context, moral judgement and commitment to make these facts tell the truth about the oppression of the Palestinians and their brave struggle for freedom and liberation. This is the least we can do in the fight against one of the world's longest injustices.

Throughout this book, readers might notice a tendency to linger on particular places and buildings. Zionism was ahead of its time in its determined focus on wining and dining potential supporters – in many ways it is the forerunner of all modern-day lobbying. Luxurious venues were chosen in order to court local elites – offering them funding if they were politicians, or other forms of assistance a prospective supporter might benefit from. I want to share the grandeur of these locations with you, so you can see for yourself how Zionism laid down its roots in Britain and the USA. But now, let's turn to the nature of lobbying.

WHAT IS A LOBBY?

Lobbying as we know it refers to the advocacy deployed to change governmental policy or alter public opinion. On both sides of the Atlantic, lobbies were initially physical places – in Britain these were the hallways of the Houses of Parliament, where MPs and Lords could mingle with advocates for various causes. The practice became notorious from the seventeenth century onwards.

On the other side of the Atlantic, would-be politicians were well aware of the British tradition of lobbying – a lobbyist was hired almost as soon as the Congress was founded, to secure better compensation for Virginia war veterans. In 1830, the foyer leading to Congress Hall became packed with people trying to influence their representatives. In other words, lobbying had become commonplace long before President Ulysses Grant described the people waiting for him in the lobby of the Willard Hotel as lobbyists.

But general definitions don't capture the scope and ambition of the pro-Israel lobby, which remains unique. Some scholars have proposed more expansive remits for lobbying. When referring to the contemporary pro-Israel lobby in the USA, Grant F. Smith suggests using the term 'Israel Affiliated Organizations'; a wider network does not necessarily work all the time or exclusively for Israeli interests but can easily be recruited to such a mission – such as the tobacco and arms lobbies in America.[4] In this way, we can comprehensively cover all the outfits that form the lobby for Israel in America. This definition works well for the lobbying groups in Britain too, including bodies that exclusively lobby for Israel and those for whom such advocacy is just one topic on their agenda; it also includes long-term projects of advocacy and those which did not survive very long due to financial or organisational problems.

Other scholars have suggested distinguishing between the formal and the informal lobby, which also offers a useful categorisation. From the very beginning of the lobbying, somewhere in the mid-nineteenth century, there were proper organisations explicitly committed to Zionism alongside ad hoc and temporary formations, both playing an effective role in selling the Zionist and later Israeli narrative as the exclusive historical and contemporary truth about the reality in historical Palestine.

Walter L. Hixson, in his meticulous history of the pro-Israel lobby in America, sees lobbying as 'conveying organized and well-funded efforts to wield political influence to advance a self-interested cause', which is a definition more of the methods than the essence of the body, but nonetheless very helpful. The money, he asserts, is raised in order to mobilise information and advocacy which in turn is used to challenge any group or individual subscribing to an opposing view to the lobby. Hixson warns us not to look at the lobby as a single, monolithic entity, but to consider it as multi-faceted groupings of ideas, individuals and organisations aiming 'to dispense pro-Israeli propaganda' and, equally importantly, to discredit anyone condemning or criticising Israel or Zionism.[5] This is another way of identifying who is part of the lobby, officially or informally.

Lobbying is an integral part of American public life – and everyone is comfortable with referring to the American Israel Public Affairs Committee (AIPAC) as synonymous with the pro-Israel lobby. But as Hixson and Smith have shown, lobbying is a lot more insidious.

Mearsheimer and Walt complement other attempts at a definition by suggesting that a lobby is a loose coalition of groups seeking to influence American policy,[6] and by extension we can say the same about the lobby in Britain. Coalitions are sometimes loose, as we shall see, but at times they are tighter and then become more powerful and influential. At the time of their book's publication in 2007, they conceived of AIPAC as the most powerful lobby in America. Hixson later expanded the parameters of the lobby by including individuals with whom AIPAC worked closely, rather than just groups.

These scholarly assessments only show the difficulties in pinning down a lobby as deeply entrenched and multivalent as the pro-Israel lobby. We hence must use the most liberal definition of lobby available to us, so that we can incorporate every individual and group devoting more or less time to advocating for Israel or Israeli interests, prompted by the government of Israel. These groupings have wilfully created a confusion, lasting to this day, between the voices and interests of British and American Jewish communities and those of Zionist and pro-Israel groups. Can such outfits as the Conference of Presidents of Major American Jewish Organizations in the USA, and the British Board of Deputies be representatives of the Jewish communities in their countries, as well as the embassies for Israel? I don't pretend to know the answer. What I do know is that combining these two functions so far has resulted in a dangerous reality where anti-Semitism is routinely conflated with anti-Zionism and concern for Jewish communities is tainted with strong anti-Palestinian sentiment and at times naked Islamophobia. I don't believe the present state of affairs has resulted in dividends either for Jewish communities here or Jews in Israel.

But the definition of a lobby is not static. The lobby changes its form, composition, orientation, methods and size as we move through time. So another way of illuminating the specificities of the pro-Israel lobby, instead of simply examining lobbying in general, is to patiently trace its genealogy up to our own time. And it all begins with Christian eschatology joining forces with an outburst of modern nationalism in Europe that bred both secular anti-Semitism and a Jewish antidote in the form of secular Jewish nationalism. These twin ideologies first appeared on the European stage, seemingly entirely irrelevant to Palestine. At that time the country was still under Ottoman rule and its population was not even aware that Christians and Jews alike were contemplating their dispossession and the takeover of their homeland. So, we have to start our story when evangelical clergymen and laymen on both sides of the Atlantic had an epiphany that it was God's will to gather the Jews of the world and transport them to a state of their own in historical Palestine.

1

The Christian Harbingers
of Zionism

Zionism began as an evangelical Christian concept and later an active project. It appeared as a religious appeal to the faithful both to aid and be prepared for the 'return of the Jews' to Palestine and the establishment of a Jewish state there as the fulfilment of God's will. But soon after, the Christians involved in this campaign politicised this 'theology of return', once they realised that a similar notion had begun to emerge among European Jews, who despaired of finding a solution to the never-ending anti-Semitism on the continent. The Christian desire to see a Jewish Palestine coincided with a similar European Jewish vision in the late nineteenth century.

For Christian and Jewish supporters of Zionism, Palestine as such did not exist. In their minds, it was replaced by the 'Holy Land' and in that 'Holy Land', from the very beginning, there was no indigenous population, only a small community of faithful Christians and pious Jews remaining after most of their co-religionists were by and large expelled by the Roman Empire or survived under hostile governances. For both anti-Semitic and philosemitic Christians, the 'return' of the exiled was an act of religious redemption.

The French philosopher and sociologist Maurice Halbwachs, who pioneered the field of collective memory, also wrote on Palestine. Patrick Hutton has summarised Halbwachs's description of the way collective memory was constructed in the case of Palestine in medieval times: 'the biblical Holy Land was an imaginary landscape conjured up during the Middle Ages in Europe and superimposed upon the landscape of

Palestine'.[1] This imaginary landscape shaped the view of the past and invoked images of the future. The past fed paintings, sculpture, novels and poetry in which time was frozen. Palestine remained as it was during Jesus' time and later it was imagined as being organically part of medieval Europe: its people donning medieval dress, roaming a European countryside. Whether these visualisations were conjured by Jews or Christians did not matter – both had nothing to do with the reality on the ground. You could take your pick and decide whether you were looking at Jewish prophets of yesteryear or saints from early Christianity. One thing was clear, there were few Arabs and hardly any Muslims in this illusory landscape.

Eschatologically, Christians envisaged Jews returning to Palestine (Zion) and building a nation, triggering the resurrection of the dead and the end of time.[2] Visionaries, politicians, pundits and travellers were drawn to this image by the thrill of discovery. Palestine was discovered and rediscovered in the imagination of these people, long before they had ever been there and in some cases continued without them ever being there.

As much as Jesus' Palestine was an imagined country, where Jesus sometimes appeared as an Aryan, sometimes as an Arab or even a black Jew, so were the Palestinians pictured first as the early Hebrews living in an ancient Christian land where nothing, nothing at all, changed from 70CE until the late nineteenth century. To this empty land in the collective Christian memory, it was easy to restore the Jews and build a future state for them, as if the country's history between the time of Jesus and his predicted return had disappeared into a black hole.

In this respect, the Christian, and later Jewish, depiction of Palestine as *terra nullius*, a land no one owned, was similar to other settler-colonial projects. But it has a special affinity with the American settler-colonial project because the settlement of North America was also derived from readings of the Bible and from the idea of pilgrimage to a holy land or to a new Jerusalem. Across the United States today you can find towns called 'Bethlehem', 'Canaan' and even 'Zion'. There were thus two 'cities on the hill', the expression American settlers had for the new colonies they built on Native American land. One they built with their own hands out of nothing, and the other was in Palestine; and from the beginning of the nineteenth century, if they were fortunate enough, they could go and see it with their own eyes. Don Peretz claims, convincingly, that the discrepancy between the imaginary 'city on the hill' and the real one in Palestine could cause serious mental disturbance among evangelical Americans who frequented Jerusalem. He found documents from the American Consulate in Jerusalem reporting scores of cases of mental breakdown of evangelical first-time visitors who were shocked to see that the modern city is a far cry from the 'city on the hill'.[3]

This fictitious concept was the basis of the early Christian lobbying for Zionism, and this forms the basis for the present Christian lobbying for the state of Israel. This kind of support at times reveals anti-Semitic undertones, since in some versions of this vision there is an unmistakable wish to convert Jews to Christianity and for Jews no longer to reside in the Western world. But even for Christian Zionists who held this view, a temporary Jewish state in Palestine became a Christian imperative. So, while Jews lobbied for a state and for its continued existence as a panacea for anti-Semitism, some of their most loyal Christian supporters sustained their anti-Semitism by encouraging the Jews to move out of the Christian West to their new coveted Jewish state in the East.

So, when and where did the first act of lobbying for Zionism take place in public and not just in the writings or visions of individuals? It all started on Queen Victoria Street in London in the summer of 1866.

QUEEN VICTORIA STREET: THE BIBLE SOCIETY

On 11 June 1866, the Prince of Wales laid the foundation stone for a grand, four-storey building, the new home of the British and Foreign Bible Society, designed by Edward l'Anson, a famous architect who could already boast the Royal Exchange building on his résumé. With generous funding from Queen Victoria and Prince William of Prussia, and an abundance of marble and granite, it represented luxury even for the British elite. Just for the ceremony, an amphitheatre with two thousand seats was put up, and guests brought flowers and flags with them. Alongside the Prince of Wales, the Archbishop of York and the Bishop of

Winchester attended to bless the construction work. These auspicious beginnings were mirrored in the finished building. It featured massive courses of granite in the outer walls and spacious staircases and halls inside the building. Bright-coloured marble, an expensive material at the time, formed the building's columns and balustrades. Some observers clearly questioned such ostentatious affluence for a Bible society; in a 1910 history of the organisation, these critics were accused of displaying the 'same grudging spirit' as the disciples during the anointing of Christ at Bethany.[4] However, none of the objections got under the Society's skin – they celebrated the Bible House's opening in 1869.

This was a particularly pleasing sight for the Society's third president, Anthony Ashley-Cooper, the 7th Earl of Shaftesbury, who had overseen the expansion of the Society since his tenure started in 1851. If a cause existed, the Earl would take it up. His philanthropy, ranging from reducing child labour to improving conditions in lunatic asylums, won him a memorial fountain. But, as time wore on, another cause would dominate his life – creating a British and Jewish state in the middle of the Ottoman Empire, Palestine. He became one of the first lobbyists for Zionism in Britain and in the modern Western world.

For him and for many who would follow a similar trajectory in the nineteenth century, the establishment of a state for the Jews in historical Palestine was seen as a religious mission. The idea that the Jews should 'return' to Palestine and build their home there had been popular among some leading evangelists even as early as the seventeenth century. The 'return' of the Jews was associated with the Second Coming of the Messiah and the resurrection of the dead – acts that would be either preceded or followed by the conversion of the Jews to Christianity.

Until the mid-nineteenth century, these were musings that had no impact on the world at large, or Palestine in particular. They became more significant when these ideas were politicised by a group of theologians who transitioned ideologically from millenarian eschatology to millenarian activism. A similar move would happen in Jewish religious circles, when Zionism appeared there. What it meant is that the faithful millennialists did not just wait for the prophecy to unfold but believed they had to be proactive in bringing about this end-of-days scenario. That is to say, the Jews had to be encouraged to move to Palestine. There was also a discussion that is beyond the realm of this book between pre-millennialists and post-millennialists around the question of whether Jesus will return to earth before the Millennium (a thousand-year golden age of peace) or whether the Second Coming would occur only after the Millennium. The return of the Jews appealed more to the former than to the latter as it could have been prophesied as one of many preliminary indications heralding the return of the Messiah before the Millennium started. In pre-millennialist eschatology, there was a certain timeline that included events such as the 'Tribulation' and the 'Rapture' into which one could situate a war against the anti-Christ and the restoration of the Jews. In the former event, the 'Great Tribulation', the world will experience a short period of natural and manmade catastrophes which will last until the 'Rapture' at the end of time, when all the Christian believers and those who were resurrected will ascend to Heaven to meet Jesus Christ. The Jews should have begun their 'return' at the very start of the Tribulation to take their rightful place in the fulfilment of the prophecy.

Judaism had a softer version of its link to the return of the Messiah, but one descended from King David and their own version of restoring the exiled Jews to their homeland. During the second half of the nineteenth century, Christian and Jewish eschatology of this kind gelled into a political project of settling Jews in Palestine. The important individuals in this respect were those Christians and Jews who were brought up with this set of futuristic visions and who searched for practical means to contribute to their fulfilment in their lifetime.

Our first chapter in the history of lobbying for Zionism is a history of prophets: very committed individuals like the Earl of Shaftesbury, who believed they were guided directly by God, and who promulgated an idea that metamorphosed into a political crusade. Once they had institutions behind them, they were able to produce a powerful and transformative narrative. Before anything else, Zionism was a narrative. Zionism thus started as a discourse before becoming a movement; this is a trajectory similar to that noted by Edward Said in his examination of the concept of Orientalism.[5] In his analysis the Orientalist discourse was based on racist and reductionist perceptions of the Orient, and once it had been employed by powerful institutions, it was translated into actions and policies that affected the lives of millions in the Arab world and beyond.

LORD SHAFTESBURY AND COLONEL CHARLES CHURCHILL

Shaftesbury's work for Zionism began long before he became president of the British and Foreign Bible Society and long before Zionism became a Jewish project. Prior to his role in the Society, he was president of another one, the London Society for Promoting Christianity Amongst the Jews, whose branch in Palestine was run by the British consul in Jerusalem, James Finn.

This consulate was opened in 1838 due to Shaftesbury's effort to persuade the British government that Palestine was of strategic importance to the Empire, since in his eyes the days of the Ottoman Empire were numbered, and the scramble for its spoils had already begun. Palestine, with Egypt and the provinces of Syria and the Fertile Crescent (encompassing the future Iraq), would be an essential link between London and its colonies in the east. The opening of the consulate was followed by the arrival of a special delegation dispatched by the Church of Scotland which was entrusted with the mission of finding out whether the Jews who were already in Palestine were willing to convert to Christianity (there was a small community of religious Jews in towns such as Jerusalem, Safed, Hebron and Tiberias – who were not interested in either Christianity or millennialism). One member of that delegation, Alexander Keith, who published a travelogue aptly titled *The Evidence of Prophecy*, was probably the first to coin the term 'a land without people for a people without land' (his son was one of the first photographers of Palestine).[6]

Shaftesbury began in 1839 to lobby in earnest for the return of the Jews to Palestine or, as he framed it, to 'restore the Jews to the holy land'.[7] He called upon the British Parliament to assist in the project, providing evidence from the Holy Scriptures that, according to his interpretation, the mid-nineteenth century was the time when the apocalypse was near and could be precipitated by the return of the Jews to Palestine. In particular, he was in the habit of quoting the Book of Chronicles, which he claimed was full of proof for the future 'restoration of Israel'. He must have been delighted to read in *The Times* that the British government was considering officially supporting this endeavour.[8]

Cognisant of the utilitarian propensity of many members of Parliament, Shaftesbury laid out more secular and strategic reasoning for such a project. This was not an easy task as the British Empire was very keen to maintain the integrity of the Ottoman Empire, lest its disintegration lead to an all-European war.

Shaftesbury argued that Britain should prepare itself for the failure of this policy. Whether Britain wished it or not, there were now, he maintained, powerful transformative developments at work that would hasten the Ottoman Empire's decline. The most important among them was the intensification of the Russian Empire's drive southward, expanding its influence and taking over territories. He also pointed to the Egyptian ruler Muhammad Ali, who, in Shaftesbury's eyes, posed an acute danger to the Ottoman sultanate's very existence. The ambitious ruler in Cairo had already occupied Palestine and Syria and seemed determined to march on Istanbul. This kind of argumentation was one that had some impact on the British prime minister, the 3rd Viscount Palmerston, Henry John Temple, who married Shaftesbury's widowed mother-in-law and was thus his father-in-law. However, unlike Shaftesbury, while supporting the idea of a Jewish state, Palmerston preferred to endorse the idea of an Ottoman Jewish Palestine as part of a European attempt to curb Egyptian expansionist ambitions.[9]

Shaftesbury wrote to his father in-law:

> 'A country without a nation' is in need of 'a nation without a country' … Is there such a thing? To be sure there is, the ancient and rightful lords of the soil, the Jews![10]

Shaftesbury alluded here to Isaiah 6:11 when describing Palestine: 'Until the cities be wasted without inhabitant, and the houses without man, and the land be utterly desolate'.

His diary tells us that in his eyes not only Palestine was a country without a nation, but the whole of Greater Syria was lacking nationhood and hence warranting absorption by the future Jewish state:

> These vast and fertile regions will soon be without a ruler, without a
> known and acknowledged power to claim dominion. The territory
> must be assigned to someone or other … There is a country without
> a nation; and God now in his wisdom and mercy, directs us to a
> nation without a country.[11]

There was a different attempt to enable the restoration of the Jews to
Palestine with the help of Muhammad Ali – rather than an effort to
oppose him. It was initiated by Colonel Charles Henry Churchill (1807–
1869), an ancestor of Winston. He was the British consul in Damascus
and his main role was to try and turn the Druze in Lebanon into British
clients at a time when European imperial powers were looking for a
pretext that would allow them to intervene on behalf of local minorities
in the affairs of the Ottoman Empire. Today the Druze are still one of
the major religious groups in the Eastern Mediterranean and live in
Lebanon, Syria, Jordan and Israel. They emerged as a separate sect from
other Muslim denominations in the eleventh century, and by the early
eighteenth century became dominant as a socio-political group in the
south of Lebanon and hence a power to reckon with in local politics and
vis-à-vis the Ottoman Empire.

While serving in Damascus in the 1840s, Churchill proposed a political plan for creating a Jewish state in Palestine. He presented his plan to Sir
Moses Montefiore, the president of the Anglo-Jewish Board of Deputies
and one of the early philanthropists of the Zionist project in Palestine.[12]

Montefiore was the first to utilise the Board of Deputies for what
would become the Zionist cause. The Board was established in 1760 by
the Sephardi community in London (the Ashkenazi community had their
own board, the Secret Committee for Public Affairs). The two bodies
merged in the London Committee of Deputies of British Jews in the 1810s
and dealt solely with the affairs of the Anglo-Jewish community.

Montefiore's conversion to Zionism was vindicated in his eyes by a
rare anti-Jewish blood libel and riots in Damascus. In 1840, after the
bones of a Catholic monk and his Muslim servant were discovered
in the city's Jewish quarter, key figures in the Jewish community in
Damascus were accused of the abduction and murder of the two, in

order to use their blood to bake the matzos (unleavened flatbread) for Passover. This allegation was supported by the French consul and was accepted by the governor of the city, leading to a brutal investigation and execution of several Jews.[13] Montefiore himself went on a mission in order to free the surviving Jewish prisoners.

But we shouldn't overstate the impact of humanitarian considerations. Montefiore supported the Zionist project quite pragmatically: the imminent end of Egyptian rule in the Levant would mean tearing up the maps of the region and starting afresh. Churchill's appeal to him made sense. In a very long letter Churchill lobbied Montefiore to push for the restoration of the Jews to Palestine:

> Let the principal persons of their community place themselves at the head of the movement. Let them meet, concert and petition. In fact, the agitation must be simultaneous throughout Europe.[14]

Churchill prompted the Jewish philanthropist to invest his own private fortune in 'regenerating Syria and Palestine' and reviving Jewish sovereignty in Palestine, which would lead the rest of Syria to fall 'under European protection'. The letter was laden with evangelical evocations such as:

> The sentiment has gone forth amongst us and has been agitated and has become to us a second nature; that Palestine demands back again her sons.[15]

Churchill planned to galvanise support through a petition from the Jewish community that already lived in Syria and Palestine and on that basis to approach European powers (even before negotiating with the Ottoman Empire).

Montefiore waited to see how far Churchill could go with his plan. The eager captain and consul was able to elicit consent from Muhammad Ali for the plan, or at least the Egyptian ruler was willing to discuss it further, but his consent became irrelevant since he soon ceased to rule Palestine.

Churchill deserves our attention since he laid the foundations for the future Balfour Declaration. The project of a Jewish state, he suggested prophetically, could be entrusted to someone like him, namely a 'public officer', who would be responsible for co-ordinating between 'the Secretary of State for Foreign Affairs and the Committee of Jews conducting the negotiations'. As it turned out, it was not to be him, but this was indeed the methodology chosen eventually.

At this point in history, we can observe two different lobbies in Britain that at that time, but not always, worked in tandem. One was the religious lobby advocating a Jewish Palestine, motivated by eschatological considerations, while the second lobbied for a British Palestine, motivated by geopolitical ambitions. The former's success hinged upon the latter's strength.

In the second half of the nineteenth century, the official strategy of Britain was to maintain the integrity of the Ottoman Empire and therefore there were no real plans for a British Palestine. The religious lobby was aiming to collaborate with a minority group among the chief policy makers who opposed that consensus and did not wish to maintain the integrity of the Ottoman Empire, but in fact prayed for its demise. They were part of a larger lobby for a British Middle East that would replace the Ottoman one.

But even when the policy continued to preserve the integrity of the Ottoman Empire, there was still enough room for deepening British involvement in Palestine, which in hindsight we can safely say ultimately helped to build the foundations for a Jewish Palestine. The principal method for doing this was to extract as many 'capitulations' from the Ottoman Empire as possible – these were a set of concessions and permits given to British citizens under pressure from the British government. When the Ottoman Empire was at its peak the capitulations were bilateral contracts with European powers facilitating easier passage and trade for European merchants, but later they were a set of agreed privileges for European subjects of the Empire.

In Palestine, these concessions enabled Christian missions to establish and expand charitable projects such as hospitals, increase the local British community and send exploratory missions to survey the country. The many British travelogues from the nineteenth century testify to this growing influence inside Palestine. As we know from Africa, these diaries and surveys usually preceded an imperial takeover. And thus visiting the place, and envisioning the return of the Jews to it, was closely associated with the expansion of British influence in the Arab world as a whole and in Palestine in particular.[16]

In order to persuade Britain's allies in Europe that extracting Palestine from the hands of the Ottoman Empire was a religious as well as a strategic imperative, the nascent Christian and Jewish lobbies for Zionism needed individuals in positions of power to reach the policy makers who could make this vision come true.

We have already met two of them, Shaftesbury and Churchill, but they were not the only heralds of Christian Zionism. Other famous figures lent their support to the restoration of the Jews to Palestine. Notable among them was Sir George Gawler, a hero of Waterloo, and later a governor of South Australia, where he experienced at first-hand settler colonialism of the kind his Empire would support later in Palestine (he was dismissed after a short while for mismanaging the Australian colony).

In 1848, Gawler wrote:

> I should be truly rejoiced to see in Palestine a strong guard of Jews established in flourishing agricultural settlements and ready to hold their own upon the mountains of Israel against all aggressors. I can wish for nothing more glorious in this life than to have my share in helping them do so.[17]

Gawler, in fact, went further than many of the early harbingers when he established a Palestine colonisation fund to help the early Zionist settlers in their new country.

Whether Christian or Jewish, lobbyists for Zionism made their voices heard by policy makers from very early on – a tactic that remains successful today, in contrast to the Palestinian national movement that even today struggles to establish a foothold amongst the international political elite. An important recruit for the early advocates was Benjamin Disraeli, the British prime minister from 1868, who in 1877 wrote an article in which he predicted a Jewish nation of one million in Palestine within fifty years.[18] As noted, the lobby was strongest when the desire for a British Palestine fused with that for a Jewish one. Disraeli in this case represented both drives. Apart from the wish to see the Jews there, Palestine had become important in his eyes ever since he led the successful takeover of the Suez Canal Company, which altered Palestine's strategic value. He was also looking for other successful ventures – imperial conflicts had not gone well for him. The British only scraped a victory against the Zulus in South Africa after five months of struggle and a remarkably high casualty rate, and although they won the Second Anglo-Afghan War in 1879, the British envoy at Kabul was nonetheless assassinated.

Alongside politicians, the support of the literati was also an important part of the concentrated effort. One of the key luminaries was George Eliot, influenced by her evangelical Christian upbringing. Her final novel, *Daniel Deronda,* articulated a desire for the 'restoration of a Jewish state', the protagonist deciding to dedicate his life to the cause.

It is said that this particular book Zionised one famous Jewish intellectual: Eliezer Perlman, who renamed himself Eliezer Ben-Yehuda. He is considered to be the father of the modern Hebrew language which became the lingua franca of the early Zionist settlers and later the state of Israel.[19]

There were some for whom restoration was only part of their agenda, but nonetheless they played a role as early lobbyists. One such person was Charles Haddon Spurgeon (1834–1892), a pastor from London who challenged the conventional hierarchy of the Anglican establishment and spread millenarianism all over Europe and beyond. He was renowned as the 'Prince of Preachers' in Europe. The future of the Jews was not his main concern, but he nonetheless played a key role in the discussion. His principal contribution was to cast aside an old debate of the Christian Zionists: should the Jews convert before or after the resurrection? This is what he wrote:

> I am not going to theorize upon which of them will come first – whether they shall be restored first and converted afterwards – or converted first and then restored. They are to be restored and they are to be converted.[20]

This was a sentiment shared at the time by the American consul in Jerusalem, Edwin Sherman Wallace, who went even further, believing that both the local Palestinians and the incoming Jews would be converted to Christianity, but was willing to see first a Jewish nation state in Palestine, as for him only the Jews had national rights in the place:

> The Jew has national aspirations and ideas, and a national future. Where if not here, will his aspiration be realized and his ideas carried out?[21]

Sometimes, this early lobbying was a mission passed on within a family. Such were the Cazalets: a grandfather and a grandson who were pillars of the early pro-Zionist lobby in Britain. The grandfather, Edward (1827–1883), was an industrialist. He made his fortune by trading with Czarist Russia and, as a pious Christian, was moved by the poor conditions of the Jews there and advocated their resettlement in Palestine. His efforts were renewed by his grandson Victor, who became a personal friend of the first president of Israel, Chaim Weizmann, and an important 'gentile Zionist' (as people like him were called by mainstream Zionist historiography later on).[22]

Also among these 'gentile Zionists' was Laurence Oliphant (1829–1888), an active restorationist who even tried to push for the establishment of the first Jewish colony in Palestine. He was a member of Parliament and a follower of Lord Shaftesbury. He decided that the best way to lobby for his idea was through the publication of a book which he sent to members of Parliament and government ministers. His book's title was *The Land of Gilead*, and it urged the British Parliament to assist in the 'restoration' of the Eastern European Jews to Palestine.[23] He was the first 'lobbyist' to pay attention to the fact that other people already lived in Palestine, but he suggested adopting the American settler-colonial 'project' of pushing the indigenous population into reservations, a project which he regarded as an apt 'solution' to the presence of a native population in Palestine.

Historians who view this chapter as part of the history of the Anglo-Jewish community, such as David Cesarani, tend to downplay the importance of any of these ideas or initiatives.[24] I disagree. I think these were the roots, planted deep in the ground, which later sustained the lobbying edifice that solidified the support of the Anglo-Jewish establishment for the colonisation of Palestine, either with full awareness of the potential disaster it would bring with it, or uninterested in the consequences of their advocacy. It is a fair question to ask whether the Judeo-Christian theological notions that were clearly used to justify the colonisation of Palestine as a religious imperative were just esoteric ideas. But I think they seeded attitudes regarding the inhabitants of Palestine that still linger potently today.

At the beginning of the next century, two impulses would shape the Christian Zionist lobby. One was a sense that Jews urgently needed rescue due to increasingly vicious anti-Semitic campaigns, at times even all-out pogroms. These were often implicitly sanctioned or initiated by local authorities, but could not take place without the enthusiastic participation of ordinary people – motivated by an open desire to drive the Jews out of Europe, particularly Eastern Europe. The second was a desire to bite into the possessions of the Ottoman Empire, prompted by the collapse of the guarded policy towards the Empire that was widespread in Europe. The fear of many leaders in Europe was that the fall of the Ottoman Empire would lead to an all-European war for its spoils. So while there was a wish to take over some Ottoman territories and weaken the Empire as a global power, there was a concurrent desire to keep it intact. The latter cautious attitude was thrown to the wind; to the millenarists this was yet another indication that the time was ripe to take over the eastern Mediterranean territories.

But the Zionist lobby didn't confine itself to Christian evangelicals. Jews, looking for a solution to seemingly intractable oppression in Europe, started to rally around the idea of a state of their own – with visions ranging from a socialist Utopia on Palestinian soil to a modern state in alliance with the Western imperial powers.

Zionism was not just a response to anti-Semitism. Some of its early thinkers were enthused by the rise in the mid-nineteenth century of both romantic nationalism and the secularisation of European societies, in the wake of the French Revolution and the Enlightenment. It was therefore an attempt to have a Jewish version of romantic nationalism and modern secularisation that, for many of these thinkers, had a better chance of maturing in the land of Old Testament Palestine than anywhere else in Europe.

Before long, the first Zionist settlers arrived in Palestine. The immediate triggers for this were the 1881 pogroms across the south-western Russian Empire following the assassination of Alexander II; these resulted in the widespread destruction of Jewish property, and many Jewish women reported rape. Jews in these territories widely believed in the government's complicity and, losing hope of emancipation under the Tsarist regime, they turned their mind to other political strategies, including Zionism.

The first settlers arrived on 6 July 1882. This was a group of fourteen Russian Jews who arrived at Jaffa Port and soon after started working as agricultural labourers in newly founded communities. Jewish intellectuals in central Europe supported these nascent endeavours from afar, one of the most important being the journalist and playwright Theodor Herzl, now celebrated as the founding father of Zionism. Under his leadership and with the help of numerous Zionist organisations that mushroomed after the increase in anti-Semitism in Europe, Zionism began to gel as an institutional movement.

Zionist Jews were able to convene an inaugural congress in Basel, Switzerland in 1897, with 208 delegates from seventeen countries. Many more congresses would follow. Even before convening the conference, the leaders of the new movement were looking for key leaders and political elites in both Europe and the Ottoman Empire to endorse the establishment of a Jewish state in Palestine. While the settlers were establishing facts on the ground, the leaders sought to create international legitimacy for them.

Christian Zionist sympathies fell short for these Jewish activists, as they seemed too remote from official government policy to make a difference. The founder of the Zionist movement, Theodor Herzl, and his successors such as Chaim Weizmann, started the hunt for influential individuals, not movements or institutions, who could make the case for Zionism at a higher level. They found the man they were looking for in William Hechler.

THE GERMANIA HOTEL: THE HECHLER CONNECTION

On 25 April 1896, Theodor Herzl was waiting for the Grand Duke of Baden (Frederick I) in the dining room of Hotel Germania in Karlsruhe, Germany. (A new hotel at the same address, 34 Karl-Friedrich-Strasse, is still there today on the corner of Lindenstrasse. The old hotel is gone, turned to dust by Allied bombing in 1944.) On the way to the hotel Herzl must have noticed the Malschbrunnen fountain – an ornate attempt to impress visitors coming into the city from the train station. At the time Herzl visited, the Kaiser himself was a regular guest of the hotel. When the Duke arrived, they moved to one of the many spacious meeting rooms on the second floor. The meeting had been made possible by the relentless efforts of a cleric named William Hechler.

William Henry Hechler was born in 1845 in India to a German missionary father and an English mother. As a young man he had already become well known in Christian restorationist circles. His interest in the cause and plight of the Jews began during the 1881 pogroms across the Russian Empire that brought him to Odessa. There he met the Zionist theorist Leon Pinsker, who would pen *Auto-Emancipation*, an impassioned plea for Jewish political nationalism, mere months after their encounter. Hechler was won round to the necessity of a Jewish state, and would spend the next thirty years trying to help establish it.

Hechler served as a chaplain in the British embassy in Vienna. In the 1870s, his star began to shine as a tutor to the Grand Duke of Baden. It would take another twenty years for Theodor Herzl to notice him – that had to wait until March 1896, over a decade after Hechler had committed himself to Zionism. In his diary, Herzl described him as a 'likeable, sensitive man with the long grey beard of a prophet' – more or less how Herzl wanted to see himself.[25]

Herzl had little interest in Hechler's theological predispositions; he bluntly told the latter that he only wanted one thing from him: a liaison with the upper echelons of the local political elite:

I must put myself in direct and publicly known relations with a responsible or non-responsible ruler, that is with a minister of state or a prince.[26]

Hechler knew immediately whom to approach: his old pupil, Frederick I, Grand Duke of Baden. Enthusiasm aside, he needed some extra money for such a mission, mainly for travel expenses, as the journey to Karlsruhe would be 'certainly a considerable sacrifice in my circum-stances'.[27] Herzl readily paid the bill. Hechler was now the first lobbyist in a long line to be funded by the Zionist movement.

The Grand Duke, Hechler's employer, succeeded in securing a first meeting with the Kaiser. It didn't go well; once the Kaiser learned that Jews whom he respected, including the Rothschild family, weren't the project's backers, he lost interest. While the Grand Duke was still eager to help, he had his own similar qualms about the cause: would his support be interpreted as wanting to expel Jews from his kingdom? Nor was he happy with losing revenue from Jewish emigration or, as he put it, from such an 'enormous exodus of money'.[28] Herzl promised him that the idea was not for the German Jews to go to Palestine (in any case it seemingly held no attraction for him either; by the time of his death, he had only visited the land once and only for a week). Herzl further explained that his movement wanted to 'drain the surplus of the Jewish proletariat',[29] and that Zionism would be an asset to the world the Grand Duke wished to preserve. He promised that Zionism would help to keep 'international capital under control'.[30] He also assured the Grand Duke that the German Jews would be happy to see the influx of Jews from the east not reaching Germany but going to Palestine. Herzl also commented that he hoped this very alarming prospect of a Jewish influx from east to west would persuade the Jews in Britain to support the Zionist project in Palestine: 'Both Germany and England were being flooded with Russian Jews; neither wanted them, no one wanted them', he explained to the Grand Duke.[31]

This was a very distorted representation of the views of the Anglo-Jewish community at the time. The Chief Rabbi Dr Adler said to the *Daily Mail*: 'I believe Dr. Herzl's idea of establishing a Jewish State is absolutely mischievous' and '[is] contrary to Jewish principles, the teaching of the prophets and the traditions of Judaism'. He was worried that people would rightly suspect Jews of lack of loyalty to their current country of residence, and he added, 'I am expressing the opinion of, with few exceptions, of the entire Anglo-Jewish community'.[32]

Herzl may have secured introductions through Hechler, but his arguments failed to convince the elites. Hechler's attempt to secure a meeting with the Russian Tsar and the British prime minister Lord Salisbury did not materialise either. At least Hechler was able to alert Herzl to the Kaiser's intended visit to Palestine in October 1897. The meeting that eventually took place between the Zionist prophet and the emperor was very brief and wholly fruitless.

Hechler, who dedicated thirty years of his life, until his retirement in 1910, to lobbying intensively for Zionism, did not live to see the establishment of the state of Israel. But his indispensability for the propagation of political Zionism in its early years is beyond doubt: he was praised as the guest of honour by Theodor Herzl at the inaugural Zionist Congress and attended subsequent ones. In recognition of his contribution, the Zionist movement provided him with a small pension up until his death.

If Hechler was first and foremost among Zionist lobbyists in Herzl's eyes, he was by no means alone. A particularly striking character is Arminius Vámbéry, a Zionist lobbyist based in Istanbul. He was a Hungarian Jew who converted to Islam, although he was always vague about his religion. What we know for sure is that he was an impressive polyglot and prolific scholar. He only met Herzl briefly in January 1900, but Herzl found out that Arminius had unrestricted access to the Ottoman Sultan, Abd al-Hamid II. A year later the Hungarian secured a meeting for Herzl with the Sultan, but this, like his meeting with the Kaiser, was futile.

Herzl knew, after three Zionist conferences in Europe and the relentless courting of European imperial powers, that he was out of luck: these elites would not support a Zionist state. He turned his attention to London and the British Empire to assist in the project of 'restoring' the East European Jews to Palestine. There, he would find a much warmer reception.

2

Lobbying for the Balfour Declaration

HERZL IN LONDON

Theodor Herzl came to London for the first time in November 1895, arriving at Charing Cross station, knowing no one and carrying only one letter of introduction to Sir Samuel Montagu in his pocket. The man in question introduced him to some members of the Anglo-Jewish elite in London; however, they failed to be impressed by Herzl or his ideas. Herzl also failed to secure an interview with Lord Rothschild. He declared that he was willing to give up the leadership of the movement in return for such a meeting.[1]

But at least he was able to secure an article in the *Jewish Chronicle* in January 1896 about his ideas.[2] This was the first time his vision of a Jewish state in Palestine hit the English-language newspapers. It may not have changed hearts and minds, but it scored Herzl an invitation for a second trip to London – and this one was more fruitful.

THE MACCABEAN CLUB AND PILGRIMAGE, 1896

His host for his second trip was Israel Zangwill, a writer and one of the early Zionist thinkers, who organised a lecture tour for him in the capital. The first stop was the Maccabean Club, named after the Jews who rebelled against the Greek Empire in ancient times.

The Maccabean Club was created in 1891 and its official aim was to form 'social intercourse and co-operation among its members, with a view of the promotion of the interest of the Jewish race'. Maja Gildin Zuckerman, a scholar of modern Jewish cultural history, noted that its interest in Palestine was explicitly an intellectual one and Herzl was thus invited as 'a Jew of letters' and not as a politician.[3] In other accounts the club is described as a proto-Zionist one, almost a branch of Lovers of Zion, an early East European colonising movement which had already settled in Palestine from 1882.

The Club emulated the nineteenth-century protocols of what were known in Britain as Friendly Societies (the first of these appeared in the early nineteenth century, as societies whose members received insurance for any mishap in the future in return for membership fees; probably the best-known one is the Oddfellows, which still exists today; some orders of Freemasons were also regarded by law as Friendly Societies). In this Anglo-Jewish order, each member had to pledge his allegiance to the Zionist cause and pay a shekel for the expenses of the order and for funding the early colonisation of Palestine, or, in the words of its charter, it was a place for persons 'of the Jewish faith who declare themselves adherents to the Zionist Movement' or similarly minded, 'non-Jewish honorary' members. The members were mainly from the Anglo-Jewish elite, or at least from the upper middle class, in London. Herzl hoped that reading a well-prepared English text would help convince his audience, but by his own account he didn't succeed. He found support among the Sephardi, Chief Rabbi Moses Gaster and of course from Moses Montefiore and his cousin Claude, who nonetheless made it clear that they were loyal British subjects helping poor Jews from Europe to settle in Palestine, but not more than that.[4]

From Herzl's perspective, the encounter with the Club left him with mixed feelings about his target audiences among the Anglo-Jewish community. His visit led one of the members of the club, Herbert Bentwich, a member of the Lovers of Zion, to organise a trip to Palestine, which he called the 'Maccabean pilgrimage' (he was the great-grandfather of the famous journalist, Ari Shavit, and the pilgrimage appears in Shavit's book, *My Promised Land*,[5] a very elegant attempt to reconcile the crimes of Zionism with a defence of its moral validity). As Zuckerman shows, the Club was now involved in a project that would serve as a model for future lobbying. In the name of the Club, but without its wholehearted endorsement, the 'Maccabean pilgrimage' induced twenty-one members of the Anglo-Jewish elite (five women and sixteen men) to travel to Palestine. They invited Herzl to join them, but he was never too enthused by the idea of visiting the place himself. However, he was very pleased with the initiative:

> Political Zionism sets to work armoured with all the means of the present day. In this sense the pilgrimage of Mr. Bentwich is of a significance which cannot be underrated. For the first time a band of modern, cultured Jews of all professions, with a distinct leading idea, make their way to the land of our fathers in order to personally explore it. It is a national enquiry commission, singular of its kind – one calculated to raise our hopes.[6]

Zuckerman, who described this mission as a 'Zionist pilgrimage', claimed that Bentwich and his friends initially regarded Palestine as a destination of religious significance and touristic interest, but not the locus of a political movement. The trip itself, in Zuckerman's view, is what turned them into Zionists.[7] They underwent a conversion, like other Jews in the West, from adhering to a faith to becoming advocates of a nationalist movement, substituting the religious interest in Palestine with a colonialist one.[8] The members of the delegation, like so many other early Zionists, were verbose, and felt the need to tell the world in great detail about their impressions, trials and tribulations. Their assessment of Palestine echoed the Zionist propaganda of an empty land waiting for the people without land.

Returning to London, some of them were now ready to serve the lobby in conveying a message that was informed by Orientalist degradation of the Palestinians, and inspired by evangelical Christianity (the trip was full of rituals which mirrored Christian pilgrimage rites performed in the 'Holy Land'). The enthusiastic pilgrims were discoursing now with the help of a new vocabulary, fertilised by the idiomatic language of Christian Zionist restorationists on both sides of the Atlantic (Palestine was, in Bentwich's words, 'our land' and he was part of 'our people' who were now bound to the land in a religious teleology).

However, as in mainland Europe, in those two years before the first Zionist Congress, Herzl found the working classes far more receptive as an audience for his ideas than those of the local Jewish bourgeoisie. He felt frustrated by his inability to communicate directly with the rich and affluent members of Anglo-Jewish society, even those who supported Zionism. Although Herzl was certainly the greatest lobbyist for Zionism, it was only his successors who established a proper rapport with the British political elite, without which the colonisation of Palestine would probably have failed.[9]

So Herzl had to look elsewhere for support, and he found it at a working men's club in London's East End.

GREAT ALIE STREET, LONDON, 1896

It does not take long to cross Alie Street in London, located in Aldgate, linking Mansell Street with Commercial Road. Despite being only four hundred metres long, it used to be two streets: Great Alie Street in the west and Little Alie Street in the east. This modest strip nonetheless has a certain notoriety as Jack the Ripper's hunting ground. In the 1890s, it was the hub of a diasporic Jewish community, who had fled the pogroms in Eastern Europe to land in London's East End.

It has a rich Jewish history and almost every building has a story to tell, although some of the original buildings are now gone. One important landmark was a new synagogue inaugurated by the Chief Rabbi of the Anglo-Jewish community, Dr Hermann Adler, at 40/41 Great Alie Street (the slow gentrification of the neighbourhood meant the synagogue fell into disuse and by 1972 the building had become the Half Moon Theatre, a left-wing fringe playhouse). At 31–37 Great Alie Street, a small eighteenth-century courthouse had become the Jewish Working Men's Club and Lads' Institute, lovingly converted by the affluent and socially conscious members of the Jewish community. Its founder was the MP for Whitechapel, Sir Samuel Montagu, who had several such projects in the area. In its early years, before it was officially opened, its main revenue came from the provision of drinks, which was not always in the workers' best interests, but it became more of a social club when the workers themselves became the stakeholders, usurping the role of the richer original patrons.

The club turned out to be a great hit with the more than 60,000 Romanian and Russian Jews who arrived in London in the last quarter of the nineteenth century, most of them penniless and precariously employed. The first cohort to join the club were artisans and skilled workers. Montagu called it a 'Palace of Delight' for workers. This may have been true of the club, but not of its annex, the Lads' Institute. It was anything but a delight for the 330 boys who dwelled there, crammed into a school they called 'the Bastille' for its lack of windows and air.

The club was closed for a while and its reopening in 1891 was memorialised by a drawing by the English School that appeared in the *Daily Graphic*. This drawing of the ceremony shows Lord Rothschild, standing in a Napoleonic pose with his hand in his jacket, announcing the inauguration. Behind him stand the Anglo-Jewish philanthropes – the men wearing bowler hats and the women sporting the latest fashions – surrounding a rabbi, dressed in the traditional Sephardi costume.[10]

It was a three-storey brick building, which had to be reached from a back alley, accessed via portico arches below a protruding staircase tower. It was squeezed between densely packed workshops and houses. The ground floor housed a library, reading room, conversation room, and billiard and bagatelle rooms. Its music hall could host 640 people. Five years after its reopening, this hall would host a historic event one Sunday afternoon in July 1896: it was chosen as the venue at which Theodor Herzl would appear on his second visit to London, ready to convince the Jewish refugees of Alie Street and its environs that they would be better off going to Palestine than staying in East London.

Posters announced the event in advance, and enthusiasm ran high. People gathered outside the hall en masse, waiting for him to speak. The people who came to hear the prophet of Zionism were too numerous to be hosted in the hall and they formed a huge gathering outside the building, eagerly waiting to hear him. Luckily for the organisers there was an open space to the rear where the masses heard the bold salvo of Herzl's lobbying campaign in London.

The listeners were captivated by his speech, but the love wasn't mutual. In his diary, Herzl derided his newfound admirers in London: 'I met an army of *schnorrers* possessing a dream' (a *schnorrer* is a pejorative Yiddish term for a beggar).[11] But it began to dawn upon him that he would need them if he wanted to make inroads into the local Jewish and non-Jewish elite.

On the same street, these new immigrants could also hear more universal and socialist messages, not confined to the Zionist nationalist agenda, and in the coming years, many among them would have to make up their minds which of the two dogmas served them best as Jewish working-class people in Britain. But at the time Herzl appeared there, working-class consciousness did not yet seem incompatible with Zionism and the prophet was warmly welcomed.

As the historian Isaiah Friedman put it, 'In London, the idea of a Jewish state had an electrifying effect on the poor Jews of the East End, but the rich Jews remained aloof.'[12] This Viennese Jew, the scion of a prosperous businessman, found an unlikely base, eager to lobby for Zionism, in the impoverished Jewish working class in London. And the ideal next stop for expanding support was the Great Assembly Hall in Mile End.

THE GREAT ASSEMBLY HALL, MILE END ROAD, LONDON, 1898

It was none other than the Earl of Shaftesbury who laid the foundation stone for the Great Assembly Hall on Mile End Road on 10 November 1883, a year before it was officially opened. In 1898, the frontage of the Great Assembly Hall was still white, unblemished by soot and filth, unlike older East End buildings. It was an elegant three-storey building which had on its ground floor two entrances, one for the gallery and a bookshop and one for a smaller hall. Above them were two grand floors, punctuated by long windows boasting satin curtains. But the frontage, opulent as it was, doesn't tell the full story about this building: it was destined to be a home for some of London's many poor. It was the project of Frederick Charrington, an heir to a brewery empire who became one of London's best-known philanthropists.

He joined the family business and the stage seemed set for a life of comfort and prosperity. He seemed to have everything that a young man could want. 'He had a pleasant disposition, was reasonably clever and extremely wealthy' is how the Tower Hamlets Mission website describes him.[13] Some go even further in portraying him as practically a saint. Here's how his 'Road to Damascus' experience went: at the age of nineteen, having read the Gospel, he felt moved to convert and become a faithful Christian. About a year later he was walking through Whitechapel and saw a poorly dressed woman with her children, trying to get her husband to come out of a public house and give her some money for food. The husband was furious and knocked her into the gutter. Charrington went to help and was also knocked to the ground. When he looked up, he saw his name on the sign above the pub and decided that he wanted nothing more to do with the brewery business. He went home and told his father that he was leaving the family business and his inheritance to devote his life to helping the poor in the East End.

He opened a school, led a fight to clean up the music halls, and became an ardent worker for the temperance movement and a member of the London County Council for Mile End. In this last capacity he ordered the construction of the Great Assembly Hall. It hosted five thousand poor and destitute Londoners who could attend a Christian service there (but would come mainly for tea prior to the evening sermon). During the week they had access to a coffeehouse, a bookshop and many social activities – it was an early forerunner of modern community centres.

Yet on 3 October 1898, during Theodor Herzl's third London tour, the city's poor were very far from people's concerns. Herzl was there to address a mass audience on the subject of Zionism. Like the Working Men's Club on Great Alie Street, a venue created for working-class empowerment became a landmark in the journey of the city's pro-Zionist lobby. These choices of venue partly reflect Zionist failure – no doubt Herzl would have preferred to address the great and good in a more salubrious location than the bustle of the East End. But they also represent a new opportunity for Zionism: an opportunity to secure a genuinely grassroots support base among ordinary Jews.

Ten thousand people came to hear Herzl speak in the hall. They occupied every seat in it. Herzl played the role of demagogue, exclaiming to the crowds: 'The East End is ours!' His audience cheered and applauded him. Having failed to get the rich Jewish bankers on his side, he used his speech to attack those very bankers as the enemies of these newly arrived Jewish immigrants. He castigated the German rabbis who opposed Zionism and coined the insult '*protestrabbiner*' – but the shoe was clearly also intended to fit the British Chief Rabbi, Hermann Adler, who had advised the Anglo-Jewish Association to 'be on our guard against fostering fantastic and visionary ideas about the re-establishment of a Jewish nation'.[14]

Yet this speech was only a dress rehearsal for a grander performance two years later: his opening speech at the fourth Zionist Congress in 1900, in the very same Great Hall.

THE FOURTH ZIONIST CONGRESS, 1900

The fourth gathering of the Zionist Congress in London was the first outside mainland Europe. At first Herzl was hardly keen on the idea of holding the event in this location, but witnessing the poverty of Eastern European immigrants in the city convinced him. These Jews, he thought, might be more amenable to moving to Palestine. He wanted to prove that Zionism was no longer just the concern of intellectuals in Basel and saw an opportunity to spread his vision for a Jewish state in Palestine. He intended to make the congress a grand affair – hoping it would be covered by the British press. In this way Zionism could reach millions in Britain.[15]

The delegates of the fourth Zionist Congress were amply compensated for being hosted in this relatively humble venue in Mile End by a seven-course meal at the Queen's Hall in Langham Place which included mock turtle, boiled salmon, roast gosling and lemon jelly. The invitation card showed a drawing of a group of Jews somewhere in the world, guided by an angel, showing them the way to Palestine (in the background one can see Roman soldiers kicking out a Jew dressed anachronistically in nineteenth-century Jewish attire; a close look at the figure shows it resembles a generic Jesus, albeit dressed as a rabbi). The wine list for all the events of the congress was made exclusively of wines from the Rothschilds' winery in the Zionist colony Rishon LeZion, called the 'Palestine Kosher Wine Company'.[16]

For all its extravagance, the Zionist Congress very nearly went ahead without its star. Herzl arrived in London on 7 August 1900 quite ill, suffering from a high fever, and he spent the initial days of his visit confined to his bed at the Langham Hotel. Herzl may have placed his faith in British politics but seemed very suspicious about British medicine's ability to provide proper treatment. The doctor had to be Viennese-trained and be a Zionist. Somehow, a doctor who met these highly specific criteria was located in the East End: Leopold Liebster. After successfully finishing treatment, Herzl was ready to move to the next stage of Zionist lobbying in Britain.[17]

Herzl delivered several long speeches during the congress. It took place against the backdrop of another wave of attacks on Jews, this time in Romania (from which a number of his listeners originated). Herzl insisted that the only preventative measure against future pogroms was a charter for a Jewish state, granted by the Ottoman Empire, which at the time controlled Palestinian territory. Other notable leaders of the Zionist movement did not believe that the aim to obtain such a charter was the sole priority of an all-Zionist Congress. They wanted to recruit resources for the colonies that were already present in Palestine and discuss practical aspects of the new idea of Jewish nationalism in Palestine (such as what language they should speak, what the aims of the educational system should be, and other aspects of the new political entity).

There was, by the way, hardly any discussion about the Palestinians, who at that point still constituted ninety per cent of the population. As in all his previous speeches, Herzl simply did not see it as necessary to discuss the people who already lived in the Promised Land. This wasn't because he didn't know they existed; he just thought that either they would welcome his ideas or, if necessary, they could be coerced to accept them. A year before, he was engaged in an intensive correspondence with one of Palestine's most important dignitaries, Yusuf Dia al-Khalidi, at times a mayor of Jerusalem and a representative to the Ottoman Parliament. Al-Khalidi had written a letter to the Chief Rabbi of France, Zadoc Kahn, in 1899, pointing out that the Jews would only be able to take over Palestine by force and suggesting that the Zionist movement should leave Palestine 'in peace'. Kahn showed the letter to Herzl. On 19 March 1899 Herzl replied to al-Khalidi in French assuring him that, if the Zionists were not wanted in Palestine, 'We will search and, believe me, we will find elsewhere what we need.'[18] Given Herzl's lack of desire to visit Palestine, let alone live there, he might have genuinely meant this as well; he was willing to explore other options. But at the congress itself, he focused on Palestine as the exclusive destination of the Zionist movement and was happy to extol the virtues of the country.

In his ambition to win British support, he flattered the self-image of the English elite with his opening remarks:

> England, great England, free England, England that looks across the seven seas, will understand us and our aspirations. From here the Zionist idea will fly ever higher; of this we may be sure.[19]

But Herzl didn't stop at praising the British Empire. He went on to suggest that a Jewish state could serve not only British interests in Asia but those of the Western world at large, saying it was in the 'interest of the civilized nations' to have a 'cultural station' in Asia. Quite simply, he played to the prejudices of his audience. The *Manchester Courier*, which reported the speech, went as far as claiming that a Jewish state would contribute 'an element of stability to Asian Politics'.[20]

The organisation of the fourth congress had been entrusted to the English Zionist Federation. It was established in 1899 and adopted a constitution committed to the 'fostering of the national idea of Israel' in Palestine. The English Zionist Federation was lauded for the successful execution of the congress. But that was by no means its core focus. From its inception, its principal mission was to gain influence in Parliament. Its early staff, sitting in Jessel Chambers on Chancery Lane, sent questionnaires to members of Parliament with the following text:

> Should you view our movement with sympathy and inform me to that effect at your early convenience, I shall be glad to advise our friends, in the constituency you seek to represent, to give all the support for your candidature, of which they are capable.[21]

A long list of those who responded favourably was published for the domestic consumption of the federation. Even some government ministers expressed their support but asked that their endorsement not be published because of their official position. This was the forerunner to modern Zionist lobbying, and calls to mind the tactics of AIPAC today on the other side of the Atlantic, promising or withholding electoral support, according to a candidate's attitude towards Zionism. As we shall see, it was more effective in the USA; in Britain what was needed was offering support for a party or a party leader rather than enlisting the services of some obscure backbencher in a constituency out in the sticks.

These tactics were invented and put into practice by Joseph Cowen (1868–1932) who was the founder and leader of the English Zionist Federation, and it was he who drafted the questionnaires. He was a relative of Israel Zangwill, who persuaded him to take part in the first Zionist Congress in Basel in 1897. Cowen became very close to Herzl and accompanied him during Herzl's audience with Sultan Abd al-Hamid II in 1901. He impressed the founder of Zionism so much that he was honoured by featuring as a character, Joseph Levy, in Herzl's *Altneuland* ('Old New Land'), a utopian novel about the making of a Jewish state in Palestine. No less crucial as a contribution to Zionism was his directorship of the Jewish Colonial Trust, which became an essential tool for the colonisation of Palestine. Such early naive fervour was not to last; later he would be part of the famous Zionist delegation that visited Palestine in 1918 and wrote back stating that the bride was beautiful but married to another man.

Cowen did not end up as the leader of English Zionism at the dawn of the twentieth century – Chaim Weizmann, who we will meet shortly, took up this position instead. But he was Weizmann's right-hand man, and ready to assist him in the negotiations of the Balfour Declaration.

This Declaration, now an infamous milestone in the history of Palestine and the greater Middle East, was not in fact a declaration but a letter – a letter to be delivered to the Zionist Federation of Great Britain. It didn't come out of nowhere, but was a destination reached after a long road of lobbying, starting from 1905. Let's turn to that now.

3

The Road to the Balfour Declaration

A 1905 photo in a local newspaper shows Lord Balfour, then the British prime minister, and the mayor of Manchester leaving the Queen's Hotel for the opening of a new technical school. A year later, the hotel was Balfour's headquarters in his failed attempt to hold his Manchester East seat as the Conservative Party leader and former prime minister. He lost by a landslide.

The hotel was built in the 1840s in the wake of the opening of the Manchester and Birmingham Railway (where Manchester Piccadilly stands today) and was created by the conversion of three townhouses into an impressive Italian-style corner building. The choice of the hotel, apart from its strategic location, may have been due to the hotel's speciality, turtle soup, a particular favourite of Balfour's (and of many his Conservative peers, including Winston Churchill and John Hope). The live turtles were imported from New York and were held in tanks in the basement, as an advertisement proclaimed:

> The hotel begs respectfully to inform the inhabitants of Manchester and its vicinity that he has just received a large cargo of Fine Live Turtles by the steam-ship America, from New York. Live Turtle on sale. Turtle Soup always ready and sent to any part of town or country.[1]

Turtle soup aside, this hotel was the venue in which crucial conversations about the future of Palestine and Zionism took place between

Balfour and Zionist leaders. His chief interlocutor was Chaim Weizmann, a leading member of the executive committee that ran the Zionist Organization after Herzl's death, who resided in Manchester as well. In his memoirs, *Trial and Error*, Weizmann wrote that Manchester brimmed with liberalism, which suited his mindset and visions.[2] He also felt at home in the prosperous and ever-growing Jewish community in the city.

Balfour's encounters with Weizmann in 1905 and 1906 would be no footnote in history – they would decisively shape the fate of Palestine and its peoples in the first half of the twentieth century.

Despite his defeat in Manchester, Balfour had no time to wallow. He swiftly fought and won a by-election for the City of London, then a safe seat for the Conservatives, to resume his position as leader of the Conservative Party, a post he retained until 1911. But he came back with a fresh political project in mind.

The reasons Balfour turned to Zionism were by no means obvious – he certainly felt no special sympathy for the plight of Jews. In 1905, the same year he met Weizmann for the first time, he supported the Aliens Act, Britain's first immigration controls, designed to stop an influx of Jews fleeing the pogroms in Eastern Europe. Some scholars suspect he was driven by anti-Semitism, both in constricting Jewish immigration to Britain and in his enthusiasm for setting up Jewish settlements in Palestine.[3] But this was nothing other than the promise of Jewish Zionists themselves: Herzl repeatedly told Britons and Germans that the Zionist colonisation of Palestine would divert the dreaded *Ostjuden* immigrants from Western Europe to Palestine.

As early as the Manchester meetings, Weizmann was able to nudge Balfour in the Zionist direction. He did so with the help of Herbert Samuel, who was a Liberal and a political foe of Balfour (and who, as we shall see later in the book, would play a very important role in the lobby), but nonetheless the two collaborated later in helping to expand the Zionist foothold in Palestine. Samuel was present at their first meeting at the Queen's Hotel, and joined the conversation.[4]

How did an émigré Jew end up meeting one of the leading politicians in the country such as Balfour? The two men were introduced by

Charles Dreyfus, then Weizmann's boss at the Clayton Aniline Company, which would go on to make key contributions to Britain's war effort. As the name suggests, he was a distant relative of Alfred Dreyfus, the Jewish military officer whose trial and condemnation polarised French society. A successful businessman in Manchester, he also presided over the Manchester Zionist Society and was a member of the city council. His role in politics didn't end there: he chaired Balfour's ill-fated election campaign in 1906. Dreyfus seized the opportunity to engineer meetings between Balfour and Weizmann.

These meetings were prompted by Balfour's wish to understand why, after Herzl's death, the Zionist movement was unwilling to discuss locations other than Palestine for its colonisation project. In 1903, while Balfour was prime minister, Herzl and the British government held serious discussions about building a Jewish state in British Uganda – the sixth Zionist Congress eventually rejected the proposal. The British colonial secretary, Joseph Chamberlain, had suggested it as an alternative to an earlier idea by Herzl to settle Jews in Al-Arish, at the time under Anglo-Egyptian rule (today the provincial capital of the North Sinai Governorate of Egypt, forty-seven kilometres west of the border between Egypt and Palestine), with a view to expanding the Jewish colony from there into the rest of Palestine, an idea that was rejected by the British Viceroy in Egypt, Lord Cromer.[5] Dreyfus himself had no objections to the Uganda plan. However, after the death of Herzl in 1904, any possibility of settling East European Jews elsewhere in the world was ruled out categorically and the movement was orientated exclusively, under Weizmann, towards the colonisation of Palestine.

This is why, in the historiography of the Balfour Declaration, the meeting between Balfour and Weizmann in 1906 is rightly character-ised as a formative moment at which Balfour was won over to support the Zionisation of Palestine. It lasted for an hour. Weizmann recalled that Balfour did not hide his obvious anti-Semitism, but the Zionist leader did not seem to be deterred by it. He surmised that Balfour's animus was reserved for particular kinds of Jews, and he had no affinity with them either. When the two men met, Balfour confessed that he had discussed the Jews with Cosima Wagner at Bayreuth (where they met several times in the late 1890s) and shared 'many of her anti-Semitic prejudices'.[6] Weizmann replied that 'Germans of Mosaic persuasion were an undesirable and demoralizing phenomenon'.[7]

At that meeting, Balfour repeated his support for settling the Russian Jews in Uganda. Weizmann responded by saying, 'Suppose I were to offer you Paris instead of London'. 'But, Dr Weizmann, we have London', Balfour replied. 'That is true', Weizmann said, 'but we had Jerusalem when London was a marsh'. 'Are there many Jews who think like you?' wondered Balfour. 'I believe I speak the minds of millions of Jews'. 'It is curious', Balfour remarked, 'the Jews I meet are quite different'. 'Mr Balfour', Weizmann replied, 'you meet the wrong kind of Jews'. Weizmann seemed to be able to persuade Balfour to accept Palestine as the only destination for Jewish immigration.[8] As a result of this change of aim within the Zionist movement, Balfour, whose key priority was most likely keeping Jews out of Britain, became a political Zionist by default.

As we shall see in later chapters, this strange concoction of anti-Semitism and ardent Zionism is still fuelling some of the advocacy in the world for Israel. In Balfour and Weizmann's discussions, neither had mentioned what the Palestinians might have to say. This too continues to this day – the rights and aspirations of these people remain disregarded.

1915–1917: IN PLAIN SIGHT

As trench warfare in Europe claimed the lives of millions of soldiers, efforts on behalf of Zionism advanced with alacrity. By this time the institutional Zionist lobby involved both individuals who were part of institutions and those who laboured independently on behalf of Zionism. Thus, in this chapter we refer to the lobby as encompassing both official and unofficial acts of advocacy, as noted in the introduction.

The principal Zionist institution during the years of the Great War was the Zionist Federation, or, to give it its full name, the Zionist Federation of Great Britain and Ireland, established in 1899. But most of the lobbying was done by several Anglo-Jewish aristocrats who now took the lead in advocacy for a British and Jewish Palestine.

As I've set out, their main challenge was to persuade policy makers in Britain that a Zionist Palestine needed to be a British Palestine – one that would be a steadfast bulwark for Britain's imperial ambitions in the Middle East. At the beginning of the war, this wasn't on the cards. Accordingly, the mission of the nascent pro-Zionist lobby in Britain was to present this goal as part of the future British strategy towards the Middle East. Sir Herbert Samuel took up this fraught task, enjoying success with his appointment as the first British High Commissioner to Palestine in 1920.

Herbert Louis Samuel was born in 1870 and enjoyed a brisk rise through the ranks of the Liberal Party, ultimately becoming its leader in 1931. He was the first non-baptised Jew in Britain to be appointed as a Cabinet minister and a leader of a party – Britain's first Jewish prime minister, Disraeli, had been baptised as an Anglican during childhood. Ironically, the very acceptance and popularity Samuel enjoyed in British politics suggests another path was possible for twentieth-century Jews in the global struggle against anti-Semitism, a path that didn't require the colonisation of Palestine.

Unlike the gentile Balfour, Samuel made no show of public sympathy for Zionism in the years leading up to the First World War. His own cousin, Edwin Montagu, remained a convinced anti-Zionist. But a wave of anti-Semitism, in which Samuel himself became the subject of false accusations during the Marconi scandal, seems to have changed his mind. At the outset of the war in 1914, he met Chaim Weizmann and affirmed his support for a Zionist state, leaving Weizmann himself astounded at the Messianism of this patrician Anglo-Jew. In many ways, we can say that Samuel was the self-appointed liaison between the Zionist movement and the British government. He was motivated by his realisation that the British government was now determined to dissolve the Ottoman Empire, provoked by the decision of Turkey to join the Central Powers in the war. Such a disintegration of the Empire required prior agreements with other members of the alliance, such as France, which were as greedy as Britain was for more territory and influence. Hence Samuel understood that it was necessary to exert Zionist pressure on the postwar map of the Arab world, if the map were to include a Jewish Palestine. As he wrote in November 1914, 'now the conditions are profoundly altered.'[9]

Immediately after Turkey's entry into the war, Samuel met the foreign secretary, Edward Grey, and said to him, 'perhaps the opportunity might arise for the fulfilment of the ancient aspiration of the Jewish people and the restoration of a Jewish State'.[10] He noted that Russia might help in this, as it would relieve Russia of its Jewish population in its current territories and in the new lands it hoped to acquire once competing empires were vanquished.

He clarified that this was not a project for Jews like himself, but for the Jews of Eastern Europe. It would succeed as 'the Jewish brain is rather a remarkable thing.' Anglo- and American Jews would take the initiative in leading the Jews of the extended Russian territories into Palestine. They were also the ones who might provide the funds for the project. 'The petty traders of past years would become a modern nation', he promised Grey.[11]

Both Grey's and Samuel's main worry was whether France would accept such an idea, but a more serious obstacle was the ambivalent position of the prime minister at the time, Lord Asquith, who seemed to see little advantage in incorporating Palestine into the British Empire in the Middle East; after all, it was 'a country the size of Wales, much of it is barren mountain and part of it waterless' – but if it were to be an Anglo-Jewish colony he would consider the idea.[12] Asquith was astonished to learn that someone like David Lloyd George supported the idea, as in his eyes the latter:

> does not care a damn for the Jews or their past or their future but thinks it will be an outrage to let the Holy Places pass into the possession or under the protectorate of agnostic, atheistic France.[13]

We can only speculate what would have happened had not the sixty-three-year-old Asquith, a father of seven children, fallen in love with a young nurse working at the London Hospital whom he met in February

1915. She was in her twenties, and he was definitely besotted by her. She was the daughter of Baron Stanley of Alderley, whom Asquith knew and liked, and she was a very close friend of Asquith's wife, Violet. Asquith professed his love in an endless stream of hundreds of letters. Ms Stanley was not quite so enamoured – her last letter to Asquith stated she was leaving him for a younger suitor, who turned out to be Edwin Samuel Montagu, a member of his own Cabinet. For some historians this affair doomed his political career. In this version, the love-stricken, inconsolable Asquith could no longer govern – those were the days when broken hearts mattered more than the affairs of the state.[14] Had this romantic fellow stayed in office, he might have thwarted the Balfour Declaration. Or in the words of Nathan Brun, writing on the centenary of the Balfour Declaration in *Haaretz*, this was 'The love triangle that changed the course of Zionism', because it pushed Asquith out of the way.[15] But this is only partially true – he remained in office for eighteen months after the end of the affair, and he also suffered the death of his young son.

The pinnacle of Herbert Samuel's activity on behalf of Zionism was persuading the Cabinet to accept a memorandum he wrote on behalf of the Zionist movement as a basis for discussing future British policy towards Palestine. In hindsight this was a far more important document than the Balfour Declaration. The document's title was *The Future of Palestine*, summarising the Zionist claims for the country.[16]

The memorandum was the result of consultation between Samuel and Chaim Weizmann. The Zionist leader, from their first meeting onwards, was delighted by Samuel's commitment to the cause. Samuel had advised him that his views reflected the positions held by many of his colleagues in the Cabinet and encouraged Weizmann to keep working quietly and continue step by step until the time was ripe to attempt an official approach to the British government.

They both agreed that realising the Zionist dream would only be possible when 'civilized conditions were established in Palestine.'[17] The message coming from the Zionist lobby in London now was that a Zionist enclave was one way in which the white man could civilise the world. This entreaty, they hoped, would convince Britain to establish a British Palestine as a precursor to a Zionist one.

Between 1915 and 1917, several discrete essential developments converged, driving the British government to announce its support for a Jewish state in Palestine. The first was the British readiness to forsake promises about Palestine they had made in negotiations with other interested parties. The vision of a joint Anglo-French or international Palestine that had been discussed between the two powers since 1912 was deserted, as was the pledge to turn Palestine, jointly with Iraq and Transjordan, into future Hashemite kingdoms, which was made during the famous correspondence between Sharif Hussein of Mecca and Sir Henry McMahon, the British High Commissioner in Egypt, in 1915 and early 1916. A recent book by Peter Shambrook put an end to a long historiographical debate that began in the 1960s on the question of whether or not Palestine was included in the British pledge to the Hashemites. Based on declassified material, it seems without doubt that Palestine was defined by Britain as part of the future Arab-Hashemite world.[18] By retreating from these alternative visions for Palestine, Britain was left with one vision: a Jewish Palestine.

It's clear that Zionism's gain in momentum from 1915 was not driven by concern for Jews alone. A curious mixture of anti-Semitism, imperialist avarice, distrust of the Muslim world and a desire to spite the French drove British policy makers into the Zionist camp.

Historians debate to this day whether, between 1915 to 1917, the tail wagged the dog or vice versa; in other words, whether British policy makers believed that supporting Zionist aspirations for Palestine would enhance the British position, or whether they were persuaded by the Zionist advocates that a Jewish Palestine would be an asset – providing an excuse to take it out of the hands of the French, limiting Hashemite power in the area and using American Jews to countervail an American president who insisted on rights of self-determination for the people living in the Ottoman Empire.

This book does not try to shed new light on the origins of the Balfour Declaration. It seeks to illuminate how the Anglo-Jewish community was successfully recruited into the Zionist lobbying machine through its effort to generate a pro-Zionist British policy that would eventually allow the creation of a Jewish state in Palestine. The historiographical debate about the Declaration's origins and significance increasingly tends to conclude that Britain would have occupied Palestine with or without Zionist pressure. And yet, the catastrophe that befell the Palestinians in 1948 was not because Britain decided – sometime between 1915 and 1917 – to take over Palestine, but because it was persuaded to make Palestine Zionist.

The key conclusion drawn by historians, from a seminal work by the Israeli historian Mayir Vereté to a recent work by James Renton, is that the leading motivation behind the now notorious Declaration was the belief that British support for the Zionist project in Palestine would strengthen British interests in the Middle East and in the world at large.[19] Renton brings a new dimension to this analysis when he asserts that Whitehall believed that:

> The Jewry was a nation derived from a general imagining of ethnic groups as cohesive, racial entities that were driven by a profound national consciousness.[20]

While this may seem positive at face value, it suggests something rather sinister: that the Jews were a nation in their own right, not part of a British nation, or indeed any other, on account of their ethnicity. One of those singled out by Renton as subscribing to ethnic ideas about Judaism was Mark Sykes, both a politician and an adviser on Middle Eastern affairs. Renton asserts that Sykes was influenced by neo-Romantic ideas of race and nationhood, which he thought applied to the new Jewish nation proposed by Zionism.[21] The role Sykes played in diverting Britain's attention to Palestine cannot be overstated. He, alongside other policy makers, turned Britain's wartime diplomacy into an existential foundation for the Zionist project in Palestine. Given the feebleness of the Zionist presence in Palestine, without Britain's imperial vision the future of Zionist colonisation on the ground would have been in grave peril.

Sykes played a key role in steering Britain into acquiring Palestine – in a clear shift away from Britain's existing policy. In the early negotiations with the French that began in earnest in 1912 about how to divide the Ottoman spoils in case of a war, Palestine still seemed to mean less than Mesopotamia, Egypt or the Arabian Peninsula for Britain. In these discussions, Britain was willing to contemplate a joint Anglo-French mandate over Palestine or even conceding it to France entirely. But the campaigns on the ground in the war, in particular the second Ottoman assault on the Suez Canal from the Sinai Peninsula, brought the message home that if Britain wanted to protect the Suez Canal, it had to rule Palestine.

At first, Sykes endorsed the vision of an Anglo-French Palestine, reflected in the Sykes–Picot Agreement of 1916. But once he deserted this vision, it had no more prominent backers in Britain and a strategy that could have changed the fate of Palestine and the Palestinians was doomed never to materialise. And thus Mark Sykes, the director general of the Foreign Office and the architect of the Sykes–Picot Agreement, transformed from a disinterested official into one of Zionism's greatest advocates.

How did this happen? A Catholic by birth and upbringing, Sykes was not influenced by evangelical restorationist ideology – his conversion to the cause was a matter of geopolitics, not faith. This was ultimately crucial in aligning the vision of a British Palestine with the Zionist project.

According to one account, his change of heart had also to do with the influence he attributed to the Zionist movement in the United States – the US government had not yet entered the war in 1916. Some of his acquaintances made the questionable assertion that American Zionists enjoyed great influence among American Jews and hence, indirectly, the American administration. This vague impression was bolstered by Sykes talking to two chief representatives of the Zionist movement in 1915, Nahum Sokolow and Chaim Weizmann; no less significant in these meetings was the role of Moses Gaster, the Hakham of the Spanish and Portuguese Jewish congregation and a former head of the English Zionist Federation.[22] He met with them regularly in 1916 and they too, like his friends, pushed the notion that American Zionist Jews could have an impact on American war policy. Sykes was not alone in being persuaded that Jews wielded immense power and had the ability to influence policy in the USA and even in Russia, where they were histor-ically oppressed.[23]

This idea was enthusiastically propagated by Vladimir Ze'ev Jabotinsky, a Zionist who founded the Jewish Legion of the British Army and was the leader of the more extreme Revisionist Zionist movement (which bred the present-day Likud Party). He wrote to British officials: 'The Jews of America, especially those of New York (1,250,000), represent a political factor of serious influence, even from the standpoint of international politics.'[24] The overstated impor-tance of American Zionists was coupled with a fear that the Zionists might seek German support instead if the British disappointed their hopes, which would have been disastrous in the eyes of the British government.[25]

Sykes and his compatriots in the British War Cabinet all had one thing in common when committing to an Anglo-Zionist Palestine: they knew practically nothing about Palestine. No one in the upper echelons of government and Whitehall was capable of questioning the assump-tions guiding the memoranda written by Samuel and similar documents produced by Zionist lobbyists and submitted to the Cabinet throughout 1915.

These were very detailed documents. They laid out a vision of a Palestine colonised by Jews from the Russian Empire as a win-win scenario. They suggested how to elicit the support of the Allied powers in the war for the project and reported that Russia indicated that it would look favourably on a Jewish Palestine.[26]

But despite their successes in persuading the government, there was still some work to be done by the lobby before they could be assured of a solid British commitment to a Jewish homeland in Palestine. The Zionist lobby had to overcome opposition to a pro-Zionist policy from two groups in 1915–1916: politicians who were reluctant to support a Zionist project, as they were aware it would be unpopular with Palestinians on the ground, and prominent Jews who dreaded the impact of such a project on the Anglo-Jewish community as a whole, worried it would mar efforts to be regarded as part of the British nation, without much regard for the Palestinian lives it would affect.

Opposition in the Cabinet was summarised by one member pleading with his peers to note that 'as long as the great majority of the inhabitants were Arabs it was out of the question [to have a Jewish Palestine]' and that not allowing the majority to decide its future would be contrary 'to the main purpose for which it had been declared that the Allies were fighting'.[27] Others opposed the idea since it was bound to generate opposition from the French and the Hashemites.

Samuel was recruited to deal with those politicians who pointed out the demographic realities as an obstacle to the idea of a Jewish Palestine. He urged the government to brush aside the inconvenient fact that the majority of those in Palestine were Arabs:

> At the same time, it was not necessary to accept the position that the existing population, sparse as it was, would have the right to bar the door to the return of the people whose connection with the country long antedated their own; especially as it had resulted in events of spiritual and cultural value to mankind in striking contrast to the barren record of the last thousand years.[28]

The final piece of the jigsaw fell into place after Herbert Asquith was replaced as prime minister by David Lloyd George. From a strategic point of view, Lloyd George took the view that a Jewish Palestine would serve British imperial interests much more effectively than an Arab one in relation to Egypt. This was an argument he was happy to hear repeated at a conference he attended in 1919 in London, where Max Nordau, a leading Zionist, promised:

> We shall have to be the guards of the Suez Canal. We shall have to be the sentinels of your way to India via the Near East.'[29]

Lloyd George, like Arthur Balfour and indeed many other senior British politicians, admired Chaim Weizmann, which increased his willingness to back Weizmann's Zionist vision. Lloyd George was a founding partner of the eponymous legal firm Lloyd George, Roberts & Co., whose services were retained by the English Zionist Federation for assistance on the Uganda Scheme, partly due to Lloyd George's close connections with the Foreign Office. But what impressed Lloyd George more than anything else seems to have been Weizmann's contribution to the British war effort.

When Lloyd George had taken the reins as minister of munitions in 1915, Britain was desperately short of acetone – a substance necessary for the manufacture of heavy artillery. The shortage came about due to the unavailability of maize, which had been blocked from reaching Britain by a German submarine siege. A mutual friend, C.P. Scott of the *Manchester Guardian,* told Lloyd George about Weizmann's chemical prowess, and the process he had designed to make acetone from horse chestnuts, which were abundant in Britain.[30] A factory at King's Lynn attempted successfully to replace the maize with chestnuts and acetone could then be mass-produced once more. The imminent crisis in weapons production had been headed off.

After becoming prime minister in December 1916, Lloyd George remembered his debt to Weizmann. The two men met mere weeks before the Balfour Declaration was issued. Lloyd George wanted to award his old friend honours for his services in the war effort, but Weizmann demurred: the only reward he wanted, he said, was a Jewish homeland – an event dramatised by George Bernard Shaw in *Arthur and the Acetone* in 1936. Foreign policy, of course, was not driven by repaying favours. But by this time, the wheels for the Declaration had been set in motion, and they were turning fast.

From September 1915, for all intents and purposes, Balfour became Weizmann's boss in the Admiralty, having recruited him to the position of honorary technical adviser. But Weizmann, although a paid employee of the British government, hesitated at first to use his position for the sake of the Zionist cause – it was Balfour, his old contact, who prompted him to take a more intensive interest and role in promoting it in Britain through his new post. According to several accounts, history again played an ironic hand here; while Weizmann the lobbyist hesitated to pressure the government to act, he was prompted to do so by the person he lobbied, Balfour. According to the diary of Blanche 'Baffy' Dugdale, Balfour's beloved niece, one day Balfour came to Weizmann's room and said: 'if the Allies win the war, you may get your Jerusalem'. These conversations, between Lloyd George, Balfour and Weizmann, helped increase governmental appetite for the Zionist project, indirectly paving the way for the Balfour Declaration.[31]

By persuading the British government that their geopolitical interests were furthered through a Jewish state on Palestinian land, Zionists managed to overcome opposition from the Cabinet by the time of the Declaration. But the second obstacle remained: the prominent members of Anglo-Jewish society who did not share the Zionist vision.

ARISTOCRATIC FEUDS ABOUT ZIONISM

The British government, composed of men who neither knew much about Palestine nor cared for it, was easy to win over compared to prominent Anglo-Jews. For the leading Jewish Zionist lobbyists in Britain, it was as important to convince their own community of the validity of the Zionist cause as it was to secure the British government's endorsement. The Anglo-Jewish community was as socially stratified as Britain in general – class distinctions were inescapable, especially in politics. While Herzl captured the imagination of Jewish immigrants in the East End, where some of them would be even more taken with socialism than Zionism later on, he failed to win over the Anglo-Jewish aristocracy that could have influenced policies from above quite significantly.

Herbert Samuel, patrician himself, understood the importance of persuading the aristocracy of Zionism and took this task up with zeal. In this effort, he was assisted by two Anglo-Jewish aristocrats, Lord Reading and Lord Rothschild, who, with others, had formed a focused lobby group in February 1915, arguing for the establishment of a British protectorate in Palestine as a basis for a future Jewish state there. Now they turned their attention to their own community.

Rufus Daniel Isaacs, first Marquess of Reading (1860–1935), like Samuel, was a Liberal politician. He served as the Lord Chief Justice of England, viceroy of India, and foreign secretary. Like Samuel, he was a practising Jew, and he became the second Anglo-Jew, after Samuel, to serve in such high positions. When he became the British ambassador to Washington in the war years, he used that position to advocate for Zionism. He published a statement in the *New York Times* (on 27 March 1918) jointly with the General Zionist Federation calling for American support for a Jewish state in Palestine. Like Samuel's, his career demonstrated that in Britain, Jews could rise to the top and perhaps didn't need a state of their own to do so.

The Readings created a dynasty of pro-Zionist lobbyists. His son Gerald Isaacs married Lady Eva Violet Melchett, the daughter of Alfred Mond (1868–1930), an Anglo-Jew from wealthy industrialist stock and the son of the German-born chemist Ludwig Mond (1839–1909), who invented the alloy nickel and founded the Brunner Mond Company, which merged into ICI in 1926. Alfred Mond was a member of the Liberal Party, although by 1926 he had broken with it in protest at its land policy and joined the Conservatives. He was a close friend of Chaim Weizmann and worked relentlessly for the Zionist cause. Eva became the Marchioness of Reading and vice president of the World Jewish Congress and the president of its British section, and later one of the main advocates of the young state of Israel.

Lord Reading, Rufus Isaacs, the father of Gerald, worked closely with Baron Lionel Walter Rothschild (1868–1937), a British banker, politician and scion of the famous banking family. It was he who received the letter from Lord Balfour which became the famous or infamous Balfour Declaration.

The Rothschilds were a banking family in Britain that was founded in the late eighteenth century in Manchester and operated as a royal house of bankers. They had branches in many countries in Europe and not all of them endorsed the Zionist project and vision. Thus, when in the late nineteenth century Herzl approached the German and Austrian branches, he was given the cold shoulder. In France, another Rothschild had his own Zionist projects; this was Baron Abraham Edmond Benjamin James de Rothschild (1845–1934), who funded the early colonisation of Palestine.

However, in Britain, members of the family such as Walter Rothschild proved to be enthusiastic Zionists. He actually should have been remembered for his achievements as an outstanding naturalist and the founder of what is now the Natural History Museum at Tring, where he assembled the biggest collection of natural history specimens ever made by one person; but he is now known mainly due to his role in the Balfour Declaration.

Walter and other Rothschild family members were close allies of the ruling class in Britain. The British branch of their bank became a potent political force when it financed some of the British expenses during the Napoleonic Wars. In 1875, the bank financed both the British purchase of the Suez Canal and Cecil Rhodes' ventures in Africa. 'Our' Rothschild was the public face of the family in Britain. He later became the president of the Board of Deputies of British Jews for one year in 1925.

Surprisingly, the main opposition to the aristocrats who advocated for Zionism came from their own relatives. Herbert Samuel's principal foe was his cousin, Edwin Samuel Montagu (1879–1924), who was part of the love triangle mentioned earlier involving Asquith and Stanley. He was a Liberal politician who was considered a member of the 'radical' wing of the Liberal Party.

Montagu saw Zionism as a 'mischievous political creed'[32] and, after the publication of the Balfour Declaration, which he considered to be anti-Semitic, he wrote his own declaration, so to speak, in which he explained his objections to Zionism (his unrelenting opposition is to some extent responsible for his cousin's agreement to include at least some reference to the Palestinians in the Declaration).

In the memorandum he wrote, he warned that:

> The Turks and other Mahommedans in Palestine will be regarded as foreigners, just in the same way as Jews will hereafter be treated as foreigners in every country but Palestine.[33]

Prophetically he also warned against establishing a state where citizenship would be granted on the basis of religion.

Probably more important than anything else was his contention that Zionism was far from being universally supported by the Anglo-Jewish community:

The sympathy, which the President of the Local Government Board suggests is widespread and deep-rooted in the protestant world, with the idea of restoring the Hebrew people to the land which was to be their inheritance, is I fear very often a thinly cloaked desire to get rid of the Jewish ingredient in Protestant populations.[34]

And he added:

I assert that there is not a Jewish nation. The members of my family, for instance, who have been in this country for generations, have no sort or kind of community of view or of desire with any Jewish family in any other country beyond the fact that they profess to a greater or less degree the same religion. It is no more true to say that a Christian Englishman and a Christian Frenchman are of the same nation.

When the Jews are told that Palestine is their national home, every country will immediately desire to get rid of its Jewish citizens, and you will find a population in Palestine driving out its present inhabitants.

As he laconically put it at the end: 'If Palestine will be the National Home of the Jews – all the voters in my constituency will tell me: "Go Home!!!"'

According to Weizmann, Montagu waged an all-out war against the Declaration and gave fiery speeches about it in Cabinet meetings. He wrote in his memoirs about Montagu that:

There was nothing new in what he had to say, but the vehemence with which he urged his views, the implacability of his opposition, astonished the cabinet. I understand the man almost wept.[35]

In 1917, however, when the British Cabinet was discussing the possibility of the Balfour Declaration, Montagu's political standing was at a nadir as a result of his deteriorating health, for which his doctors failed to find a satisfactory medical explanation. In Lloyd George's government, he served as secretary of state for India, and the long letters and memos he composed regarding Palestine did not move the Cabinet away from its support for the Zionist colonisation of Palestine.

In the 1922 election, Montagu lost his seat in the House of Commons and found himself out of politics altogether. Two years later, on 15 November 1924, he died an embittered and defeated man, suffering from a then-unidentified illness, likely to have been sepsis or encephalitis.

Insurrection in the Rothschild family arose thanks to Lionel Nathan de Rothschild (1882–1942). Lionel was a major in the British army, a banker and a Conservative politician, who, with others, co-founded the Anti-Zionist League of British Jews in 1917. The League was formed in opposition to the Balfour Declaration, immediately after its publication. It included Sir Philip Magnus and Montagu. It had only eighteen members but every single one of them was an influential politician and, up until it ceased its activities in 1929, it was the most important counterweight to the British Zionist lobby.

The League did not object to individual Jewish emigration to Ottoman Palestine, should those Jews be welcomed there, but was categorically opposed to their arrival there as a nation – horrified by the idea that the nationality of Anglo-Jews would be questioned because of Zionism. They published their views in a journal called the *Jewish Guardian*, edited by Laurie Magnus, becoming the anti-Zionist equivalent of the pro-Zionist journal the *Jewish Chronicle*. There was an additional battlefield between the two journals. The *Jewish Chronicle* endorsed enthusiastically the Marxist and Bolshevist ideas that many Jewish immigrants brought with them from Russia, whereas the League was fiercely anti-communist. Moreover, the League, very much like the senior officials in the Foreign Office, erroneously equated Zionism with Bolshevism (in the case of the Foreign Office, this assumed ideological affinity led to a hope that the Balfour Declaration would pave inroads into the new Bolshevik government that was about to rule Russia).[36]

Opposition to Zionism and to Anglo-Zionist alliance also came from institutions within the Anglo-Jewish community. One such institution was the Anglo-Jewish Association (AJA), established in 1871 by a former editor of the *Jewish Chronicle*, Abraham Benisch, and Albert Löwy, a Reform rabbi from London. It devoted its activities to helping Jews around the world who suffered from anti-Semitism. From its inception, it was a trusted institution within the community; in 1878 it established a Conjoint Foreign Committee with the Board of Deputies.

By 1917, both the Board of Deputies and the AJA were led by Anglo-Jews who opposed the Zionist project. The Board's president was David Lindo Alexander and the AJA was headed up by Claude Montefiore. The two men disagreed on many issues but they were united by their antipathy to Zionism and its definition of Judaism.

Their hostility led them to try to pre-empt the Balfour Declaration by penning a joint statement on 17 May 1917 which they sent to *The Times*, but it was only published a week later. This may well have been due to the pro-Zionist sympathies of *The Times*'s editor – the delay diminished their statement's impact as Weizmann had already made public announcements alluding to the British government's forthcoming support for a Jewish state in Palestine.[37]

One of the main reasons for the opposition to Zionism among prominent Anglo-Jews was their sense that they were British, not a separate nationality in Britain. Unlike elsewhere in Europe, Anglo-Jews had no memory of pogroms, and by 1890 Jews had achieved full legal emancipation in Britain. Although Britain became the hub of Zionist lobbying, its emergence and expansion had little to do with the actual experience of anti-Semitism in Britain, nor was it seen as a remedy to oppression in Britain. Zionist lobbying in Britain, whether led by Jews or non-Jews, had more to do with the strategic vision of the Empire's future in the Middle East than with the affairs of Jews in Britain.

The very lively and still ongoing historiographical debate about the surge of anti-Semitism in Britain during that period indicates how marginal Zionism was when it came to public awareness of local anti-Semitism, which indeed was there, in particular between 1912 and 1914. Discussion about it was triggered by two scandals: the Marconi scandal and the 'Purchase of Silver for India' scandal. The Marconi affair was a series of allegations against the famous communication company claiming that it won the tender issued by the British Post Office for a telegraph network unfairly and illegally. The postmaster was Herbert Samuel, and it was alleged that he preferred a Jewish-owned company, headed by the first Lord Reading's brother, Godfrey Isaacs, at the time when Lord Reading was the attorney general. Co-conspirators were named as Lloyd George, who was chancellor of the Exchequer at the time, and Lord Alexander Murray, the Liberal chief whip. Pre-deal, they all bought shares at a ridiculously low price, only to double their earnings after the deal was done. A parliamentary committee rejected most of the allegations, but the popular press pointed to a 'Jewish connection'.

Coinciding with this was the 'Purchase of Silver for India' scandal. The India Office purchased silver bullion for the minting of Indian rupees. The purchase was surprisingly entrusted to a private bank and not, as was customary, the Bank of England. The private bank was the Samuel Montagu & Co. Bank. Several members of the Montagu family were both in the Bank and in the India Office, another ground for spreading rumours of a Jewish conspiracy. Remember that Herbert Samuel was related to the Montagus, which did not help. And it went on and on, exposing more people involved, with family connections of one sort or another to the Montagus. Again, investigation found most of the allegations invalid or unsubstantiated.[38] The leading anti-Semite journal in the country, *The Eye Witness*, soon to be called *The New Witness*, led the attack.

In the end, both affairs had more to do with the corruption intrinsic to Britain's liberal capitalist system at the time than anything related to the Jews. But whatever historians say about anti-Semitism around the time of the Balfour Declaration, it's obvious that it did not lead to any increase in support for Zionism. None of those named in the scandals felt helpless or unable to withstand the storm, and indeed they were able to stay in public office after the scandals broke. Britain was and remained a safe place for poor Jews in the East End and successful ones in the West End.[39]

Neither the absence of widespread anti-Semitism nor the presence of vociferous anti-Zionist campaigns stopped the British government from supporting Zionism. In fact, the British government got involved in the campaign to win support inside the Anglo-Jewish community and among Jewish communities around the world. Just before the Declaration was made, the British government and the Zionist movement joined forces to propagate the new alliance among Jews around the world, so that it would gain wide support once it was declared. This institutional collaboration between the British government and Zionism was in many ways as significant as the Balfour Declaration itself. The propaganda arm of the British government, the Ministry of Information, recruited one of the leading activists of the Zionist movement to help persuade Jewish people across the globe to support the Declaration. His name was Albert Montefiore Hyamson, a civil servant in the Post Office. From 1900 onwards he wrote extensively in various newspapers about Zionism. His main writings appeared in the British Palestine Committee newsletter, which was the major publication of the lobby. He was an able and persuasive writer. Lloyd George stated that one of Hyamson's articles in the *New Statesman* stimulated his interest in Zionism.[40] In April 1917, Hyamson was made the editor of the *Zionist Review* (the newspaper published by the English Zionist Federation).

The idea that Hyamson would become the head of a Jewish Bureau within the Ministry of Information was put forward by Jabotinsky. And hence Hyamson swiftly became both the Ministry and the Zionist Federation's best propaganda asset. One of his more impressive outputs was a film called *The British Re-conquering Palestine for the Jews*, made after General Allenby had entered Jerusalem, following its occupation in December 1917. The film was sent to Jewish communities and organisations around the world.[41] On the cover of a book he wrote, titled *Palestine: The Rebirth of an Ancient People*, readers were told that this book enumerated 'the benefits the recent Jewish colonisation of Palestine has brought to the land'.[42] To the land, of course – not to the people. Hyamson also made Jabotinsky the official British journalist for Zionist affairs in Palestine. For his efforts Hyamson was later awarded a post in the first British Mandatory government by Herbert Samuel when he became the High Commissioner of Palestine. This was indeed a dazzling career that began with humble Zionist advocacy, moving to a role in British strategic consultation about the future of Palestine and then being part of the administration running the colonised country, and all this within four years, when Jews constituted only slightly more than ten per cent of the population in Palestine.

But it seems to me the most important achievement of lobbyists such as Weizmann and Hyamson was the successful recruitment of Lloyd George to the Zionist cause, and persuading him that the strategic aims of the British Empire and that of the Zionist movement were one and the same. The scene was set for putting the final touches to one of the most famous documents in the history of modern Palestine.

THE FINAL DRAFTING OF THE BALFOUR DECLARATION

With the advance of the British forces, aided by the Anzac troops, on the ground in Palestine, the preparation for the Declaration gathered momentum. All these politicians in whom the lobby invested were now ready to push the process forward. Sykes was promoted in January 1917 into the War Cabinet Secretariat with responsibility for Middle Eastern affairs. In that month, he began intensive meetings with both Nahum Sokolow and Chaim Weizmann.

In March 1917, in a meeting with Balfour, Weizmann observed that it was 'the first time [that he] had a real business talk with him'.[43] Contrary to an earlier prediction by Balfour, the French began to be less enthusiastic about a British Palestine; a similarly cold reception was also given in Rome where the Vatican voiced its own qualms. Nahum Sokolow was now recruited by Sykes to be part of the negotiations with the French and 'educate' them about Zionism. He was a persuasive person apparently, and did the job. He also convinced Pope Benedict XV in May 1917 to endorse this vision (helped by growing support for Zionism within the Italian Jewish community). The next stop was America, but I will leave the tale of lobbying for the Balfour Declaration and Zionism on the other side of the Atlantic for chapter 5.[44]

In June 1917, the lobbyists for Zionism and all the senior British policy makers began drafting what became known as the Balfour Declaration. The initial draft was prepared by leading Anglo-Zionists.

A parallel document drafted by the Foreign Office was consigned to the dustbin of history as it did not satisfy the Zionist movement.[45] On the 17th of that month and parallel to these final efforts, the Anglo-Jewish Board of Deputies was transformed into an advocacy group supporting the Zionist initiatives in Britain. On that date, under pressure from the *Jewish Chronicle*, a vote was taken in the joint committee of the Board and the Anglo-Jewish Committee. Sixty-one members voted in favour of the Zionist project in Palestine, fifty-six voted against and six abstained. The president of the Board, David Lindo Alexander, resigned, and the elder brother of Herbert Samuel replaced him. In many ways he should have been the recipient of Balfour's famous letter, both as the president of the Board and also as a pro-Zionist. But someone, speculated to be either Weizmann or Herbert Samuel, felt that the Board was still too divided about Zionism for the letter to be assured of a warm reception. And so Rothschild is the addressee of the letter, so convinced of Zionism that he wrote to *The Times* to complain about the Conjoint Foreign Committee's anti-Zionist statement.

On 31 October 1917, the War Cabinet finally approved the Zionist drafting of the Declaration, and it was announced a few days later in the House of Commons. It was an unprecedented diplomatic statement: a promise by the British government to the informal head of the Anglo-Jewish community, to build a homeland for Jews in Palestine. Of course Anglo-Jews like Rothschild had no intention of packing up and emigrating to Palestine.

On Sunday 2 December 1917, a month after the Declaration was handed over to Lord Rothschild and read in the House of Commons, a thanksgiving for the Declaration, led by Lord Rothschild and attended by Herbert Samuel and Chaim Weizmann, among others, was hastily organised at the Royal Opera House. One report even noted an Arab speaker from Palestine, although this does not seem to be corroborated by other sources.

The Declaration was the first tangible success of the lobby. Building a Jewish state in Palestine was now recognised as an imperial British interest. This meant that from the moment Britain gained actual control over Ottoman Palestine, it would help to build the infrastructure for a Jewish state there.

Britain completed the occupation of Palestine in the winter of 1918 and initially imposed military rule until the international community, through the League of Nations, finished its deliberations on how to divide the Ottoman spoils in the Arab world between Britain, France and Italy. By 1920, it became clear that the League and Britain's allies in the Great War consented to Ottoman Palestine becoming a British Mandatory state, in which Britain was free to decide how to run it and how to visualise its future.

In this respect, the Balfour Declaration as a letter was not that important; it only became a crucial factor in the future of Palestine and the Palestinians once it was incorporated into the Mandate charter in 1922. Armed with the new charter, when Herbert Samuel was appointed in 1920 as the first High Commissioner of Palestine, he was able to retain, at least until the end of his term in office, the pro-Zionist orientation of British policy towards Palestine.

4

Lobbying in Britain During the Mandate

WINNING OVER THE LABOUR PARTY IN THE 1920s

Dollis Hill is a huge green lung in north-west London, in the borough of Brent. Once it was located in the middle of the countryside – but now urban sprawl means it's in London's Zone 3, and well-served by the Jubilee Line. By the 1920s, the original Edwardian terraced houses were accompanied by semi-detached houses and a small business centre.

It had made it onto the map a hundred years earlier, when the Finch family consolidated a number of local farms on the eponymous hill into a single estate, and built Dollis Hill House as their residency. Lord Aberdeen bought the house later and hosted William Ewart Gladstone for long periods as his esteemed guest. In his honour, following the prime minister's death in 1896, the estate's parkland became Gladstone Park, a name it still carries today. It is yet another important landmark in the history of the pro-Zionist lobby in Britain.

It was still quite rural in its appearance when a very non-bourgeois group, at least in aspiration, Poale Zion in England (the Workers of Zion in Hebrew), located its headquarters in house number 14, which was one of the neighbourhood's new houses built on Gladstone Park Gardens.

Poale Zion was a Zionist ideological movement that tried to fuse Zionism with socialism, as advocated by its founding ideologue Dov Ber Borochov. He wrote Poale Zion's first programme in 1906, *Our*

Platform, where he presented the class structure of Jewish society as an inverted pyramid. In his analysis, Jews are destined for an anomalous economic position in modern capitalist society, because the Jews, as an immigrant population, are divorced from nature – the 'national material patrimony' which is the precondition for the development of the forces of production. As the Jews have no territory, they accordingly have no peasantry, and moreover, they remain a distinct national group because the majority nation does not allow entry of the Jews into agriculture or other basic industries, in order to safeguard its control of the material territory. Jews can only enter into fields of industry not yet occupied by the majority nation – hence their over-representation in consumer industries like needles and tobacco, and their chronic poverty. This means their position is intrinsically precarious, for the moment the majority nation is capable of entering that industry on its own, the foreign nationality 'is entirely isolated from any possibilities to access on the economy of the land in which it lives'.[1] Palestine would be the future focus of a wave of Jewish immigration by historical necessity, and as the land was a 'semi-agricultural' economy, Jews could move into the basic industries and create the means of production. Like so many ideologues of the socialist Zionists, he assumed there would be no resistance to this process from the native inhabitants of Palestine. Jewish territorial autonomy in Palestine would be the first step to socialism.

This workers' Zionism emerged after the General Jewish Labour Bund, which organised workers across the Russian Empire, came out against Zionism in 1901. Workers in the Pale of Settlement (the boundaries of allowed Jewish residence), stretching over south Russia and parts of Poland, founded societies on the basis that the solution to the plight of Jewish workers lay in a new state. In 1905, it acquired a clear identity when the 'Territorialists' (i.e. those who believed a Jewish state could form in any location, including Uganda) withdrew from the nascent organisation – now Poale Zion consisted purely of those committed to a Jewish Palestine. It was founded as a separate organisation on Purim 1906, in the storeroom of a Jewish bakery in Poltava.

Poale Zion's founders became some of the leading thinkers behind the early Zionist project. Intellectually these pioneers gave birth to the leadership of the Mandatory Zionist movement and later the state of Israel, which included the indisputable leader of the movement and the state, David Ben-Gurion. Later Poale Zion merged with other groups and founded Mapai in 1930, the ruling party in Israel until more or less 1977 (it would appear later with different names, such as the Labour Movement, the Labour Party and Maarach [the alliance] from the mid-1960s). From its establishment, it was led by Ben-Gurion as a socialist Zionist party that gradually deserted socialist values for the sake of building a Jewish nation in Palestine. By the end of the Mandate, its leaders regarded themselves as part of the social democratic world and thus in close affinity with the Labour Party in Britain.

The mixture of Zionism with socialism quickly spread among Jewish activists worldwide. In the same year as the first Warsaw group appeared, a branch of Poale Zion was opened in New York and a year later in London, Leeds and Vienna. In 1907, the Palestine branch of Poale Zion was established. And where Poale Zion did not have a presence, similar Zionist socialist parties were set up by Jewish communities, including in Canada, Ukraine, France and Russia. The French branch of Poale Zion became part of Leon Blum's Popular Front which dominated the left camp in French politics in the interwar period. In the Russian Empire, it grew exponentially, due to widespread fervour following the 1905 Revolution, and the strong existing base of Jewish labour organisations.

Initially, London was hardly the centre of activity for Poale Zion and similar groups. Divided on Uganda as a settlement option, the British branch only reunified after Herzl's death, when Uganda was definitively ruled out of the question. Meetings would take place anywhere from Krakow to Stockholm, but never in England. In 1917, this changed. London transformed into Zionism's centre stage as it became clear that a Jewish Palestine hinged upon British support. The house in London came to life and directed the actions of the pro-Zionist lobby in Britain. The main task of Poale Zion in England was to find a way of working in tandem with the Labour Party and influence its policy towards Palestine.

By 1917, the Zionist movement had two sites of leadership: one in London, led by Chaim Weizmann, and one in Palestine, where

Ben-Gurion emerged as an alternative leader and at times Weizmann's nemesis. Usually they worked in unison for the same goal. Their rivalry concerned who would lead the global Zionist movement, not the movement's objectives.

Even before the Balfour Declaration, the Zionist leadership in Palestine pressured its advocates in Britain to build an alliance with the Labour Party, as it was hoped it had more of an ideological affinity to Zionism, at that time still associated with a strong socialist orientation. The task was entrusted to the British branch of Poale Zion, guided by Poale Zion in Palestine. David Ben-Gurion, who in those years began to position himself as the leader of the Jewish community in Palestine, was personally responsible for co-ordinating the work of this group of young men and women who believed that socialism and Zionism were compatible. For that purpose, he spent much time at the London headquarters, taking direct charge of the campaign.[2]

Poale Zion made a firm alliance with Sidney Webb, the founder of the Fabian Society, and Arthur Henderson, the leader of the Labour Party after the outbreak of the First World War. And with their help, the lobby began to influence Labour's policy towards Palestine more effectively, at least until 1945. A quick browse in the Central Zionist Archives shows that many of the letters sent in the 1920s to the British government and in particular to the Labour Party, attempting to impact Britain's Palestine policy, were headed with the Dollis Hill address, signed by Weizmann or Ben-Gurion.

Although the Zionist colonies in Palestine were growing steadily, it was still difficult to persuade Jews from around the world to go and settle there. Globally, most Jews did not see settling in Palestine as a solution to anti-Semitism. They either hoped for a better future in Europe or cast their eyes farther afield to faraway destinations such as the Americas, China, South Africa and Australia. Similarly, despite the Balfour Declaration, as we have seen, ten years later British policy makers in London and Palestine were also not convinced that Palestine was the obvious and exclusive safe haven for Jews around the world.

However, this unpromising outlook in terms of Jewish emigration to Palestine didn't concern the Zionist lobby in Britain. Their priority was to maintain the support of the British political elite. It was non-partisan in pursuing this, working equally hard to persuade the Labour Party and the Conservative Party to continue their support for the next stages in the colonisation of Palestine.

In this respect, the lobby, and in particular Poale Zion, had some impressive achievements. On 5 February 1920, Poale Zion, now called the Jewish Socialist Labour Party, had its application to affiliate to the Labour Party accepted by the party's Organisation Subcommittee.

From that period, we have an intriguing record of the Poale Zion meeting at which it was decided to pursue affiliation. The meeting was summarised by one of the leaders of the Zionist movement from Palestine, Moshe Sharett (a future foreign minister and prime minister of Israel); his notes reveal the methods deployed by the nominally socialist Zionist lobby at this early stage. Sharett's report shows the group was already involved in elections in various constituencies, helping the Labour candidate, hosting balls (*neshafim* in Hebrew) for potential supporters, fundraising, and participating in local trade union work. Alongside advocacy for Zionism, this was also an opportunity to build financial institutions, such as a bank, and trade in the local stock exchange in an attempt to raise funds for the colonies in Palestine.[3]

The affiliation bore fruit very quickly; in the very same year the group achieved a real coup: the Labour Party Conference voted unanimously in favour of the resolution, 'Palestine for the Jews'. It was proposed by Jacob Pomeranz, the secretary of Poale Zion. The following year, a similar resolution, proposed once again by a Poale Zion delegate, was carried unanimously once more. And when Labour first took office in 1924, the secretary for the colonies, James Henry Thomas, a completely unapologetic imperialist, told the House of Commons that the government had determined 'after careful consideration of all circumstances, to adhere to the policy of giving effect to the Balfour Declaration'. Labour supported the League of Nations' Mandate that gave Britain control of Palestine and was wholeheartedly committed to the establishment of 'a Jewish autonomous Commonwealth' in the country.[4] The wishes of the Arab population, both Muslim and Christian, counted for nothing. There was to be no self-determination for the

Palestinian people. But the Palestinians began to make their voices heard, even if they were ignored in London.

PALESTINE RESISTS

On the first anniversary of the Balfour Declaration, Palestinians demonstrated in large numbers all over Palestine against it. From that moment onwards, a consolidated Palestinian national movement led by a younger generation of urban professionals and intellectuals, alongside traditional heads of rural and urban clans, commenced an anti-colonialist struggle. For nine years, 1920–1929, their activity consisted of petitions, and participation in negotiations with the British government, while building a democratic political structure, where parties could elect their representatives to an annual national conference. The consensual position was clear: total rejection of the Balfour Declaration, and opposition to Jewish emigration to Palestine, the Zionist purchase of land and colonisation. They demanded that Britain adhere to twin principles, on the basis of which the West had promised to build a new world after the First World War. The first was democracy and the second was the right of self-determination. The Palestinian leaders felt that while these principles were respected in Palestine's neighbouring countries, such as Lebanon, Syria and Egypt, they were not implemented in Palestine.

Matters came to a head in April 1920 in Palestine – following several provocations on the part of the British government and the Zionists, including the dismissal of the Palestinian mayor of Jerusalem and the installation of a Zionist deputy mayor. On 4 April, Palestinians congregating for the Nabi Musa festival started rioting and ransacked the Jewish quarter of Jerusalem. In 1921, there were riots in Jaffa and Petah Tikva, driven by the widespread feeling that the British administration prioritised Zionist interests over the interests of all Palestinian inhabitants.

An uneasy peace followed for a few years until violence erupted again in 1929, triggered by a large Zionist demonstration at the site of the Western Wall – where the Prophet Muhammad tied up his mythological steed Al-Buraq before he ascended to Paradise in the Muslim tradition, and the wall of the Temple in the Jewish tradition. Palestinian Muslims retaliated and by late August 1929, there were confrontations across Palestine, including Jerusalem, Safed and Hebron.

But this uprising wasn't just about a holy site. More than a decade after British rule began in Palestine, local society could feel the negative impact of the Zionisation of the country: workers were driven out of the labour market and farmers were evicted or forced to emigrate to towns where makeshift slums began to appear. They either lost their land when it was sold by their landlords to the Zionist movement or had to seek a new future due to poverty in the countryside, caused both by Zionist settlements there and by British disinclination to invest in rural areas. About 8,000 Palestinians were evicted in these early stages and thirteen villages were depopulated.[5]

The eruption of violence on a large scale in Palestine in 1929 led to a rethink in London about British policy towards the country. The land without people, which was how Palestine was perceived by Zionist leaders and those supporting the colonisation of Palestine, turned out to be full of people who categorically rejected the transformation of their homeland into a Jewish state and were even willing to engage in an armed struggle against the endeavour. It was now much more difficult to lobby for a transfer of Jews from Europe to a Palestine that increasingly proved to be resistant to the idea that the 'Jewish problem' of Europe would be solved at its expense.

The rethink was informed by a royal commission of inquiry headed by Lord Shaw, which in 1930 recommended severe limitation on Jewish immigration and an end to Zionist purchase of lands, and suggested that Britain would help build a state that respected the Palestinian majority in the land. This was a total U-turn from the Balfour Declaration and it became a White Paper, authored by Sidney Webb, now secretary of state for the colonies. Another inquiry, the Hope-Simpson commission, also affirmed its support for a reorientation of British policy in Palestine.

The lobby faced its first serious challenge to its work in Britain; and yet surprisingly it took it only one month to reverse the reversal! Within that month, the prime minister, Ramsay MacDonald, clarified in the

House of Commons that the paper did not mean withdrawal from the Balfour commitment, and, more importantly, repeated this commitment in a letter to Chaim Weizmann – but also stated clearly that it did not annul the White Paper. Both the Zionists and the Palestinians, however, interpreted it as a reversal of the paper, which is probably more significant.

This swift retraction puzzles scholars to this very day and some scholars, such as Carly Beckerman-Boys, claim the reversal had nothing to do with Zionist lobbying and much more with the fact that it would have been too expensive to change course and invest in building a proper Palestinian state in the future.[6] This consideration might have played a role, but there is also clear evidence, as several scholars have clearly shown, that Weizmann was intransigent in exerting pressure on the British government.[7] One person in particular was willing to heed Weizmann's call for action against Webb (now Lord Passfield) and the government's new policy, and this was the former prime minister Lloyd George, who helped in the campaign, and was rewarded by an invitation to be a keynote speaker at one of London's most prestigious venues: the Savoy Hotel.

THE SAVOY HOTEL, 1931: THE EMPTY LAND REVOLTS

One good reason to have a lobby meeting, for any group, in the London Savoy in 1931 would have been the head chef, François Latry, who had upped the culinary ante of the luxurious hotel since his appointment in 1919. Latry revelled in extravagance: his creations included crayfish stuffed with foie gras and braised turbot in very expensive vintage burgundy.

When the members of the English Zionist Federation came to meet the former prime minister Lloyd George in the hotel ballroom in 1931, the Savoy represented the pinnacle of opulence – it was the very first hotel with amenities like air-conditioning, telephones and twenty-four-hour room service.

It's no accident that the English Zionist Federation chose to host Lloyd George there; it was an overt demonstration of power. After a sumptuous meal, the former prime minister delivered the keynote speech of the evening. Extracts from the speech were screened later on the Pathé newsreel. He was visibly moved not just by the honour of being invited to address the Federation but by a much more permanent tribute bestowed upon him by the Zionist movement:

> Words can hardly express the gratitude I feel to you for the enduring honour you have conferred upon me by attaching my name to a colony in the Vale of Jezreel.[8]

This was the colony of Ramat David in Marj ibn Amir, which the Zionist movement renamed the Jezreel Valley. The kibbutz was built on land bought in 1926 from an absentee landlord in Beirut, the Sursuq family, and the tenants (from the village of Ma'alul that was later destroyed in 1948) living there for centuries were evicted to make way for the new settlers. This was the first substantial act of Zionist ethnic cleansing under the Mandate. Lloyd George opened his speech by boasting deep and detailed knowledge of the Jezreel Valley and Canaan, as he called Palestine, which of course he had never visited.

It is not surprising that Lloyd George referred to Palestine as Canaan. He was raised in a pious environment, brought up in the Church of Christ, one of several denominations that emerged from the Restoration movement in America. It was distinguished by its refusal to permit musical instruments in religious services and its insistence that there were no Christian doctrines outside what was written in the Bible. In his memoirs he claimed that as a grown-up he outgrew these early religious convictions, but from 1917 onward, his language remained laden with biblical allusions. Upon hearing of the British invasion into Ottoman Palestine, he remarked: 'we have entered the land of the Philistines … that is very interesting. I hope we shall conquer the Philistines.'[9] From there it was easy to deduce that the Jews should replace the Philistines, namely the Palestinians. The Jews, in his eyes, were not members of a religion but of a nation defined by the Bible.

The speech was a brilliant summation of Lloyd George's role in bringing about the Balfour Declaration. He proudly told the audience how he secured the Declaration after the First World War ended, as he presided over the councils of the Imperial Cabinet which:

> gave expression to that policy, and secured for it the sanction of our allies ... I was the principal delegate of the British Empire at San Remo where the Mandate for Palestine received its final shape and was conferred upon Britain.

He took care not to claim all the credit, sharing it with Herbert Samuel:

> I had the privilege on behalf of the British Empire, of offering to another distinguished Jew the position of the first *Hebrew Governor of Jerusalem* for over 2,000 years, and worthily did he fulfil the expectations which were formed of him on his appointment.[10]

The speech also exposed how much Lloyd George internalised the Zionist mythology of 'the land without a people':

> Few countries have ever been so badly let down. As the result of centuries of strife, neglect and misrule a land of great natural fecundity had been reduced, as to the greatest part of it, to a stony and swampy wilderness.

In fact, it was a particularly harsh version of that myth:

> A land of great natural beauty had been stripped of its verdure, starved and left bare and haggard to the eye. It was not a home for any people, but a ruin; at best it was a site for a home.[11]

Lloyd George castigated Lord Passfield's actions and policies. He stressed that he saw no need for any curbs on Zionist colonisation, as it helped everyone in the land to thrive and prosper. And no less importantly:

The Jews surely have a special claim on Canaan. They are the only people who have made a success of it during the past 3,000 years.

Such a full-fledged unequivocal commitment would become a benchmark for the future. Anyone who did not fully endorse this narrative would not be considered a friend of Zionism, or later of Israel. This would become painfully clear in the way Zionist leaders treated former allies when they were unable to recruit them to work against the British government in the final days of the Mandate.

After this stirring speech by Lloyd George, Chaim Weizmann followed, sharing his recollections of how they first met and heaping praise on the former prime minister for being won over to the Zionist vision. He presented a rose-tinted description of the first meeting between the two men, but it suited the celebratory atmosphere of the meeting: having the most senior Liberal politician take the side of Zionism was no small achievement. The next step was to secure support from the two other political forces in the country: the Labour and Conservative parties; it became clear that the Palestinian resistance would intensify and with it British doubts about the Palestine policy could recur. In order to expand the network of support for Zionism, the lobby also had to deepen its influence among British trade unions, as well as leading politicians such as Lloyd George.

THE LOBBY, ZIONISM, MARXISM AND SOCIALISM, 1930–1948

As the Labour Party solidified its commitment to Zionism in policy terms, Poale Zion gained new influential advocates in the party, like Ernest Bevin, then general secretary of the Transport and General Workers' Union (TGWU) – although largely out of pragmatism. His support was due to the efforts of a special emissary from Palestine, Dov Hoz, who arrived in 1928, in order to expand the network of Poale Zion to reach everyone influential in the labour movement and the party itself. Hoz convinced Bevin that in order to win a by-election in Whitechapel, the Labour parliamentary candidate, chosen by the TGWU, needed to support Zionism and oppose the Labour government's own White Paper proposing to limit Jewish immigration to Palestine. With one eye on the votes needed to keep the seat, Bevin promised that all MPs backed by the TGWU would oppose the White Paper. Labour won, and the alliance was cemented: Bevin spoke at the farewell party for Hoz when the latter's mission was completed in 1931.[12]

It was to prove a brief departure. Hoz had to return to London in 1934, after Moshe Sharett, then head of the Political Department of the Jewish Agency, was worried that the lobby was not working properly. He complained that the Zionist Executive, the directorship of the World Zionist Organization that Herzl founded in Basel in 1897, had lost contact with public opinion and influential figures in Britain, and had neglected its ties with the new generation of leaders who had emerged in the Labour Party. With the emergence of a Zionist leadership in Palestine, represented by the Jewish Agency, the two bodies – the Jewish Agency in Palestine and the World Zionist Organization seated in London – had parallel assignments and missions, not always clearly defined. Broadly speaking, the Jewish Agency took charge of the affairs of the Jewish community in Palestine and the World Zionist Organization had responsibility for lobbying for Zionism throughout the world. However, the lobbying mission was also entrusted to the Political Department of the Jewish Agency; Dov Hoz felt that this duplication weakened the effectiveness of the lobby.

Nevertheless, the Labour Party was successfully courted by the pro-Zionist lobby between 1920 and 1945. In other words, Zionist socialism seemed to be a legitimate ideology in the eyes of many British socialists and particular Anglo-Jewish socialists. However, the equation of both ideologies was not accepted by everyone. Poale Zion in Manchester began their history as more of a socialist group than a Zionist group and part of other radical and anarchist formations, fighting for workers' rights and identifying themselves as communists. In the 1920s, it was quite brave to openly be a Jewish communist, compared to the comfortable position of being defined as a Jewish Zionist. Identifying Jews with Communism was the bread and butter of anti-Semites all over Europe

– Adolf Hitler claimed that the Jews were responsible for the Bolshevik Revolution, while Goebbels asserted that the Jews invented Marxism.

In Britain, Zionism was considered by some of its supporters as a healthy antidote to Bolshevism. This position was articulated plainly by Winston Churchill in an article he wrote in 1920, entitled 'Zionism versus Bolshevism: A Struggle for the Soul of the Jewish People'. The Jews for Churchill were a 'mystic and mysterious race ... both divine and diabolical'. The diabolical ones were the Bolsheviks, who were also depicted as sinister individuals and terrorists, and whether they were British or leading the revolution in Russia, they were cut from the same cloth. Thus, in his mind, Zionism was the cure for this diabolical Judaism. Churchill called upon the Jews who had not become Zionists, whom he defined as 'national Jews', to join forces with the Zionists against the 'Bolsheviks'. Moreover, he wrote: 'a Jewish state under the protection of the British crown' would thwart the Bolshevik threat both for the Jewish people and for Britain.[13]

For a while members of Poale Zion in places such as Manchester dwelled in the liminal space between Zionism and Marxism; but eventually the majority of the members of this branch made a final choice and preferred Zionist colonisation to world revolution.[14] Nonetheless, a sizeable number made their way to the Communist Party, as illustrated by the most famous individual transition of this kind by Ben Ainley,[15] and later by Tony Cliff's even more famous journey from Zionism to Communism. Communism, with its active propaganda against Nazism and Fascism, seemed a more urgent cause than colonising a land that most young Jews in Britain had never set foot in. In part, the threat of Communism prompted Zionist leaders to emphasise the compatibility of Marxism and Zionism and even to go as far as depicting Zionism as the major drive against feudal exploitation in the Arab world in general and in Palestine in particular.

The admixture of Marxism and Zionism did not appeal to the liberal Zionist leader of the world movement, Chaim Weizmann, but he recognised its utility in appealing to the Jewish working class. For a while Weizmann joined a culture group active in the working-class East End, led by one of the most important members of Poale Zion, Kalman

Marmor, then a chemistry teacher in London. But Weizmann never warmed to socialist Zionism. He ridiculed the new movement's statements as 'meaningless phrases and sheer stupidity'.[16] After the First World War, middle-class Zionists like Weizmann would understand that diplomacy was vital. In the 1920s, Jewish workers remained the only demographic willing to emigrate to Palestine and construct a new nation. These 'socialist' Zionists were ready to build Jewish settlements in Palestine – and they weren't too concerned about them being socialist ones. Zionists of every political stripe were now united in being part of a project of settler colonialism in Palestine, which began expanding significantly on the ground through increasing ethnic cleansing projects in the east and inner plains of Palestine, by the purchase of land from absentee or local landlords. The villages that existed on these lands for centuries were seen as a minor obstacle at best. This affected at least eight villages and eight thousand Palestinians in Wadi al-Hawarith and Marj Ibn Amir.[17]

At the same time as Zionism was making enthusiastic efforts to overcome the historic hostilities of working-class Jews to the project, European socialist parties began to reappraise their attitude to Zionism. Until 1914, the socialist Second International took an assimilationist perspective on the Jewish question – Jews were part of the working class, who perhaps spoke a different language and had distinct customs, but were not a nation in their own right. The right of nations to self-determination, a popular formula in response to national oppression under the Tsarist and Austro-Hungarian Empires, did not apply to them. When Poale Zion and two other territorialist Jewish parties sought recognition at the Stuttgart Congress in 1907, the decision was delegated to the Russian section: the Russian Social Democrats promptly rejected their application. But once the First World War broke out, major socialist parties experienced a change of heart, dropping their commitments to internationalism. This went hand in hand with a reconsideration of Zionism – in 1919 the recently reconstituted Socialist International's steering committee passed a resolution sponsored by Poale Zion recognising the right of Jewish people to a national life in historical Palestine. The old hostility to Zionism was left as the preserve of the new Communist International. When a left-wing offshoot of Poale Zion, the Socialist Workers Party in Palestine, sought to affiliate with the Comintern, its application was rejected on account of its refusal to denounce Jewish immigration into Palestine.

Socialists, by contrast, had made their peace with colonialism. After the war, the European socialist movements proved to be as colonialist in their approach as were their governments and rulers.[18] As a contemporary observer noted of the parties at the forefront of the Brussels Congress in 1928:

> The Labour party of England, and the socialists of France, Holland, and Belgium, are against policies which would seriously disturb the basic relations of their home countries with their colonial dependencies.[19]

And so European socialists didn't simply gloss over the colonialist aspect of the Zionist project; they lauded it as a way of bringing superior civilisation to the Arabs. As Labour leader Ramsay MacDonald claimed, 'the Arab population do not and cannot use or develop the resources of Palestine.'[20] Only the Communists maintained that Zionism was 'the expression of the exploiting and great power oppressive strivings of the Jewish bourgeoisie, which makes use of the Jewish national minorities in Eastern Europe for the purpose of imperialist policy to insure its domination.'[21]

Zionist actions on the ground were colonialist to the bone, but under the guidance of Weizmann, Zionist diplomacy made a conscious effort to portray the settlements and the purchase of land as the authentic fulfilment of both socialism and rightful Jewish nationalism. He understood that during the First World War, Herzl's discourse about the Jewish colonisation of Palestine was no longer palatable to an international audience. He and other leaders gradually abandoned the early vocabulary of the founding fathers of the movement: phrases like 'Jewish Colonies', 'Jewish Colonisation' and 'Jewish Colonialism' no longer appeared in their speeches or writings. They now emphasised the plight of Jewish workers, the socialist society that pioneer settlements were building, and the necessity of economic development in Palestine:

music to the European socialist movement's ears. But Labour Party support didn't satisfy them. To ensure the future of Zionism, regardless of the composition of the British government, they needed to enlist the support of the other major political party in Britain, the Conservatives.[22]

COURTING THE CONSERVATIVE PARTY

While efforts in the 1920s were focused on the Labour Party, the lobby did not pay much attention to the Conservative Party that was in power for many periods during the time of the Mandate. The main reason for this seeming neglect was that during the 1920s, at least until the outbreak of violence in 1929, Palestine experienced relatively 'quiet years' and thus British policy, be it Conservative, Liberal or Labour, was quite solid and consistent.

Moreover, at that time there was a small group within the Conservative Party, which we can describe as 'Conservative Zionists', that operated during the interwar years, including Winston Churchill and Victor Cazalet. However, the party's attitude to Zionism was not uniform. There were some, such as Colonel Claude Lowther, MP for Lonsdale, who displayed open disdain towards Zionism, tinged with anti-Semitism. In the House he asked sardonically: 'Since when has Palestine become a new home for the Jews, and is not this a great blow to Brighton?'[23]

And yet those members who did support Zionism were important figures in British society. The Cazalets were a case in point in this respect. Edward Cazalet had already promoted the 'return' of the Jews to Palestine in the 1870s, and his son Victor Alexander chaired the House of Commons' Palestine Committee, a committee dedicated to a Zionist Palestine, where he advocated strongly for a Jewish state in Palestine. He was a close friend of Balfour and Weizmann. He went as far as saying during the Second World War, a week before his death in a plane crash:

> I would gladly give my life for the establishment of a Jewish state in Palestine, as I am ready to give my life for the preservation of the

British Empire … Whatever happens, the Jews *must* have a permanent home.[24]

Another important Conservative Zionist was Leopold Charles Maurice
Stennett Amery (1873–1955). He was a journalist and a Cabinet minister, both in the 1920s and in the Churchill war ministry. He helped to
draft the Balfour Declaration and encouraged Jabotinsky to form a
Jewish Legion that would participate in the occupation of Palestine. As
colonial secretary, he pushed for the creation of white-dominated colonies, including in Palestine; a proposal that was removed from the political agenda by the outbreak of the first significant Palestinian revolt
against the pro-Zionist British policy in Palestine in 1929.[25]

Zionism was packaged as a successful socialist enterprise in barren
Arab lands for the Labour Party, and as a paragon of constitutional
democracy for the Conservative Party – a tidy solution to the European
'Jewish question' that dovetailed neatly with British imperial interests. It
would all have worked well had it not been for the fact that the indigenous population of Palestine cared very little if the settlers were liberals
or socialists, or whether the person pressing the boot against their face
clutched the Bible or *Das Kapital*. And they rebelled against the attempt
to turn their homeland into a Zionist haven, posing serious challenges
to the pro-Zionist lobby in Britain. But early on, and before 1948, the
Palestinians were not engaged in any kind of advocacy that could match
the ever-growing pro-Zionist lobby in both Britain and the USA.

THE PALESTINIANS CONTINUE TO RESIST

One fine April day in 1930, two old ladies were anxiously watching the
trains coming into Victoria Station. One of them was holding a flag that
none of the travellers in the station could have recognised: the flag
of the Sharif of Mecca's small army that fought alongside Britain during
the First World War, led by the legendary T.E. Lawrence, who hoped
that Britain would grant the Sharif's family, the Hashemites, a fair share
in the spoils of the defeated Ottoman Empire. They were waiting for
Hajj Amin al-Husayni, the Mufti of Jerusalem and the President of the

Supreme Muslim Council, acting as the informal leader of the Palestinian community, on his visit to London to discuss the future of Palestine with the British government.

The rather humble welcome party attested to the weakness of the pro-Palestinian lobby in London at the time. They took their guest to the Café Royal near Piccadilly Circus and waited for several hours for an interview at the Colonial Office to discuss the British policy in Palestine. His visit coincided with that of another important guest from Palestine, the president of the Jewish Agency, Chaim Weizmann, who was received by an official delegation and was immediately granted interviews with practically anyone he liked in government before ending the day at the Zionist headquarters.

The Palestinians had nothing equivalent to the Zionist lobby and their leadership had no idea what a powerful enemy they were facing. However, the Palestinians didn't need to lobby in London and Europe to cause the Zionists serious problems. What mattered were their actions on the ground.

British attempts before 1929 and after to bring the two sides to some sort of agreement all failed miserably. Further Zionisation of parts of Palestine, and British crackdowns on any attempt to build a Palestinian national movement, led to an even a bigger revolt than the one in 1929; namely, the Arab Revolt, which erupted in 1936.

In April 1936, Palestinians began to demonstrate en masse against what they deemed was a pro-Zionist policy of the Mandatory government; the British responded with arrests of most Palestinian leaders, while the informal head of Palestinian society, Hajj Amin al-Husayni, manged to escape before he was arrested.

The wave of arrests triggered guerrilla warfare, very much inspired by the activities of a Syrian preacher called Izz ad-Din al-Qassam, who arrived in Haifa after taking part in a Syrian rebellion against the French mandate. In the name of Islam, he encouraged a large number of Palestinians who had lost their jobs and farms as a result of the increase in Zionist settlements and Zionist takeovers of the labour market in the towns, to take part in armed struggle against Britain and the Zionist movement. He was killed by the British army in 1935, but his call for an armed struggle was heeded by many, leading to widespread guerrilla attacks on British installations and personnel.

The British responded with a ruthless repertoire of collective punishments: demolition of houses, closures of whole communities, destruction of parts of villages and cities, arrests and executions. Eventually, the government needed to use the RAF to quell the revolt, which it finally succeeded in doing at the beginning of 1939.

Although officially Britain pursued a brutal policy of repression against the Palestinian revolt of 1936 that lasted for three years, the revolt's intensity and perseverance caused a number of British policy makers to retreat from their early support for the Zionist project. A few of the 'gentile Zionists' showed signs of disenchantment with the project which they had fully supported in the past, after they visited Palestine and realised that the reality there differed from the image that had been sold to them.

From the outburst of the first wave of violence in April 1920 up to the eruption of the Arab Revolt in April 1936, it became clear to British policy makers that building a Jewish state in Palestine was bringing Britain into conflict not just with Palestinians, but with the Arab world as a whole.

During the three years of the Arab Revolt, British policy at first was still loyal at least in principle to the Zionist project, but by 1939, policy makers became outwardly hostile towards the project.

In August 1936, the British government dispatched a commission of inquiry chaired by Robert Peel, a former secretary of state for India and a judge, assigned with the mission of trying to find a solution to the ongoing conflict. In July 1937 his commission suggested partitioning Palestine into a Jewish state, constituting roughly seventeen per cent of Palestine, and an Arab entity that would be annexed to Transjordan, while the airports, ports and holy places would be under British rule. Until then, Peel and his colleagues suggested severe limitations on further Zionist purchase of land and immigration.

The Peel Commission, taking stock of the situation at a comparatively early stage of the Arab Revolt (the end of its first year), was regarded by most Zionist leaders on the ground as reasonable: articulating support for a future state, indicating a willingness to discuss transferring the population, proposing the annexation of the 'Arab parts' of Palestine by the Hashemites in Transjordan and all in all expressing a strong anti-Palestinian-nationalist position and a preference for the 'good Arabs' (in the eyes of both the British and the Zionist movement). This report deviated from the line adopted by previous commissions of inquiry and turned out to be the exception that proves the rule. Within two years, a new commission that was asked to translate the report into more practical guidelines, the Woodhead Commission, re-orientated British policy in the opposite direction. The new commission advocated a harsher attitude towards the Zionist project in Palestine and attempted to take into account the aspirations of the native Palestinians.

Following the Woodhead Commission's recommendations, the visionary parts of the Peel Commission report were for the time being discarded by the British government, but its recommendations for the short term, namely severe limitation on Jewish immigration and Zionist purchase of land, were endorsed by the government in a 1939 White Paper.

In this White Paper, the new policy was now clearly charted by Malcolm MacDonald, the secretary of state for the colonies; it was presented to the House of Commons in May 1939 and obtained its approval. The paper called for the establishment of a binational state in Palestine within ten years, limited the quota for future Jewish immigration and restricted the purchase of land. It further re-interpreted the Balfour Declaration not as a commitment to transforming Palestine into a Jewish state but merely declaring the desirability of a Jewish homeland within a future state. While the Zionist leadership saw the White Paper as the annulment of the Balfour Declaration, the British government saw it as a clarification of the Declaration.

The Zionist leadership in Palestine reacted furiously. The White Paper was decried by the local Hebrew press as the 'Black Paper', the 'Paper of Deceit', and many other choice epithets. The lobby was now called into action again, facing one of its most difficult periods during the British Mandate. The lobby pinned its hopes on Chaim Weizmann to come to its rescue once more. After all, he was credited with annulling the 1930 White Paper. He began to work more intensively in London (gradually ceding the leadership of the community in Palestine to the determined and ruthless Ben-Gurion who was working on the ground there). Weizmann was assisted in his endeavour to bring about a U-turn in British policy by the *Guardian* journalist Harry Sacher, and business-men Simon Marks and Israel Sieff, who later ran the quintessential British clothing retailer Marks & Spencer. They and others who formed an entourage around Weizmann moved the centre of lobbying from the house in Gladstone Park Gardens on the periphery of London to a more central place in the West End on Great Russell Street.

'77': THE GREAT RUSSELL STREET LOBBY HQ

If you stroll along Great Russell Street next to the British Museum, on the corner of Bloomsbury Street, you will pass by no. 77, named Bloomsbury House. You will notice the blue plaque stating that the architect Thomas Henry Wyatt (1807–1880) lived and died here. Today it is an office building and its illustrious former tenants include the head office of the publishing house Faber & Faber. But before that it was the headquarters of the Zionist lobby in Britain, from 1920 to 1965.

It had three floors and was identical to the other buildings in this row of Victorian housing. The English Zionist Federation moved into the building in 1920 and was then joined by the Jewish Agency, the body permitted by the Mandate to serve as the 'government' of the Jewish community in Palestine. Two other important Zionist organisa-tions were based there as well: the World Zionist Congress and the Jewish National Fund. This cohabitation created confusion between bodies running the affairs of the Jewish community in Palestine and those lobbying for Zionism in Britain:

> It was sometimes difficult to discern where the one [meeting of one
> of the three bodies] began and the other ended. Officials intermin-
> gled; meetings were often held jointly.[26]

Despite the number of influential organisations housed there, the envir-onment was hardly glamorous. The rooms had little light in them, and it lacked proper sanitation facilities, according to the recollections of Abba Eban, a senior member of the political department of the Jewish Agency and a future minister of foreign affairs in Israel.[27]

From its headquarters on Great Russell Street, the lobby – now integrated properly into the political structure of Zionism on the ground in Palestine – was first asked to help raise funds to sustain the colonisation of Palestine. In 1938, in a memorandum sent to the Evian Conference on Jewish refugees, born out of the visible disaster Nazi Germany began to inflict on the Jews of Europe, the Zionist leadership tried to direct some of the funding offered to solve the new problem of Jewish refugees in Europe towards the settlement of Jews in Palestine, in the process exposing the important role the Anglo-Jewish community played in building the infrastructure for further colonisation. Between 1920 and 1938, the office in London was able to raise about £14 million and opened a special bank for that enterprise: the Anglo-Palestine Bank.[28]

The main body for lobbying and raising money in the interwar years was the Jewish National Fund. It upgraded the work of the lobby to a new level. It also offered a more professional approach to lobbying. Here is how one of its main publications advised activists on how to lobby efficiently in the modern era:

> Commercial propaganda essentially aspires to achieve the same goal we are trying to achieve, and that is to arouse as many people as possible for a known purpose to do something they would not have done without the propaganda.[29]

They aimed for Zionism to become ubiquitous and inescapable:

> We must inundate the Jewish people with slogans and pictures, to rivet their attention, to create an atmosphere of unrest ... in every place a Jew sets foot in: in communal centres, lodges, places of business, society and union centres, the offices of charity organizations, mutual aid societies, rabbinical offices, libraries, theatres, bath houses and rest houses, shelters, hospitals, pharmacies, clinics, synagogues, seminaries, schools, doctor's waiting rooms, restaurants,

hotels, pensions … leave no place where there is no illustrated poster with a clear and brief text.

As noted, lobbying was carried out by two Zionist bodies which did not always work in tandem. The Jewish Agency, under David Ben-Gurion, dispatched Dov Hoz once more to try and recruit Labour to fight against the shift in British policy (he passed away by the end of 1940). The World Zionist Organization had its own representative in London, Berl Locker, who worked closely with Chaim Weizmann in trying to divert Britain from its policy of restricting Jewish immigration and purchase of land.[30] Weizmann also tried to use his connection to the local Anglo-Jewish aristocracy to help in this respect, and this is where Blanche Elizabeth Campbell Dugdale comes into the picture, the niece of Lord Balfour. As we've seen, lobbying is built and sustained by both individuals and institutions, and in some cases individuals can play a decisive role due to their personal political influence, even if they have no official institutional affiliation. 'Baffy', as she was known to her friends, was one such person.

'BAFFY': THE SAVIOUR WHO DID NOT DELIVER

Uncertainty about the British policy in Palestine meant that the Zionist lobby had to expend more effort. This enhanced effort was spearheaded by two of the chief lobbyists of the late 1930s: Blanche Elizabeth Campbell Dugdale and her desperate aspiring lover Walter Elliot. They attempted to synchronise their endeavour to change British policy on Palestine in no other place than the Savoy Hotel.

Baffy was a writer whom Chaim Weizmann called 'an ardent, life-long friend of Zionism'.[31] Her attempts at a writing career culminated in a two-volume biography of her uncle, Arthur Balfour. Her day job consisted of roles in naval intelligence and in the League of Nations. Walter Elliot (1888–1958) was a Scottish politician of the Unionist persuasion, who served both as a member of Parliament and as a Cabinet minister in various governments. He was a decorated hero of the First World War, leaving the army with the rank of colonel. Later in life he was the Rector of the University of Aberdeen and then of the University of Glasgow.

They met regularly at the Savoy for Zionism and light flirting. They were called to act when the Peel Commission returned from Palestine and was about to publish its conclusions in a special report. The lobby was apprehensive about what this report would entail. After all, the commissions of inquiry that London dispatched to Palestine all came back with similar concerns, warning against the disastrous impact Zionism had on the local Palestinian community, and recommending, with different degrees of conviction, a U-turn in British policy towards Palestine.

At midnight before the publication of the Peel Commission report in 1937, Elliot showed Baffy the first draft of the recommendations that were appended to the report, several hours before anyone else saw it. Some authors such as Nick Reynolds believe that Elliot leaked this document more because of his love for Baffy than out of devotion to Zionism, and therefore was not a spy but rather someone who 'sailed close to the wind'.[32]

The romantic/political meeting took place at the Grill Room of the Savoy.[33] To Baffy's disappointment, after she passed the documents to the Jewish Agency, the Agency responded the next day that it could live with these recommendations and thanked the two loyal lobbyists for the advance warning. Baffy's diary tells us that she was more critical of the report and hoped that with her connections she could water down the parts of the report that were less favourable to Zionism. But it seemed unnecessary given that David Ben-Gurion responded positively to the report.

But when the Woodhead report's recommendations were publicised as the 1939 White Paper, Baffy and Elliot were called once more to action. Alongside others in Great Russell Street, at first they were quite sanguine about their chances of influencing British policy. The success of the lobby in annulling the 1930 White Paper gave the Zionist lobbyists confidence they could do it again. But British policy did not change until the end of the Mandate. Once the clouds of war began to appear on the European continent, Britain became painfully aware of the need to build alliances in the Arab world, whether genuinely or cynically – and the Arab world demanded a less pro-Zionist policy in Palestine.

Baffy and Elliot were helpless and could not change British policy. Faced with a new European war, Palestine slid down the priority list. But nonetheless the lobby set Baffy and Elliot some small tasks. One of them was to try and help the Jewish Agency to persuade the British government to support the establishment of a Jewish brigade in 1941 that would fight alongside the Allies and gain experience as a military force. At first, it seemed the government was amenable, and Elliot wrote that this decision was 'Weizmann's greatest achievement since the Balfour Declaration'.[34] But by November that year, the British government reversed its decision. This failure signalled the demise of Weizmann as a central figure in the Zionist project.

Walter Elliot continued to be an important member of the lobby after Israel was established in May 1948. He was asked to help push for British recognition of the Jewish state (Britain was slow in recognising Israel *de jure* and only accorded it *de facto* recognition). His main contacts, however, were with the Conservative Party and not with Labour, which was in power until 1951. In July 1948, he tried to recruit Winston Churchill for such a mission, but Churchill seemed to be fed up with the whole issue and defined the Anglo-Israeli relationship as such a 'hell-disaster that I cannot take it up again or renew my efforts of twenty years'.[35]

A NEW ROLE FOR THE ANGLO-JEWISH COMMUNITY

As we've seen, the various Zionist agencies were somewhat porous – without defined boundaries. By 1938, the project's leaders decided to establish a clearer hierarchy: the Zionist leadership in Palestine would strategise and the lobby in London would help to implement that strategy. For years, the Anglo-Jews who were part of the '77' headquarters believed erroneously that they were also part of the Zionist leadership and therefore had a say in strategising for the future of the Jewish community in Palestine. It took some time for notable leaders of the Anglo-Jewish community, who had devoted their lives to Zionism, to adjust to the reality that they were now relegated to the margins of the project, as mere propagandists for Zionism in Britain.

On 18 May 1938, in an afternoon meeting at 77 Great Russell Street, the penny dropped. It was during a meeting of the advisory political committee of the World Zionist Organization, the body representing the Anglo-Jewish community in running the Zionist project. The most loyal heads of the Anglo-Jewish community took part in this meeting; these people had committed their energy and wealth to the Zionist cause. But now they found themselves demoted to clerks in a newly formed lobby office. The chair was Lord Reading, who was, as we've seen, one of the most influential Jews in Britain.

It is interesting to look in closer detail at two of the Anglo-Jewish leaders. The first is Leonard Stein, born in Manchester and educated in Oxford. He was the ultimate Anglo-Zionist devotee upon whom the Zionist leadership in Palestine could rely. He was the political secretary of the World Zionist Organization (1920–1929) and legal adviser to the Jewish Agency (1929–1939). As his role in the lobby came to a close in 1939, Stein returned to being more active in purely Anglo-Jewish affairs.

The second is Osmond D'Avigdor Goldsmid, born in 1877, the scion of the Goldsmid baronetcy – the first Jewish family in England to enjoy hereditary titles. He was educated at Trinity College in Cambridge and had a pre-war career in finance. He was involved with the lobby from its very early days. He began with a very active role in organising the Jewish Colonization Association (JCA), founded in 1891 by Baron Maurice de Hirsch. This was a project involving the settlement of Russian Jews in agricultural communities in North America, South America and Palestine. Soon the two first locations were dropped and the JCA became an important driver of the colonisation of Palestine, alongside the Jewish National Fund. By 1900, this was a project overseen by Baron Edmond James de Rothschild. In 1924, Goldsmid founded a new organisation, reflecting the explicitly Zionist focus: the Palestine Jewish Colonization Association (PICA), which purchased land in Palestine (today, PICA's lands belong to the state). The JCA and PICA more or less fused into one body in 1933 and Goldsmid is recorded in their official history as one of the founding fathers of the body that resulted from the merger of these two colonisation agencies. Supplementing the Jewish National Fund, they would later become crucial tools for building Jewish settlements following the destruction of Palestinian villages in 1948.

Going back to the meeting in 77 Great Russell Street in May 1938, it is easy to discern from the minutes that the atmosphere was bleak. Most agreed that the Jewish Agency had failed to consult this body, the political advisory committee, at a pivotal moment for the Zionist project in Palestine. The members angrily pointed out that nobody sought their advice when the Woodhead Committee arrived in Palestine – a committee prepared to override the Peel Commission's pro-Zionist recommendations and propose a more stringent policy towards Zionist immigration and land purchases in historical Palestine.

Since the very beginning of 1938, the Zionist leadership in Palestine pushed the under-secretary of state for the colonies, William Ormsby-Gore, to accelerate the procedures and reaffirm Peel's support for the foundation of a Jewish state in Palestine, even if only on a small portion of land. None of the loyal members of the lobby in Britain were asked to take part in it, nor were they informed about the content of the meetings between the Zionist leadership in Palestine and the Woodhead Committee.

One of the members is recorded in the minutes as saying that he and Sir Avigdor were embarrassed by being treated in such a manner. The representative of the Jewish Agency tried to calm them down, but to no avail. This era of British Zionism had come to an end. Zionism was no longer spearheaded by well-assimilated Anglo-Jews with inherited wealth and occasionally peerages, but by a forceful leadership in Palestine.[36]

There was a silver lining to these affronts to patrician sensibilities: Zionism was no longer a minority position among the Anglo-Jewish community, and its leading institutions were more sympathetic to the cause than they ever had been.[37]

What became of the old Anglo-Jewish leadership? They were gradually replaced by an entourage that accompanied Chaim Weizmann when he came to Britain, including the famous historian Lewis Namier and Baffy. The rest of the team in '77' was now, as one visitor put it, relegated to 'propaganda'.[38]

As far as the Zionist leaders on the ground in Palestine were concerned, '77' was an embassy, not a headquarters. They encouraged the advisory committee to invest in galvanising the Anglo-Jewish community behind the Zionist project. And the advisory committee applied themselves to this with real fervour – at long last persuading the Jewish Board of Deputies to give their full-fledged support to a new homeland in Palestine.[39]

LOBBYING FOR ZIONISM DURING THE HOLOCAUST

By the time Europe woke up to the threat of Nazism, most Jewish organisations had settled on Zionism as the preferred strategy for overcoming anti-Semitism. In these years Zionism had transformed 'from an alternative into a dominant strategy', as Sharon Gewirtz and other historians have argued.[40] Moreover, as Richard Bolchover commented, active Jewish participation in the British war effort was associated with the Zionist image of a new, modern and secular Jew in the minds of Jews and non-Jews, further increasing sympathy for Zionism during the Second World War.[41]

The first indication of this change was the creation of a group within the Board of Deputies that attempted to associate this avowedly non-political body with the World Jewish Congress, a landmark American Zionist organisation. The last non-Zionist president of the Board of Deputies, Neville Lasky, fought a losing battle against the Zionisation of the Board and in December 1939 he was replaced by the Zionist activist, Professor Selig Brodetsky. At the outset of the Holocaust, every significant Jewish body in Britain had become pro-Zionist.

This coloured their reactions as the Nazis conquered more and more of Europe. Until 1943, Nazi atrocities were not at the top of the Jewish community's agenda – in the UK, the debate about Zionism was far more vociferous than the question of what was happening to Jews in occupied Europe. When evidence of an ongoing genocide became undeniable, Jewish organisations turned their full attention to it. Yet they saw it all through one lens: Zionism.[42]

The reason there were always inhibitions affecting Zionist, or Anglo-Zionist, engagement with the plight of the Jews of Europe before and during the Holocaust was not necessarily because of lack of care, but more due to natural human limitations of energy, resources and time. The Zionist leadership on the ground in Palestine provided one example of how to navigate between concern for the Zionist colony and apprehension about the fate of the Jews facing the danger of extermination in Europe. For them, the priority was undoubtedly the survival of the community in Palestine, as shown by the works of critical Israeli historians such as Tom Segev and Idith Zertal.[43] Rescuing the Jews of Europe had to be closely associated with the fate of the community in Palestine. This was epitomised by David Ben-Gurion's position one month after Kristallnacht, the first mass Nazi pogrom of the German Jews. On 7 December 1938, he addressed a Labour Zionist meeting, saying:

> If I knew that it would be possible to save all the children in Germany by bringing them over to England, and only half of them by transporting them to Eretz Yisrael, then I would opt for the second alternative. For we must weigh not only the life of these children, but also the history of the People of Israel.[44]

This attitude – that only Zionism could save the Jews from the unfolding catastrophe – was indisputably bolstered by the refusal of the West, especially Britain and the USA, to take in Jewish refugees en masse. This Western and Anglo-American reluctance was on full display during the Evian Conference of July 1938. Delegates from thirty-two countries, one after the other, expressed regret about the plight of Jewish refugees in Europe, but in the same breath apologised for not offering a haven for these Jews and declaring their inability to increase their countries' immigration quotas, in most cases citing the worldwide economic depression. The representatives spoke in general terms, not about people but about 'numbers' and 'quotas'. In the end, only one country at the conference, the Dominican Republic, officially agreed to accept refugees from Europe. (Dictator Rafael Trujillo, influenced by the international eugenics movement, believed that Jews would improve the 'racial qualities' of the Dominican population.)[45] A handful of other countries accepted Jewish refugees in the 1930s: Bolivia, Switzerland

and the Shanghai International Settlement (up until the Japanese conquest). Britain somewhat reluctantly increased the number of permits for Jewish immigration into Palestine, but not on anything approaching a sufficient scale.

By 1943, the Zionist lobby in Britain openly connected the Holocaust with immigration into Palestine. It pressurised the British government to allow limitless Jewish immigration into Palestine, arguing for it as the only solution to the crisis in Europe. Initially Britain demurred – knowing that Palestinians would resist, as they had between 1936 and 1939. But it was faced with a dilemma of its own making: it had no desire to admit large numbers of Jews into Britain, and the USA closed its gates as well.

Historians still debate the motives for Britain's unwillingness to admit more than a very small number of Jewish refugees – and even then with stringent conditions attached. Declassified documents have shed new light on this. Louise London's *Whitehall and the Jews*, based on the newly available material, shows clearly that British self-interest consistently limited humanitarian aid to Jews.[46] Asylum was severely restricted during the Holocaust, little attempt was made to save lives, and admissions often required the intervention of individuals. After the war, the British government delayed announcing whether refugees would obtain permanent residence, hoping to avoid long-term responsibility for large numbers of homeless Jews.[47] There was one exception: the Kindertransport operation, whereby Britain allowed Jewish welfare organisations to rescue about ten thousand children, up to the age of seventeen, from Nazi Europe and raised them in British families. Their parents were left to die.

Under international pressure, Britain and the USA convened another international conference in April 1943 on the subject of Jewish refugees, in British-controlled Bermuda. To the great dismay of the Zionist lobby, the British delegation refused to link the discussion of Nazism with Jewish immigration into Palestine. Shortly after the Bermuda conference, a special ad hoc committee was convened in the House of Commons for the issue to be considered by MPs, some of whom declared that they were representing the Zionist lobby in Britain in the Commons debates. The discussion had limited political impact, but it revealed much about Zionism.

ZIONISM COMES TO THE HOUSE OF COMMONS

At the time, British MPs had no power to influence the immigration policy that the British rulers of Mandatory Palestine had settled on: controlled immigration in the hope of limiting Palestinian resistance to the continued Jewish colonisation of their homeland, while not opening the gates for the Jewish refugees fleeing Europe. Those on the committee who demanded a change in the policy repeated the Zionist narrative of Palestine's emptiness and the country's potential capacity to absorb Jews in their millions.[48] For instance, George Ridley, Labour MP for Clay Cross, argued:

> I plead also that we should fling wide open the doors of Palestine. The absorptive capacity of modern Palestine is undoubtedly high. The Jews there have turned the desert into a fertile country, and the absorptive capacity of that fertile country has been lifted in consequence. I am assured that there is a man-power shortage and that Palestine would gladly take about 30,000 families or 70,000 people. The Palestinian has his father, mother, sisters and brothers, in the hell's cauldron that we call Europe; he waits feverishly to receive them. Whatever we can do to unite them we should regard it as our fundamental duty to do. The White Paper quotas, which seemed to mean so much five years ago, now mean little, and we ought not to be limited in a period of grave crisis by figures which were fashioned in other circumstances.

In Ridley's parlance, 'the Palestinian' meant the recent Jewish settler, not the indigenous resident. All Britain could do in response to Nazism was to fill Palestine with new Palestinians.

He was supported by John Mack, Labour MP for Newcastle-under-Lyme and a Zionist activist, who told the committee: 'it has been my lot to speak on behalf of the Zionist Federation of this country'. He brushed aside the possibility of native Palestinian objections to the scheme:

> Allusion has been made to the Arab reaction which might take place, I believe it is not as formidable an obstacle as has been suggested. It

has been grossly exaggerated, and behind that exaggeration there is a certain amount of Nazi controlled propaganda. We must relax that White Paper. We must say that if Jews can get into Palestine in excess of the numbers in that White Paper every facility will be afforded them to do so, because, searching the four corners of the earth, I bid fair to say, that this country and the United Nations will find no more noble and gallant allies than the brave Jewish people who are making their splendid contribution to the cause of which we are so proud.

Mack was opposed by the Conservative MP Colonel Sir Lambert Ward, who took it upon himself to represent the position of the British government in Palestine. Letting a large number of Jewish immigrants into Palestine was 'absurd in the case of an agricultural country, if anything rather smaller than Wales'. Moreover:

> The difficulty there is that one has always been up against the antagonism of the Moslems, and a largely increased immigration would probably increase the friction.

Some MPs took the compassionate approach when faced with these difficulties, suggesting that Britain ought to take more Jewish refugees in. A mixture of anti-Semitism and xenophobia prevented Whitehall from allowing that to happen. Ward represents the government position here again – if large-scale immigration into Palestine was undesirable, large-scale immigration into Britain was inconceivable:

> One of the great difficulties in admitting large numbers of refugees to this country is the fact that a very considerable proportion of the population does not want them. It has been said – I should not like to say whether it is true or not – that to admit a large number of refugees of the Jewish religion might easily fan the smouldering fires of anti-Semitism which exist here into a flame. Many people regard that as absurd, but from my own experience I am not at all sure there is not something in it. From almost exactly this date three years ago until the beginning of the year I was working with the Home Guard in the East

End. The zone for which I was responsible comprised the Boroughs of Benthal Green, Stepney and Poplar and some of the outlying districts of their boroughs. There was undoubtedly in existence a very definite anti-Semitic feeling. When it came to the selection of officers, or non-commissioned officers, one was always up against that problem. One heard it said directly anything went wrong that the Jews were to blame – quite untruthfully. If there was any question of a black market, it was said, untruthfully, that the Jews were largely doing it. When that terrible disaster took place at a shelter three or four months ago the rumour was put about that it was panic on the part of the foreign Jews. It is quite untrue, as was shown by the fact that only something like 5 per cent of the casualties were members of the Jewish religion.

Louise London has proven that the charge that anti-Semitism would increase if too many Jewish refugees were granted entry was stated throughout the war period, by both government officials and the established Anglo-Jewish community.[49] Moreover, the prospect of any kind of immigration stoked economic anxieties, as it still does today.

Confronted with this mixture of responses, Mack, the representative of the English Zionist Federation so to speak, surprisingly ventured his own solution, which would never have been approved by the Zionist leadership in Palestine:

I would say that as a positive solution, the Government of this country should announce to the world a statement that refugees who can escape by whatever means should be granted temporary asylum in Britain …

I believe that if this country is bold and courageous, if this country is prepared above all other countries – and its record is as great as that of any other country – to say to the Jews of the world, 'Come ye into this country as a temporary refuge, and those Jews who temporarily take refuge in this country will be able after the war to go to Palestine,' the very German Jews themselves would be glad of the opportunity of going to Palestine. If the Government will recognise that to be its true policy, it will be not merely carrying out a great eleemosynary principle, but will perform a deed which will preserve the name of this country for time immemorial as the greatest and most wonderful benefactor of all mankind.

In his view, the refugees were to be admitted on a temporary basis, on the understanding that they would leave Britain for Palestine in the near future. While in reality some 40,000 remained in Britain, this had not been the government's intention. Asylum was to be for a limited time and was granted in the hope that most of the refugees would seek other countries in which to settle permanently.

The debate in the House was not intended to result in the implementation of new policy; it simply enabled MPs to express the views of both the Zionist lobby and the British government (in Palestine and in London). The views of Palestinians were notably absent. Even so, British policy was informed by the fear of Palestinian resistance – and the British were unwilling to acquiesce to Zionist demands in the middle of the war.

The pro-Zionist lobby succeeded for a while in forming a front with many in the Jewish community who were not necessarily pro-Zionist. Together they authored a petition to the British government requesting an increase in the quota for immigration into Palestine as the first priority, and if this proved to be impossible, then exploring further options in places such as Jamaica, Cyprus and Kenya.[50] This unity was mirrored by a similar development on the other side of the Atlantic. In hindsight, this was no passing alliance, but helped pave the way for the gradual Zionisation of other Jewish organisations on both sides of the Atlantic, as we shall see. When the war was over, the lobby could rely on the new supporters to push forward the Zionist project.

FACING THE ATTLEE GOVERNMENT, 1945–1948

The dissolution of the Churchill war ministry was welcomed by the leaders of the Jewish Agency in Palestine, who hoped that the newly elected Labour government would be more sympathetic to Zionist aspirations in Palestine. As we have seen, the Zionist lobby invested huge amounts of time and effort in securing strong ties with Labour over decades, so the disappointment when the Attlee government turned out to be lukewarm at best was correspondingly immense. Zionists had good grounds for high expectations. Just a few years before, in February 1940, the National Council of the Labour Party condemned the war coalition for treating Palestine as a colonial possession and not as a mandated territory.[51] The Labour Party continued to support the Zionist project and at its 1940 party conference unanimously adopted a resolution reprimanding the British government's restrictions on Jewish land purchase and immigration. The war created a groundswell of sympathy for Zionism across the party, which passed resolutions one after the other demanding that the Jewish Agency 'be given authority to develop to the full capacity of Palestine to absorb immigrants'. The Liverpool Labour Party and the Liverpool Trades Union Council (TUC) pledged 'the wholehearted support of the Labour movement in the fight against anti-Semitism and for safeguarding the Jewish future in Palestine'.[52]

But, despite all the promise, the Attlee Labour government (1945–1951) proved to be a mixed bag as far as the Zionist lobby was concerned. Many members of the parliamentary party itself were strongly pro-Zionist and used the *Tribune*, the Left Labour Party publication that was founded in 1937, to air these views. Among the pro-Zionist party members, Richard Crossman stood out. He played a crucial role in persuading the Anglo-American Committee of 1946, the last international effort to solve the conflict in Palestine, to connect the fate of the Jewish survivors of the Holocaust with a future Jewish state in Palestine. This link was later confirmed by UNSCOP, the special committee appointed by the UN to investigate a solution for Palestine.

Crossman denied vehemently that he, or his colleagues who shared his views, were influenced by a Zionist lobby:

> No British government is embarrassed by a Jewish 'pressure group' nor did the Labour party put a Zionist plank in its platform for purely electoral purposes … the Party's Palestinian policy was the result of profound conviction that the establishment of the national home is an important part of the Socialist creed.[53]

Crossman portrayed Zionism as representing socialism in Palestine. This counterintuitive representation of affairs came directly from the propaganda of the Zionist Labour movement in Palestine, in which local landlords and dignitaries were denounced as capitalist oppressors, unlike the new landlords and settlers. The Labour Party, wrote Crossman, was 'unanimous in denouncing Conservative support for the corrupt Pashas and Effendis' of the Arab world.[54] This portrayal bore no relation to reality. Moreover, in the Arab world as a whole, it was the British Labour Party that courted the 'corrupt' effendis and rejected the progressive movements of liberation. Some in the lobby used a cruder version, accusing the Palestinians of supporting both Fascism (on the basis of an interview with Oswald Mosley in the Palestinian newspaper *Al-Difa*) and Communism (since the Palestine Communist Party supported the Palestinian struggle); later critics of Israel would be defamed in a similar way as being simultaneously fascists and communists.

But the government also included Ernest Bevin as foreign secretary, with his eyes firmly focused on serving British interests in the Arab world, and with no particular enthusiasm for building a Zionist socialist Utopia. He drew the ire of Zionists in the party and outside for firstly wanting Palestine to remain a mandated territory for the time being, and secondly refusing to countenance unlimited Jewish immigration into Palestine – notoriously he sent *Exodus 1947*, a ship containing around 4,000 Jewish refugees on its way to Palestine, back to France. Crossman was joined by other senior members of the party in accusing Bevin of waging a war against Zionism in 1947–1948 and went as far as blaming him for incidents of anti-British Zionist terrorism.[55]

Bevin was not responsible for the ferocity of the Zionist terrorists but he did make some unsavoury remarks about Jews. At one stage he said that Americans wanted more Jewish immigration into Palestine because 'they do not want too many of them in New York.'[56] In 1945 he said he was:

> anxious that the Jews in Europe shall not over-emphasise their racial position ... if the Jews, with all their sufferings, want to get too much at the head of the queue, you have the danger of another anti-Semitic reaction through it all.[57]

Bevin here was echoing prime minister Clement Attlee's policy in terms of the logistical challenge of repatriating over six million displaced people at the close of the Second World War – especially the last million who had no home to go back to. Both Britain and the US were reluctant to be seen to be giving the Jews 'special treatment'. Yet Bevin's lack of tact opened him up to accusations that he harboured anti-Semitic views.

Crossman was not alone in criticising Bevin. He was supported by Stafford Cripps, then chancellor of the Exchequer, who was an unlikely ally of the Zionist lobby. He was associated in the lobbyists' minds with his aunt, Beatrice Webb, a known critic of the pro-Zionist policies of the British government. But he gained the confidence of the lobby and assiduously supported Zionism in the pages of the *Tribune*. 'It would be criminal', he wrote, 'to snatch from the Jewish race the last hope of having even a tiny territory that they may call their own'.[58] Readers today may be surprised that Cripps referred to the Jews as a race, but Zionism necessarily implied viewing Jews as a distinct national group or even as a race, rather than as full citizens of Britain.

Around Crossman and Cripps, a formidable pro-Zionist group of devotees emerged who would have more impact later, in the days of the Harold Wilson government. The group included politicians such as Arthur Henderson (the son of the former Labour leader) and Tony Benn (who later became a severe critic of Israel). Sometimes whole families were recruited for the cause, such as the Greenwoods (the father Arthur and his son Anthony) and the Janners (Barnett and his son Greville).

In 1947, this pro-Zionist lobby inside Labour publicly rebuked Ernest Bevin's impertinent questioning of 'the whole validity of political Zionism'. Like Crossman, they accused him of triggering Zionist violence, since his policies left the Zionist movement on the ground no option but to resort to terrorism against the Mandatory forces and government.[59] After 15 May 1948, this section of the lobby continued to condemn Bevin as Israel's arch-enemy, waging a war against the Jewish state – a critique that seeped into the rather lukewarm obituaries some of his colleagues wrote after his death in 1952.[60]

Incidentally, the lobby tried to recruit Winston Churchill to directly reprimand Bevin regarding his Palestine policy. However, after losing the 1945 elections he was even less interested in Palestine. His private papers are full of letters from the lobby asking him to take a leading role against Bevin's policies. He did not seem to oblige, probably having lost interest in the question following his fall from political power.[61]

Up until May 1948, Bevin's position carried the day, and other Labour activists, like Christopher Mayhew, a junior minister in the Foreign Office, and Fenner Brockway, a socialist and pacifist, objected to the Zionist campaign.

Caught between these two sides, the position adopted by the Attlee government until 1948 did not conform to the wishes of the Zionist lobby and hence enraged them. But if the lobby couldn't win over the Labour government, it still had another avenue for making its voice heard. It turned to the Trades Union Congress (TUC).

THE TUC AND THE LOBBY

Before the end of the Mandate, the lobby made one last effort to try and change the Attlee government's policy, by trying to recruit the TUC to its mission. The mission was entrusted to the international department of the Histadrut, the Zionist trade union organisation in Palestine. It was not an easy task since the TUC did not have a clear position on Palestine. But the lobby was hopeful it could be convinced, because the TUC had had strong and friendly ties with the Zionist movement in Britain and in Palestine, from the time of the 1917 Balfour Declaration.

On 28 December 1917, at a joint conference, the Labour Party and the TUC summarised the achievements of the Great War, before it had even ended. The final document included bombastic declarations about the need to continue the drive for 'the complete democratisation of all countries' and a call to abandon 'every form of Imperialism', even going as far as to appeal for 'the entire abolition of compulsory military service in all countries' – all promises that both outfits, the party and the TUC, failed to stand by in years to come. Section F of the document declared:

such of the Jewish people as desire to do so may return [to Palestine] and may work out their salvation, free from interference by those of alien race and religion.[62]

As John Newsinger wryly observed, many worthy promises were made, but only the one to Zionism was kept.[63]

Based on this happy recollection of past friendship, the Histadrut sent its own emissaries to add pressure on the Labour government – even though the TUC had previously dashed expectations by refusing to oppose the 1939 White Paper that restricted Jewish immigration into Palestine.[64]

Since then, there had been some positive indications that raised the hopes of the lobby that the TUC was open to modifying its position. The TUC Congress invited the Histadrut to join the World Trade Union Conference in London in February 1945. The Histadrut represented Palestine alongside a Palestinian union, the Palestine Arab Workers Society. However, the Palestinian delegation felt betrayed by the World Trade Union Conference, as it passed a resolution supporting a Jewish homeland in Palestine. The resolution was a huge achievement for the Zionist leadership, but it did not help to change British policy on the ground.[65]

But although the Zionist lobby was grateful for the TUC's support, it didn't really need it anymore. The British government had made the decision to leave Palestine in February 1947 and began the process of disengaging. Both sides in historical Palestine knew that the British attitudes now counted for less and less. By 1948, Britain became less relevant to the future of Palestine, and it became clear to the Zionist lobby that the United States was a far more important arena. As we shall see in the next chapter, lobbying in the United States did not emerge upon the establishment of the Israeli state. It had a long history, stretching back to the second half of the nineteenth century, like its counterpart in Britain. We will trace its journey from being an evangelical fringe project to becoming a force to be reckoned with.

5

Early Zionist Lobbying in the USA

THE BLACKSTONE–SCOFIELD LEGACY:
THE EARLY CHRISTIAN ZIONIST LOBBY

The British pioneers of Zionism in the second half of the nineteenth century operated on the margins of Christian theology, but their co-thinkers in America would take the world by storm. These evangelicals described themselves as 'restorationists' – hoping for the return of the Jews to Israel as a fulfilment of biblical prophecy, and of God's promise to Israel. It evolved as a raw idea that was shaped and reshaped by moving back and forth from one side of the Atlantic to the other. This constant dialogue between British and North American evangelical communities produced what would eventually constitute the ideological infrastructure for a potent American political Christian Zionist movement in the twentieth century.

Even before this transnational interchange existed, there were individual restorationists in the USA. Some public figures in America expressed support for the idea. President John Adams wrote, 'I really wish the Jews again in Judea as an independent nation', and famous novelists, such as Herman Melville, followed suit.[1] Among the various denominations prevailing in North America in the seventeenth century, the Puritans in particular were enthused by this idea. They prayed for the 'return' of the Jews to 'their homeland' as part of their ceremonial gatherings. The Jews for them were a 'nation'. Redefining Judaism as a nation, not as a religion, became an important concept in the development of political Zionism. One of the most fervent early supporters, David Austin of New Haven, even built docks and inns for launching large-scale Jewish emigration from North America to Palestine.[2]

John Nelson Darby's arrival in North America invigorated support for this initially esoteric theological idea. He was an Anglican minister from Dublin and was known as one of the founders of the evangelical movement known as the Plymouth Brethren, which regarded the Old Testament as the supreme authority for the church and its faithful.

Darby's theological, or rather eschatological, viewpoint is crucial for our narrative. He was a restorationist, a pre-millenarian and the mind behind Dispensationalism: a theology which dictated that history was divided into 'dispensations' for God's chosen people, the Jews. There were seven dispensations since the time of innocence of Adam and Eve, and the nineteenth century was within the period of the sixth dispensation, between the crucifixion and a future rupture leading to the last dispensation, which would include the restoration of the nation of Israel as part of a wider divine period leading to the thousand-year reign of Christ.

For our purposes, we only need to discuss why this new theology translated into enthusiastic American support for Zionism. And there's nothing more apt than Darby's own explanation for why he advocated the return of the Jews to Palestine and the creation of a modern Jewish nation – one deserving a homeland and independence in Palestine. His lucid presentation of these ideas made him the ideal torch bearer from one side of the Atlantic to the other.

So, let me try and summarise Darby's take on the role of the Jews, Palestine and Christianity. The Jews were and are God's chosen people and will receive in time the fulfilment of God's Old Testament promises (in the late nineteenth century, the fortunate receivers of these prophecies were to be the Jews who lived in Russia; later Darby's successors would confer these prophetic promises on all the members of the Zionist movement and after 1948 on the Jews of Israel). When Christ returns to earth and establishes the millennial kingdom, the nation of Israel will be born again and acknowledge its role in the crucifixion of Christ. Until then – and this is crucial – the Jews are the chosen people and enjoy God's protection (and the unconditional support of evangelicals), especially in returning to Palestine.

Darby and his friends influenced both the Christian and the Jewish Zionist movements. They inspired Jewish intellectuals seeking a remedy for anti-Semitism and contributed to the emergence of the Zionist movement in Eastern Europe. This influence came about through the popularisation of Darby's views, disseminated by his American students, among the early Zionist leaders. Herzl heard about him through Hechler, who was a great admirer of Darby.[3]

Secondly, and probably more importantly, their theologies stimulated a more institutionalised restorationist movement which appeared in the USA in the 1880s. Its members met regularly, spreading the word and extending its reach. Its first meaningful meeting took place in 1884 on Lake Ontario.

THE QUEEN'S ROYAL HOTEL: THE FIRST AMERICAN LOBBY

Today you cannot find the Queen's Royal Hotel in the town of Niagara-on-the-Lake. But the Queen's Royal Park is still there, off Ricardo Street, and stretches along the Niagara River, very near the spot where the river falls into Lake Ontario. The view is spectacular: the Niagara Fort on one side, the lake on the other. This scenic panorama could also be admired from the Queen's Royal Hotel's famous verandas, now hidden under the green lawns of the new park.

The elegant hotel was opened in 1868. A local website displays a photo of the hotel as it was seen by 'visitors arriving by boat' who 'would have been very impressed when the hotel came to sight – a magnificent four-storey building, white with green shutters and trim, dominating the Niagara River Bank'. Visitors could reach the hotel from the river and walk through a long veranda into the dining room and reception. By all accounts, it was regarded as one of the best hotels in North America. The hotel was demolished during the Great Depression, but until then its pavilion was an important venue for big conventions. At one such convention, the Christian Zionist lobby in America was founded, a year after the hotel opened for business.

A group of American evangelicals, impressed by Darby's message, launched the Believers' Meeting for Bible Study. The first meeting was small, but from 1883 to 1897 it became an annual event known as the Niagara Bible Conference, propelled forward by the energy of a Presbyterian minister from St Louis, James H. Brookes.[4]

Brookes served as the editor of the journal *The Truth*. David Rausch, who called the pioneers we meet in this chapter 'protofundamentalists', describes this publication as the 'granddaddy of protofundamentalist publications'.[5] Anything that wasn't discussed on the lake was explored seriously in the pages of this publication. 'Is Israel a Nation or a Sect?' asked one article that accentuated the new idea of Judaism as nationalism rather than as a religion, at a time when most Jewish intellectuals in Europe shunned the idea. It also prompted other contributors to associate the restoration with encouraging Jewish immigration, in particular from Tsarist Russia to Palestine.[6]

These early notions paralleled those aired by the early Jewish Zionists whose movement began to flourish roughly at the same time. Although coming from different angles, both movements interpreted Jewish prayers such as 'next year in Jerusalem, the rebuilt' as an indication that the Jews were a scattered nation working for their return to Palestine. Brookes's role was to present this interpretation as a religious imperative for the followers of evangelical Christianity to help realise this Jewish aspiration.[7]

This meeting was lavish – the connection between luxury and lobbying had already been established. Brookes himself wrote on the subsequent meetings in the journal *The Truth*, in which the return of the Jews to Palestine was a major theme:

> The place ... becomes more beautiful as the years go by, and it would be difficult to find a spot better suited to the quiet and prayerful study of the Sacred Scriptures. The building in which the Conference meets, overlooking Lake Ontario and the River Niagara, and surrounded by green trees, is secluded from the noise of the world; and so excellent were the arrangements for the accommodation of the guests, both in Queen's Royal Hotel and in the boarding houses of the village, that not a word of complaint was heard from anyone.[8]

The Niagara meetings were called Bible meetings, and resulted in a form-ative document in 1891: the Niagara Creed. This was a statement composed of fourteen fundamentals that were meant to guide the faithful into the future and which included the call for the 'restoration of Israel'.[9]

By 1900, the conferences petered out, but the Niagara Creed lived on, encompassing the fundamentalist movement, and moulding impor-tant churches and theological centres such as Moody Church, founded by Dwight Moody, and Biola University as future pro-Zionist bastions, which remain core parts of the institutional backbone of the Christian Zionist lobby for Israel today.

The Christian lobby's American origins shed light on the nascent coalition that would eventually justify the colonisation of Palestine at the expense of the indigenous people there. An important pillar of this coalition was the white settler-colonial community of the United States, whose elite segments were now easily convinced of the religious basis of another settler-colonial project, this time in Palestine.

A different contribution to the formation of a Christian Zionist lobby in the USA was provided by the tycoon William Eugene Blackstone. Sometime in the early 1870s, he had an epiphany that led him to devote all his time, and his considerable wealth, to the restora-tion of the Jews to Palestine – a vision and a mission he articulated with great pathos in a bestseller he wrote in 1878, called *Jesus is Coming*. In this and other publications (some of them even in Yiddish!) he pushed forward two propositions, which echoed the beliefs of the other fore-runners of Christian Zionism on both sides of the Atlantic. The first was a genuine concern for the fate of the Jews in the Russian Empire. The second was a belief that their salvation did not lie in their immigration to the West, but only to the Holy Land.

Blackstone convened a conference in 1890 to discuss the 'past, present and future of Israel'. The venue chosen was not as lavish as the others; it was the rebuilt First Methodist Episcopal Church in Chicago, known as the Clark Street Methodist Church due to its location on the famous street. It had been badly burnt during the Great Fire of 1871 in which around seventeen thousand buildings were destroyed, and had been reconstructed a few years later. The meeting was more of a workshop than a conference, with the attendees seriously deliberating on what could they do for Zionism.

A year later in 1891, Blackstone solicited signatures from prominent American politicians and businessmen for a petition now known as the Blackstone Memorial. Among the many luminaries were John D. Rockefeller, J.P. Morgan, and the chief justice of the US; it was submitted to the American president. The Memorial was very much a follow-up to the Niagara meetings. It called upon the Ottoman Empire to receive Jews from Russia and allow them to settle in Palestine, as small groups of Jews had already been doing from 1882 onwards.

Blackstone was groundbreaking in one way: he used the term 'Israel' to refer not only to the Jewish people, but also to the land of Palestine. He hence anticipated and influenced the discourse of the Jewish Zionist lobby in the near future:

> We believe this is an appropriate time for all nations, and especially the Christian Nations of Europe, to show kindness to Israel. A million exiles, by their terrible suffering, are appealing to our sympathy, justice and humanity. Let us restore them to the land of which they were so cruelly despoiled by our Roman ancestors.[10]

The very same ideas would appear five years later in Theodor Herzl's book, *Der Judenstaat*. Blackstone wrote:

> As the powers [of Europe] gave Bulgaria to the Bulgarians ... they should now give Palestine to the Jews. Does not Palestine as rightfully belong to the Jews?[11]

Blackstone laid another important foundation stone for later Zionist propaganda about Palestine when he stated in 1891 that the general 'law of dereliction' did not apply to the Jews in relation to Palestine:

> for they never abandoned the land. They made no treaty; they did not even surrender. They simply succumbed, after the most desperate conflict, to the overwhelming power of the Romans.[12]

Brick by brick, Christian Zionists in America helped to concoct a historical narrative that would serve the broader Zionist movement in legitimising its right to colonise Palestine. Even if Blackstone remained an obscure figure to the mainstream US population, the people who signed the Blackstone Memorial year after year hailed from the political and economic elites of the country. It's no coincidence that President Harry Truman quoted the Memorial when he was the first world leader to recognise Israel in May 1948.

FARWELL HALL AND THE PROPHECY CONFERENCES

Alongside the Bible conferences, a different kind of gathering was energising Christian Zionism in late nineteenth-century America. These were the Prophecy Conferences. One of the first took place in Chicago shortly after the Great Fire of 1871.

Farwell Hall on Madison Street, east of LaSalle, was more commonly known as the Young Men's Christian Association Building, proudly opened in 1866. The association was a successful venture; in fact, it grew so much that it needed this majestic building, hailed as 'one of the chief architectural ornaments of our city' by the *Chicago Tribune*.[13] Its rebuilding after the fire was even more beautiful – and much more modern. 'Such is the hall, the largest and finest in the United States, perhaps in the world', boasted the local newspaper.[14]

Rather aptly, the new building had three images on the long-arched windows, one featuring Moses looking at the Promised Land, and the second Abraham, standing over his son Isaac, on the verge of sacrificing him. The third featured Jacob wrestling with the angel. For an audience who knew their Bible well, the meaning was obvious – the angel had said, 'Your name shall no longer be called Jacob, but Israel.' Of course, in reality, the angel had not called for the colonisation of Palestine, but like many other verses in the Bible, it was seized upon for the Christian Zionist cause. A sacred text had been turned into a divinely sanctioned, and indeed divinely ordered, political programme.

There, in this glorious, renovated hall, more than three thousand people gathered for the second Prophetic Conference. It distinguished itself from all preceding conferences in the USA in one way: it was the first time the restorationists became advocates not just of a mere dream, but of a real settler-colonial Jewish project in Palestine. On that occasion, one of the keynote speakers was Professor Ernst Ströter, who presented scholarly arguments, rather than theological ones, for a more practical interpretation of the imperatives in the Bible supporting the Zionist colonisation of Palestine. In his speech he claimed:

> the closing decade of this nineteenth century has brought an awakening of the national spirit and a revival of national hopes and aspirations – not indeed in Reform Judaism, but among the downtrodden masses of Jews in Eastern Europe, which only waits for the breath to burst forth in a blaze of unquenchable enthusiasm that will startle the world.[15]

At the third Prophetic Conference in Allegheny, Pennsylvania, in 1895, the message was repeated in even clearer terms. The speakers now referred to Palestine and Israel interchangeably, and this terminological looseness would appear later in the major publications and writings of the Christian Zionists.

The next phase of building this kind of theological and ideological infrastructure was establishing early contact with the Jewish Zionist movement itself. Blackstone became involved in the initial discussions with the Jewish Zionist movement and even tried to influence some of its decisions. When he learned that Herzl seriously considered, for pragmatic reasons, directing Zionist colonisation to Uganda, after failing to secure a charter from the Ottoman Empire for a Jewish Palestine, Blackstone was despondent. He dispatched in haste his famous Bible to Herzl, entreating him not to forsake Palestine. Blackstone marked in the Bible every passage 'that referred to Palestine, with instructions that it alone was to be the site of the Jewish state.'[16] Herzl kept the Bible, and it is on display at the Herzl Museum in Jerusalem. This was the only correspondence between the two men, but as David Borg writes, it 'provided a political entrée to a young movement that lacked it'.[17]

Blackstone's work at the Prophecy Conferences was aided by similar efforts invested in the same cause by Cyrus Scofield, another household name among early Christian Zionists. A lawyer from Michigan, he was mentored by Moody and became in many ways his successor. Unlike Blackstone, he did not experience an epiphany at the height of his success, but was forced to resign as a district attorney after 'questionable financial transactions'. After some time in jail, he found God and Zionism.[18]

Initially Scofield's perspective, put forward mainly in a journal he edited, *Our Hope* (the successor to *The Truth*), was to focus on Herzl as the new prophet. His colleague, William B. Riley, declared of Herzl's movement that 'I frankly confess it may shortly prove to be more significant than all the other movements',[19] and Scofield described it as the beginning of the fulfilment of restoration.

But Scofield was to go further still. He became famous for his own edition of the Bible, *Scofield's Bible*. Maidhc Ó Cathail goes as far as to claim that *Scofield's Bible* 'made uncompromising Zionists out of tens of millions of Americans'.[20] Published in 1909, it was an annotated version of the King James Bible that interprets the holy book as a Zionist manifesto that predicted the state of Israel and urged Christians in the USA to protect that state once it came into being unconditionally and if need be with their life. We will return to Scofield and his Bible when examining lobbying for Israel in the USA much later in the 1980s – such was its lasting influence. As recently as 2015, John Hagee, the founder of Christians United for Israel, declared this Bible the foundation on which 'fifty million evangelical bible-believing Christians unite with five million American Jews standing together for Israel'.[21]

The core group of the American pro-Zionist lobby in the 1930s and the 1940s was cut from the same cloth as the group that worked for the idea of the return of the Jews in the previous century. This lobby became more immersed in premillennialism (including Dispensationalism) and expanded its base among conservative American Protestants.

A leading member of this group was Jacob Gartenhaus. He was an Orthodox Jew from Austria, primed to become a rabbi. After moving in his twenties to New York, he recalled that he 'found Jesus' and he converted as a young man to Christianity, attracted to it by one of the veteran missionary outfits in the USA, the Southern Baptist Theological Seminary, and became there the head of the Department of Jewish Evangelism. This department was the origin of much pro-Zionist propaganda and was motivated by what Gartenhaus defined as his deep conviction 'that Zionism is going to win whether anybody likes it or not'; he warned that to oppose Zionism is akin 'to opposing God's plan'.[22]

Frank Norris was an even more energetic campaigner in this period. He marked himself out by personally pressuring President Truman to adopt a pro-Zionist policy in the crucial years of 1947 and 1948 as Israeli statehood hung in the balance. Earlier on, he was a very well-known and controversial novelist, attacking the big companies and standing up for workers and farmers, but also preaching against the degeneration of modern life. Critics of his work were quick to notice strong elements of anti-Semitism in his portrayals, stemming from a cultural Darwinist perspective that had also influenced Nazi ideology.

The ascendance of international Jewish Zionist bodies in 1940s, many of which became American branches of London-based Zionist organisations, meant that the lobbying baton was slowly passed from Christian Zionists to Jewish Zionists. Both remained active, as there was no competition between the two lobbies. In the eyes of the messianic Christians in America, the creation of the state of Israel in 1948 was the final and decisive proof that the divine apocalyptic schemes were about to materialise in front of their eyes: the return of the Jews, their conversion to Christianity and the Second Coming of the Messiah.

Obviously, there were other Christian denominations in the USA that adopted a different attitude towards the realities in Palestine; some are still active today. In the period under review, roughly 1880 to 1948, they made their views heard, but they were unable to match the appeal of the Christian Zionist lobby.

THE ALTERNATIVE LOBBY AND ITS DEMISE

If you ignore a 'no entry' sign on your right when you ascend towards the Jaffa Gate in the old city of Jerusalem and take the forbidden turn alongside the old Ottoman wall, driving through the Citadel, you will reach one of Jerusalem's hidden gems. On the mountain's slope looking west lies the old Gobat School. Samuel Gobat was an Anglican bishop who built a boys' school there in the mid-nineteenth century, which became the main preparatory school for the Palestinian elite. Today it is an American college and, around it and among the beautiful buildings left behind by the Anglicans, modern-day Americans have planted posters supporting the idea of a Greater Israel (that is, the claim that Israel has the right to annex both the West Bank and the Gaza Strip, which Israel occupied in 1967) and a Zionist Jerusalem, which would not have shamed the most ultra-Right Zionist settler movement in Israel. Gobat came to Palestine, as some Americans do today, because he believed that the return of the Jews would precipitate the Second Coming of the Messiah and the unfolding apocalypse. But, unlike his contemporary successors, he fell in love with the local population and helped bring them into the global educational system. His missionary objectives then took second place to his pedagogical ones. His efforts helped the embryonic Palestinian national movement to emerge.

Gobat was initially the intellectual heir of John Nelson Darby and Edward Irving, the fathers of premillenarianist eschatology in the first half of the nineteenth century. He was not alone in pursuing one thing and finding something very different; like King Saul searching for the donkeys and finding his kingdom, he was searching for Zionism and found the Palestinians.

Both those Americans who came to convert the Jews and restore them to Palestine, and those who supported the local Palestinian aspirations, were educated in the same locations. One such place was the Andover Seminary in Newton, Massachusetts. Newton was once a city itself; today it is part of greater Boston. Newton is a circular suburb and at its centre, in a typical New England wood, lies the theological seminary of Andover. In its early days, it hosted a Presbyterian brotherhood who wished to bring 'the word of God to the heathen'.[23] Two hundred and fifty enthusiastic boys were enlisted for the purpose; a decade later, they were in Palestine and the surrounding area, trying to convert to their kind of Christianity a society that had already encountered the Jesuits and the Greek Orthodox missionaries who had arrived years before. The Andoverians built institutes that, in time, would become the American universities of Cairo and Beirut, the alma maters of the Arab nationalist movement's first generation of leaders. The gospel they brought was thus not only that of Jesus, but also that of the youngest state in the world, just liberated from the British colonialist yoke. The historian George Antonius, author of the famous work *The Arab Awakening* and a senior clerk in the British Mandate government in Palestine, asserted that these missionaries were the principal agents of modernisation and nationalisation in the formative period of the modern Middle East.[24] With the advent of a more complex theoretical view of how nations are born, the role of the Presbyterian missionaries was diminished, but they are still regarded as meaningful facilitators in the upsurge of nationalism in Egypt and the Eastern Mediterranean.[25]

This ambivalence in the American theological view, between a premillenarianist vision and identification with the awakening Arab peoples, continued until the First World War. We find, at the end of the nineteenth century, a debate between the two positions. On one side stood William Blackstone who, in the famous 1891 Niagara Creed mentioned above, demanded from President Benjamin Harrison that the US should 'consider the condition of the Israelites and their claims to Palestine as their ancient home'.[26] On the other side stood the American consul in Jerusalem, Selah Merrill, who attempted to counter-balance the growing influence of the 'return of the Jews' notion. Merrill wrote to the president that, in his view (which was shared by his friends, the Muslim notables of Jerusalem), Zionism was neither a holy nor a religious phenomenon but, rather, a colonialist project that, he predicted, would not last, because it pertained to the Jewish Eastern European world and was totally alien to the Arab world. While his analysis was apt, his prediction was disproven by the events that followed.[27]

The premillenarianists seemed to gain the upper hand as the years went by. However, the 'Merrills' had one powerbase – the State Department. More importantly, they were the precursors of individuals and groups that on rare occasions tried to mitigate the pro-Zionist American policy with some consideration for the Palestinians' aspirations and well-being. The State Department established a Near East

Division in 1909 (which actually also covered Russia, Germany and Austria-Hungary because of their involvement in the region). The division did not take kindly to Zionism and saw it, in the words of one US diplomat from that department, 'as an illustration of the purely Hebraic and Un-American purposes for which our Jewish community seek to use this government'.[28] The Near East Division was also aware that the Ottoman Empire did not favour the Zionist project in Palestine. Merrill was still in office when the division was founded, and he provided his own view on the matter in a rather succinct manner: 'Palestine is not ready for the Jews. The Jews are not ready for Palestine.'[29]

There was neither interest in nor knowledge about Palestine, only recognition of a pre-existing indigenous population – and that it would serve American interests to remain aware of that. More importantly, there was a sense among others in the State Department that this part of the world interested other allies of America, so meddling didn't seem necessary. Thus, when the Zionist Literary Society, one of the first Jewish Zionist organisations, out of many more to come, requested an interview with President William Howard Taft in 1912, the secretary of state, Philander Knox, declined their request, explaining that:

> Problems of Zionism involve certain matters primarily related to the interests of countries other than our own ... and might lead to misconstructions.[30]

American policy remained quite aloof from Palestine until the outbreak of the First World War, as was the American Jewish community in general, which, unlike the Christian one, did not follow the colonisation of Palestine closely nor did they deem it the fulfilment of God's will.

In the years leading up to the war, the affairs of the American Jewish community were run by several institutions, the most important of which was the American Jewish Committee. It was founded in 1906 by German Jews, who were part of the more affluent sector of American Jewish society.

The American Jewish Committee embodied the American Jewish community's indifference, and even hostility, toward Zionism. As another organisation, the Union of American Hebrew Congregations, argued following the first Zionist Congress in Basel: 'Zion was a precious possession of the past ... but it is not our hope of the future. America is our Zion.'[31] Those who shared the view of the American Jewish Committee saw themselves as Americans who happened to be Jews, and not as Jews who were temporarily stranded in America while they waited for Israel to be built. They were not oblivious to the plight of Jews in Eastern Europe and did what they could to persuade the USA to accept these Jews if they could and wanted to come over. But their rescue efforts were not orientated towards Palestine – regardless of whether these humanitarian activists were wealthy liberals, socialists or ultra-Orthodox Jews.

Their pro-Zionist rivals in the American Jewish community were part of a smaller outfit named the Federation of American Zionists, founded in 1897 (it changed its name to the American Zionist Federation in 1912). It was founded by a group of young Jews in New York who enthusiastically endorsed the call for the Zionist colonisation of Palestine by the inaugural Zionist Congress. They were first-generation young Jewish immigrants who returned to Europe for their studies and were caught in the spell of the first and second (convened in 1898) Zionist Congresses in Basel. It was an umbrella organisation of 152 societies, with a membership of 8,000. It had a monthly magazine, *The Maccabean*, and occasionally published pamphlets with titles such as 'Judaism and Zionism', 'The Aims of Zionism' and 'The Progress of Zionism'. Its first president was Richard Gottheil and its first secretary was Stephen S. Wise, of whom we will hear more later. It had a sub-federation in the West of the USA called the Knights of Zion, which nonetheless had its headquarters in Chicago. The American Zionist Federation exists to this very day with head offices both in the USA and in Israel.

Richard Gottheil did not remain active for long. He was born in Manchester, England, but was raised as a child in the USA in a Reform rabbi's family in New York. From an early stage in his life, he was interested in scholarly work and pursued an academic career in Europe, culminating in a doctorate in Semitic studies from the University of Leipzig in 1886. He became a supporter of Zionism after attending the second Zionist Congress in Basel and came under the influence of Theodor Herzl. He was in many ways coerced to become the president of the Federation of American Zionists (1898–1904) as he seemed to prefer academic life to that of public advocacy for Zionism. This may explain his abrupt disappearance from the scene in 1904 after Herzl's death. As we shall see, Stephen Wise became a permanent and prominent voice in the Zionist lobby.

Among its first members was the distinguished and famous figure of Louis Dembitz Brandeis, a pillar of American law and eventually associate justice in the American Supreme Court. Brandeis rolled into the American Zionist Federation in 1912 when he was fifty-six years old, at the peak of his popularity as a lawyer with a reputation for taking on big business and the establishment. A particular friendship with Jacob de Haas, who used to be Herzl's personal aide, played a role in the conversion of Brandeis to Zionism. He was the first of many progressive Americans who failed to see the real nature of the colonisation project in Palestine, and would later become known as the PEOPs: Progressive Except on Palestine.

During the First World War, the locus of Zionist activity was in Europe – moving away from Germany and landing forcefully in Britain. American neutrality did not weaken the Zionist leadership's determination to win the USA over to their side. Brandeis was selected by the leadership in London to help turn the USA into a Zionist powerhouse by elevating the importance of Zionism in the eyes of the American public.

Brandeis was willing to take on this assignment, which forced him to alter how he spoke about American society: previously a great believer in the 'melting pot', he now talked about a 'salad bowl' of multiculturalism and nationalities. This shift from viewing the American Jews as members of society who happened to belong to that religion, to seeing them as members of a national group, raised questions of the dual nationalism of American Jews very early on, should they opt for the Zionist definition of Judaism. Brandeis was one of the early Zionists trying to pre-empt potential questions about the loyalty of American Jewish Zionists to America, a phenomenon later called the 'dual loyalty problem':

> Let no American imagine that Zionism is inconsistent with patriot-
> ism. Multiple loyalties are objectionable only if they are inconsistent
> … Every American who aids in advancing the Jewish settlement in

Palestine, though he feels that neither he nor his descendants will ever live there, will likewise be a better man and a better American for doing so ... There is no inconsistency between loyalty to America and loyalty to Jewry. The Jewish spirit, the product of our religion and experiences, is essentially modern and essentially American.[32]

One wonders whether he thought this verbal sleight of hand did the trick, or whether he truly believed this was a valid elucidation of a conundrum to which there are still no good answers. He used to invent bizarre aphorisms such as: 'To be good Americans, we must be better Jews, and to be better Jews, we must become Zionists.'[33] In any case, he was advocating Zionism as a solution for other Jews, not those living in the West, and in this spirit he heeded a World Zionist Organization request to play a major role in persuading the American administration to support the pro-Zionist policy of the new rulers of Palestine: the British.

AMERICAN SUPPORT FOR THE BALFOUR DECLARATION

The war, and more importantly the British Empire decision to stand behind the Zionist project through the Balfour Declaration, gave more substance to the actions of the American Zionist Jews when they were urged by the World Zionist Congress in London to help pressure President Woodrow Wilson publicly to support the Balfour Declaration. Brandeis was chosen by the World Zionist Congress to lead the campaign to support the Declaration even before it was made, and he was privy to the lobbying efforts in Britain in the months preceding the Declaration.

The lobby hoped that Brandeis's friendship with President Wilson would secure American endorsement of the Balfour Declaration. At first this seemed straightforward. Presbyterians all over America at that time gave their full support for the idea of a Jewish homeland in Palestine even before the Balfour Declaration was made. For instance, the Presbyterian General Assembly passed a resolution in 1916 favouring the idea.[34] By the end of the First World War, Christian Zionists moved from the evangelical margins into the more established churches and mainstream Presbyterians were Zionised. But support didn't just come from the

Christian lobby; secular organisations like the American Federation of Labor also declared support for a Jewish state in Palestine – despite most of the Jewish delegates at the Federation's conference opposing it.

However, Brandeis very soon learned that official endorsements by the White House or the State Department were not that easy to obtain. Brandeis was now asked by the pro-Zionist lobby in London to endeavour even harder to elicit such an official endorsement from President Wilson, because the State Department consistently demurred. He was implored by Chaim Weizmann to demand official American sponsorship of the Declaration and the policy behind it. Weizmann wrote to him on 8 April 1917:

> An expression of opinion coming from yourself and perhaps other gentlemen connected with the Government in favour of a Jewish Palestine under a British protectorate would greatly strengthen our hands.[35]

Pressure on Brandeis also came from James de Rothschild, the leading Anglo-Jewish aristocrat campaigning for the Balfour Declaration. He sent a cable to Brandeis on 25 April 1917 urging American Zionists to do all they could to secure President Wilson's approval of the British and Zionist plans for Palestine. His telegram read:

> Unanimous opinion only satisfactory solution Jewish Palestine under British protectorate. Russian Zionists fully approve. Public opinion and competent authorities here favourable … It would greatly help if American Jews would suggest this scheme before their government.[36]

After the Declaration was made, the American Zionist Federation took to the streets, probably for the first time ever, demonstrating on behalf of Zionism. There was enough enthusiasm, at least among the sizeable Jewish community in New York, to support the Declaration in public, and in relatively large rallies consisting of several thousand people. These demonstrations called on the American president to back the Declaration. At first it seemed like an easy task. In one of the many rallies that took place in New

York during the months of November and December 1917 in the wake of the Declaration, the American ambassador to Istanbul, Abram I. Elkus, and the consul in Jerusalem, the Reverend Otis Glazebrook, attended the rally, giving the impression that their presence indicated an official American endorsement for the Declaration. The main banner of that rally cried out for the participants to celebrate 'the British promise to return Jerusalem and the Holy Land to the Jewish People' and a message came from the White House in response, through the words of the president: 'in Palestine shall be laid the foundation of a Jewish commonwealth'.[37]

But the official American position was more ambivalent. The American secretary of state at the time, Robert Lansing, and other senior American diplomats did not share President Wilson's apparently positive reaction to the Balfour Declaration. Wilson saw a new Jewish homeland as part of his broader commitment to the right of oppressed minorities to self-determination (that is, to form a new state) – but not everyone in the American administration had such a rose-tinted view. In fact, as we shall see later, Wilson's commendation of the Balfour Declaration was given against the advice of Lansing. It was Zionist pressure that led Wilson to bypass and humiliate American diplomats. Lansing was only informed of the decision to back the Declaration in December 1917 – in a blow to his authority, this was a day after he advised the president to take a more cautious approach in the name of the American national interest:

> My judgment is that we should go very slowly in announcing a policy for three reasons. First, we are not at war with Turkey and therefore should avoid any appearance of favoring taking territory from that Empire by force. Second, the Jews are by no means a unit in the desire to reestablish their race as an independent people; to favor one or the other faction would seem to be unwise. Third, many Christian sects and individuals would undoubtedly resent turning the Holy Land over to the absolute control of the race credited with the death of Christ.

> For practical purposes, I do not think that we need go further than the first reason given since that is ample ground for declining to announce a policy in regard to the final disposition of Palestine.[38]

Wilson was probably being honest when he explained to Lansing that while one could have formed 'an impression that we had assented to the British declaration regarding returning Palestine to the Jews', this was never an official policy.[39] Wilson had never made a public endorsement of the Declaration, which allowed Lansing to continue to act as if the president's private endorsement had no weight. On 28 February 1918, Lansing wrote to Wilson opposing a request by several Zionist organisations in the USA to be issued passports to take part in a Zionist commission sponsored by Britain to tour Palestine. In his letter, Lansing wrote that the United States had never accepted the Balfour Declaration and should not sponsor an organisation with distinctly political goals. Wilson agreed with his secretary of state.

You may be able to detect that Lansing's approach was not so much driven by sympathy for the Palestinians as it was by a distaste for Jewish people. We will encounter this again and again when analysing the individuals and organisations that opposed the pro-Zionist and later pro-Israel lobby. There were a few who weren't expressly anti-Semitic, but simply viewed the issue through the narrow lens of American interests – the Palestinians were irrelevant. An even smaller minority were concerned with the rights of the native inhabitants of Palestine. As the century wore on, these noble, initially lone figures would be joined by many more.

The struggle between the State Department and the pro-Zionist campaign continued. It received a new impetus with the establishment of a new body, which not only attempted to exert more pressure on the administration but also tried to dominate the political discourse on Zionism in the American Jewish community: this was the American Jewish Congress, founded at the end of 1918.

THE AMERICAN JEWISH CONGRESS

At half past two in the afternoon, on 15 December 1918, a new American definition of Judaism was born: it was not just a religion, it was a nationality, entitled to self-determination and a nation state to call its own. And what could be a better venue than the place where the American nation was born too: the historic Independence Hall in Philadelphia?

Four hundred delegates came to the opening ceremony to declare the rebirth of the Jewish nation; they then moved to the Opera House.

The Metropolitan Opera House was another impressive station on the journey of Zionist lobbying on both sides of the Atlantic. It was opened in November 1908 and widely acclaimed across the USA. The neoclassical façade and white brick exterior contrasted nicely with the nearby red brick and brownstone houses on North Broad and Poplar Streets. It was a visionary project on a grand scale conceived by the impresario Oscar Hammerstein and designed by the architect William H. McElfatrick in 1907 as the residence for Hammerstein's opera company, the Philadelphia Opera Company. Two years later Hammerstein's son sold it to the New York Metropolitan Opera, the building taking the name Metropolitan Opera House. It now functions as a church and a concert venue.

Looking at the building today, it's scarcely possible to imagine how such an ambitious structure was constructed in the short span of nine months. And the timeline was extremely tight. Workmen only removed the ladders and brushes hours before the first performance on 17 November 1908. It is said that the paint of the lobby's columns was not yet dry when the first violinist's bow touched the string for the overture of *Carmen* by Bizet.

The American Jewish Congress's inauguration rivalled the dramatic operas typically hosted by the venue. The organisation was founded as a popular reaction against the American Jewish Committee, now casti-gated as an affluent, elitist and conservative group of German Jews who could not speak for American Jewry. The new body, the Congress, brought together the liberals, the new immigrants – many with socialist tendencies – and the new disciples of Zionism under one roof.

What all these people had in common was not just their embrace of the Zionist dream but their sympathy for the project of redefining Judaism as a faith of equality, progress and modernisation for Americans as a whole. In the same breath it associated this noble idea with a demand for the lifelong commitment of Jews and non-Jews in America to the Zionist project in Palestine. Being a good Jew meant believing in democracy, equality and Zionism. This is the first time Judaism came to be defined in terms of national identity – but not consistently so. It was a national identity in Palestine and Eastern Europe, but not in Britain, Canada or the USA. In other words, Jews were a national minority in Eastern Europe, and a proper nation in Palestine, but Judaism was only a religion in Britain, Canada and the USA. The explanations for this distinction were curious at best, and totally irrelevant at worst. But given the rise of brutal and violent anti-Semitism after the Great War in parts of Eastern Europe, the Congress's principal public call that emerged from this inaugural event was the demand to recognise the Jews as a national minority in various East European countries and in Palestine as the best way of coping with these increasing threats.

The demand for national rights for Jews in Palestine was accompanied by a plea to the American government to help build a Jewish nation state there. In a way there were now several varieties of Jewish nationalism; the most understated was in America, and the most full-blooded was the version intended to be nurtured in Palestine. But perhaps these nuances were lost on the four hundred delegates who voted in favour of supporting the Balfour Declaration, stressing far more than Balfour himself, or for that matter the Zionist leadership in Britain or in Palestine, the need to safeguard the rights of non-Jews in the future. Genuine belief in noble ideas such as equality – either from the liberal right or the socialist left – did not contradict unconditional support for the colonisation of Palestine.

The convention in Philadelphia was a break from past American Jewish attitudes towards Zionism. But those who attended it constituted a mere fraction of American Jews; it was estimated that a minority of about 20,000 of America's 2.5 million Jews sympathised with Zionism at this time.[40]

Among those gathering in Philadelphia, there was an impressive representation of the younger generation; but among them were also some older members of the community and quite famous figures such as Brandeis, whom the lobby in London continued to pressure to secure an official and public presidential endorsement of the Balfour Declaration, although he still could not obtain a definitive response.

For those who attended the founding of the American Jewish Congress, the ambivalence in American policy carried little weight and was not of any real interest to the convenors and leaders of the embryonic body, which, alongside the American Zionist Federation, would become a pillar in the pro-Zionist lobby in the USA up to 1948. Indeed Wilson's (albeit vague) support for the Balfour Declaration was the recurring theme in the Congress's deliberations.

Colonel Harry Cutler, the chair of the administrative committee of the American Jewish Congress's inaugural meeting in Philadelphia, opened the first session. He introduced Rabbi B.L. Levinthal, head of the United Orthodox Congregations of Philadelphia, who offered the opening prayer – one of the first to infuse the traditional Jewish prayers with the political message of Zionism. God was asked 'to secure a safe refuge for our people in the land of our fathers'.[41]

Letters of congratulations were read one after the other. The first letter came from a delegate who could not be there and ended with the following paragraph:

> I am especially glad to know that Palestine, the cradle of civilisation, is about to become the home of the people who once so proudly possessed it. In that enterprise I wish you all good and God-speed. Yours very truly.[42]

Speakers such as Professor David Werner Amram greeted the Congress in the name of the Jews of Philadelphia and stressed that for him Zionism was a project that would ensure equality for all in Palestine 'without regard to religion, race or sex'. And:

> So far as it lay in our power to declare the principles upon which a new state in Palestine should be erected, we said in no uncertain words that Christians and Mohammedans should enjoy every right and every privilege that is enjoyed by any Jew.[43]

As with the Balfour Declaration, such statements gave the impression that the Jews had a significant presence in Palestine at the time and that they were part of the indigenous population. In reality, the Jews were less than ten per cent of the population, and nearly half of them were settlers who had just arrived in Palestine. As for the aspirations of the local population at the time of the conference, they were clearly articulated by the nascent Palestinian national group, the Muslim-Christian Associations, which demanded an independent Palestine on the basis of their Wilsonian right to self-determination. And yet, there was a striking difference between Anglo-Jewish support for Zionism and the sentiment expressed at the Congress. All mentions of support for Balfour were immediately followed by a caveat about the need to consider the aspirations of the other people in Palestine. In their speech delegates tried to drive the message home in various formulations such as this:

> In Palestine the Jews have pledged themselves to recognize the rights of every people and of every creed. The Jews of America know what it means to live in harmony and unity with their fellow-citizens whatever their nationality or origin may be.[44]

Respecting the rights of other nationalities remained important to them, even though it was an impossible promise within Zionism, both in its ideology and in practice. The Zionist movement aimed to build a democratic Jewish state. This could only work if the majority of its inhabitants would choose a Jewish state – a very unlikely outcome if historical Palestine's demographic make-up remained the same.

In any case this came out in the final resolution:

> The American Jewish Congress, speaking for the Jews of America expresses its appreciation of the historic and epoch making declaration addressed by His Majesty's Government on November 2, 1917, to the Jewish people, through the Zionist Organization, in which it approved of the establishment in Palestine of a national home for the Jewish people and pledged to use its best endeavors to facilitate the achievement of this object – it being clearly understood that nothing shall be done which may prejudice the civil and religious rights of non-Jewish communities in Palestine or the rights and political status enjoyed by Jews in any other country.[45]

But when it came to grassroots members, the discourse was much more in line with that heard in Britain or in Palestine: 'America is our sanatorium, but Palestine will cure us altogether', as one delegate put it.[46] This was expressed mainly in the form of personal stories of conversion to Zionism:

> Before this war, I was in Palestine, and I saw the hills which beckon to our people. Now that Palestine is to belong to us, we must be united. There must be room in Palestine for the conservative and for the radical. Palestine must be the mother of us all.[47]

Or, as another delegate put it:

> Our doubt bound us with heavy chains. Now we know our future. We have won our nation and our country. Now we get new strength, and we know that the Jewish nation will accomplish much. The great demonstration that witnesses the adoption of the Palestine resolution gives us spirit for the future.[48]

And finally, in the words of another delegate:

> Only give to the Jews the right to return to their Mother Zion and they will show the world that they are again the holy and mighty people.[49]

Eyes were turned in this respect to the socialists who attended the Congress in large numbers. Zionism and socialism may have worked in tandem in Palestine or in Britain, but in America, Zionists weren't allied with the socialists by default. At the Congress, the socialists made an effort to show that the two ideologies were compatible. They were encouraged by the support for the Balfour Declaration by the British Labour Party. One delegate commented:

> Several years ago, I wrote an article and I said that the Jews were entitled to their language, their religion and their country. In the Socialist circles it was looked upon as a bit of treachery. Since that time there is no Socialist opposition to the idea. A year ago the

Socialist Internationale adopted a resolution warmly endorsing Palestine as a homeland for the Jews. At about the same time the Jewish National Socialist Bureau adopted a similar resolution. I began to preach Socialism when I was 17 years old. I am now sixty and I hope to die a Socialist. It may be that I will die a Socialist in Palestine.[50]

This delegate vastly overstated the support of the 'Socialist Internationale' for Zionism. There was no meeting of the pre-1914 Socialist International members during the war, as the French refused to meet the Germans, and hence those on opposing national sides met separately. These references to Balfour and Palestine should be read against the overall discussion in the first Congress about Judaism being a national identity in Palestine as elsewhere. If it applied to America, the delegates immediately detected the catch – they might be accused of dual loyalty, so they hastened to explain:

The clouds of doubt have been dispelled. The misconceptions that have clung about the Zionist aims have been cleared away. No one believes any longer that the renascence of the Jewish people and the ultimate re-establishment of the Jewish commonwealth is a movement to drive all the Jews into Palestine or in the slightest degree to impinge upon their exclusive loyalty to the country of their birth or naturalization. No one expects or desires that all Jewry shall be gathered together in that small land. Through practically all of their history Jews have been scattered. In the ancient days but a nucleus of them constituted the Jewish nation in Palestine. In our days and generation and in the centuries to come no one expects that more than a nucleus of our people will be gathered together in their national home. Those who are so gathered will, however, be sufficient in numbers truly to be representative of the Jewish people.[51]

This was a statement no one among the Zionist leaders and activists on the ground in Palestine would have concurred with, as the delegates who phrased it probably realised. But it was a statement which was deemed a good strategy for allaying the concerns of the American public and the enemy from within – the American Jewish Committee; this paradox, and the fear of dual nationality, were at the centre of the Committee's rejection of Zionism.

Statements like this of course did not solve the conundrum that unfolded when Judaism was discussed more fully as nationalism, and, as James Loeffler rightly notes, this ambivalence continued to trouble the community until 1945. By default, knowingly or not, the American Jewish Congress was rejecting those who decided to assimilate into non-Jewish societies, but at the same time had no idea how to implement the idea of Jewish nationality on the ground in the USA. Again in Loeffler's words: 'American Jews fell conspicuously silent about their own political identity at home',[52] while loudly promoting Jewish nationhood elsewhere.

The American Jewish Congress demanded that two countries in particular should grant their Jewish communities the status of a national minority: Poland and Romania. The Congress stated that in these two countries, there was 'an urgent need' to recognise the Jews as a national group, with national rights as the best means to oppose growing anti-Semitism in those countries. The nation state for both these national groups would not be forever their home countries, as their true home was being built in Palestine.

After the inaugural meeting, the leaders of the emerging lobby, unlike the rank and file of the Congress, were still preoccupied by the absence of clear American support for the Balfour Declaration. They were mainly annoyed by the ambiguity caused by the strong objections of the State Department, preventing an unambiguous statement on the issue by the White House.

The State Department was loyal to the worldview that President Wilson envisioned in his speech at Mount Vernon in 1918, as it aided the president in his endeavours to translate this vision into reality during the peace negotiations after the war. The American president wished to exploit the results of the war to dissolve the mammoth colonial empires in the name of the right to independence and self-determination. In the Wilsonian vision, the Arab peoples too were entitled to enjoy national freedom and be part of a brave new world. Wilson suspected that Britain and France wanted to replace Turkish and Austro-Hungarian imperialism with European colonialism. He therefore asked the Peace Conference in Versailles to send a commission of inquiry to the Arab world to ascertain the peoples' aspirations there.

The main aim of the State Department under the guidance of the secretary of state, Robert Lansing, was to persuade the president that the right to self-determination for the Palestinians was incompatible with Zionism. Lansing wondered how Wilson's commitment to self-determination could be 'harmonized with Zionism, to which the President is practically committed'. But it wasn't only in the Department that such queries were raised. The president's own legal adviser, David Hunter Miller, stated that 'the rule of self-determination would prevent the establishment of a Jewish state in Palestine'.[53]

Lansing convinced the president to include Palestine in the tour of the commission of inquiry, and now the president had to choose the right people for that mission.

THE KING–CRANE LEGACY AND ITS DEMISE

In the heart of Ohio lies the town of Oberlin. At the beginning of the nineteenth century, it was still a typical mid-west American village, surrounded by cornfields stretching for miles. Both rural and remote, it would have escaped a place in the collective American memory had it not been for a unique theological college that was established there in 1833, away from the ivy towers of the east and west coasts. Oberlin College was opened by clergymen – but of an unusual kind. Its members were motivated by a commitment to peace and equality, both in the USA and in the world at large. In its early years, the college fought against racial segregation and discrimination against women in American academia. There, Henry King taught for many years but, as was common for researchers then, he did not specialise in one particular area. At first King was attracted to theological education, then mathematics and finally philosophy. In 1902 he became the college's president; then, during the First World War, he left this comfortable position to become the head of the YMCA in Paris. In the photo gallery of the college, one can see a tall man with a Groucho-like moustache decorating his long face, sitting next to a thin, long table made to fit this tall man's proportions. This was taken at the Paris YMCA. It was while there in France that King was asked by his good friend, President Woodrow Wilson, to become involved in world politics and head his commission of inquiry to the Arab world.[54]

King's partner for heading the mission came from a very different place: Turkey. In the north-eastern part of Istanbul, the University of Boğaziçi overlooks the Bosporus Strait. Its buildings, clinging to the hill slopes that descend to the banks of the strait, resemble those of Oberlin College, which is no surprise as they too were built by American clergymen. This campus was opened in 1839 and was first named Robert College.[55] It survived the Great War, which positioned the US and Turkey as enemies, remaining an American cultural centre at the heart of Istanbul. Charles Crane, a businessman from Chicago and a diplomat of sorts, was the campus's main trustee. He was about to invest more time in it as part of his plan to expand an all-American campus system in the Arab world, when he too was called on by President Wilson to assist King in his Middle East peace mission.[56] Crane gladly agreed to take part in what was an effort to enhance the independence of the Arab peoples according to the principle of self-determination.

This was a tall order, as most of the Arab world had already been divided into new nation states by the colonialist powers, even before the war ended. The particular part of the Arab world due to be visited by the commission had already been carved up by Britain and France in the Sykes–Picot Agreement of 1916. However, like President Wilson, they hoped to quell colonialist hunger by bulking out the dish with a bit of liberalism. It was still necessary to understand the real ambitions of the people living in the areas that Britain and France co-ruled. And thus, despite demonstrable hostility from Britain and France, the Versailles Peace Conference (representing the ten victorious countries that won the war) agreed to delay the decision about the final make-up of Syria, Lebanon and Palestine until the report by the commission was completed.

King and Crane enlisted seven experts in different fields and set out for the area on 10 June 1919, staying there for forty-two days. They visited more than 1,500 locations – an amazing achievement for such a small delegation. In Palestine, they met urban elites, Jewish settlers and Christian missionaries. They were in Jaffa, Rishon LeZion, Jerusalem, Ramallah, Nablus, Jenin, Nazareth, Haifa and Acre until they returned to Turkey on board the US navy destroyer *Hazelwood*. They commended the sincerity of the urban and rural inhabitants of Palestine. They discovered that most of them were happy to be part of a pan-Arab independent Syria, although quite a few of the urban inhabitants hoped that an independent Palestine would eventually be established. They mainly knew what they did not want: a Zionist presence, the Balfour Declaration and a British or French mandate. King and Crane's final report refrained from taking set positions, except on one point: it clearly stated that Palestine's non-Jewish population was emphatically against Zionism and that to subject them to 'unlimited Jewish immigration' would be a 'gross violation' of their rights.[57]

Two of the experts disagreed with the report on this point and produced their own minority report, which better reflected the American and British positions on Palestine. Their report stated: 'Zionism was in the best interest of the land and its people … and this trumped all other considerations'.[58] They were assisted by a Zionist effort on the ground to find 'good Arabs' who would welcome a Jewish state in Palestine, but these manipulations, as they are described by Andrew Patrick, did not impress those who authored the major report's rejection of Zionism.[59]

In Paris and London, the report was viewed suspiciously, not only because of its rejection of Zionism, but mainly due to its attention to the right of self-determination for the Arab nations in areas coveted by the two European powers. As Michael Reimer noted, 'the French and British and even some Americans argued that a sound decision could be made in Paris [that is, at the Versailles Peace Conference] about Syria without consulting the Syrian population'.[60] Without such 'sound decisions', such a report could challenge the Anglo-French network of secret agreements, already set up in 1912, that divided up the greater Syria area

(Palestine, Lebanon, Syria and Jordan) between themselves. The Balfour Declaration was thrown into the deal, granting the establishment of a Jewish homeland in Palestine as well as the creation of a Hashemite kingdom in Transjordan.

The report was only published in 1922 – long after President Wilson, the only world leader then sympathetic to Arab self-determination, had left office on account of a debilitating stroke. The report was submitted to the League of Nations and was immediately shelved and ignored.

Charles Crane blamed the Zionists and the French for the burial of the report, but it seems that the State Department was unable to over-come the lack of interest both in the White House and on Capitol Hill to involve America any further in the affairs of the Arab world. Nor was there anyone making a concerted effort to challenge the passive support the US Congress lent Zionism.

As far as the American Jewish Congress and the American Zionist Federation, the two principal pro-Zionist lobbies at the time, were concerned, the key issue was not whether the report was published, but preventing it from having any impact. Without much pressure being applied, the US Congress was already mostly pro-Zionist. This provided an important lesson on the power of inertia – the more people who took Zionism for granted, the less need there was for the lobby to cajole politicians into voting the right way.

Several historians lamented the failure of the report. If heeded, wrote Martin A. Smith, it could have led to the creation of a unitary state in Palestine (rather than a partition) and may even have helped to establish a greater Syrian state.[61] Andrew Patrick goes further, stating that the people of the Middle East were not taken seriously in 1919, leading to cycles of violence that are still with us today. Lori Allen, in a recent book, is even more scathing in her judgement. She doubts even the sincerity of King and Crane themselves because they were ingrained in a deeply Orientalist mentality and therefore conceived of the Arabs in general as a 'race' inherently incapable of forming democratic national states.[62]

With the suppression of the report, the formerly energetic American involvement in the Middle East petered out, and with it, the only

American scheme in modern times that attempted to build a new Middle East according to the wishes of its inhabitants and not the interests of Washington and its allies. Sparks of this positive energy would intermittently flicker among the more pro-Arab American diplomats and officials of the State Department, but it would never again materialise into a concerted strategy to allow Arab self-determination. This was particularly true in Palestine's Mandatory period. When experts were asked by President Franklin D. Roosevelt to provide an assessment of the Zionist movement, they wrote: 'It has never been considered [by the US government] that the realization of a Jewish National Home was connected with safeguarding American rights and interests.'[63] But they mainly recommended pursuing a neutral policy and clandestinely assisting the British. This line held until 1942, when the Zionist leadership in Palestine succeeded for the first time in eliciting overwhelming support from the American Jewish community. This was immediately translated into pressure on the White House to abandon its neutrality towards the future of Palestine. A powerful lobby began its work, encouraging whoever was sitting in the White House to discard any ideas akin to those proposed by King and Crane.

It did not happen overnight. For a while King and Crane's legacy lingered on and their heirs were a group of professional university graduates who staffed the State Department sections dealing with the Near East. These were the famous 'Arabists'. We will turn to their surprising impact on US policy later.

However, the influence of 'Arabist' ideas, which would have orientated the USA to side with the Palestinian liberation movement, never fully materialised. The forces that countered the 'Arabists' gradually blunted the influence of professional diplomats on American policy towards the Arab world as a whole and towards Palestine in particular. This counter force consisted of the pro-Zionist Jewish and Christian lobbies, working in tandem even before 1948. The basis for this co-operation was the rise of a new generation of Christian Zionists during the first half of the twentieth century. The number of their disciples grew exponentially, enthused by their fiery sermons, first broadcast on radio and then screened on television, reaching millions with the simplistic message of a religious imperative to support Zionism and its actions on the ground unreservedly. Their positive view of Zionism was reinforced by the growing tension between the Christian missionaries and the Islamic religious establishments in the Eastern Mediterranean. The missionaries, who once preached for liberation from European colonialism, hoped that American Christianity and not the Islamic tradition would become the leading light of the new nations, a mission in which they failed. In many ways, the second and third generations of missionaries became the first 'Orientalists' – in the more negative sense of the term. But forty years before Edward Said's *Orientalism* brought widespread attention to this group, another Edward was warning of the dubious impact of the missionary. This was Edward Earle, a Princeton professor, who wrote in *Foreign Affairs* in 1929 that:

> For almost a century American Public Opinion concerning the Near East was formed by missionaries. If American opinion has been uninformed, misinformed and prejudiced, the missionaries are largely to blame. Interpreting history in terms of the advance of Christianity, they have given an inadequate, distorted, and occasionally a grotesque picture of Moslems and Islam.[64]

The missionaries presented an even more distorted picture when they focused on Palestine. Their descriptions faithfully presented their immense disappointment at their first physical encounters with the Holy Land. Like Mark Twain, they found it difficult to digest the gap between what they discovered and the vision of a Christian biblical country that the Holy Scriptures had led them to imagine. Very much like the Zionists who would follow them, as well as the British and Germans who came with them, they did not perceive the locals as a nation or a group with rights or claims to the country, but rather as, at best, an exotic spectacle and, at worst, an ecological nuisance. The Zionist movement, similarly uninterested in the local population except for the inconvenience they represented, immediately won their support, although it would take years before this link became a solid alliance between Christian fundamentalism and the state of Israel – an alliance that would greatly affect American policy in the Middle East as a whole. Before that could happen, Zionism had to become more popular among the American Jewish community. Before the outbreak of the Second World War, this was a slow process. But from then onwards, there was no stopping the rapid Zionisation of the American Jewish community.

THE FINAL STRUGGLE FOR THE BALFOUR DECLARATION

As late as 1922, the head of the Near East Division, Allen W. Dulles, wrote: 'Ex-President Wilson is understood to have favoured the Balfour Declaration, but I do not know that he ever committed himself to it in an official and public way.'[65] But by that time, it seems the lobby was less interested in the position of the State Department; it turned its attention to the United States Congress and was able to garner unequivocal support for the Balfour Declaration. Its success there taught future lobbies for Israel an important lesson: if, as a lobbyist, you encountered ambivalence about Zionism, and later Israel, at the level of the executive or diplomatic branches, you could counter their hesitation by approaching the legislative arm of the administration, which was more susceptible to pressure and advocacy. And thus, the first ever application of this tactic, namely bypassing an equivocating president and unco-operative State Department by approaching Capitol Hill, took place on 11 September 1922. On that day, Congress passed a joint resolution favouring a Jewish homeland in Palestine. The words of the resolution practically echoed the Balfour Declaration; both houses declared:

> That the United States of America favours the establishment in Palestine of a national home for the Jewish people, it being clearly understood that nothing shall be done which may prejudice the civil and religious rights of Christian and all other non-Jewish communities in Palestine, and that the Holy places and religious buildings and sites in Palestine shall be adequately protected.[66]

The Zionists loudly trumpeted the resolution as another Balfour Declaration, evidence that their quest had official support. After all, it had been sponsored by Senator Henry Cabot Lodge and Representative Hamilton Fish, and signed by President Warren G. Harding. However, during the debate leading up to the ratification of the resolution, a number of speakers had emphasised that it was merely an expression of sympathy by Congress and that the resolution in no way would involve the United States in foreign entanglements. This was the interpretation adopted by the State Department, who made it clear that the declaration in Congress was meaningless and did not affect American policy towards the future of Palestine.

There were other challenges after Philadelphia. Some of the pillars of the new lobby gradually withdrew from public life. One was Brandeis, who seemed unable to find a common language with a younger, more eager generation.

After the Philadelphia founding of the American Jewish Congress and the resolution in Capitol Hill, the upward trajectory was linear. Over the next decade, pro-Zionist organisations grew in number and in membership and some began to collaborate with the Christian Zionist lobbying groups. One of the main organisations pulling the discrete threads among Christians and Jews and weaving them into a more powerful lobby was the Pro-Palestine Federation, founded in 1930. It saw pressuring the British government to remain loyal to the Balfour Declaration as its principal aim. It joined forces, during the Second World War, with two other new bodies: the American Palestine Committee and the Christian Council on Palestine, working for similar aims. The number of Zionist organisations with Palestine in their name is liable to mislead: these were separate institutions which, moreover, used 'Palestine' in the sense of a new Jewish homeland. Now Palestine is the name of the disinherited nation of Palestinians.

The work of these Christian organisations concluded the saga around the Balfour Declaration. In December 1942, sixty-three senators and 182 representatives of the House, marked the twenty-fifth anniversary of the Balfour Declaration with a special proclamation in Congress that confirmed that the US endorsed the Declaration.

6

American Zionists and the Holocaust

As in Britain, Nazism and the Holocaust made American Zionists confront an existential question: what should they do about Jews desperately fleeing for their lives? As in Britain, it was a question of energy, resources and time. Researchers now suggest that American Zionists preferred prioritising the survival of the Jewish community in Palestine to promoting sanctuary in America out of ideological commitment.

Like most other countries, the United States did not welcome Jewish refugees from Europe. The Johnson–Reed Act of 1924 severely restricted immigration from Eastern and Southern Europe, while tightening enforcement – a devastating blow to Jews attempting to flee anti-Semitic governments. It restricted their previous quota numbers and limited legal immigration routes for Jews hoping to escape Nazism.[1] The ongoing rise of Nazism and Fascism in Europe did not change this policy. At the 1938 Evian Conference, the USA demonstrated no desire to open its gates. The government faced no pushback for its indifference to the fate of Jewish refugees. In 1939, eighty-three per cent of Americans were opposed to further immigration, and humanitarian concerns took a backseat to economic anxiety.[2]

In the wake of the Great Depression, many in the USA feared the burden that immigrants would place on the nation's economy; refugees, who in most cases were prevented from bringing any money or assets with them, were an even greater cause for alarm. Indeed, as early as 1930, President Herbert Hoover reinterpreted immigration legislation barring those 'likely to become a public charge'[3] to include even those immigrants who were capable of working, reasoning that high unemployment would make it impossible for immigrants to find jobs.

This hostile policy also stemmed from prejudices that conjured imaginary threats allegedly posed by the refugees to American national security – apprehensions that had no basis in reality. Government officials from the State Department to the FBI, as well as President Franklin D. Roosevelt himself, all subscribed to this conspiratorial accusation. While economic concerns certainly played a role in Americans' attitudes toward immigration, so too did feelings of fear, mistrust and racism above all. The ever-growing American institutions deemed to be responsible for the nation's security conceptualised immigrants as either potential communists or Nazis. All in all, in the face of the human catastrophe that so many in Europe experienced during the Second World War, America's conduct was dismal. As Daniel Gross puts it, 'the United States had a poor track record offering asylum' during the time of Nazi domination of Germany and Europe.[4] The most notorious example and consequence of this callous policy occurred in June 1939 when the German ocean liner *St Louis* and its 937 passengers, almost all of them Jewish, was turned away from the port of Miami, forcing it to return to Europe. More than a quarter of its identifiable passengers perished in the Holocaust. If we look at the visa quotas offered by the USA, we see similar indifference to the fate of Jews at work. In late 1938, American consulates were flooded with 125,000 applicants for visas, many coming from Germany and the annexed territories of Austria. But national quotas for German and Austrian immigrants had been set firmly at 27,000.[5]

Most of those who needed sanctuary in the USA were Jews and most of those turned away were Jews. Deborah Lipstadt wrote that the hostile official policy was born out of anti-Semitism, and this is substantiated by other research.[6] The anti-Semitic argument was propagated by leaders such as Father Charles Coughlin, known as the 'radio priest', a pioneer in political broadcasting who reached millions of people with each broadcast. In addition to his religious message, Coughlin preached anti-Semitism, accusing the Jews of manipulating financial institutions and conspiring to control the world. There were other leading voices such as Gerald Smith, a well-known evangelical priest, and the industrialist

Henry Ford, who each in their own way became prominent figures in spreading anti-Semitism.[7]

This official position and the news from Europe gave a different momentum to the Zionist movement in America. The Zionist activist Stephen S. Wise urged the movement as a whole to take advantage of the new developments and used them to strengthen the lobby in North America. Wise was born in Hungary to a Conservative Jewish family but emigrated at a very young age with his family to New York. In New York he received Reform Jewish education – both Conservative and Reform Judaism were indifferent to Zionism at best, and hostile at worst. However, this did not prevent him from becoming one of the most important lobbyists for Zionism in the USA before 1948. Like Gottheil, the first president of the Federation of American Zionists, he too was captivated and enthused by the new ideas of the movement as a young delegate at the first Zionist Congress in Basel. With other friends experiencing the same excitement of participating in the creation of a 'new Jew', when returning to New York, he founded, in the very same year as the Basel Congress, the New York Federation of American Zionists – a body that would grow into the Federation of American Zionists, of which he became the first secretary. The young disciples of Zionism were rewarded by a new invitation to the second Zionist Congress in Basel, working closely with, and totally mesmerised by, Theodor Herzl and his revolutionary vision of Judaism. Wise's influence only grew from there.

From 1935 onwards, through appointment to senior positions in the American Zionist Federation, Wise became the leader of American Zionism and, in the words of Donald Neff, he 'awakened [the move-ment] from its long slumber'.[8] Wise also enjoyed the friendship of President Franklin D. Roosevelt and had free access into the White House. Roosevelt was an easy convert: Chaim Weizmann recorded a conversation with him in which he promoted the idea that Palestine as a whole should be Jewish, and he reportedly said in a February 1940 meeting with Weizmann: 'What about the Arabs? Can't that be settled with a little baksheesh [bribe]?'[9] Weizmann took his meaning to be that the Palestinians should be paid off as an incentive to leave the land.[10]

As long as the Zionists did not demand that the USA open its gates, they had an ally in the White House. American Zionists, like their British counterparts, saw Palestine as the panacea for the plight of the refugees. While after the war, Jewish human rights organisations such as the American Jewish Joint Distribution Committee would help Jewish refugees to be admitted to the USA, in the late 1930s it was mainly Christians who strove to change American policy. Martha and Waitstill Sharp challenged the strong tide of anti-refugee opinion when they agreed to travel to Europe to help victims of the Nazi regime.[11] They were among a small number of Americans who worked to aid refugees despite popular sentiment and official government policies. Most rescue and relief works were carried out under the auspices of aid groups such as the Unitarian Service Committee (created through the Sharps' work), the American Friends Service Committee (run by the Quakers), the Committee for the Care of European Children and the American Jewish Joint Distribution Committee.

Some American government officials also recognised the existential danger facing Jewish communities in Europe and looked for ways to bring more refugees into the country. At a time when having the right 'papers' determined a refugee's chance of survival, immigration policy was crucial. In 1939, Senator Robert Wagner, a Democrat from New York, and Congresswoman Edith Nourse Rogers, a Republican from Massachusetts, sponsored a bill that proposed to admit 20,000 more German Jewish children, outside the existing quota for German-origin migrants. The bill resulted in a rancorous public debate, and vehement opposition by nationalist and anti-immigration groups, and therefore it never reached a vote in Congress.[12]

Like the Zionist leadership in Palestine and their British counterparts, American Jewish organisations only became more focused on rescuing Jews from 1943 onwards, when the horrors of the Holocaust became brutally clear. This new realisation led to a temporary unity of the non-Zionist and Zionist Jewish organisations as part of an effort to save Jews from Nazism, in the form of the Joint Emergency Committee, and also prompted the American government to be more proactive by joining Britain at a special conference convened in Bermuda in 1943 to discuss refugee policies.

The location of Bermuda, under British rule, was suggested by the US State Department – to avoid the spectacle of Zionist demonstrations by the American Jewish Congress in New York. The Zionist lobby hoped for clear support for sending the refugees to Palestine and the non-Zionists anticipated a more humane Anglo-American approach to the question of Jewish refugees. Both were disappointed. The British refused to lift the cap on Jewish immigration into Palestine, and the US refused to admit more Jewish refugees. They could not even agree to send food packages to concentration camps. As Jews faced extermination in Europe, neither Britain nor the US was willing to put their lives ahead of domestic and political interests. One reason for the US's intransigence on the question of refugees was that American Zionists never seriously pushed for more Jews to be admitted into the US. The principal message of American Zionists continued to be that the salvation of Jews lay in unlimited Jewish immigration into Palestine, leading to its eventual colonisation. The scholar Aaron Berman even goes as far as to argue that the Zionisation of American Jews disabled any serious Jewish effort on behalf of the Jews of Nazi Europe.[13] It seems hard to dispute that while individuals were doing their best, the organisations, under Zionist influence, were passive. Critics of his work claim it would not have made a difference. This may be true – even the most rigorous efforts on the part of America's Jewish minority might not have sufficed to overcome the American public's rigid opposition to immigration of any kind. But the purpose of this analysis is to demonstrate the moral cartography of the American Zionist lobby: a cartography in which indirectly pressuring the British state to allow more immigration into Palestine took precedence over rescuing Jews through any other means, even when other means were more viable. After all, why care too much about the Bermuda conference when the Biltmore conference had already taken place, one year before?

THE DEFINING AMERICAN ZIONIST MOMENT: THE BILTMORE CONFERENCE

The New York Biltmore Hotel might have seemed at first glance a particularly imposing railway station – designed by the architects

Warren and Wetmore, who also designed the city's iconic Grand Central Terminal right next door. The neoclassical hotel boasted two towers, each adorned with two pillars at the centre of their façade, visible from the streets below. The twenty-six-storey hotel was an eclectic edifice with a 'stone base with arch openings, a grey brick mid-section and terracotta loggia and projecting cornice', towering above other buildings nearby.[14] It was one of the first buildings in New York history to use air rights – that is, developing property on a platform above the railway lines. Turkish baths, pools, a golden clock in its main lobby and a Palm Court were some of its attractions, but its most brilliant feature was the Italian Garden, on the rooftop of the sixth-storey setback, overlooking Vanderbilt Avenue and the Grand Central Terminal (in winter, it became an ice-skating rink).

Its history can boast some scandal; Zelda and F. Scott Fitzgerald honeymooned there so boisterously that they were asked to leave, and 'meet me under the clock' was a watchword for hopeful lovers. But in the hotel's dining rooms, a different kind of romance reached a new peak – between Zionism and the American Jewish community, a love story that continues to this very day. The Zionist leadership in Palestine, now at loggerheads with Britain, chose this venue to convene one of its most important strategic meetings between 6 and 11 May 1942.

The dining room was arranged so it could function as a conference hall. The rows of chairs faced an elevated platform, at the back of which an unconventional American flag stretched like a theatre screen. On its two sides were the regular Stars and Stripes flag on the right and the Zionist flag (which later became the flag of Israel) on the left. Next to this impressive display stood two comparatively meagre palm twigs, stuck into huge pots, and they completed the decorative set for this historical event.

On the podium there were two rows of chairs and tables, the upper one for the more important guests and speakers, and in the middle was a lectern for the orators. The guests included Chaim Weizmann, the president of the World Zionist Organization and the Jewish Agency, and David Ben-Gurion, the chairman of the Zionist Executive, as well as heads of all the Zionist and pro-Zionist organisations in the American Jewish community.

It was a doubly formative event. First, it was a crucial moment in the history of the Zionist movement on the ground in Palestine. At Biltmore, the Zionist leadership moved away from co-operating with British policy, demanded the whole of Palestine and sidelined Zionist diplomats such as Weizmann. Diplomacy was now obsolete – force was the order of the day.

But second, it was also a defining moment for the lobby in the USA. As the official publication of the American Jewish Congress (AJC) put it:

> The fact that such a major event occurred here and not in London or Jerusalem, hitherto the headquarters for Zionist political work, clearly indicates that the United States has become the main center for Zionist political activities.[15]

The leading star of the conference was Abba Hillel Silver. He was born in Lithuania to a rabbinical family (his grandfather and father were rabbis). From very early on as a teenager in New York he joined in Zionist activities and became a Reform rabbi during the First World War in Cleveland, Ohio, presiding over the largest Reform congregation in America. He gave his first speech in 1907 when he was merely fourteen years old, just a few years after his family had arrived from Lithuania.[16]

His leadership was marked by a constant apprehension that general concern for Jewish suffering would undermine the Zionist project in Palestine:

> Our overemphasizing the refugee issue has enabled our opponents to state that, if it is rescue you are concerned about, why don't you concentrate on that and put the politics aside ... It is possible for the Diaspora to undermine the Jewish state, because the urgency of the rescue issue could lead the world to accept a temporary solution ... We should place increased emphasis on fundamental Zionist ideology.[17]

Silver was critical of the previous leadership and regarded their approach as too soft:

> We'll force the President to swallow our demands! The gentle, patient and personal diplomatic approach of yesterday is not entirely adequate for our days.[18]

He declared:

> We are going to respond to every attack upon our people, to every libel and every slander, by more Jewishness, by more schools and synagogues and by more intensive and loyal work in Palestine.[19]

For a while, his abrasive style did the Zionist cause no favours: presidents and administrations considered him unsavoury and rude. As Nahum Goldmann described him:

> He was an Old Testament Jew who never forgave or forgot … He could be extremely ruthless in a fight, and there was something of the terrorist in his manner and bearing.[20]

What presidents disliked was what grassroots activists went wild for. At the 1942 Biltmore Conference, he was a star, and every motion he moved was accepted almost unanimously. To a huge roar of applause, he demanded that the attendees assist:

> those who have given their tears and their blood and their sweat to build for them and for us and the future generations, at long last, after the weary centuries, a home, a national Home, a Jewish Commonwealth, where the spirit of our entire people can finally be at rest.[21]

As Walter Hixson writes, in many ways he had waited all his life for this moment.[22] Silver's main task was to expand the Zionisation of the American Jewish community. All the Zionists in America endorsed the

Biltmore programme, calling for the creation of a Jewish common-wealth encompassing all of Mandatory Palestine, and the mission now was to obtain similar backing from the Jewish community as a whole.

At Biltmore, the American Jewish community was asked to provide unconditional endorsement of the next steps of the Zionist project in Palestine. Some members of the two leading organizations helping to convene Biltmore, the American Jewish Congress and Hadassah, felt some discomfort about such a request for allegiance, but on the whole, the rank and file followed the leadership's cue on this. Hadassah was also known as the Women's Zionist Organization of America and its claim to fame was its philanthropic work in the field of medicine: it raised funds for hospitals in the Jewish community in Palestine and later in Israel, but was also an important participant in Zionist lobbying on gender issues, which would be perfected and become more sophisti-cated in the years to come. Like the American Jewish Congress, Hadassah adopted a carte blanche commitment to the Zionist project and a promise to continue pressuring the USA to support its main mission of protecting cultural Jewish life in America.

Institutionally, this accelerated Zionisation also manifested in the opening in May 1942 of the Jewish Agency's office in Washington DC – an embassy to all intents and purposes, but one which also co-ordin-ated lobbying for Zionism in the USA (the Jewish Agency registered as a foreign lobbying agent with the Department of Justice in 1939). This was triggered by a visit to the USA by Moshe Sharett, the chief of the Political Department of the Jewish Agency in Jerusalem, and he insti-tuted the American office formally under his direct authority. *In situ*, it was run by Nahum Goldmann, in co-operation with leaders of the American Zionist Organization such as Louis Lipsky and Stephen Wise.

Alongside the old organisations representing Zionist factions on the ground in Palestine (such as Poale Zion and HaMizrachi, a religious Zionist movement organised under the slogan of 'Torah and Labour'), a new lobbying group was born after the Biltmore Conference, named the American Zionist Emergency Council (AZEC, referred to in some sources as AZC). This is a later name; it was first called the Emergency Council of Zionists in America. It functioned until 1949. It had a membership of well over 171,000 by 1940.[23] AZEC would eventually evolve into AIPAC and, like AIPAC, it turned out to be the principal umbrella outfit leading the lobby and dominating its agenda. Immediately after the Biltmore Conference, it focused its efforts on enlarging the membership and the influence of the lobby in America; its first task was to reconnect with the Christian Zionists.

RECONNECTING TO CHRISTIAN ZIONISM IN THE 1940s

The Christian Zionist ideology changed somewhat during the Second World War; its mysticism was now complemented by a realist foreign policy regarding the future of Jews in Palestine. This new orientation was driven by Reinhold Niebuhr, a minister hailing from a German immigrant family. He began his theological life under the spell of socialism, before becoming one of the important thinkers of neo-conservative realism, which represented a new school of thought in international relations, justifying its ideas with allegedly scientific analysis of the pros and cons of aggressive American policies. More importantly for our topic, Niebuhr was the father of 'Christian Realism'. On one hand, this theological position rejected the literal interpretation of the Scriptures by fundamentalists, but on the other hand, it chastised those deemed to be 'Liberal Christians', who subscribed to notions of egalitarianism, anti-colonialism and anti-imperialism. Niebuhr ridiculed these more humane Christians and described them as 'naïve Christians'.[24]

There was now also a Christian Realist logic for supporting Zionism and later Israel; it was a crucial bastion in the battle against the Soviet Union and its allies in the Arab world. The future Israel could not ask for more: it was now both the fulfilment of a divine wish and the shield of the Western world and its democracies in the Middle East.

For ordinary Christians in America, which by that time was the most religious nation on earth, what they learned in Sunday School was enough to persuade them to follow Zionism blindly; they had no need for the intellectual Christian Realist analysis that appeared in Niebuhr's books, such as *The Children of Light and the Children of Darkness*, published in 1944. It was the curriculum of Sunday Schools that informed their worldview, carrying the message that the Jews were the chosen people, who had to be protected unconditionally until the return of the Messiah. Christian Realism would be an important part of the ideological infrastructure that sustained support for Israel later on, as a bridge between the fundamentalist Christian Zionists and the neo-conservative right.

AZEC made light work of reinforcing the pre-existing connections with Christian Zionist bodies and recruiting them in the last days of the Mandate as pressure groups to ensure the maintenance of American support for Zionism in Palestine. This enterprise was pushed forward with the help of two groups: the American Palestine Committee, a Christian 'organization of persons in public life sympathetic to the Zionist program', and the Christian Council on Palestine, a pro-Zionist group composed of Christian clergymen.[25]

The American Palestine Committee was the more important group of the two. It was established in 1931 by several Protestant churches and it advocated reuniting the Jewish people with the 'land of its ancient inheritance.' One of its principal adherents, Senator William King, a Democrat from Utah, asserted that it was the duty of the United States in its 'pre-destined role of arbiter of world affairs' to embrace the Zionist cause. The American Palestine Committee was involved in the 1940 elections, when it began to look for bipartisan endorsements, and it succeeded in enlisting both the future president Harry Truman, who was at the time a Democratic senator from Missouri, and the Republican presidential nominee Wendell Willkie, a senator from Indiana. The American Palestine Committee had its own particular take on the Zionist project in Palestine, as it argued that colonisation would be beneficial to the Palestinians because it would lead to modernisation. But otherwise, it was the same song sung by earlier Christian Zionism: 'The Christian world must rededicate itself to the heritage it has received from Judaism, the mother faith of Christianity.'[26]

The hope was that these new Christian outfits would help recruit money for the Zionist project in Palestine, and AZEC worked closely with the American Jewish Congress on this front. The collection of funds was carried out through the same appeals campaign as for rescuing Jews from the Holocaust. The plea was for money that was needed to save Jews, whether they went to South America or to Palestine. This unified effort was known as the United Jewish Appeal (UJA) – short for the United Jewish Appeal for Refugees, Overseas Needs and Palestine. The archive of the UJA details how the money was distributed, and it seems that roughly a third of the contribution went to Palestine during the war years. Later this campaign would be accompanied by more explicit fundraising for Israel, known as the United Israel Appeal, where one could buy bonds, translated into money, exempted from tax and, as we will learn, sometimes channelled back to the USA, to fund the lobbying work over there.[27]

CONFRONTING RIVAL JEWISH ORGANISATIONS

AZEC was very close to the mainstream leadership of Zionism and some of its time and energy was devoted to fighting the right-wing Zionist faction of Herut (led by Menachem Begin), known at the time as the Revisionists, whom AZEC found to be too anti-British and violent. The Revisionists had many small outfits such as the League for a Free Palestine, Friends of a Jewish Palestine, the Emergency Committee to Save the Jewish People of Europe and many others. AZEC fought them hard and publicly, issuing a 'Warning to the Zionists of America':

> Do not be misled by this group's publicity – remember that full page advertisements will not rebuild the Jewish National home. Mobilize public opinion behind the accredited Zionist bodies.[28]

However, the real mission was not so much suppressing right-wing Zionism but Zionising the faint-hearted Jews, who were still not convinced or enthused by the movement for a new Jewish state. The leaders of AZEC felt that their sister organisation, the American Jewish Congress, was not active enough on this front and took the lead as the most prominent Zionist organisation in the USA. The history of lobbying on both sides of the Atlantic was like a never-ending relay race, where the baton was passed from one organisation as it petered out to a new one poised to take the leadership role. In the 1940s, the star runner was, inevitably, Abba Hillel Silver.

Under his leadership, AZEC initiated a new venture after Biltmore, aimed at luring non-Zionist outfits to be part of a new federated alliance called the American Jewish Conference, and recruited Henry Monsky, the president of B'nai B'rith, allegedly a non-political body that became more Zionist than ever before, to help convince more American Jews to become Zionists.

The non-Zionist organisations were willing to participate in the American Jewish Conference, but stipulated two conditions: first, that Silver would not speak at the inaugural meeting of this new body, and second, that there would be no reference to a Jewish state in Palestine at that meeting. Silver accepted those conditions but found a way to get around them: he made a contribution from the floor about the Jewish state in Palestine. The conference voted overwhelmingly to support the Biltmore plan but the American Jewish Committee, still non-Zionist, walked out in protest. Sixty-four American Jewish organisations embraced the resolution. Silver was pleased; throughout the years of the war, he was able to marginalise non-Zionist Jewish organisations that he claimed 'divided the Jewish community', while his organisation represented 'the overwhelming majority of American Jews'.[29]

The American Jewish Conference recruited other more veteran organisations and together convened, again in Philadelphia, in May 1943 under the banner 'The National Conference for Palestine of the United Palestine Appeal'. Its main message was condemnation of the 1939 White Paper, which restricted severely Jewish immigration into Palestine and Zionist purchase of land there, and it called upon the government of the United States to ask Britain for assurances:

> that Jewish immigration into Palestine shall not be abridged nor shall the purchase of land by Jews be restricted.[30]

On the occasion of a visit to the USA in May by Prime Minister Winston Churchill, all Zionist groups joined in appealing to him to keep Britain's promise to establish a Jewish national home in Palestine and to repudiate the 1939 White Paper. Upon arrival, Churchill was greeted by full-page newspaper advertisements, paid for by the Zionist Organization of America and published on 18 May 1943, demanding bluntly: 'Mr. Churchill, drop the Mandate!'[31]

From this point on, readers will learn about numerous organisations and alliances and federations. But one stands out above all: AZEC, the forefather of the modern AIPAC, which is still hugely influential today. It differed from all the other organisations and umbrella organisations that already populated the lobby. It no longer sought to convince American Jews alone of Zionism – it wanted to win over the American public as a whole.

BUILDING THE FUTURE AIPAC MODEL, 1944–1948

After the second meeting of the American Jewish Conference, AZEC established a model that AIPAC would adopt later. It had a reasonable budget and fourteen professionally staffed departments to galvanise American public opinion in support of the Zionist colonisation of Palestine. It opened a permanent bureau in Washington in 1943 to co-ordinate all its national activities. The journalist Donald Neff rightly attributes all this success to Abba Hillel Silver:

> In the process he created the modern Israeli lobby, the most pervasive and powerful special interest group in foreign affairs in the United States.[32]

A new era of lobbying began, led by Silver and others, that began to break away from a strategy which almost exclusively pinned its hopes on the Democratic Party. Silver thought otherwise. He believed in well-organised and large-scale lobbying and pressure on candidates of both parties. For this he established the 'Community Contacts Committees', later known as the Emergency Committees (ECs), working with grass-roots Jewish America and, more importantly, with local politicians of all parties:

> The first task will be to make direct contact with your local
> Congressman or Senator ... The support and understanding of the
> Congressman should be won, not on the basis of a vague sympathy
> towards the plight of the Jews or because of presumed local political
> obligations, but because he himself has been convinced by reason
> and logic of the justice of our cause.[33]

Everyone was a potential target for lobbying, including union members, wives and parents of servicemen, and Jewish war veterans.

The ECs orchestrated campaigns of mass petitions and flooded Washington with letters – all this had to be done 'in the quickest possible time'. Members of ECs were asked to work through synagogues and other Jewish organisations. They were instructed to cultivate relations with clergymen and develop personal contacts with radio stations and the press. The ECs were instructed to arrange speakers for organisations interested in postwar planning, and for clubs such as the Rotary Club, Kiwanis Club, Exchange Club and Lions Club. AZEC sent ECs a manual, entitled *Confidential Bulletin*, teaching them how all of these tasks should be operationalised on the ground – a 'dummies' guide' for the Zionist lobbyist.[34]

The trade unions were also targeted (and this was a worthy investment, as these unions would be AIPAC's first allies in its early years). To enlist their support, yet another body was founded: the American Jewish Trade Union Committee for Palestine, which included many important leaders of the trade unions in America. The sense among the Zionist leaders in America was that this particular target was fully achieved, as was testified in front of the House Committee on Foreign Affairs:

> American organized labor – twelve million strong – unreservedly
> and unequivocally supports the aspiration of the Jewish people for
> the establishment of their homeland in Palestine.[35]

Like its successor AIPAC, from 1944 the AZEC held annual gatherings, inviting all the ECs, which by that year, as one scholar put it, 'were to be one of the most effective instruments for vocalizing Zionism'.[36] A leader of AZEC stated proudly:

> For the next several years these Committees were to operate with such phenomenal effectiveness as to startle even a Washington grown blasé about lobbying. At a single telephone call, they went immediately into action. More than one Government official and newspaperman expressed his astonishment at the speed and efficiency of the execution.[37]

The main weapons were letters and petitions, and in particular the former. This tactic is still deployed today. Decades later, I was interviewed by Stephen Sackur on the BBC World Service flagship programme *HARDTalk*. I was given a very hard time by him, for which he apologised at the very end of the recording, explaining he had to take a tough line otherwise the BBC would be inundated with a barrage of complaints.[38]

These utterly devoted and tireless bands of local Zionists of all parties hounded local editors for favourable comments, and arranged forums for the Zionist cause in churches, schools and civic societies. They solicited statements from political candidates, sent deputations at their own expense to Washington to interview congressmen and senators, and at critical junctures flooded the White House, the State Department and congressional offices with literally thousands upon thousands of letters and telegrams. They organised local branches of the American Christian Palestine Committee, for whom speakers and seminars were arranged.[39]

As Doreen Bierbrier writes:

> In the 1944 Zionist campaign for the abrogation of the White Paper, more than 3,000 non-Jewish organizations – unions, churches, Rotary, Lion, Elk, and Kiwanis clubs, YMCAs, ministers' associations, orders of the Knights of Pythias, and farm Granges – passed pro Zionist resolutions, circulated petitions, and sent letters and telegrams to the Administration and their Congressional

representatives. In Meriden, Connecticut, alone, whose entire Jewish population did not exceed 1,500 persons, more than 12,000 letters on the subject of Palestine were reportedly dispatched to President Roosevelt and the State Department. Similar expressions to Washington emanated from 200 non-Jewish organizations in Colorado, from petitions signed by 60,000 persons in South Bend, Indiana, and from Leominster, Massachusetts, 1,000 telegrams. Congressmen expressed 'amazement' at such substantial non-Jewish interest in distant Palestine.[40]

The other method, which AIPAC would perfect, was targeting individual politicians early in their careers. What they were asked to do was to secure pro-Zionist resolutions from state legislatures and hundreds of municipalities which represented more than eighty-five per cent of the American population. Congressmen were the primary targets of the members of the local ECs. In October 1944, AZEC reported that out of the 535 members of the seventy-eighth Congress, 411 endorsed the Zionist call for immediate American action to sanction a Jewish commonwealth. Representatives of every state, totalling eighty-six per cent of the Senate and seventy-five per cent of the House of Representatives, further affirmed the Jewish right to settle in Palestine, unhampered by arbitrary British restrictions.

Efforts were also made to organise grassroots support from the wider American public. An effective channel for Christian goodwill toward Zionism was provided by two Christian organisations I have mentioned before, the American Palestine Committee and the Christian Council on Palestine. Directives were issued to the ECs urging them to prepare a list of all Christian notables in the community and send it to AZEC, along with a brief note on each prospective candidate. An invitation to join the American Palestine Committee was signed by Senator Robert Wagner and then sent to each prospective member. When there were enough members to form a local chapter of the American Palestine Committee, they were inaugurated by a nearby Jewish Emergency Committee. All the expenses incurred in such operations were paid by AZEC.

Through this generous financial support, the American Palestine Committee was able to recruit an impressive number of members. I reiterate that the word 'Palestine' here had nothing whatsoever to do with the Palestinians in Palestine; it referred only to the Jewish colonies and settlements. By 1946, the organisation had a membership of 15,000, organised into seventy-five nationwide local chapters. The membership was drawn largely from representatives of law, business, education, social service and public life. These local Christian chapters were often organised by the chairmen of the Jewish AZEC and the local ECs. Or put differently, the American Palestine Committee, which was nominally a Christian grouping, was de facto run by American Jewish Zionist organisations.

By March 1944, the American Palestine Committee was able to have a formidable national conference in support of Zionism attended by the vice president, Henry A. Wallace. The Christian Zionist bodies had their own national conference in November 1945 with representatives from thirty countries, including the future president of Chile, Gonzáles Videla.

But lobbying efforts didn't end here: Zionists looked to garner support in university campuses. This was the role of the Committee for Intellectual Mobilization run by Rabbi Milton Steinberg. Zionism had not attracted widespread campus support during the 1930s, since more liberal and socialist movements dominated intellectual circles in America. After the Second World War, Jewish academics became more interested in Zionist ideology and a number of them began to support it publicly. However, surveys taken in 1941 and 1946 on college campuses 'reveal that Zionist opinions were less prevalent among Jewish students than among adult Jews'.[41] Nonetheless, parts of the academic community were mobilised. A petition was presented to the US Congress in January 1945, signed by 150 college presidents and deans, and 1,800 faculty members from forty-five states. The petition declared support for the reconstitution of Palestine 'as a free and democratic Jewish Commonwealth' open to unlimited immigration and colonisation. Nonetheless, the intellectual community of America never appeared to endorse Zionism wholeheartedly.[42] As late as February 1947, AZEC had difficulty in persuading mainstream media to publish its loyal writers. They failed to get pro-Zionist articles published in *Harper's* and *Foreign Affairs*. As we shall see, this would change dramatically after the June 1967 war. But the pre-1948 Zionist lobby had its own major publication: *Palestine*, which was later joined by another, called *Palestine Affairs*. AZEC lobbied writers and academics to write pro-Zionist fiction and non-fiction, disseminating the books for free through the ECs. Among these were *His Terrible Swift Sword* by Rev. Norman MacLean, *American Policy Toward Palestine* by Carl J. Friedrich, and *To Whom Palestine?* by Frank Gervasi. One book, *Palestine, Land of Promise* by Walter Clay Lowdermilk, made the best-seller lists of several newspapers.[43] Nowadays the lobby's impact on many American campuses is limited – it regards them as lost causes in the propaganda battle. Over the past century, American academia has developed at least some powerful anti-Zionist voices.

Next the newspapers and the radio were targeted. The American press was generally sympathetic to the plight of European Jewry – the mission of the lobby was to translate this humanitarian sympathy into support for the colonisation of Palestine. More urgently, AZEC made a huge effort to galvanise the press against the 1939 White Paper of the British government, which recommended significantly restricting Jewish immigration into Palestine and land purchases. More than 350 anti-White Paper editorials appeared in prominent American newspapers during the council's campaign. The council placed full-page advertisements in the largest English and Yiddish newspapers. It was possible to buy airtime in North America, and in 1943 both AZEC and the Zionist Organization of America purchased 182 hours on American radio and 50 hours in Canada. *Palestine Speaks* was the flagship programme of this effort and its anchors were Hollywood stars such as Joseph Cotten, Eddie Cantor and Edward G. Robinson.[44]

And finally, building on this multidimensional strategy, AZEC added the organisation of mass rallies and conventions, framed as 'large scale gatherings' by the leadership. There was a strict directive from Abba Hillel Silver and the leadership not to waste time and energy on smaller gatherings. Quite frequently, up to 1948, it was Madison Square

Garden and big urban parks that were the venues for these mass rallies on behalf of a Zionist Palestine. The rallies were a mixture of the old model of rabble-rousing speeches and the glamour and star power of Hollywood and Broadway musicals. The first of these grand spectacles in Madison Square Garden took place in 1943.

It was called *We Will Never Die*, arranged by a group called the Committee for a Jewish Army, a Zionist organisation led by emissaries from the paramilitary Zionist groups in Palestine to advocate for a Jewish state in Palestine as the only answer to the extermination of the Jews by the Nazis.

It was written by Ben Hecht and produced by Billy Rose, while Kurt Weill wrote the music. A young Marlon Brando was there with Paul Muni and Edward G. Robinson on the set. The poster for the play showed Jewish soldiers, donning American military fatigues, but also representing the Zionist militias in Palestine, as all of them wore bands on their shoulders with a Star of David on it. In one scene, one of these soldiers saved an Orthodox Jew from the hands of a Nazi soldier. The pageant was a great success and toured the country from coast to coast. The premiere was attended by the First Lady, Eleanor Roosevelt, and by almost all the members of the Supreme Court.[45]

It was the first, and perhaps last, time that the Holocaust would be turned into a musical. It began with a prayer for two million Jews who had been killed in Europe, as news of the camps had trickled in from the continent. Twenty actors dressed as rabbis were presented as escapees from Europe, reciting the Jewish prayer of 'Shema Israel' together. They stood in front of the Ten Commandments of the Old Testament, appearing as ten separate high tablets. In the next scene Paul Muni and Edward G. Robinson, two of Hollywood's most well-known stars at the time, listed the names of prominent Jews throughout history, beginning with Moses and ending with Supreme Court Justice Louis Brandeis, Sigmund Freud and the twenty Jewish Nobel laureates. Harsher scenes followed depicting life in the concentration camps, and the victims would appear in the final scene testifying in front of an imagined postwar peace conference. In a subsequent production of the same show on the stage of the Hollywood Bowl a few weeks later, the Zionist anthem *Hatikvah* (which became the Israeli national anthem) was added to the scoreline to counter Nazi songs at the end of the show.

The American Jewish Congress leadership felt uncomfortable about this kind of emotive advocacy and some performances were cancelled under pressure from them. But one hundred thousand Americans turned up to see a musical memorialising the victims of a Nazi genocide that had not yet ended. This genocide served as the ultimate proof that Jews needed their own state and their own army.

After the pageant, more conventional displays of Zionist presence were held. The peak of this activity was a convention in October 1945. A photograph of that convention captioned 'Americans for a Jewish Palestine' says it all. The hall of this meeting was packed, with 22,000 sitting inside and 45,000 standing outside, and in a rally a day earlier in Madison Square Park it was reported that 200,000 people had been part of a new Zionist show of force. The banner dangling from the third floor read 'Fed up with false promises' and 'Six million Jews dead is enough'. On the second floor, two huge photographs, one next to the other, juxtaposed an image of a concentration camp with one showing a happy Zionist settler in Palestine.[46]

A year later, at a pageant in March 1946, John W. McCormack, House majority leader, in a speech phoned from Washington to Madison Square Garden, accused Great Britain of directing the might of its Empire 'against those wretched survivors, whom Hitler did not quite succeed in exterminating', and of using lend-lease weapons to spread imperialism.[47]

At that event, Senator James M. Mead said that:

> The conduct of the mandatory power and its administration in Palestine is in sharp contrast to the endless chain of commitments by the United States and the United Kingdom.[48]

He further exhorted Americans:

> to erase the blot on our conscience left by the callous massacre of six million Jews, which could have at least been partially averted had Palestine not been hermetically sealed to escaping Jews.

J. Howard McGrath, the solicitor general of the USA, the fourth-highest position in the American Department of Justice, and a future attorney general, declared in the meeting that the 'time has come for the Jewish Nation to reclaim Palestine.'[49]

Even before this convention, a cable was sent on its behalf to the British government, and its final section read:

Taking gravest possible view position and disastrous consequences announcement enforcement such policy [stop] proper immediate reaction Jewish general American opinion may perhaps still avert the catastrophe [stop].

In addition, 250,000 notices were sent out. 'Telephone squads' contacted as many people as possible. Letters were sent to 700 rabbis asking them to make announcements concerning British policy and the forthcoming rally.

In the wake of the meeting, 'An Open Letter to Mr. Attlee' (the British prime minister at the time) was placed in forty newspapers throughout the country. Abba Hillel Silver and Stephen Wise issued strong statements to the press declaring 'that the Jewish people would resist to the bitter end the reported British decision to continue the White Paper policy.'[50]

Mass demonstrations were also conducted in thirty other cities throughout the nation. An emergency conference of EC leaders was held in Washington three days later. The 531 delegates received instructions from Silver for further action and were enlightened by an analysis of the political situation in Palestine by one Emanuel Neumann, a senior activist and one of the heads of the World Zionist Organization in the USA. That same day, two-thirds of the Senate had an audience with constituents who had participated in the Madison Square Garden conference. Two days previously, ten senators spoke on the Palestine issue in the Senate. On 16 October (two weeks after the conference), seventeen representatives spoke on Palestine; thirty-four more did not have time to speak, but their speeches were placed in the Congressional Record. It was estimated that 411 members of the Senate and the House, out of 535, made pro-Zionist statements.[51]

All of the above activities were planned and executed within a time span of approximately one year between October 1945 and October 1946 – a very busy year. Yet another open-air rally was held in Madison Square Park towards the end of October 1946. An estimated 250,000 attended to express solidarity with the Jewish colonies in Palestine – making it the largest Zionist demonstration of all time. It ended with a specifically Christian Conference in Washington which was organized by the staff of AZEC.

By 1948, the people who established AZEC could look back proudly at their work since 1943. They had founded the political arm of American Zionism, which became one of the strongest pressure groups that had ever existed in America until then, leaving barely any room for Jewish public life outside the realm of Zionism, and this was long before the appearance of AIPAC. Yet their success in the public sphere had barely any impact on American state policy towards Palestine. In the 1940s, they were sowing the seeds, but those seeds would bear fruit in the early 1960s – and laid the foundation for American policy from the post-Kennedy era to today.

THE RISE OF ISAIAH LEO KENEN

In the American Zionist lobby's relay race, the baton was now handed over from Silver and Wise, following Silver's retirement and Wise's death, to Isaiah Leo Kenen. His Zionist activism began when he was a junior staffer in Silver's Cleveland offices.[52] Kenen was a young journalist from Toronto, working for the *Toronto Star*, who moved to Ohio in 1926. He left journalism behind and began to study law but did not practise it for long. In 1941 he decided to be publicly involved in pro-Zionist activity and soon became the president of the Cleveland Zionist District, which was part of the Zionist Organization of America. In the 1940s he also served as a director of the Jewish Agency's information department until the establishment of the state of Israel when he joined the new state's delegation to the UN, where he would set a new lobbying institution, AIPAC, in motion in 1953. For him, the eventual triumph of the Israeli state represented the defeat of Hitler, and a challenge to

America and other Western democratic states who did nothing to save the Jews from the Holocaust:

> Our Jewish community faced a challenge in 1942. Numbed and helpless bystanders as Adolf Hitler waged his demonical war against the Jewish People, embittered by our failure to rouse the democracies to deter Hitler, to rescue and open doors to those who might be saved, American Jews assumed their responsibility during World War II. Despite the opposition of the Department of State, they made a commitment to establish an Independent Jewish state where Jews could live in freedom and security.[53]

Nowhere in his writing, from his early career to the end of it, does he mention, or show concern for, the Palestinian victims of the project he so wholeheartedly supported, and to which one might even say he devoted his life.

Kenen was intensively involved in the 1944 electoral campaign when for the first time he practised a methodology that would become the hallmark of AIPAC. In February, he reported that lobbying for the creation of the Jewish Commonwealth had 'profoundly impressed the Capitol, evoking many assurances of support from Congressmen'.[54] This was part of the overall effort of AZEC to be involved in an American national election campaign in a systematic way for the first time. That it was a successful first attempt can be seen from the fact that both major political parties endorsed the idea of a Jewish state in their platforms. Kenen worked mainly with the Democratic Party. It was Abba Hillel Silver who began building an alliance with the Republican Party that would grow to be the main base of the pro-Israel lobby in America today. In this he was assisted by Benzion Netanyahu, a professor at Cornell University, a right-wing Revisionist Zionist and father of Benjamin Netanyahu.[55]

At this point US lobbying efforts didn't affect the reality on the ground in Palestine, as the British Mandate was still making the key decisions. But Washington could have had some impact. It took part in the last international initiatives searching for a solution. The first was a joint Anglo-American committee of inquiry assembled in Washington in January 1946 which, after three months, published a report about the conditions of the people in Mandatory Palestine and recommendations for the future. The American representatives were hoping to de-politicise the question of Palestine – through this lens, the Jewish presence was a humanitarian concern, not the groundwork for a colonisation project. This was an unrealistic approach, based on either total ignorance of Zionism's aims or total disregard for Palestinian aspirations. The recommendation was to allow 100,000 Jewish refugees to enter Palestine and to rescind the restrictions imposed on land purchase by the 1939 White Paper in preparation for a settled future – namely a long-term continuation of British rule. A more detailed programme for continued British rule appeared later in another joint Anglo-American inquiry, the last of these, led by the British Cabinet minister Herbert Morrison and the American ambassador to London, Henry Grady. In July 1946, this small group suggested a federalised Palestine under British trusteeship.

By that time, both initiatives proved to be pointless. The Zionist movement in 1946 was willing only to negotiate about space and not sovereignty. There were certain parts of Palestine they were willing to concede, about one-fifth of the country. The leadership had already begun to contemplate how to get rid of the Palestinians in the remaining coveted eighty per cent of Palestine. The Palestinian leadership demanded the same freedom and self-determination promised to the rest of the Arab world – a unitary democratic state, where they would constitute two-thirds of the population and would consider what status they would give to the Jewish settlers who arrived before the Second World War. The deadlock in the negotiations pushed Britain to decide to leave Palestine and entrust its future into the hands of the United Nations in February 1947.[56]

As far as the pro-Zionist lobby in America, under Kenen's leadership now, was concerned, these two initiatives in 1946 went quite unheeded. And this is not surprising; the powerbase that AZEC had built was not bothered with these overtures and continued to supply the goods: consistent support, no questions asked, for a Jewish state in

Palestine with the blessing of America.[57] The lobby had a different mission now: to assess and counter possible voices in the USA that might push Washington away from a clear pro-Zionist position.

OTHER VOICES

A Gallup Poll taken in 1945 found that seventy-six per cent of Americans supported the Zionist colonisation effort in Palestine;[58] thus, it is unsurprising that it is not easy to find many dissenting voices in the three years leading up to the establishment of Israel – either rejecting a pro-Zionist policy or demanding even more proactive American support for Zionist actions in Palestine.

We might have expected some pro-Palestinian voices within the Arab American community, which was 100,000 strong at the time. Its most important organisation was the Institute of Arab American Affairs, founded in 1945. But at that moment in time, it didn't concern itself with the future of Palestine, and was not a force to be reckoned with. This early generation of immigrants were hesitant in voicing their opposition to America's Palestine policy or the Zionist lobby.

As for American Christian opposition to Zionism, it became more vocal once the news began to arrive from Palestine in February 1948 that the Zionist forces had commenced the ethnic cleansing of the Palestinians. A new body, jointly convened by anti-Zionist Jews and Christians, appeared that month: the anti-Zionist Committee for Justice and Peace in the Holy Land. Among its founders was Kermit Roosevelt, an 'Arabist' from the State Department, who was later involved in clandestine operations in the Arab world, including the toppling of Mohammad Mosaddegh in Iran. The committee also included less morally compromised figures such as Virginia Gildersleeve, Rabbi Morris Lazzaron, Garland Evans Hopkins and Henry Sloane Coffin.

As Doreen Bierbrier has observed, the American oil companies could have been another counterforce that ought to have posed a serious challenge to the American Zionist lobby. Certain oil companies, notably the California Standard Oil Company and the Texas Oil Company, which were operating in Saudi Arabia under the name of the

Arabian American Oil Company (ARAMCO), had a large stake in maintaining their position in the Arab countries. American support for a Jewish state and the visible dispossession of the Palestinians increased the hostility of societies in many parts of the Arab world toward American industries in the region. However, the oil companies did not become part of the anti-Zionist lobby, partly because such an act was pre-empted by the well-established advocacy of lobbyists. Benjamin Akzin, the director of the Washington bureau of AZEC, who emigrated to Israel and became dean of the humanities at the Hebrew University, sent reports of meetings he had with representatives from the oil companies and informed the leadership in Palestine that despite their sympathy with the Palestinians, the oil magnates decided not to be proactively anti-Zionist. One of them told Akzin that in any case, King Ibn Saud of Saudi Arabia was more dependent on the USA than vice versa. Akzin's conclusion was that the oil companies were not afraid that the Arabs could inflict serious consequences on them. This view was reinforced by a conversation Akzin had with Abe Fortas, the under-secretary of state in the Department of the Interior, who said to him:

> Even the oil companies hardly believe that strong American backing
> of Zionism would result in a permanent endangering of American
> oil interests.[59]

At the time the Zionist lobby was reaching some landmark moments in its history the Jewish community in the USA was already the largest in the world (around five million). So, it stands to reason that there were some non-Zionist American Jews at the time, but they were not always organised or institutionalised. The only noteworthy rival to the pro-Zionist lobby, the American Jewish Committee, was still struggling to constitute a counter force, but as the state of Israel became a fait accompli, they became more Zionist. By 1948, a small outfit, the American Council for Judaism, was the only Jewish organisation that still publicly opposed Zionism in America. The Council was launched in 1943 and took in some of the leading members of the dwindling American Jewish Committee. It had a modest membership of 15,000, who gradually became anti-Zionist to the bone, insisting that Judaism is a religion and not a nation and therefore categorically opposed to the idea of a Jewish state in Palestine.

There were parts of the Zionist lobby that were even more aggressive than AZEC, and these were affiliated with the Revisionist movement, led by Menachem Begin in Palestine and Peter Bergson in the USA. Bergson formed an organisation called the Hebrew Committee, which AZEC told the American press was a 'pistol packing group of extremists', while Abba Hillel Silver called them 'vestigial oligarchs … little foxes … busily at work trying to spoil this vineyard which American Israel has planted'.[60] Such abrasive language, using the idiom of biblical condemnations (and evoking the Song of Solomon), was thus not only reserved for anti-Zionist Jews or Christians, but also for rivals within the movement itself.

But all in all, AZEC was on top of things on the eve of the establishment of Israel. No lobby in the USA could match them for sheer organisational resources. For the lobbies on both sides of the Atlantic, the declaration of the state of Israel in May 1948 was the crowning achievement of a long-term historical project. They felt, in some way, that they had made it happen. The foundation of Israel marked a new era in lobbying: first, the lobby in Britain played a crucial role in solidifying and sustaining the new state, until the 1967 Arab–Israeli War. After 1967, the American lobby exerted enormous influence to keep American policy on an almost unconditionally pro-Israel track. Let's look at these efforts on both sides of the Atlantic.

7

Lobbying for Israel in Postwar Britain

In the mid-1920s, the architect Austen St Barbe Harrison began planning a new residence for the British High Commissioner in Palestine. The previous one had been badly damaged in an earthquake and the Empire that still believed it would rule Palestine for many years to come searched for a fitting palace for its most senior representative on the ground.

Harrison was the chief architect of the public works department in Mandatory Palestine from 1922 to 1937. There are still several impressive landmarks associated with his name today in what used to be historical Palestine (among them the Rockefeller Archaeological Museum in East Jerusalem). But the High Commissioner's Palace was the jewel in his crown. Harrison belonged to an imperial and colonialist architectural school of thought known as the 'regionalist credo', infusing local styles with a European one; New Delhi showcases the best examples of this style. Anyone visiting the residence today will find replicas of arches, high ceilings and decorated pillars inside – poor imitations of the grand houses of the local urban elite nearby. The exterior has a much greater resemblance to government buildings in early twentieth-century London than anything to be found in the Arab world. It lacked the beauty and elegance of the homes of the Arab Ottoman elite so familiar to those who visited nearby Palestinian neighbourhoods. 'A crusader castle for today' is how one reviewer described it when it was opened to the public at large.[1] This style of architecture was deliberately chosen to reflect the idea of the British as the 'redeemers' of

Jerusalem, following in the footsteps of the crusaders. The same reviewer wrote that the new residence:

> represents the fulfilment at long last of a dream that set the medieval world aflame. The view over the sacred city commanded by these windows floated fantastically and unattainably before the eyes of our forefathers, whose dust now lies beneath a cross-legged effigy in churches scattered over the length and breadth of our land.[2]

Christian Zionism thus still fuelled the imagination of the new British rulers of Palestine, and there could not be a better spot overlooking the city than this one. The unique panorama that the site commanded made it an extraordinarily successful choice. To the south and east spread the sublime landscape of the Judaean desert, with its bare hills and rugged wadis, painted by magnificent hues of red during sunset.[3] This was the imagined landscape of Christ's earthly lifetime, if you insisted on looking only in that direction. Any other direction showed you a city with dwellings inhabited by people of many faiths, still unaffected by the architectural monstrosities Israel would build there after 1967.

The building was opened in 1931 and its last resident was Sir Alan Cunningham, the last High Commissioner of British Palestine. Cunningham was as pleased with the abode as were his predecessors; he said it was a fine example of the fusion of 'modern progress with treasured antiquity.'[4]

On 14 May 1948, Cunningham left this impressive residence on the way to Haifa. Before he left, he signed the termination of the Palestine Mandate in his office, at the centre of the pavilion, as he watched, helpless, as 'Jewish terrorism' intensified all around him. More than a month later, on 22 June 1948, he told a Chatham House audience about his last day. He thought that even then he could make a final effort if only the Zionists had been willing, as the Palestinians were, to allow him to play the role of mediator for the last time:

> The Jews prevaricated and did not comply with my invitation to come to see me (the first time they had done this in the whole of my

time in Palestine). It is a melancholic business presiding over such an occasion, but I sincerely trust we can feel that we left with dignity, using all our efforts to the last for the good of Palestine.[5]

Britain did not rule with dignity; nor did it leave with it. It created a vacuum that led to the ethnic cleansing of the Palestinians and the creation of the state of Israel on the ruins of Palestine. Britain began to play a minor role in the post-Mandatory arrangement and therefore there was no need for an active lobby on behalf of the new state. The one person considered to be the arch-enemy of Israel and Zionism, whose effigy I even remember burning as a child in Haifa, was Ernest Bevin, Britain's foreign secretary.

Up to the end of the Mandate, Bevin rejected the idea of a Jewish state and preferred a British-controlled federation between Palestine and Transjordan. But very pragmatically and ironically, after the 1948 war, he became the main lobbyist for Israel, accepting the Jewish state as a fait accompli, and saw his main task as ensuring it did not join the Eastern Bloc in the ensuing Cold War. Under his pressure a British *de facto* recognition of the state of Israel turned into a *de jure* one, paving the way for the sequence of events that led to the Suez fiasco in October 1956, in which Israel, Britain and France colluded in a failed attempt to bring down a new and revolutionary regime in Egypt.

But at the time, Bevin, with the full support of his prime minister, Clement Attlee, pursued a British policy that outraged the Zionist leadership in Palestine. This policy changed dramatically within the year of 1946, but still was deemed anti-Zionist. At the beginning of the year, Britain still entertained the idea of remaining for a long time in Palestine, without allowing any side to have its independence. Then, an economic crisis, the intensification of Jewish terrorism against British targets in Palestine, and new ideas about the need to shrink the Empire led to a different policy altogether. By the end of the year, Britain preferred to abandon its claims to Palestine and leave it all in the hands of the UN.

The British policy makers were never themselves very clear about what they expected the UN to come up with. The lobby was not particularly interested either. Neither the policy at the beginning of 1946 nor the policy at the end openly declared support for a new Jewish state. Unknown to most members of the pro-Zionist lobby, Britain was already deeply involved in secret negotiations in 1946 between the Jewish Agency and Amir Abdullah of Transjordan and accepted both sides' wishes to divide Palestine between themselves after Britain left.[6]

When the UN appointed a special committee to suggest a solution for Palestine in February 1947, UNSCOP, Britain did not follow it too closely, since it gave preference to the ongoing secret Transjordanian-Zionist negotiations. UNSCOP recommended partitioning Palestine into Arab and Jewish states. This became UN General Assembly Resolution no. 181, called the Partition Plan. Britain abstained in the General Assembly – a position that was regarded by the lobby as a rejection of the idea of a Jewish state.

The Arab League and the Palestinian leadership categorically rejected the idea of partition, while the Zionist movement accepted it. It was decided by the UN that Britain would end the Mandate on 15 May 1948. In the period from the adoption of the resolution (29 November 1947) until the end of the Mandate, British policy focused mainly on securing a swift and safe withdrawal of all British personnel, while still secretly advising the Transjordanians in their secret negotiations with the Jewish Agency. They succeeded in preventing the Arab world from intervening militarily in Palestine until the end of the Mandate. But on the other hand, the British army watched indifferently when, in that particular period, the Zionist forces commenced systematically planned ethnic cleansing operations, which I have described in *The Ethnic Cleansing of Palestine*, that emptied most Palestinian towns and turned a quarter of a million Palestinians into refugees before May 1948.[7]

The lobby, however, was focused on one assignment: how to pressure the Attlee government to support the Zionist demand for a Jewish state. Since Bevin refused to make such a commitment until May 1948, he became the arch-enemy of the lobby.

It was Ian Mikardo, then a young Labour MP, who led the charge against Ernest Bevin's policy in the very last months while the Nakba (the Palestinian term for the 1948 ethnic cleansing, meaning 'the catastrophe') was already unfolding. Known as 'Mik', he was a long-serving

Anglo-Jew in the Labour Party. Mikardo was an ardent Zionist. The Zionist leadership in Palestine needed a counter force within the Labour Party in the crucial year of 1947 when, in both London and Washington, Zionist policies and demands were not always accepted and validated. Violence on the ground led the Americans to doubt the wisdom of the November 1947 UN Partition Plan, which, instead of leading to a solution, ignited a kind of civil war and saw the beginning of Zionist ethnic cleansing operations on the ground. The lobby feared that Britain would be pro-active in demanding an alternative to the partition of Palestine.

Mikardo led a proper revolt in March 1948, with the threat of a 'no confidence' vote in the Labour government due to what he called its 'pro-Arab' policies.[8] It is telling that Bevin is not remembered at all as pro-Arab by Palestinians to this day. Instead, he's seen as the epitome of perfidious Albion.

Bevin was targeted by Israel's advocates in the years leading up to the establishment of the state. There was no official pro-Israel lobby at the time; it was too early for that. But those who saw themselves as Zionism's champions in the UK instrumentalised allegations of anti-Semitism, in a manner they still do today, in order to demonise their opponents. Their opponents were not simply people who were pro-Palestinian – the net was wide enough to catch anyone who didn't unconditionally accept the claims of the aspirational Jewish state. Thus, Ian Mikardo claimed that Bevin's Palestine policy was distorted by the 'fanatical hatred he developed for the Jews.'[9] Christopher Mayhew, a close colleague of Bevin about whom we'll read more later, contested these claims:

> [Bevin] wasn't racially prejudiced, not at all … He was emotionally outraged by the tactics of Zionism – by their terrorism, by their deception, by the monstrous pressure brought on the British government by the American government as a result of the pressure of the American Jewish community.[10]

What is surprising is the continued hostility towards Bevin and total mistrust in his policy, even after it transpired that he led the British government to recognise Israel *de facto* in 1949 and supported the ongoing attempts of Jordan and Israel to reach a bilateral agreement that continued until the assassination of King Abdullah I in 1951 – probably a result of these negotiations. In the next few years, the lobby looked for new allies against these perceived anti-Israel policies in two areas. They found one in the trade union movement and the other in a small group in the parliamentary Labour Party. The latter would be the nucleus of Labour Friends of Israel.

THE TUC AND ISRAEL, 1948–1953

The TUC's policies in the period 1948 to 1967 were all in all pleasing as far as the pro-Israel lobby was concerned. The task of recruiting the TUC to Israel's side was entrusted to Israel's own TUC, the Histadrut. In London, the Histadrut's emissaries soon expanded their remit beyond the bilateral contacts with the TUC and established their own advocacy enterprise targeting the Labour Party as a whole. The task was taken over in 1949 by Schneier Levenberg. He was a lifelong Zionist and Labour Party member. He multitasked in several positions at the same time: he was the London representative of the Jewish Agency as well of the Histadrut; he was the chairman of both the Palestine Labour Political Committee and Poale Zion. He co-ordinated his work in the TUC with the Israeli Legation in London. His direct boss, so to speak, was Reuven Barkat, the head of the international section of the Histadrut. What was unique about the presence of the Histadrut in Britain was that most of its activities had very little to do with workers' rights, as we shall see, and were much more focused on influencing political decisions made by the British government or the Labour Party on questions of importance to the Israeli government.

Levenberg's advocacy group invented a new method of lobbying that would become very popular with the pro-Israel lobby in the USA – organising free visits to Israel in return for TUC invitations to Israeli politicians to visit Britain. The first trip was organised by Levenberg, under the instruction of Barkat, at the end of 1949. The delegation was received with the greatest formality; they met with the president of

Israel, the prime minister, members of his Cabinet and leaders of the Histadrut, as well as visiting schools, kibbutzim and factories. Part of the strategy was to use this tour to influence the head of the British Legation (it was not yet an embassy), Sir Alexander Knox Helm, who was not known for his positive views on Israel.

'It was a huge success', reported one member of the delegation, Sam Watson, the Durham miners' leader, who added:

> I came as a friend but somewhat ignorant of what that State was trying to accomplish and left as a friend, much better informed, much clearer in their conception of Israel's hopes and desires.[11]

In 1950, the Labour Party reciprocated and invited a Histadrut delegation to Britain. The only objection to that visit came from the Foreign Office, learning that Mapam, the second-largest party in Israel in those days, and strongly affiliated with Moscow, would also be represented in the delegation, but the visit took place anyway.[12] Clement Attlee, the prime minister, declared that the visit of the Israelis had done much to promote friendly relations between Britain and Israel.[13] Many more visits organised by the TUC and the Histadrut would follow.

Was there any concern at all for the fate of the Palestinians in general, or the Palestinian workers, who in those years began to be exploited as a semi-proletarian force building the Jewish state on the ruins of Palestine? It seems the Foreign Office was much more troubled by the conditions of the Palestinian working class in Israel than the TUC. But even Ernest Bevin felt that the important question about the '1948 Arabs' (the Palestinian citizens of Israel) was less about their well-being and more about their loyalty to the Jewish state. This Palestinian minority lived until 1966 under harsh military rule, based on the British colonialist Mandatory regulations, which robbed them of many basic civil rights. Often their villages were put under curfew. In one case, villagers in Kafr Qasim were not notified about any curfew and were late in returning from the fields. Consequently forty-three men, women and children were massacred by Israeli border police.

The connection with the TUC, and with American trade unions, enabled Israel to prevent a 1953 international trade union conference in Stockholm from passing a resolution endorsing the Palestinian refugees' right of return, and also to hinder the relationship with other Arab trade union delegations. The aim was to foster an anti-Arab trade union coalition, with the TUC and the Histadrut at its centre, a task entrusted to the labour attaché at the Israeli embassy in London; this was the first ever such position Israel had anywhere else in the world. In those days Britain also had a labour attaché in its Tel Aviv embassy. The British attaché in Tel Aviv was a diplomat, while the Israeli one was a member of the Histadrut.

The TUC and Labour were seen as more natural allies of the lobby in the early part of the Conservatives' long period of power (1951–1964) than the ruling party. From 1951 to the end of 1955, the Churchill government and the first year of the Eden government, the Conservative policy was ambivalent towards Israel. The worst period for the lobby, in a way, was 1955, when Britain joined the USA in pressuring Israel to make significant concessions in order to enable peace with Gamal Abdel Nasser in Egypt. Within a year, the Eden government made a U-turn and depicted Nasser as the new enemy of civilisation in the Middle East, joining forces with Israel to try and topple him. Amid such a whirlwind of ups and downs, it is no wonder that the lobby found the Labour Party a safer bet as its ally. However, Eden wavered when it came to the drastic idea of going to war with Israel against Egypt. Let us look at this erratic period in more detail, as it impacted on the lobby's work in years to come.

ALLIES ON THE PATH TO SUEZ

Guildhall, the ceremonial and administrative centre of the City of London, hosts many events throughout the year, the most notable being the Lord Mayor's Banquet, which is held in honour of the immediate-past Lord Mayor of the City of London and is the first to be hosted by the new Lord Mayor. In keeping with tradition, at this banquet the British prime minister makes a major speech on world affairs, delivered in the medieval Great Hall, built at the turn of the fifteenth century, with a high arched ceiling and two huge, Gothic stained-glass windows emblazoned with the name of past Lord Mayors.

In what follows, we will read about three speeches by British politicians on world affairs. All three sent shockwaves that reached Israel and unnerved the Jewish state's lobby in Britain. On all three occasions, Israeli's intransigence and unwillingness to compromise for the sake of peace was publicly condemned.

The first such speech was delivered by Anthony Eden on 9 November 1955 in the Great Hall. The only Israeli journalist present on that occasion reported an impressive attendance of 1,000 people listening to what he described as a very nervous prime minister.[14]

Eden alluded in his speech to a project the British Foreign Office and the American State Department had been working on for several months before the speech, called Operation Alpha. The project was in essence a 'road map' for peace between Israel and Egypt based on two principles: a land bridge between Egypt and Jordan that would be carved out of the Naqab Desert (the Israeli Negev), and a discussion of the repatriation of the Palestinian refugees. These basic principles, if agreed by Israel, would form the basis for concluding peace treaties between Israel and its Arab neighbours. Eden was quite forthright that if Israel adopted a policy of rejectionism, it would lose Britain's friendship and support.

It was the brainchild of Sir Evelyn Shuckburgh, the under-secretary of state in the Foreign Office responsible for Middle Eastern affairs. However, the real father of the project was the Egyptian president Gamal Abdel Nasser. After coming to power, he pursued a realistic policy which accepted Israel as a fait accompli and a necessary evil that had to be tamed and confined, since he believed it was planning to expand territorially both in historical Palestine and beyond into the lands of its Arab neighbours. He commenced secret negotiations with the Israeli foreign minister, Moshe Sharett, beginning in 1953 and further intensified the contact when Sharett became Israel's prime minister for a year and a half during 1954 and 1955. During these negotiations Nasser suggested a plan very similar to the Alpha project.[15]

For a while Sharett went along with Nasser's ideas, not accepting them, but willing to negotiate on their basis. However, his nemesis, David Ben-Gurion, as prime minister, and for a short while out of power, had his henchmen in Sharett's government and they foiled these negotiations: the defence minister, Pinhas Lavon, and the general chief of staff, Moshe Dayan. Together, the two initiated a series of provocations against Egypt, the most important of which were an attack in February 1955 on the Egyptian army in the Gaza Strip that ended with thirty-seven dead Egyptian soldiers, and later the establishment of a terrorist network of Egyptian Jews meant to plant bombs in cinemas and libraries associated with the West (so as to damage Nasser's relations with the West).[16]

By the time Eden made his speech, Nasser had lost faith in Israel's willingness to make peace and Sharett realised his inability to challenge Ben-Gurion's aggressive policy towards Egypt. The reason Eden at that time sided with Egypt was his wish to create an anti-Soviet alliance in the Middle East with Turkey, Egypt and Iraq at its centre. For a while, the Americans backed this idea of an alliance, which was named the Baghdad Pact, of loyal Middle Eastern states, without Israel, which came at the price of forcing of Israel to compromise territorially and agree to at least partial repatriation of Palestinian refugees.

Eden came to the Guildhall, quite enraged about the American retreat from its support for the Baghdad Pact. Sir Evelyn had no doubt who was to blame for this 'American backsliding', as Nigel Ashton called it: 'This is becoming an almost blatant piece of Israeli pressure, exercised through the State Department's lawyers.'[17]

Eden's speech, and the other two that are mentioned later in this chapter, posed an immediate challenge to the lobby and of course to Israel, not only because of the inferred condemnation of the Jewish state, but mainly because of the warm welcome the speech received in Egypt. Nasser and his prime minister gave interviews to British newspapers such as the *Observer*, praising Eden and saying his speech offered a very good basis for negotiation.[18]

Officially, Israel was quick to condemn the speech and reject any idea of territorial compromise. Sharett in many ways was now forced to be Israel's intransigent face appearing both in the British press and in direct negotiations with the British Foreign Office.

The lobby responded in two ways; one was the publication of a number of articles in the *Jewish Chronicle*, depicting the speech as 'unhelpful' but in language that was quite diplomatic. A more severe criticism of possible British pressure on Israel to compromise was heard in the House of Commons, led by Denis Healy, the famous Labour leader and MP for Leeds East, during a special session devoted in the House to the speech, attended by Eden and his foreign minister, Harold Macmillan. It was held on 12 December 1955, about a month after Eden's speech.[19]

In that discussion Healy stated:

> It seems to me that on every single count the Prime Minister's initiative in his Guildhall speech was most unfortunate and calculated only to make the existing situation more difficult to solve.

and:

> In this situation I suggest that the initiative of the Prime Minister in his speech at the Guildhall was a gross blunder which has made the problem infinitely more difficult to deal with.[20]

The lobby relied mainly on Labour MPs and in particular those on the Left. In 1955, in the pages of the *Tribune*, the party's Left sided unequivocally with Israel's retaliatory raids into the Gaza Strip against Palestinian guerrillas; counterintuitively it was much more hawkish in its approach than the Conservative government of Anthony Eden and the Israeli government headed by Moshe Sharett. The *Tribune* sided with David Ben-Gurion, and scolded his former foreign minister, Sharett, for his efforts to reconcile with Egypt. The *Tribune* endorsed Ben-Gurion's intransigent attitude towards Egypt, both in and out of office, culminating in the joint ill-fated Suez operation – collusion between Israel, France and Britain that failed to topple Egypt's leader, Gamal Abdel Nasser.[21]

Before the Suez crisis in 1956, being a supporter of Israel in the Labour Party was an easy and popular choice. But it would cease to be a rose-strewn path as the crisis imposed strains on its pro-Israel wing. In the summer of 1956, Eden changed his attitude towards Nasser. The Egyptian president despaired of getting British support for either negotiations with Israel or for proper economic and military aid for building a new Egypt. Moreover, while Britain was willing to withdraw its army from Egypt proper, it insisted on staying in the Suez Canal Zone. In response, in July Nasser nationalised the canal, and Eden began to collude intensively with France and Israel with the aim of overthrowing the Egyptian president. On 29 October 1956, Israel, France and Britain attacked Egypt from the land, sea and air; Israel occupied most of the Sinai Peninsula and British and French troops landed in the Suez Canal area (around Port Said), before American and Soviet pressure brought an end to the operation and a few months later forced all the participants in the invasion of Egypt to withdraw.

Against this background the Labour Party had to make up its own mind on the evolving crisis. The official party line was to oppose the prime minister Anthony Eden's adventurism and imperialism in Egypt and the rest of the Arab world. But the party was divided, as was the British political system as a whole. In fact, neither the Left nor the Right of the party had a fixed position on Suez, and thus many on the Left in the party identified with the right-wing Hugh Gaitskell's statement that he 'spoke for England' when he condemned British aggression towards Egypt. The TUC's campaign, run jointly with the party under the slogan 'law, not war', represented the moral stance that should have been taken.[22] On the other hand, the TUC president, Charles Geddes, endorsed Britain's policy of belligerence but was unable to force the main body of the TUC, the General Council, to adopt a resolution reflecting this.[23] Geddes was supported by most of the backbench Labour MPs and there is no doubt that Geddes's close relationship with the Histadrut, the Israeli TUC so to speak, played an important role in his support for the British government's collusion with France and Israel in the attempt to bring Nasser down. As Ronnie Fraser points out, the leadership of the TUC ironically regarded Israel as a far more important player than Egypt or the Arab world in the new world the British Empire left behind. Many members of the TUC tended to support Israel as they were particularly impressed by the growing Israeli influence in the decolonised parts of Africa.[24]

But more was still needed to overcome Labour's opposition to this military adventure. The brunt of this burden fell mainly on senior Israeli politicians. The campaign to elicit British co-operation was led by the newly appointed Israeli foreign minister, Golda Meir, fresh from her abortive attempt to become the mayor of Tel Aviv. She recalled that some of her comrades in the Israeli Mapai Party were worried that Labour 'swallowed Nasser's line whole'.[25] Under her guidance, the principal message to the Labour Party was that Palestinian 'terrorism', namely the Palestinian Fedayeen (the nascent Palestinian guerrilla movement that began launching its operations in the early 1950s mainly from the Egyptian-controlled Gaza Strip) posed a danger to the British Empire in the Middle East as a whole. Members of the party were flooded with information kits prepared in Israel. According to one report, the Israeli ambassador in London managed to persuade Hugh Gaitskell to change his view and begin to toe the Conservative government's aggressive line towards Nasser and the Palestinian liberation movement. This is not verified by any reliable source, but we do know that Gaitskell, notwithstanding his opposition to Suez, had a very close relationship with the Israeli ambassador in London, Walter Eytan.

While the Israeli government deluged Labour with warnings about the terrible threat of Palestinian 'terrorism', the local lobby also played a part in pleading with Labour to refrain from disrupting the new scheme between Israel and Britain against Nasser's Egypt. Poale Zion, by that time also known as the Jewish Labour Movement, took up the mantle in this saga. This group sent representatives to every public debate on Suez it could attend, pointing out that Israel felt Labour was a truer friend than the Conservative Party (emphasising that Labour was more sympathetic when it came to questions of supplying arms to Israel) and that there was a kindred sisterhood between the two 'socialist parties' defending the 'socialist' state of Israel. In fact, according to June Edmunds, the view of Poale Zion was that Labour had the potential to be more pro-Israel than the Conservative government itself in years to come – a hunch that proved correct during Harold Wilson's years in office.[26]

The fact that Poale Zion, a pre-1948 organ of the Zionist movement, born of a now obsolete desire in the distant past to fuse Marxism and Zionism, a long-forgotten aim that had no relevance to the state of Israel, was still there in the 1950s is quite bewildering. Its very existence in the post-state era explains why it was not always easy to say when such a body represented socialist Jews in Britain or was an advocacy group for Israel. It was both affiliated to the Board of Deputies and the state of Israel (through membership of the English Zionist Federation). After the establishment of the state of Israel, it would have been logical for it to pack up its things and go home: after all, its goals had been achieved. But like the Jewish National Fund, the Jewish Agency and a number of pre-1948 Zionist organisations in the USA, it continued to function, despite the creation of a proper state, as all were deemed to be crucial parts of the pro-Israel lobby infrastructure in the world. In the case of these bodies, including Poale Zion, such a reality required them to tweak their original mission statements. They could not go on promoting the idea of a Jewish state in Palestine (or a socialist Jewish state in the case of Poale Zion) and therefore began to propagate a new message: that they existed in order to protect the right of self-determination of the Jewish nation in Israel. At the end of the day, Poale Zion did not fight for socialism either in Britain or in Israel. It was part of a lobby meant to arrest any potential anti-Israel orientations in the Labour Party in Britain and strengthen the relationship between the Labour Party and its pro-Israel Jewish constituencies.

At that time the Jewish Agency, which mediated between Israel and the pro-Israel lobby groups in London, such as the English Zionist Federation, was annoyed by the way known pro-Israel members of Parliament such as Barnett Janner toed the party line and voted against the government's Suez policy in the house. The English Zionist Federation tried to defend Janner and explained to the Jewish Agency how Parliament works. He was, they wrote, 'one of the most loyal, one of the most passionate Zionists in the country'.[27] But as we shall see time and time again, Israel accepted nothing less than unconditional and unreserved support. To ensure such undivided loyalty, a new body was established: Labour Friends of Israel.

THE MAKING OF LABOUR FRIENDS OF ISRAEL

The Pathé newsreel, a regular prelude to the movies in Britain, announced the start of the 1957 Labour conference with these words: 'Leaders and delegates of the Labour party gather in Brighton for their annual conference ... when they are all inside, Brighton is so quiet you can hear the sea, almost'. The peace and quiet on Brighton's beaches only accentuated the tense drama unfolding inside the conference hall at the beginning of October 1957.[28]

The most vociferous debate was about Britain's H-bomb. The slimier side of politics was exposed when one of the most high-profile figures on the party Left, Aneurin 'Nye' Bevan, who was expected to champion unilateral disarmament, spoke against it, famously saying it would 'send a British Foreign Secretary naked into the conference chamber'. His followers were shocked. Many heckled him, shouting 'shame', 'nonsense' and 'rubbish'. This spelled the end of his leadership of Labour's radical wing.[29]

Bevan is best known now for founding the NHS, but he also exerted considerable influence on Labour's foreign policy during the first Attlee government and beyond. In this capacity, he played a crucial role in establishing the pro-Israel lobby in Britain as the fledgling state asserted itself, and steered Labour onto pro-Israel lines.

Why did this socialist firebrand somehow overlook the injustice inflicted on Palestinians in the name of Zionism? In oral recollections, Bevan attributed his commitment to Israel as born out of an intimate friendship with Chaim Weizmann that developed throughout 1945. A less rose-tinted account credits the relentless Harold Laski, a tireless Zionist lobbyist in Labour, for his recruitment to the cause. Laski, with others, was already liaising with Bevan during the war to try to secure his support for a Jewish state in Palestine. Less high-minded motives may have also been in play. Zionism was a thorn in Ernest Bevin's side as foreign secretary, and Bevan may have spotted an opportunity to undermine his biggest internal opponent in the party.[30]

Whatever lay behind it, by the mid-1950s Bevan had become one of the Labour Party's more committed Zionists, writing in the *Daily Herald* that:

> When the Arab says that the Jew should find a home anywhere except in Palestine, he asks something the Jew cannot concede without mutilating his racial personality beyond endurance.[31]

Bevan and his wife, Jennie Lee, were among the group who founded Labour Friends of Israel (LFI). Bevan's early enthusiasm was whetted after visiting Israel in 1954. Although he was sensitive to the degradation of poverty in Britain, he chose not to notice the destroyed Palestinian villages and towns he passed, nor did he inquire why the remaining Palestinians were subjected to brutal military rule and quartered in ghettos (the term the Israeli army gave to quarantined quarters of what remained of urban Arab neighbourhoods). None of this even merits a mention in his reports on Israel. This was the beginning of the Labour journey into the most pro-Israel chapter in its history, in which Israel enjoyed unquestionable legitimacy and moral authority.

What mattered to him is articulated clearly in a report Jennie Lee wrote after their trip to Israel, describing the state as a socialist paradise. The crowning glory of this paradise was the kibbutzim, where Lee found:

> the kind of passion that socialist workers everywhere who have had their own experience of victimization and of exile through poverty should particularly understand.[32]

The kibbutzim they visited were built on the ruins of Palestinian villages, whose villagers would have understood the 'experience of victimization and of exile' much more than the settler kibbutzniks.

LFI's first action was to organise a huge public rally, led by senior Labour leaders such as Herbert Morrison and moderated by the first chair of LFI, Anthony Greenwood, in Brighton, as a fringe event at the party conference.

This new organisation was a joint initiative by the English Zionist Federation, Poale Zion and Mapai in Israel. The leading figure behind the initial attempts to build a reliable pro-Israel base within the Labour Party was Ian Mikardo. By the 1950s, he was an influential member of the National Executive Committee of the party. Later, in the 1970s, he was also chairman of the party for one year and remained active in leading roles both in the Labour Party and in the European social democratic scene up to the early 1990s. The latter arena, the social democratic Western European milieu, was where Israel built a shield of immunity not only as 'the only democracy in the Middle East' but also as the 'only social democracy in the Middle East'. Both assertions were highly questionable given the settler-colonial nature of the Jewish state and its policies towards the Palestinians wherever they were.

'Keep Left' was Mikardo's slogan, and 'Left' meant support for Israel. He was very close to the left wing of the Israeli Left party, Mapam, and genuinely seemed to believe that Israel was a paragon of socialism. Mikardo managed to recruit leading members of the Labour Party, such as its treasurer, Anthony Greenwood, and Glenvil Hall, the chair of the parliamentary group, to be part of the new outfit.[33]

The core group of early members also included former leading figures in Zionist institutions in Britain such as Barnett Janner, who headed the English Zionist Federation in Britain since 1940 and served as the president of LFI from the 1950s to the 1970s.

A close and early associate of LFI was the labour attaché at the Israeli embassy, who now had a stronger base for building a pro-Israel group in the TUC, which was instrumental in preventing British arms sales to Egypt in 1955 – further alienating Nasser from the West.[34]

By 1956, there was a change of guard in the TUC and a new and more radical leadership, headed up by Frank Cousins, launched twin campaigns for disarmament and protecting the Labour-built post-1945 welfare state. But even a shift to less hawkishness with regard to weaponry did not undermine existing TUC support for Israel. The lobbying method was the same: a VIP invitation for the new TUC leadership to visit Israel to ensure their loyalty. The British ambassador to Israel concluded: 'the Israelis must be well satisfied with having arranged this visit and with its results', and his labour attaché added that the two new TUC leaders – Frank Cousins was joined by Fred Hayday, the chair of the TUC's International Committee – had left him 'in no doubt of their sympathy and support for Israel'. Back in London, comments by these two TUC officials prompted the Foreign Office's Sir John Moberly to describe the duo as 'well and truly brainwashed'.[35]

Until the June 1967 war, LFI and other lobbying groups had very little to do as successive British governments granted Israel anything it wanted, more or less. This included a generous supply of arms and absolute support for Israel's position in the UN. This was also a period of reorganisation and post-traumatic recovery for the Palestinian national movement that was unable, at that moment in time, to be a forceful presence in either the regional or the international arena as it would after 1967.

You might have observed I have said very little in this section about lobbying in the Conservative Party. The reason is twofold. Firstly, as Israel was run by a labour party (namely Mapai), its leaders still believed that Labour would be the main political body representing Israel's position in Britain. Secondly, the Conservative governments in that period, in power for nearly all of the 1950s, pursued policies the Israeli government regarded as pro-Israel to the bone. Advocacy had been rendered redundant.

The lobby was free to concentrate all its energies on the Labour Party. And they needed to. On the day war broke out in June 1967, a new figure came onto the stage. He voiced unprecedented doubts about Israel's claims and propaganda, becoming one of the first Labour politicians to side openly with the Palestinian struggle. His name was Christopher Mayhew.

THE ENEMY FROM WITHIN: CHRISTOPHER MAYHEW

On 5 June 1967, war erupted. According to the modern Israeli narrative, Israel launched a pre-emptive strike against an Arab world on the verge of embarking on a war of annihilation against the Jewish state. These days, Israeli historians admit, as they must in the face of the overwhelming evidence, that Israeli radio lied the day the war started. The Arab armies had not invaded Israel; Israel was not acting in retaliation.

Recent scholarship has changed the historiographical picture of the processes that led to the war. Some historians point to Nasser, who wished to pressure the world to reopen discussion on the Palestine question and, more importantly, was convinced that Israel planned further territorial expansion into Jordan and Syria, states that Egypt was bound to assist in case of aggression. His fears were confirmed when, from the spring of 1966 up to June 1967, Israel aggressively militarised its border with Syria, consistently encroaching on the no man's land outlined in the 1949 armistice agreement. It was committed to bringing down the regime in Syria and sought out a pretext to take over the Golan Heights so that it could better defend its settlements below in the Hula Valley. Recurrent military skirmishes on the land and in the air, combined with the Soviet conviction that an attack on Syria was imminent, pushed Nasser into a series of actions which included removing the UN from the Sinai Peninsula, dispatching his army into it, and blockading the Tiran Straits, the maritime route to Israel's small harbour in Eilat.

But historiography too often blames Nasser's actions and neglects to look at how Mapai, then the ruling party, was influenced by an expansionist faction for a 'Greater Israel', pushing for a military takeover of the West Bank since the mid-1960s. Adherents to the Greater Israel ideology saw the West Bank as the heart of the nation, and considered the Jordan River an essential buffer against Arab military threat. The pre-1967 boundaries were denigrated after the June 1967 war as the 'Auschwitz borders', to use the extreme terminology of Abba Eban. The influence of this faction meant that Israel flatly refused to back down in Nasser's game of brinkmanship – and many exit points were missed.[36]

On Monday 5 June 1967, Sir Robin Day walked into the BBC *Panorama* studio to discuss the burning issue of the day: the onset of the June 1967 war. On that morning, the Israeli air force destroyed the air forces of the neighbouring Arab countries and invaded the West Bank, the Gaza Strip and the Sinai Peninsula. Wearing his bow tie, he entered to the familiar music of 'Openings and Endings' by Robert Farnon and took his seat in front of a panels of discussants. In the background was the familiar, pale and shabby-looking globe in black and white. Sitting alongside him at a round table, with microphones in front of them, were his three guests: Christopher Mayhew; Jeremy Thorpe, the leader of the Liberal Party; and Duncan Sandys, the Conservative member of Parliament, waiting anxiously for Sir Robin's first round of questions.[37]

Thorpe and Sandys reiterated the perceived British consensus: Israel's actions were in self-defence and peace was desirable. Christopher Mayhew, however, disregarded the script. He stated, 'I think there is an Arab case as well as an Israeli case', and openly questioned Israel's official announcements and their self-exculpatory narrative. Mayhew observed that 'the Israelis are the aggressors' who began that war, while he pointed to Nasser's policies as contributory factors.[38]

LFI leapt into action – any recognition of Arab grievances was treated as an attack on Israel. On 7 June, LFI published a statement blaming the Arab states for the war and, more importantly, wrote to the chief whip of the Labour Party complaining that *Panorama* had given the false impression that 'Mayhew's views represented the position of the Parliamentary Labour Party'.[39] Pro-Israel ministers in the government went even further: they framed Mayhew's tame comments as fanatically pro-Arab; he was lucky not to be, on that occasion, accused of being an anti-Semite. This would happen later.

Some writers, such as James Vaughan, who appraised Mayhew's work from a pro-Zionist point of view, attributed Mayhew's commitment to Palestine as being more anti-Zionist than pro-Palestinian because of attitudes he developed while he was Ernest Bevin's under-secretary of state in the last years of the British Mandate. Both he and Bevin were a target for death threats by the Irgun, a Zionist paramilitary organisation.[40] While this was undoubtedly traumatic, I do not think this was the reason for his lifelong commitment to the Palestinian cause; it only hardened his resolve. His experience made him warn other critics of Israel not to fear Israeli pressure or succumb to intimidation. In this vein, he offered support to the foreign secretary, Lord Carrington, during a period of strained Anglo-Israeli relations:

'Although Begin and Shamir have spoken rudely about you', he observed, 'they have not threatened to assassinate you as they did to

> Ernie Bevin and me in the old days. Their manners are improving as
> the years go by and we should be truly thankful'.[41]

Like so many before him and many more after him, what shaped Mayhew's
perception was witnessing the reality of Zionism for himself – the bitter
truths that no lobbying could refute or whitewash. Mayhew became an
advocate of Palestinian rights during a visit to the Palestinian refugee
camps in Jordan in 1953. In particular after 1967, many visitors to the
occupied territories became activists on behalf of Palestine, sometimes
even after only short visits to the place. Israel's brutal policies became
harsher and visible to such an extent that even many of those who participated in organised guided tours that were intended to persuade them to
immigrate, in the case of Jewish visitors, or to become ambassadors for
Israel, in the case of non-Jews, experienced a change of heart and became
active on behalf of the Palestinians. The lobby in years to come in Britain
and the USA was unable to challenge such personal transformations.

A second trip in 1963, this time to Israel, reinforced Mayhew's
convictions. We hear him using language now common among academics and human rights organisations when referring to Israel. He framed
the Israelis as 'colonial settlers': settler colonialism became the dominant paradigm in Palestine Studies in this century.[42] Meetings with Israeli
leaders at the time did very little to change his mind. On these meetings,
Vaughan writes:

> He found the Prime Minister, Levi Eshkol, to be 'brash and aggres-
> sive' and dismissed Foreign Minister, Golda Meir, as 'a disappointing
> woman rather superficial in mind and temperament'. Meir, he
> remarked, related to Palestinians solely as 'drivers, gardeners and
> houseboys' and possessed a 'colonial settler's attitude' similar to that
> of British settlers in East Africa.[43]

This proved rather prescient: in 1972, Meir categorically denied the
existence of the Palestinians as a people.[44]

Mayhew attributed his failure to obtain a position in the Foreign
Office after the 1964 general election to the Israelis whispering in Harold

Wilson's ear: 'Of course, the Israelis complained to my party leader about my attitude on this visit in 1963 ... and this had a considerably adverse effect'.[45] He may have strengthened his commitment to the Palestine cause, but it came at a steep price – he had to accept a position as minister for the Navy, a far cry from where he wanted to be in the new Labour government.

As the years went by, Mayhew's views solidified and he articulated them more forcefully, leading to increasingly vitriolic attacks by the lobby. In December 1967, he argued, during an exchange with Immanuel Jakobovits, the Chief Rabbi of the United Hebrew Congregations of the British Commonwealth, that British Jews were perfectly entitled to support the Israeli government against the British government when this seemed right to them, but that neither the Chief Rabbi nor the pro-Zionists among the Anglo-Jews should act 'almost as if he [the Chief Rabbi] and they were Israeli nationals' and he warned that 'any suggestion that a particular section of the British people has rights and duties in respect of a foreign government which the rest of the people do not have is dangerous.' Jakobovits accused Mayhew of 'sowing the seeds of strife and bitterness' and denied the charge of dual loyalty, to which Mayhew responded:

> You deny that members of the Jewish community in Britain ever do this [i.e. waver in their national loyalty]: I myself, out of a very long and intimate experience, assert that they do.[46]

But an even greater challenge to Zionism arose in the very same month the war of 1967 erupted – this was once more a public speech, the second out of three, reminiscent of Eden's Guildhall speech, this time delivered by Britain's foreign minister, George Brown.

A NEW BOGEYMAN: GEORGE BROWN

Israel had been accepted as a member state of the UN in May 1949. Before its formal acceptance, its experiences of General Assembly meetings were mixed, to say the least. As we shall see in the next chapter, when the UN was still hosted by the small town of Lake Success, the reception for Zionists was not uniformly warm. But after Israel was accepted as a member state in May 1949, its delegation was well treated and it happily took part in the meetings convened in the new Manhattan building, its green glass shimmering by the river. On 21 June 1967, the Israeli delegation took its usual six seats – three for full delegates and three for their alternates, behind tables facing a raised speaker's rostrum and podium, watched by the secretary general of the UN who presided that day over the assembly. What they would hear would make them wish they had earplugs rather than earphones.

On the podium stood the most senior British diplomat at the time, George Brown. Not a very tall man, with large round black spectacles, he was not renowned for his oratory powers. But he was about to give a speech about Israel and Palestine unparalleled in the history of British diplomats at the UN and reminiscent of Eden's Guildhall speech in November 1955. Yes, this was the second of the three 'outrageous' speeches the lobby had to fight against.

The astounded Israeli delegation heard Brown almost apologising for the way Britain had empowered Israel in its annexationist policies in the past and promised that this would come to an end. In fact, expansionism was a recurring theme in his speech. His acknowledgement of Israel's expansionism meant that this rather unremarkable orator made statements about Israel and Palestine never heard before or since.

This was a very structured speech. Brown began by stating that Israel was in danger of violation of article 2 of the UN Charter:

> All members shall refrain in their international relations from the threat or use of force against the territorial integrity or the political independence of any state.

He warned that war could not be an excuse for territorial expansionism. In very strong terms he demanded an Israeli withdrawal from the territories it had occupied in the June 1967 war. He devoted considerable time to condemning Israeli policies in East Jerusalem (Israel unilaterally annexed East Jerusalem *de facto* immediately after the war and ethnically cleansed part of the Muslim quarter that was near the Wailing Wall). He stated:

They will be taking a step which will not only isolate them from world opinion, but will also lose them the sympathy that they have.[47]

Prophetically he warned that Israel would officially annex East Jerusalem and hoped that this could still be averted. He was less accurate in his prediction when he warned Israel that the world would not tolerate such an annexation; it did and still does. But he was right in warning his listeners of a new refugee crisis, and the precarity of living under an occupying power.

For the pro-Israel lobby in Britain, this was a real moment of peril, when the UK might have U-turned on its policy altogether. The official Israeli response was harsh, and Brown was portrayed as a traitor. The lobby in Britain needed to spring into action.[48]

The Israeli historian Moshe Gat wrote:

Israel had listened to Brown's performance with mounting shock and disbelief. Furious, it damned the speech as a transparent, indeed shameless attempt on Britain's part to ingratiate itself with the Arab states at Israel's expense.[49]

Israel was unable to control the narrative it wanted the world to accept: a small state defending itself against the whole Arab world. Brown challenged this narrative significantly. Golda Meir, Israel's former foreign minister, even went so far as to brand Brown a Judas.[50] This was followed by similar remarks by Israel's prime minister, Levi Eshkol, who declared Brown to be one of Israel's worst enemies. Under his orchestration, a smear campaign began first in the Israeli press and then in the Anglo-Jewish one. 'From Bevin to Brown', cried the headlines.[51]

George Brown (1914–1985) was a mercurial, outspoken and intelligent diplomat and politician. His political rise was handicapped by his alcoholism, but as foreign secretary in the first Harold Wilson government, he played a crucial role in post-1967 diplomatic efforts to deal with the consequences of the June 1967 war. He, and anyone else who wished to be involved in this effort, faced the thirteenth government of Israel, the most united government Israel has ever had (including all the

Zionist and Orthodox parties), which decided in advance that peace was not a priority.[52]

Brown pushed a British policy that aimed for Israel's withdrawal from the territories it occupied in the June 1967 war, including the West Bank and the Gaza Strip. He and other ministers in Wilson's government were worried about Britain's deteriorating relationship with the Arab world following the 1956 Suez fiasco. Brown focused on establishing good relationships with the Arab oil-producing countries. Foreign Office documents also mention the need to secure a friendly environment to enable free passage to the Far East and, more than anything else, prevent Soviet influence from growing in the Arab world.[53]

Brown's speech went down with Israel like a kick in the guts. He indirectly blamed Israel for using force in order to expand its territory. However, even harsher judgements of Israel were made in private Foreign Office documents. In a minute sent by the Office to the Cabinet, a senior official wrote:

> We have now examined that evidence [and] have come to the conclusion that the Israelis fired the first shot and take the view that it was reprehensible of them not [to] wait for the efforts we and others were making to extricate them from the admittedly impossible situation in which the UAR [United Arab Republic] had placed them.[54]

In retrospect, this document had hugely significant implications. The Americans and the British accurately read Gamal Abdel Nasser's ambitions on the eve of the June 1967 war. He exerted pressure in order to reopen diplomacy about the future of post-Mandatory Palestine and genuinely believed Israel was about to attack Syria. Washington and London identified some strategies that would have prevented the situation from spiralling into a war, most importantly a concentrated diplomatic effort. But the intransigent Israelis were not interested in conciliation; they viewed the whole situation as a golden opportunity to create the 'viable' and 'natural' Israel, namely the one that included the West Bank, which they had failed to build in 1948; now they could rectify what the government called '*bechiya ledorot*' – literally meaning 'generations to come will cry', and in essence meaning a lamentable missed opportunity (to create the Greater Israel).[55]

Viewed more objectively, Brown was far from being anti-Israel, but he was not pro-Israel enough in the eyes of the Israelis. In fact, he had equally good relations with Arab leaders and Israeli politicians before the famous speech – he simply prioritised British interests before his relationships with either. Eric Moonman, a Labour MP, took it upon himself to spearhead the attack on Brown, accusing him of 'taking sides' against Israel. At a Jewish ex-servicemen's rally in Southend, he called Brown's speech 'a serious embarrassment' because Brown 'aggressively departed' from the neutral policy of the government, and accused him of giving 'harsh and arrogant advice' to the Israeli government.[56] Of course this was all nonsense, but it undermined Brown's image in the eyes of some pro-Israel Labour MPs.

And yet at the end of the day, the personal assault on Brown petered out and the lobby and the Labour Party renewed their positive pre-1956 relationship. Ultimately, the foreign secretary had little power compared to the prime minister. And Israel could not ask for a better friend than Harold Wilson.

THE TOP LOBBYIST: HAROLD WILSON

In hindsight, the Brown affair was insignificant. His stance was the exception that proved the rule. What mattered was his prime minister Harold Wilson's attitude, and he was pro-Israel to the bone.

Wilson was committed to Israel both as prime minister (1964–1970; 1974–1976) and as leader of the Opposition (1970–1974). Why was Wilson so committed to Israel and even its principal sponsor in British politics throughout his career? In many ways it was an unlikely position – and even astonished veteran supporters of Israeli like Ian Mikardo, who stated:

> I don't think Harold … [had] any doctrinal beliefs at all. Except for one, which I find utterly incomprehensible, which is his devotion to the cause of Israel.[57]

Mikardo told the audience at the close of LFI's annual dinner in October 1975 – the last Wilson would attend before shocking the country by suddenly resigning the premiership the following spring – that the prime minister was 'not only Israel's most important friend in the Labour party, but also her most consistent friend.'[58] Wilson's long-standing former political secretary, Marcia Falkender, claimed he had 'in many ways a romantic' view of Israel and was attracted to it as a 'wonderful experiment in socialist politics.'[59] Wilson was also close to Chaim Herzog, the Israeli ambassador to the UN at the time, Teddy Kollek, the mayor of Jerusalem, and Abba Eban. To Wilson, they were 'social democrats who made the desert flower.'[60] Abba Eban recalled:

> Among European statesmen whom I have known, some have stood out in the special preoccupation that Israel evoked in their hearts. Harold Wilson is preeminent among these.[61]

For another of the former prime minister's close Israeli comrades, Shimon Peres, Wilson was 'a true friend of Israel.'[62]

Wilson, like his successors Tony Blair and Gordon Brown, was the product of a religious upbringing. On the question of Israel, as on many other questions, Labour leaders owed more to Methodism than to Marx. The combined effort by LFI and Wilson's practically religious pursuit of pro-Israel objectives managed to silence the more Palestinian voices in the party. The threads that connected Wilson to the evangelical Christian Zionists of the nineteenth century are unveiled in Wilson's book, *The Chariot of Israel*. According to Roy Jenkins, a long-time member of Wilson's government, this book was 'one of the most strongly Zionist tracts ever written by a non-Jew.'[63] Wilson talks about his Christian Nonconformist upbringing; as he put it, his devotion to Israel was 'in part a response to the teaching of religious history.'[64]

Wilson was intent on granting Israel exceptional treatment in Britain's foreign policy. He told his biographer, Philip Ziegler, that when he assumed the leadership of the Labour Party he was determined to 'expiate Bevin's sins.'[65] James Callaghan, who succeeded Wilson as prime minister, recalled that when Wilson appointed him as foreign secretary,

Wilson said he would give him a free hand 'with the exception of two areas – Israel and South Africa', the latter because of Wilson's detestation of apartheid and the former 'because of day schools and Sunday schools, chapels, churches, kirk and conventicles'.[66] By the late 1990s, anti-apartheid stances could not be squared so easily with the pro-Israel one; in particular when Nelson Mandela declared that South Africa would be not be free until Palestine is free. But during the Wilson years, opposing apartheid in South Africa and condoning the oppression of the Palestinians did not seem like mutually exclusive moral positions and thus Israel could rely on the British prime minister. Bluntly, the lobby had a lot of spare time in those days.

Wilson's ties to Israel strengthened after his youngest son, Giles, went to volunteer in the Yagur kibbutz after 1967. Like Mikardo before them, the Wilsons did not know, or did not want to know, that this kibbutz extended over the ruins of a 1948 Palestinian village named Yajur.

Wilson's greatest contribution was to solidify LFI, making it a powerful actor in influencing British foreign policy towards the Middle East. Israel's most loyal ally in British politics held powerful positions, twice as a prime minister, and long terms in office as a leader of the Opposition. He used his time in power to solidify Labour's pro-Israel stance and prevent any internal opposition from gaining a foothold. As a consequence, Labour would not have a pro-Palestinian leader until 2015.

Wilson asserted that his views represented the overall position of the Labour Party and thus confidently stated that one could not find 'a political party to be more committed to a national home for the Jews in Palestine than was Labour'. And he added: 'since 1917 … this theme had been incorporated in Labour's statement of war aims' and 'had been reiterated eleven times from then to May 1945'.[67]

So, in the immediate aftermath of Brown's speech, the lobby was in two minds on how to approach the Wilson government. After all, Harold Wilson was never suspected by Israel and its lobby as being behind Brown's policy, although Brown was acting with the full knowledge of the government. The government fully supported Brown when he suggested that Britain would vote in favour, twice during the month of July 1967, of a Pakistani resolution in the UN condemning in strong terms Israel's annexationist policies in East Jerusalem (the Israelis were determined to officially annex East Jerusalem and 'unite' the city very soon after the war ended). But, under pressure from Wilson, Brown was forced to meet with Abba Eban, the Israeli foreign minister, and try to quell Israeli criticism and provide a softer version of the British position.[68]

But Wilson wasn't able to present the party as wholly behind Israel as he claimed it was (and indeed wanted it to be). The pro-Israel lobby in Britain, in the wake of Israel's expansion after the 1967 war, for the first time felt it couldn't be complacent.

One person who definitely felt that the Labour Party was not yet a safe space for pro-Israel politicians was Eric Moonman. As we've seen, he spearheaded the assault on Brown. He would represent a new phenomenon in lobbying for Israel on both sides of the Atlantic: individuals who believed they had a better idea than others about how to lobby for Israel. We will meet a number of these individuals when we discuss lobbying for Israel in the twenty-first century – in most cases not only do they act independently of the more institutionalised endeavours; they obstruct the more co-ordinated work. Moonman conjured up multiple projects along these lines. The first was in 1972. He persuaded the European Jewish Congress to let him work on their behalf in creating a group of experts who would be tasked with professionalising the Israeli propaganda machine. He asserted that the lack of professionalism was the reason Israel's message was not received well in many parts of the world. Accordingly, he recruited professional PR people and strategists. The group had the rather long title of 'West European Public Relations Group for Information on Behalf of Israel'; its main funder was the Israeli Foreign Ministry.[69] Not much came out of this initiative and in 1975 Moonman moved on to become the chairman of the Zionist Federation, working once more within an established advocacy group.[70] His first public act was to protest against a visit to London by two executives of the Palestine Liberation Organization (PLO). The PLO was founded in 1964 by the Arab League and grew in prominence after the June 1967 war, when the Fatah faction dominated it and pushed aside the Arab League chair, Ahmad al-Shukeiri, replacing him with Yasser Arafat. At that time the PLO did not recognise the legitimacy of the existence of the state of Israel. In the early 1970s, the organisation's more hardline factions took to actions like plane hijackings and bombings of non-military targets – tactics that the broader organisation did not publicly endorse. Protests were largely Moonman's speciality; he could boast of few other achievements.[71]

But why did Moonman turn into a one-man lobby for Zionism, dissatisfied with the more established outfits that had enjoyed great success? Fundamentally, he was a Labour man. And within Labour, an incipient pro-Palestinian lobby was starting to take shape: the Labour Middle East Council.

PALESTINIAN LOBBYING IN THE LABOUR PARTY, 1967–1974

In the late 1960s, a new body appeared, the Labour Middle East Council (LMEC), founded by Christopher Mayhew. The inspiration for LMEC came from the successful establishment, in the immediate aftermath of the June 1967 war, of the Council for the Advancement of Arab-British Understanding (CAABU), a cross-party organisation for the promotion of Arab and particularly Palestinian interests. MPs Ian Gilmour (Conservative) and Colin Jackson (Labour) served as chairmen. The early members of CAABU also included Mayhew and other Conservative politicians such as Sir Anthony Nutting and John Reddaway and journalists such as Michael Adams. In a letter to Mohamed Hassanein Heikal, the editor of Egypt's *Al-Ahram* newspaper, Mayhew defined LMEC's purpose as being to build up 'an effective resistance to the powerful Zionist propaganda and pressure ... [that] so far dominated the Labour movement.'[72]

The historian James Vaughan depicts LMEC as a powerful lobby, but even by his own account, it's obvious that LMEC had no chance of equalling the edifice built by LFI. During the 1970s, three attempts by LMEC to affiliate to the Labour Party formally were rejected by the National Executive Committee. The pro-Israel lobby was strong enough to ensure that these appeals would be rejected as 'Palestine' was not recognised as a state and the PLO was still regarded as a terrorist organisation. This was an absurd situation, as Poale Zion, which was founded before Israel existed and by this point functioned as a Zionist youth movement in Britain with no Israeli equivalent, remained on the Labour Party's books as an affiliate organisation. Mayhew expressed bewilderment when he wrote to all Constituency Labour Parties criticising the Labour Party for continuing to accept Poale Zion as an affiliated group while refusing to recognise 'a body pledged to a more balanced approach and to the support of United Nations' resolutions'.[73] LMEC was unsuccessful in its approach to the TUC. In April 1969, Mayhew invited the TUC to send representatives to LMEC's first major conference. The TUC declined, citing the short notice given, but it did express a willingness to receive any LMEC documents produced in support of the event.[74]

Failure to gain acceptance as a formally affiliated Labour Party organisation or within the TUC did not hamper LMEC's lobbying activity. In June 1972, an LMEC policy statement entitled 'British Policy on the Middle East' was distributed to the foreign secretary, the shadow foreign secretary, the International Committee of the Labour Party and all Labour MPs. This statement attributed the failure to achieve a peace settlement to 'Israeli intransigence and American bias' and proposed a British policy based on dissociation from American leadership in the region, a strong commitment to UN Security Council Resolution 242 (which called upon Israel and the Arab states to establish peace based on the principle of Israeli withdrawal from the territories it occupied in the 1967 war in return for normalisation with the Arab states) and a warning to Israel that Britain would not tolerate settlements in the occupied territories. A draft resolution based on these principles was dispatched to all Constituency Labour Parties with an invitation for them to consider submitting the statement to the annual party conference.[75] However, LMEC, recognising the power of the pro-Israel lobby in the party, refrained from advocating British recognition of the PLO.

A very benign statement in 1973 by the party's National Executive Committee was the peak of its success. This balanced statement is still regarded by the pro-Israel lobby as evidence of anti-Zionist sentiment in Labour. The National Executive Committee issued a statement which, whilst expressing sympathy and understanding for 'Israel's single-minded determination to preserve her security', sensibly warned that 'a total reliance on military strength can only lead to the kind of grimly militaristic and rigid social organisation which disfigures so many other countries already', and that:

> A concern with security cannot justify the retention of territories occupied during the conflicts with her Arab neighbours, nor their integration into Israel's economic structure.[76]

In the period from 1967 to 1977, the Foreign Office shared LMEC's frustration with the USA, concerned it was becoming a dishonest broker, using Britain in the UN in a Machiavellian way to try and impose on the Arab world a post-1967 settlement, crafted by Henry Kissinger to Israel's order.

This is not surprising. The grim reality of an oppressive occupation spoke louder than any lobbying on either side – and it began to reach the ears of Labour members. The PLO and anti-Zionist Jews who left Israel contributed to a lucid presentation of a narrative that ran counter to the Israeli one.

The bitter truths, combined with the advocacy of the Palestinian and pro-Palestinian groups, started to influence even avowedly pro-Israel organisations such as the TUC. As we have seen, it was Israel's own TUC, the Histadrut, that had been entrusted with the task of eliciting the TUC's support for the Zionist project in Palestine.

Up until the 1967 war, the Histadrut felt it had an ally in the TUC. But the re-emergence of the Palestinian liberation movement caused grassroots members to question the Israeli narrative. A telling case study, a year after the 1967 war, illuminates the issues the Histadrut had in keeping the TUC on its side. On 23 July 1968, Palestinian guerrillas hijacked El Al Flight 426 from Rome to Tel Aviv and diverted it to Algiers. Although the Algerian government released all the non-Israeli passengers almost immediately, they refused to release the Israeli passengers, the crew and the airplane. While this was going on, the TUC was approached by the Histadrut: a very intriguing campaign began there to try and compare the rights of the Israeli passengers to those struggling throughout the world for social justice. One European Union federation that was easy to recruit was the Deutsche Gewerkschaftsbund. But appeals to other trade union bodies in Europe were made in vain. These organisations failed to accept the Israeli portrayal of the situation.[77] It was one of the first instances when the Histadrut could not win over the TUC. This trend would accelerate when the PLO moved away from armed struggle and focused on diplomatic campaigning.

After 1967, some members of the TUC began to doubt its pro-Israel stance. In January 1968, George Foggon, who by then had left the Foreign Office and become the director of the London office of the International Labour Organization, reported a conversation with the secretary general of the TUC, Frank Cousins, in which the latter had expressed 'disappointment' with Israel and concern about elements of Israeli policy: 'They have not been too happy about a number of aspects of Israel's policy since the Six Day War', noted Foggon, particularly 'since they saw the refugee problem in Jordan and had an opportunity to talk with some of those still crossing from the West Bank'.[78] Remember this is the same Cousins who was enchanted by Israel after his first visit to the state. Cousins's message was substantiated by reports at the time from foreign journalists and representatives of the International Red Cross on Israel's ethnic cleansing policy in the West Bank, including shooting over the heads of those crossing the River Jordan to encourage them to leave.

In retrospect, Mayhew and activists who worked with him, such as Ghada Karmi and other members of LMEC, laid the foundations for more significant pro-Palestinian networks later in the twentieth century and in the twenty-first. Between the announcement of its formation at the Greater London Regional Conference in April 1969 and the mid-1970s, it was able to build an infrastructure to provide information that was not available in the mainstream media or academia. Through conferences, newsletters and recruitment of new members, it created a nucleus that would later counteract, to some extent, the huge influence of the pro-Israel lobby on Labour.

In July 1974, thoroughly disillusioned with the impossibility of working for Palestine in the Labour Party, Mayhew defected to the

Liberals, establishing the Liberal Middle East Council, a group that would attract the support of future party leader David Steel.

However, these clashes between pro- and anti-Israel advocacy groups should be seen in context, given the fact that Britain in any case played second fiddle to the Americans, who now with full force imposed their will and ideas on what became known as the 'peace process', the first phase of which ended in dismal failure. But by that time, Labour was out of power, suffering defeat in the 1970 general election. To their great surprise, the pro-Israel lobbyists found out that, unlike Wilson, the new Conservative government ruling Britain for the next four years was much more sympathetic to Brown than Wilson was, and their foreign minister, Sir Alec Douglas-Home, was about to deliver the third of the three speeches that took the lobby by surprise, after Eden and Brown's speech, and triggered an angry response.

YET ANOTHER ENEMY OF THE JEWISH STATE: ALEXANDER DOUGLAS-HOME

At the height of the February 1974 election, a classic gentleman entered Thames TV studios for an interview with Eamonn Andrews, one of Britain's most respected journalists. Alec Douglas-Home was already one of an endangered species on the political scene then, and now his kind is extinct altogether.

Douglas-Home was about to retire, and this was in many ways an attempt to sum up his career to that point. He was asked by Andrews to enumerate the high points of his career as foreign minister. After naming a few of them, he added:

> And I think the last one I would name would be the speech I made in Harrogate which had some influence on the Arab–Israeli War and how it would be solved and the improvement of our relations with the Arab countries, as a result.[79]

On 31 October 1970, in front of the council of regional associations of the Conservative Party in Harrogate, Yorkshire, Douglas-Home laid down his ideas of how to approach the reality that unfolded in historical Palestine after the June 1967 war. He was helped by a team in the Foreign Office and won the full support of the prime minister, Edward Heath, for what became an important announcement. The most crucial message in that speech was that Britain could no longer 'ignore the political aspirations of the Palestinian Arabs'.[80]

These are his words:

> How can these tensions be resolved? An equilibrium is needed in the Middle East which both sides would be prepared to accept. The actual issues in dispute are of a kind which can be solved. The fabric of a settlement consistent with the Security Council Resolution of November 1967 which would be fair and should be workable can easily be produced. Agreed solutions on all the separate elements would have to be incorporated into a formal and binding agreement which would be endorsed by the United Nations Security Council. But like the Resolution of November 1967, any such settlement must be based on two fundamental principles: the inadmissibility of the acquisition of territory by war and the need for a just and lasting peace, in which every state in the area is guaranteed the right to live in security. This means as the Security Council Resolution said, that Israeli Armed Forces must withdraw from territories occupied in the conflict; and that, on the other hand, the state of belligerency which has existed in the Middle East must be ended and the right of every state to live in peace within secure and recognized boundaries, free from threats or acts of force, must be recognized.[81]

He further emphasised the importance of recognising a 'legitimate aspiration – resettlement in dignity and honour' and Palestinians' desire for a 'means of self-expression' as essential elements of his government policy.[82]

For years afterwards, his speech remained significant in convincing Britain to acknowledge Palestinian aspirations. Today, it may surprise readers to learn that the pro-Israel lobby in Britain had to work harder during the time the Conservatives were in power and less so when Labour was the government of the day. In the twenty-first century, both governments had pursued a policy that was broadly acceptable to the lobby.

Douglas-Home was consistent in his support for Palestinian rights. In other appearances, he reiterated the main points he had made in Harrogate. In his statement to the House of Commons on 22 October 1973, when referring to the Harrogate speech, he repeated his government's view that 'the question of the Palestinians must clearly form part of a complete and long-term settlement'. Otherwise, according to Douglas-Home, 'the settlement would not stick.'[83] Although in his Harrogate speech and in the British Parliament, Douglas-Home did not mention anything about either a Palestinian 'homeland' (a term used later publicly in 1976 by the Labour secretary of state, Anthony Crosland) or a 'state', he thought that this could be an outcome of the peace process. In his autobiography, Douglas-Home recalled that when he drafted the speech, he thought:

> Now that Egypt and the Arab countries have been purged of their humiliation by achieving a stalemate in battle; and now that there is a possible solution for the resettlement of the Palestinians in an independent State on the West Bank of the Jordan, the prospects of a permanent peace look to be more helpful than for some time past.[84]

Douglas-Home further annoyed Israel by his refusal to expel the PLO representative, Said Hammami, from his seat in the Arab League Office in London. He stated:

> I should not wish to provoke the very hostile reaction that would undoubtedly be caused in the Arab world if we were to expel the representative of an organisation which has now been recognised by almost all the Arab states as the sole legitimate representatives of the Palestinians and whose organisation sits as a full member of the Arab League.[85]

Douglas-Home seemed to be the only senior British politician, after Brown, who interpreted UN Resolution 242 as a demand for

unconditional Israeli withdrawal to the 5 June 1967 borders and applied
it to all the territories Israel occupied during the war. He declared:

> Secure and recognised boundaries should be based on the Armistice
> Line which existed before the war of 1967 subject to minor changes
> which might be agreed between the two countries.[86]

Later in his autobiography, Douglas-Home recalled that when he
drafted the Harrogate speech, he had thought that a future peace was
bound to involve substantial withdrawal of Israeli forces (with minor
adjustments) from the occupied Palestinian and Arab territories:

> I was well aware that it was impossible to please both sides. Predictably
> the Arabs were welcoming and the Israelis angry; the more so as they
> had thought that I was sympathetic to them in the fight for their exist-
> ence. In the latter feeling they were right; and the speech stemmed from
> the conviction that their only hope of survival in an age of missiles lay
> in abandoning their conquered Arab territories, and in retiring behind
> their 1967 frontiers which would then be policed by the United Nations,
> and would probably require an international guarantee.[87]

Douglas-Home did not stop there. He was the only British foreign
secretary to challenge the dishonest brokery of the Americans,
which became visible in the early 1970s. His diplomats shared his
frustration with the American position and its hesitation to pressure
Israel into concessions. The British ambassador in Washington, Lord
Cromer, gloomily reported in November 1972 that the US was only
looking for an interim solution in Palestine, whereas Britain wished
for a more comprehensive one. This was not solely out of concern
for the Palestinians. In the background of all of this we should
remember that, since the devaluation of the pound in November
1967, the grim economic reality led to a strategic decision to end
whatever was left of the Empire in January 1968, in particular east of
Suez.[88] In light of this, there was a need for a new Anglo-Arab
understanding.

These were peculiar times, when the British Foreign Office was keen to show the Arab world that it was pursuing a policy independent of American influence. This era also saw early contacts between Britain and the PLO in the UN behind the scenes, more in tandem with Arab and African positions than that of the USA and Israel. The relationship between Britain and Israel deteriorated further when Israeli commandos used falsified British passports in their raids on Beirut in 1973.

In this extraordinary period, it is important to mention another unique contribution by Douglas-Home. He was the only British foreign secretary to openly discuss the right of return of the Palestinian refugees that were expelled by Israel in 1948 (British policy until then supported the idea of resettling the Palestinian refugees in the Arab world and ignoring their aspirations and demands for return). Douglas-Home stated that those refugees who wished to return to their homes and were ready to live in peace with their neighbours should be permitted to return – a verbatim quotation of UN Resolution 194. This was a position that even the civil servants in the Foreign Office were reluctant to recommend. They asserted, based on their surveys, that many Palestinian refugees wished to settle in the West Bank and Gaza once the Israeli occupation was over. I am not sure this was an accurate assumption but, in any case, the Foreign Office declared that the British government could not support any plan for a Palestinian population in these areas and therefore there was no need for a British declaration of support for the right of return.[89]

The Israeli reaction to Douglas-Home's policies mirrored their indignation at Brown. Once more the press at home and the lobby in Britain were recruited to express Israel's outrage. Three years later, the rage continued. In 1973, Abba Eban went as far as insinuating that the Harrogate speech encouraged the October war and the joint Egyptian–Syrian attack on Israel.[90] But Douglas-Home was the least of the Israeli government's problems: what was really insuperable was that the prime minister Edward Heath agreed with him on his approach to the issue. In Cabinet meetings, it was nonetheless noted that the British public was angered by the oil embargo and in general there was 'public sympathy for Israel and concern for her survival'. John Davies, the chancellor of the Duchy of Lancaster, regarded this concern as unwarranted and deliberately played up by the British media, which:

> appeared to be excessively open to Israeli influence and put only one side of the case and ignored the Government's consistent endeavours … that there could be no lasting settlement in the Middle East while they sought to protect their own frontiers by holding Arab territories through force of arms.

He explained why it would be a difficult mission:

> There was, however, a large and active lobby at work in this country to further the Israeli cause; and it was difficult for a balanced viewpoint to get a hearing.[91]

Because of the lobby, at Cabinet meetings discussing the reaction to the speech and the Heath government's overall policy, it was suggested that the problem was:

> that the Government's attitude to this question was not fully appreciated either by the Jewish community in this country or by public opinion at large

and therefore:

> No effort should be spared to make it understood; and for this purpose, it would be valuable for members of the Cabinet to be fully briefed on the issues, the facts and the considerations underlying the Government's policy.[92]

Unlike the Labour government that would follow it in 1974, the Cabinet remained loyal to the path charted by Douglas-Home in the Harrogate speech. Lobbying was not enough to alter the course of the Conservative government. In another Cabinet meeting at the beginning of 1974, it was agreed that the political aspirations of the Palestinians could only be fulfilled within a state of their own. To this day, not a single British government has fully adopted this position.

Heath refused to deliver arms to Israel during the 1973 October war, mostly out of fear of the Arab oil embargo, but also because he believed in the European Economic Community (EEC) and was happy to follow the new tendency in Europe to heed at least some of the Palestinian aspirations. Heath also refused to allow US intelligence gathering from British bases in Cyprus and barred the US from using any British bases to resupply Israel or refuelling in Britain.[93]

In the case of Heath and other Conservative ministers, this refusal to conform to Israel's demands was not driven by moral principles, but by a cynical concern for Britain's energy supply and security. However, it was one of the few rare moments in twentieth-century British foreign policy when the Palestinians were recognised as a wronged party. Needless to say, the government didn't go as far as accepting all the PLO demands in those years, nor was there a willingness to end the Israeli occupation of the West Bank and the Gaza Strip. But while on the other side of the Atlantic, Palestine was synonymous with terrorism, in Europe the climate was very different. The Heath government's statements about Palestine coincided with the British decision to join the EEC and Britain was immediately drawn into supporting the new body's policy. In 1973, the same year Britain officially joined, the EEC published the Brussels Declaration, stating that 'in the establishment of a just and lasting peace, account must be taken of the legitimate rights of the Palestinians'. As we know now, nothing came of these fine sentiments: the occupation entrenched itself, the settlements expanded and the incremental ethnic cleansing of the Palestinians continues to this day, accompanied by harsh policies of collective punishment and oppression.

Heath's government also allowed the PLO to open its office in London. In a concession to pressure from Israel, Douglas-Home promised the Israeli foreign minister on 29 June 1972 that the PLO 'will [not] enjoy any kind of official or quasi-official status from the government'.[94] But even this limited conciliatory gesture towards the Palestinians worried Israel: the Israeli government now appealed to pro-Israel members of the Conservative Party to act. Accordingly, a new organisation in the pro-Israel lobby in Britain entered the fray: Conservative Friends of Israel (CFI). This move was initiated by the MP for Bury and Radcliffe, Michael Fidler, who was the first Jewish mayor of Prestwich and president of the Board of Deputies from 1967 to 1973. CFI's first patron was Anthony Eden, a zealous convert to Zionism after his humiliation in the 1956 Suez Crisis, extending his hatred of Gamal Abdel Nasser to the rest of the Arab world. The party leader who followed in 1975, Margaret Thatcher, also gave her blessing to the new outfit. In time, as we shall see, CFI would become a powerful lobby group in its own right. But for now, during the Heath government, CFI was insignificant; however, this brief interlude of Palestinian sympathy in British government would not last for long when Labour returned to power.

HAROLD WILSON TO THE RESCUE, 1970–1975

Unable to gain a foothold inside the Conservative Party for now, the Israeli government sought to apply pressure through the leader of the Opposition, their trusted ally Harold Wilson. Out of government he was even more unequivocal in his support for the Zionist lobby. He persistently complained about the government's anti-Israel bias, which he claimed was apparently manifested in allowing Egyptian pilots to train in the UK, while prohibiting the USA from resupplying Israel from British bases and making it difficult for the Israelis to obtain spare parts for their British-made Centurion tanks. In truth, the Heath government imposed an embargo on both the Israeli and the Arab sides. But Israel did not tolerate being treated equally.

Wilson's crucial task in the eyes of the lobby was to nip the emergence of a pro-Palestinian lobby among the party's Left in the bud. Wilson was aware that among the more progressive circles within his party, Israel's militarism and more visible oppression of the Palestinians had created an informal pro-Palestinian internal lobby.

This informal lobby evolved around the Labour Middle East Council, which continued to pursue pro-Palestinian policy after the departure of its founder. One of the main areas where LMEC tried to create some balance in the approach towards Palestine was the BBC. There it initiated a campaign spearheaded by Andrew Faulds. He was a broadcaster as well as a Labour MP. With others he established a Palestine Action Group at the BBC. Its greatest success was the broadcasting on 26 November 1976 of an episode of BBC Two's *Open Door* series, devoted to the Palestinian refugees' right of return. Faulds presented the programme, inviting guests such as the pro-Palestinian Labour MP from Bristol David Watkins, and Peter Hain, who in those days was part of the anti-apartheid campaign in Britain.[95] A few days after the broadcast, Ghada Karmi, who was a prominent member of the Action Group and today a renowned scholar and campaigner for Palestinian rights, reported that Abu Lutuf (Farouk Qaddumi), the 'Foreign Secretary' of the PLO, had praised the programme as 'the best film he had ever seen on the Palestine issue' and CAABU's John Reddaway also congratulated Faulds for making 'a notable contribution towards the exposition and defence of Palestinian rights'.[96]

The pro-Israel retaliation was led by the Israeli press. The popular Israeli tabloid *Yedioth Ahronoth* reported: 'last weekend, the most extremist anti-Israeli programme ever shown on Western television was screened by the BBC'.[97] They needed to come down hard on it, as this first ever exposé about the victims of the Nakba generated public support. The Palestine Action Group received many letters of support, membership queries and donations. In Scotland the programme hit a nerve; members of the Scottish National Party saw similarities between what they deemed was the English oppression of Scotland and the Palestinian plight. Faulds welcomed the solidarity but distanced himself from the comparison, as he objected to Scottish independence.

The commitment of such politicians and intellectuals to Palestine revealed the early signs, noted at the time by the *Jewish Chronicle*, that lobbying for Israel would have to move its target from the Left to the Right as 'Israel is no longer the automatic beneficiary of socialist sympathies'.[98] This remark was premature. For a quite a while, well into the 1980s, socialists in the British Labour Party sided with Zionism. It was a period in which lobbying was practically unnecessary – as Labour leaders, in opposition and in government, gave unquestioning, whole-hearted support to Israel.

As a result of this pressure from Israel, pro-Palestinian politicians suddenly found their political careers destroyed. The first was Andrew Faulds. In 1973, due to the outcry from the lobby, Wilson dismissed Faulds from the Shadow Cabinet because he had openly questioned the loyalty of Jewish members of the party who sided unconditionally with Israel. Or as Wilson put it, '[Faulds] impugned the patriotism of Jewish Members of the Parliament ... by implying that they had dual loyalties.'[99]

But Wilson could not prevent the emergence of a pro-Palestinian group of Labour activists – he could only limit their influence. Looking back at this record, we can now understand better why the pro-Israel lobby felt as if it were facing a doomsday scenario when, in the next century, a pro-Palestinian politician became leader of the Labour Party and its candidate for prime minister. The emergence of a pro-Palestine group in the Wilson era sowed the seeds for the new, powerful generation of activists in our own era – right up to Jeremy Corbyn himself.

But the lobby still felt very strong and focused when Wilson returned to office in 1974, ending Heath's four years in power. His second term in office was received with great relief by the lobby. His first mission was to try and move on from the 'bad days' of Brown and Douglas-Home. But he did not stay long enough to 'expunge' this 'negative' influence. He shocked the country and the Queen when he decided to resign in 1975 and was replaced by James Callaghan, who remained in office until 1979. Even after his resignation, and in his years in the Opposition after the 1970 Conservative election victory, Wilson continued to work within the framework of LFI and was its president for a while.

His first trip overseas after he resigned was to Israel, where he received an honorary doctorate from the Hebrew University and, more importantly from a Palestinian perspective, he visited and officially opened a forest on the border between the West Bank and Israel, half-way between Jerusalem and Hebron, that had been donated by the Anglo-Jewish community, named Park Britannia, where his and Richard Crossman's contributions to Zionism are recognised. It was 15,000 *dunam* (roughly 15,000 square metres) of mainly pine trees planted over the ruins of seven Palestinian villages and their lands: Zakariyya, Ajjur, Dayr ad Dubban, Ra'na, Kidna, Bayt Jibrin, and Dayr Nakh-khas. The forest was paid for by the Jewish National Fund (JNF). At the time nobody paid attention to the unique role the JNF played in the history of Zionism and Israel, or, more importantly, Britain's relationship to it (which was recently exposed in meticulous detail by Uri Davis).[100] Suffice it to say here that for most of the time since its founding, the UK branch of the JNF has enjoyed charitable status and resulting subsidies from British taxpayers. The JNF branch in Israel (Keren Kayemet LeYisrael) functions as an arm of the Israeli state in the enforcement of an apartheid system of land control and population segregation and has played a major role in the refinement of this system over the years.

Wilson fully supported the JNF and was either oblivious to or ignorant of its role in building Jewish settlements and planting forests over the ruins of hundreds of Palestinian villages that Israel destroyed in 1948. In retirement, Wilson took up the role of president of Labour Friends of Israel. Its then director, Valerie Cocks, recalled: 'I never had to ask him to say anything pro-Israel – it came naturally. He spoke about Israel in the most loving, warmest possible way.'[101]

THE LABOUR GOVERNMENT, 1975–1979

Wilson's successor James Callaghan continued the re-orientation of British policy away from the Brown and Douglas-Home legacies. But not immediately. As foreign minister in Wilson's second government (1975–1976), he did not share Wilson's unconditional support for Israel. While he was foreign secretary, his official line was very much supportive of the Palestinians. In this capacity he wrote in *The Times* on 13 February 1974 that the Palestinians had to play an important role in any future solution, and this was followed by an even more explicit statement in the House of Commons (as part of the Queen's Speech debate on 30 October 1974):

A provision must be made for satisfaction of the needs of the Palestinians, by which I mean not only the rights of individual

Palestinian refugees, as was laid down for so many years by the General Assembly, but also the legitimate rights of Palestinian people.[102]

Callaghan later wrote in his memoirs that whilst Labour would not perform a 'U-turn' in its relations with Israel, he emphasised that the party recognised that the Palestinian people had legitimate aspirations.[103] Britain's representative at the time in the UN, Lord Ivor Richard, in his speech to the General Assembly on 22 November 1974, echoed this sentiment:

> It has long been my government's view that in any debate on the Middle East the views of the Palestinian people must be listened to. Indeed, I said so myself on 14 October in this Assembly ... I said, 'the British government has made plain many times its belief that no peace settlement in the Middle East is possible that does not take account of the legitimate rights of the Palestinians. The British Foreign Secretary has several times spoken of the need for any settlement to provide for a personality for the Palestinian people. It follows, therefore, that we consider it right that the view of the Palestinian should be heard.' I would reaffirm that position today. Whatever else can be said of this debate, it would seem that a Palestinian voice has been heard clearly and unmistakeably in this Assembly.[104]

Callaghan was even willing to support the idea of a Palestinian state in public. He also made it clear as foreign secretary that Britain disagreed with Israeli claims that occupation of the territories was vital for its security.[105]

However, when he became prime minister in 1976, Callaghan charted a different course, aiming to erase both the Brown and Douglas-Home legacies. Callaghan made sure that many of Douglas-Home's statements on Palestine would be altered or jettisoned altogether, in particular those referring to a Palestinian state and possible recognition of the PLO, a line religiously adhered to by his own foreign secretary, David Owen.

As prime minister, Callaghan shaped British policy towards the peace negotiations brokered between Israel and Egypt by the American president, Jimmy Carter, leading to the 1978 Camp David Accords. Callaghan adopted a pro-Israel stance, cultivating close relations with the Israeli leadership, and was unwilling to chastise Israel for its increased settlement activities in the West Bank and the Gaza Strip. In this respect, Callaghan's government departed from the established British policy to the point that Britain abstained and did not endorse United Nations Security Council Resolution 446 in March 1979, which condemned continuing Israeli settlement activity. This stance damaged Britain's relations with Egypt and Jordan, two Arab states committed to normalising relationships with Israel.[106]

Was this return to Wilsonian policies the outcome of intensive pro-Israel lobby activity in Britain? The answer seems to be no. As early as the 1920s, the Zionist lobby had entrenched itself among Britain's political elite, further fortified by the founding of Labour Friends of Israel in the 1950s. The dividends of decades of hard work were being reaped in the 1970s – support for Israel was by now second nature to senior British politicians, the default foreign policy. Only when events on the ground became excessively brutal and inhumane – and visibly so – could the automatic consensus be shaken.

If we understand how inertia and self-censorship guided Britain's privileging of Israel in its foreign policy – to the extent that Israel did not have to exercise any active pressure – we can begin to understand why the Palestinian liberation movement lost faith in changing British and Western policy through diplomatic means. The wish to attract attention and remind the rest of the world that Palestine is still fighting for its existence led to desperate actions by the liberation movement's militant fringe, including targeting Israeli civilians. The Munich Olympics massacre in 1972 and the Zion Square refrigerator bombing in 1975 made headlines across the world. Those leading the Palestinian revolution believed that only dramatic events and operations like this could bring international attention to their cause and force the world to respect their right to defend themselves. With time, these actions became redundant, and were regarded by the Palestinians themselves as counter-productive because even without such actions, colonised and occupied Palestine became much more well known. The flow of information was far more effective in changing public opinion in the world, and in the West in particular, about the plight of the Palestinians.

In any case, Douglas-Home's candid commitment to Palestinian statehood was watered down by David Owen. In March 1979, when debating the issue of the peace negotiations in the Middle East in the House of Commons, Owen was already faithfully toeing the American line, referring to 'Palestinian autonomy' in the West Bank and Gaza as the sole 'solution' to the 'conflict'; a discourse that we now know in hindsight had very little do with Palestinian aspirations or the reality on the ground. Menachem Begin, Israel's prime minister (1977–1982), was responsible for introducing the idea of Palestinian autonomous rule in the West Bank and the Gaza Strip, offering self-rule, without sovereignty or economic independence, and spread over a bifurcated space, controlled from the outside by the Israeli army and secret service – a kind of Bantustan model.

Owen explained that it was his government's policy that:

> We believe there must be a Palestinian homeland if there is to be a comprehensive peace settlement. We see as the first step towards that settlement full autonomy on the West Bank and Gaza.[107]

The Labour Cabinet was fully aware that by adopting the notion of autonomy and not statehood, they were erasing Douglas-Home's legacy. Under American pressure, which I will analyse in the next chapter, the government adopted the most unfavourable interpretation of the EEC's continued support for a change in the Western world's position on Palestine. The subject arose in London when, in June 1977, at the time that Britain held the presidency of the EEC, the European Council declared 'the need for a homeland for the Palestinian people'.[108] Until the 1977 Camp David summit between Anwar Sadat, Menachem Begin and Jimmy Carter, which gave rise to the bilateral Israeli–Egyptian peace treaty two years later, there had been no American request for Britain to tame the EEC's bolder position in standing by the Palestinians.

In March 1977 Jimmy Carter made America's most pro-Palestinian declaration ever, baffling the government in London. In any case, this short-lived American deviation from its dishonest brokery escaped the notice of British policy makers. They interpreted the American position as far more rigid than it was at times, asserting that Washington wanted London to balance the pro-Palestinian tendencies within the EEC.[109]

On the surface, the lobby was quite redundant during the days of Callaghan, even taking into account Callaghan's personal dislike of Israel's leader Menachem Begin, who was previously *persona non grata* in London due to his terrorist past. Nonetheless David Owen could not stop singing the praises of Begin and fully endorsed Israel's manipulation of the discussion about Palestinians in occupied territories to focus on the futile question of autonomy.

Callaghan's own rejection of the PLO mirrored Wilson's overall pro-Israel attitude on this question. Of course, the anti-PLO stance was also encouraged by the civil service in the Foreign Office. Its senior advisers recommended avoiding any recognition of the PLO and advised against any rapprochement. Wilson, in an interview he gave to the American TV network ABC's flagship show, *Issues and Answers*, stated:

> But so far as this [recognising the PLO] is concerned, we cannot negotiate with men who have got blood on their hands, and they know it well.[110]

The 1970s were a unique period in the international arena, when the question of the PLO's legitimacy showed how Europe and the USA were miles away from post-colonial Asian, African and South American views of Palestine. At this time, Third World liberation movements viewed the liberation of Palestine as part of the struggle for a decolonised world. This was the decade when decolonisation and the battle against apartheid were at their peak, and so was solidarity with the PLO. But Callaghan as foreign secretary stated in the House of Commons:

> The leaders of the PLO have not yet recognised the existence of the state of Israel. In those circumstances, I find it difficult to meet them.[111]

However, it should be said that more junior members, as well as the Labour electorate, did not share this categorical rejection. The minister of state for foreign affairs, Frank Judd, wrote a letter to his parliamentary colleague John Gorst, emphasising that although Britain did not recognise the PLO:

> We believe that the views of all Palestinians, including the PLO must be taken into account in reaching a just settlement.[112]

However, this didn't signal any concrete change in policy – Judd knew there was an easy way to defuse any potential Israeli wrath. Immediately after he wrote the letter, he explained to Andrew Faulds, who had hoped this indicated a change of heart in Whitehall, that Britain ruled out any contact with the PLO if it did not accept UN Resolution 242, asking for peace with Israel in return for Israeli withdrawal from the June 1967 occupied territories, and amended its Charter, which according to him denied Israel's right to exist.[113] Put simply, in principle Britain wanted to hear the views of the PLO, but considered its opinions null and void.

One way of undermining the PLO's growing international legitimacy that was popular with the Israeli Labor Party was to try and push forward the 'Jordanian option', an idea dating back to the early 1920s. The option meant a search for an understanding about the future of the West Bank and the Gaza Strip with the Hashemite Kingdom, rather than seeking a solution that would satisfy the Palestinians. This notion was the basis for tacit negotiations between King Abdullah and the Jewish Agency on the eve of the Nakba, when, in return for limited participation by the Arab Legion (the Transjordanian Army) in the war effort, Jordan was granted free access to the West Bank. After 1967, Israel offered Jordan either functional co-operation in ruling the occupied territories or geographical partition; in both cases Israel offered too little, and quite often Abdullah's grandson, Hussein, sensed correctly that most of these offers were not genuine. In any case, the Jordanian option collapsed in 1988, when King Hussein ceded the West Bank for all intents and purposes. But at the time of the Callaghan government, Britain served as the location for secret talks between the then Israeli foreign minister, Moshe Dayan, and King Hussein at the house of the king's personal physician in London.[114]

Callaghan's rejection of the PLO was sweet music to Israeli government ears; no less satisfying was his attitude towards the illegal Judaisation of the West Bank and the Gaza Strip. As Nigel Ashton remarks, on settlement, Callaghan was even more supportive than the Wilson government.[115] So, what was the role of the lobby, if the Callaghan government delivered the goods, especially compared to its US counterpart (which, as we shall see, was more fickle)?

The most active lobby group in the Callaghan years was Labour Friends of Israel. Regardless of the unambiguous position communicated by Downing Street, LFI was still unconvinced that Callaghan went far enough in being pro-Israel. Despite the government's evident hostility to the PLO, LFI constantly demanded that it reiterated its negative position.[116] But the LFI had nothing to worry about. Structural support for Israel was solid enough to ensure Callaghan's obedience. As Ashton writes:

> Callaghan's position was a product of the extensive links between the British Labour Party and Israel which had been built up during the 1950s and 1960s, most notably through the Socialist International organisation, but also between the Trades Union movements, and as a result of the backing of the British Jewish community for Labour during these years.[117]

Thus, David Owen sent occasional letters to Eric Moonman, the chair of the LFI, such as the one he wrote on 27 November 1978:

> I can assure you that there is no question of our 'recognising' the PLO, so long as their formal position remains that they refuse to accept Israel's right to exist.[118]

With the return of the Conservatives to power in 1979 under the leadership of Margaret Thatcher, the lobby could look back with satisfaction on the last five years of the Labour governments. At a time

when in Africa, Asia and South America the PLO was gaining legitimacy and popularity, Britain under Labour seemed to be as loyal to
Israel as the USA, and at times even more loyal, as we shall see. Once
again, it is difficult for the historian to credit the lobby with these
anti-Palestinian British policies. The success of the pro-Zionist effort
that began at the turn of the century meant that the lobby's inheritance was a well-oiled machine for advocacy, and a political culture
where uncritical support for Israel was the norm. Whenever Israel or
the PLO were discussed, political obedience and self-censorship had
already been assured.

THE THATCHER YEARS

When looking at the recollections of members of the pro-Israel lobby or
Israeli officials dealing with advocacy during the time of Margaret
Thatcher, it seems that they took the Iron Lady's support for Israel for
granted. However, in the early years of her government, Thatcher was
unable, or perhaps unwilling, to heed recurrent requests by the lobby to
keep a tight leash on the Foreign Office, which the lobby considered
'anti-Israeli' in essence. The crime of this assortment of civil servants
was their infrequent challenges to some of Israel's policies in the occupied territories – tantamount to siding with the enemy in the eyes of the
lobby.

There was a rumour in the Foreign Office that Thatcher was regarded
as a naturally pro-Israel politician because of the 'Finchley Factor'; in
other words, she had to satisfy her North London constituency for
thirty-three years, including the eleven years of her premiership, and
this constituency had a sizeable Anglo-Jewish majority living in it.

Civil servants recall that upon her election as leader of the
Opposition in 1975, the Foreign Office felt it should pre-empt any ill
feelings in the Arab world where she might be deemed as being 'a prisoner of the Zionists'.[119] Thatcher was a founding member of the Finchley
Anglo-Israeli Friendship League and of the Conservative Friends of
Israel. She did not differ in her approach compared to those who
preceded and succeeded her; there is no indication in any of the

documentation of any wish on her behalf, or the Foreign Office's behalf, to change her predecessor James Callaghan's basically pro-Israel orientation. So in other words, she was no more or less pro-Israel than her predecessors in the office.

According to some accounts, her admiration for Israel stemmed from her veneration of Judaism – whether this was genuine or opportunistic, it definitely existed on paper.[120] Azriel Bermant is the only scholar who has comprehensively looked at Thatcher's relations with Israel, and he assumes that her attitude was born out of a pragmatic approach; on this view, Israel was part of the world she belonged to and she saw herself as its defender.[121] The lobby was hence capable of forgiving her when she criticised certain Israeli policies. Occasionally her government's attitude to Israel prompted some rebuke by the lobby, but since she never accompanied her criticism with any meaningful action, it made little difference at the end of the day.

Like her predecessor, Thatcher disliked Menachem Begin, but this personal distaste did not suffice to propel her to alter British policy in any significant way. The Venice Declaration by the nine-member EEC was her first challenge in managing relations with Israel. This landmark declaration acknowledged the right of the Palestinians to self-determination and called upon international diplomacy to include the PLO in any future negotiations on the fate of the occupied territories. The declaration was made just one year into her premiership – meaning it had largely already been decided by the time she came to power. On the face of it, the declaration was meant to allow Europe to play a far more active role in the peace effort than ever before. Thatcher was asked by the Americans to safeguard Washington's leading role in the 'peace process', which was a request meant to disarm any serious European challenge to that policy. She was willing to fulfil this request to a certain extent, but not fully. Despite American requests, Thatcher readily endorsed the Venice Declaration and stood by her decision right up to the end of her term in office – in her memoirs, she described the decisions at Venice as striking 'the right balance'.[122] However, for Menachem Begin, balance was most unwelcome. He penned an enraged letter to her:

Madam Prime Minister. Did anybody since the days of Hitler and Goebbels, Goering, Rosenberg and Streicher ever declare more plainly and more precisely that the endeavour is to destroy both our people and our state again ... And yet, the great, free, democratic countries of Europe assembled and asked us, the elected representatives of the people of Israel, the USA, and all other nations to recognise that organisation as a future partner in 'peace' talks. This is not only astonishing: As I said, it hurt us deeply.[123]

When it came to foreign policy he didn't like, Begin never waited too long before bringing up the Holocaust. He also complained that Britain was selling arms to Jordan but not to Israel. Although the Foreign Office offered to help draft a response, Thatcher decided not to respond at all.[124]

In hindsight, it's clear that the Venice Declaration wasn't worth the paper it was written on. More significantly, Britain was not the prime mover behind the Venice Declaration. In fact, informally, Britain warned other EEC members, as did the Americans, that it would be difficult to pursue a 'peace' policy which the Israelis would reject out of hand. As Nigel Ashton remarks, Britain took it upon itself to 'balance' the pro-Arab stances brought to the various EEC forums by the French.[125]

But the pro-Israel lobby in Britain was not privy to behind-the-scenes diplomacy and operated on the assumption that it constantly had to ensure support for Israel in Britain through intensive work, in tandem with Israeli diplomats in London, to mobilise the local Jewish community to neutralise the impact of the Venice Declaration. The campaign was orchestrated by the Israeli ambassador, Shlomo Argov, who began a new chapter in the activity of the lobby – a joint assault by the embassy and the pro-Israel Jewish outfits on any senior British politicians who were depicted as entertaining 'pro-Palestinian' views. As a celebratory *Jewish Chronicle* article put it, Argov recruited the Anglo-Jewish community against the 'pro-Palestinian' ministers in Thatcher's government so that the latter would feel 'the wrath of the local community and [be] ill at ease'. More dryly it stated:

The Israeli Ambassador viewed Anglo-Jewry as an asset to be employed to counter policies that were detrimental to Israel.'[126]

Argov believed this was the only option left. In a cable to Israel's Foreign Ministry, he wrote:

> We should not be afraid of making noise – it will embarrass the British more than it will embarrass us … It would be easier and more convenient to limit the campaign to the diplomatic sphere. It would be a lot more complicated and arduous to conduct a public campaign but this is the only sphere where we have room for manoeuvre and action, including the need for the mobilisation of the Jewish community.[127]

This was another milestone in the process that transformed Anglo-Jewish institutions into advocacy groups for Israel, justifying this transformation by equating criticism of Israel with anti-Semitism – a ploy that would be used to devastating effect later on.

The lobby under Thatcher hence devoted its time to attacking positions that actually represented the traditional British view on Palestine since 1967. Britain agreed notionally to PLO involvement in peace talks, but on conditions that were unacceptable to the PLO at the time. Consequently in practice there was no official contact with the PLO. Thatcher was fully aware of the campaign and seemingly took little notice of the lobby's indignant protestations – the British policy of deliberate inertia was hers too.

So once more, the lobby wasn't actually needed to maintain Britain's pro-Israel attitude, regardless of the outrage whipped up. Thatcher's sympathies were fully revealed when she became the first serving British prime minister to visit Israel in 1986.

During her premiership, Thatcher showed support for Israel's position all in all and her trip to Israel also gave her a great admiration for the state's achievements. Despite her general support for Israel, a more forensic examination of her policies allows us to see areas in which she was quite outspoken in condemning Israel's actions. Like Edward

Heath, she did not hesitate to raise the spectre of arms deals and embargos when conducting tougher conversations with the Israelis. After Israel's bombing of the Iraqi nuclear plant at Osirak in 1981, Thatcher described this operation as 'a grave breach of international law' and a 'matter of great grief'.[128] Following the Israeli invasion of Lebanon in 1982, Thatcher joined other European countries in imposing an arms embargo on Israel, which lasted until 1994.

These condemnations and other stances Thatcher adopted were pragmatic more than anything else. The National Archives contain correspondence between Thatcher's close circle, prompted by her and the Foreign Office, about the viability of a Palestinian state, very shortly after she took office. The discussion revolved around envisaging a Palestinian version of the South African Bantustans, closely attached to Jordan, as the fulfilment of both Jimmy Carter's and Margaret Thatcher's public promises to respect Palestinian political rights and sovereignty, contributing later to what Dana El Kurd described as a total misuse and manipulation of the concept of sovereignty in relation to Palestine.[129] In this correspondence, the Harrogate speech reappears as a benchmark: 'the crux of the matter with Israel is that we believe since Harrogate that the 5 June 1967 borders are the ones to respect'.[130] From our vantage point today, we can see how deluded the Foreign Office was in thinking its assertions even mattered.

So while the Labour governments up to 1979 did all they could to erase the 'dangerous' legacy of the Harrogate speech, informed by the pro-Israel lobby inside Labour, pragmatic Conservatives understood that there was no need to do so. Only Lord Carrington, the foreign secretary under Thatcher, stood out in his approach to the Palestine question. It seems that his endorsement of Palestinian aspirations for independence and self-determination were born not only out of Conservative pragmatism but were also motivated by genuine concern for the Palestinians under the ongoing Israeli occupation. His sincere commitments affected Thatcher's own attitude at times. Such a moment transpired when Thatcher met in 1986 with Palestinian leaders from the West Bank and the Gaza Strip in the British consulate in East Jerusalem, preceded by a confrontational meeting between Thatcher and Yitzhak Rabin, then the Israeli minister of defence, in which the British prime minister pleaded with him to ease the oppression of the Palestinians. Thatcher described the meeting with Rabin as unproductive in contrast to her warm and constructive meeting with the Palestinian side. For once, the lobby did not bother to respond. They understood that a few kind words from a British prime minister were irrelevant.[131]

This was just as well. From the very beginning of her term in office, Thatcher found the hysterical Israeli reactions to any hint at changing policy unacceptable. Frequently she didn't even deign to respond to them. After all, there was no point – she had no desire to break the British consensus on this question. Thatcher functionally followed the same pro-Israel policies as her predecessors. Once again, this was not due to pressure from the pro-Israel lobby in Britain, but rather due to the much earlier success of the pro-Zionist lobby, before 1948, in making support for a Jewish state in Palestine into a British national interest, one that all governments had taken for granted since 1948.

However, as in many parts of the West, civil society in Britain was far less content with the consensus and underwent a dramatic shift towards supporting the Palestinian cause and struggle. This process began in 1967 and gathered momentum in the 1970s and 1980s.

MOVING THE BATTLE TO CIVIL SOCIETY

On 6 June 1982, the Israeli army invaded Lebanon, using an attempted assassination of the Israeli ambassador in London, Shlomo Argov, as a pretext. Ariel Sharon, the Israeli defence minister and the architect of the invasion, blamed the PLO for the attempted killing and linked it to the continued rocket launching from south Lebanon into Israel that intensified in 1981 (although the Americans by that time had secured a shaky ceasefire between the two sides).

Declassified documents reveal that Sharon was frustrated by his inability to create a pro-Israel leadership as an alternative to the PLO in the occupied West Bank and Gaza Strip. He asserted that destroying the main PLO base, which was located in Beirut and southern Lebanon, would better facilitate his search for collaborators. As the invasion evolved, Sharon entertained another ambitious plan, to install a pro-Israel Maronite president in Beirut, and hence widened the scope of the invasion, which also led to a direct clash with the Syrian army. More importantly, this strategy deepened the divide in Lebanon between Phalangists, who were mainly militant Maronite Christians, and the Palestinians living in refugee camps in the south of Beirut and southern Lebanon. This exploded in a most horrific way in September 1982, when the Phalangists, under the watchful eyes of the Israeli army, massacred between eight hundred and two thousand refugees living in two camps in the south of Beirut: Sabra and Shatila.

The invasion was a brutal affair, which included constant shelling and air bombardment of Beirut and led to the flight of hundreds of thousands of Lebanese from the south to the north. The Israelis remained in many parts that they invaded more or less until the year 2000, and established harsh military rule that included infamous prison camps such as Khiam, where Palestinians and Lebanese were tortured and imprisoned without trial. At the same time, the Lebanese resistance, led by the Shiite minority residing mostly in the south of Lebanon, inflicted a high number of casualties on the Israeli army that eventually forced the Israelis out of Lebanon.

The scenes from Lebanon played out on every TV screen in British homes and energised those within British civil society to institutionalise advocacy for the Palestinians. One of the first sectors where this unfolded was the trade union movement. We've seen that at the time of the activity of LMEC in the late 1960s, it was impossible to establish a Friends of Palestine group with the TUC. In the wake of the invasion, this was now possible, and this new group appeared, led first by the dynamic George Galloway.

Supporters of Israel characteristically ascribed the successes of the Palestine group in the TUC to the lack of an efficient pro-Israel lobby within the TUC – a bizarre conclusion given the intense lobbying since the 1940s. But it was easier to blame the messenger for this failure rather than re-examine the message. The Histadrut regarded the Palestine group within the TUC as a real menace and sent a special envoy from Tel Aviv, Yonah Yagol, to coach pro-Israel TUC members and with them established the Trade Union Friends of Israel. Yagol sent exaggerated reports back to Israel, whose readers might have got the impression that violence was the main method used to persuade members of the TUC to care about Palestine.[132]

It was not only the invasion of Lebanon that challenged lobbying for Israel in Britain. Even before the invasion, the rise of the right-wing Likud Party caused uneasiness among the Anglo-Jewish community, to the extent that British officials could hear reservations expressed within the Anglo-Jewish Board of Deputies about Menachem Begin and Ariel Sharon's policy towards the Palestinians. This is why Thatcher could truthfully report to King Hussein that she thought she had allies in the Anglo-Jewish community against Begin's policies.

The shift to the right in Israel and the demise of liberal Zionism accelerated British public opinion's turn against Israel and towards tentative support of the Palestinian cause. The Thatcher years exposed a gap between the shenanigans of official policy towards Palestine on one hand and the seismic change in public opinion on this topic on the other. It first appeared forcefully in Britain, but the USA would follow their lead. So while Thatcher's policy remained loyal to British precedent, civil society demonstrated growing sympathy for the Palestinians, accompanied by a new willingness to confront Israel's actions with the same spirit of enthusiasm shown by the anti-apartheid movement of solidarity with the African National Congress.

This paradoxical situation moved the lobby to direct its attention to local civil society. Old outfits such as the veteran English Zionist Federation, now called the Zionist Federation of Great Britain, were once more called upon to disseminate the Israeli point of view to the public, while at the same time working hard to convince Anglo-Jews to emigrate to Israel – a contradictory message, if there ever was one, priding themselves on being part of good old British democracy and at the same time encouraging Jews to leave Britain for Israel. While this anomaly rattled the Board of Deputies, plunging it into an identity crisis between being an embassy for Israel and a parliament for Anglo-Jews, the Zionist Federation easily found its groove and embraced advocating Israel to civil society in general, rather than just the powerful.

Under the energetic leadership of Eric Moonman, the Zionist Federation singled out sections of the British press as the first target in the attempt to arrest the swelling of pro-Palestinian sentiment in British civil society. This began in 1977. In June that year, the *Sunday Times* published a front-page story and a four-page 'Insight' investigation reporting on the torture of Palestinian prisoners in the occupied territories. The Israeli embassy in London called the assertions a 'vicious slander as it is insulting to the only democracy and free judiciary in the area'.[133] The embassy's response was misleading. Amnesty International and many other human rights organisations, notably the Public Committee Against Torture in Israel, corroborated the brutal methods used by Israeli persecutors in the interrogation of Palestinians in their own research.[134]

Moonman made three complaints about the report in the *Sunday Times* to the Press Council – the start of a pernicious trend in which Britain's media watchdogs would be swamped by endless complaints from Israel's would-be defenders, even when the British media was indubitably pro-Israel. In his complaints, Moonman demanded that the press seek a response from Israel before publishing articles about its policies. At the time, it was fruitless – his complaints were rejected and ignored.

In those days, Moonman's every whim was not endorsed by the Anglo-Jewish community as a whole. Moonman's nemesis in this respect was the *Jewish Quarterly*, a publication founded in 1953 that focused on Jewish concerns at home and abroad. The editor of the *Quarterly* doubted the wisdom of Moonman's paranoid campaign and questioned his assertions about growing anti-Semitism in Britain. But Moonman was powerful enough to force the editor of the *Quarterly* to resign, one of his rare victories in his lobbying mission.[135] Encouraged by this success, Moonman went on to institutionalise a body that would target the British media and police its attitude towards Israel, and this was BIPAC: the British-Israel Public Affairs Committee.

BIPAC AND THE END OF THE THATCHER ERA

Moonman created BIPAC while he held office in the Board of Deputies and modelled it on the USA's AIPAC. In essence, BIPAC was an attempt to liberate Anglo-Jews from the bipolarity suffered by many bodies that failed to navigate successfully between representing Jewish concerns in Britain on the one hand and working for Israel as advocacy groups on the other. This challenge didn't stem from their internal doubts about the validity of their activism – they were true believers – but emerged as a result of a shift in British public opinion towards Israel, in particular among the Left and Liberal parts of the political spectrum.

Moonman was helped by Zelda Harris, who was listed as number five on the *Times of Israel* Aliyah 100 list. This meant that her life story had been one of the more significant, persuasive and exciting stories of Anglo-Jews who made Israel their home. Published in the *Times of Israel* and *Jerusalem Post*, Harris told a stirring tale of emigrating to Israel after the horrors of the Holocaust had converted her to Zionism. But this is not the main reason she was number five on the Aliyah list; she did something more important than emigrating to Israel at a relatively young age – she helped to fund BIPAC after, according to those who nominated her, the British public became 'hostile' in the wake of Israel's invasion of Lebanon in 1982.

Harris can be seen as the person who institutionalised a programme of propagandist visits to Israel by those who were deemed to be policy makers and public opinion formers, with the hope of making them advocates for Israel upon returning to Britain. This work began in 1983 and lasted until 1999.

BIPAC shot to public attention two years after its establishment. It led a public campaign against the arrival of two PLO members within the PLO–Jordanian delegation invited to London by the government in 1985. The delegation was disinvited, but it is not clear whether BIPAC's campaign was the reason (according to the *New York Times*, the delegation refused to sign a joint statement that did not match the PLO's position).[136] The Thatcher government made a great effort afterwards to apologise to Jordan and Saudi Arabia for the cancellation of the visit. Thatcher mainly wanted to smooth over any ruffled Saudi feathers as she was about to close the al-Yamamah deal: a £5 billion arms deal with the Kingdom, signed in February 1986.[137]

Thatcher herself was defiant about the deal during a meeting with Israeli journalists on 30 September 1985:

> No, I do not believe Saudi Arabia will ever attack Israel, ever, ever, ever. Saudi Arabia is really quite a bastion for stability in the Middle East and, as you know, she has taken a very statesmanlike position on many things that could have destabilised the Middle East, a very statesmanlike position. She too is entitled to defend herself.[138]

BIPAC was less interested in preventing Saudi Arabia from receiving a huge supply of British armaments and much more concerned about what Israel deemed was the quid pro quo for the deal: allowing PLO members to come to London as part of the joint delegation. Even then, the event's insignificance was apparent, but BIPAC charged into a crusade nonetheless, hoping to flex its muscles.[139]

BIPAC was not as effective as the pro-Israel lobby in general; that is, those working for the Israeli cause in the Israeli embassy, the Board of Deputies and the Zionist Federation. At the end of the day, BIPAC proved to be one of the less successful lobbying ventures, closing down in 1999 due to a lack of funds. It probably failed because other bodies engaged in lobbying for Israel did not welcome its existence. It had some success when it was headed by Michael Sacher, the vice president of Marks & Spencer and president of the Joint Israel Appeal (Britain's foremost Zionist fundraising body). His central role in the more general lobbying for Israel benefited BIPAC, but once he left the outfit, BIPAC was unable to recruit the necessary budget to run its ambitious plan to discipline the British media and was closed down.[140]

One notable failed project of BIPAC was the announcement of a modest £500 prize, partly funded by the World Zionist Organization, to anyone who would write a pro-Israel op-ed – it was a one-off competition, and it was given to the famous children's writer Lynne Reid Banks, who is a staunch supporter of Israel. She received it for writing an article in the *Guardian*.[141]

Ironically, a year before it disappeared into thin air, BIPAC was highly praised by the *Jerusalem Post* as 'having a significant impact on the often-hostile media and on the political echelon over the past two decades'.[142] The paper was very impressed with an esoteric publication called *BIPAC Briefing*. BIPAC's most important claim to fame was its success in persuading senior Arab journalists to travel to Israel under its auspices. It also prided itself in having strong institutional links to the military industry and security apparatuses of Britain. In its last year, it boasted that it had managed to install some of its staff among the 'top strategic advisors' of Jordan, Turkey and Israel as well as among consultants to a major conference in London dealing with world affairs.[143]

Ultimately, BIPAC did not influence world security or British policy towards Israel. After all, it was active during the time of a British prime minister who outlasted four Israeli prime ministers: Begin, Peres, Shamir and Netanyahu. Thatcher had similar problems with all of them, but in essence her policies were pro-Israel and did not require much work on the part of the pro-Israel lobby in Britain. Her successors, John Major, Tony Blair and Gordon Brown, similarly gave no cause for concern, but civil society continued to pose a problem.

This was the reality that characterised British policy in general towards Israel ever since 1948 up to the end of the twentieth century. As we shall see, this picture did not differ much from that on the other side of the Atlantic. American and British policies in the past enabled the Zionist colonisation of Palestine before 1948, tolerated the 1948 ethnic cleansing of Palestine, legitimised the state of Israel after the Nakba, and by actions, rather than words, accepted the Israeli takeover of those parts of historical Palestine (the West Bank and the Gaza Strip) that the Jewish state failed to acquire in 1948. The means used by Israel to police the millions of Palestinians, from apartheid through to occupation and ethnic cleansing, moved societies on both sides of the Atlantic to question not only Israel's policies, but also its ideology and foundations. The lobby was now asked not just to defend a policy here and there, but the very legitimacy of an active settler-colonial state among people who no longer bought into the myth that Israel was the only democracy in the Middle East.

8

Lobbying for Israel in Twentieth-Century America

FROM FLUSHING MEADOWS TO LAKE SUCCESS: THE FIRST CHALLENGE TO THE LOBBY

After its birth in 1945, the United Nations sought out appropriate venues in which to convene the meetings of its main bodies, such as the General Assembly and the Security Council. One of its first locations was the former New York City Pavilion in Flushing Meadows–Corona Park in Queens, which hosted the World's Fair from 1939 to 1940 (today it is the home of the Queens Museum).[1]

On 5 May 1947, *Time Magazine* sent a reporter to Flushing Meadows. 'What do you want to go to Flushing Meadows for, honey?' a Manhattan taxi driver asked the reporter. 'I'm going to the United Nations', she said. 'Well', he said with a wink, 'that used to be quite a lovers' lane in my day.' The reporter wrote a week later:

> The flats of Flushing were no lovers' lane last week. At UN, the quarrelling sons of Shem had gathered to dispute the title to their ancient dwelling place. The problem of Palestine engrossed the 55-nation tribunal of the General Assembly.

The reporter summed up the American position:

> The US also played coy. First it heartened Zionists by opposing full discussion of the Palestine case this session. Then it disappointed

them by voting against admission of the Jewish Agency to the Assembly floor.[2]

Flushing Meadows is where the Jewish state was recognised on 29 November 1947 after Britain entrusted the question of Palestine to the hands of the UN in February 1947. The pro-Zionist lobby in America took a central role in those nine months in 1947 in which the UN offered its own vision for the future of post-Mandatory Palestine. It did not only focus on the American position but was also involved in influencing the positions of other UN member states.

The main challenge was to interest the USA in taking a central role in these deliberations. For Washington, the most pressing issue on the international agenda was the future of Germany, and for that, it did not need the new international organisation. Interestingly enough, the Soviet Union was not deeply involved either. Both the Americans and the Soviets wanted the UN to focus on regional conflicts in which the superpowers' interests did not clash: Palestine was one such place. Both superpowers thus agreed to take a backseat when the UN decided to send an inquiry commission that did not include either an American or Soviet member. In fact, the Soviets suggested at first that the two superpowers would quickly settle the issue between them, as they shared a similar point of view: namely that there should be a Jewish state somewhere in historical Palestine, but a committee would work out the details; however, the Americans refused, fearing that this would allow the Soviets a leading role in post-Mandatory Palestine. The result was a commission made up of eleven members with little knowledge and experience who decided the fate of Palestine and devised a plan that led to disastrous consequences on the ground.

The commission of inquiry was boycotted by the Palestinian leadership and the Arab League and welcomed by the Zionist leadership. The pro-Zionist lobby was fully recruited to be part of the process. This was possible because leading members of the lobby also held official positions within the diplomatic core of the Jewish Agency in America. Thus when, in April 1947, UNSCOP arrived in New York to hear the voice of at least one Palestinian who was willing to appear before it

– Henry Cattan, a lawyer from Jerusalem and a member of the Arab Higher Committee (the official political leadership of the Palestinian community from 1934, which was eventually replaced by the PLO); his counterpart was Abba Hillel Silver, wearing the cap of the representative of the Jewish Agency in the USA.

It was clear there were two possible outcomes of UNSCOP's deliberations; it could either support the idea of a Jewish state on the soil of historical Palestine, or regard Palestine as a binational democratic state, in which case the overwhelming native Palestinian majority would determine the future of the country. The Truman administration, which until then had kept quite a low profile in the negotiations, was encouraged by the Zionist movement to put pressure on countries to vote in favour of the first option. As for the eleven members of the committee, it was clear even before they convened that many of them supported the idea of partitioning Palestine into two states.

This impression was reinforced when, on 14 May 1947, Andrei Gromyko, the Soviet deputy foreign minister, announced his government's support for a Jewish state in Palestine. This was a very important moment for the lobby, which had closely watched the dispute between the State Department, which was opposed to partition, and the White House, which leaned towards it.

In any case, by the beginning of November 1947 UNSCOP was ready to submit two reports for the UN General Assembly to vote upon: a minority report proposing a binational state, with a Palestinian majority and identity, and a majority report recommending the partitioning of the country into an Arab state and a Jewish one.

The State Department was fully supportive of the minority report, and the secretary of state, George Marshall, was also willing to endorse it, but the lobby was in constant contact with the president, who in any case leaned towards partition. Marshall was torn between Loy Henderson, the director of the Office of Near Eastern and African Affairs in the State Department, and the president. Had it not been for Truman's insistence on supporting partition, Marshall would have led the US policy against it.

The question facing the lobby was how the USA would help the Zionist movement in the crucial month of November 1947 to ensure that the General Assembly would vote for the partition resolution. The UN secretariat determined that an ordinary majority was not enough; there was a need for a two-thirds majority. The debate in Flushing Meadows on partition began on 26 November 1947. The Zionist delegation was surprised to hear the representative of the Philippines speaking against the resolution; they had counted his as an assured vote in its favour. The lobby concluded that the US had not done as it promised, by failing to exert enough pressure on a country that was utterly under its domination. A similar surprise unfolded when the representative of Haiti, also under American influence and considered an 'assured vote', spoke against the Partition Resolution.

Thanksgiving night fell on 27 November, and the lobby's main activists recalled that they could not enjoy their turkey because they were busy beseeching the president to intensify his pressure on stubborn states such as the Philippines and Haiti. These two countries, together with Ethiopia and Liberia, were needed to achieve the two-thirds majority.

Issa Nakhleh, the representative of the Arab Higher Committee, wrote to the secretary general of the UN later in February 1948 about how ashamed the Haitian delegate was when he eventually had to vote for partition. Here is an excerpt from his letter:

> The Delegate of Haiti on Wednesday made a very strong speech against partition, on instructions from his government. On Saturday he circulated a note to the delegations explaining that he is voting for partition in accordance with fresh instructions from his government. The Haitian delegate did not find words to describe his shame and he was seen in tears in the lobby and Delegates' lounge. Being a sincere and noble man, he could not hide the fact that his government surrendered to pressure and was forced into changing its instructions to him.[3]

In September 1947, the lobby concluded that only the USA could get the two-thirds majority and now, forty-eight hours before the vote, the lobby's networks of contacts had to make the final push. The lobby and the official representatives of the Jewish Agency spent the last forty-eight hours alternating between Temple Emanu-El and Chaim Weizmann's suite at the Waldorf Astoria. Most of the meetings were at the temple, which was one of the world's biggest synagogues, still there today on East 65th Street and Fifth Avenue: a huge limestone building, combining Byzantine and early Romanesque features with Moorish and Art Deco style.

In those hours, even non-Zionist Jews were recruited, such as a very reluctant Bernard Baruch, a tycoon who made his fortune by speculating on sugar and later became one of America's leading industrialists. He was asked to put pressure on the *New York Times* to publish an op-ed condemning those countries which still considered abstaining or voting against partition. 'I went along', he told a friend, but 'the whole thing makes me sick.'[4]

Two people were crucial in this final push: Sol Bloom, a pro-Zionist Congressman from New York, and David Niles. Niles was the president's special assistant on minority affairs, and at the time he was, as David Friedman writes, 'a little known or appreciated Jewish advisor to the president, and the rest is history' – meaning that, at least in his eyes, Truman's support for partition and recognition of Israel owed much to Niles, who worked 'against the experts'.[5]

Niles provided the lobby group in New York with information on the mood in the White House. It seemed that the administration was willing to use its connections with the stubborn countries to persuade them to vote in favour of partition; but in order to do that, prominent members of the American Jewish business community had to be recruited to help with the mission.

The members of the lobby and of the Zionist delegation to the UN used Niles to convey messages to the White House about their own independent attempts to pressure stubborn member states. This autonomous action outraged some of the White House and State Department staff. Matt Connelly, the private secretary to the president, wrote a memorandum to the president, conveying to him a complaint from under-secretary Robert Lovett that 'our case is being seriously impeded by high pressure being exerted by Jewish Agencies. There have been indications of bribes and threats by these groups'.[6] They threatened Liberian politicians that they had the power to thwart an American promise to help develop Liberia's natural resources. Pressure on Liberia also came from Harvey Firestone, the owner of the famous tyre company, who recalled he was asked to persuade the Liberian president to vote in favour of partition.[7]

There were similar promises of loans and financial help to Haiti and political assistance to Nicaragua. Lovett reported that the Nicaraguan delegate to the UN informed him that he was offered political bribes: 'In the case of Nicaragua, the delegate was told by some of these groups that if he went along these groups would see to it that they were recognized by the United States'.[8]

It is interesting that Lovett reported these complaints, as the Philippines delegate claimed Lovett pressured his government to vote in favour. The 'bribes', so to speak, offered in return for voting for partition, were a mixed bag: money for political leaders, American recognition for fledgling states and American aid for local development projects. All these goodies were promised on behalf of America by either leading members of the American Zionist community or official American representatives. The countries approached included China, Ecuador, Paraguay and Greece.[9]

The World Jewish Congress took part in these negotiations; it was a veteran organisation founded in 1936 to co-ordinate pan-Jewish diplomacy for Jewish communities in need. It was also a Zionist organisation in its own eyes, and in the eyes of those who worked with it. Its records, however, do not reveal the context of the conversations with the foreign delegates.[10]

When the forty-eight hours were over, it was clear that the lobby had done its job. Despite serious reservations from the State Department, pro-Israel advocates enjoyed the taste of victory. On 29 November, two-thirds of the members voted in favour of a programme that disregarded the Palestinians' aspirations, which included the right to self-determination, the building of a democratic state covering all of historical Palestine and the integration of the country within the Arab world. The resolution adopted by the two-thirds majority of the General Assembly,

Resolution 181, offered the Palestinians less than half of their homeland and asked them to be in economic union with the future Jewish state (while allowing citizens of both states to vote in whichever state they chose). It also devised a timetable for British withdrawal from Palestine (to be completed by 15 May 1948) and a map demarcating the borders of both states.

This was not precisely the Zionist vision – the movement wished to build a state over a much larger part of Palestine and share the land, if at all, with Transjordan and not the Palestinians. The movement also rejected the idea of an international Jerusalem, which it wished to make the capital of the Jewish state. However, as research has shown recently, this diminished version of the Zionist dream was accepted since it was clear that the Palestinians and the Arab world would reject it anyway, and what would matter would be who had the power to take over the Mandatory state.[11] The importance of the UN resolution for the Zionists was its recognition of the Jewish state, not its partition map or arrangements. The Zionist leadership had already made final preparations for taking by force as much of Palestine as they could and leaving as few Palestinians in it as possible.

When further discussion on Palestine moved to a different location, Lake Success, the picture changed dramatically and with it the American position towards Zionist aspirations in Palestine. Contrary to what its name suggests, Lake Success on Long Island was an ancient arena of defeat – that of the Native American Montaukett Nation, who were destroyed in the overall genocide of Native Americans. Like so many other locations in the USA, this, too, is named after the chief of the defeated tribe, Sacut. By the twentieth century, it was chiefly home to the military industrial complex: with industrial plants producing bomber planes, missiles and gun turrets. In 1946, the fledgling United Nations approached the mayor of this seemingly unpromising town and asked to rent some of the industrial areas, including huge hangars, as a temporary home.

The inevitable result in the months that followed, from December 1947 to February 1948, was the unfolding of a civil war in Palestine. It began with Palestinian demonstrations and sporadic attacks on Zionist colonies and transportation. The Zionists used these attacks as a pretext to launch large-scale ethnic cleansing of the Palestinians from the areas allocated to them by the UN Partition Resolution from 29 November 1947. At the beginning of February, under the noses of the British, the first three Palestinian villages, around the ancient Roman town of Caesarea, were occupied, and their entire population was expelled.[12]

It was clear to foreign representatives on the ground that the Zionist forces were now preparing a huge attack on the major urban centres of Palestine in order to destroy the Palestinian elite and economic centres. These developments led the State Department to rethink its previous strong support for the UN partition plan.[13]

The reappraisal of the American position was led by the 'Arabists' in the State Department and the secretary of state, Dean Acheson, who persuaded President Harry Truman that the partition plan wrought havoc and destruction, instead of promoting peace. They suggested an international trusteeship for Palestine to allow a rethink about its future, while consulting all parties concerned.

This was the culmination of a long process in the State Department, whereby the reality unfolding in Palestine forced a radical rethinking of priorities. A key figure driving forward this alternative American approach to the Palestine question was Loy Henderson, the director of the Office of Near Eastern and African Affairs between 1945 and 1948. He would be demonised as an anti-Semite for his efforts by pro-Israel journalists. While previously State Department officials like Selah Merrill were apprehensive about what *could* happen to the Palestinians, Henderson and his allies found their reservations vindicated by what *had* happened – namely the violent dispossession of hundreds of thousands of Palestinians on the ground. In February 1948, President Truman accepted Henderson's suggestion to offer international trusteeship as an alternative to the partitioning of Palestine.

In a hangar in Lake Success this new American policy, or rather this U-turn in American policy, was revealed to the world. Here, on 19 February 1948, the American representative to the UN, Warren Austin, expressed America's wish to annul the partition plan and replace it with a new peace plan for Palestine. It was a short declaration that had three points. The first was that it was obvious that the partition plan could only be implemented by force. The second was that there was a need for a ceasefire, and the third was a suggestion that international trusteeship would be imposed on Palestine pending an agreement by all sides on its future.[14]

This apparent change of heart in American policy sent shockwaves through the Zionist world in Palestine and beyond. The American Zionist Emergency Committees (AZEC), then the most significant organisation in the Zionist lobby, had laboured long and hard to secure American support for the Partition Resolution in November 1947. It was mobilised by its energetic prime mover, Isaiah 'Si' Kenen, who understood that if a State Department or a president is being difficult, you can always exert pressure on Congress. Kenen had already built up an impressive network of connections on Capitol Hill before 1948 and used his influence on senators and members of the House to push the White House to reaffirm the principle of partition in Palestine.

Until this perilous moment, President Truman had been the lobby's hero – orchestrating the American diplomatic campaign to secure the necessary majority in the UN for Resolution 181. The president of B'nai B'rith had declared that Truman 'would go down in history' as a hero to Jews worldwide. The veteran Zionist Chaim Weizmann expressed his 'profound sense of gratitude' directly to Truman.[15] After Austin's UN speech, all these accolades were on the line.

There is an ongoing historiographical debate about Truman's attitudes towards, and perceptions of, Zionism. There are those who attribute his overall pro-Zionist policy to the effective work done by the lobby, and there are those who depict him as a moral politician deeply moved by the horrors of the Holocaust and informed by his Baptist upbringing. It is quite possible that each of these factors played a role in shaping his views, but let's focus on his interaction with the lobby in his years of presidency.

After the new American policy was declared, the lobby went directly to the top. They demanded unconditional US support for the partition plan, and for a Jewish state in Palestine. Moreover, the lobby called for the mutual arms embargo imposed on the Zionist forces, Egypt and

Jordan to be lifted – for the Zionist side only. Without these arms, Weizmann argued disingenuously, the Jewish community in Palestine would be exterminated. Eleanor Roosevelt, a trusted ally, was also enlisted to pile pressure on the White House and to insist on providing Jewish forces with the most cutting-edge US weaponry.[16]

President Harry Truman knew very well what was in store for him. Although the proposal of trusteeship instead of partition was conceived by the State Department, Truman had no objections to it. By this point, he had developed an antipathy towards the Zionist leaders in his country, such as Abba Hillel Silver, whom his Jewish advisers invited into his chambers every now and then to complain about the State Department. Harry Truman later recalled:

> I do not think I ever had as much pressure and propaganda aimed at the White House as I had in this instance. The persistence of a few of the extreme Zionist leaders – actuated by political motives and engaging in political threats – disturbed and annoyed me.[17]

Truman believed that people such as Silver prevented the US from playing a constructive diplomatic role, which could have ended the violence in Palestine. Almost every scholarly work on that moment in the history of Palestine credits Chaim Weizmann as the one who persuaded Truman to return to the old policy. In his memoirs, Truman describes Weizmann as one of the wisest men he ever met. The crucial meeting between the two on this question was arranged by Truman's friend and former Jewish business partner from Kansas City, Edward Jacobson. When Jacobson and Weizmann left the Oval Office on 18 March 1948, Truman told them, 'you two Jews have put it over on me', meaning they had forced him to desert the State Department's new policy.[18]

Pleasant or not, the pressure worked – it had, after all, been an election year. The next step was to persuade Truman to recognise Israel on 15 May 1948. The president's adviser, Clark Clifford, recalled that Truman had been under 'unbearable pressure to recognize the Jewish state promptly'.[19] His advisers cautioned against such a quick response, but he ignored them. Walter Hixson believes that Truman embarked on this path because he was a devout Baptist, inspired by the teaching of the Bible, rather than realpolitik considerations; an analysis shared by Irvine Anderson: 'Truman's biblical background at least predisposed him to favour prompt recognition'.[20] In a recent book, Jeffrey Herf depicts those who opposed the lobby as a bunch of self-serving clerks wishing to appease the Arabs, as this course of action would be in the USA's best interest. I would look at it differently: as one of the last points at which the catastrophe taking place in Palestine counted as much as Zionist aspirations in the USA's foreign policy calculations.[21]

Whatever the reasons were for Truman's policy, the lobby and the new state had to deal with one challenge after another as the international community worked out the fate of post-Mandate Palestine. After winning round Truman, the Israeli state still had to resolve the future of Jerusalem and, even more pressingly, the fate of Palestinian refugees, who were all too fleetingly the subject of international concern.

UN initiatives in 1949 sought to rectify the horrific consequences of the body's decisions in 1947 – although the effort was doomed from the outset. The UN now tried to make Israel submit to the more unpleasant terms of the Partition Resolution: namely to make Jerusalem a *corpus separatum*, an international zone governed by the UN. To tackle the mass displacement caused by the expulsions of Palestinian Arabs in conquered territory, the UN passed Resolution 194, a General Assembly resolution adopted on 11 December 1948, which, among other clauses, affirmed the right of return for refugees and created a new body to pursue what it deemed as reconciliation efforts: the Palestine Conciliation Commission (PCC). Israel viewed this body with hostility from the very beginning. It had adopted a similarly antagonistic attitude towards a previous mediator, Count Folke Bernadotte, and rejected all his suggestions for compromise. He was assassinated in September 1948 by Zionist terrorists – an act that served the Israeli government well, although it probably had nothing to do with this.

The PCC was made up of three members: an American, a Frenchman and a Turk. In May 1949, it decided to convene a conference in Lausanne, Switzerland, to which it invited Israel, a Palestinian delegation and delegations from Lebanon, Egypt, Syria and Jordan. It was clear that the

PCC hoped to solve the conflict on the basis of three principles: partitioning historical Palestine, internationalising Jerusalem and allowing the refugees to return. For that to happen, the PCC had to pressure Israel to give up a sizeable part of the territory it occupied in 1948 and accept the repatriation of the refugees.

The challenge for the pro-Israel lobby in America was to find a way to ease the pressure on Israel on the question of the internationalisation of Jerusalem and to undermine the attempts of the PCC to force Israel to compromise. The first American PCC representative was Mark Ethridge, who from the onset of the reconciliation effort viewed Israel as belligerent and analysed correctly its disinclination to be involved in any meaningful peace talks. Israel did more than just decline to co-operate with the peace efforts: it was busy demolishing the Palestinian villages its army occupied, and moved its capital from Tel Aviv to Jerusalem in clear violation of the UN resolution.

The Christian lobby group, the American Palestine Committee, duly sprang into action – aiming to get America to endorse Israel's blatant violations of the UN's policies. This group co-ordinated opposition to the United Nations' efforts to internationalise the city of Jerusalem, which was divided between Israel and Jordan in the 1948 war. However, they failed to convince American decision-makers, who insisted that the city's future could not be decided by either Israel or Jordan. As Israel's government defied the terms of the UN resolution, many countries chose to place their embassies in Tel Aviv, and not in the contested territory of Jerusalem. The US followed suit and refrained from opening an embassy in Jerusalem – right up until 2019, in the days of the Trump administration. Yet this was at best a token gesture of support for the UN's decisions – the US took no other steps to prevent Israel from making Jerusalem its capital, regardless of the censure of the international community.

The US approached the refugee problem in a similarly ambivalent fashion. The State Department's position in principle was that repatriation of the Palestinian refugees was the preferred solution to their plight; the root cause of the conflict was hence the 1948 ethnic cleansing of Palestine, even if this was not stated directly. Under its guidance, the

Palestinian right of return was the backbone of the new UN peace initiative attempted in 1949. Then, as they had in February 1948, the White House and other bodies involved in formulating US policy on the question of Palestine at first accepted the Department's lead. One month was noteworthy: May 1949. In that month, the US demanded that Israel must allow the repatriation of hundreds of thousands of Palestinian refugees, regardless of the cause of their flight and not even pending the conclusion of a final settlement. On 29 May 1949, the US ambassador to Israel, James McDonald, conveyed a very sharp letter from President Truman to the Israeli prime minister, David Ben-Gurion, which made an explicit threat of severe sanctions if Israel did not adjust its policies. This was accompanied by a threat to suspend a grant promised to Israel to assist it in the absorption of new Jewish immigrants who arrived from Europe.[22]

For a short while the relationship between the two states seemed at risk – and the lobby panicked. The grant had been the final product of a concerted and successful effort by the various bodies that were part of the pro-Israel lobby. In January 1949, Truman was persuaded to award Israel a $100 million grant, and at first it seemed it would be provided with no strings attached. However, four months later, the US pursued a more complex approach due to its involvement in the Lausanne conference.

Mark Ethridge, the American representative in this body, felt he had the freedom to pursue a tougher policy towards Israel's intransigence. He used his position at the conference to exert pressure on Israel to allow a sizeable repatriation of nearly a million Palestinian refugees and worked for the resettlement of the rest in neighbouring Arab countries. He also believed that the partition plan now, in 1949, would be accepted by both the Arab world and the Palestinians as a basis for peace negotiations. His most impressive achievement in this respect was persuading the head of the Israel delegation to the conference, Walter Eytan, director general of the Israeli Foreign Ministry, to sign with all the Arab delegates a protocol on 12 May 1949. The protocol stated that on the basis of the Partition Resolution and Resolution 194 (calling for the return of the refugees), peace negotiations would commence between all sides concerned. A day later, the Israeli prime minister David Ben-Gurion forced Eytan to declare

Israel's withdrawal from the protocol – this was the day Israel was admitted to the UN as a member state, and Ben-Gurion felt there was no need for any more gestures towards the international organisation.[23]

Nonetheless, Ben-Gurion understood that while he may not need to appease the UN, he could not afford a direct confrontation with the USA. In June 1949, Israel conveyed the impression that it was about to give in to pressure both on the issue of repatriation of the refugees and the internationalisation of Jerusalem, but asked for time to deal with some technical aspects of the requests. In the meantime, conflicts broke out in different parts of the globe as the Cold War began to heat up; hence, until the end of Truman's administration, that pressure slowly petered out and the PCC was robbed of any meaningful say in the future of Israel or Palestine by 1951. A long period of inactivity on the diplomatic front ensued. The result was that officially America's UN delegation continued to support the Palestinian right of return, while in practice any mechanism for fulfilling this right had been neutered.

Truman remained president until 1953 and in his final three years in office, the Israeli government had some work for the lobby to do. The liaison between the government and whoever was part of the formal or informal pro-Israel lobby in America was Abba Eban. He co-ordinated the work from his seat in the Israeli embassy in Washington, where he had been appointed as an ambassador in June 1950. Eban convened an 'utterly private and unofficial' caucus regularly to implement the Israeli government's agenda. He preferred such a small group – any larger and they would 'hesitate to speak personally in a really confidential way'.[24] The group included one of the leaders of the American Zionist Federation, Louis Lipsky, and David Niles, among others. Others in Eban's informal advisory group included the Democratic fundraiser Abraham Feinberg (of whom I will talk more later in this chapter) and representatives of Jewish communities from around the nation. This 'unofficial' group would evolve into a major player in the lobby: the Conference of Presidents of Major American Jewish Organizations.

The various missions for advocacy included pressure to continue financial assistance to Israel, which was overstretched by the influx of more than a million new Jewish immigrants. The 1950 Law of Return made every Jew in the world a potential citizen of Israel, while the government wanted to build both a welfare state and a strong army. Truman was persuaded to pursue a policy of emergency financial help to Israel for the resettlement of these immigrants. Kenen was called to co-ordinate the campaign on Capitol Hill that ended with a $150 million grant to Israel, despite protestation from the State Department's senior officials, who rejected what they called the 'favouritism' shown towards Israel.[25] There was the same division of labour as we saw in the 1944 elections: Kenen being the liaison with the Democratic Party and Silver with the Republican one.

During Truman's term of office, the 'Arabists' of the State Department exercised significant influence over the Palestine policy, even if they couldn't alter Truman's overall pro-Israel stance. Evan Wilson commented that 'the early months of the Truman presidency represented the last time the State Department exercised a dominant role in our policy on Palestine',[26] and yet the 'Arabist' legacy also seemed to influence Truman's successor, Dwight Eisenhower, who was elected in 1953, and remained a force to be reckoned with during the administration of President Kennedy.

The State Department was the number one enemy of the pro-Zionist lobby in the USA during all three administrations, from Truman, through Eisenhower and up to Kennedy's term in office. To counter this influence from the moment it was detected by the pro-Zionist lobby in the USA, there was a need for a new outfit, much stronger and more efficient than any of the previous Zionist organisations in the land. And this is how AIPAC came into being in the early 1950s. But before that happened, AZEC needed to confront the new Eisenhower administration, which the Israeli government deemed as led by an unsympathetic president and two very hostile brothers: one was the secretary of state and the other the director of the CIA: the Dulles brothers.

FACING EISENHOWER AND THE DULLES BROTHERS

In January 1953, it seemed that the new president Dwight Eisenhower had not given up on finding a reasonable solution to the million

Palestinian refugees displaced after Israel's 1948 ethnic cleansing. He was heard more than once talking about the need to allow their repatriation. Moreover, unlike his predecessor Truman, Eisenhower distinguished between the American need to provide humanitarian aid to the refugees in their camps and adherence to principled American support for the right of return.

His secretary of state, John Foster Dulles, visited the area and reported that allowing the return of refugees was still physically possible. In fact, Dulles wanted more – he aspired to revise the previous administration's policy towards Israel and condemned the Truman administration for acquiescing to 'the wishes of the Zionists in this country', which 'had created a basic antagonism with the Arabs'.[27] He was about to reverse the lobby's earlier success by steering American policy on Jerusalem and the refugees away from its pro-Israel bias. He was less successful in pushing forward his own peace plan, the Alpha plan. In order to build a pro-American alliance in the Arab world, he assumed that Israel needed to concede territory in the south, allowing a land bridge between Jordan and Egypt and repatriating refugees; numbers were not specified (as readers may recall from the previous chapter, the Alpha project was a co-initiative with the British Foreign Office and was revealed to the world by the British prime minister, Anthony Eden, in his Guildhall speech in November 1955).

The Israeli prime minister at the time, David Ben-Gurion, pleaded with AZEC to foil the project, especially after he received indications that Gamal Abdel Nasser might agree to it (in fact, in the British press the Egyptian president welcomed the project, as it was based on his own ideas for a solution), while, at the same time, the Czech Republic was about to sign an arms deal with Egypt.[28]

AZEC explored every possible avenue. It targeted public opinion, working in tandem with the Israeli embassy and distributed information kits showing the danger of the new American strategy towards the Middle East and Israel. In a last-ditch attempt to change the course of that policy, Kenen met Dulles to persuade him to change his views, but to no avail.

But the real coup, and the best option, was winning over the Houses of Congress. These offered a more pro-Israel line of thinking. Israel demanded the resettlement of the refugees in the Arab world. This idea was discussed in earnest in both Houses of Congress, and it was suggested by Congress that the USA should support the resettlement of Palestinian refugees on both sides of the River Jordan. President Eisenhower agreed, but informed Congress that this would provide a solution for only 300,000 refugees, and therefore the rest should be repatriated. In any case, the Palestinians and the Arab states hosting the refugees did not endorse the plan and Israel rejected it, both because of its element of return and since it did not wish to see so many refugees on the River Jordan, preferring that they resettle as far from Palestine as possible.

QIBYA: HOW TO DEFEND ISRAELI WAR CRIMES

Thirty kilometres north of Ramallah lies the village of Qibya, an ancient village dating back to the Roman period. It was spared during the 1948 Israeli ethnic cleansing – and few outside Ramallah had even heard of it, until the Qibya Massacre in 1953. Israeli commandos, under Ariel Sharon, massacred sixty-nine villagers there and blew up forty-five houses, a school and a mosque, as retaliation for a Palestinian guerrilla attack in the Israeli town of Yehud in which an Israeli woman and her two children were killed.

The Israeli massacre was condemned by the State Department and by Jewish communities around the world. The State Department declared that economic aid to Israel would be suspended, not only due to the massacre but also because of other Israeli raids into the West Bank, which violated the 1949 Israel–Jordan armistice agreement of April 1949.

Kenen was mortified, less by the massacre itself and more by its potential for collateral damage to the lobby. He stated that the massacre 'undermined the moral position of the Jewish people ... discredited the premises of our propaganda and has given the color of truth to Arab propaganda.'[29] He embarked on a damage control campaign, the principal message being that American policy was one-sided. Retrospectively, he seemed to relish the need to face a serious challenge like this, which enabled the lobby to 'spring back to life and action in a crisis.'[30] This leap involved extending AZEC's networks to include churches and colleges, where AZEC previously had less presence. Particularly important recruits were the Jewish councils across the country, tasked with making sure that their local news media received Israeli propaganda.

As historian Doug Rossinow argues, AZEC reacted to the aftermath of the Qibya Massacre by creating the Conference of Presidents of Major American Jewish Organizations (COP), convened by Nahum Goldmann, the president of the World Jewish Congress, which became a force to reckon with inside the lobby. Consequently, instead of generating moral outrage against Israel, the official American condemnation of the massacre produced closer unity between non-Zionist and Zionist Jewish bodies in America. This may seem counterintuitive; a civilian massacre ought to have increased hostility to Zionism. Yet the instinct of non-Zionist organisations was to defend Israel's legitimacy, regardless of the morality of its conduct.[31]

This new unity was badly needed. Oppositional voices started to appear on the stage: the American Friends of the Middle East (AFME), founded in 1951, and the American Council for Judaism, founded in 1942 by a group of Reform rabbis, were leading the criticism of Israel. The AFME was encouraged to form by Allen Dulles, the secretary of state's brother and director of the CIA. He and Henry Byroade, the assistant secretary of state for the Near East, were looking for a force to counter the pro-Israel lobby, and help them pursue the policies they deemed best for the American national interest. The lobby coined the term 'Byroadism': 'meaning a toxic mix of anti-Semitism and Arabphilia'[32] – which would be thrown at anyone not loyal enough to Israel among the senior diplomats of the USA. A similar accusation was directed at British politicians not toeing the pro-Israel line on the other side of the Atlantic. This allegation was usually directed unjustly towards officials who opposed Israel's policies on the basis of their expertise on the Arab world in general and Palestine in particular. Even at this early stage, many predicted accurately that the plight of the Palestinians would continue to drive resistance to Israel and American policies in the Middle East.

Byroade warned prophetically that Israel aimed to have 'complete control of the Jordan River' and had total disregard for the UN, and declared that Israeli policy would 'preclude a reasonable settlement'.[33] He also cautioned that Israel would be immune from any genuine criticism of its intransigent policies if it were to win the propaganda battle. Byroade, however, was deserted by the Dulles brothers by the end of 1953. Even these two brothers were afraid to confront Israel with such an accusation, and Byroade was demoted and reassigned as the American ambassador to Egypt. Both brothers were still convinced that the lobby for Israel undermined the American national interest and that it operated in an ethically dubious way in its attempt to influence American policy towards the Middle East, even if it did not violate any laws. A year later, they would learn that this lobby was even more powerful than they thought, when the 1954 mid-term elections came.

However, President Eisenhower did not share Byroade's apprehension and asserted that there was no substantial Zionist lobby in the US – 'Zionist lobby' being his phrase of choice for the grouping. On 28 October 1953, he wrote to Dulles:

> The political pressure from the Zionists in the Arab-Israeli controversy is a minority pressure. My Jewish friends tell me that except for the Bronx and Brooklyn the great majority of the nation's Jewish population is anti Zion.[34]

He added, 'I should inform Israel that we'd handle our affairs exactly as though we didn't have a Jew in America'.[35] The large proportion of non-Zionist Jews in his administration informed this perspective, which was welcomed by the State Department's civil servants and was supported by a number of other government agencies.

But Eisenhower was in for a rude awakening about the lobby's aggressive tactics during the mid-term elections. The lobby wanted candidates to support an embargo on military aid to Arab states and upgrade financial and military aid for Israel. The demand did not go down well with the executive branch of the administration. Eisenhower reacted by promising to 'continue our present policy of impartiality' and vowed not to 'be deterred by political pressures … in connection with the forthcoming elections.' Dulles pledged he would 'not allow himself to be stampeded' into arming the Israelis, explaining that it would 'be interpreted throughout the Arab world that we have capitulated again. All we have tried to do will be lost.' Dulles even summoned Abba Eban to exhort Israel not to interfere in the elections, complaining about:

> Israeli Embassy activities which seemed clearly to go beyond the bounds of what was proper for a foreign government in that they involved domestic political action.[36]

He received a vague promise from the Israeli ambassador, far from satisfying in Dulles' eyes. He now had a further source of concern: during the mid-term elections, a more powerful lobby than AZEC appeared. AZEC evolved into a new body, the American Israeli Public Affairs Committee (AIPAC).

THE MAKING OF AIPAC

AIPAC appeared at a time when lobbying in the USA became more professionalised, and closely connected to economic interests and American identity politics. Success in the American political system was practically guaranteed if you had affluent backers, on one hand, and a well-defined identity group behind you, on the other.

AIPAC took a similar line to other powerful lobby groups, which were led by politicians weaponising collective identities for the sake of a fruitful political career. The master of such identity politics and the person who inspired AIPAC was the ultimate New Yorker politician, Fiorello H. La Guardia. He was born in the Bronx in 1882, the child of an Italian immigrant and a Hungarian Jew. This double ethnicity became a useful political tool during La Guardia's career in the American labour movement, culminating in his becoming a member of the House of Representatives and mayor of New York. At every stage of his political career, until he died in 1947, he drew on his ethnic identity cards – Italian or Jewish – to enhance his chances of being elected to coveted positions. He mastered Italian and Yiddish, and some claim his Hebrew was not at all bad. His legacy was such that those who followed him understood how useful instrumentalising identity politics was within the overall political scene. La Guardia unashamedly accused opponents of trying to undermine the position of ethnic groups he happened to represent at the time: first the Italians in New York (in East Harlem), then the Jews in Brooklyn and, even later, he represented the Irish wherever they were.[37] In the 1950s, the next generation of politicians focused on the three 'I's – Israel, Italy and Ireland – as safe bets in local electoral races. From this angle, American foreign policy reflected the domestic ethnic balance of power. And within this framework, the official new pro-Israel lobby was born.

Political aspirants aiming to exploit ethnic identity for their careers had long been associated with the phenomenon of lobbying. The original lobbies in the early nineteenth century were rooms outside the chambers of state houses which hosted people who came to influence policy. The term was later applied to the foyer leading to Congress Hall. In the 1830s it became packed with people trying to influence their representatives in person; hence the term that is today associated with slickly run outfits doing much the same. Since 1830 onwards, many congressmen and women have spent time talking with lobbyists. Lobbying produced inevitable corruption, which, in turn, prompted some lawmakers to find ways of limiting this kind of manipulation. The first law, passed in 1946, stipulated clear regulations for lobbying. The most important of them were tight restrictions on representing a foreign country.[38] A few years later AIPAC, according to its critics, would violate this rule regularly and repeatedly.

AIPAC was built on these twin legacies of identity politics and political lobbying. In his memoir *All My Causes*, Kenen recalls that he operated a very small version of AIPAC in 1944, under the name of the American Zionist Committee for Public Affairs, which was defined as the lobbying arm of AZEC.[39] After the creation of the state of Israel, he changed its name and registered the new body as the American Israeli Public Affairs Committee in 1951. He began to register it as a foreign agent working for the Israeli Ministry of Foreign Affairs – but never completed the process, realising that registering AIPAC in such a way would limit the new lobby's sphere of influence and risk legal violations. He strategically understated the link to Israel and portrayed AIPAC as a public body working for AZEC. But very soon the arm of the new body consumed the mother organisation and replaced it.

AIPAC as we know it today was finally shaped in 1959, and throughout the process of finalising it, Kenen believed that significant 'anti-Israeli' policies by the administration could only make the group stronger and more influential. This conviction seemed to fuel the journey ahead, beginning in 1954 with AIPAC's first ever attempt to affect the result of the mid-term elections in America.

Kenen boasted of having 300 candidates from thirty-six states, as well as twenty-five senators, in the lobby's pocket, willing to heed the lobby's request to impose an embargo on arms sales to the Arab states. Indeed, the impact of AIPAC (still working as part of AZEC) on the mid-term 1954 elections was impressive, but despite the election of many pro-Israel candidates, it seemed that as long as Eisenhower and Dulles were shaping American foreign policy, neither Kenen nor the new AIPAC could rest on their laurels. They were constantly urged by Israel to intensify their efforts to change American policy. It is difficult to judge how successful they were. On the one hand, Eisenhower despairingly admitted in 1958 that he did not have a free hand in pursuing policies towards Israel, to the detriment of the American national interest. On the other hand, twice in his term of office, he bluntly ignored Israeli pressure to take its side in policy towards the Arab world. In fact, on those two occasions, in 1956 and 1958, his administration took a very harsh position towards Israeli policies and forced Israel to revise its actions on the ground. In a matter of seven years, Israel was twice threatened with American sanctions.

As mentioned, in October 1956, Israel colluded with Britain and France in an attempt to topple Gamal Abdel Nasser, the president of Egypt, following his nationalisation of the Suez Canal and his support for the Palestinian guerrilla operations against Israel from the Gaza Strip. During the attack on Egypt, Israel occupied the Gaza Strip and the Sinai Peninsula and its actions were condemned by both the USA and the USSR. In 1958, in the wake of the 14 July Revolution in Iraq, in which officers terminated the pro-Western Hashemite rule, Britain and the USA feared that Jordan and Lebanon would be next to fall to what they defined as Arab radicalism. Israel offered to occupy parts of the West Bank to save them from falling into 'radical' Arab hands, should the Hashemites also lose Jordan, but their offer to help was declined by the Americans.

When Kenen looked back at that period, he credited the lobby with preventing the administration from turning punitive threats into actual sanctions. Such a retrospective assessment disregards the success of the Americans in forcing Israel to withdraw from the Sinai Peninsula and the Gaza Strip in 1956 and the very assertive rejection of David Ben-Gurion's desperate wish to turn Israel into a Western ally in the Anglo-American campaign against progressive and revolutionary forces in the Arab world in 1958. Without Israeli help, which was conditional on Israel taking over the West Bank, American and British forces assisted the young Hashemite king of Jordan, King Hussein, to retain his throne.[40]

Kenen and Abba Eban redoubled their efforts after these two crises unfolded. They realised there was a need for even more systematic and professional groundwork among the American media and inside the legislative arm, if future presidents and their secretaries of state were to adopt similarly critical policies towards Israel.

Parallel to these efforts, Kenen issued a new publication under the name of the *Near East Report*, which became the pro-Israel lobby's mouthpiece (funded partly by Israel).[41] As Walter Hixson writes, this was not just a ploy to disseminate the message of the lobby more efficiently; it was also a way of circumventing tax issues that every now and then had preoccupied AZEC when it came to tax exemptions for funding and contributions. Kenen understood that once he finalised the legal status of AIPAC around 1957, he had a problem. Because of its legal status, AIPAC could not legally receive contributions from Jewish and non-Jewish organisations that supported it, if they wanted the contributions to be tax-free. However, they could purchase endless copies of the new publication, which they did, thus adding to the coffers of AIPAC. By 1949, the *Near East Report* had a circulation of 20,000 paid subscribers.[42]

The first visible result of Kenen's call to arms was action taken by Jewish members of the dockers' union, who boycotted Arab ships in American harbours in order to prevent American aid reaching Arab states that did not recognise Israel. Then, around 1960, came the first of many pro-Israel initiatives on Capitol Hill, pushing for more anti-Arab legislation; in particular a demand to boycott products from countries belonging to the Arab League, as a response to the Arab League's boycott on Israel.[43]

On the way to finalising the formal organisation and orientation of AIPAC, Kenen focused on mobilising support by pressuring any upcoming politician from the most local level possible up to the congressional level. This was the lobby's proverbial ace, at least in Kenen's eyes. Detective work was needed to find out voting patterns and prospective candidates' vulnerabilities, as AIPAC perfected the system of offering help and then threatening to withdraw it. Kenen had an index card system that located politicians on a spectrum between 'leaning away' to 'active champions' of Israel.[44] No electoral candidate escaped his meticulous mapping.

The old method of letter writing was resurrected – to the media and to politicians. 'Make sure that also Christians write the letter', Kenen proposed.[45] And like the old Jewish and Christian Zionist methodology of the late nineteenth century, dinner parties in opulent venues were arranged to maintain constant contact with key stakeholders. The biggest prize was a private function with the ambassador Abba Eban. As we shall see, the British lobby would mimic these tactics in the 1990s, helping to secure formidable allies in the British Labour Party.

A journal, a think-tank and a grassroots network now constituted the visible face of AIPAC, which was ready to take up the mantle as the leading force in pro-Israel lobbying in the USA. Before it could assume this role, it needed the blessing of two places. One was the Conference of Presidents of Major American Jewish Organizations, which provided not only legitimacy, but also another avenue through which tax-free financial donations could be channelled legally, or nearly legally, to

AIPAC. The other place was Israel. After obtaining Israel's favour, nobody could stop AIPAC from overshadowing all other organisations. There were many other groupings, but AIPAC formulated the strategy for the lobby as a whole, and dominated the discussion about Israel.

AIPAC needed a clear, conventional administrative structure. The structure included an executive committee at the top, accountable to a national council, and slowly other branches were built, focusing on education, media and similar fields of activity.

Key targets were also more clearly prioritised. The most important mission was to control the legislators in both Houses of Congress – accompanying them during their election campaigns and, no less importantly, after their arrival on Capitol Hill. It was more than just benignly tagging along with the new elected representatives – it was making sure they toed the line. As Hixson puts it:

> Everyone in Congress quickly learned that AIPAC, backed by local councils and Zionist groups across the country, was monitoring their every move on Middle East policy.[46]

A second priority was to focus on the growing film industry and in particular the power of Hollywood. The magnates of the industry were recruited, and the jewel in the crown for pro-Israel film production was the 1960 film *Exodus*. An Aryan-looking Paul Newman represented the new Jew fighting nameless savage 'Arabs' and bringing Holocaust survivors to make Palestine's desert bloom. This B movie was adapted from a similarly mediocre and propagandising novel by Leon Uris. But it had an impact. Several historians, such as Amy Kaplan and Michelle Mart, believed that *Exodus* had immense influence on American public opinion by presenting the narrative of Israel as a small nation defending itself against Arab aggression, and one that only could be saved with the help of America, as the leader of the democratic world.[47]

The pro-Israel pageants of the 1940s had already effectively weaponised visual art. Now AIPAC wanted to outdo those huge events in Madison Square Garden. There was a need, its captains believed, for annual shows of this kind. These came in the form of the now familiar annual AIPAC conferences – events that became staples on the calendar of any serious presidential candidate.

The first of these was convened in 1960, but it was overshadowed by another meeting that took place at the Statler Hilton Hotel in New York City on 26 August 1960. This was an event organised by the American Zionist Federation and its keynote speaker was Senator John F. Kennedy.

He began his speech by referring to pre-Zionist Palestine as a 'wasteland', and thus his listeners knew that he would be loyal to the Zionist narrative in the rest of his speech. He recalled visiting Palestine in 1939 and seeing there, as he put it, 'the neglect and ruin left by centuries of Ottoman misrule'.

He proudly mentioned attacks on him on Egyptian radio for saying 'Israel is here to stay', but also expressed his wish to be the mediator, should he be elected president, and to facilitate peace between Israel and the Arab states since 'I have always believed that there is no real conflict or contradiction between the genuine aspirations of the Arab nations and the genuine aspirations of Israel'.[48]

He received a standing ovation, but whoever was part of the lobby of course waited to see what his policies would be once he sat in the White House, which he did in 1961.

TAMING JOHN F. KENNEDY

AIPAC had high hopes for a change in American policy when John F. Kennedy won the election, and the Eisenhower era came to an end. After all, a number of pundits believed that Kennedy narrowly won against Richard Nixon because of the Jewish vote. Two of Kennedy's funders worked long and hard after the election to try and keep Kennedy on the 'right' track. These were the men responsible for recruiting the Jewish vote for him: Myer Feldman and Abraham Feinberg.

Myer Feldman was from Philadelphia and had a career in the army and in financial regulation before he was recruited as a legislative adviser by Kennedy's team during the election, remaining as a presidential adviser after the election. In private, he often met with David Ben-Gurion, Israel's prime minister, and Golda Meir, Israel's foreign minister.

Feldman denied that these meetings affected any of his recommendations to the president. His most important mission was to try and avert any decisive move by Kennedy against Israel's development of nuclear capacity and weapons at the Dimona plant in the Naqab Desert. Feldman's advice was vehemently challenged by the CIA and its director, Richard Helms.[49] At first Kennedy was willing to take this matter seriously and he grasped the risks of Israel's desire to become a nuclear power. In the past this had pushed Israel into an alliance with France in developing its nuclear capacity, until Charles de Gaulle changed his attitude towards Israel in the wake of the 1967 war. The US president, mainly in classified correspondence, used harsh language to describe what he saw as Israeli tactics to try and deceive the Americans and prevent them from inspecting the Dimona plant. AIPAC and Feldman began an opposing campaign, depicting Kennedy as an 'appeaser' of the Arab world. However, Kennedy's efforts to curb Israel's nuclear ambitions and its intransigence regarding Palestinian refugees were cut short by his assassination.

What is clear is that Kennedy was not alone in his efforts. The director of the CIA, Richard Helms, long before 1967, worried that Israel's aggressive policy, motivated by territorial expansionist ambitions, would lead to a military confrontation with Egypt's Nasser. Another ally was Kennedy's secretary of state, Dean Rusk, who complained to the president that Feldman was working too closely with Israeli politicians. He described the relationship as 'improper' and told Kennedy that a number of diplomats in Washington were worried that Feldman had become 'the primary White House staff influence'.[50] Others were aware that Feldman had a small group of advisers, including the new Israeli ambassador in Washington, Avraham Harman, who convened regularly to figure out what should be demanded as policy from the president.

Such a consultation took place when the president was asked to intervene in the question of arms sales to Israel. The particular focus was on the Hawk missiles, surface-to-air anti-aircraft weaponry that the White House put on hold, as a means of pressuring Israel to halt its National Water Carrier Project; the diversion of the River Jordan's water for the carrier ignited an endless series of clashes with the Syrian army that contributed to Egyptian–Syrian and Soviet anticipation of an imminent attack by Israel on Syria in May 1967, which pushed Nasser into a series of actions that Israel considered *casus belli* and in reaction launched its attack that began the June 1967 war.[51]

Kennedy's boldest move stemmed from his genuine interest in reopening the discussion on a just solution to the Palestinian refugee problem. He contemplated a new UN initiative that might include the return of refugees to Israel. In a panic, Ben-Gurion began to recruit historians in Israel to concoct a fabricated Israeli narrative of a voluntary Palestine flight in 1948, in an attempt to prove that Israel had no moral responsibility for the refugee problem. A number of Israeli scholars were willing to play along with this historiographical charade. In the end, the initiative went nowhere and after Kennedy's assassination disappeared.[52]

It was not easy for Kennedy to ignore Feldman. He was an invaluable asset during the election campaign against Richard Nixon. Feldman fastidiously uncovered Nixon's darker side, helping to undermine the reputation of Kennedy's opponent in the national elections, producing a damning collection of evidence known as *Nixopedia*.[53] He was instrumental in helping Kennedy defeat Barry Goldwater's promising campaign as an independent candidate in the presidential elections. In short, he did all the dirty work.

Feldman was assisted in his assignment by Abe Feinberg – a very different and rather noble figure in comparison. He epitomised the PEOP (Progressive Except on Palestine). As a rabbi from New York, he had an impressive record as a human rights campaigner. He spoke eloquently and publicly against racism, apartheid in South Africa and American imperialism in Vietnam, advocating nuclear disarmament. He even went to Montreal to join John Lennon and Yoko Ono in their famous and bizarre 'Bed-in for Peace' and sang with them *Give Peace a Chance*. The chance was not to be in Palestine. After all, he was a principal fundraiser and facilitator in the service of AIPAC, toiling away to exert pressure on Kennedy to announce that Israel and the USA enjoyed a 'special relationship'; a slogan that every American president would have to include in speeches while visiting Israel, attending an AIPAC convention or receiving official Israeli guests. In the days of Kennedy, it was only a slogan. It was borrowed from the Anglo-American alliance that defeated Hitler – but who Hitler was in this scenario was left deliberately unspecified. After Kennedy, this unholy marriage was sealed with financial and military aid.

Kennedy's ideas were not the only challenge facing AIPAC during his term in office. Probably even more of a problem was the fact that not all of AIPAC's actions conformed to the legal requirements for lobbying. Tax policies and funding practices were sailing close to the wind, and one particular American politician, the Democratic senator J. William Fulbright, of Fulbright Scholarship fame, believed these practices profoundly undermined the American national interest. He would pay dearly for his convictions.

THE FIRST POLITICAL VICTIM: THE FULBRIGHT AFFAIR

James William Fulbright was born in Sumner, Missouri, but grew up in Arkansas, where he studied history and excelled on the local American football team. A longer spell in Oxford in England made him one of the most Anglophile politicians of his time. He came from the world of humanities, where the history of the world at large and that of human rights attracted his attention. He added to this a legal career which he undertook in the mid-1930s and from there he joined the Department of Justice. His impressive career continued as a lecturer in law and as the youngest-ever president of an American university, the University of Arkansas. In 1942, we find him as a Democratic representative in the House and in 1945 in the Senate, pushing forward educational programmes that are still benefiting American and foreign students today.

At critical junctures of twentieth-century history, he made the right choice: opposing Hitler, rejecting McCarthyism, criticising Kennedy's adventurism in Cuba, seeking détente with Russia and advocating disarmament of nuclear weapons. His one big mistake was to support the initial American invasion of Vietnam, but he quickly came round to a more moral position – and became an important voice against the war.

He served in many administrations, from Eisenhower to Nixon, but his political career quickly hit a ceiling. AIPAC couldn't stand him due to his constant criticism of Israel's policy towards the Palestinians and his belief that, because of that, the USA was abandoning its friends in the Arab world. The enmity only deepened when he questioned the legality of AIPAC's operations in the USA.

Fulbright's main axe to grind was his concern about how foreign countries influenced US foreign policy. But he had a particular interest in Palestine and Israel. Like the Palestinians themselves, and so many other people in later years, he saw the 1947 UN partition plan as unfair and unjust as it did not respect the principles of democracy and the Palestinians' right to self-determination. He clashed earlier on with AIPAC, when it organised the boycotting of Arab ships on the docks, which he called 'irresponsible intervention into US foreign policy making'.[54] Later on, during 1960, he spotted initiatives on Capitol Hill on behalf of Israel, such as pressuring Egypt to open the Suez Canal for Israeli shipping. He claimed it had nothing to do with US foreign policy interests and that it was the result of 'the existence of a pressure group in the US which seeks to inject the Arab–Israeli dispute into domestic politics'.[55] He also argued quite sensibly that such pressure would only strengthen Egyptian determination not to allow such passage – and he was completely vindicated. His concluding remarks on that particular incident, regarding the Arab conviction that the USA would always take the side of the Israelis, merit remembering:

> This Arab conviction, for which I regret to say history affords some justification, is the greatest single burden American diplomacy has to carry in the Middle East.[56]

Just when AIPAC thought the coast was clear for its activities, Fulbright, as the chair of the Senate Foreign Relations Committee, decided to investigate AIPAC's financial affairs. Although his sympathies with Palestine indicate he considered AIPAC detrimental to the American national interest, it seems the only possible way to curb its impact on American policy was through allegations of tax evasion.

He alleged that AIPAC was in violation of the Foreign Agents Registration Act, which was meant to limit funding from other nations being used in political campaigning. He commenced hearings and produced damning evidence. The three hundred pages produced by the investigating body revealed that various pro-Zionist organisations used tax-free United Jewish Appeal money, meant to help poor communities in Israel, in order to fund AIPAC's activities in the USA. Over four years, the lobby had raised $5 million, tax-exempt, from the Jewish community in the US.[57] Some of the money was recruited from two known mobsters, Aaron Weisberg and John Factor, known as 'Jack the Barber'.[58]

Fulbright's committee drew on FBI wiretaps and subpoenaed documents which revealed how subscription to the *Near East Report*, the mouthpiece of AIPAC, was used as a source for funding and circumventing tax issues for the donors. But the brazen violation of financial regulations occurred through AIPAC's relationship with the Jewish Agency in Israel. This obsolete pre-Mandatory Zionist body played two roles after the founding of Israel: Judaising the lands in Israel and funding the lobbying abroad.

The system was quite complicated. Some of the money that AIPAC needed came directly from Israel; for instance, Kenen was paid quarterly payments of $5,000 for his labour. But most of the money was extracted from American Jewish donors who purchased Israeli bonds. Ostensibly these donors received shares in operations in Israel, allegedly focusing on social issues and helping communities in need, but some of the money funnelled back to AIPAC, from Israel, through the services of a new body, the Jewish Agency American Section, registered in the USA. In fact, Fulbright's committee found out that none of the money was ever delivered to the deprived citizens of Israel. Instead, it went to the Israeli state and, from there, immediately back to the US – directly into Zionist organisations. For instance, for eight years, eighty per cent of the budget of AZEC (of which AIPAC was officially the lobbying branch) came from the Jewish Agency in Israel.[59] Fulbright had been on the hunt for these violations, and he found them. Between 1955 and

1962, in this way the Jewish Agency American Section received $5 million from American donors – money intended for deprived people in Israel.

The money raised was also used to fund trips to Israel, organised by the American Christian Palestine Committee, as well for funding Hebrew Culture Chairs at American universities.[60]

As Alfred Lilienthal revealed in 1995, these masked funds 'touched almost every aspect of Jewish and Christian relations'[61] and oiled the machinery for pressuring both the American media and politicians to adopt a pro-Israel stance.

One very important outfit funded by Israel, with American Jewish money, was the Jewish Telegraphic Agency (JTA). This was another outfit that was initially concerned with Jewish affairs in general, in this case global Jewish affairs, which gradually became a mouthpiece for Israel and part of the lobby in the USA. It was founded in 1917 with the mission of informing world media about issues concerning Jewish communities worldwide. Until the twenty-first century, it was highly loyal to the Israeli narrative, but, like many other progressive Jewish outfits in the USA, it became more critical of Israel during the Netanyahu era, and sharply distanced itself from AIPAC: 'We respect the many Jewish and Israeli advocacy organizations out there, but JTA has a different mission – to provide readers and clients with balanced and dependable reporting', which it began to do, to such an extent that the lobby created an alternative news agency in 2010, the Jewish News Service, which was loyal to Israeli right-wing politics.[62] But in the 1960s the JTA's reporting displayed utter fidelity to the Israeli narrative.

Fulbright became the pro-Israel lobby's arch nemesis and had to be deposed by any means possible. AIPAC immediately started turning the screws on the new president, John F. Kennedy, and his vice president, Lyndon B. Johnson. Kennedy's Jewish affairs adviser Myer Feldman told the president that 'The Jewish community is very uneasy about this Investigation.'[63] The pressure worked only partially when Fulbright agreed, reluctantly, to hold his committee hearing behind closed doors.

But that didn't mean AIPAC's misdeeds would be kept secret. A summary of the damning report that concluded the investigation appeared in *Newsweek* on 12 August 1963. The uproar was immediate and public. The memory of the Fulbright hearings meant that AIPAC would foil his career at every turn.

The last straw for AIPAC was Fulbright's refusal to join a group of fifty-nine senators and 238 House representatives in appearing in an ad published in the *New York Times* (on 11 May 1969) attacking the UN position on the conflict – namely condemning the UN's call for Israel to withdraw from the areas it occupied in the 1967 June war and expressing concern for the plight of the Palestinian refugees. His later opposition to large-scale funding for Israel was already assumed by AIPAC to be inevitable, as would be in their eyes his doubts about the wisdom of granting Israel a $2 billion grant in the aftermath of the October 1973 war:

> Instead of rearming Israel, we could have peace in the Middle East at once if we just told Tel Aviv to withdraw behind its 1967 borders and guarantee them.[64]

The campaign against him became an AIPAC model. The *Near East Report* accused him of being 'consistently unkind to Israel and our supporters in this country.' Everything was done to ensure that he would not be re-elected. Lobby money poured into the campaign coffers of his rival, Arkansas Governor Dale Bumpers, in the May 1974 Democratic primary election. Anyone standing against him was financed and supported.[65]

In the words of Lilienthal:

> On behalf of Arkansas Jews, Little Rock attorney Philip Kaplan announced that 'Fulbright is a Neanderthal.' Philip Back, Arkansas chairman of Bonds for Israel, said that the Senator's statement that Congress was controlled by Israel was 'uniformly disliked by Arkansas Jews, and he should be retired to private life.' A Bumpers lieutenant boasted to the *Chicago Tribune:* 'I could have bought central Arkansas with the offers of money from the Jewish community – they came particularly from people in New York and California who have raised a lot of money in the Jewish community for political purposes.'[66]

From that time to this day, the road to the Capitol has been scattered with candidates, from the elite of American politics, whose careers have been similarly torpedoed by AIPAC. In this manner, AIPAC manipulated Congress policy with such successful results that very few have since dared to follow in Fulbright's footsteps.

As noted, less draconian means were used by AIPAC to deal with Kennedy. On occasion, he showed willingness to confront Israel, but at the end of the day, he laid the foundations for a fortified alliance between the two states. In retrospect, Kenen regarded Kennedy as a president who did not dare to deviate too much from Eisenhower's unwelcome policies towards Israel. Kennedy 'disappointed' him because he did not introduce any significant change to his predecessor's policy, and he was relieved when Lyndon B. Johnson took the reins. Kenen seemed to agree with Johnson who told him after Kennedy's assassination, 'you have lost a great friend, but you have found a better one.'[67]

A TRUE FRIEND: LYNDON JOHNSON

In his memoirs, President Lyndon B. Johnson paid tribute to the wisdom of his favourite aunt. One of her recommendations was the following:

> Lyndon, always remember this, don't ever go against Israel ... The Jews are God's people, and they are always going to be ... that's their land ... and nobody is going to take it away from them.[68]

Perhaps thanks to this aunt, Israel and its lobby found him to be a more reliable ally than they could have ever expected to be sitting in the White House. Johnson's term in office was a quiet time for the lobby.

If Johnson's dear aunt gave him a nudge in the right direction, Myer Feldman held his hand the whole way through. He continued to serve as adviser on Jewish affairs or, as he described it, as 'Prime Minister on the question of Israel [in the White House]'.[69]

He was badly needed. Johnson's tenure coincided with David Ben-Gurion's worst nightmare: the Palestinian issue returned to the forefront of Middle Eastern politics, challenging the ostensible 'peace process'. At least in the corridors of the UN, people changed how they discussed Palestinian nationalism – talking about liberation and rights. One of Feldman's first missions was to ensure that the president didn't learn these new words. 'Palestine went out of existence in 1948', he reminded the president.[70]

As he had for Kennedy, Feldman masterminded Johnson's campaign against Barry Goldwater, resulting in a landslide election victory in 1964. Shortly after, the lobby tried to remove Dean Rusk, Feldman's *bête noire* under Kennedy, from the State Department, but this foundered. Hence the State Department under Rusk and the CIA under Richard Helms continued to advise the new president to prioritise America's national interest over the demands of Israel. But did the president take their words to heart? Quite often, it seems, AIPAC could whisper more closely in his ear.

AIPAC didn't solely rely on Feldman as a counterweight to Rusk and Helms. Its predecessor, AZEC, had already laid the foundation for a formidable advocacy system on Capitol Hill. Congress could now easily be won round, either to help the president against his officials or to make sure he did not deviate from a pro-Israel policy. We can see this when we look closely at the evergreen discussion on the extent to which military aid to Israel should be upgraded. The lobby utilised Congress to press Johnson to arm Israel with America's latest weaponry, and to prevent him from sending these same arms to the Arab world, in particular Jordan, his favoured state. In the latter case, AIPAC failed, and modern arms were also shipped to Jordan.

Failure did not always spell disaster. The lobby used the arms sales to Jordan as a pretext for demanding more arms for Israel. Even today this quid pro quo continues to be plan B for the lobby: you either stop arms sales to the Arab world, or you concede but demand compensation for Israel. Even after the Abraham Accords – a set of peace agreements between Israel, the UAE, Bahrain and Morocco – were concluded in 2020, arms deals for Arab countries continued to be balanced by more aid to Israel, making sure the arms race never ended. Indirectly, AIPAC's insistence on arms for Israel in the 1960s contributed to greater Soviet involvement in the Middle East, intensifying the region's transformation into a Cold War arena.

As the region increasingly descended into a military arms race between Israel and the Arab world, the hallmark of Johnson's administration was passivity. Every now and again the president would talk the talk – but not once did he take action. Israel persisted in being wilfully opaque about the development of its nuclear capacity, which even Johnson couldn't ignore, and pursued a brutal retaliation policy against Palestinian guerrillas in the West Bank as well as against the Jordanian army. One such operation turned into a collective punishment (although with a relatively small number of civilian casualties) when the army demolished 125 houses, a clinic and a school in the village of Samu in November 1966 in the Hebron area.

Walt Rostow, one of Johnson's senior advisers, wrote to the president, revealing Israel's aggressive role in bringing about the June 1967 war:

> I'm not suggesting our usual admonition against retaliation. We'll maintain that posture … but retaliation is not the point in this case. This 3,000-man raid with tanks and planes was out of all proportion to the provocation and was aimed at the wrong target. In hitting Jordan so hard, the Israelis have done a great deal of damage to our interests and to their own: They've wrecked a good system of tacit cooperation between Hussein and the Israelis … They've undercut Hussein. We've spent $500 million to shore him up as a stabilizing factor on Israel's longest border and vis-à-vis Syria and Iraq. Israel's attack increases the pressure on him to counterattack not only from the more radical Arab governments and from the Palestinians in Jordan but also from the Army, which is his main source of support and may now press for a chance to recoup its Sunday losses … They've set back progress toward a long-term accommodation with the Arabs … They may have persuaded the Syrians that Israel didn't dare attack Soviet-protected Syria but could attack US-backed Jordan with impunity. It's important that we strengthen the hand of those within the Israeli Government who feel this is not the proper way to handle the problem. Even members of the Israeli military now doubt that retaliation will stop the cross-border raids, though they see no better solution.[71]

In the UN, the American delegate joined his British counterpart in strong condemnation of the operation as a 'clear violation of solemn obligations undertaken by Israel in the General Armistice Agreements'.[72]

The Israeli government reacted by ordering AIPAC to communicate its displeasure at how the US was behaving in the international arena. But AIPAC dragged its feet on this – they realised Johnson was too big an asset to risk alienating, especially for the sake of empty talk. The *Near East Report* assured its readers that the tough American position was a clever trick to tame the Soviet attempt to dominate the Arab world.[73] American reaction to the massacre in Samu was pathetic and contributed to the young King Hussein's decision to join Egypt and Syria in a military alliance, defending him both from domestic anger about his pro-American stances and from future Israeli aggression. The simmering tension on Israel's borders was close to boiling point.

AIPAC's propagandising and lobbying in the White House only made things worse from there. On the eve of the 1967 war, AIPAC convinced the president to withhold a critical wheat package from Egypt, then the US food aid programme's largest per capita consumer. This decision caused Gamal Abdel Nasser to lose hope that the USA had any intention of enabling a positive resolution to the conflict between Israel and the Arab world.[74]

AIPAC DURING THE 1967 WAR

By May 1967, the tensions on Israel's border and the war rhetoric from all sides began to impact on the American Jewish community. I have described in the previous chapter the gap between the Israeli historiographical explanation for the outbreak of the war and more recent historiography. In the former version, the war was caused by a wish in the Arab world, led by Gamal Abdel Nasser, to destroy the state of Israel; in the latter, Nasser's brinkmanship policy aimed at forcing a diplomatic process to solve the Palestine question and defending the Arab world from Israeli expansionism. His policy created a situation which allowed Israel to implement a plan it had devised in 1963 to take over the West Bank, the Gaza Strip and the Golan Heights and establish the Greater Israel.

In May 1967, however, the American public and in particular the American Jewish public bought into Israeli propaganda claiming that Egypt was about to embark on a destructive war against Israel. Also, most Israelis at the time were convinced that they were facing the imminent danger of an all-Arab war of annihilation against the Jewish state.

In this fraught situation, AIPAC capitalised on the panic generated by Arab, and in particular Egyptian, war rhetoric. This was a moment when it could also enlist more critical Jews, who were on the Left and were involved in movements that opposed American intervention in Vietnam, by persuading them that Israel faced an existential threat. It was, as Jonathan D. Sarna and Jonathan Golden put it, 'the paralyzing fear of a "second Holocaust"'.[75]

Huge demonstrations in New York and other cities expressed this horrifying message – haunting the minds of many American Jews. The Israeli ambassador Avraham Harman declared that Israel was facing 'a genocide'.[76] Ultimately, however, American Jewish apocalypticism was counterproductive. These chilling scenes led Abba Eban to urge his fellow ministers in the Israeli government to put an end to such shows of solidarity. In a Cabinet meeting, he warned ministers that such portrayals of a trembling, victimised Israel undermined confidence in Israel's government and demoralised its Jewish population, at a time when Israel wanted to mobilise for an imminent war. AIPAC needed to put a lid on the hysteria it had unleashed – urgently, he argued.[77]

As we reach 5 June 1967, it turns out that a few exit points from the crisis emerged; in particular, an American intelligence community message to Israel. In their eyes Nasser, as Abba Eban put it, wanted a victory without war.[78] This analysis was shared by quite a few Israeli ministers. The 'victory' was a new diplomatic effort to solve the conflict. But as one Israeli military historian put it: the Israeli army was 'spoiling for a fight and willing to go to considerable lengths to provoke one'.[79]

President Johnson was also convinced that Israel was trigger happy but did very little to pressure it to de-escalate the tensions. A warning to Israel not to threaten Syria, giving Egypt the sense that the USA also understood the Egyptian point of view and was not unilaterally siding with Israel, would have helped to scale down the conflict. Instead, the dispatch of the Sixth Fleet of the US Navy to near Egypt's territorial waters looked like a sign of American aggression rather than part of an international effort to help solve the conflict.

Another exit point could have been attempted, had the Americans taken a clearer position on the UN decision to withdraw from the Sinai Peninsula and the Gaza Strip. The Egyptians were using the pressure on the UN to make a point, not as part of military preparations, but the UN secretary general and some of the countries involved in the UN forces there, such as Canada, either misunderstood the Egyptian position or panicked and unnecessarily withdrew without negotiation, which the Egyptians did not expect.[80]

Johnson woke up in the middle of the night to the news that Israel had launched pre-emptive air strikes on Egyptian airfields. He was aware that in Washington, CIA and State Department experts were still talking about an international armada that would go through the Tiran Straits, hoping it would be accompanied by a new diplomatic process. Privately Johnson had insisted to both Israeli diplomats and to AIPAC leaders that Egypt's actions did not justify war – a deeply troubling position for AIPAC. In fact, although it did not change the outcome of events, AIPAC failed to persuade its favourite president to make a clear-cut statement of support for Israel. The State Department still insisted publicly that the USA was working together with its allies and the UN in search of a diplomatic solution to end the crisis. But AIPAC's real success didn't lie in Johnson's official stances; more simply, its lobbying ensured that no one would sanction Israel for escalating military hostilities. Even more importantly, with the help of AIPAC, it was clear that whatever Israel did, the USA had no intention of obstructing it.

But it may seem that this carte blanche had limits – which were breached when the Israeli air force bombed an American spy ship called *Liberty*, killing thirty-four navy personnel and wounding more than a hundred. Israel apologised, explaining it away as a case of mistaken identity – scarcely plausible given that the Star-Spangled Banner flew high on the deck.

AIPAC realised that it could not prevent President Johnson from admonishing Israel in public for its assault on the ship. All it could do was damage control, as it was clear that even the usually pro-Israel mainstream media would find it hard to swallow the Israeli explanation. Israel's reasons for attacking the ship are still debated today. It probably had to do with information the spy ship was able to collect that might have tarnished Israel's international reputation. Most scholars assume that the ship had gathered intelligence about an Israeli massacre of Egyptian soldiers and about the expulsion of Palestinians from the Gaza Strip, which Israel wanted to conceal. But we still need further substantiation of this reasonable, and in many ways only acceptable, explanation. The most important task for AIPAC was to dissuade members of Congress who wanted an official inquiry from making this demand – a goal they successfully achieved.[81]

HELPING TO CREATE THE GREATER ISRAEL

After six days of fighting, Israel became a regional mini-empire. It ruled over the Syrian Golan Heights, the West Bank, the Gaza Strip and the whole of the Sinai Peninsula, all the way west to the banks of the Suez Canal.

The lobbying for this new Greater Israel was led by Kenen at first. He once more entered the arena as the prime mover, co-ordinating not only the actions of AIPAC, but also those of other lobby organisations, be they formal or informal. The defeat of 1956, when Eisenhower forced Israel to withdraw from the Sinai Peninsula, still rankled; he was determined that Israel would not be asked to make such a concession again. His task was to ensure that the dissenting voices on Capitol Hill regarding Israel's need to withdraw unilaterally from the territories it occupied would remain in the corridors and would not reach the assemblies.

For that purpose, he enlisted a new actor, the Anti-Defamation League, originally founded in 1913 by B'nai B'rith to fight against anti-Semitic smears in the media. Now the body followed the age-old trajectory of becoming a front for Israel. It betrayed its original charter and mission. Its original name was the Anti-Defamation League of B'nai B'rith and since its founding it had been active in the struggle to protect Jewish civil rights; for instance, when Leo Frank, an American Jew, was wrongly accused of murdering a thirteen-year-old employee at his workplace. He was spared the death penalty but lynched later.

After 1967, combating anti-Semitism against American Jews ceased to be its main task – now, cheered on by AIPAC, it sought to portray certain 'anti-Israel' actions as anti-Semitic. It propagandised against any attempt to pressure Israel into withdrawing from the occupied territories.

Kenen recalled that after the June 1967 war, the wheels of the lobbying machine were especially well-greased, as the events had prompted many American Jews to donate generously to AIPAC. But as in the case of Truman and 1948, AIPAC did not just target Congress but also used its contacts with the small entourage of the president's friends. Every possible avenue had to be taken; every lobbyist knew what was at stake here. With not one Israeli settler in the West Bank or in the Gaza Strip, the international community considered full withdrawal entirely achievable. This was the time when the ruler of Jordan, King Hussein, made a *mea culpa* statement in several interviews; namely that it was a mistake to involve Jordan in the war. That kind of statement made it easier for Israeli policy makers to accept him as a suitable partner for a postwar arrangement for the future of the West Bank. But Israel had no intention of withdrawing from the West Bank, so they offered the king peace for peace. The thirteenth government of Israel represented every stripe of Zionist and Orthodox parties. All were united on one point: the necessity of creating a Greater Israel. The lobby now needed to win round Israel's allies to this position.

Hence the appeal to the president's friends. The most important among them was Abe Fortas, a Supreme Court judge, born and raised in Memphis, who became very close to Johnson, a friendship forged when Fortas represented Johnson in a legal skirmish that was bitterly fought during the president's second nomination. He was a something of a folk hero: a musician as well as a *pro bono* defence lawyer fighting for the rights of petty criminals, which earned him some fame when he came to the rescue of Clarence Earl Gideon in court, who was charged with breaking and entering a pool hall and was initially denied legal counsel. This affair was covered in a book and a film, both titled *Gideon's*

Trumpet. It did not end there; he fought for children's and students' rights as well. How did such a stalwart champion of the oppressed end up in AIPAC?

It seems that he was, indeed, another PEOP; namely someone who regarded Israel as a progressive cause, even if the facts on the ground challenged such support for the Jewish state. Immediately after the 1967 war, it was probably difficult to ascertain how abusive the Israeli policy was toward the Palestinians. Leading American newspapers did report the expulsion of a large number of Palestinians from the West Bank just after the war, but did not show any interest in discrimination against the Palestinian citizens of Israel, or the illegal annexation of East Jerusalem (which included the ethnic cleansing of Palestinians from the old city). And the fact that Israel was still adamant about not allowing the 1948 refugees, and for that matter those of the 1967 war, to return was not a topic that would have interested famous people like Fortas. So perhaps it was easy for AIPAC to recruit him and use his credentials to ensure Johnson would not exert undue pressure on Israel to withdraw.

Another friend was Mathilde Krim, known for founding the American Foundation for AIDS Research and for her numerous scientific accomplishments, including developing a method for the prenatal determination of sex. She was born in Italy and grew up in Switzerland, where, as a young woman, she smuggled guns for the Zionist paramilitary group Irgun for the fight against British rule in Palestine. Having married an Irgun member, she was pro-Zionist to her bones. Like many close friends of the Johnsons, she often spent time in the White House guest room, and this is where she was when the June 1967 war erupted. Walter Hixson tells us that she was privy to secret documents shown to her by the president pertaining to policies towards Israel.[82] She had become close to the president through the contacts her second husband Arthur B. Krim cultivated with the Democratic Party. Krim was a New York attorney, head of United Artists, the film company, and the founder of Orion Pictures. From an early age he was active in the Democratic Party and became an adviser to presidents Kennedy, Johnson and later Jimmy Carter.

Despite all these contacts, AIPAC had to concede that the USA was now necessarily a major player in the so-called 'peace process'. The lobby would hence occasionally engage in some verbal sparring with the government when it made a strongly worded policy statement – but these statements amounted to nothing on the ground. From 1967 until today, the USA has acted as dishonest broker, as aptly described by both Naseer Aruri and Rashid Khalidi.[83] US policy featured occasional outbursts against particularly egregious aggression by Israel, but nothing was done to curtail it.

Strong tones of rebuke could be heard from Washington when Israel unilaterally annexed East Jerusalem, flagrantly violating international law. Israeli documents from the time reveal many outraged missives from the president and from the American ambassador in Tel Aviv condemning the early Judaisation of greater Jerusalem, which included ethnic cleansing of the Palestinians from various parts of the old city and from nearby neighbourhoods, dramatically altering the city's landscape and identity. But the American government never put its money where its mouth was. AIPAC took the credit for the USA's remarkable reluctance to act, but they exaggerate their own influence. Earlier Zionist and later pro-Israel efforts had already entrenched inertia as the standard approach. While it was easy to reprimand Israel in writing, there was no political will to stand in its way.

AIPAC's real service in the last years of Johnson's term in office was in pressuring the US to provide the cutting-edge weaponry it produced to Israel (such as the F-4 Phantom jet fighters, to which very few armies outside the USA had access; these took the Israeli air force to a new level). Experts, whether in the CIA or the State Department, warned that such a supply would make the US the main arms provider of Israel in the eyes of the Arab world. Their warning was unheeded and the USA became the main supplier, but it did not impact on the Arab-American relationship that much. After much effort by AIPAC, constantly stoking fear about the Arab threat, Israel received its first sixteen Phantom jets in late 1969. They deployed these long-awaited jets to devastating effect when bombing Beirut in 1982.

As we can see, the political elite were the main target of the lobbying endeavours in the Johnson era. As the administration's sympathies were unambiguously with Israel, there was little need to smear recalcitrant politicians or scheme to remove them from office. There was also no reason for AIPAC to be particularly worried in the immediate aftermath of the June 1967 war about undercurrents in American civil society, which were not yet easy to detect, that might shift sympathy to the occupied Palestinians and away from Israel. Both Arno Mayer and Noam Chomsky recalled a reasonable level of freedom when talking about Israel and the Palestinians until 1967.[84] A seismic change in what could be said about Israel only took place after it had won the June 1967 war. Mayer observed that in American academia, Israel was seen as rather a niche interest, and most Jewish academics were involved in different fields. After Israel's victory in the 1967 war, its empire in miniature finally invoked national pride in some American Jews.

IF JOHNSON WAS A FRIEND, NIXON WAS A HERO

Richard Nixon was a Republican president elected after a relatively long period of Democratic occupants in the White House. AIPAC, as well as many political groups within the American Jewish community, were loyal to the Democratic Party, and thus the election of a Republican president took them into uncharted territory.

On the surface, Nixon had no real need to be co-operative. As a Republican president in the late 1960s, it was clear to him that the Jewish vote went to the Democrats. However, as a new president he needed the support of Congress, and Congress only grew more and more intertwined with the lobby when it came to policies towards Israel and the Middle East as a whole. This meant that the lobby would have leverage and a way of influencing his policies on Israel and beyond.

Lenny Ben-David, who worked as an intern for AIPAC in those years, gives us a taste of why the election of a Republican president like Nixon did not much change the influence AIPAC already had in Congress. The lobby's work on Capitol Hill in those days was run from a relatively small office, headed by Kenen, working with ten staff members, who were not always paid their salaries on time due to the relatively small budget ($300,000 annually) that Kenen had at his disposal.

However, it was an effective operation. Kenen 'didn't have to prowl' the halls of Congress to meet with elected officials and twist arms. He consulted with two handfuls of congressional titans, and they set the legislative agenda and rounded up the votes on the Hill. Many years later, Kenen's work in those years was summarised by the neo-conservative Israeli think-tank, the Jerusalem Center for Public Affairs:

> Kenen supplemented his direct relationship with senior Members of Congress with the 'key contacts' on his telephone Rolodex and mailing lists of local Jewish community leaders and politically active friends of Israel across the United States. When a legislative issue or foreign aid vote was pending, AIPAC would mail out an alert or even a 'mailgram' to them, the new postal conveyance of the time.

> Long-serving chairmen of important committees possessed the power to promote legislation or crush it and the ability to do the same to the career of a junior committee member. Once a chairman decided, that was final. Their positions were protected by their *droit d'seniority* [*sic*] – until younger Members of Congress finally rebelled.[85]

There was another reason for optimism that a Republican president would not change course regarding Israel and Palestine, and that was the appointment of Henry Kissinger as the president's national adviser. After a stellar career at Harvard University as a professor for International Relations, Kissinger joined politics as adviser to other Republican candidates until he was recruited in 1968 by Nixon.

Kissinger was a dedicated Zionist by the time he entered the White House. He had visited Israel six times before taking up the position, establishing an important network of contacts with its leaders.[86]

The first manifestation of Kissinger's influence on policy towards Israel appeared in what became known as the Nixon Doctrine. With other members of the president's entourage, Kissinger helped the president to author a new doctrine for defending the American national interest, and when the president spelled out this doctrine, it included a total reliance on Israel as the main pillar of US policy in the Middle East. Moreover, he pledged to guarantee Israel 'a margin of technological and military superiority' over the Arab world. The *New York Times* wrote back then that 'the pledge marked a significant shift in the methods to be used in advancing America's Middle-East policy'.[87] His doctrine also included turning a blind eye to Israel's nuclear capacity destabilising the region by instigating a nuclear arms race there.[88]

However, there was another presidential appointment that worried AIPAC: William Rogers as secretary of state. He was someone who was never close to the lobby and was an enigma as far as his position towards Israel was concerned. A lawyer by profession, his appointment in 1969 surprised many, owing to his lack of previous experience in world affairs. Kissinger constantly ridiculed his deficiencies on this front – mainly because he coveted the job for himself.

What worried both Kissinger and AIPAC about Rogers was that he seemed to listen carefully to the advice of the professionals within the State Department, including the remaining 'Arabists' in the Near East Department. Together with these veteran diplomats, Rogers devised a simple plan for peace between Israel and the Arab states that were involved in the June 1967 war, based on the formula of 'land for peace': the more land Israel would withdraw from, the more formal the peace with the Arab states would be. This was also the spirit of UN Security Council Resolution 242, which advocated such a formula for peace in the wake of the June 1967 war.

AIPAC was busy in Congress undermining every step taken by Rogers, who was willing to work in tandem with the UN to implement Resolution 242 as the basis for a solution. As we've seen, the November 1967 resolution called upon Israel to withdraw from the territories it occupied in the June 1967 war to enable peace talks, as well as calling for a just solution to the refugee problem. The peak of that campaign was AIPAC's annual conference in April 1969, which began with a statement by 227 members of Congress, who rejected the 'land for peace' principle and demanded 'Arab recognition of Israel first' as a

precondition for any discussion.[89] And as always in such annual conferences and those to come, the request was for more and better arms to be
supplied to Israel. Nixon heeded these appeals.

Rogers was not deterred and on 9 December 1969 he announced his
nine-point peace plan, spelling out a future Israeli–Egyptian peace
based on total Israeli withdrawal from the Sinai Peninsula and seeking
a joint arrangement for the Gaza Strip. It was quite similar to a plan
proposed a year before by the UN mediator, Gunnar Jarring. Jarring
was appointed after the UN Security Council adopted Resolution 242,
which failed after being rejected by both sides, but Rogers believed that
if it were packaged as an American initiative rather than a UN one, it
would have a better chance of success.

Both AIPAC and Kissinger castigated Rogers's plan as naive due to
his lack of experience in Middle Eastern affairs. Kissinger preferred
behind-the-scenes negotiations, with baby steps towards a non-aggression agreement between the two sides. Experienced or not, Rogers's
peace plan was logical and hence doomed to fail.

This was more than just a discussion about the right policy; Rogers
was Kissinger's nemesis all along. Simply put, Rogers had got the job
Kissinger wanted. AIPAC was an important ally for Kissinger in this
rivalry.

AIPAC went to war against the plan. AIPAC's main lobby partner in
those years, and years to come, was the Conference of the Presidents of
Major American Jewish Organizations. It had its own repertoire and
modus operandi. In this era, this outfit was responsible for the discourse
about a second Holocaust facing Israel in June 1967. Even after the war,
it would occasionally generate panic about the Jewish state's fate as a
result of Rogers's peace plan and demand that American Jews be alert
and operate under a constant state of emergency. Hence, in 1969 it
convened a 'national emergency conference' in Washington at which
the 'American Jews' expressed their horror towards the existential
dangers implied by the Rogers Plan.

The main speaker was Max Fisher. He was a philanthropist from
Pittsburgh, born into a Russian Jewish immigrant family. In another
light, his was a story that proved Jews didn't need Zionism to flourish

– they could be enormously successful Americans. But like many American Jews, he seemed to see the state of Israel as an insurance policy to keep in his back pocket. Be that as it may, Fisher made his money in the oil business, real estate and banking, donating generously to mainly Jewish causes, but in retrospect his chief vocation was, as the title of his biography puts it, being the 'quiet diplomat'.[90] In his case this meant simultaneously advising the government of Israel and successive American presidents on how best the US could serve Israel's interests. There on the podium in Washington, his credentials were proudly announced: he was a member of the Republican Party and adviser to Nixon, as well as a chairman of the United Israel Appeal a year earlier (the main body channelling funding from American Jews to Israel). The list was long, and his presidency of the Council of Jewish Federations was mentioned, as well as his seat on the board of governors of the Jewish Agency and other Zionist organisations in America. With such impressive titles behind him, he read aloud a personal pledge from the president to support the Israeli demand for Arab recognition of the Jewish state as a pre-condition for any bilateral talks with Arab countries and rejecting any UN (and by association William Rogers's) proposed peace initiatives.[91]

Congress was successfully galvanised, with House representatives and senators parroting what they read in AIPAC's main publication, the *Near East Report*, as if it were the Bible. The two-fold prize arrived in 1970: Nixon withdrew his support of Rogers's peace plans and compensated Israel for the unpleasant period with another huge arms deal, a package of $500 million, and an agreement to provide more Phantoms. The *Near East Report* called the deal 'the major 1970 development in US-Israel relations'.[92]

Congress was not the only target of the well-orchestrated campaign against the Rogers Plan. As mentioned, both Kissinger and AIPAC suspected that the 'Arabists' in the State Department were the main source of information and inspiration for the Rogers Plan. Kissinger saw them as 'inherently anti-Israel' and wished to replace them with more pro-Israel officials in the State Department, and among the advisers around the president.

The campaign to replace those less favourable to Israel was partly successful. It began with the appointment of two prominent American Jews who acted, according to the *New York Times*, as 'conduits between Richard Nixon and the American Jewish Community'. They were Arthur Burns and Leonard Garment. Burns was a famous economist who would later be the chairman of the Federal Reserve and Leonard Garment was a well-known attorney; both served as 'counsellors' to the president.[93]

What these advisers succeeded in doing was to replace the one diplomat in the State Department who for them was the epitome of an 'Arabist' determined to subscribe to the wrong policies: Parker Thompson Hart, the assistant secretary of state for the Near East. He had served as a senior diplomat in most of the Arab capitals and spoke Arabic. He was too pro-Arab in the eyes of AIPAC and Kissinger, although he was professional to the bone. Under the pressure of the lobby, he was replaced by Joseph J. Sisco, who was a Sovietologist and not an 'Arabist', and never served abroad, and thus was more susceptible to accepting the notion that Israel was a bulwark against Soviet expansion in the Middle East.

Despite the replacement of Hart, the 'Arabists' still played a role during Nixon's term of office. As the *New York Times* summarised their situation in 1971:

> For the time being, the Arabists are a relatively happy bunch. President Nixon, Secretary Rogers and Assistant Secretary Sisco are all pushing for a settlement in the Near East. As never before, the official ear is cocked for any suggestions from down the line.[94]

This was probably why AIPAC was also busy after 1971 until the end of the Nixon term in office in trying to balance the influence of those they deemed anti-Israel actors, be it professional diplomats or captains of the military and oil industries.

The essence of the dispute AIPAC and Kissinger had with the remaining 'Arabists' and with Rogers was about the Palestinian issue. This was when the Palestinian national movement re-emerged in the refugees' camps, taking over the mantle from the Arab League, and reminded the world that the Palestinian nation still lived. This was when a growing number of people could see the brutality of the Israeli occupation for themselves, up close. This was when Israel's propagandists around the world found it difficult to paint Israel as the victim and the underdog in what became known as the Arab–Israeli conflict. Politicians such as Rogers, with a modicum of integrity, were willing to view the 'conflict' from both sides. Simply trying to be balanced, as many politicians learned to their peril, was condemned as anti-Israel. The lobby sought to rein in naive politicians like Rogers and ensure that no one dared to look at the Palestinian side of the question again.

From 1971 President Anwar Sadat of Egypt offered the same formula to Israel that had already been offered by his predecessor, Gamal Abdel Nasser, and rejected: peace for full Israeli withdrawal from the Sinai Peninsula. Israel rejected Sadat's peace proposals and moreover took action on the ground that hindered any future agreement between the two states, including building Jewish settlements at the northern and southern ends of the Sinai Peninsula.

The failure of the plan led to a war of attrition between Israel and Egypt, which consisted of artillery duels over the Suez Canal and widespread Israeli aerial bombardments of wide areas west of the Suez Canal, displacing a million Egyptians from the canal area.[95] During that time Rogers was content with trying to persuade the two sides to agree to a ceasefire – achieving this in 1971.

The military escalation, which occurred not only on the Suez Canal but also on Israel's border with Jordan (where the PLO and Israel were involved at the same time in another war of attrition), caused Nixon to view Rogers's efforts at pacifying the region more favourably. More importantly, Nixon began to suspect that Kissinger might not be putting the American national interest first in this case.

He almost made a U-turn in 1971, telling anyone who was willing to listen that Israel was deceiving him and had no interest in achieving peace. Kissinger, he lamented, had fallen prey to their machinations as he was Jewish.[96] Hence the staggeringly large-scale military aid, decided upon by Congress, was temporarily withheld. The prime minister of

Israel, Golda Meir, attempted to change Nixon's mind, but Nixon refused to budge. Encouraged by the détente with the USSR and the American–Chinese rapprochement, Nixon wanted some tangible results in ending hostilities in the region. With Nasser out of the way and Egypt's new leader Anwar Sadat distancing himself from the Soviets, the time was ripe for a change. Nixon wanted to help Sadat win legitimacy in the West, by triggering an incremental Israeli withdrawal from the Sinai Peninsula through disengagement agreements. However, Meir and her defence minister, Moshe Dayan, were still in a triumphant and euphoric mood and rejected out of hand any proposal for an Israeli withdrawal from Sinai in return for bilateral peace with Egypt. As a goodwill gesture, Nixon withdrew his objection to yet another huge arms deal with Israel, hoping it would encourage the Israeli government to adopt a more positive posture towards the disengagement process. It did not matter, in Nixon's own analysis, because Congress was totally loyal to AIPAC:

> In the Middle East the problem is Israel ... Israel's lobby is so strong that Congress is not reasonable ... We have to have policies which don't allow an obsession with one state to destroy our status in the Middle East.[97]

In October 1973, in collaboration with Syria, Sadat led his army in a surprise attack that was meant to retake the Sinai Peninsula by force. He did not succeed and eventually the Israeli army repelled the Egyptian forces and invaded a small part of the western bank of the Suez Canal. However, their success in defeating the Egyptians' surprise attack came at the cost of a high number of casualties, and was only possible because of massive military supplies organised by Kissinger during the early part of the Egyptian offensive, in which the Egyptians managed to get a long way into the Sinai Peninsula.

In retrospect, Kissinger regretted his opposition to the peace plan. When he met a group of Jewish leaders at the Hotel Pierre in New York in June 1975, he told them: 'I am sorry that I did not support the Rogers effort more than I did ... [which] would have prevented the 1973 war.'[98]

'Land for Peace' was an idea that might have worked, and eventually did work, only in one place, the Sinai Peninsula, and this only after Israel suffered a military defeat during the October 1973 war, a conflict from which Israel in the end emerged relatively successful, with the full backing of the US and in particular that of Henry Kissinger. In the case of Palestine, where it mattered more, there was never a chance for such a formula to work, vis-à-vis either Jordan or the Palestinians. The Israeli Labor Party (1948–1977) viewed any diplomatic conversation on 'Land for Peace' as a tolerable nuisance, since it did not prevent Israel from colonising the occupied territories. Their successor, the Likud Party, which came to power in 1977, dispensed with the talk and nonetheless survived and thrived. Whenever more realistic, or more honest, American policy makers repeated the naive mistakes of Rogers, attempting to take a balanced view, their good deeds did not go unpunished. They were scolded and called to order by AIPAC.

In the aftermath of the war, Israel had been far more willing in 1974 to follow Kissinger's lead and enter in a meaningful way into an incremental disengagement process not only in the Sinai Peninsula but also in the Syrian Golan Heights, conceding some territory for the sake of tacit non-aggression agreements. Ironically, only when the right-wing Likud Party came to power in 1977 was this process completed; but the laurels for this American achievement were bestowed upon a new president and a new secretary of state.

After the October 1973 war, Kissinger conferred more regularly with the prime movers within the pro-Israel lobby in America: AIPAC and the Conference of Presidents of Major American Jewish Organizations. He consulted with these two bodies, boasting about his achievements, which grew exponentially: with every meeting, he promised a greater quantity and quality of American arms supplies to Israel.[99] This was a quantum leap in arming Israel, whose army now enjoyed the highest amount of American military aid outside NATO. These armaments had rescued the Israeli army from a early defeat in the 1973 war, when Kissinger arranged an airlift, even bigger than that offered to besieged Berlin in 1948.

After the Watergate scandal and the impeachment of President Nixon, American involvement in diplomacy and in the Middle East decreased somewhat compared to earlier periods, and the new president, Gerald Ford, although known to be pro-Israel, did not seem to show any particular interest in the affairs of either the Israelis or the Palestinians.

However, Ford remained intransigent on one point – there would be no legitimisation of the PLO, in accordance with the views of Israel's prime minister since 1974, Yitzhak Rabin. Henry Kissinger, in close communication with AIPAC, made no attempt to change the Israeli administration's mind on this. In conversations with Jewish community leaders, Kissinger declared he hoped to 'isolate the Palestinians', and turn the other Arab states away from the Palestinian cause.[100]

It is possible that this relatively low-key involvement enabled other ideas to evolve besides Pax Americana. I have already described the scene in the UN during this period in the previous chapter: a newly decolonised world seeking to get involved in the Palestine question, though direct contact and legitimisation of the PLO. As a result, alongside the armed struggle, the PLO pursued a new diplomatic initiative to be included as a legitimate partner in any discussion on the future of Israel and Palestine. This also impressed the European Union and resulted in the 1980 Venice Declaration, which located the Palestine issue at the heart of efforts to solve the Arab–Israeli conflict.

However, the new Israeli prime minister of 1974, Yitzhak Rabin, and the new US president, still running his foreign policy under the guidance of Kissinger, who still consulted with AIPAC on these matters, were not interested in changing Israel's intransigent policies on the Palestine issue.

THE SIX-MONTH 'WAR OF NERVES', MARCH–SEPTEMBER 1975

Where the Ford administration did have an issue with Israel was with the difficulty of bringing Egypt and Israel to sign a disengagement agreement: a partial Israeli withdrawal from Sinai in return for an Egyptian commitment to solve any outstanding issues through talks.

Israel prevaricated, under pressure from its settlers in the Sinai Peninsula and its overall reluctance to withdraw.

President Ford called it 'stalling' and wrote that the Israeli tactics 'frustrated the Egyptians and made me mad as hell'.[101] He was equally harsh at the time in a famous telegram he wrote to the Israeli prime minister, Yitzhak Rabin:

> I wish to express my profound disappointment over Israel's attitude in the course of the negotiations ... Failure of the negotiation will have a far reaching impact on the region and on our relations. I have given instructions for a reassessment of United States policy in the region, including our relations with Israel, with the aim of ensuring that overall American interests ... are protected. You will be notified of our decision.[102]

The key word here is 'reassessment'. On the face of it, it's a mundane-sounding word, but in the context of the particular vocabulary that emerged over the years for describing the American–Israeli relationship, it assumed a far more ominous meaning. The reason for this is that there's a basic assumption that the American–Israeli relationship is so solid that there is no need for 'reassessment', but if the need arises, something fundamental in the relationship between the two states must have changed. The declaration of this reassessment was made in March 1975 and by September Israel had signed the agreement with Egypt. But within this half-year, according to Ford, a 'war of nerves' raged between him, Israel and AIPAC allies in Congress.[103]

Although there was a threat of sanctions during 1949 and in 1956, the concept of reassessment was used for the first time by Ford. As I finished writing this book, the term reappeared as a possible American reaction to the right-wing Israeli government elected in November 2022. As Rabin noted much later, the term sounded quite 'innocent' but in essence it 'heralded one of the worst periods in American-Israeli relations'.[104]

The president explained to Congress that reassessment meant suspending military aid to Israel – in particular reassessing Israel's request to receive F-16 fighter jets, to which the USA had previously responded favourably.

We might well be surprised that Ford was 'shocked', in his own words, at the refusal of so many members of Congress to support his 'reassessment'. Was he unaware of how powerful AIPAC was by then? According to Arlene Lazarowitz, although AIPAC by then had an impressive and effective presence on Capitol Hill, it did not have clout, as yet, in the White House, which may explain Ford's bewilderment. Lazarowitz also points out that by the time of the reassessment, other less prominent advocacy groups, such as the Conference of Presidents of Major American Jewish Organizations, B'nai B'rith and Hadassah, were still reeling from the June 1967 war, and were easily recruited by AIPAC to join in forming a public campaign against the reassessment.

If the president was surprised at AIPAC's reaction to the reassessment, it should be noted that AIPAC was also astonished that a president, known to be pro-Israel throughout his political career, would embark on such policy. A few months earlier, in December 1974, Ford, in the company of Kissinger, had met twenty leaders of the American Zionist community and assured them that he would pursue a pro-Israel policy.

After the president's announcement of the reassessment, AIPAC began an intensive campaign to bring an end to it. AIPAC was by no means the only aggressive member of the anti-reassessment campaign. Recall the American Jewish Committee – a non-Zionist group at the beginning of the twentieth century, but utterly Zionised after the 1967 war. It warned the president:

> If 1975 turns out to be the year of intense pressure on Israel, there will be a very serious reaction among American Jews. We will go directly to Congress, and 1976 [the election year] is not that far.[105]

But what mattered was AIPAC's ability to put sustained pressure on Congress. The peak of this campaign was a public letter signed by seventy-six senators from both parties to the president that was published in the *New York Times* on 22 May 1975, warning the president that if the USA did not provide the necessary weapons to Israel it could lead to another war. It was not meant to be published as it was sent as a private letter. Ford was convinced that the Israeli prime minister Rabin leaked the letter to the press and scolded him for that in a meeting between the two men, but Rabin did not admit to being behind the leak.[106]

In Ford's eyes, the letter was particularly offensive to Egypt and its president Anwar Sadat, who had co-operated fully with American policy throughout. Ford told the Egyptian president that the letter was 'distorted out of proportion' and was signed by ignorant politicians: 'half of them didn't read it and a quarter did not understand the letter'.[107] Ford was true to his word when he told Sadat he would not capitulate to Congress on this issue. Israel eventually signed the agreement. But something else happened and this would repeat itself several times in the future: a successful executive policy to which AIPAC was opposed had to be sweetened later on, more often than not by a generous aid package for Israel. This time it was a $2 billion supply of arms to Israel, with free oil shipments. In the years to come, money and military aid would do the trick.

We now know that there was always a good chance for some sort of pacification between a pro-American Egypt and a pro-American Israel. But the heart of the matter in the Middle East was the Palestine question and during the Ford years, the USA undermined every possibility for meaningful progress on this issue.

So, on the face of it, while the UN and the EU began to be more attentive to the Palestinian side in the conflict, the USA seemed to be unconditionally loyal to Israel. Yet the lobby's faith in consistent American support would soon be shaken, albeit only for a short while, when Jimmy Carter won the presidential elections in 1976. As a candidate he seemed to be an ideal Democratic president that the lobby could trust, but in his first year as president he opted for a different approach, rooted in humanitarian principles, rather than narrow geopolitical interests. The lobby prepared to mobilise to resist any potential change of tack – if they were losing trusted friends in the White House, they needed to make new ones.

A RIVAL IN THE WHITE HOUSE: THE CARTER YEARS

The town hall in Clinton, a small town in Worcester County in mid-Massachusetts, located on 242 Church Street, could have been a historical landmark in which a new American policy towards the Palestine issue was forged – a turn of events that could have altered the course of history in the Middle East as a whole in the last quarter of the twentieth century. However, as with so many other locations, it is destined to be forgotten – a landmark that never was. The presence of a formidable and effective lobby ensured that the USA's unequivocal support for Israel would continue as it ever had. The catastrophe continued unabated.

Visitors cannot miss this hall in a town of roughly 15,000 people. At its centre rises a rectangular tower, dividing the relatively small building into two parts. The tower soars into the sky, looking down on a red-tile roof. At the top, there's an open section, surrounded by thin white pillars. It was built in 1909, replacing Clinton's old town hall which had burned down two years earlier.

But rather than becoming a landmark in Palestine's history, its claim to fame remained its role in America's industrial upsurge that began in the mid-nineteenth century and ended with the 1929 depression. In 1828 the Bigelow brothers, Erastus and Horatio, started an industrial revolution that altered this rural community and introduced it, and the county around it, to the modern world. Erastus, a mechanical genius, invented a power loom for manufacturing coach laces, counterpane cloths and gingham plaids. Horatio was a marketing entrepreneur, and the brothers captured a firm hold on the textile industry, not only in Clinton but also all over Worcester County and other parts of Massachusetts.

Perhaps because of this illustrious history, many presidents have honoured this town with a visit. Carter's arrival on 16 March 1977 was the eighth visit by a sitting American president to the greater Worcester area. George Washington and John Quincy Adams were here in the early years of the new republic, while Theodore Roosevelt and William Howard Taft arrived as the nineteenth century edged into the twentieth. In 1932, Herbert Hoover campaigned in Worcester for a second term, and FDR visited four times from 1934 to 1944. Lyndon B. Johnson gave the 1964 commencement address at the College of the Holy Cross in Worcester. After Carter, Bill Clinton came twice, once to honour the six firefighters killed in the deadly Worcester Cold Storage and Warehouse Co. fire in December 1999. In 2014, President Barack Obama gave the commencement address at Worcester Technical High School. Forty years ago, as the *Evening Gazette* reported, Carter's goal was to stay close to the people in an 'ordinary town'. Instead, he told the gathered crowds, he had discovered that the town of Clinton was 'extraordinary'.[108]

The Jimmy Carter we know today is an elder statesman, a Nobel laureate, a man revered for his tireless devotion to peace and human rights as well as his efforts to combat homelessness. In his nineties, as this book is written, he still teaches Sunday school every week in his hometown of Plains, Georgia, and volunteers for Habitat for Humanity. He continues to be involved with the Carter Centre, which he and his wife Rosalynn founded in 1982 as a non-profit, non-partisan organisation whose goal is 'to resolve conflict, promote democracy, protect human rights and prevent disease and other afflictions', according to the Carter Library website. Indeed, the former president has only taken time off to receive treatment for metastatic melanoma, with which he was diagnosed in 2015.

In 1977, however, when he visited Clinton as part of a campaign to connect with the American public, President Carter was just beginning his first and only term in office. Most of the critical moments of his presidency – the Camp David Accords, the seizure of American hostages by Iranian revolutionaries – were yet to come. There were other pressing issues that year; inflation and unemployment were high, the country was in the middle of an energy crisis and people were having trouble paying their bills. His anticipated talk at the town hall was meant to focus on these issues.

After Air Force One landed in nearby Hanscom Field, Carter made his way to the home of Edward and Catherine Thompson on Chestnut Street, where he stayed the night, delighting the local community with his obvious humility. 'We didn't even know he was up until we heard the shower running (about 7 a.m.)', an excited and grateful Catherine Thompson told the *Gazette*'s reporter, Christine R. Dunphy.

Carter delivered his speech on 16 March in Clinton town hall in front of a packed house, with hundreds more listening outside. Standing next to a lectern with a drawing of the pre-colonial landscape on it, together with emblem of the president, and of course next to the American flag, he outlined his future plans as the new president. Between his short talk and the questions from eighteen representative residents, the president called for federal income tax and welfare reform, a reduction in the arms race with the Soviet Union, and help for Vietnam veterans looking for jobs. He talked about 'abortion, the Israeli situation, oil spills and the draft', wrote the *Gazette* reporter Leonard J. Lazure.[109]

The Central Massachusetts audience was, Carter recalled, the first to applaud his opposition to abortion, four years after the passage of *Roe v. Wade*. He pledged to work to 'provide family planning services so that every child born would be wanted.' As we know, what he endorsed back then in terms of family planning services was wiped out by the Supreme Court during Donald Trump's tenure. Carter's domestic reforms stuck only in part and the American economy did not take off under his presidency, although he created jobs and reduced the national deficit. He is remembered as the president who established the Department of Education and attempted to forge, unsuccessfully, a national energy policy. But in the end he was not judged by his domestic policies, but rather by his foreign policy, which he hoped would focus on peace in the Middle East.

And yet, he could not have known back then in Clinton how much of his legacy would be examined through the lens of his achievements and failures in pursing American policy in the Middle East: a mixed bag that included, on the one hand, a dramatic and historic bilateral peace between Israel and Egypt, and, on the other, a terrible fiasco and miscalculations that began when he was faced with the abduction of American citizens by Iranian revolutionaries.

Beyond addressing immediate domestic crises, Carter wanted to put forward a new, just foreign policy, especially in the Middle East. He declared, 'There has to be a homeland provided for the Palestinian refugees who have suffered for many, many years.'[110] Although Palestinians today regard a 'homeland' as a poor substitute for an independent and sovereign state, it was back then a dramatic break from previous American policies that ignored the Palestinians as a legitimate national group altogether.

AIPAC was caught completely off-guard – they had lauded Carter's candidacy as soon as he announced it, and had high hopes for his future presidency. His presidential campaign included a pledge that the US would not negotiate with the PLO until it recognised Israel's right to exist – the key demand of AIPAC. Like every other candidate, he retained the mainstay of US policy: supplying arms to Israel and vetoing any attempt in the UN Security Council to condemn the various violations of international law by the Israeli occupying forces in the West Bank and the Gaza Strip.

To AIPAC officials, he seemed ideal. As governor of Georgia, he visited Israel frequently, and his evangelical Christianity ensured that he associated the return of the Jews to the Middle East with safeguarding the state of Israel. More pragmatically, Carter enlisted the help of Zionist lobbies in his campaign and in return supported harsh legislation against American companies that complied with the Arab boycott on Israel. Since 1951, members of the Arab League had officially refused to trade with companies around the world that traded with Israel, although a number of companies found ways of bypassing the boycott and managed to trade with both Israel and the Arab world. His predecessor in the White House, Gerald Ford, and his rival in the elections, as we have seen, had a bumpy ride on the way to the 1976 elections after initiating the six months of 'reassessment'. It did not help that he relieved some of the restrictions imposed on these Arab states in his short term at the helm. Ford's policy was used by Carter in his campaign as proof of the alleged anti-Israel bias of the Republican candidate and his party, and helped Carter to win Jewish votes and funding. He also surrounded himself with several Jewish advisers and appointed them to senior positions in his campaign team.[111]

AIPAC had every reason to be happy with Carter. But they didn't realise his closest allies thought rather differently to him. In 1975, his national security adviser, Zbigniew Brzezinski, and William B. Quandt, his adviser on Middle Eastern affairs, were working in the Brookings Institution, attempting to forge the Democrats' Middle East policy. Their conclusions were outlined in the report *Toward Peace in the Middle East*, which called for Israel's withdrawal to its pre-1967 borders and provision for self-determination for the Palestinians. This became Carter's blueprint for his foreign policy.[112]

Unsurprisingly, AIPAC whipped up outrage when the report was published in 1975 – the same time as Gerald Ford was considering a 'reassessment' of Middle East policy. But it largely believed it had neutered the threat, and it hoped that Carter would walk a different path from his predecessors. The Clinton speech was a nasty shock. But it would not be the last one. In later encounters, Carter repeated his new stance in even stronger language and reiterated his determination to alleviate the plight of the Palestinians.

What gave Carter the courage to make such radical statements? There is a scholarly consensus on this question. This was a president who listened to his advisers and was willing to learn. Unlike some of his predecessors, he took part in the traditional White House meetings to reassess foreign policy that occur after the inauguration of every new administration.

He had his own views, which were obscured in his campaign, but emerged somewhat later after he was in office. He regarded the Palestinians as another disenfranchised people like the African Americans and saw parallels between the segregation policies in the south of the USA and the treatment of the Palestinians by Israel.

By deploying a new vocabulary, he alarmed the pro-Israel lobby, accustomed to their narrative being accepted unreservedly. He talked about Palestinians and the PLO in neutral terms, rather than describing them as terrorists. He was encouraged by those around him to go beyond words and seek direct contact with the PLO, which he was willing to attempt. The close entourage that encouraged him to deviate from previous American policy was led by Harold Saunders and William Quandt, members of his National Security Council, as well as Cyrus Vance and Zbigniew Brzezinski. Carter later recalled how much he learned from them about the predicament of the Palestinians.

This was Carter in March 1977. It seemed that at last a US president was willing to take a stand and seek justice for the Palestinians. But these expectations would be frustrated and AIPAC had an important role to play in their demise. But Carter himself can't evade blame for shying away from the battle, and not pursuing his just policy to a more successful outcome.

FORSAKING THE PALESTINIANS

In AIPAC's collective memory, Carter's drifting back to traditional American policy on Israel, after a few months in the wilderness, was due to the lobby's successful campaign. The lobby undeniably played an important part in this transformation, but it can't claim all the credit. Carter lost his patience with the Palestinians, demanding from them a clear acceptance of Resolution 242, which was an unreasonable concession as it meant that the future of the West Bank and the Gaza Strip would be in the hands of Israel, Jordan and Egypt. The PLO demanded that it should be the only representative of the Palestinians in any negotiation on the future of historical Palestine. Carter's demand thus contradicted the idea of legitimising the PLO as a partner in the peace process – it seems in hindsight that he regretted his impatience, but at the time, his early determination petered out and there was no significant change in American policy. His lack of resolve created a vacuum, which was filled immediately by local actors, such as Egypt, diverting the diplomatic effort away from the Palestine question to a bilateral agreement between Israel and Egypt, at the expense of the Palestinians.

Carter was enthused by this new direction, forsook the Palestinians and became the mediator who celebrated with Egyptian president Anwar Sadat and Israeli prime minister Menachem Begin, at the successful Camp David Summit in September 1978. On 16 March 1979, an agreement was signed and the three-way handshake on the White House lawn made the history books. The agreement had two basic features. One dealt with the bilateral relationship between Israel and Egypt, based on full Israeli withdrawal from the Sinai Peninsula in return for full diplomatic relations between the two states. The second was a promise to discuss the future of the occupied Palestinian territories in a process that would be led by Israel and Egypt.

This agreement expunged the future of Palestine from Carter's presidential agenda. He was initially willing to go further towards a just solution to the Palestine issue than any president before him, but the half-mile he covered was not sufficient to change the reality on the ground. For the purposes of this book, it is important to examine more closely the role of AIPAC in Carter's swift retreat from the path he first embarked on in the Clinton speech in 1977 to its total desertion in September 1978.

AIPAC's aim was to guarantee that whatever complexion different administrations gave to American policies towards Israel, the overall outlook would not alter in any significant way. America would continue to furnish Israel with as much military aid as possible and provide international immunity against any global condemnation or rebuke.

When it came to these two principles, military aid and international immunity, American policy was a zero-sum game. There was nothing new about it. From the very beginning of lobbying for Zionism until today, there remains no option for reserved, conditional support. As Congressman Paul Findley would opine some years later, one's support had to be 100 per cent; give ninety per cent support and they'd allege you were an anti-Semite (as will be demonstrated a bit later when we look at his particular clash with AIPAC).[113]

On these two fronts, military aid and international immunity, the lobby had no issues with Carter. It entered a new field of activity when it decided to add a third dimension to its activity: controlling the narrative on 'Palestine' and the 'Palestinians' or, in other words, fighting against any attempt to legitimise the Palestinian narrative.

The day Carter pronounced the word 'homeland', he became the lobby's enemy. To accord the Palestinians any consideration whatsoever was completely taboo – and Carter went even further, by daring to broach the issue of displaced Palestinian refugees once again. It didn't matter that he had made no political commitments; the very mention was enough to send AIPAC into overdrive.

AIPAC's printers relentlessly churned out data, articles and booklets, assisted by Israeli and pro-Israel academics. This anti-Palestinian propaganda then flooded the White House. The most important weapon in AIPAC's arsenal was a 1977 'Report on Middle East Refugees' by Joan Peters, who claimed that as Syria had 100 per cent employment, Palestinian refugees ought to resettle there. She later became notorious as the author of the bestselling 1984 book *From Time Immemorial*, which made the implausible claim that most Palestinians only arrived in the land in the 1930s, and moreover, that the expulsion of 'Arabs' in 1948 was merely a population exchange, as their numbers equalled the number of displaced Jews in Arab countries. By the time of the book's UK publication, her stock had fallen; even pro-Israel scholars could not ignore the serious errors in her scholarship.[114]

AIPAC fêted Peters's report, to counteract Carter's reference to the refugees as people displaced by force. Carter's team perceived a just solution to the Palestinian refugee problem as the key for any future comprehensive settlement of the Palestine question. The new administration's effort began with organising an ambitious conference in Geneva, involving all the parties concerned with Palestine, and aiming to deal with all outstanding issues around the Palestine question, including the future of the 1948 and 1967 Palestinian refugees (numbering five to six million at the time). Israel, and by extension AIPAC and other pro-Israel lobby groups, categorically rejected this approach. They tolerated Nixon and Kissinger's step-by-step approach that led nowhere and was bound to drag on while the occupation of the Golan Heights, the West Bank and the Gaza Strip could be further entrenched and expanded. At this time, the Sinai Peninsula was still under Israeli control, but there was Israeli willingness after the harsh October 1973 war to recognise it as Egyptian territory that would eventually be returned to Egypt.

The new approach was 'dangerous' in the eyes of AIPAC as it could reopen old wounds: refugees' right of return and the future of Jerusalem. The lobby headed a coalition that included the Anti-Defamation League and B'nai B'rith, intent on teaching the president 'the actual facts', in the words of Morris Amitay, then AIPAC's director. He even had a textbook for the president, *Myths and Facts*, published by *Near East Report* in 1976.[115]

The campaign against Carter reached its peak in July 1977. An ad hoc formation of pro-Israel leaders of the American Jewish community met with Carter, Vice President Walter Mondale, Cyrus Vance and Zbigniew Brzezinski. Needless to say, no Palestinian delegation would have been able to enjoy such a privilege.[116] If the White House were committed to balance, the best they could achieve was meeting with Arab-American organisations, but they only did so in December 1977. By this time, American policy was following the lead of the Israeli and Egyptian governments – as Begin and Sadat sought to reach a settlement between their two states. The US had lost interest in reigniting discussion about the fate of Palestine and the Palestinians.

At this July meeting, Carter experienced first-hand the zero-sum-game approach of the pro-Israel lobby. He was taken aback by their criticism. After all, regardless of any sympathies he might have towards the Palestinian refugees, he unambiguously opposed the establishment of a Palestinian state, only proposing limited autonomy for Palestine in a Jordanian–Egyptian-controlled West Bank and Gaza Strip. His call for Israeli withdrawal from the Golan Heights and the Sinai Peninsula in return for bilateral peace conformed to the terms of UN Resolution 242, which had been unanimously agreed upon only one decade earlier.

The lobby may have been effective enough to persuade a president frustrated with the lack of any progress in his peace efforts to abandon his attempt to change American policy, but this can hardly be put down to its one-dimensional propaganda campaign. What mattered was that by the time Carter reached the White House, AIPAC had a vice-like grip on Capitol Hill. Consequently, neither the House nor the Senate had any appetite for radical change.

The lobbyists did not get the assurances they wanted at the 1977 meeting. Luckily for them, Carter's initiative for a new Palestine policy did not take off either. Regional actors such as Anwar Sadat and Menachem Begin cast Carter in a new and attractive role: the facilitator of a historic bilateral Israeli–Egyptian peace agreement, but they had no inclination to involve him in futile talks about Palestinian autonomy in the West Bank and the Gaza Strip. The USSR was willing to co-operate with him at an international conference in Geneva (which in the end was foiled by Israeli intransigence), but he couldn't overcome domestic resistance to any change in direction regarding Palestine.

Carter was eventually persuaded to meet leaders of the Arab-American community in December 1977, the first time a US president had done so. The Arab-American delegation sought to counter the new orientation towards Egypt instead of Palestine by demanding the participation of the PLO in the diplomatic process. However, any attempt to convince the president to change American policy towards the PLO fell on deaf ears. As we have seen, a PLO that did not recognise Israel, or accept Resolution 242 as a precondition for any American contact with it, was deemed a terrorist movement that could not be included in the 'peace process'.[117]

In hindsight, we can see how, despite all efforts by AIPAC and its allies in the pro-Israel lobby coalition, there was a nucleus of support for the Palestinians within the Democratic Party that opened up lines of communication with the PLO for the first time. Communication between the two was initiated by the veteran diplomat George Ball, who served in the UN and the State Department, and the journalist Landrum Bolling, who was a committed activist for peace and social justice throughout his life. They were both part of Carter's inner circle and were in charge of these back-channel meetings with the PLO. There were others who mediated, such as congressmen James Abourezk and Paul Findley. The latter would pay a high price for this role, as we shall see, when he became AIPAC's enemy number one. These behind-the-scene discussions enabled the American ambassador to the UN, Andrew Young, to meet with PLO representatives. Some American diplomats were fortunate to talk to Issam Sartawi, one of Fatah's leaders, who commenced a direct dialogue with progressive Israelis on the ground, before he was assassinated.[118] None of these contacts led to any fundamental change in American policy, but the pro-Israel lobby nonetheless couldn't tolerate it.

Despite the actual influence Palestinians exerted on American policy being close to nil, the very attempt to exert such pressure was deemed a hostile act. The lobby needed to confront it, and assert its dominance over American policy. The concrete ups and downs in the 'peace process' were not necessarily reflected in the intensity of AIPAC's campaigning. The lobby was not concerned with whether the 'process' was moving forward smoothly or was stuck; what mattered was identifying any potential reservations about unwavering American support for Israel – and swiftly moving to defuse the threat.

This becomes apparent in the way the lobby tried to prevent Carter from playing the role he did in helping to finalise the bilateral agreement between Israel and Egypt. The most prominent representative of the pro-Israel lobby in his administration was Edward Sanders, who served as a senior adviser. He was a Los Angeles attorney and for a while the president of AIPAC. Sanders was instrumental in winning Jewish support for Carter in the election campaign.[119] He advised the president to adopt a low profile in the process and avoid trips to the Middle East. In the eyes of the lobby and its representative in the White House, Carter had one role: to please the Jewish electorate. In a January 1978 memo, Sanders wrote:

> If involvement in the Sadat–Begin peace process is too public, the Administration runs the risk of being blamed whenever difficulties arise ... We believe that a visible substantive American role is unnecessary ...
>
> The President has scored markedly at home by voicing explicit opposition to an independent Palestinian state (any diminution of that position would be harmful) ... Needless to say, serious domestic problems could occur if assistance to Israel is curtailed.[120]

But Carter did not heed the advice, visiting both Cairo and Jerusalem in March 1979. The final peace treaty would be signed on 26 March 1979, in Washington DC. However, even if AIPAC and its supporters in government couldn't prevent Carter mediating between Israel and Arab states, it did ensure that American policy still had support for Israel as its bedrock. As he negotiated the Israel–Egypt treaty, Carter promised to Israel that the US's military relationship with them would take on 'new and strong and more meaningful dimensions'.[121] Carter may have been sincerely committed to peace in the region; however, sincerity was not enough to overcome the pro-Israel bias long since baked into US policy.

CARTER'S *MEA CULPA*

In 2006, Jimmy Carter published his book, *Palestine: Peace Not Apartheid*.[122] The book cost him dearly: he was accused by pro-Israel groups and individuals of falsifying history and of being anti-Israel. Some even went as far as condemning him as an anti-Semite. The very use of the word 'apartheid' in the title, which today is more acceptable regarding Israel, was not common at the time, and definitely was not used by former presidents.

It is written as a memoir, covering his involvement in the Palestine issue since his first visit to Israel in 1973 up to the establishment of the Carter Centre in Atlanta after he retired from the White House. He did not cease to be involved in Palestine; in the 1990s and early 2000s he was part of an international team that monitored elections in the occupied West Bank and Gaza Strip.

He regrets not doing enough for Palestine, and attributes his failure to the power of the lobby which ensures that Israeli policies cannot be opposed by the USA, even by the US president:

> Israeli government decisions are rarely questioned or condemned, voices from Jerusalem dominate in our media, and most American citizens are unaware of circumstances in the occupied territories.[123]

Nothing could have prepared him for this reality. He had never been anti-Israel; his upbringing led him to believe strongly in Israel before he became president:

> I was excited and optimistic about the apparent commitment of the Israelis to establish a nation that would be a homeland for the Jews, dedicated to the Judeo-Christian principles of peace and justice, and determined to live in harmony with all their neighbours.[124]

Carter is vaguer about how far he was responsible for excluding the PLO from the peace negotiations. He repeats the fact that he demanded the PLO recognise Israel and accept Resolution 242, but seems to rethink whether this was the right attitude. At that time, he finally concludes that the PLO 'was out of diplomatic bounds ... still officially classified by the United States as a terrorist organization'.[125]

The second half of the book relates to events after his term in office. For the sake of this book, it is noteworthy that Carter believes Israel had already been involved in building an apartheid system when he was in office, but he was not aware of this at the time. Today, the apartheid framework is extended to describe both Israel and the occupied territories. Yet despite his convictions, Carter's hands were tied with regard to actually doing anything to change the situation. Reading the book, one gets the impression that Carter faced two apartheid regimes, one in South Africa and one in Israel, and despite his great ambitions as the leader of the foremost global superpower, he was quite restrained in influencing his country's policies to challenge both these apartheid regimes. Neo-conservative advocacy groups in America deemed South Africa an asset in the Cold War and restricted Carter's wish to be more pro-active against the regime in Pretoria. Despite declaring the protection of human rights as the main guideline of his foreign policy, the USA continued to support other dubious regimes around the world. His hands were tied even more tightly when facing apartheid in Israel by a pro-Israel lobby that was willing to destroy anyone's political career should they dare to confront Israel in any significant way.

Faced with spiralling inflation, a major energy crisis in 1979 and the humiliation of the United States after fifty-two Americans were held hostage for over a year by Iran, Carter lost the 1980 election by a landslide. The lobby could breathe a sigh of relief. His successor, Ronald Reagan, had no aspirations to be a peace-maker, and so the lobby's influence could grow uninhibited. But Reagan's penchant for arms deals with the Arab world soon started causing them problems.

RONALD REAGAN: THE GOLDEN YEARS OF THE LOBBY

You can't miss the McDermott Building, home of the eponymous legal firm at 500 North Capitol Street in Washington. A glass building with nine floors and a new roof deck, it was built in 1922 and renovated in

2012. It stands at the east end of the city, very near Independence Avenue and of course Capitol Hill. This proximity was needed for the third-floor occupants in suite 300: the AIPAC headquarters in Washington.

It was not the only AIPAC building in town, but it was more or less until 2009 its hub. In their book on the lobby, Mearsheimer and Walt publish several recollections of politicians invited there as part of what was called 'briefing', but was more of a 'grilling' of prospective candidates who were offered AIPAC's financial and political help in their campaign during the Reagan era in the White House (1981–1989).[126]

The lobby also had offices in other high-rises nearby on several blocks, forming a mini-empire, most of which could not be easily identified as AIPAC's bases. If you were perceptive enough, or interested enough as I was in the 1980s, you would realise you had entered the AIPAC zone by detecting a tightly guarded building with uniformed officers and remote-controlled entrance doors. The remaining staff members were located in seven geographical regions around the United States plus an office in Jerusalem.

'A gigantic fist: do it our way or you will pay the price.' This was the power of the pro-Israel lobby during the Reagan years, according to AIPAC's vice president.[127] And yet it soon found a policy it couldn't bulldoze, although it made a formidable attempt to direct its 'fist' against it.

The American military's latest toy, the Airborne Warning and Control System (AWACS), was offered to Saudi Arabia, together with an upgrade of their F-16 fighter jets, alongside other military supplies, in the largest foreign arms sale in US history up to that point. AIPAC reacted much more fiercely than Israel did – not least because Israel had clandestinely co-operated with Saudi military intelligence services since the 1960s. AIPAC, by its very nature, vastly exaggerated the threat of any policy that could even slightly disadvantage Israel. It also leapt at the chance to prove its usefulness.

The battle over AWACS, which Reagan won against AIPAC, was a bizarre spectacle of AIPAC's capabilities and deficiencies. It was led by Dale Bumpers of Arkansas, who won a seat as AIPAC devoted itself to demonising his rival, Senator Fulbright, in the early 1970s. Goaded by

AIPAC, he accused the White House of intimidation when it refused to retract the deal with Saudi Arabia:

> They [White House staff] do not have to make public promises. They know how things are done around here ... if you wish to desperately get something for your state, they do not have to say a single word ... you simply feel the pressure.[128]

This alleged 'intimidation' on the part of the White House seems like a friendly gesture compared with the brutal means AIPAC employed against the few congressmen and senators who dared to show only reserved support for Israel in the 1980s. In response to AIPAC's histrionics, Reagan made endless efforts to find a compromise with the organisation, as if it were a superpower in its own right. He beseeched friends such as the Jewish ambassador to Italy, Max Raab, Senator Rudy Boschwitz and others to mediate between him and AIPAC's leaders – negotiations that resulted in a 'compensation deal' for Israel, considerably adding to the immense amount of military aid the US already provided to Israel.[129] As Secretary of State George Shultz told a packed and cheering AIPAC convention in 1987: 'America's support for Israel has never been stronger or more steadfast.'[130]

This aid package was achieved through the efforts of a new recruit to AIPAC, who became known as the chief lobbyist on Capitol Hill, Douglas M. Bloomfield. He was enlisted in 1981 and served the lobby for nine years. Before that he was the representative of the World Jewish Congress in Washington, co-ordinating an American investigation into the role of Swiss banks in hiding gold and property seized by the Nazis during the Second World War. He was the legislative director of the lobby and in this role he was responsible for developing and guiding strategy on Capitol Hill to secure military and economic aid to Israel.

His political trajectory is one shared by many of those who would become important figures in the lobby. Like him, they would begin as a staffer in the office of a House representative or senator before joining AIPAC. First, Bloomfield was a member of the staff of a prominent House Representative, Benjamin S. Rosenthal. Similar trajectories were followed by Richard Perle (who later led the neo-conservative group that advocated the invasion of Iraq in 2003, and was an important supporter of Israel, while serving in the Department of Defense), who was part of Henry Jackson's office; Morris Amitay (who replaced Kenen as AIPAC's president in 1974), who was part of Senator Abraham Ribicoff's office; and finally Tom Dine (the executive director of AIPAC between 1980 to 1993) who was a member of Senator Ted Kennedy's staff.[131]

That the US sold AWACS to Saudi Arabia didn't change anything in the grand scheme of things. Nonetheless, AIPAC's own peculiar sense of self-importance led it to react very strongly to its failure to stop the Saudi deal. There was a sense that the lobby needed to find a better way to convey the strategic importance of Israel to the USA. To that end, Tom Dine, one of AIPAC's leaders throughout the 1980s, hired a former RAND Corporation strategist, Steven Rosen, as AIPAC's director of research and information. RAND was one of the biggest non-partisan American think-tanks, funded mostly by the government. Rosen's principal mission was to inundate policy makers with an endless number of pamphlets about Israel's strategic value compared to what the Arab world could offer. He went quite far, to put it mildly, in describing Israel's potential ability to face not only the Arab world but also the USSR. He told an audience of senior American naval officers that Israel would 'require no more than 1200 combat sorties to destroy the entire Soviet fleet in the region'.[132]

Researcher Helena Cobban believes that this new energy and orientation overwhelmed the Department of Defense to such an extent that it accepted a strategic relationship with Israel that exceeded the Department's own preferences, but, as she writes, 'they now saw no realistic way to avoid it'.[133] This is probably why the keynote speaker at the AIPAC 1988 annual convention was the defence secretary, Frank Carlucci, rewarded for publicly justifying this 'strategic' alliance that used American taxpayers' money to subsidise Israel's defence needs.

Consequently, despite an apparent 'defeat' for the lobby, the president did not change the balance of power on Capitol Hill in any meaningful way, nor did he wish to do so, and he would have failed if he had tried. As Cobban reminds us:

By the mid-'80s Congress did not need to be pushed by what was everywhere referred to as simply 'the Lobby', in order to tilt markedly toward Israel on a whole range of issues. Many members of Congress had long been used to applying different standards to actions undertaken by Israel and those undertaken by any other government, including their own, across a wide range of issues.[134]

All the AWACS affair did was demonstrate to the lobby that even the most sympathetic administration would not pander to every whim of AIPAC. This may explain why during the Reagan years, AIPAC doubled its lobbying efforts, targeting those who were unwilling to show unconditional support for Israel much more effectively. And thus the 30,000-strong membership had invested so much effort in terrorising potential anti-Israel candidates that in doing so they inadvertently allowed some of the actual policy making in Congress to pass unnoticed. Senators such as Charles Percy of the Republican Party, who were suspected of being unwilling to provide unconditional support for Israel, were deposed. We can, in fact, select any year since 1963 and find similar victims of AIPAC's campaign. In 1983, AIPAC succeeded in ending the political career of Paul Findley, a member of the House since 1961 and one of the few critics of Israel's policy in the occupied territories. Later, others whose loyalty to Israel was suspect were affected in a similar way, including the Democratic African American members of the House Earl Hilliard and Cynthia McKinney, as we shall see.[135]

Paul Findley, who wrote a book about his trials and tribulations and also gave interviews on the topic, has provided a forensic testimony of what it meant to be on the receiving end of the pro-Israel lobby's campaign.[136] In general, he noted that in the 1980s, AIPAC weaponised anti-Semitism, even before the state of Israel did so, to silence critics of Israel on Capitol Hill. He called it 'the reckless use of the charge of anti-Semitism'.[137] Readers will recall how in the first half of the twentieth century, supporters nicknamed 'the gentile Zionists' were severely criticised by the pro-Zionist lobby in Britain for deviating from blind obedience to the Zionist strategy on the ground in Palestine.

In an interview he gave to the *Journal of Palestine Studies*, Findley listed a number of American politicians whose careers, he asserted, were shot down for not being loyal enough to Israel in the eyes of the lobby: 'Charles Percy of Illinois, Walter Huddleston of Kentucky, Congressman Paul (Pete) McCloskey of California and me'.[138] They lost their seats, and their absence led to the silence of any voices critical of American policy towards Israel and Palestine:

> Now there's no one on Capitol Hill who feels it's worthwhile to speak out. All are convinced they'll pay a price if they do. They look at what happened to Percy.[139]

When Percy was interviewed many years later, he recalled that naively he could not believe that 'Israel has more power than that of the senators of the USA and the President of the USA'. In 1984, he paid the price for the lack of faith he had in the lobby's might. As it did in the case of Fulbright, AIPAC here too approached Percy's rival in the next elections, the Democrat Paul Simon, in order to unseat Percy. As Tom Dine recounted, 'We told him [Simon] run! We can help you; the committee will help you!'[140] Simon corroborated this in his autobiography. Dine thought the ability to persuade someone to run as a rival candidate became a new AIPAC strategy in the 1980s, although, as noted, it had a precedent in Fulbright's case. From that moment, Dine proudly declared, 'AIPAC was feared!'[141] Jonathan Weisman of the *Washington Post* referred to these tactics back then in the 1980s as a hunting season in which AIPAC was 'taking people out', including Jewish members of Congress.[142]

Findley believed that AIPAC's methodology was distinguished by its meticulous attention to detail. AIPAC and other groups such as the Anti-Defamation League published lists of 'enemies' of Israel, intended to 'intimidate journalists, professors, news media people, people in public life, and retired diplomats from speaking out on the Middle East'.[143] He further noted that AIPAC had 'a network on the campuses throughout the United States and trains college students in methods to keep critics of Israel off campus' and 'instructs students in how to harass speakers who do come on campus'.[144]

According to him, this effectively silenced Israel's critics in the USA:

> A colleague of mine passed the word to the lobby that I was thinking
> about an amendment to the aid bill and within a few minutes, two
> other members of the committee had calls from their home districts
> from pro-Israel constituents who had been informed about this
> 'Findley Amendment' and were worried about it and wanted a
> report. The congressmen came to me asking questions. It was a
> dramatic illustration of the effectiveness of the lobby in getting infor-
> mation, passing it out quickly, and getting a reaction from the
> precincts very rapidly. The lobby helps its friends; and it has almost
> instant access to members of the House and Senate. One of the
> lobbyists told me candidly that he can walk in and see just about any
> congressman he wants. No other lobbyists that I know of can do that.
> Most lobbyists figure they're lucky if they can get in to see two legis-
> lators a day. Not so with Israel's lobby ...[145]

AWACS was not the only bone of contention between AIPAC and
President Reagan. A debate evolved around the president's Middle
East peace plan, introduced in his first year in office. The peace plan
was devised by George Shultz, the secretary of state, and was
condemned by Menachem Begin, the Israeli prime minister. The
Reagan plan was relatively mild by today's standards. It opposed
Palestinian statehood in the West Bank and the Gaza Strip and at the
same time rejected Israel's annexation of these territories, proposing
instead a fully autonomous 'self-governing Palestinian authority'
linked to Jordan.

Israel's refusal to play along did not undermine its strong strategic
alliance with the USA. The Reagan years were also a period of dramatically increased strategic co-operation between the two countries.

THE LEBANON WAR, 1982

If the Israeli invasion of Lebanon in June 1982 was a seminal event in
the history of Israel, Palestine and the Middle East, and one that had

some impact on British policy towards Israel/Palestine, it did not have any lasting effect on American policy.

A year before the invasion, America was involved in attempts to prevent further deterioration on the Israeli–Lebanese border, an area of friction since the PLO moved to southern Lebanon in 1970 after being expelled from Jordan. The president entrusted the mission to a veteran career diplomat, Philip Habib. He failed to pre-empt the invasion and became the facilitator of the arrangements in Beirut after the end of hostilities during the summer of 1982. Quite extraordinarily his role in expelling the PLO further, to Beirut, and allowing the Israelis to stay on Lebanese soil for a long time, won him the Presidential Medal of Freedom – the highest official honour given to an American citizen by the president. It was not the first or last time those who failed to bring peace and justice to historical Palestine were rewarded with prizes.

At first, the US interest in this particular crisis was military. Israel shared Soviet weapons captured in Lebanon with Washington, along with lessons learned in confronting Soviet-built Syrian planes and air defence systems. American policy during the crisis pleased AIPAC. A week after the Israeli invasion of Lebanon, on 14 June 1982, Morton Silberman, the president of AIPAC, wrote to President Reagan:

> We are also proud of the stand you and your Administration took during the Lebanon crisis. It was clear that your Administration, unbending to foreign pressure and true to your commitment to combat terrorism, permitted Israel to effectively carry out its operations. As a result, a major source of international terrorism has been dealt a severe blow, and American interests have been enhanced. All American friends of Israel express deep appreciation for your support of our ally, Israel.[146]

The hope was that the president would continue this support after Israel's invasion of Lebanon commenced. As noted in the previous chapter, the pretext for the invasion was an attempt to assassinate the Israeli ambassador in London, Shlomo Argov. Nothing connected the incident to the

PLO, but it sufficed for the Israeli minister of defence, Ariel Sharon, to launch the attack. He broke a ceasefire Israel had with the PLO, and misled his leader and mentor, Menachem Begin, into thinking that he was aiming for a short-term and limited invasion, while he was actually planning to take over as much of Lebanon as possible and install a pro-Israel puppet Maronite president – one who would be forced to sign a peace treaty with Israel and secure its northern border.

It seemed likely that the lobby and the president would see eye to eye on the Lebanese situation, but realities on the ground cast some doubts on this unity of purpose. At the time when Reagan entered the White House, AIPAC was 50,000-strong and, apart from the AWACS affair, had an excellent relationship with the new president. However, the Israeli invasion of Lebanon proved to be a death-trap for both the Israeli army and the American soldiers who joined a multi-national UN peace-keeping force (MNF) established in August 1982 as an attempt to observe a *de facto* agreement by which the PLO leadership moved to Tunis and the Israeli forces withdrew to the south of Lebanon.

The first batch of eight hundred American Marines landed in Lebanon in August alongside French and Italian soldiers. Israel was reluctant and slow to withdraw from Lebanon, and proper resistance to its presence began, led by a new Shiite outfit: Hezbollah. These guerrillas also opposed the presence of the MNF and in October 1983 let the Americans know what they thought about their continued presence. Nobody in Lebanon interfered with the MNF when it oversaw the eviction of the PLO from Beirut in 1982; but nobody wanted them to stay there longer. A suicide bomber drove into the MNF's American headquarters, killing 241 American soldiers.

This calamity did not convince Reagan to withdraw American military forces from Lebanon, and AIPAC insisted on the necessity of them remaining there. But as the Israeli presence continued, it became more difficult to justify such a long military presence in the eyes of the American public. A new batch of Marines, coming directly from the invasion of Grenada, found themselves engaged in military confrontations with Hezbollah and the Syrian army. There were more casualties, and now Congress, reacting to their increasingly vociferous electorate, overwhelmingly demanded a complete American withdrawal. By 1984, Reagan caved in and ordered the full withdrawal of the American forces. The death of so many Americans was something Congress could not overlook and, since it did not directly relate to Israel, here the lobby could not change the consensual wish to bring the boys back home, so to speak.

The American blunder in Lebanon provided an opportunity for the 'Arabists' in the State Department and the CIA to remind policy makers in Washington that it might have been better to listen to them and their objections to supporting Israeli adventurism in the Middle East. During the early Reagan years, they had the ear of James Baker, at the time Reagan's chief of staff. This is why AIPAC targeted him as a potential problem as early as 1984. The lobby sent a memo asking for the White House to host, as it often did at the request of AIPAC, 'a cocktail party for their [AIPAC] "Capital Club" (read "heavy hitters")'. The memo noted that a similar request the year before had led to an event hosted by the vice president, George Bush Sr, and his wife. And the memo stated the main reason for the request:

> As we discussed, this social event might provide an opportunity for Jim Baker to develop ties with the AIPAC leadership that would benefit this Administration.[147]

Baker, as we shall see, would not be impressed by such tactics. He was not the only one: during the Reagan years, the lobby identified a hated trio: Vice President George H.W. Bush, Secretary of Defense Caspar Weinberger and Baker. For a while, Jeane Kirkpatrick, the ambassador to the UN, was also deemed to be a member of group. Very early on in Reagan's term, the Israeli air force bombed Iraq's nuclear reactor. AIPAC thought the president did not mind, which might have been the case, but Kirkpatrick collaborated with her Iraqi counterpart on a unanimous Security Council resolution condemning Israel, and the Reagan administration embargoed F-16 deliveries to Israel as a consequence.

But as long as Reagan was in the White House, running his crusade against the USSR, AIPAC saw him as a friend. He told an annual meeting of AIPAC that the USA and Israel had established a Joint Political Military Group, focused 'on the threat posed by increased Soviet involvement in the Middle East' – which was a bizarre statement at a time when there was hardly any Soviet influence left in the region. More important for AIPAC were promises to establish a Free Trade Area between Israel and the USA – but these were less successful in materialising. However, even these disappointments were sweetened by Reagan's public references to Yasser Arafat (the chairman of the PLO since 1968 and the leader of its Fatah faction) being 'anti-American' (which did not prevent the continued search for back channels with the PLO by the State Department).[148]

While AIPAC could confidently assume that the president was on their side and at their disposal, they had more serious problems facing the Jewish electorate of the Democratic Party on one particular issue – the continued alliance between Israel and apartheid South Africa. Here is how one of the top officials explained it to a worried congregation of the AIPAC rank and file:

> It is in this context [sic] to remember that Israel, at the request of the US government, has acted as a surrogate for Washington in the supply of arms, for example, missile boats. Geo-political interests are often counter to moral democratic imperatives in foreign policy, and this certainly is one clear instance of such a collision course. To summarize this point: Most Western countries trade with South Africa as do Arab, African, Asian, Latin, and Communist countries. Israel's percentage is miniscule. Israel's relationship with South Africa developed in large part because of the Arab boycott and of the constant threat from its Arab neighbors supplied by the United States, other Western countries, and the Soviet Union. This prevented Israel from having the luxury of choosing its trading partners. Finally, Israel's military relationship did not emerge in isolation.[149]

This analysis significantly underplayed the relationship between the two countries. South Africa was one of Israel's closest military allies and Israel was the most important supplier of arms to the South African army.[150] But these rather morally dubious arguments worked for quite a while to whitewash Israel's long-standing support for the apartheid regime in South Africa. More importantly, AIPAC echoed Israel's leadership's assumption that moral arguments or values were not very helpful in galvanising support for Israel in the USA. As former AIPAC director Morris Amitay declared at a 1983 conference:

> Moral authority has very little influence in politics. Few would attempt to convince a congressman to vote for an aid bill for Israel with an appeal on behalf of Israel's 'moral authority'. Rather, I would make an appeal based on Israel's value.[151]

The lobby not only escaped moral rebuke but was also pardoned for its alleged espionage work. In 1984, the FBI investigated AIPAC for spying and theft of government property.[152] The documents stolen from the State Department were mainly taken in order to pressure members of Congress on the various issues interesting AIPAC and Israel. This long-running espionage was chiefly meant to provide Israel with intelligence on the American response to Israel's request for a Free Trade Area. The Israelis suspected rightly, as it would transpire much later, that this was not a particularly favourable and efficient agreement compared to other free trade pacts the USA signed over the years. The scandal petered out relatively quickly as the FBI made the mistake of charging an Israeli diplomat, who happily accepted the charge, as an AIPAC employee. He had diplomatic immunity and escaped to Israel.[153] Today such an act would be more thoroughly investigated no doubt, but under a presidency that saw complex deals connecting the Islamic Republic of Iran, Israel and the Contras in Nicaragua, this was a relatively minor misdemeanour.

AIPAC also survived the Jonathan Jay Pollard affair. He was a young Jewish man from Texas who tried to enlist in the CIA in 1977. He was declined as a polygraph test showed he had faked some of his academic credentials. He fared better when he applied for a position in 1979 to work in the Navy intelligence service. His tendency to look for material beyond his remit got him into trouble and he was suspended for a while before he was assigned within this intelligence service in 1984 to a new anti-terrorist task force as an analyst.

In this new role he initiated contact with Aviem Sella, a senior officer in the Israeli air force who was on sabbatical in the USA, and offered to provide Israel with hundreds of thousands of documents on issues that the American intelligence community was reluctant to share with their Israeli counterparts (such as America's ties with South Africa, American free trade agreements and information the Americans had on the Soviet Union, the Arab world and the Palestinians). Seymour Hersch claims Pollard offered the same material for money to Chinese and Pakistani agents who declined the offer.[154]

Sella knew that Israel's national intelligence agency, Mossad, might have been uneasy about directly assisting an American Jew spying on its behalf on Israel's most loyal ally. Therefore, Sella handed over the material to a relatively new secret agency, called LATAM, an acronym in Hebrew for the branch for special assignments, run by Rafael Eitan. It operated alongside Mossad and it proved to be receptive and willing to handle the new mole. Officially it was established to protect Israel's nuclear industry, but it soon undertook missions even Mossad found too risky; one of them was spying on the USA. Pollard was paid by LATAM; $30,000 was deposited into a secret account in Switzerland and he was promised more at the end of his mission. His generous financial remuneration undermined his argument in court, after he was found out, that he acted from altruistic motives.

But he was not a very careful spy, and he was caught in 1985. He tried to reach the Israeli embassy and request asylum but was denied entry and spent a long time in jail until he was pardoned by President Obama in 2015.

Nonetheless, it should be stressed that AIPAC had very little to do with Pollard. In fact, in 1981, when the AWACS controversy erupted, Pollard offered his services to AIPAC's leaders, who found him to be too eccentric, and hence unreliable, to be employed by them. He was quite insistent and tried in vain several times to renew contact.[155] But the affair was a challenge to AIPAC, as the whole question of the dual loyalty of American Jews resurfaced as a result, and pleas by Israel to release him over the years did not help either. In hindsight, AIPAC's strategy of saying as little as possible about the affair was vindicated. Interest died out when more important issues occupied both Israel and the USA in the final years of the Reagan administration.

For Israel, AIPAC's main role in the Reagan years was to help alleviate the pressure brought about by its own economic crisis that erupted in the mid-1980s. The state was hit by hyper-inflation (up to 1000%) and needed American financial support. AIPAC was able to cultivate Shultz as its main delegate in the effort to push Congress to increase aid to the Jewish state.

Towards the end of the Reagan era, a significant changing of the guard took place in AIPAC. In essence, and in relative terms, more moderate leaders were replaced with more hawkish and neo-con members of the lobby and, more importantly, those who were strong believers in the need for AIPAC to be bipartisan were removed and substituted with pro-Republican personal.

The first one who was forced to resign was Douglas Bloomfield – as mentioned, he had been dubbed 'top lobbyist for AIPAC' in the 1980s. His official title was that of legislative director of AIPAC, a position he had held since 1981. He received two weeks' notice to pack his things and leave. His nemesis in AIPAC was Steve Rosen, another top official, who was steering AIPAC away from its bipartisan aspirations and image. Rosen allied with powerful members in the lobby such as its chairman, Robert Asher, and its president, Edward Levy Jr. These two were now openly calling the faithful to vote for the Republican Party, a campaign they intensified when the Reagan era came to an end, and George Bush Sr became 'their candidate'.[156]

The internal strife led to more resignations. A pro-Israel representative warned the organisation (via *Associated Press*):

> The partisanship that is perceived as creeping into AIPAC's decision-making will hurt them in the long run. They have to understand that the real bedrock of Israel's support is the Congress. Administrations come and go. We're pretty constant and reliable.[157]

The issue, it seems, was not only the drift towards the Republican Party, but also a takeover by businessmen, as pointed out by Amitay, who left the group in 1980:

> The organization should be professionally run. When real-estate dealers and land salesmen try to make the decisions, they are asking to be co-opted by the administration ... Why should (Secretary of State) George Shultz listen to AIPAC?

He added:

> To me, this is so fundamental. It is beyond personalities, beyond partisanship. Now damage is being done to the lobbying arm of the organization.[158]

AIPAC AND THE AMERICAN–PLO RAPPROCHEMENT, 1988–1989

The American relationship with the Palestinians in general and with the PLO in particular moved along two separate tracks in the 1980s. The administration had maintained backdoor contact with the PLO ever since 1981 which culminated in the American recognition of the PLO at the end of 1988. At the same time, Congress, under strong pressure from AIPAC, embarked on series of legislative measures meant to prevent any rapprochement between the USA and the PLO. It should be obvious that the official recognition marked another failure of the powerful lobby. Alas for the Palestinians, this failure did not change their reality: by the end of that decade, and for many decades to come, they continued to live under a ruthless occupation and oppression, whether they dwelled in the West Bank or the Gaza Strip, or lived in refugee and exile communities where they were second-class citizens.

But it is also an intriguing chapter that exposes the power of the lobby and its limitations. Both these tracks have to be understood against the background of two momentous events that occurred within that decade: the Israeli invasion of Lebanon in 1982 and the outbreak of the first Intifada in 1987. These events caused a shift in some sections of American civil society, including among progressive Jews: a new under-current that would also influence both the orientation of the lobby and its ability to influence American policy.

But it seems that both the administration and AIPAC did not notice this undercurrent before 1987; their opposing politics were motivated by different factors. AIPAC became closer in that year both to the Republican Party and to the right-wing parties in Israel, and acted more in accordance with this more extreme Zionist worldview which had never put much faith in any kind of reconciliation with the Arab world or with the Palestinians. As for the administration, we should recognise that until 1987 it was the PLO that initiated the contacts, and the American response was not negative but could hardly be described as enthusiastic. The PLO chairman felt, although not everyone around him agreed, that after the expulsion from Lebanon and without a super-power to support the liberation struggle, it was time to be part of the Pax Americana.

The contact with the PLO that began in 1981 was conducted through a mediator named John Edwin Mroz, an expert on the Middle East who worked for a New York-based foundation. It was overseen by Alexander Haig, the secretary of state at the time, who entrusted the assistant secretary of state, Nicholas Veliotes, with representing the administration in these negotiations. When George Shultz replaced Haig, he continued the effort throughout 1982 up to the Israeli invasion of Lebanon and the expulsion of the PLO to Tunis in June of that year. Mroz met Yasser Arafat and his two deputies, Abu Jihad and Abu Iyad, and all three conveyed the message that the PLO was willing to declare the end of the armed struggle in return for American recognition of the PLO.[159] The talks continued uninterrupted until 1984.

There was a certain lull in the discussions in the next few years. It should be remembered that officially Congress had already banned any contact with the PLO in 1975, so all the conversations were informal.

Until that time, Congress moved in the opposite direction, under the guidance of AIPAC. It seems that around 1985, the lobby wanted, or was directed by Israel, to nip in the bud any possibility of a new

American policy towards the PLO. In 1985 it prodded Congress to codify a policy prohibiting negotiations with the PLO, and a few days after the outbreak of the first Intifada, AIPAC succeeded in pushing forward an anti-terrorism act that defined the PLO as a terrorist organisation. Its official publications, the most important of which were its annual policy reports, still commended the president for his refusal to recognise the PLO or to negotiate with it and urged him to look for an alternative Palestinian leadership.[160]

With that AIPAC showed it was either unaware of how far the administration was leaning the other way or decided to ignore the shift. But it was not only countering the administration's policy; it also did not align with the way the first Intifada was received in American civil society. Public opinion in the USA for the first time began to shift dramatically towards supporting the Palestinians and questioning the past depiction of the Palestinian liberation struggle as terrorism.

Within one year, hesitant American–PLO negotiations ended with an official American recognition of the PLO. This accelerated process is well described by Muhammed Rabi, who at the time headed an independent educational NGO in Washington. Rabi was part of a team at the Brookings Institute, headed by William Quandt, that in July 1988 had already prepared a detailed document that urged the American administration to officially recognise the PLO. At the very same time, a similar plea came from the Swedish foreign ministry, which also intensified its contacts with the administration and with progressive Jewish voices in America with a similar aim, and offered to mediate between the PLO and the USA.[161]

After the November 1988 elections, both the president, Ronald Reagan, and the president elect, George Bush Sr, endorsed more warmly the Swedish offer to mediate between the secretary of state, George Shultz, and Yasser Arafat, also using the historic declaration of independence by the Palestinian National Council (the PLO's parliament) on 15 November 1988 as a landmark that justified an American U-turn. In the declaration the PLO's legislative body accepted the two-state solution as the basis for continued negotiations. While the meeting of the legislative body was taking place, American officials in Algeria took over negotiations with the PLO from the Swedes, and the road to official American recognition was open.

The end result was that less than a month later, on 14 December 1988, President Reagan issued the following statement:

> The Palestine Liberation Organization today issued a statement in which it accepted United Nations Security Council resolutions 242 and 338, recognized Israel's right to exist and renounced terrorism. These have long been our conditions for a substantive dialogue. They have been met. Therefore, I have authorized the State Department to enter into a substantive dialogue with PLO representatives. The Palestine Liberation Organization must live up to its statements. In particular it must demonstrate that its renunciation of terrorism is pervasive and permanent.
>
> The initiation of a dialogue between the United States and PLO representatives is an important step in the peace process, the more so because it represents the serious evolution of Palestinian thinking towards realistic and pragmatic positions on the key issues. But the objective of the United States remains, as always, a comprehensive peace in the Middle East.
>
> In that light, we view this development as one more step toward the beginning of direct negotiations between the parties, which alone can lead to such a peace.[162]

What caused the American change of heart? First of all, the American negotiators extracted from the PLO chairman agreement to the conditions that had been insisted upon ever since the days of Jimmy Carter. The PLO accepted Resolutions 242 and 338 and more or less renounced terrorism, while very few among the Palestinians accepted that their armed liberation struggle was terrorism. It was not predicated on the recognition of Israel, quite cleverly, as no Palestinian leader would have been able then, or even later, to become a Zionist.

One of AIPAC's former leaders, Douglas Bloomfield, asserted that this recognition occurred partly out of frustration with the government

of Yitzhak Shamir and partly as a favour to the incoming Bush administration. Israel's 1984–1988 unity government of Likud and the Maarach
(meaning 'the Alignment', a joint bloc comprising the Israeli Labor Party
and the Left Zionist party Mapam) was replaced by a right-wing government that showed no inclination whatsoever to be part of a peace process.
Both Shultz and James Baker were outraged by its intransigence and its
aggressive support for the expanded Judaisation of the West Bank.[163]

Cheryl Rubenberg offered a different explanation for the new policy
in 1989. She claimed that the American recognition of the PLO was not
done in good faith – the purpose was not to 'facilitate a just and permanent solution to the Palestine–Israel Conflict'.[164] Rubenberg made a
valid point that also is relevant to the eventual decision of Israel to
negotiate with the PLO in 1993. Both the Americans and the Israelis
hoped that negotiations with the PLO would bring an end to the uprising in the occupied territories that had erupted in December 1987, and
was not initiated by the PLO. The hope was that by promising the PLO
a role in running some aspects of Palestinian life, the chairman of the
PLO would at least tame his movement's desire for national self-determination. Moreover, the gesture of recognising the PLO was meant to
improve America's image in the Arab world, and depict Washington as
an even-handed mediator.

Whatever the real motives were, in December 1988, Israel and
AIPAC faced a new reality. It took the lobby by surprise because earlier
in 1988, it had still been able to galvanise Congress to take even more
draconian measures against the PLO. In March 1988, Congress enacted
a law that had been passed in 1987, ordering the closure of the PLO
observer office in New York – this was the office of the Palestinian delegation that participated in the UN sessions. This time the Arab-
American community did not remain passive. The Arab-American
advocacy groups, together with the Arab ambassadors to the UN, took
the matter to the International Court of Justice in The Hague, with the
support of the UN, and won the case when the Court ordered the USA
not to shut down a body that was affiliated with the UN.[165]

Bloomfield tells us that a top aide in the Israeli prime minister
Yitzhak Shamir's office called the leader of AIPAC, urging 'Israel's

friends on Capitol Hill' to start a 'firestorm' of protest against the move. The firestorm was never ignited and the whole campaign turned into a storm in a teacup.[166] However, anyone in AIPAC endorsing the administration's move was immediately ostracised. Many scholars have overlooked the impact the recognition of the PLO had on the Democratic old guard of AIPAC's founding fathers, most of them deemed redundant by Rosen. They saw no reason to be more pious than the president on the issue of the PLO. One such person, Tom Dine, called for the creation of an independent Palestinian state alongside Israel on C-SPAN and was duly fired. He was not the only one purged at that time.

Reagan, with Shultz's help, by then enjoyed such a high level of trust in the pro-Israel camp that the decision to recognise the PLO went unchallenged. What was once unacceptable had become the norm, setting the stage for ambitious but largely unsuccessful peace efforts by succeeding administrations. It was not AIPAC that doomed these efforts to failure; Israel moved to the right, and the various American initiatives continued to disregard the basic aspirations and rights of the Palestinians.

And yet I think that the most formidable challenge for AIPAC was not the policy of the administration. Presidents come and go, and so do Secretaries of State. But public opinion is not a pendulum that sways easily from one side to the other. It is affected by trends that have longevity beyond that. It was clear by the end of the 1980s that the progressive Jewish voice was not part of the constituency of AIPAC anymore. More Democrats found it difficult to approve of a lobby that was identified only with the right wing of Israeli politics. The most important constituency that still could be relied upon was the Christian Zionists. Before they make a grand re-entrance in the 1980s, let's rewind to the 1970s, and look at the fate of the lobby in that decade.

WITH GOD ON THEIR SIDE: JEWS AND CHRISTIANS FOR ISRAEL, 1970

Ominous music was heard all over cinemas in America. Kids who skipped school to go to the movies regretted their escapades. Troy Fidler was nine years old when he was taken to the Fox Theater in Bakersfield, California, to watch Orson Welles's *The Late Great Planet Earth*. 'This movie was scary', he remembered; Joel Decoster had a similar recollection: 'the movie scared the s...t out of me when I first saw it as a teenager.'[167] These children and the faithful Christians and folks who loved science fiction fell silent when on the screen they could see a bunch of 'Arabs', which transpired very soon to be ancient Hebrews, chasing a Gandalf lookalike, who surprisingly leapt effortlessly over a steep rock, before reaching a dead end and facing his pursuers, who, with one blow to his head, kicked him over into the abyss. If this was not enough, these ancient Hebrews continued to stone the poor fellow. In the next scene Orson Welles rediscovers the skull of the hunted man and declares him to be the old Hebrew prophet Jeremiah, who suffered such a brutal death because he was thought to be a false prophet. Wrongly so, Welles assures us, since his apocalyptic prophecies would be fulfilled to the letter in the 1980s.

Thus begins the film, *The Late Great Planet Earth*, adapted from Hal Lindsey's book of the same title which sold millions of copies in a short time and was a blockbuster hit all over the USA.[168] Born in Texas, Lindsey was enrolled, from a very early age, in the religious education system in the south of the USA. The Israeli victory in the June 1967 war turned him into a preacher who combined pro-Israel stances with fundamentalist Christian fervour. He sprang to public attention with the publication of that book in 1970. He was one of the early televangelists, working at TBN. He had to leave the network in 2005, rumoured to have been forced to do so as his constant support for Israel coupled with virulent Islamophobia was too much to digest, even for that network. He moved to the Angel One and Daystar networks which were very happy to broadcast his messages. He later returned to TBN with his own show, albeit self-funded.

The next scene of the film shows the prophet Jeremiah as the epitome of Hollywood's image of a modern-day poet: a slim, slightly bearded, handsome young man conversing with God. The rest of the film, like the book, narrates the establishment of Israel in 1948 as the first landmark in a new trajectory that would lead to the end times and the Second Coming of the Messiah, in accordance with biblical prophecy.

Apart from the establishment of Israel, most of these predicted events did not transpire at all, such as Lindsey's warning that the creation of a dreary and bureaucratic ten-nation Western European confederacy would wreak mayhem and disaster on the continent. Lindsey's anti-European integration rhetoric, though, could have made him a star on the Leave campaign bus during the UK debate on Brexit, as he framed what he called the European confederacy as the new Antichrist. He lacked the divine insight needed to prophesy the fall of the Soviet Union – in his later book, he suggested it would endure until the end of time itself.

The fact that most of his prophecies were not fulfilled did not puncture Lindsey's popularity and he continued to play a crucial role within the Christian Zionist lobby for Israel. Year after year, solidarity with Israel was spearheaded by Christians who wanted to see the state as a battlefield for the final confrontation between the forces of Good and Evil.

Lindsey was not content with books and a film. He organised and led frequent trips to the site where the battle was supposed to occur: Tel Megiddo, on the ruins of the Palestinian village of Lajjun which was destroyed in 1948. He would usually take with him about two hundred of his flock. On his visits, he was allowed by the Israelis to enter the Megiddo Prison, a notorious incarceration camp where many Palestinian political prisoners were held. The prisoners were employed by the prison as diggers; they exposed a well-preserved mosaic which had adorned the floor of what may have been, according to Lindsey and the Israeli archaeologists, 'the Holy Land's oldest church'.[169] Among the sixty prisoners employed, one prisoner was hailed on Israeli and American TV as a happy amateur archaeologist. The fact that he was there as a political prisoner did not seem to trouble the Christian Zionists.

The film and the tours were very much the product of a new wave of Christian identification with Israel after the June 1967 war. After the war, the Christian and Jewish lobbies were working more in tandem than ever before. But it took some time before the Jewish lobby was willing to be associated so clearly with such fundamentalist outfits. The hidden, but staunch, anti-Semitic element within the millenarian dogma deterred the pro-Israel lobby at first from joining forces too visibly with the expanding network of Christian fundamentalist organisations. But it was difficult to withstand the temptation. With the election of Menachem Begin and Likud in 1977, all this changed. Menachem Begin, ironically one of the most nationalist leaders of Israel, who represented more than anyone else the idea of the proud new assertive Jew, led the way to a new alliance with Christian Zionists. He was helped by an enthusiastic young Likudnik, Benjamin Netanyahu, who had just returned from his studies in the USA and joined the party's leadership, beginning his ascent to its very top.

In 1978, one year into Begin's first ever term in office (after being in opposition since the creation of the state of Israel in 1948), the Likud government declared its intention to strengthen the connection with Christian fundamentalists. Their anti-Semitism was absolved. Christians who were never anti-Jewish, but dared to criticise Israel, became the new Christian anti-Semites.

After Likud came to power, and as the occupation of the West Bank and the Gaza Strip continued, it was difficult to galvanise support among progressive American Christians or Jews. Israel moved to the right, and so did the lobby. Therefore, the lobby, whether Christian or Jewish, had to rely on neo-conservatism, fundamentalism and right-wing American politics. To celebrate this new marriage a new venue was established, the International Christian Embassy Jerusalem, and the matchmaker was Netanyahu.

The embassy was located in the neighbourhood of Qatamon in West Jerusalem. Before 1948, this quarter housed the urban Palestinian elite of the city and in many ways of the country as a whole. When the Israeli takeover of West Jerusalem commenced at the beginning of January 1948, this part of the city was subjected to weeks of heavy Zionist artillery shelling that forced women, children and elderly residents to flee. After the Haganah, the main Zionist military militia, occupied Qatamon on 1 May 1948, its elegant houses were looted but not demolished, unlike the houses in nearby Palestinian villages. One Jewish nurse recalled the widespread pillage:

> For days you could see people walking by carrying looted goods ... I saw them walking by for days. Not only soldiers, civilians as well. They were looting like mad. They were even carrying dining tables. And it was in broad daylight, so everyone could see.[170]

The emptied houses were offered to senior clerks in the Israeli government and to foreign countries as locations for their embassies. One of its most beautiful villas still stands today on 20 Rachel Imenu Street. It was built in the 1930s by the Palestinian contractor Ibrahim Haki. It's distinguished by its façade of six arches and a carefully cultivated garden. The family who lived there sold the house to the Czech Republic, which stationed its consulate there until 1948. After the Nakba, Ivory Coast took it over as an embassy, until the Israeli violation of the UN resolution on the internationalisation of Jerusalem forced it to move the embassy to Tel Aviv. The Shalom Hartman Institute took it over and in 1997 it became the International Christian Embassy Jerusalem (it had already opened in 1980 elsewhere in the city). In return for having a place for its work, which Orthodox Jews suspected was proselytising, the Embassy raised funds to help finance Jewish immigration into Israel from the Soviet Union as well as the construction of Jewish settlements in the West Bank.

The appointment of Benjamin Netanyahu as Israel's ambassador to the UN in 1984 strengthened the connection between Israel and American Christian Zionists. He served in this position for four years. In his second year on the job, he declared in front of the annual convention of Christian Zionists that their support for Israel was a superior moral deed. That night he endeared himself to his Christian fundamentalist audience. The churches did not stop at warm words; they established a specific organisation, Christians United for Israel, which focused on helping Israel inside the US – later to be exploited by Netanyahu when he became prime minister.[171]

The Reaganite foreign policy of the 1980s and its accompanying ideological narrative – which claimed that this American president and his British counterpart, Margaret Thatcher, were leading a hawkish West into decisive victory over the great Satan in Moscow – further reinforced Christian Zionism. It was also fed by a TV revolution that bowdlerised the American value system and collapsed fundamentalist Christianity into the dimensions of the small screen. Flamboyant men appeared as preachers and succeeded, in the typical discourse of this shallow medium, in conveying even more simplistic messages from the Christian Zionist pulpit.

This is how the tele-preachers of Christian fundamentalism became the face of the pro-Israel lobby in the 1980s. Famous evangelical conservative preachers such as Jerry Falwell and Pat Roberson were leading the way: 'to stand against Israel is to stand against God', they declared (although it should be noted that earlier on some of this discourse had also been adopted by Martin Luther King).[172]

In 1980, Jerry Falwell received the Jabotinsky Centennial Medal from Menachem Begin. The various groups that fell into the category of Christian Zionism won an unprecedented place in the Israeli political system. So, despite vigorous opposition from the Orthodox Jews in Jerusalem to any missionary work in the city, Falwell and his friends shifted the focus of Christian Zionist activity to Jerusalem. Ever since, every few years, the city has hosted the main convention of the American Christian Zionists – a body that has adopted a host of resolutions call-ing upon Israel to pursue an expansionist policy in the occupied terri-tories and encouraging the US to wage continuous war against Islam and the Arab world. These positions were taken long before the US was attacked by Al-Qaeda.[173]

The Israeli invasion of Lebanon in 1982 opened up another location for the Christian Zionists. Until the Israeli withdrawal in 2000, the southern part of Lebanon was designated by Israel as a security zone, run by the South Lebanese arm of a local militia commanded by Maronite officers overseeing a group of Druze, Shiite and Maronite soldiers. It was dismantled after the Israeli withdrawal and many of its officers moved to Israel. Within that 'security zone', Christian fundamentalists were allowed to open a TV station, Hope TV. This station was bought in 1982 by the Christian Broadcasting Network; it broadcast from Marj Ayyun in South Lebanon until 2000, when it moved to Cyprus after Israel was forced to leave the south by Hezbollah. Its official name is Middle East TV (METV) and it still operates today. It began by broadcasting WWF wrestling competitions and soon moved on to televangelism. It targeted children with animated films about Jesus and his fight against the 'evil' Jewish priests throughout his life, but its prime-time programmes called upon the faithful to show unconditional allegiance to the Jewish state.

During the time of the Reagan administration (1981–1989), this kind of joint Christian and Jewish lobbying for Israel went on unhindered. Netanyahu integrated the Christian fundamentalists into Israeli *Hasbara* ('propaganda') – in this case a state PR attempt to manage views of Israel abroad. A few months before he was elected to his first prime ministerial term in 1996, the Christian university he helped to establish in Jerusalem published the following proclamation:

God the Father, Almighty, chose the ancient nation and people of Israel, the descendants of Abraham, Isaac and Jacob, to reveal His plan of redemption for the world. They remain elect of God, and without the Jewish nation His redemptive purposes for the world will not be completed.

Jesus of Nazareth is the Messiah and has promised to return to Jerusalem, to Israel and to the world.

It is reprehensible that generations of Jewish peoples have been killed and persecuted in the name of our Lord, and we challenge the Church to repent of any sins of commission or omission against them.

The modern Ingathering of the Jewish People to *Eretz Israel* and the rebirth of the nation of Israel are in fulfilment of biblical prophecies, as written in both Old and New Testaments.

Christian believers are instructed by Scripture to acknowledge the Hebraic roots of their faith and to actively assist and participate in the plan of God for the Ingathering of the Jewish People and the Restoration of the nation of Israel in our day.[174]

This rhetoric became somewhat watered down during the days of Reagan's successor in the White House, George Bush Sr. For a short while, the gods of petroleum, cement and neoliberalism competed successfully with the divinities of Christian Zionists and their representatives on earth.

LOBBYING UNDER BUSH SR: BETWEEN OIL AND GOD

George Bush Sr was part of an American elite that for years sustained the connection between power and money as its launching pad for successful political careers. His family were embedded into the revolving door that existed between the upper echelons of the Republican Party and big business. ARAMCO and the huge construction and cement company Bechtel provided employment for George Shultz and Caspar Weinberger who served Republican administrations. It may have been expected that these oil, cement and armament profiteers would steer American policy away from a battle between God (Israel) and Satan (the Arab world, the Soviet Union, critics of Israel, etc.). In some ways they were more critical of Israel than the Democrats, but in the end they did not cause a shift in American policy.

This military-industrial nexus had representatives in high positions in the administration: a secretary of state here and a national security adviser there. Some of the captains of the arms industry, of course, benefited from military aid to Israel. But others did not fail to see the prospective financial wonderland just waiting for them to reach out in the Arab world. But these industrialists had no impact on American policy. No wonder Mearsheimer and Walt were so deeply frustrated when they saw such people, with their own impressive think-tanks and presence in the Ivy League, retreating helplessly in the face of AIPAC's charge forward. No wonder that in their seminal work they attributed such immense political powers and financial might to the pro-Israel lobby in Washington.[175]

But AIPAC can't take full credit for blunting this complex's ability to influence American policy. Throughout its history the oil complex did not try to sway American policy on Israel in any direction, contrary to

AIPAC's fears. As we've learned, the early oil companies did not stand in the way of pro-Zionist policy before the creation of the state of Israel and during its early years of statehood. The famous 'Five Sisters' (Standard Oil of California, Standard Oil of New Jersey, Standard Oil of New York, Texaco, and Gulf Oil) had drilled oil in the Arabian Peninsula since the 1920s and depended on the goodwill of local rulers and governments to protect their share of the royalties and profits that petroleum offered. It seems that until 1967, American policy on Israel and Palestine did not undermine the American bonanza in the Arab world.

Once Israel occupied parts of Arab states in 1967, backing Israel *and* maintaining strategic interests in the Arab world became a far more difficult juggling act. And yet the nationalisation of oil production all over the Arab world in the 1950s and 1960s undermined American profits much more than America's policy towards Israel. Despite clandestine operations led by the CIA to prevent large-scale nationalisation, it was now widespread, and it reduced the earnings of the American companies somewhat but did not disrupt the flow of oil to the USA in any significant way.

The pro-oil lobby in America, arguing for a more reserved position towards Israel, lost any efficacy it might have had when the oil-producing Arab states declared an embargo on oil shipments to the West in 1973. But when it transpired that this step was not meant to assist the Palestinians but to bring up oil prices, the embargo became a fleeting episode. After all, such aggressive tactics are the bread and butter of the capitalist system. And when prices stabilised, to the satisfaction of all concerned, the oil-producing Arab states began formulating a definite pro-American policy. The lesson was clear: American administrations found they could ensure oil flow from Saudi Arabia and, at the same time, categorically reject any sensible peace proposals made by the Saudi crown for solving the Arab–Israeli conflict. Saddam Hussein also contented himself with warlike anti-Israel rhetoric while shipping oil to the US. Only the Iranian Revolution made life difficult for the Americans but, to confront the new regime in Tehran, the Americans did not need Israel. They preferred to have Saddam Hussein as a bulwark, arming and financing him accordingly. Saddam was also led to believe that all his obsessions, including the return of the 'lost' Kuwait to Iraq, would be supported. In October 1989, after the eight-year Iran–Iraq War, April Glaspie, the American ambassador in Baghdad, recommended that Bush Sr issue a presidential decree ordering a significant improvement in the bilateral trade and oil relationship between the two countries. So, the US purchased one billion dollars' worth of Iraqi crude oil annually.[176] Until 1991 therefore, Iraq, rather than Israel, was deemed America's ally against the Islamic Republic of Iran.

One of the legacies Reagan left to his successor George Bush Sr was the recognition of the PLO. Since this move was welcomed warmly by America's allies in the Arab world, it was clear that the Bush administration would endorse it as well. And thus, discrete processes, such as the downfall of Soviet Union, the rise of the Islamic Republic of Iran and the first Intifada, led the new administration, for the first time since 1949, to focus on Palestine as the core issue in the region.

This new focus coincided with the rise of Israel's most right-wing government ever, one that rejected any compromise on Palestine. While ignoring that government's protests, the Bush administration engaged in a real dialogue with representatives of two Palestinian power bases: the PLO in Tunis and the Palestinian leadership in East Jerusalem, seated in Orient House. The two bases were perceived as 'moderate', not only by 'Arabists' in the State Department, but also by members of the White House. It was the first time since 1948 that any Palestinian group had been treated in such a way. This was a rare moment of all-Arab consensus on how to solve the conflict – on the basis of the two-state solution – and how to pursue the normalisation of the oil supply to the US. Everyone was happy, apart from Israel and AIPAC. In particular, the pragmatic stance of the Palestinian leadership in Orient House troubled Israel. Its government reacted with a policy of harassment and extensive construction of illegal settlements inside East Jerusalem. Officially America responded angrily, including a public rebuke from Secretary of State James Baker to the Israeli government. The pro-Israel lobby reacted on two levels: on Capitol Hill it undermined the alliance with Iraq, aided by its think-tank, the Washington Institute for Near East Policy, and in the public arena it tried to demonise the Jerusalemite Palestinian leadership as terrorists.[177]

It was easier to tarnish the positive image of Iraq built by the US ambassador on the ground. In 1991, AIPAC took a proactive role in trying to affect American policy beyond Israel.[178] AIPAC took centre stage in the American public debate in the wake of the Iraqi invasion of Kuwait and joined the almost universal American condemnation of that invasion. The US was not above invading other nations to serve its interests; while they were condemning Iraq, the US military had troops in Grenada and Panama. AIPAC created an anti-Iraq atmosphere long before Saddam Hussein's army invaded Kuwait, but the US ambassador in Baghdad concealed this from him, even suggesting that the US would not oppose the invasion. When Iraq did invade Kuwait, the option of sanctions was not even brought forward – it had to be military action. The president had been led to this uncompromising policy by a number of experts on the National Security Council and the Pentagon who had known links to the AIPAC-run Washington Institute for Near East Policy.[179]

The second goal, the demonisation of the Palestinians, proved to be tougher – not so much because of any particular change of heart among policy makers in Washington towards the Palestinian liberation struggle, but more because of dividends promised to those Arab states willing to be part of the anti-Saddam alliance. The Bush administration recruited Arab allies for a military operation that repelled the Iraqi forces and made promises in return that linked the post-invasion solutions with a peace conference on Palestine that was eventually convened in Madrid in 1991. Ironically, linking the fate of Kuwait with that of Palestine had been one of Saddam's demands to begin with.

WHEN YOU ARE SERIOUS ABOUT PEACE, CALL US: A FINAL SHOWDOWN WITH JAMES BAKER

On 10 June 1990, in front of 1,500 attendees, AIPAC's thirty-first annual conference commenced. In the huge ballroom of the veteran and mammoth Washington Sheraton Hotel, the day began with the screening of a film that praised Israel's successful absorption of the million or so immigrants who had arrived from the former Soviet Union.

In between clips of panoramic scenes from Israel, showing a flourishing country with no mark of any Palestinian presence, happy immigrants were interviewed telling more or less the same story: their arrival was the fulfilment of a two-thousand-year dream of returning to the ancient homeland. Given the fact that at least forty per cent of them were not regarded as Jews by the Israeli rabbinical institution (and some of them indeed practised Christianity after arriving in Israel) and that most of them either wished to move later to the USA or chose Israel as a capitalist haven when fleeing from the chaos after the collapse of the Soviet Union, this was a somewhat disingenuous message. But it was one that was hammered home by the main speakers of the day. As Tom Dine put it in his keynote speech, the film showed that this new immigration to Israel revalidated the Zionist project: 'Right before our eyes, this exodus is reaffirming the Zionist ideal and is reminding us why Israel is so precious to the Jewish people everywhere.'[180]

The new president of AIPAC, Mayer 'Bubba' Mitchell, noted that it validated another crucial claim of Zionism, that Jerusalem was the capital the Jewish people had craved for the last three thousand years: seeing these 'Jews realize their dream of "next year in Jerusalem" excites our imaginations on a daily basis'.[181]

The last point enthused the audience. Even before the end of the film, the delegates stood up, applauded loudly and joined in with the final score, singing *Jerusalem of Gold* by Naomi Shemer – a song first performed mere weeks before Israeli took over Jerusalem in the June 1967 war.

There were two reasons for this particular emphasis on Russian immigrants. The first was financial. AIPAC, on behalf of Israel, had requested a $10 billion grant to help resettle these immigrants and a $400 million loan to build housing for them (money that could and did eventually also go to the Jewish settlements in the occupied territories). Secondly, this was an attempt to shift the agenda in the public mind away from talking about the new rapprochement between the administration and the Palestinians, be it the PLO in Tunis, or the leadership of the Palestinians in the occupied territories. AIPAC wanted to present Israel as a continuous miracle, while depicting the Palestinians as terrorists intent on destroying the 'the only democracy in the Middle East'.

These messages were supported fully by half of the Senate who made it to the conference and were treated to a sumptuous banquet. They were also endorsed by two senior members of the executive who opposed Bush and Baker's advances towards peace with the Palestinians: Vice President Dan Quayle and Defense Secretary Dick Cheney. They all stood behind the recalcitrant Yitzhak Shamir, who refused to enter into any meaningful talks with the Palestinians, declaring that the status quo was the best Israel could hope for.

Some of senators were particularly outspoken when they rose to speak during the banquet, attended by more than two thousand people. Republican senator Bob Packwood from Oregon encouraged the stubborn Shamir not to cave in to pressure to concede territory: 'My policy would be – not one inch!' The guests ate it up, and he roused them further by shouting, 'If we fight, we will win!' His flair for dramatics won him a standing ovation. The governor of Virginia, Douglas Wilder, went on the attack against any gestures towards the PLO: 'We read his [the President's] lips about the PLO, now it's time for him to read the lips of the American people: "No more terrorists; no more negotiations with avowed terrorists"'.[182]

Tom Dine concluded the conference by reminding Congress of what was expected of it on an annual basis: 'the single most important message for you to convey to your legislators is how vital Israel's $3 billion aid package is to US interests in the region'.[183]

The message of AIPAC to James Baker was clear: do not link the promised grant to Israel with progress in the peace process. The apprehension was that Baker might do that. One year earlier, in his speech at AIPAC's thirtieth conference in 1989, he told the lobby that Israel should abandon its expansionist policies and added, 'lay aside, once and for all, the unrealistic vision of a greater Israel ... forswear annexation, stop settlement activity, allow schools to reopen, reach out to the

Palestinians as neighbours who deserve political rights'.[184] President Bush was quick to congratulate him on a candid and fair speech. He echoed Baker's call on the Israelis to stop the settlements.

He and Baker were the first American politicians to refer to the Jewish settlements in the West Bank and the Gaza Strip as a major obstacle to peace. However, neither they nor those who followed suit went beyond verbal condemnation; nothing practical was done to stop the Judaisation of these two areas.

The conference ended on 12 June 1990. The next day, Baker dropped a bombshell, giving the impression that Israel was now a belligerent state in American eyes and that US economic aid to Israel might be suspended. He appeared in front of the House Committee on Foreign Affairs, and rebuked Israel for its intransigence. He told Israel that the US would cease to pursue Middle East peace talks unless Israel stopped delaying proceedings. Or, as he put it bluntly: 'The phone number [for the White House switchboard] is 202-456-1414. When you're serious about this, call us'. Concretely, he demanded that the Shamir government accept the American offer to commence direct talks with the Palestinians that would lead to elections in the West Bank and the Gaza Strip of a local leadership that would continue the negotiations. So far, he told the House, Israel had rejected the plan and continued to build settlements.[185]

Baker's outburst was planned no doubt, but was uncharacteristic of someone most interviewers described as cold and emotionless.[186] But its immediate impact quickly vanished: two months later Saddam Hussein ordered his army to invade Kuwait, interpreting a conversation he had with the American ambassador in Baghdad as providing him with the green light for such an operation. He also assumed that occupation of another country was something Israel was licensed to carry out by the Americans. In his mind, he, as a loyal ally, ought to receive similar treatment.

Obviously, he was wrong, and President Bush organised an international coalition, including Arab countries like Jordan and Syria, although not Israel, to push Iraq's forces out of Kuwait. In an attempt to break the Arab alliance against him, Saddam Hussein launched forty-two Scud missiles into Israeli territory, hoping that Israel would retaliate and Arab countries would then withdraw their support for the US coalition. But the Israelis were persuaded not to respond. William Quandt made an intriguing remark about the link between Kuwait and Palestine, similar to views expressed by Saddam Hussein: 'it is difficult to imagine him [Saddam] making such an audacious move as the invasion of Kuwait, if Israelis and Palestinians had been engaged in peace talks.'[187]

Saddam Hussein lost the battle, and the Arab allies of the coalition were rewarded with an international conference on Palestine, the brainchild of James Baker who saw the war as an opportunity to do more than just tell Israel to call the president when it was ready. Bush's popularity soared after the war, and both he and Baker felt even more defiant against Israeli rejectionism and AIPAC's power in Congress. If Israel wanted a grant and a loan, it had to attend this conference.

In September 1991, the pressure on Israel grew. This time the president took the lead. In a press conference on 12 September, an angry Bush pounded on the table, directly accusing AIPAC of working against him; he described the lobby as a 'powerful political force' fighting against 'one lonely, little guy'. He was an American David battling against an AIPAC Goliath which prevented him 'from doing his job'. He reminded the Israelis that American troops manned the anti-missile systems that brought down the Scuds from Iraq, and risked their lives in doing so – an exaggeration, but a potent one.[188]

The pressure worked and Israel joined other countries in a Middle East peace conference in Madrid, which gathered there in the final days of October 1991. In one of the 3,418 rooms of the Royal Palace in Madrid, the largest palace in Europe, the conference assembled for an opening session. Its history stretched back further than its status as the seat of the Spanish monarchy: it was built on the site of the palace of the Umayyad Emir of Cordoba, Muhammad I.

Delegates from Lebanon, Syria, Egypt, Jordan and Israel were greeted by the Spanish king, and the co-hosts of the conference: President Bush Sr and President Mikhail Gorbachev.

Indirectly AIPAC was at least able to influence the question of who would represent the Palestinians. It did so through its connection with a new neo-con group of strategists who had already held senior positions in the Reagan administration. This particular group grew up around the Washington Institute for Near East Policy which was founded in 1985; the Institute's founding director was Martin Indyk, who had been a deputy research director at AIPAC.

Indyk was born in London into an Anglo-Jewish family, but grew up in Australia. He was attracted to Zionism at an early age and volunteered in a kibbutz in the wake of the October 1973 war – an experience he described as 'a defining moment in my life'.[189]

In Australia, he obtained a doctorate in international relations and after emigrating to the USA in 1982 he joined AIPAC. He had clear twin objectives in those days: a harsh policy in the Middle East towards anyone who did not co-operate with the USA, alongside solidifying the alliance with Israel. This strategy's first great success was in mitigating the US tendency to respond more favourably towards Palestinian aspirations after the first year of the first Intifada (1988) at the end of the Reagan era. In the 1988 report published by the Washington Institute for Near East Policy, *Building for Peace: An American Strategy for the Middle East*, the team under Indyk's leadership recommended more aggressive and coercive American policy towards the Palestinians and the region at large. The reason: 'the Palestinians seem to believe they can achieve more than is possible or, from the US viewpoint, desirable.' Two out of the four conditions for negotiations were the following:

> Any Palestinian participant must accept UN Resolutions 242 and 338, renounce terror and recognize Israel's right to exist [and] There should be a prolonged transitional period in which the intentions of the Palestinians to live in peace with Israel and Jordan could be tested.

Based on this paper, the Institute succeeded in ensuring that there would be no official invitation to the PLO. In contrast, the Reagan administration, as we've seen, went into negotiations with the PLO without these preconditions. So officially, the Palestinians were part of a joint Jordanian-Palestinian delegation. But there was also an informal PLO delegation. The Palestinians were led by a trio: Haidar Abdel Shafi from the Gaza

Strip, Faisal Husseini from Jerusalem and Hanan Ashrawi from Ramallah – all three were in constant contact with the PLO leadership in Tunis.

If you wanted to gauge the chances of the conference, all you had to do was observe the Israeli delegation. Prime Minister Yitzhak Shamir and Deputy Foreign Minister Benjamin Netanyahu did not manage to hide their disdain throughout the conference. The expression on their faces said it all: we were forced to be here, and we are just waiting for this ordeal to end. Shamir in fact flounced out in protest before the end and refused to allow his foreign minister, and nemesis in the Likud Party, David Levy (a Moroccan Jew who was much more interested in peace with the Palestinians), to attend.

The Palestinians on the other hand impressed the Americans as being pragmatic and very capable politicians. They came well prepared after working with experts in Orient House in Jerusalem, who were divided into teams, known in Arabic as the *Tawaqim*, toiling over detailed plans covering every aspect of a future independent Palestinian state in the West Bank and the Gaza Strip. Their ability to present their point of view was assisted eloquently in English by prominent American-Palestinian scholars who left their ivory towers to help the diplomatic effort, including the legendary Ibrahim Abu-Lughod and Edward Said. Their appearances at the time on American media won many over to the Palestinian side and accentuated the belligerent image of the Israeli government.

And yet the conference did not yield a solution in the long run or an end to the Israeli occupation. But it did cost Shamir the 1992 Israeli national elections and allowed Yitzhak Rabin to become Israel's prime minister once more. The attempt of the convenors to maintain momentum by creating bilateral working groups between Israel and the Arab states did not take off, and it did not help that Baker resigned in August 1992 to run Bush's presidential campaign.[190]

The ambassador to Israel, William Andreas Brown (1988–1992), described how unpleasant it was to be in his position at that time, but he had to 'soldier on' nonetheless. This gives an indication of the nadir to which the American–Israeli relationship had sunk in the early 1990s. Nevertheless – and this is highly important – Israel eventually received the grant, the peace process stalled, the settlements expanded and, as Brown put it, 'the worst sufferers in this whole process were Palestinians'.[191]

AIPAC was vindictive and during the election campaigns of 1992 attacked James Baker at every possible opportunity. The tabloid *New York Post* collaborated gladly with the ex-mayor of New York, Ed Koch, in smearing Baker. In March 1992 the *Post* ran a front-page headline: 'Baker's 4-Letter Insult: Sec'y of State Rips Jews in Meeting at White House'. This was reported by Koch who quoted Baker's dismissal of AIPAC's anger at his policies, by saying: 'F*** 'em. They didn't vote for us'. After the word 'they', the *Post* had added in brackets 'the Jews'. Needless to say, this was categorically denied by Baker and the president, which did not prevent lobbyists from suggesting he might be an anti-Semite. Interestingly, Jack Kemp, a former congressman who had heard the alleged statement and told Koch about it, apologised to Baker years later and claimed that Koch had 'mischaracterized' it.[192]

In any case, the Democrats were back in power in 1992. Both Israel and its lobby needed to face continued American scrutiny on the Palestine question. Some of the Israeli electorate embraced America's interest in the issue, but a more influential portion vehemently opposed American attempts at oiling the wheels of the peace process. AIPAC followed the lead of the latter.

LIBERAL ZIONISM IS THE NEW ENEMY:
THE CLINTON YEARS

Bill Clinton's arrival in the White House coincided with the 1993 Oslo Accords – a landmark agreement between Israel and the PLO – and Yitzhak Rabin's government's endorsement of the two-state solution. The illusion that Israel was reverting to more mainstream politics and away from right-wing Likud rule meant that, at least as far as a Democrat like Bill Clinton was concerned, Washington and Jerusalem saw eye to eye on the progress of the peace process. The only issue domestically for Clinton was AIPAC's close association with the Likud Party, in opposition between 1992 and 1996. The new administration had to walk a tightrope to manage its strategic affiliation with Israel's labour government, while not antagonising the lobby at home.

Even when the party was out of government, Likud still exercised an enormous amount of sway over AIPAC's policy, as it did over the Christian Zionists. In hindsight, AIPAC's concerns about a dramatic U-turn in American policy under Clinton were unwarranted. Progressive policies domestically did not automatically lead to progressive policies on Palestine. It seemed worrisome because the Clinton administration was far more cynical than ideological when it came to Palestine. This was a result of the impact that American academia managed to have on American policy from time to time. Usually, as Noam Chomsky has shown, this academic establishment simply provided scholarly scaffolding to policies from above.[193] But the boom in Peace Studies, Conflict Management Studies and the like introduced the world of financial businesses to the world of 'peace business'. Quantitative and qualitative methodologies were employed to prove relatively simplistic hypotheses of how best to maintain conflicts in 'low fire' or 'low intensity' mode, and how to use known tactics of compromise from the industrial world in the attempt to settle decades-long hostilities. However, these conflicts were driven by real injustices and moral principles that were quite immune to Madeleine Albright's assertion that you can build a solution on the basis of the maxim that everything that is visible is divisible: land, resources, blame and control. The long colonisation of Palestine and the concomitant oppression experienced by Palestinians proved to have much that was invisible to Western eyes and hence indivisible. Justice and the rule of international law were required, not smart hacks from the finance industry.

But even this academic approach, perhaps because it implied the division of land, worried AIPAC. They had no reason to be concerned, as time would prove these new conflict resolution theories did not harm Israel's interests. In fact, on the ground they had an even more negative impact on the Palestinians than the openly unsympathetic policies pursued by the previous administrations. New policies based on these academic hypotheses created the false impression that it was a historic moment when the USA finally recognised the Palestinians and their aspirations. As it turned out, anyone who cultivated hopes in this direction swiftly had them dashed by actual developments in the real world.

The group of academics and experts who were running the 'peace business' in Washington, through a revolving-door employment policy, deserve closer examination, as they reappear not only in abortive attempts to solve the so-called Arab–Israeli conflict, but also other conflicts in which America ended up intervening. I call their approach the Morgenthau and Waltz legacy.

I will use this context as an introduction to the Clintonian approach to peace, before analysing AIPAC's response to it. I will show that the progress of the peace process as a diplomatic effort, and as it unfolded on the ground in Israel and Palestine, had nothing to do with the way AIPAC's response developed. AIPAC was not interested in the peace process, neither in diplomatic negotiations nor as a transformation on the ground. It was focused on maintaining its own power.

THE MORGENTHAU AND WALTZ LEGACY

In 1943, the German refugee Hans Morgenthau became naturalised as a US citizen. He had arrived in 1937, taught at the University of Kansas and then moved to the University of Chicago. No other refugee apart from the German Henry Kissinger affected American foreign policy as much as he did. His book *Politics among Nations*, published in 1948, provides a clue to his future influence. Morgenthau likened foreign policy to policy in the business world – that is, decision-making free of sentiment or moral values and entirely based on cost/benefit considerations and balances of power. The young state of Israel was one of the first to take up his approach. Throughout October 1948, at the height of Israel's ethnic cleansing of Palestine, Morgenthau advised David Ben-Gurion on a host of political issues. The first prime minister of Israel decided to reward the academic guru by naming a destroyed and evicted Palestinian village after him. The village of Khirbat Bayt Far became Tal Shahar, a translation of Morgenthau ('morning dew') into Hebrew.[194]

Twenty years later, Kenneth Waltz followed suit. He spent most of his teaching years at the University of California, Berkeley, where he became the doyen of international relations as an academic discipline. His claim to fame was a book, *Theory of International Politics*, published in 1979, in which he challenged some of the basic assumptions of Morgenthau's realist approach; hence, while Morgenthau is referred to as the father of 'realism' in international relations, Waltz is the father of 'neo-realism'.[195] Waltz argued that, in the field of international relations, there are no clear patterns of conduct because of the absence of a point of gravity, and thus states act within an international anarchy that dictates and limits their options. Most states seek to maintain the status quo, and those who wish to change it do so mostly due to domestic factors, and not because the international system allows them to do so. Translated into practice, states' policies are still based on cost and benefit, but there are more unexpected factors which limit the effectiveness of this approach. His work still constitutes the ideological infrastructure of most studies in international relations research centres in America. From these centres graduated the American diplomats who were selected to conduct the peace process in the Middle East, guided to overlook issues such as justice or morality in the process and to take as few risks as possible. This suited Israel very well and disadvantaged the Palestinians considerably.

The first administration to appoint such a team was that of Richard Nixon, though it was not until the first Bush Sr administration that the existence of such a group became public knowledge. Various experts, some from the State Department and others from the National Security Council and academia, translated the realist and neo-realist theories into actual policies.

Under Nixon and Ford, this academic group of officials endorsed the 'Jordanian option' put forward by the Israeli Labor Party and peace camp: namely, looking for a solution that disregarded the Palestinians and their aspirations. The idea was that a territorial or functional partition between Jordan and Israel of the West Bank and the Gaza Strip would be the basis for a successful peace in the future. Very much like the Jewish parable, they were looking for a lost key where there was light and not where it was lost.

The first Intifada, and the lack of real intention on the Israeli side to concede control to Jordan in the West Bank, persuaded King Hussein to opt out of the 'Jordanian option'. The academic advisers of the Bush Sr administration now began looking to integrate the Palestinians into the negotiations more fully and the idea of a two-state solution began to dominate the research, the thinking and eventually the policy itself.

When Bill Clinton came to the White House, he brought a group of experts with him that helped to devise his administration's interpretation of why there was a conflict and the optimal solution to it.

The 'Clinton boys' laid down four neo-realist guidelines for a solution. These guidelines also permeated the approach of FAFO, the institute for peace in Oslo that assumed the role of mediator between the PLO and Israel in late 1992, leading eventually to the Oslo Accords.

The first guideline was that a peace process has to be based on the local balance of power in the contested area. Thus, when a search begins for the components of a prospective solution, these have to be adapted more to the viewpoint of the stronger party and less to that of the weaker party. We can clearly see, from the very beginnings of the attempt to construct a Pax Americana in Israel/Palestine – more or less since 1969 – that what the Americans marketed as a peace plan was a formula meant to satisfy the Israeli point of view. The result was a constant and curious disregard of the Palestinian point of view and, more importantly, of what American experts had themselves earlier defined as the heart of the problem: the refugee issue. So during the days of the Clinton administration's involvement in Palestine, the refugee issue was written out of the peace script. It is hard to think of a similar concentrated diplomatic effort in modern times that has evaded the root problem of a given conflict. The inevitable collapse of the peace efforts at subsequent stages has not altered the basic American position.

The second, stemming directly from the first, is that only the stronger party in the conflict should be consulted when the features of a prospective solution are sought. But within that stronger party, the mediators should seek out the 'peace camp': its viewpoint is the most flexible element on the side of the stronger party. And its viewpoint has to be imposed on the weaker party. The essence of peace-making thus became, first, to detect a 'peace camp' in Israel at every given historical moment, and then, to attempt to force its view on the Palestinians.

Until 1977, the Israeli Labor Party was that camp. Then, until 1984, the 'moderate' wing of the Likud Party won the title while it was in power. In the days of the Israeli unity government (1984–1988), it was not a party so much as a collection of political figures that, in the eyes of the American experts, represented the political centre in Israel. In the twenty-first century, Ariel Sharon (in power from 2001 to 2007) embodied this camp for the Americans, as did his successor Ehud Olmert, who replaced him as the head of the new party Sharon established: Kadima (2007–2009). Kadima, which did not survive for long, was the dream party for any American mediator who wished to implement the third guideline in peace-making; that is, that conflicts had be 'managed', not resolved. 'Management', according to the neo-realists, meant maintaining the conflict as a 'low intensity confrontation' – which meant violence would continue to be part of the reality on the ground, but would be tolerable, if not in the eyes of its victims, then at least in the eyes of the mediating superpower.

It became much more difficult to find such a peace camp after 2009, and the Obama administration mainly had to deal with the new reality in Israel – the disappearance of the peace camp and the total shift of the political system as a whole to the right. Obama's successor, Donald Trump, threw all principles to the wind and made no more effort to mediate in the Palestine question.

The final guideline was that the peace process has no history. Every attempt began afresh from a starting point that assumed there had never been such attempts in the past. Such an approach disables any learning process – crucial for anyone facing complex human problems of ethnic and national conflicts. This approach suited the interests of those who led the Zionist peace camp in Israel. When the US returned to the politics of Palestine in 1967, the Zionist peace camp's understanding – that 1967 was the day the conflict broke out – became rooted in the American perception of the conflict and its origins. As the stronger party was preferred over the weak, the Israeli denial of the 1948 Nakba and its role in the ethnic cleansing of Palestine was endorsed by the American peace negotiators. Therefore, the peace process became an effort to find a solution to the question of the areas Israel occupied in 1967. The year 1948 was excluded from the peace agenda and, with it, the Palestinians were first pushed out as participants, to be replaced by the Hashemites of Jordan; then Palestine was reduced to twenty-two per cent of its original space and 'Palestinians' were only the people living in that twenty-two per cent (the West Bank and the Gaza Strip).

It took until 1988 for a new Israeli and, in turn, new American approach to develop. The decline of the Soviet Union lessened the image of the PLO as a Soviet agent and eased the onset of PLO–American negotiations. These negotiations culminated in an American recognition of the PLO in 1988. The Israeli peace movement declared that it was now willing to enter negotiations with the PLO.

Again, there was a fusion of discrete historical processes, which matured during the Clinton administration. Never before had academics in the field of international relations been given such a free hand in engineering a peace process as Dennis Ross (who, during the Regan years, was a senior member of the National Security Council) and his friends during the Clinton days. The disastrous fruits of the theoretical games they played with the lives of Palestinians and Israelis are still with us. Moreover, if we sum up all the guidelines, their main failure was in overlooking the root problem.

Ignoring a root problem and focusing on its symptoms is as wrong in politics as it is in medicine. Think of the way Americans reacted to the 9/11 attacks, ignoring America's own role in creating Al-Qaeda, or the Clintonian policy towards crime in inner cities. A 136-page report published by the Police Foundation at the time, under the title *Inner-City Crime Control*, suggested the following: 'Instead of focusing on what causes crime, we focused on what can be done to control it.'[196] Much easier to ignore the racism and neo-liberal policies of impoverishment that are the core causes of rising crime and opt instead to tackle only the symptoms of the problem by sinking funding into police forces and expanding the network of community organisations.

The four guidelines were put to the test during the time of the Oslo Accords. The peace camp was now the Rabin Labor Party government.

The bargain was the same – Israel was willing to withdraw from only part of the occupied territories. The sole change concerned the new 'weak' participant: the PLO. It was asked to accept not only part of the territories, but also only part of the authority in them. In addition, it was asked to give up the refugees' right of return and its claim to Jerusalem. Meanwhile, the reality in the occupied territories changed as well – the settlement project expanded to such proportions that it simply underscored the humiliating nature of the new Israeli proposal for peace.

It is true that, in the very same period, the 1980s and 1990s, American peace-makers could have listed a number of achievements in the realm of Israeli bilateral relations with Jordan and Egypt. Ironically, these peace treaties were concluded because of minimal American involvement in the negotiations. The formula for their success – if the 'cold peace' between Israel and its two neighbours can be described as such – was that the treaties did not relate to the Palestine question.

The Madrid Conference of 1991, in the eyes of the Palestinians, deviated from this legacy and guidelines as, at least on paper, it gave them a voice and did not ignore the root causes of the Palestine problem. It also was accompanied by a vanishingly rare American public reprimand of Israeli brutality in the occupied territories.

However, this deviation did not last for long. Bill Clinton did not continue Bush Sr's tougher stance against Israel, and the Israeli Labor Party, coming back to power for the first time since 1977, returned to the old guidelines, ignoring what had happened in 1948 and trying to impose Israel's idea of 'peace' onto the Palestinians.

At the end of the day, Bill Clinton proved to be easier prey than AIPAC suspected. A typical Democrat, he was of the opinion that without the Jewish vote he could not win presidential elections. The victory of the 'peace camp' in the Israeli elections in 1992 enabled Clinton to pursue an explicitly pro-Israel policy that, ostensibly, did not neglect Palestinian interests. Indeed, Clinton invested much time and energy to the question of Palestine. But the people he appointed to produce a 'road map' for peace were mostly Jewish: the remaining 'Arabists' who had a foothold in these issues were pushed out. Without the 'Arabists', it was easy to advance, on 30 June 1993, a policy paper that stated that Israel should have a free hand in 'developing' (read: uprooting and colonising) East Jerusalem. So, the illegal settlements of the past became the integral neighbourhoods of the present. The door was opened for the settlement of 200,000 Jews in the eastern part of the city and the commencement of the transfer of its 200,000 Palestinian inhabitants.

Such an approach did not, on the face of it, require deep American involvement. But although in many ways the Oslo Accords began with minimal American involvement, it did become nonetheless an American show. In fact, for the troubled President Clinton, it was the only show in town. And, at first, it looked likely to work, since the Israelis and the Americans found a Palestinian leader who was willing to succumb to pressure, so completing the process: a plan for peace conceived in the Israeli peace camp, dictated to and accepted by the Palestinians. The plan was for limited Palestinian control over a small part of the West Bank and the Gaza Strip, without dismantling Jewish settlements or stopping their expansion, with no return of refugees and without a Palestinian political presence in Jerusalem. As we know now, this was possible because the Palestinian leader Yasser Arafat believed that this state of affairs was temporary and that the Israeli architects of the Oslo Accords would be loyal to their promise, after five years of an interim agreement, to proceed to the establishment of a fully sovereign Palestinian state. He misread Israel's intentions and interpretation of the 1993 Oslo Accords and also could not predict that Likud would return to power in 1996. The Israeli interpretation was at best a reduced Palestinian Bantustan as the final product of the 'peace process'.

When did Arafat realise that he was cheated? We do not know. Was it when he was in the Sinai Peninsula in 1994, when he had to be almost physically coerced by Egyptian president Hosni Mubarak to sign the Oslo II Accord, which translated vague ideas of the September 1993 Declaration of Principles into a new and oppressive reality on the ground? According to Oslo II, Arafat would lead an authority ruling sixteen per cent of the West Bank and part of the Gaza Strip as a municipality, while acting on Israel's behalf to suppress any Palestinian opposition to the new deal.

Maybe it was then that he understood he had been taken for a ride. What is clear is that at one point he realised that Oslo meant the expansion of Israeli settlements, and the enclaving of Palestinian 'autonomous' areas within a matrix of settlements, military bases and highways, without any solution for Jerusalem or the refugee problem. Perhaps the realisation dawned during the grotesque show Clinton staged much later, in 2000, when he was again physically pushed into a hut in Camp David and asked to sign a Palestinian letter of surrender to neo-realist logic. The surrender text included a final solution that consisted of a Palestinian Bantustan in part of the occupied territories and peace for Israel. Even for the fragile Arafat, this was too much. He resisted, and the rest, as we know, is history.

A sterile version of this sequence of events was repeated after the second Intifada broke out in October 2001 – a spontaneous response to the huge disappointment of the years of negotiations since 1993. American mediators attempted in vain to revive their 'road map' – leading to nowhere. Israeli colonisation deepened and produced a particularly desperate resistance, which, in turn, produced the brutal 'retaliation' so familiar to us today. And instead of Dennis Ross and his team asking themselves who in Israel was benefiting economically from the occupation as a possible explanation for the lack of progress, along came 9/11. The ensuing narrative was easily plotted: Islamic terrorism, linked to the attacks on America, had hijacked the Palestinian political movement. This explained the inability of the Palestinians to take part in a reasonable and sensible Pax Americana.

Ariel Sharon and, after him, Ehud Olmert composed another Israeli version of peace in 2006: disengagement from Gaza, while leaving the Palestinians even less territory than was promised to them in Oslo in 1993 and Camp David in 2000. The new prescription was a lasting peace based on a Palestinian state stretching over sixteen per cent of historical Palestine, with no real sovereignty or economic independence and, of course, with no solution to the fate of Jerusalem or the refugee problem. Again, the developing reality on the ground was grimmer than the words on the page. Gaza became a huge prison camp, bombarded and starved, with the American administration blindly standing by.

AIPAC UNDER CLINTON

When we present the facts like this, the insincerity of Israel's position during and after the Oslo Accords seems obvious. For AIPAC, however, the process of the Oslo Accords and their aftermath constituted an existential threat to Israel, and they fully subscribed to Likud's view that any withdrawal from the occupied territories was tantamount to national suicide. In the eyes of AIPAC, Clinton's participation in this process made him potentially a pro-Palestinian president who had to be tamed and reoriented back to traditional American support for Israel. As we've seen, the way AIPAC decided who Israel's enemies were often had very little to do with the actual policies, which were frequently to Israel's advantage – they decided simply based on how obedient an administration was to the lobby. America's endorsement of the Oslo Accords was not a milestone on the road to peace for AIPAC, but a testimony to its own failure to influence America's policy.

Accordingly, Clinton's first year in office, hailed in the Middle East as the arrival of a new opportunity for peace, was regarded by AIPAC and other bodies comprising the pro-Israel lobby in the USA as ominous. AIPAC adopted Likud's hostile attitude towards the 1992 Rabin government and towards its attempt to reach peace with Syria and the PLO.

Bill Clinton was aware of AIPAC's apprehensions. To win over the lobby, Clinton appointed someone very dear to the lobby, Martin Indyk, as his chief Middle East adviser. As mentioned, he served the lobby for eight years before being invited by Clinton to join his team as a special adviser on the Middle East in the National Security Council. He would later become the American ambassador to Israel. During his eight years in AIPAC, he was the executive director of the lobby's most important institution, the Washington Institute for Near East Policy. With such a CV, Indyk was a true advocate of Israel in the White House team – and Clinton hoped this would placate the lobby. Ironically, the term in the White House transformed Indyk's approach and he became more dovish in his views. Today he serves on the board of the liberal New Israel Fund executive board, a funding body that supports the Palestinians in Israel and civil rights organisations in Israel – it is constantly targeted as an anti-Israel organisation by AIPAC.

The lobby was particularly anxious about the secretary of state, Warren Christopher, especially in conjunction with the new professionals in the State Department, who favoured liberal Zionism rather than AIPAC's brand of right-wing politics. Christopher's main 'sin' was previously serving in the Carter administration. He was held responsible for Carter's brief flirtation with a progressive policy on Palestine.

Indyk's appointment would not help to mend AIPAC's rift with the administration. What did help to smooth some of the tensions was the adventurist Clintonian policy towards Iran in the mid-1990s, which suited both Israel's and the lobby's agenda; the USA regarded the regime in Tehran as being behind some of the more daring actions taken against American targets around the world. When Iran was the topic, meetings between the president and AIPAC were quite pleasant. In May 1995, Clinton appeared before the World Jewish Congress and announced his intention to impose sanctions on Iran.

But AIPAC needed more to show it was still a force to reckon with in Washington. And it got this when Bill Clinton was the first serving president to address AIPAC. But the conference soon discovered Clinton expected them to return the favour. Clinton devoted the first part of his speech to Yitzhak Rabin, talking prophetically about the high personal price the Israeli prime minister would pay for trying to make peace. He ended his speech by returning to its main theme – support for Rabin:

> Stand with this brave man in his attempts to make peace. And let's don't [*sic*] stop until the job is done.[197]

AIPAC by then was almost entirely an extension of Likud, so this went down like a lead balloon. But Clinton wanted another quid pro quo on top of that – he expected support for his more conciliatory relationship with Russia. While the televangelists were still referring to Russia as the representative of the Antichrist on earth, Clinton praised Russia for the swift disarmament of its nuclear arsenal. He curried some favour with his listeners by adopting an aggressive tone towards Iran and describing some of cutting-edge military equipment and technology the USA supplied to Israel.[198] Keith Weissman, a leading analyst in AIPAC in those days, recalled that AIPAC's main goal was to prevent American aid to the newly established Palestinian Authority and the method deployed was, according to another AIPAC official, demonisation of the Palestinians as terrorists.[199]

But AIPAC did make an attempt to appease the president. For the first time some Arab journalists were invited to its conference. At least some of its leaders contemplated the future of a meaningful Pax Americana under Clinton and were willing to temper their criticism of the peace process to allow for that. But events removed all need for moderation. Only a few months after AIPAC convened, Yitzhak Rabin was assassinated by a right-wing extremist. Netanyahu won the following election, and with that, Likud was back in charge.

At the end of the day, AIPAC's thirty-seventh annual conference was just words. AIPAC granted Clinton its support for the Oslo Accords, and in return received promises from Clinton that he would sanction Iran, consider moving the American embassy to Jerusalem and provide large-scale military aid to Israel.

Clinton's second term in office was a different story. On one hand, these were the golden years of the Christian Zionist lobby and the onset of its honeymoon with Netanyahu's Likud Party, which was about to dominate Israeli politics in the next century. AIPAC soon took the role of second fiddle not only to that of the Christian Zionist lobby, but also to that of the neo-con movement.

In the 1990s, the neo-cons became a force with which the lobby wanted to work more closely. Their various think-tanks developed close links with the Likud Party, in power between 1996 and 1999. Already then their independent view was that Israel should repudiate the Oslo Accords and that the USA should go to war against Iraq. One such advocacy group was the Institute for Advanced Strategic and Political Studies, with offices in both Washington and Jerusalem. A typical publication of this body was entitled *A Clean Break: A New Strategy for Securing the Realm*, which advocated that Israel repudiate the Oslo Accords and seek permanent annexation of the West Bank and the Gaza

Strip. Even more provocatively, it urged Israel to support Jordan in advocating restoration of the Hashemite monarchy in Iraq and the elimination of the regime of Saddam Hussein – 'an important Israeli strategic objective in its own right.'[200] The report was in fact commissioned by Benjamin Netanyahu and the team of well-known neo-cons was led by Richard Perle.

The *Clean Break* paper appealed to Likud's general strategic vision. A pre-emptive war against Iraq would legitimise the principle of using force to solve diplomatic and political problems, which Israel has done on several occasions, most notably in the wars of 1956, 1967 and 1982. Two days after receiving a copy of the *Clean Break* paper, Netanyahu delivered an address to a joint session of Congress, embracing several of its propositions. The *Wall Street Journal* published excerpts from the paper the same day and editorially endorsed it on 11 July 1997.

For its part, on 26 January 1998, the Project for the New American Century (PNAC), another neo-con outfit, dispatched a letter to President Bill Clinton urging that he launch a war against Iraq. The signatories included the crème de la crème of American neo-conservatism: William Kristol, Dick Cheney, Lewis Libby, Donald Rumsfeld, Paul Wolfowitz, Elliot Abrams, and Zalmay Khalilzad. Unhappy that Clinton did not heed their advice, the same group repeated their proposals in letters to the Speaker of the House, Newt Gingrich, and the Senate majority leader Trent Lott on 29 May 1998. The result of efforts by PNAC and others was the passage of the Iraq Liberation Act of October 1998, which announced the switch in US policy on Iraq from disarmament to regime change. This legislation was adopted weeks before Clinton ordered the UNSCOM inspectors out of Iraq and launched Operation Desert Fox – four days of intensive bombing.[201]

By 1998, AIPAC was closely associated with the neo-con perspective on American policy in the Middle East, as was the Likud Party. AIPAC's shift to the right, in America and in Israel, deepened its internal divisions, which translated into a decline in funding from the American Jewish community.

Towards the end of both Netanyahu's first term in office and that of Clinton, the American administration began to be impatient with the Israeli prime minister. The White House foreign affairs spokesperson noted that:

> The ball is not in the Palestinian court; the ball is in the court of the Israelis to try to work with the Palestinians and work with us to come to a second 'yes'. We have a 'yes' from the Palestinians and we are looking to get ourselves in a position where the Israelis can say 'yes' as well.[202]

US pressure bore fruit and a reluctant Netanyahu joined Yasser Arafat and a very ill King Hussein of Jordan to sign some agreements. The most important of these was the 1998 Wye River Memorandum, an agreement on redeployments of Israeli forces and closer co-operation between the Palestinian Authority and the Israeli security services against attacks by Hamas and Palestinian Islamic Jihad, a group founded in 1981 and heavily influenced by the Iranian Revolution.

These efforts were largely in vain – Netanyahu's outlook meant that for all intents and purposes, the Oslo Accords were dead. It was to be expected that Netanyahu's insincere commitment to honouring Israeli commitments under Oslo would lead to some rebuke from the Clinton administration. But this amounted to nothing more than some minor expressions of dismay.[203] What mattered was that Clinton continued to supply brand new military equipment to Israel and intensified the collaboration in joint military exercises.

AIPAC had virtually nothing to do and yet it continued to criticise the State Department, which was bizarre since its policies were pro-Israel compared to those of previous years. Since the days of the Nixon administration, when Joseph Sisco became assistant secretary to the Bureau of Near Eastern Affairs (the NEA succeeded the old Near East Division), the State Department had transformed from a powerbase of 'Arabists' into a department closely linked to liberal Zionists both in the USA and in Israel. The process was continued by Henry Kissinger who staffed the relevant section of the State

Department with liberal Zionist Jews and sympathetic non-Jews. It culminated with the appointment of Dennis Ross and Martin Indyk, both former employees of AIPAC, by Clinton. As the scholar Leon Hadar put it, Indyk and Ross 'virtually guaranteed that the American approach to Israel would never run against the consensus in the American-Jewish community'.[204]

Indyk and Ross were not Likudniks, unlike those who replaced them in AIPAC – and hence AIPAC had cause to be disappointed with them. 'Pro-Israel' and 'enemy of AIPAC' are not mutually exclusive terms. However, the right wing in Israel, once in power, indicated in a war of words that these officials were hostile to Israel. Neither side took this verbal sparring to heart, as American policy continued to favour Israel in every meaningful way possible.

As it approached the twenty-first century, the lobby faced old and new challenges. The most important of these was the seismic change in American public opinion, including within the Jewish community, towards Israel's policies in historical Palestine. As Kenen told his disciples back in 1957: challenges only made AIPAC more aggressive and determined, in a century when it lost the moral high ground but still had a lot of money, political influence and powerful Christian Zionist allies.

AIPAC did become more aggressive, but the challenge facing it became more formidable. Israel couldn't shield its reputation, and the image of its lobbies abroad, from the consequences of its brutal actions: a daily tale of demolitions, political arrests, closures (*seger* in Hebrew) of villages and towns, abuse of civil and human rights and the killing of Palestinians, including women and children. Up until the cataclysm of 9/11, Israel's moral standing was on the decline. But when planes flew into the World Trade Center, everything changed. America reacted with a surge in anti-Arab sentiment, and aggressive, and disastrous, military interventions in the Middle East. The window of opportunity for reconsidering the US's relationship with Israel was now closed. It would take a long time to reopen.

9

Lobbying for Israel in Twenty-First-Century America

HOPE AND DESPAIR: THE BUSH JR ERA, 2001–2009

As we've seen, the Clinton administration steered discussion of Israel and Palestine into dangerous waters – for AIPAC at least, if not for Israel itself. Its official recognition of Palestinian interests, even if it amounted to empty words, was not to AIPAC's taste. Even if its former staff were in charge, their liberalism now clashed with AIPAC's alignment with the right. But things were now set to change. The very beginning of the twenty-first century breathed new life into the work of the lobby, beginning with the second Intifada in 2000 – which effectively killed off the Oslo Accords for good. Even though the Intifada was triggered by the failure of the Camp David Summit, Clinton did not apportion any blame to Israeli intransigence, choosing to blame Arafat instead. But he himself was on his way out.

The 2000 presidential elections would be a landmark in AIPAC's history. For the first time, both presidential candidates addressed its annual convention. Al Gore needed AIPAC's financial and political support, and hence the outgoing Democratic administration headed up by Clinton was reluctant to put any pressure on Netanyahu or his successor Ehud Barak (in government from 1999 to 2001) to change their position. This yet again illustrates how the lobbying infrastructure in the USA, as well as in Britain, became so embedded into political life that active exertion wasn't necessary. Gore and Clinton did not need to be reminded by AIPAC or any other unit in the elaborate lobbying infrastructure that their policy towards Israel could influence their success in the domestic elections.

Al Gore's and George Bush Jr's messages to the delegates seemed indistinguishable. Both speeches reiterated the commitment to a strong Israel; both condemned the trial of thirteen Jews in Iran who were tried as spies for Israel. They both backed a peace process and accordingly they both were greeted with the same loud applause. They differed on one issue: Bush promised to move the embassy to Jerusalem (although he got it wrong and promised 'only' to move the ambassador – this could have been interesting) and Gore did not mention the issue at all. As the US had chosen to respect the 1949 UN resolution regarding the international status of Jerusalem, the American embassy was based in Tel Aviv. Although Congress had backed moving the embassy to Jerusalem, the Clinton administration declared such a move counterproductive.[1]

A more nuanced variation in the two speeches involved Bush's reference to Clinton's peace efforts hitherto. Bush indirectly scolded Clinton's identification with the so-called 'peace camp' in Israel when he promised not to interfere in Israeli domestic politics.[2] Bush, however, was still associated with his father's harsher attitude towards Israel and thus may have felt in 2000 that he was less favoured than Gore among that audience.

If that convention made observers believe that AIPAC was finally going along with the Clinton philosophy of supporting the 'peace camp' in Israel without changing Israel's actual policies, it all changed in the wake of a series of events at the end of 2000 and into 2001. In October 2000, the second Intifada burst out, triggered by an uninvited visit by Ariel Sharon, then the leader of the opposition, to Haram al-Sharif, the holy site of the Al-Aqsa Mosque. It was caused by frustration about the new map of disaster and oppression the Oslo Accords created on the ground. This dissected the West Bank into a large number of Palestinian enclaves connected by roads monitored by Israeli checkpoints, where Palestinians were abused daily and coerced into serving as collaborators, and allowed Israel to encircle the Gaza Strip with barbed wire, turning it into a dense open prison. Peace was no longer on the agenda.

This was followed by the 9/11 attack on the twin towers of the World Trade Center in New York and the Pentagon in Washington. This period turned out to be more comfortable for AIPAC and the pro-Israel lobby at large. They now had a new president in the White House: George W. Bush Jr.

It seems that he was able to disassociate himself from his father among the American Jews who voted Republican. His message was appealing: 'My support for Israel is not conditional on the outcome of the peace process', or in other words he supported the Israeli rejection of the Palestinian demands.[3] A few months into his term in office, the AIPAC mouthpiece the *Near East Report* noted that the 'Bush administration backed Israel's stance that political negotiations cannot resume amid the continuing violence, which was launched by the Palestinians'.[4]

After 9/11, the hawks were back in charge of AIPAC, and they were quick to reassert their authority. The lobby began commodifying a narrative that linked terrorism with Islam and Palestine. Unconditional support for Israel was now a pillar of the new 'war on terror'. The question was: how would the new Republican administration deal with the situation in Palestine and what would be its basic attitude towards Israel?

FORSAKING PALESTINE YET AGAIN

Bush's main desire was to distance himself from the Israel/Palestine issue as far as he could, but the circumstances did not always allow it. His reservations about taking any kind of strong stand are indicated by his refusal to renew the position of a special envoy to the Middle East (the last one was Dennis Ross). But developments on the ground ruled out such an aloof approach. Daniel Zoughbie's title for his book, describing the endless haphazard changes in Bush's policy every time he had to respond to a new challenge in the real world, was apt: *Indecision Points*.[5]

AIPAC was not the only body closely watching the new president; other actors on the scene revealed themselves when the president decided to appoint Daniel C. Kurtzer as an ambassador to Israel. The Christian Zionists, together with Morton Klein, president of the Zionist Organization of America, objected to the appointment. A hawkish group called Americans for a Safe Israel, founded in 1970, called upon the president to find 'a Bible-believing Christian' instead of Kurtzer, who was an Orthodox Jew. In their eyes, this appointment probably implied too much distance from their idiosyncratic reading of the Bible as a book that adjures Israel to annex the West Bank and Gaza Strip. As their website states:

> AFSI was founded in 1970 as an American counterpart to the Land of Israel Movement, asserting Israel's historic, religious, and legal rights to the land re-claimed in the 1967 War.[6]

They had their own candidate, Edward E. McAteer, founder of another Christian Zionist outfit, Religious Roundtable, and close friend of the televangelist Jerry Falwell, who told the press he was interested in the job. As for Klein, he described Kurtzer as someone who 'praised Arafat and the PLO as moderates' and hence unsuitable for the job. However, this campaign failed since AIPAC did not join it, and thus Kurtzer's appointment was approved.[7]

After 9/11, Bush found himself facing an Arab world that demanded a reward for collaborating with the American 'war on terror'. Another challenge was the intensification of violence on the ground in 2002, when a suicide bomber entered a hotel in Netanya during a Passover seder, killing thirty civilians and injuring 140. This led to Operation Defensive Shield, in which Israel practically reoccupied the whole of the West Bank and the Gaza Strip, using tanks and aircraft in the process, culminating in the massacre of many in the Jenin refugee camp in April 2002. These developments prompted the Bush administration to take a deeper interest in de-escalating the conflict in this area at least. In the background was a clear Saudi initiative in 2002, supported by the Arab League, offering recognition of Israel in return for a genuine two-state solution.

The Bush administration sent several envoys, who here and there obtained short ceasefires, meetings between the sides and plans for more diplomacy in the future, but in reality changed little.

AIPAC was called into action when President Bush sharply urged Israel to withdraw immediately from the newly occupied spaces run by the Palestinian Authority. 'Do it without delay', he exhorted the Israeli prime minister, Ariel Sharon.[8] The response was a huge demonstration organised by the lobby in Washington on 5 May 2002, demanding that the president stop pressuring Israel, a message also passed on by leading neo-conservatives and Christian Zionists (two important constituencies of the president's electoral power). Bush changed the tone of his next public references to the situation in Palestine. The lobby also recruited the majority leader of the House, Tom DeLay, to organise a similar appeal from Republican members.[9] The overall message was clear: give Israel a free hand to quell the second Intifada.

By June 2002, Bush and Sharon were on the same wavelength. The president implored the Palestinians to elect a new leadership, a call well received by AIPAC and Israel. But unexpectedly, Arafat and the neighbouring Arab countries snatched this opportunity, which was followed by an American commitment to a 'road map' that would lead to a Palestinian state. Arafat appointed a prime minister to run the affairs of the Palestinian Authority, Mahmoud Abbas. The Arab world backed these moves and responded positively to the idea that a step-by-step 'road map' would lead eventually to the establishment of an independent Palestinian state in the West Bank and the Gaza Strip. But at the same time the harsh Israeli oppression continued, as did the Palestinian guerrilla attacks against civilians inside Israel, and there was no move towards such a 'road map'. In September 2003, Mahmoud Abbas resigned, and America was engaged in a new imperialist adventure: the Anglo-American invasion of Iraq.

THE CHRISTIAN AND JEWISH CHEERLEADERS FOR THE IRAQ WAR

John Mearsheimer and Stephen Walt allege that AIPAC's involvement in building consensus in the US administration for the invasion of Iraq in 2003 was both central and indisputable.[10] This is true, but there was another group, nascent in the Reagan, Bush Sr and Clinton administrations, pushing for war with Iraq: the neo-conservatives. Eventually, Israeli politicians, AIPAC and the neo-conservatives worked in tandem and formed a powerful pressure group in favour of invading Iraq.

Let us begin with the Israeli impact. At first, as Mearsheimer and Walt point out, Israel under Ariel Sharon was sceptical about such an invasion and preferred to see American action against Iran, but he was persuaded that Iraq was only the first step and Israel lent its support to those in the administration who advocated such an action.[11]

As early as August 2002, Sharon told the Knesset's foreign affairs and defence committee that Iraq was 'the greatest danger facing Israel'. In the same month he warned the Bush administration that postponing the attack would allow Saddam to accelerate his weapons programme.[12]

From that moment onward, Israel's top propagandist, Benjamin Netanyahu, was enlisted in the campaign to persuade people in America of the validity of the invasion. 'The urgent need to topple Saddam is paramount', he told the American Senate in 2002, adding that such a campaign 'deserves the unconditional support of all sane governments'.[13] Later he wrote op-eds for the *New York Times* and the *Wall Street Journal*, entitled 'The Case for Toppling Saddam', and stated: 'nothing less than dismantling his regime will do.'[14]

Another recruit was Shimon Peres, Israel's foreign minister, who told CNN: 'Saddam Hussein is as dangerous as Bin Laden' and therefore the USA 'cannot sit and wait'.[15] Last but not least, Ehud Barak, the former Israeli prime minister, suggested in an op-ed in the *Washington Post* that the Bush administration 'should, first of all, focus on Iraq and the removal of Saddam Hussein'.[16]

AIPAC amplified these efforts by the Israeli state and boasted about their role. Howard Kohr, the CEO of AIPAC, told the *New York Sun* in January 2003 that one of AIPAC's greatest successes was in lobbying Congress to approve the initiation of a war. And indirectly, the publisher of *US News & World Report*, Mortimer Zuckerman, chair at the time of the Conference of Presidents of Major American Jewish Organizations, used his magazine to call for a war. Jewish leaders of official outfits such as the American Jewish Committee and Reform bodies were all putting pressure on the administration to invade. The sentiment was summarised succinctly by Gary Rosenblatt, editor of the *Jewish Week*:

> Washington's imminent war on Saddam Hussein is … an opportunity to rid the world of a dangerous tyrant who presents a particularly horrific threat to Israel.

He went on to say: 'the Torah instructs that when your enemy seeks to kill you, kill him first.'[17]

AIPAC began lobbying for the war from the end of December 2001 until the use of force was approved by Congress in 2002 and the war commenced. It published a *Briefing Book* for its membership and congressional offices, presenting information and analyses. It contained the following statement:

> As long as Saddam Hussein is in power, any containment of Iraq will only be temporary until the next crisis or act of aggression.[18]

Its newsletter, the *Near East Report,* had in its 'editor's comments' on 7 October 2002 a totally unfounded analysis of Saddam Hussein's involvement in the 9/11 attacks. At times it was hinted by AIPAC that Yasser Arafat was part of the conspiracy. Years later the 9/11 commission report stated clearly:

> to date we have seen no evidence that these or the earlier contacts ever developed into a collaborative operational relationship. Nor have we seen evidence indicating that Iraq cooperated with al Qaeda in developing or carrying out any attacks against the United States.[19]

There were other strong indicators of how AIPAC influenced American policy on Iraq. On the eve of the war, after the USA failed to get UN approval, Rep. James Moran (Democrat, Virginia) told a meeting of his constituents that:

> If it were not for the strong support of the Jewish community for this war with Iraq, we would not be doing this.[20]

Leaders of the organised Jewish community of greater Washington, along with several of Moran's fellow congressional Democrats, seized upon these remarks and forced the representative to issue a rather pathetic retraction.[21] Though this incident had no practical policy implications, the brief media furore that followed Moran's comment exposed the ambiguity in the pro-Israel lobby when it came to assessing its own role in pushing America towards a war in Iraq. They could not deny that it was in Israel's interest – which they represented in the USA – to persuade the USA to go to war. On the other hand, the moment the war became less popular, they didn't want to look like they had anything to do with it. The best way forward was to accuse congressmen such as Moran of anti-Semitism and hope it would distract everyone from looking too closely at the issue. Moran's swift apology demonstrated how much Congress representatives felt the need to toe the line – allowing the lobby to manage its own image in the eyes of the public.

AIPAC's impact on the decision to go to war should also be viewed in light of its connections with American neo-conservatism. Even before the invasion, a group of neo-conservatives, strongly linked to Israel's Likud Party, became influential in shaping George W. Bush's Middle East policy. We should remember that AIPAC did not represent American Jews as such, but only a small portion of them, and secondly, among the people who influenced Bush's policy in the Middle East and pushed for the war, there was a large number of non-Jews, most prominently Dick Cheney and Defense Secretary Donald Rumsfeld. The link between the most hawkish elements of the pro-Israel lobby and the second Bush administration was based on a convergence of interests and ideology.

The neo-cons did not need any prompting from AIPAC; they had been pushing for a war since the early 1990s. They pursued the invasion more zealously after 2001 and tried to substantiate their advocacy for war on a professional basis through research in many think-tanks and institutions. Like amoebas, these outfits transmuted or reappeared as new bodies. After the 9/11 attacks, the same personalities could be found on the Defense Policy Board, which emerged as an advocacy group calling upon the White House to remove Saddam Hussein by force. They carried out their own erroneous research that linked Saddam Hussein with Al-Qaeda. They even claimed there had been a meeting between Iraqi intelligence and the hijackers in Prague prior to 9/11. The Czech intelligence services have adamantly denied that such a meeting ever took place.[22]

This all led to the infamous open letter written by the Board to President Bush on 20 September 2001 that stated:

> Even if evidence does not link Iraq directly to the [September 11] attack, any strategy aiming at the eradication of terrorism and its sponsors must include a determined effort to remove Saddam Hussein from power in Iraq ... Failure to undertake such an effort will constitute an early and perhaps decisive surrender in the war on international terrorism.[23]

The neo-con movement was far more ambitious than AIPAC and its expectations of the American administration and visions of the future were not confined to Israel – they were dreaming of changing the entire Middle East region, remaking it in their image. Their ideal scenario was a region transformed by force and coerced into being subordinate to the West, or at least domesticated by the West (within this imagined political cartography one can find a Greater Israel, stretching over the whole of historical Palestine). The neo-cons rejected the Oslo Accords, as well as the idea of a Palestinian state. The links now among opposing Palestinian statehood, supporting apartheid Greater Israel and endorsing an aggressive policy in the region as a whole up to and including the invasion of Iraq ought to have prompted more serious criticism from within the American establishment. So why did no dissident tendency emerge?

The graduates of the Washington Institute for Near East Policy – Dick Cheney, Donald Rumsfeld, his deputy Paul Wolfowitz and Richard Perle – got Colin Powell onside and pushed for a military attack on Iraq. At the same time, another, more consensual assault on Al-Qaeda was contemplated in Afghanistan. Each one of these figures would participate in the annual AIPAC conference. And each time they spoke, they reaffirmed unconditional support for Israel's policy vis-à-vis Palestine and the Palestinians.

Since these prime movers of the neo-con lobby for war and Israel's annexationist policies were partly employed in outfits associated with AIPAC, we can see how a coalition of sorts became a powerful voice eventually persuading the White House to occupy Iraq in 2003. This was a pseudo-academic coalition that advised the Bush administration on the basis of 'research' to forgo any meaningful attempt to facilitate a peace process and adopt an aggressive policy in the Arab world. In tandem with AIPAC, this group presented the invasion of Iraq first and foremost as an action to defend Israel against weapons of mass destruction allegedly developed by Saddam Hussein, rather than retribution for 9/11.[24] The lack of evidence for such weapons did not trouble their consciences too much.

Dick Cheney, who was part of the entourage supporting the war in Iraq, was also a moving spirit behind a group that supported similar action against Iran. This was a body he created called Freedom's Watch, which worked in conjunction with the Jewish Republic Coalition, formerly known as the National Jewish Coalition that was founded already in 1985. Its other close partner was the American Enterprise Institute for Public Policy Research, a veteran neo-con institution. Freedom's Watch, according to the *New York Times*, tried to convene a private pressure group that would urge the administration to wage war against Iran.

Years later, when the British Parliament demanded explanation from its former prime minister, Tony Blair, for his ill-fated decision to join the war, he told an inquiry commission about a meeting he had with Bush in Crawford, Texas, in April 2002, where Israeli officials were present and the Israeli connection to a prospective action against Iraq was discussed. He recalled that 'the Israel issue was big at the time'.[25]

It took only a year for the world to realise that the invasion of Iraq wasn't all it was cracked up to be, and that bragging about the lobby's role was inadvisable, to say the least. But the work of the lobby, in its neo-con, Christian Zionist and Jewish stripes, set a precedent for how administrations related to the lobby for the next decade.

Despite the seemingly universal consensus about the invasion that AIPAC sought to portray, the reality is that the American Jewish community at large did not support the war. Sadly, as Jewish community bodies had been co-opted to such an extent by the Israeli state, they no longer had a vehicle to express their opposition.

The Israeli government, neo-cons and Christian Zionists, all of whom AIPAC closely collaborated with, helped make the invasion of Iraq possible and must be held responsible for the catastrophes that followed: civil war, state collapse, the rise of the Islamic State and the ongoing refugee crisis. AIPAC and Israel encouraged the American propensity for bellicose Middle Eastern policies. But as soon as the war erupted, AIPAC had to navigate carefully between its enthusiasm and the growing opposition to the war once the first coffins of American soldiers arrived from both Iraq and Afghanistan. This difficulty of this navigation was clearly displayed at AIPAC's 2003 convention.

WAR ON IRAQ IS GOOD FOR ISRAEL

There were two interlinked issues that troubled the organisers of the 2003 annual conference of AIPAC: firstly, the administration's support for the 'road map' that would lead to the establishment of an independent Palestinian state in the West Bank and the Gaza Strip, and secondly, the question of how to downplay AIPAC's enthusiasm for the war at a time when it could well become as unpopular as the Vietnam War in the 1960s.

AIPAC's leadership suspected that their guest of honour, President George Bush Jr, would repeat his support for a 'road map' as an attempt to appease the pro-American camp in the Arab world. Just before its 2003 convention, AIPAC, even more than the Israeli government, reacted nervously to Bush's attempt to build an international coalition in Iraq by promising a 'road map' after a Palestinian prime minister 'with real authority' had taken office. This was a convenient ploy by Israel's government to make progress conditional on something that was always subjective – and hence always up for debate – in this case demanding a prime minister with 'real authority' in a territory he could have no real authority over.[26] American policy makers followed suit and obfuscated any promise of a vision for justice for Palestinians to the point that the gestures were meaningless. This was illustrated by a string of contradictory statements that voided each other. Thus, in March 2003 the State Department spokesman, Richard Boucher, said that the 'road map' was non-negotiable, while other State Department and National Security Council officials explained immediately after this that everything was open for further discussion.[27]

But AIPAC's worries were dispelled when they realised that the adventure in Iraq delayed any clear American policy on the 'road map'. On the eve of the convention, AIPAC leaders informed the media that they had been heartened by the White House's reluctance to embrace the 'road map' during the Iraq crisis and its willingness to delay its implementation at Israel's request.[28]

But AIPAC wasn't happy to rest on its laurels; it couldn't risk someone genuinely committed to the peace process whispering in the president's ear. It took the precautionary step of calling repeatedly for congressional legislation that would codify the condition that Bush stipulated in his 24 June 2002 speech, in which he called for an interim Palestinian state, but only after a complete cessation of violence against Israel and the replacement of the Palestinian Authority leadership, as legally binding.[29] AIPAC convinced lawmakers in the House but not in the Senate to offer such legislation and place it inside bills related to funding offered to the Palestinian Authority and other Palestinian organisations. The theory was that legislation that held Bush to the parameters of his June speech could offset the influence of the 'road map'. In the words of AIPAC's president, Amy Friedkin: 'We will be lobbying for support for the road map that implements the president's June 24th vision.'[30] This was a redundant exertion on AIPAC's part; it was simply an assertion of their own power. American aid did flow into the West Bank and the Gaza Strip, and this was a part of American policy that AIPAC was unable to stop; however, suggestions about moving Israel onto the 'road map' leading to a two-state solution were only hollow words, and everyone knew it.

In any case, the Iraq War put any talk of a 'road map' out of sight and out of mind. 'I don't think there will be that much talk about the road map,' said Morris Amitay, former executive director of AIPAC, to the Jewish press on the eve of the 2003 conference, 'unless the war is over by then, everything will be focused on the war.'[31] The war did not end with the deposition of Saddam Hussein. Iraq still feels the repercussions now.

The invasion also meant that the 2003 conference was a muted affair. There was a widespread belief that Israel, via AIPAC, had played a crucial role in the decision to invade Iraq without a mandate from the UN – and AIPAC didn't want to make that connection any stronger.

'I believe that we don't have to choose between being pro-Israel and being a patriotic American', Amy Friedkin told the Jewish press.[32] But nonetheless the US held back from stating Israel's role openly, and it shied away from proclaiming its work in protecting Israel from attacks in Baghdad. The *Jewish Telegraph* summarised the dilemma in the following way:

> In a perfect world, AIPAC would highlight the role Israel has played in US efforts against Iraq, and the job the United States has done to protect Israel from possible attacks from Baghdad. In the real world, however, the United States has tried to downplay Israel's role – even keeping it off the list of countries in its 'coalition of the willing' – to prevent a potential backlash from the Arab world.[33]

In reality, Israel was part of the 'coalition of the willing', the forty-nine nation states that the administration identified as supporting the Anglo-American assault on Iraq. When AIPAC met for its 2003 convention, it was reluctant to declare an official position on the situation in Iraq, to avoid intensifying the aspersions already being cast. But AIPAC's website was happy to boast about 'Israeli weapons utilised by Coalition forces against Iraq', referring to the Israeli Hunter and Pioneer drones and Popeye air-to-surface missiles used in Iraq.[34]

Although the war was controversial in American civil society – sparking some of the biggest protests the country had ever seen – the pro-Israel lobby practically unanimously supported the invasion. Abraham Foxman, national director of the Anti-Defamation League, said: 'There was no need for Jews to get ahead of the curve' on Iraq by speaking out before the White House decided whether to go to war, and added 'but now that the United States has invaded Iraq, it is appropriate for the Jewish world to support it'.[35]

Amy Friedkin echoed the consensus of the lobby, conscious of the advantages of Middle East issues now making the daily headlines: 'We are very aware that we are at war', Friedkin told the *Washington Post*, and 'while we are celebrating the relationship of the United States and Israel, we need to support American troops and support the efforts for democracy to be built in the Middle East.'[36]

Accordingly, AIPAC's 2003 conference was the one place Colin Powell, now notorious for presenting the falsified report about Iraq's weapons of mass destruction, could find a warm reception. Powell was personally addressed by Silvan Shalom, Israel's foreign minister at the time, who attended the conference. Shalom praised Powell for the attack on Iraq.[37] In his speech, Shalom imbued America's invasion with significance that even Powell might have struggled to agree with:

> Even as we speak, allied forces are engaged in combat in Iraq. While Operation Iraqi Freedom is advancing, it is not a simple undertaking and involves high risks. The tyranny of Iraqi rulers today has its roots in ancient Babylon of biblical times. The prophet Jeremiah referred to the dangers posed by Babylon, Iraq of today, to the region, and to God's punishment for the cruel despots of the land of two rivers. Some would say Jeremiah prophesied current events. He said, and I quote, 'I will raise against Babylon an assembly of great nations from the north country, for she has sinned against God.'
>
> Tonight, I would like to offer our prayers for the safety of the heroic men and women of the coalition forces. Your courage and bravery are for a great and historic cause. Success in Iraq will pave the way for new hope in the Middle East, for new hope for Israel, for new hope for the rest of the world.
>
> Freedom, democracy, and human rights should no longer be foreign terms for the people of the region. Believe me, nothing will make us happier than knowing that Israel is no longer the sole democracy in the Middle East.[38]

Although Israeli guests could be unabashed in their support for the war, AIPAC's leadership had to walk a tightrope – given that anything from a third to a half of the US public had reservations about the war. 'The war inhibits your desire to want to trumpet the relationship at a time when the United States and Israel are downplaying it', said Doug Bloomfield, former legislative director for AIPAC. But conference attendees 'can highlight common values and common issues', he added, in an attempt to justify the huge enthusiasm on the floor for the invasion.[39]

The invasion wasn't AIPAC's only image problem in 2003. Its bipartisanship was seen by many as a façade for its complete commitment to the Republicans. Any dissent from the floor from Republican consensus was swiftly shut down by lobby officials. When Leon S. Fuerth, the former national adviser to Al Gore, expressed his misgivings about the utility of imposing democracy by force on a foreign country, he was scolded by the moderator, AIPAC's Steve Rosen, who declared: 'God willing, we're going to have a great victory in Iraq', and was cheered loudly by the attendees.[40]

Conscious of these tensions, Israel also advised AIPAC to tone down their embrace of the war in public debate in the US. 'We do not need to shout', advised Eyal Arad, who used to be Ariel Sharon's campaign's adviser, realising that the Bush administration did not wish to expose Israel's role in the discussions and preparations for the assault.[41] But in Israel itself, there was no need for moderation.

American taxpayers might have seen the war as a dubious use of their dollars, but AIPAC saw it as a time to raid the federal piggy bank. It was decided to use the 2003 conference to encourage Congress to approve the White House's proposal for $1 billion of military aid and $9 billion in loan guarantees for Israel. The argument was that it was a small percentage of the overall anticipated $100 billion expenditure for the Afghanistan and Iraq campaigns.[42]

By that time such congressional support was obtained by a well-oiled advocacy machine whose actions were aptly depicted in Mor Loushy's documentary, *Kings of Capitol Hill*. In the film, you can see on Capitol Hill side rooms rented informally by AIPAC in which members of both Houses were introduced to potential donors for future electoral campaigns (donors who represented groups and firms that had nothing to do with Israel), while, at the same time, the guests were briefed by AIPAC on the positions they should hold vis-à-vis American policy towards Israel and the Middle East.[43]

Extra aid to Israel could have gone down badly in the midst of war, tax cuts and a deficit, but the pro-Israel lobby knew the wheels of the perpetual motion machine they had spent decades building were still turning, and it would ensure that there would be bipartisan support from congressional leaders on military aid to Israel, even at that difficult moment in American fiscal history. It did not always get what it was asking for. When it sought $4 billion in military aid, it had to be content with only a quarter of that amount. AIPAC president Amy Friedkin told the Jewish press that AIPAC would lobby for whatever package the Bush administration and Israel would agree to.[44]

After the conference, and throughout 2004 up to the November elections, AIPAC still had one reservation: the Bush administration was still making public endorsements of the two-state solution and declaring its adherence to the basic guidelines adopted by other members of the Quartet to which America belonged: Russia, the UN and the EU. The Middle East Quartet, as it is known, was established in 2001 in the wake of the second Intifada and as part of the international effort to secure a ceasefire. A year later in Madrid it was officially declared as an initiative to bring about the two-state solution to the Israeli–Palestinian conflict, and it located its headquarters in East Jerusalem.

AIPAC's objection to this solution was voiced in the wake of an unusual lament by Bush about the undue force used by Israel against the Palestinians. AIPAC, together with the Conference of Presidents of Major American Jewish Organizations, and supported by Christian Zionist organisations, made sure Bush was brought back to toe the line expected of him. These organisations initiated a number of mass demonstrations, and invited Benjamin Netanyahu as a key speaker at them, to demand that Palestinian actions against the ongoing occupation would be seen as pure terrorism. A similar message was sent from Sharon to Bush. In the words of Tom Friedman from the *New York Times*, while Sharon had Arafat under house arrest in Ramallah, 'he's had George Bush under house arrest in the Oval Office'.[45] Bush was quick to adopt AIPAC's preferred descriptors for Palestinian resistance once again.

But by the 2004 elections, they didn't need to worry, as neither candidate troubled themselves with the fate of the Palestinians. Both candidates, George Bush and John Kerry, depicted the Palestinian liberation struggle and its guerrilla warfare as terrorist activity, equating it with Al-Qaeda in Afghanistan and with Saddam Hussein in Iraq. This was a very shaky argument. As evidence, both candidates resurrected the 1985 killing of Leon Klinghoffer by Palestinians, who had hijacked the cruise ship he was on, and the more recent beheading of the American journalist Daniel Pearl in Afghanistan in 2002. The fact that Daniel Pearl was murdered by Pakistani fundamentalists, not Palestinian guerrillas, seemed not to register. Bush had another noticeable blind spot: namely, over three thousand Palestinian deaths at the hands of the Israeli army since the turn of the millennium.

George Bush returned to AIPAC for the first time as a sitting president for their 2004 annual convention. His forty-eight-minute speech was interrupted by twenty-four standing ovations. It was mostly about his alleged success in Iraq and how much Israel benefited from American aggression there.[46]

Bush's words need no interpretation:

> AIPAC is doing important work. I hope you know it. In Washington and beyond, AIPAC is calling attention to the great security of challenges of our time. You're educating Congress and the American people on the growing dangers of proliferation.[47]

Moreover, flush from celebrating 'victory' in Iraq, Bush compared Jerusalem to Baghdad as two cities that needed to be liberated from terrorism and from 'the enemies of freedom', and for that he received a standing ovation. His remarks were even more welcome when he once more reiterated the possible connection between Palestinian 'terrorism' and the new 'war on terror'.

When Bush declared: 'for the sake of peace and security, we ended the regime of Saddam Hussein', the applause reached a crescendo, and it rose to an even higher volume when he finally found a way to connect Saddam to 'terrorism against Israel' by informing the audience that 'the [Iraqi] regime sponsored terror; it paid rewards of up to $25,000 to the families of Palestinian suicide bombers'.[48]

But the audience noticeably cooled when the president reiterated the US's commitment to establishing a democratic and viable Palestinian state, although to reassure them, he quickly added the qualifier that for that to happen the Palestinians needed to renounce terrorism first and get rid of their corrupt leadership.

From 2002 until the end of Bush's term in office, American political and public engagement with Israel and Palestine moved along three different tracks. The first was official negotiations with the Israeli government. For most of the time the dealings were with Ariel Sharon as prime minister, until he suffered a severe stroke in 2006 and was replaced by Ehud Olmert.

All in all, Israeli policy, in particular from the moment Sharon decided to disengage from the Gaza Strip in 2004 (namely pulling all the Jewish settlers out of there and leaving the Palestinians to take over), was quite well co-ordinated with American–Israeli actions at a governmental level.

AIPAC was ambivalent towards Sharon's policies and in particular the disengagement from Gaza. Most of its members sided with the opposition to the disengagement, but the organisation hesitated to oppose an Israeli government and an American administration that fully supported its policies.

What mattered more to AIPAC was its own role in the new political set-up in Israel. And its main efforts were less aimed at changing Israeli policies or persuading Bush not to support them, and much more focused on maintaining its vital role in shaping the American–Israeli relationship.

This is why it did not attack the government of Israel at its annual conference in 2005. At the conference, AIPAC found an effective way to show its continued vitality and usefulness. It stated its role as ensuring that Congress would find a way of compensating Israel for the 'concession' it made in Gaza, thus continuing to build on the foundations that

AIPAC and its predecessor, AZEC, had established since the mid-term elections in 1944.

The second track was AIPAC's attempt to control the narrative on Palestine in American civil society and to arrest the avalanche of solidarity with the Palestinians, which accelerated when activists depicted Israel as a pariah state and demanded that the administration act accordingly. For the first time, large sections of the African American and Native American communities were recruited to the global solidarity network with Palestine. The third track was the lobby's appeal to Christian Zionist and neo-conservative groups to increase their influence on American foreign policy. This Judeo-Christian Zionist lobby was fighting with all its might the shift towards supporting the Palestinians that had intensified among Democrats and progressive sections of the American Jewish community.

AIPAC JOINS THE ROAD MAP TO NOWHERE, 2004–2005

In March 2004, the Israeli prime minister had just announced the 'Gaza disengagement' plan – meaning the Jewish settlers departed and anyone could step in to fill the power vacuum. What Israel didn't plan on was Hamas winning the elections for the legislative assembly created by the Oslo Accords in both the West Bank and the Gaza Strip in 2006. It could justifiably claim to be the new authority in the Gaza Strip. It was powerful enough to repel a Palestine Authority attempt, backed by Israel and the USA, to topple it. These elections hence heralded a bloody and disturbing chapter in an internal Palestinian conflict that separated the West Bank from the Gaza Strip, while the latter became a military battlefield between Israel and Hamas (aided by organisations such as Islamic Jihad).

This development wasn't as much of a blow to Sharon's strategy as we might expect. Disengagement meant he was free to punish the Strip without worrying about incurring collateral damage to Jewish settlers. Nor was he deterred by a developing clash within Israeli Jewish society bringing the state to the brink of civil war in the eyes of many, due to widespread and violent demonstrations by the right in Israel against

disengagement. Sharon claimed that disengagement – entirely implemented on his initiative and not from any impetus from Palestinians –
was a national trauma that could never be repeated again; in other
words, Israel would never disengage from the West Bank. He was not
the first to resort to such gaslighting, presenting himself as a man of
peace willing to concede territory, while in essence he tightened Israel's
grip on Gaza from the outside and excluded totally the West Bank from
any future negotiations. Menachem Begin had sacrificed the Israeli
settlements in the Sinai Peninsula for the sake of the Greater Israel, and
now Sharon had sacrificed the Gaza Strip for the consensual version of
the Greater Israel, incorporating the West Bank.

On 14 April 2004, President Bush wrote a long letter to Prime
Minister Ariel Sharon praising his decision to disengage from the Gaza
Strip.[49] He also approved of the construction of the separation barrier
within the West Bank and between the West Bank and Israel (one which
was categorially condemned worldwide and partly declared illegal by
the International Court of Justice). Bush wrote as if there were a promise that this wall would be temporary, pending a peace agreement. All
boded well towards the beginning of 2005, although AIPAC still did not
regard Sharon as the ideal leader for Israel and waited impatiently for
Likud to return to power.

The close ties between AIPAC and Likud could have made it a
powerful voice in America against disengagement from Gaza. But as
noted, the lobby cared about its power much more than about developments on the ground. And as long as Sharon and Bush recognised its
power, they were welcome at AIPAC's biggest ever annual convention in
2005. Although his popularity with the lobby had waned, the Israeli
prime minister remained AIPAC's guest of honour at its key event. It
was a mutually beneficial set-up – AIPAC got the prestige of Sharon's
presence, and Sharon obtained AIPAC's official approval of the disengagement plan, despite its unpopularity among other members of the
pro-Israel lobby. Disapproval of the plan mainly came from Morton
Klein, the president of the Zionist Organization of America, once a
force to reckon with, but with greatly diminished power in the twenty-
first century.[50] For the first time in its history, AIPAC was congratulated

by organisations traditionally opposed to it within the American Jewish community, such as Americans for Peace Now, the sister organisation of Peace Now in Israel.

It was clear that when Sharon was about to talk to the 2005 conference, he would face some opposition from the floor, but not from AIPAC's leadership.

AIPAC'S BEST YEAR YET: 2005

The Walter E. Washington Convention Center, in Mount Vernon Square in Washington DC, was only two years old when AIPAC met there for its 2005 annual conference. The centre is a 210,000 square-metre complex and is run by Events DC, the entertainment authority for the District of Columbia. The firm Thompson, Ventulett, Stainback and Associates commissioned the centre from the architects Devrouax and Purnell. They specialised in 'superblocks' – gigantic edifices that were a spectacle in themselves – and this was one of their largest ever projects.

On 23 May 2005, you would have found it difficult to reach the convention centre. Police cars blocked every intersection leading to it. Entry was limited to those escorted by motorcade or a designated bus.

The five thousand fortunate attendees enjoyed endless quantities of food and the company of the top politicians in the country. Twenty-six thousand kosher meals, 32,640 hors d'oeuvres, 2,500 pounds of salmon, 1,200 pounds of turkey, 900 pounds of chicken, 700 pounds of beef and 125 gallons of hummus were there to feed everyone for the three days of meetings – as AIPAC boasted in its press releases.[51] It also crowed that AIPAC was at that time one of the four top lobby groups in America with a membership of over 100,000.

The distinguished guest list was also heralded as a huge success. The Israeli guests of honour were headed by Ariel Sharon. He told the conference that his disengagement plan would strengthen Israel's security and expressed his confidence in the US president's 'road map'. Some attendees loudly heckled his speech – they were forcibly ejected from the conference hall by security personnel.

A source who refused to be named told the *Jewish Journal*: 'the real story is that they [AIPAC] were forced to make a statement supporting it [the disengagement] as part of the price of getting Sharon to speak to them [at the conference]'. The journalist attracted his readers' attention to the fact that 'the mood in the hall was sceptical – this was evident every time a speaker mentioned it [the disengagement] – but they had no choice.'[52]

Another journalist covering the event concurred with this description and reported that anyone praising Sharon from the rostrum got limited applause. Many delegates wore orange buttons, an Israeli symbol indicating support for the Gaza settlers. When Secretary of State Condoleezza Rice lauded Sharon's policy of withdrawal, she received faint applause.[53]

As for the other American politicians, readers can get a sense of how they were received from the following quotation from the *Jewish Journal*:

> During AIPAC's famous 'roll call' congressional guests were greeted with ovations ranging from the tepid to the tumultuous (Sen. Lincoln Chaffe, R-RI, widely seen as cool towards Israel, produced barely a ripple: Sen. Max Liberman, D-Con, almost brought the house down).[54]

The conference was attended by a larger number of members of Congress than any other event, except for joint sessions of Congress and the State of the Union address. Had it been an election year, the sitting president would quite probably have headed the group of VIPs.

For the first time in AIPAC's history, only the US national anthem was played at the conference, while *Hatikvah*, Israel's national anthem, was dropped. That led attendees at the 2005 conference to speculate that the decision to drop Israel's national anthem was an attempt by the group to show its loyalty to the US government, given the growing doubt about this among some sections of American society.

Senate Majority Leader Bill Frist (Republican, Tennessee), Senate Minority Leader Harry Reid (Democrat, Nevada), Speaker Dennis

Hastert (Republican, Illinois) and House Minority Leader Nancy Pelosi (Democrat, California) took to the podium to pledge their continued support for Israel.[55]

Condoleezza Rice was the first speaker in the morning, and she was followed by congressional leaders, debating American foreign policy. Those taking part in the debate, Rep. Jane Harman (Democrat, California) and the administration's informal foreign policy adviser Richard Perle, engaged in a neck-and-neck battle to persuade their audience that they were more pro-Israel than their interlocutors.

For instance, Harman tried to curry favour with her audience, most of whom were Republicans, by reminding them that she had an aide who once worked for AIPAC and schmoozed the audience by commending them for being 'very sophisticated'. To top it all, she joined the crowd in celebrating Yasser Arafat's death as 'a blessing'.[56] But after half an hour of this, Harman could not keep up. Perle provoked cheers from the crowd when he favoured a military raid on Iran, saying that 'if Iran is on the verge of a nuclear weapon, I think we will have no choice but to take decisive action.' When Harman said the 'best short-term option' for dealing with Iran was the UN Security Council, the crowd reacted with boos.

Words were accompanied by histrionics. AIPAC's multimedia show, 'Iran's Path to the Bomb', was displayed in the convention centre's basement.[57] The exhibit, worthy of a theme park, began with a narrator condemning the International Atomic Energy Agency for being 'unwilling to conclude that Iran is developing nuclear weapons' (it had similar reservations about Iraq) and the Security Council because it 'has yet to take up the issue'.[58]

In a succession of rooms, visitors saw flashing lights and heard rumbling sounds. Next to them were contraptions that were meant to be yellowcake uranium pieces alongside a presentation of a plutonium reprocessing plant. As one observer put it, there were as many nuclear warheads around as there were gallons of hummus.[59]

And yet this penchant for spectacle could not hide the fact that this was an ambiguous moment in the history of the lobby. A year before, AIPAC had dismissed its policy director and another employee, in reaction to the FBI probing the possibility that they had passed classi-fied US information to Israel. Larry Franklin, a former senior analyst on the Pentagon's Iran desk, could have received a prison sentence of nearly thirteen years for passing top-secret information to Steve Rosen and Keith Weissman, who worked for AIPAC at the time.[60] These two AIPAC officials were charged under the Espionage Act. In 2009, however, US Justice Department prosecutors overruled the FBI's advice to take the pair to trial and instead dropped the case.

This was more than just a momentary embarrassment. Although AIPAC had successfully navigated its way out of the dangerous waters of the Pollard affair, it once more had to convince the American public that it was not simply an arm of Israeli diplomacy.

The annual conference avoided mentioning these rather inconven-ient matters; most of the delegates probably did not feel any sense of panic. Again, as Dana Milbank observed, none of these issues kept the powerful 'from lining up to woo AIPAC'.[61] In the conference, in fact, other bodies appeared to show solidarity with AIPAC. Abraham Foxman of the Anti-Defamation League said that they were there because 'there is a cloud over AIPAC' and so 'it is important for leaders of the American Jewish Community to be here and show support'.[62] Another delegate dismissed altogether the FBI probe into the affairs of AIPAC and told journalists the delegates were only focused on Iran.

On the face of it, it looked like a moment when AIPAC had reached a pinnacle of success. Since 1949, the US had passed to Israel more than $100 billion in grants and $10 billion in special loans. According to the estimate suggested by Mearsheimer and Walt, by 2005 total American aid to Israel was $154 billion and was worth more when accounting for the favourable conditions attached to loans.[63]

Other bodies that were not part of the administration annually transferred $1 billion to Israel. As Naseer Aruri notes, this is larger than the amount of money transferred by the US to North Africa, South America and the Caribbean put together. Their joint population amounts to over one billion people; Israel's population barely reached nine million in 2007. Over the last forty years, roughly $8.5 billion had been given to Israel for military purchases.[64]

Despite this, AIPAC continued to target politicians whom it deemed potentially anti-Israel. In 2002, the pro-Israel lobby successfully targeted African American representatives Earl Hilliard (Democrat, Alabama) and Cynthia McKinney (Democrat, Georgia), leading to their defeat in the Democratic primaries.

Hilliard was the Alabama congressional Democratic run-off candidate in 2002. He ran successfully in the previous five campaigns. His criticisms of Israel, it should be noted, were very tame, but enough to bring the wrath of AIPAC upon him. He refused to condemn the Palestinian freedom fighters as terrorists and had visited Libya in 1979. Although he was supported by the African American caucus on the Hill, AIPAC was stronger than that caucus. Consequently, his opponent, Arthur Davis, won the election. Davis received $300,000 from AIPAC – in stark contrast to the modest $1,000 Hilliard received from Arab-American organisations.[65]

In the next three years leading up to the election of President Obama, the good times just kept rolling for the lobby. The unholy trinity of Christian Zionism, neo-conservatism and American Jewish lobbying still had immense impact on legislation, elections and policies concerning Israel and Palestine. The Second Lebanon War in the summer of 2006 and the first of many brutal Israeli assaults to come on the Gaza Strip triggered a new phenomenon in 2007, a liberal Zionist counter-lobby, J Street; a precursor of the more fundamental challenges that would face the lobby, and in particular AIPAC, in the Obama years and even during Donald Trump's bizarre term in office.

More problematic for AIPAC was the rise of the pro-Palestinian network of solidarity, emerging around campuses, trade unions and small communities, reacting to the extraordinary cruelty of Israel's retaliation following the second Intifada. AIPAC was swift to try to nip these initiatives in the bud. Every local initiative for active solidarity with Palestinians was confronted with a storm of outrage by the 'Jewish community'; in actuality, the lobby. One early case of AIPAC's deep involvement in a very localised affair was the lobby's intervention in Somerville in the Greater Boston area. It was an early prototype for AIPAC's later modus operandi.

THE SOMERVILLE DIVESTMENT PROJECT: 2003–2004

The city of Somerville, in the metropolitan Boston area, is located north of Cambridge in Middlesex County, now numbering over 80,000 inhabitants, famous for its culture of arts and live music and its vibrant student population.[66] Until 2003, it had no link whatsoever to the Israel/Palestine question. But in the space of one summer, it became a crucial battleground, where Palestine solidarity clashed with Israel's claim to moral legitimacy.

A young high school teacher, Ron Francis, founded the Somerville Divestment Project at the College Avenue Methodist Church. The Project group approached the aldermen (the city councillors) to try and persuade them to declare support for divestment from Israel; more specifically the Somerville Retirement Board, which managed the pensions of the city employees, was asked to sell its Israeli bonds and any stocks in American companies doing military business with Israel. Eight of the eleven aldermen were persuaded by the moral argument and were about to vote in favour of such a resolution. The pro-Israel lobby sprang into action: a flood of letters to the *Somerville Journal* convinced the mayor Joe Curtatone to threaten to veto the resolution. The Israeli Consulate General in Boston, as well as other lobbying organisations, began to organise locally and nationally to prepare for a public debate on 8 November 2004. Each participant had two minutes to talk – the pro-divestment speakers group had many Jewish members (constituting forty per cent). While Iftah Shavit, an ex-Israeli, supported the project wholeheartedly in an article he wrote, the lobby invited ex-military Israelis, studying or working nearby, to tell the board how unsafe they felt because of the project.

In this David and Goliath battle, it would be David who came out the loser. The council rejected the proposal, with only one of the aldermen, Denise Provost, remaining faithful to their initial support. Nonetheless, this event in a small American city is worth revisiting. Whether the board of the city endorsed the project or not, it would not have changed anything on the ground in Palestine. And yet the pro-Israel lobby mustered all its might to defeat a symbolic gesture by civil society. This small group of Americans only wanted to signal their moral contempt for the actions of the Israeli state.

Denise Provost felt it was the implications of her courageous stance in 2004 throughout her political career that brought her to the Massachusetts House of Representatives, representing the 27th Middlesex District between 2006 and 2020. In her campaign for this post, her rivals constantly reminded the electorate of her 'anti-Israel' stance, and rich businessmen associated with the lobby funded them in the elections. She lost some votes because of this, but managed nonetheless to represent the working-class Middlesex 27th District. Her stance required fortitude, as, like so many before and after her, she was warned that the moral positions she subscribed to were tantamount to political suicide, which was probably true for a number of politicians at the local, state and federal levels.

Initiatives such as the one in Somerville began to blossom in many other parts of the United States, organised by Americans of Palestinian origin, African Americans, Native Americans and other minority groups showing solidarity with the oppressed Palestinians and working in tandem with growing pro-Palestinian activism among American Jewish society. They would become an even more serious challenge to AIPAC after 2004, in particular, as we shall see, after the second Israeli invasion of Lebanon in 2006. It was not easy for AIPAC, as the images emerging from the Second Lebanon War became emblematic of the devastation Israel could wreak, further eroding Israel's moral legitimacy in American civil society.

As Walter Hixson tells us, the need to defend Israel's image against the clear evidence of its brutality brought AIPAC even closer to Christian Zionist bodies such as Christians United for Israel, led by an owner of a Texan megachurch by the name of Reverend John Hagee, who became a personal friend of Netanyahu, and was amply rewarded by being invited by him to attend, with President Trump, the opening of the American embassy in Jerusalem in 2018.[67]

The need to airbrush the horrific features of occupation and siege also brought AIPAC closer to the right wing of the Republican Party. By the end of the Bush years, bipartisanship was widely seen as a pretence on

AIPAC's part – it seemed firmly aligned with the Republicans. And this brings us to the third track AIPAC was moving on, alongside action vis-à-vis the president and civil society – cementing its connections with twenty-first-century Christian Zionists and the American extreme right.

CHRISTIAN ZIONISM FOR THE TWENTY-FIRST CENTURY AND THE WAR ON ISLAM

For the hard core of Christian Zionists, Operation Shock and Awe, the Anglo-American assault on Iraq in April 2003, looked like a scene out of their own doomsday scenarios. This was the wrath of the Hebrew God that was joyously received by Christian Zionists as well as messianic Jews in Israel, who uncovered a theological basis for the dubious links between Islam, terror and Palestine. The old bestseller *Scofield's Bible* was revived and offered a contemporary fundamentalist reading of Old and New Testaments – interpreted to command support for Israel as a literal article of faith.

After 9/11 this theology had adopted a clear anti-Islamic line. In his important work on the subject, Stephen Sizer has revealed how Christian Zionists constructed a historical narrative that described the Muslim attitude to Christianity throughout the ages as a kind of genocidal campaign directed against both Jews and Christians.[68] What were once hailed as moments of Islamic triumph – the Islamic renaissance of the Middle Ages, the *Convivencia* in Al-Andalus, the golden era of the Ottomans, the emergence of Arab independence and the end of European colonialism – were recast as the satanic, anti-Christian acts of heathens. In this new historical view, the US became St George, Israel his shield and spear, and Islam their Dragon.

This new presentation of the old idea of Israel being on the side of Christ and its enemies as the modern Antichrists was delivered in the twenty-first century through a multimedia franchise run by Christian Zionists called the Left Behind Project. It started as sixteen bestseller novels written by Tim LaHaye and Jerry B. Jenkins, resurrecting the ideas of the Dispensationalists, as if nothing had changed in the intervening century and the apocalyptic prophecies still held as true as ever.

The Antichrist this time was 'global communities' which represented hatred towards the forces of Christ. From its first film, *Left Behind: The Movie*, screened in 2000, to the latest version in 2014 with Nicolas Cage, through to a PC game, the franchise has made far-fetched Dispensationalist prophecies easily digestible for the American public.[69]

The introduction to the PC game *Left Behind* says it all, reflecting the power of informal lobbying. It enjoins players to support Israel and the equally sacrosanct imperative to identify the Muslims, the Palestinians and the liberals of the world as Antichrists who intend to destroy Israel, unless America defends it.

The following extended quotation is from the fan-made Wikipedia description of the PC game, which defines Israel for the players (who need to help the Jewish state if they want to save the world). It refers to both the film and the game and explains that Israel is:

> the land God has given to the descendants of Abraham, Isaac, and Jacob by a perpetual covenant … Jews are considered part of Israel. The enemies of Israel, particularly Muslim countries, refer to Israel as Palestine due to the desire of their national leaders wanting to drive its inhabitants 'into the sea' since it became a nation in 1948. Up until this day, the land has remained in constant dispute between the Israelis and the Palestinians.[70]

Under a futuristic interpretation of the Book of Revelation in the Bible, God has not yet fulfilled some of the Old Testament prophecies related to Israel. The plot of the *Left Behind* series is based on this interpretation and depicts how the authors believe God may fulfil these prophecies in the future.

In the next game in the series, *Rapture*, it is God that defends Israel from the Russians, a rescue operation predicted in the prophecy of Ezekiel chapter 28. In the next instalment, *Tribulation Force*, on another front, Israel reaches a seven-year agreement to exchange knowledge with Nicolae Carpathia and the Global Community (a liberal feminist Satanic coalition led of course by a woman). Israel provides the Global Community with its knowledge of fertilisers(!), and in return, but not in good faith, the Global Community's feminist leader deviously lures Israel into believing that it can rely on the Global Community to defend it. It is clear that this a terrible mistake by Israel, because the Global Community is pro-Russian and pro-Palestinian and, above all, it is a bunch of Antichrists masked as progressive people. And betrayal does come when Nicolae desecrates the temple in Jerusalem. But not to worry: Jesus comes back and defeats the horrible Nicolae, despite the fact that she heads up a massive army (yes, in the battle of Armageddon). And it goes on and on for another battle with Satan's army. The real final chapter in this trajectory is not to be found in the books, the PC games or the film, although it should be part of them: the conversion of the Jews to Christianity (or their barbecuing in Hell).[71]

As we can see, the basic notions of Christian Zionism have not changed in the twenty-first century. It continues to interpret the prophetic texts as foretelling the establishment of the state of Israel. A Lifeway poll conducted in the United States in 2017 found that eighty per cent of evangelical Christians believed that the creation of Israel in 1948 was the fulfilment of a biblical prophecy that would bring about Christ's return, and more than fifty per cent of them said that they supported Israel because it is important for the fulfilment of biblical prophecy.[72]

Christian Zionists were also instrumentalised through a more familiar method of persuasion, used in the past by both secular and religious lobbies: trips to Israel. These trips were no longer just pilgrimages to the holy places of Christianity; instead they involved collective prayers in the very heart of the Holy Land, apparently giving them a better chance of being heard by God, beseeching him to defend Israel against its enemies, ranging from Russia to progressive humanism.

Islam had gradually replaced Russia as the arch-enemy. Christian Zionists in America now saw their main task as defending Israel from its regional enemies. One of the common ways of showing such a commitment was through these prayer pilgrimages. The most notable of these was a project involving tours to Israel under the banner 'Day of Prayer for the Peace of Jerusalem'. The origins of this initiative lay in the 1990s, when Dan Mazar, the publisher and editor of a Christian Zionist mouthpiece called *Jerusalem Christian Review*, organised the 'World

Prayer for Peace in Jerusalem'. This event was broadcast on all the major US TV networks (including CNN) and among the faithful participants were former president Ronald Reagan and the Australian prime minister Bob Hawke, alongside Billy Graham, Pat Robertson, Jerry Falwell and other Christian fundamentalist household names.[73]

The concept was taken up by two Pentecostal evangelical leaders, Jack W. Hayford and Robert Stearns. They formed an organisation called Eagles' Wings, the purpose of which was to combat various 'dangers' to the Judeo-Christian world, such as secular humanism and radical Islam. And again, the best way to 'combat' these dangers was by showing unconditional support for Israel. In 2006, the two advocates claimed that 150,000 churches around world collaborated in staging these days of prayer.[74]

All these activities were supported by the Israeli Ministry of Tourism and the Israel Allies Foundation (IAF). The IAF is an umbrella organisation of all caucuses within parliaments around the world committed to maintaining Israel as a Jewish state and making Jerusalem the united and eternal capital of Israel.

All the caucuses are modelled on the one in the Israeli Knesset called the Christian Allies Caucus. From the Israeli Knesset, the IAF co-ordinates the work of politicians around the world who are tasked with galvanising support for Israel in their respective parliaments, which include both Houses on Capitol Hill (although their US branch was somewhat redundant, given the plethora of pro-Israel outfits on the Hill). The Christian Allies Caucus website outlines several red lines it has vowed never to cross, such as never doubting Israel's sovereignty over the whole of Jerusalem.[75] It has branches in the Philippines, South Korea, Brazil, South Africa, Japan, Australia, Finland, Italy, Canada, Costa Rica and Malawi; altogether by 2021 it had fifty affiliated groups. The perks include tours of Israel.[76]

The prime mover behind the initiative on the Israeli side was Avigdor Lieberman, the leader of the hard right Russian immigrant party, Yisrael Beiteinu. Accordingly, the IAF drifted to the right, co-opted by settlers in the occupied West Bank and by politicians who supported the transfer of Palestinians from the West Bank to Jordan. Its main funder was Irving

Moskowitz (who made his money from a diverse portfolio including hospital and casino construction). He passed away in 2016, but his family continued to aid the settlers' projects in the occupied West Bank and, in particular, efforts to de-Arabise greater Jerusalem.

Under the influence of scholars such as Samuel Huntington, the Knesset sought to situate support for Israel as part of a 'clash of civilisations' narrative in which the caucuses contribute to the defence of the Judeo-Christian heritage, legacy or civilisation. This was especially bizarre in light of a millennium of Christian persecution of Jews, from expulsions to pogroms to outright genocide. This now became the hegemonic discourse. Jews and Christians in the lobby for Israel were now committed to protecting 'Judeo-Christian values'. These 'values' really amounted to nothing more or less than unconditional support for Israel. As one of its leading figures, Uri Bank, told the Knesset:

Evangelical Christians are powerful in their countries and they love Israel, but they haven't been taught how to leverage that in our favor ... That is what we're doing.

His colleague Benny Elon added:

The Christian world is Israel's most strategic ally both existentially and spiritually. Existentially, they stand up against radical Islam and their desire to destroy the state of Israel. Spiritually, Christians are our partners in the clash of cultures between our values and those of radical Islam.[77]

With the growing power of the conservative wing of the Republicans, along with what became known as the 'Tea Party group', the discourse on Israel was now increasingly determined by Christian fundamentalism. A candidate for the Republicans' 2016 presidential nomination, Ted Cruz, a senator from Texas and the son of an evangelical minister, made various references to heroic chapters in Jewish history, such as the rebellion against the Greeks at the end of the biblical period. Muslims, in his eyes, were the 'Greeks' against whom Israel now had to defend itself. After one of his speeches in New York in front of a Zionist group, one of the organisers noted, with satisfaction:

> He's aligned with the Jewish people. He's aligned with the Jewish calendar. He understands Jewish history. He understands that Jews, even though they have small numbers, persevere and are victorious ... because God is on Israel's side. He understands that.[78]

This Christian fundamentalist discourse is also popular among Latin American neo-conservatives. For both Christian fundamentalists and neo-conservatives, Israel is crucial for the defence of America; either because this is God's will, or because Israel is the bulwark against the new enemies of twenty-first-century America: Iran, Russia and 'Islamic terrorism'. Combined, religion and neo-conservatism make an incredibly dangerous mixture. Incidentally, Cruz's loyalty to Israel did not pay off, and he was thoroughly beaten by another ultra pro-Zionist, Donald Trump, in the elections for the Republican candidacy in 2016.

But before we reach the Trump era, when both Christian Zionists and neo-cons had a field day, they and AIPAC had to face a new political star that appeared on the horizon in the Democratic Party, and AIPAC immediately wanted to get its claws into him. AIPAC, after all, has no political allegiances beyond unconditional support for Israel.

History never really repeats itself. But let's think of a relatively unknown Democratic nominee, who first happily receives help from AIPAC to win the presidency. However, after the election, he bitterly disappoints them – even if he has done nothing that changes the balance of power in Palestine. Two names come to mind. The first is Jimmy Carter. The second is Barack Obama.

ANOTHER ENEMY IN THE WHITE HOUSE: THE OBAMA YEARS

The day after Senator Barack Obama gained the Democratic nomination for president, he took to the stage at AIPAC's conference to dispel any doubts they might have had and reassure the group's supporters that he was 'a true friend of Israel'. He added:

> I want to say that I know some provocative emails have been circulating throughout Jewish communities across the country. A few of you may have gotten them. They're filled with tall tales and dire warnings about a certain candidate for president. And all I want to say is – let me know if you see this guy named Barack Obama, because he sounds pretty frightening.[79]

Obama reminisced at length in his speech about his childhood, and recalled how the elders in his family, such as his grandfather and great-uncle, served during the Second World War, pointing out that since then he had been aware of and concerned about the horrors suffered by the Jews during the Holocaust.

He also pledged to move the American embassy from Tel Aviv to Jerusalem: 'Jerusalem will remain the capital of Israel and it must remain undivided', he told the AIPAC conference. (But as often happens with presidents, his actions, including those regarding Jerusalem, didn't quite live up to his promises on the campaign trail.)

However, events on the ground made it very difficult for AIPAC to accept Obama as a friend, although this may also have been connected to his African American background and his vociferous opposition to the war in Iraq.[80]

The consistent orientation taken by Israel, ever since Netanyahu came to power on the basis of a coalition of Israel's extreme right, exacerbated the oppression faced by the Palestinians, who by this point had been subject to a colonial project for over a hundred years. A new landmark in this policy of brutalisation was Operation Cast Lead.

On 27 December 2008, a three-week Israeli assault on Gaza began, which left more than 1,400 Palestinians dead and the Strip ruined, with many Palestinians losing their homes, wounded and traumatised. Israeli forces killed four of their own soldiers and lost another six, along with three civilians. This was televised carnage, and the humanitarian crisis that followed was even more high-profile. The Israeli siege continued and made it very difficult to rebuild, treat the injured and re-establish any kind of normality.

A UN commission of inquiry, officially known as the UN Fact Finding Mission on the Gaza Conflict, was dispatched to the area under the chairmanship of Judge Richard Goldstone, a South African Jew. While condemning Hamas for committing war crimes, it accused Israel of targeting Palestinian civilians intentionally. Since Israel came out of this report very badly, Goldstone was boycotted by his community in South Africa; he was not allowed to attend his grandson's bar mitzvah ceremony at the local synagogue.[81] This may explain why in an op-ed in the *Washington Post* he refrained from accusing Israel of intentionally killing civilians, but the other members of his commission responded with an article in the *Guardian*, restating that this was their major finding.[82]

Somewhat surprisingly, Obama was quite tame in his reaction to Cast Lead, never blaming Israel directly, so this was not an immediate cause for friction with AIPAC. It was his next step, a historic speech he gave on 4 June 2009 in Cairo (and which won him the Nobel Peace Prize), that provoked AIPAC. He was the first president to refer to the 1948 catastrophe and rebuked Israel for its 'intolerable mistreatment' of the Palestinians. He promised he would support the Palestinians in their desire to establish their own state.[83]

That same year Benjamin Netanyahu won the elections in Israel and began a second term in office. Since his last term he had established strong connections with Christian Zionists and the Republican right – and like AIPAC he made no pretence at bipartisanship. This did not bode well for the relationship between the two men. From the moment Benjamin Netanyahu was elected in 2009, their relations soured over the Israeli prime minister's blatant lack of commitment to finding a solution to the Israeli–Palestinian conflict.

Both the Israeli government and AIPAC correctly assumed that Obama would talk the Clintonian talk when it came to Palestine, but had no intention of walking the walk. After all, the personnel in the State Department were practically the same as in Clinton's time. So Obama would allow Israel's actions in Palestine, including expansion of the settlements, Judaisation of large parts of the West Bank, and the harsh siege of the Gaza Strip. His tolerance would extend to defending Israel in the UN and providing it with international immunity.

The talk was indeed there. His statements throughout 2009 called upon Israel to freeze the settlements in the West Bank. AIPAC reacted by organising a petition signed by seventy-six senators and 329 representatives rejecting the call. But the president was forceful enough to extract from Netanyahu a freeze on new housing projects, which he did not intend to fulfil, an infraction which went unpunished by any action by the Obama administration. But vice president Joe Biden was genuinely irritated that the violation of this commitment was announced while he was on an official visit to Israel at the end of 2010.

Obama's secretary of state Hillary Clinton's role was to sweeten the pill every time a harsh condemnation by the president was issued, and the same happened after Biden's visit. AIPAC might have attempted to reciprocate in kind but it was outflanked by its strongest ally in American politics, the Christian Zionists, who did not hesitate to weaponise racism in the struggle against Obama's entirely meaningless 'commitment' to a two-state solution. This African American president was a far cry from their biased image of an American leader. Alongside the Christian Zionists, Glenn Beck, a conservative political commentator who became notorious for his claim that Obama had 'a deep-seated hatred for white people or the white culture', joined in the battle against a two-state solution. His message in 2010 sounded like something from the Christian Zionist/AIPAC heyday:

> They are going to attack the center of our faith, our common faith, and that is Jerusalem. And it won't be with bullets or bombs. It will be with a two-state solution that cuts off Jerusalem, the old city, to the rest of the world. It is time to return inside the walls that surround Jerusalem and stand with people of all faiths all around the world.[84]

Beck organised mass demonstrations to convey this message, both in the USA and in Jerusalem. But most importantly of all, his diatribe had endless repeated reruns on *Fox News*.

As described in the first volume of Obama's memoirs, *A Promised Land*, he was essentially bullied by Netanyahu and his supporters during his term in office.[85] To his detriment, he failed to stand up to this pressure effectively. Netanyahu, meanwhile, made little effort to hide his animosity toward Obama throughout his presidency, going so far as to publicly fête his presidential challenger Mitt Romney in the 2012 US elections.

As for AIPAC's role, its impact can clearly be seen in Obama's memoirs. This book is a valuable source that provides the president's detailed descriptions of his experience as the target of a well-orchestrated campaign. He opens up about the influence of the pro-Israel lobby on US lawmakers. His memoir pointedly describes the difficulties that he and, by his own admission, any US lawmaker faced in pushing through policies opposed by the Israeli government and its allied domestic lobby groups.[86] Obama paints a stark picture of a US political system that, in a limited but serious way, has been compromised by foreign influence.

The main message from Obama's memoirs is familiar. Any criticism of Israel by US lawmakers, even when Israel had gone against US policy, was subject to the lobby's wrath. Those who criticised Israeli actions 'too loudly' risked being labelled 'anti-Israel' or even 'anti-Semitic'. They could have to contend with a 'well-funded opponent' when elections rolled round. It did not help that seventy per cent of American Jews gave Obama their vote. He had no chance with AIPAC, as they had decided a priori that Obama did not feel his outward support for the Jewish state in his 'guts'.[87]

'By the time I took office', Obama wrote, in a section reflecting on the troubled US history of mediating the Israel/Palestine conflict, 'most congressional Republicans had abandoned any pretence of caring about what happened to the Palestinians.'[88] Religious commitments had led many white evangelical Republican voters to blindly support the Israeli government in everything. Obama went on to say that meanwhile, due to electoral and ideological considerations inside the Democratic Party, 'even stalwart progressives were loath to look less pro-Israel than Republicans.'[89]

Obama might have been thinking about the ordeal his nominee for secretary of state for defence, Chuck Hagel, underwent when his nomination was discussed in Congress. During his hearing before Congress, he was grilled by pro-Israel Congress members about an interview he had given to Aaron David Miller in 2006 when he said: 'the Jewish lobby intimidates a lot of people [on Capitol Hill]'. Using the word 'Jewish' instead of 'Israel' opened the door to accusations of anti-Semitism. He went through what Stephen Walt described as the 'circus' of a *mea culpa* and had to prove his loyalty to Israel in order to salvage his nomination.[90]

At the heart of the problem, as Obama described it, stood a nexus of pro-Israel lobbying groups and activists in DC that exerted pressure on his presidency at every turn, despite the fact that he considered himself 'fiercely protective' of Israel and had provided it with strong economic, political and military support. Obama didn't seem to think that he was the only one facing this predicament. As he wrote:

> Members of both parties worried about crossing the American Israel Public Affairs Committee, a powerful bipartisan lobbying organization dedicated to ensuring unwavering US support for Israel.[91]

'I'd delivered on my promise to enhance US–Israel cooperation across the board', Obama pointed out, lamenting the apparent lack of gratitude in response to this support.

> Nevertheless, the noise orchestrated by Netanyahu had the intended effect of gobbling up our time, putting us on the defensive, and reminding me that normal policy differences with an Israeli prime minister – even one who presided over a fragile coalition government – exacted a political cost that didn't exist when I dealt with the United Kingdom, Germany, France, Japan, Canada, or any of our other closest allies.[92]

As Israel's own political drift to the far-right continued, Obama went on to write, AIPAC also maintained a forceful insistence that:

There should be 'no daylight' between the US and Israeli governments, even when Israel took actions that were contrary to US policy.

This created a serious dilemma for any US politician trying to maintain
a commitment to liberal principles, let alone those leaning towards the
left in any meaningful way. The consequences of crossing AIPAC and
other pro-Israel organisations could be dire for any US politician.

Obama described one case in detail which illustrates the kind of
pressure he was exposed to, when in 2011 he repeated his call on Israel
to freeze settlements. 'White House phones started ringing off the hook'
after Obama asked Israeli leaders to freeze settlement activity; he added
that he was the target of a 'whisper campaign' that characterised him as
hostile to Israel.[93] His own Jewish supporters were forced to fight back
against this whisper campaign alleging Obama's private hostility toward
Israel, which was supposedly proven by his friendships with a few
Palestinian academics and periodic expressions of sympathy for those
living under Israeli occupation.

These recollections are worth comparing with Obama's speech
delivered to the annual AIPAC conference in 2011. Obama did all he
could to stress his commitment to 'a strong and secure Israel' as an
American national interest and continued to describe Israel in terms
that were familiar and pleasant for AIPAC's conference attendees: 'Israel
lives in a very tough neighbourhood', which 'I saw first-hand' – referring to a visit to Sderot, the Israeli development town hit by Qassam
rockets launched from the Gaza Strip. He further boasted of his contribution to the security collaboration in developing the 'Iron Dome', the
anti-rocket defence system, and described it as the best solution for the
'tough neighbourhood': 'It's why we're making our most advanced technologies available to our Israeli allies.'[94]

He received a large round of applause when he defined the course of
future sanctions on Iran; little did he know this would be the main bone
of contention with AIPAC in his second term in office. He went further
by fully adopting the Israeli position on Palestinian unity. Any agreement between Hamas and Fatah, he declared, 'is dangerous' and he
repeated the compulsory mantra for any pro-Israel politician: 'Hamas is

a terrorist organization'. In those days, there was an additional demand: the unconditional release of the captured Israeli soldier Gilad Shalit – with no mention of the thousands of Palestinian political prisoners held by Israel.

There was an indirect clash with Benjamin Netanyahu's position on the Palestine question. Obama referred in his speech to the two-state solution, adding, to applause, a pledge for a 'land swap' and a 'demilitarised state' at an undetermined point in the future.

In Obama's second term, Operation Protective Edge in 2014 brought a new challenge to his relationship with Israel. From 8 July to 26 August 2014 Israel launched its largest operation so far against Hamas in the Gaza Strip, which, as with the operations that preceded it, turned the Strip into a disaster zone, and compounded the already unbearable living conditions caused by years of Israeli siege. The death toll was higher than ever before; 2,300 Palestinians, sixty-six Israeli soldiers and six civilians died during the operation.

Events like this intensified the pro-Palestinian impulse in American society and alternative media, and sometimes fed through to mainstream media in a muted way, but AIPAC initiated frequent legislation and congressional declarations from August 2014 until the end of the year, aimed at justifying the Israeli assault as a war of self-defence. These warm words were accompanied by action. Even before the Israeli assault ended, on 4 August 2014, Congress passed legislation with an overwhelming majority providing Israel with an additional $225 million on top of its annual aid. It should be stressed that this was a bipartisan initiative.[95]

So powerful was this campaign that Obama's new secretary of state, John Kerry, had to repeatedly scold both sides in Congress and demand that they show restraint. He expressed sorrow for the situation, while his delegation in the UN cast veto after veto on any attempt to condemn Israel in the Security Council.

But there were red lines for the president, as with all presidents, and they were drawn when a deal with Iran on its nuclear capacity was seriously put on the table. While Palestinians may have hoped that the key conflict between Barack Obama and AIPAC and the pro-Israel lobby at large would be the Palestine issue, they were disappointed by the end of his two terms in office. Obama did clash with the lobby – but Iran was the issue, not Palestine. AIPAC mobilised over an attempt to conclude a final agreement in which Iran was willing to freeze, or at least slow down, its nuclear development in return for removal of the sanctions regime that had hitherto been led by the USA.

THE NETANYAHU–AIPAC SHOWDOWN
WITH OBAMA ON IRAN, 2015–2016

On a hot summer day in July 2015, Palais Coburg in Vienna played host to an array of international statesmen. Already over a century old, the palace was redolent of Old World opulence, though now fitted with every modern amenity. It was designed in 1839 by the architect Karl Schleps in neoclassical style, and required high levels of constant maintenance over the years to protect it from the soot that urban modernisation brought with it to many parts of the city. It took five years to build and was finished in 1845. It is located on the site of the city's Braunbastion (brown bastion), dating back to 1555, which was demolished shortly after Palais Coburg was built. It was soon dubbed Spargelburg (the 'Asparagus Castle') by locals in the Austrian capital on account of its thin freestanding columns. The last Sachsen-Coburg-Koháry to own the building was Sarah Aurelia Halász, the widow of Philipp Josias von Sachsen-Coburg-Koháry, who lived there until her death in 1994, although she had sold it to a realtor in 1978. Following renovations in the 2000s, it became a luxury hotel.

The hotel's white façade was polished, and its interior sparkled as it waited to receive a large number of world dignitaries, dropped off by a succession of black saloon cars. The VIP guestlist was headed by the American secretary of state, John Kerry. It was not easy for journalists to see who was arriving, as a green glass screen covered the elegant front entrance to the hotel. But they could still appreciate the beauty of the two storeys, with the asparagus-like columns separating stylish windows. On the roof stood six statues, holding the old palace's marble emblem. The guests occupied all thirty-three suites that the hotel offered.

The Austrian government went out of its way to make life as comfortable as possible for the negotiation teams. The government footed the guests' bills and offered Austria's trademark wafer biscuits and chocolate *Mozartkugeln* free of charge. Between meetings, the guests were treated to buffet breakfasts, lavish brunches, lunches and dinners every day. As an industrious *Guardian* reporter noted, the Iranians, the Americans and the British seemed to think that their own cuisine was superior (completely inexplicable in the case of the latter group) and each brought their own food: the Iranians green raisins and pistachios, the Americans ten pounds of strawberry-flavoured Twizzlers, twenty pounds of cheese strings and thirty pounds of mixed nuts and raisins. The British team shuttled between Vienna and London, returning with Marks & Spencer biscuits. Only the French seemed to enjoy the local food and even raided the famous wine cellar in the hotel.[96]

But it was not that comfortable. The eighteen days of negotiations were held amid an unprecedented heat wave and, like most continental hotels, the Coburg had yet to adapt to the reality of global warming, so its air conditioning system was relatively weak. So this was a real effort on behalf of diplomats and politicians, most of whom were over sixty, with all the challenges that come with age.

But their efforts bore fruit and, after toiling literally day and night, they put the final touches to what became known as the 'Iran nuclear deal', after agreeing on its principles earlier, on 2 April 2015 in Lausanne, Switzerland. There the USA joined the EU, Russia and China in declaring and signing a deal with Iran that was meant to orient its nuclear capabilities towards peaceful goals. President Barack Obama said this was 'a historic understanding' and called it a very good deal.[97]

This ended a two-year effort by the Obama administration, which had begun in March 2013 when the US commenced a series of secret talks with Iran in Oman. The election of Hassan Rouhani, considered a 'moderate' by the West, as president of Iran accelerated the process and the rapprochement between the two countries. When Rouhani spoke on the phone with Obama in September that year, this was the first ever contact between American and Iranian heads of state – a historic moment.

An interim agreement had already been signed in Geneva in November 2013, called the Joint Comprehensive Plan of Action, and this paved the way for the Vienna agreement.

For President Obama the hard work was only beginning. He knew that he would have to use a presidential veto to overcome the Republican majority in Congress, who also had several allies in the Democratic Party when it came to the Iran nuclear deal. He had the support of 150 Democratic House members, which was the number he needed to sustain the veto.

The main campaign against the deal was run by AIPAC, with some other constituent parts of the formal and informal pro-Israel lobby. AIPAC created a new group: Citizens for a Nuclear Free Iran. The group was furnished with $20 million. Its prime movers were anonymous, and when the *New York Times* approached two people in the new group to inquire about its financial resources, those involved stated they were not authorised to disclose more detailed information about it.[98]

AIPAC spent large sums of money in the effort to thwart the deal. Forty million dollars were invested in this campaign. Most of the budget was spent on TV ads in the states where undecided lawmakers resided; but in many cases, the lobbyists flew to these states to exert direct pressure on the legislators living there. Sanguinely but wrongly, *The Nation* magazine believed that this act nearly destroyed AIPAC. It did harm the lobby, but in a less disastrous way than predicted by *The Nation*.[99]

This campaign was demanded and orchestrated by the Israeli prime minister, Benjamin Netanyahu, who, like a good general, came to the battlefield himself, armed with insinuations of anti-Semitism and Islamophobia, doomsday scenarios and puerile graphic representations of the Iranian danger sketched on a drawing board.[100] He came to a joint meeting of the two Houses of Congress without an official invitation in March 2015, an appearance brokered by Israel's ambassador to the United States along with House Speaker John Boehner (Republican, Ohio). This uninvited appearance was seen by the president and the Democratic Party as an insulting breach of diplomatic norms. Many Democrats boycotted Netanyahu's speech, as they rightly pointed out that this was part of a bid to win yet another Israeli national election. However, this show of protest by about fifty Democrats did not prevent his attendance. He gave a speech in front of a joint session of Congress. The grand rehearsal for this speech took place in front of the AIPAC 2015 annual conference in Washington. He also made a webcast, asking the American Jewish community to do all it could to thwart the Iran nuclear deal.[101] Most pundits, at the time, believed that this combative speech to Congress in March went down so badly that the deal was sure to be approved.

In the aftermath of this visit, AIPAC began intensive lobbying against the Iran deal. It was directed solely at the Republican Party, as any effort directed towards the Democratic Party proved to be a total failure. The lobby persuaded only two Senate Democrats, and a handful in the House, to join its campaign, while Obama secured more than the thirty-four Senate votes needed to ensure that opponents wouldn't be able to collect the veto-proof two-thirds majority to block the deal.

Obama fought back ferociously. He did not mince his words when he found out that AIPAC had invested almost $40 million in the campaign against the Iran nuclear deal. He likened those opposing his deal to those who created the drumbeat of war in the run-up to the invasion of Iraq in 2003.

He told AIPAC officials he would 'hit back hard' against particular ads published by AIPAC that frustrated him. AIPAC had used several organisations to spread its ad campaign, which it called the 'blitz campaign'. One such group was Secure America Now, which published an ad showing an interview with a woman whose husband was killed by an IED in Iraq, allegedly produced in Iran. The woman says: 'and now President Obama would do a deal that lets Iran get a nuclear weapon.'[102] Obama enlisted the help of twenty-nine of America's most eminent scientists and nuclear policy experts, including five Nobel Prize winners and many other luminaries, to strongly endorse the Iran nuclear deal on the pages of the *New York Times*. Richard Garwin, Siegfried Hecker (the former head of the Los Alamos National Laboratory), Freeman Dyson, Sidney Drell, and many other household names, theoretical physicists and arms control experts professed their support.[103]

AIPAC was strong enough to intimidate a few of those who wanted to ally themselves with the president. Congress's Jewish lawmakers came under some of the most intense pressure from anti-deal activists. Rep. Steve Cohen (Democrat, Tennessee), who announced his support for the deal in August, described weathering a barrage of attacks from passionately opposed constituents and others on social media, who questioned his religion, his intelligence and called him a *kapo* – a term used to describe prisoners of Nazi concentration camps who were assigned to supervise forced labour – as they pressurised him to oppose the deal. Cohen and others were quite confident that AIPAC's language was escalating due to encouragement by Ron Dermer, the Israeli ambassador in Washington. What they learned from him was what every liberal Zionist, Jewish or not, would eventually grasp in twenty-first-century America and Britain: support has to be total. As Cohen put it: 'This is it, take it or leave it, and if you're on the other side of it, you're wrong.'[104] However, Cohen thought AIPAC's crude methods of pressurising him and his colleagues backfired and mainly blamed Dermer for worsening AIPAC's position by association.

A similar conclusion was reached by Chris Coons, a Democratic representative from Delaware, who was targeted by the very aggressive AIPAC campaign against particular politicians who hesitated. In his case too, the bellicosity did not bear any fruit. As Coons told the *Washington Post*:

> Senators who have been comparably torn on this with whom I've spoken – where the ads in their states are much more aggressive than the ones here – it has backfired … instead of making them feel compelled to vote against the deal, it has made them feel resentful.[105]

Whether or not he was helped by Netanyahu's belligerence, Obama could celebrate a rare victory against the most powerful lobby in Washington. Obama secured enough backing in the Senate to protect the pact from efforts to dismantle it. Everyone was quick to declare the end of AIPAC's influence on Capitol Hill. Had the White House indeed won a lasting victory in securing the future of the Iran deal? Had AIPAC lost its claim to iron-clad influence over lawmakers on issues pertaining to Israel? In hindsight, we know the answer to both these questions is no. But in 2015, people saw it differently.

Robert Wexler, a congressman from Florida and later the director of the Center for Middle East Peace, thought that AIPAC had become irrelevant and out of touch with the new realities in America, as had Netanyahu:

> Prime Minister Netanyahu knows the America that elected Ronald Reagan president. He's completely unfamiliar with the America that elected Barack Obama president. And they are in fact very different Americas.[106]

The director of J Street, Jeremy Ben-Ami, thought the same about AIPAC:

> It used to be that AIPAC could deliver votes in a situation like this by emphasizing the political cost of going against them. That no longer works as well as it used to, with Democrats in particular, who recognize that the majority of their supporters in the Jewish community support this deal … The days of AIPAC being able to present itself as the sole voice of American Jews on these issues are over.[107]

Indeed, the showdown over the Iranian deal was a milestone in the history of AIPAC. It was the first time that AIPAC had to contend with a competing lobby of any significance: J Street, which sided with Obama's policies both on Palestine and on Iran. More and more alternative voices began to add to the clamour for justice in the public sphere. These voices had always been there, but before they could not be heard over the noise of the pro-Israel lobby.

COUNTER-LOBBIES

J Street was founded in the latter half of 2007. Its message was simple: being pro-Israel meant being pro-peace. It was promoted as an antithesis to the new discourse that Benjamin Netanyahu was propagating in

Israel, and that AIPAC had adopted, which equated liberal Zionism with anti-Israel stances and even anti-Semitism. It resembled what AIPAC could have been, had it not entrenched itself on the hard right of the political spectrum.

Its stated goal was to push the US into the role of an exclusive peace broker for a two-state solution, in a form accepted by liberal Zionist parties in Israel. Their efforts misfired somewhat when they opposed the recognition of Palestine as an independent state in the UN in 2011.[108] It is therefore very difficult to detect any clear policy of theirs on the Palestinian issue. On the one hand, J Street has devoted a special section on its website to proudly listing all the times it has condemned the Palestinian Authority.[109] On the other hand, in January 2011, it recommended to President Obama not to veto a Security Council resolution condemning Israel's settlement policy. By 2012, J Street became more positively involved in supporting the idea of a Palestinian state – a position that manifested itself in their effort to block two Republican members of the House who were trying to pass legislation against American support for the Palestinian Authority and helped to foil this initiative, which also cost the two Republicans their seats in the next election.[110]

Given the background of its main funders and fundraisers (such as Alan Solomont, the principal fundraiser for the Democrats), it seems J Street's main purpose was to fill the vacuum in American Jewish politics produced by the overt hostility of AIPAC towards the Democratic Party.[111] Even if liberal Zionism seemed to be in decline in Israel, J Street asserted that it was still a relevant political tendency in the US.

J Street's mode of action imitated AIPAC's methods, namely associating funding and support for political candidates with the hope of winning their loyalty to the lobby's policies. By 2016, J Street had invested several million dollars in such activities that, according to its own report, related to 124 candidates. Like AIPAC, J Street had its Educational Fund and its own student union. One striking difference from AIPAC was its willingness, indeed its desire, to receive donations from non-Jewish sources including the Lebanese American businessman Naseer Beydoun.[112]

J Street funding equals roughly a tenth of AIPAC funding. It is difficult to gain a clear picture of either lobby's budget. According to
American law, organisations are promised confidentiality on the question of funding – the last publicised budget of AIPAC was in 2013, when
it was stated to be $66 million dollars,[113] and today the estimate is $300
million. In the case of J Street, a public discussion about its funding was
less about the amount and more about the source. The tabloid
Washington Times claimed that George Soros donated around fifteen
per cent of the lobby's budget (it is illegal to receive financial support
from foreign interests in America).[114] As long as Benjamin Netanyahu
was in power (2009–2021), it was not clear who J Street represented, as
the Israeli government refused to work with it. Naftali Bennett's shaky
coalition government of 2021 included parties that had close ties with J
Street, a political constellation that gave more credence to the idea of a
liberal Zionist lobby; however, this was only a brief interlude before
Netanyahu returned to power. It remains to be seen if liberal Zionism
will exert any influence at all, in either Israel or the US.

J Street was not alone in acting as a counterweight to AIPAC. During
Obama's presidency, Arab-American and Palestinian-American organisations began to put forward their own narrative, which found more
and more listeners. So far, they have not been able to shape policy in the
same way that the pro-Israel lobby has. But at certain times, they have
been able to make significant interventions – and so they merit examination, starting from their origins in smaller groups under the administration of Bush Sr.

After a relatively long silence, the 'Arabists' made their voices heard
again in support of Palestine during George Bush Sr's term.
Unfortunately, they held only junior positions and played no role in the
decision-making process that shaped American policy in the Middle
East in the period between the Oslo Accords and Netanyahu's second
term in office (1993–2009). In 2003, the veterans among the 'Arabists'
dispatched an impressive petition that accused George Bush Jr of
severely damaging the American national interest by occupying Iraq
and uncritically backing Israeli policies.[115] However, the impact of this
was blunted – American policy had proceeded along pro-Israel lines for

too long for it to change course so rapidly. By the time of the Bush Jr presidency, they could not have woken America up.

Nonetheless, this dissenting foreign policy perspective was further strengthened by the establishment of the American Educational Trust (AET), known for its publication, the *Washington Report on Middle East Affairs*. The AET was founded in 1982 by retired US foreign service officers as a counter-lobby to AIPAC in order to influence US policy not only towards Israel, but towards the Middle East as a whole. Like the 'Arabists' before them, their message was based on profound knowledge of the area and its history and culture. Among them were former ambassadors, officials from various government agencies and members of Congress (although just a handful of the latter).

The AET was also very effective in unearthing more clandestine activity by AIPAC – but the pro-Israel lobby was more apprehensive of J Street. AIPAC tried to counter the new lobby by founding a specific action group to challenge the new kid on the block. William Kristol gathered a group of right-wing Republicans in 2010, declaring it was inspired by J Street, mainly as the model of a relatively small advocacy group that makes big waves. The 'big wave' Kristol wanted to create was equating any and every criticism of Israel with anti-Semitism. This ploy would be perfected on the other side of the Atlantic, as we shall see. But this strategy never needed to be realised in full in the US, as by 2015 Israel demanded that every member of the lobby focused their attention on Obama's Iran policy. Once again the pro-Israel lobby had to enlist the Christian Zionists, who regarded Obama as the new Antichrist and were happy to oblige.[116] However, the AET and J Street were part of a broader coalition that integrated into the Palestine solidarity movement in civil society, and on university campuses in particular. After the repeated Israeli assaults on the Gaza Strip in 2006, 2008–2009, 2012 and 2014, resulting in the deaths of thousands of Palestinians, this movement gathered momentum. At the heart of this movement were young Americans from Muslim, Arab and Palestinian backgrounds, working in tandem with progressive Jews, African Americans, Native Americans and other groups of committed students through a network of Palestine solidarity groups. These are incrementally changing the political landscape of American campuses to this day.

And yet with all these counter-advocacies, and Obama's brave performance in his showdown with Netanyahu on the Iran deal, we have to remember that this victory required a presidential veto. Dependence on the presidency would be a risky strategy for AIPAC's opponents. When Trump entered the White House, AIPAC took pride of place in American policy once more, and the clock was set back on further negotiations with Iran. Like the AWACS deal under Reagan, the Iran nuclear deal was a bitter reminder of AIPAC's limitations, but they were confident in their ability to bounce back. Nevertheless, clear harm was done: this affair further damaged AIPAC's relationship with the Democratic Party. Whenever there is a Democratic president, like Joe Biden at time of writing, there is potential for AIPAC's influence to lose its edge – although we are still waiting for that happen.

On the other hand, if AIPAC had not been so self-centred, it would have noticed that the really important thing for the pro-Israel lobby was that Israel benefited from huge aid deals during the Obama presidency, including a mammoth $38 billion package during its final year.

This is why AIPAC's utter intransigence about Iran was bizarre – under Obama, Israel received more generous military aid than it had at any point since 1948. And yet when the showdown on Iran unfolded, his largesse to Israel was forgotten entirely. The lobby, with all its sixty-five years of experience behind it, was willing to be consumed by the ambition of one man who saw the battle over the Iran deal as his ticket to staying in his comfortable abode on Balfour Street – the official residence of the Israeli prime minister.

Was there an alternative? Yes, but it required a Herculean amount of political will. We got a hint of what Obama's presidency could have looked like in the administration's parting gesture when the USA abstained during a vote on a December 2016 UN Security Council resolution, condemning Israel's continued settlement-building activities in the occupied West Bank and East Jerusalem. Previous administrations would have voted against such a condemnation as a matter of course. It was Obama's last action on Palestine, and he could only find the will to do it when his presidential career was over.

The new president, elected in one of the most controversial contests in US history, was ready to turn a new page in the government's relationship with AIPAC. And AIPAC was only too happy to overlook his unfortunate statements about Jews.

A TROUBLED RELATIONSHIP, FOR AIPAC
BUT NOT FOR ISRAEL, UNDER TRUMP

The final ad in Donald Trump's successful campaign to win the presidential elections in 2016 showed images of Jews, such as the billionaire George Soros and the Federal Chair Janet Yellen, as representing global power that corrupts governments. This dovetailed with an outrageous comment by the candidate in the wake of a neo-Nazi rally in Charlottesville, asserting that of those involved were 'very fine people'.[117] There were some who felt that these reckless remarks may have given some encouragement to those associated with the Pittsburgh synagogue shooting which killed eleven people.[118]

On the face of it, Trump's conduct did not bother AIPAC, to the point that they invited him to their conference in 2016. However, unlike the Israeli government, which, under Netanyahu, had many outspoken anti-Semitic allies such as Viktor Orbán, the prime minister of Hungary, AIPAC could not easily ignore anti-Semitic allies.

Trump's anti-Semitic rhetoric and action caused several individuals and organisations affiliated with AIPAC to ask the lobby not to invite him. These groups included the Workers' Circle, IfNotNow, and an ad hoc group, Jews Against Trump, that distributed a petition stating that 'As Jews and as Americans, we condemn hate speech in all its forms.'[119] The Workers' Circle's petition stated: 'We are horrified by your invitation to Donald Trump to speak at the upcoming policy conference and we call on you to withdraw it immediately.'[120]

IfNotNow is a group of young Jews opposed to AIPAC's views. Its website describes the group as 'a movement of American Jews' calling to 'end US support for Israel's apartheid system and demand equality, justice and a thriving future for all Palestinians and Israelis'.[121] Unsurprisingly, they used the harshest words against the president:

> If there is anyone who should stand up to a neo-fascist who threatens and intimidates minorities it's the American Jewish community. American Jews have long fought for freedom and dignity for all people because of our history of persecution by strongmen who blamed us for society's woes.[122]

A day before Trump spoke, the Union for Reform Judaism, representing the largest Jewish denomination in North America, stated:

> The Reform Movement and our leaders will engage with Mr Trump at the AIPAC Policy Conference in a way that affirms our nation's democracy and our most cherished Jewish values. We will find an appropriate and powerful way to make our voices heard.[123]

Petitions were followed by a mass demonstration outside the convention hall under the banner 'Come Together Against Hate', whose organisers declared their intention to walk out on Trump's speech:

> We are committed to saying that Donald Trump does not speak for us or represent us, and his values are not AIPAC's values. They are not the values of the Jewish community.[124]

But this criticism did not lead to a disinvitation; neither did Trump's populist diatribes against rivals in the Republican Party such as Ted Cruz and John Kasich and the Democratic frontrunner Hillary Clinton.

Indeed, anti-Trump critics were voices in the wilderness. The rank and file of AIPAC, and most of its leaders, warmly welcomed Trump, who stated, 'I am a newcomer to politics, but not to backing the Jewish state.' Every sentence he uttered about what he had done for Israel was received with loud applause.

Most of his speech was devoted to how he would deal with Iran. He accused Iran of funding 'terrorism' not only in the Gaza Strip but also in the West Bank. The rest was a tirade about the way Hillary Clinton and Barack Obama had treated Israel: 'very, very badly'.

Believe it or not, he needed to read this particular sophisticated line from the teleprompter and did not utter it off the cuff. But he could not resist veering off script to describe Hillary Clinton, formerly Obama's secretary of state, as a 'total disaster'. To the apparent embarrassment of some of the senior officials of AIPAC, Trump received a roar of approval when he called Barack Obama 'maybe the worst thing to happen to Israel'.[125]

The next section of the speech was a total fabrication of a scenario in which the UN would impose a solution on Israel and only Trump would be able to stop it. He characterised the Obama years as 'the days of treating Israel like a second-class citizen'. He accused the Palestinian Authority of fomenting a culture of hatred towards Jews and claimed that 'Already half of the population of Palestine has been taken over by the Palestinian ISIS and Hamas' – points taken from Netanyahu's speeches. More ironically, he claimed that 'Israel does not name public squares after terrorists'. As an Israeli, I can name many, many squares named after Zionist terrorists in Irgun and Stern – but of course they are heroes of the Jewish state.

He closed by reverting to personal invectives against Clinton and Obama and got the AIPAC crowd to give him a standing ovation. Judging by the body language of AIPAC leaders during that diatribe, it seems it made them squirm in their chairs somewhat.

It is possible that those who opposed his invitation did not make their voices heard because of a pre-warning they received from AIPAC in the form of an email sent to conference attendees, stating that any vocal disruption of Trump's speech would result in a permanent ban from AIPAC events. The email reads in part:

> You are welcome to disagree with a speaker, but you are expected to do so silently and respectfully, in a way that reflects the higher order values of AIPAC and of yourself as an activist. If you choose to disrupt the program, understand that you will be removed, your conference credentials will be taken, and it will be the last AIPAC event you attend.[126]

As a president, Trump was divisive and promised to implement policies that contradicted the value system that most Jews in America regarded as sacrosanct. His promises to round up immigrants and build a wall on the Mexican border caused unease among many who attended the 2016 convention. Officially AIPAC denounced Trump's blunt criticism of Obama at the conference. The day after Trump's show, AIPAC's president, Lillian Pinkus, broke away from the planned agenda to distance the organisation from Trump's remarks. 'Last evening, something occurred which has the potential to drive us apart, to divide us', Pinkus said, and added:

> We say unequivocally that we do not countenance ad hominem attacks and we take great offence against those that are levied against the president of the United States of America from our stage. Let us take this moment to pledge to each other that in this divisive and tension-filled political season ... those who wish to divide our movement from the left or from the right will not succeed in doing so.[127]

She concluded by remarking that Trump's outburst undermined the group's efforts to broaden the base of the pro-Israel movement, and stated that 'We are disappointed that so many people applauded a sentiment that we neither agree with nor condone.' She seemed to forget that AIPAC itself had invited Trump onto the stage.

If you were an AIPAC leader, you could always do both: condone and condemn in the same sentence. In reality, AIPAC was overwhelmingly satisfied with Trump and his proposed policies, including the pledge to move the US embassy to Jerusalem – a promise he fulfilled during his first year of presidency – and his objection to the Iran deal.

Indeed, it should have been easier for AIPAC and the pro-Israel lobby in general when Donald Trump was elected. He and those around him should have epitomised the unholy trinity of neo-cons, pro-Israel Jews and Christian Zionists. But it was more complicated than that. His political messaging, from before he became the Republican nominee, through to his unsuccessful 2020 campaign, had unavoidable anti-Semitic undertones. In 2018, during the mid-term elections, Soros once more starred in Trump's anti-Semitic rhetoric, when he accused the billionaire of secretly funding immigration to the USA.[128]

But AIPAC ignored this. After all, this was the president who moved the American embassy from Tel Aviv to Jerusalem, took the US out of the Iran nuclear deal and recognised Israel's sovereignty over the occupied Syrian Golan Heights.

We know now that the Trump administration not only killed the Iran deal by withdrawing from it; it also provided immunity for a more aggressive Israeli policy towards Iran, which gave the green light for operations such as the assassination of the Iranian nuclear scientist, Mohsen Fakhrizadeh, which was probably carried out by Israel with possible US support. This was a sledgehammer blow against the Iran nuclear deal. Shortly after, President Donald Trump withdrew from the deal, which was signed by Iran, on the one side, and the US and four other permanent members of the United Nations Security Council, and Germany, on the other, as part of a broader campaign to undo Obama's achievements in office.[129]

In 2018, a video was leaked of Netanyahu boasting about coaxing Trump into pulling the US out of the nuclear agreement: 'We convinced the US president [to exit the deal], and I had to stand up against the whole world and come out against this agreement', Netanyahu said in the video, aired on Israel television.[130]

This is what really mattered for Netanyahu, and hence AIPAC had to continue to swallow Trump's anti-Semitism quietly. AIPAC refused to condemn Trump's adviser, Steve Bannon, despite the allegations of anti-Semitism surrounding him.[131] One person who made allegations about Bannon was his ex-wife, who recalled that when they were considering which school to send their daughters to, he rejected any school that had Jews in it and he said that 'he doesn't like Jews and that he doesn't like the way they raise their kids to be "whiney brats" and that he didn't want [his] girls going to school with Jews.' Bannon denied he ever made these remarks. What he could not deny was his statement in a document that warned of an Islamic jihad against America, which he presented to Trump, and in which he described the 'American Jewish Community' as among the 'unwitting enablers of Jihad'.[132] At the end of the day, Trump was an asset in the eyes of the pro-Israel lobby – they did not need to worry about what he did in office. They could turn their attention to an issue that had become increasingly pressing: the shift in American public opinion towards sympathy for the Palestinians, a process that began in 2001 and has accelerated ever since.

THE END OF TRUMP'S TERM

While Netanyahu could only be pleased with Trump's policies, the president did not forget the rebuke he had received from AIPAC's leadership for his violation of the code of conduct in attacking President Obama. He therefore snubbed AIPAC for the rest of his presidency, and did not appear again in person at its annual conferences.

For $600 you could attend the 2017 annual AIPAC conference. But for that money you could only listen to Vice President Michael Pence repeating the president's promises to move the American embassy to Jerusalem. You could also hear Senator Kamala Harris (later Biden's vice president) singing the praises of the Israel government and AIPAC. She and other Democrats were courted by the leadership, if not by the rank and file. It was good to see Democrats, said Lillian Pinkus, the president of AIPAC. But you could also encounter, at the entrance to the conference hall, a small group of members of IfNotNow carrying a banner that read 'Jews won't be free until Palestinians are. Reject #AIPAC. Reject occupation.'[133]

This particular annual conference attempted to showcase its support among the Black community, including Ethiopian Jews, to negate the impression created by Black Lives Matter that younger Black activists were largely supportive of Palestine. To counter this, a special event for African Americans was organised by the Israel Project (a pro-Israeli lobby group founded in 2002 by Jennifer Laszlo Mizrahi, a PR adviser and businesswoman who decided to add to AIPAC's efforts with her own organisation, which lasted until 2019). This was held in the unique setting of the restaurant Rosa Mexicano, located in the Capitol's Penn Quarter, in the restored 1924 Hecht Company building, an architectural marvel with fourteen-foot wraparound windows. It was the first branch of Rosa Mexicano – a renowned Mexican chain – to open outside New York City in December 2003. The Project invited anyone who was part of a Black community for a special dinner. After the meeting the Project widely publicised this alleged all-Black support for Israel.[134]

Despite these efforts, African Americans, including Black Lives Matter activists, and Native Americans became important members of the informal rainbow coalition showing solidarity with the Palestinian struggle for liberation. The alliance between Black liberation in the States and the Palestine solidarity movement has strong historical roots: the Black Panthers met with the PLO in Algiers, and republished PLO speeches.

The 2018 annual AIPAC conference celebrated the move of the embassy, but again Trump was not present, and this time Mike Pence's star was eclipsed by Nikki Haley, the American ambassador to the UN. But the keynote speaker was Benjamin Netanyahu, who appeared in person as he needed AIPAC for his domestic campaigns. He was losing popularity in Israel. In his thirty-minute speech, he compared Trump to the Babylonian King Cyrus who allowed the Jews to return and build the second temple.[135]

Leading Democrats did not lag behind in invoking the Old Testament as a way of showing unconditional support for Israel. The prominent Democratic politician and Senate Minority Leader Chuck Schumer blamed the deadlock in Israel and Palestine squarely on the fact that the Palestinians had the temerity to not believe in the Torah:

> Of course, we say it's our land, the Torah says it, but they don't believe in the Torah. So that's the reason there is not peace.[136]

No Christian Zionist or neo-con could have put it better.

Here too, and this time in growing numbers, protesters demanded that the conference be shut down. Around 500 demonstrators chanted, 'Hey, hey, ho, ho, AIPAC has got to go!' (a new iteration of a chant that dates back to the 1950s).[137]

The 2019 annual conference was a different affair, marred not just by protesters outside the building, but by some of the Democratic candidates vying for the presidential nomination choosing not to appear at the conference, as had long become conventional. But as for Trump's sour relationship with AIPAC, it was all forgotten when Trump was reinvited to the 2019 conference, in a showcase of the 2020 candidates. Although he did not appear in person, he was undoubtedly the favourite candidate. But some cracks in this relationship had become clear, despite the very strong alliance between the White House and AIPAC during his presidency.

AIPAC was still trying to preserve some vague semblance of bipartisanship. For instance, it opposed a move by Israel and Trump to bar the Democratic representatives Ilhan Omar and Rashida Tlaib from entering Israel. Omar and Tlaib, the first two Muslim women elected to Congress, have frequently criticised Israel's treatment of Palestinians and expressed support for the Boycott, Divestment and Sanctions (BDS) movement. They have frequently been joined by Alexandria Ocasio-Cortez in a brave trio condemning Israeli policies. That support was cited by the Israeli government as the basis for blocking them from entering the country.

The BDS movement is a Palestinian non-violent resistance movement promoting all these three modes of actions against Israel to pressure it to respect the basic civil rights of the Palestinians that are rooted in international law: the right of the refugees to return, the right of people not to live under occupation or siege in the West Bank and the Gaza Strip and the right of the Palestinians in Israel to live in full equality. It was inspired by the anti-apartheid movement that galvanised support for the African National Congress's liberation struggle. Since its inception in 2005, it has been very successful in reinvigorating the dormant solidarity movement and persuading unions and churches around the world to rethink their financial connections to Israel. One of its more successful campaigns was an academic boycott which led to dozens of student unions, universities and professional academic associations giving up official contact with Israeli academia. It was able to persuade leading global cultural figures in music, literature, poetry and theatre to follow suit. These included, among others, Arundhati Roy, Iain Banks, Judith Butler, Naomi Klein, Ken Loach, Angela Davis, Roger Waters, Elvis Costello, Gil Scott-Heron, Lauryn Hill, Faithless,

MK King, U2, Bjork, Zakir Hussain, Jean-Luc Godard and Snoop Dogg.

It is noteworthy that the BDS movement is supported by 150 NGOs and outfits within Palestinian civil society. AIPAC tweeted in response to the decision of Israel to disallow Omar and Tlaib's visit:

> We disagree with Reps. Omar and Tlaib's support for the anti-Israel and anti-peace BDS movement, along with Rep. Tlaib's calls for a one-state solution. We also believe every member of Congress should be able to visit and experience our democratic ally Israel first hand.[138]

And the head of the American Jewish Committee, David Harris, put out a statement siding with AIPAC, saying that 'Israel did not choose wisely' in this decision. Harris wrote:

> While we are under no illusions about the implacably hostile views of Reps. Omar and Tlaib on Israel-related issues, we nonetheless believe that the costs in the US of barring the entry of two members of Congress may prove even higher than the alternative.[139]

Among the detractors was the New York Democratic Representative, Eliot Engel, who also called the move a 'mistake', saying in a statement that this decision would 'only strengthen the anti-Israel movements and arguments' and that it depicted Israel as if it was 'closing itself off to criticism and dialogue'. Engel said he told Israeli ambassador Ron Dermer his views on the move. Even Senator Marco Rubio thought it was a mistake, as did another friend of AIPAC, Ted Deutch, the Democratic Representative from Florida, who said he was 'disappointed' with Israel's decision, and questioned Trump's encouragement of the move in a tweet.

Although this particular Trumpian move led to protests from unexpected politicians and organisations, it did not indicate a fundamental change of attitude in Congress regarding the Palestine question. Omar and Tlaib are still constantly attacked by AIPAC with all the traditional smears and strong allegations that the lobby has deployed in the past against critics of Israel. Even when their right to travel to Israel was defended by AIPAC, each rebuke of Israel's decision was immediately qualified by a condemnation of the two representatives.[140]

However, what was really important in this affair was not AIPAC's defence of American democracy, but the potential shift in the young Democrats' perceptions of Israel. No amount of money invested by AIPAC would change the views of Ilhan Omar or Alexandria Ocasio-Cortez about Israel. As Natan Sachs, at the time the director of the Centre for Middle East Policy at the Brookings Institution in Washington, observed:

> The Democratic Party now has a younger generation that views the Israel–Palestine conflict through the lens of human and civil rights rather than a question of security and terrorism.[141]

The shift was visible at AIPAC's annual conference in 2019. As mentioned, most of the Democrats seeking the party's nomination in 2020 did not participate in it. This act was supported by seventy-four per cent of the party members according to one poll (while a March 2019 Gallup Poll found that only twenty-six per cent of American Jews approved of Trump's presidency). Elizabeth Warren, Kamala Harris, Bernie Sanders, Beto O'Rourke, Pete Buttigieg and Julian Castro all stayed away. Bernie Sanders summarised for all of them the reason: they would not support an organisation that provided a platform for 'leaders who express bigotry and oppose basic Palestinian rights'.[142]

These decisions not to attend were made after prominent liberal group MoveOn.org called on all Democratic candidates vying for the party's presidential nomination to boycott the conference. Iram Ali, campaign director for MoveOn.org, wrote in a statement:

> It's no secret that AIPAC has worked to hinder diplomatic efforts like the Iran deal, is undermining Palestinian self-determination, and inviting figures actively involved in human rights violations to its stage.[143]

The very familiar last-minute routine on the opening day of an AIPAC annual convention was carried out as usual on 24 March 2019. The technicians added the finishing touches and readied the Washington Convention Center for the AIPAC meeting that would conclude on 26 March. The LED panels were lit up for a final check, showing two inter-linked Stars of David, one red, one blue, and at the point at which they intersected, they shone together as a sparkling purple light, signalling bipartisanship – a rare commodity in America by 2019.

The 2019 convention was one of the first ones when AIPAC openly and officially identified with the extreme right-wing settler movement in Israel. How far AIPAC, and for that matter Israel, had moved to the right could be seen from the invitation given to Oded Revivi, a leader of an illegal Jewish settlement council in the occupied West Bank, to the conference. A very grateful Revivi told the *Jerusalem Post*:

> AIPAC has finally realised that they cannot ignore half-a-million people living in Judea and Samaria, who are becoming more and more attractive to the audience of AIPAC.[144]

Ahead of the event, there was anxiety among conference organisers that turnout would be low and would expose AIPAC's decreasing popularity. Those fears were not borne out: the halls were packed and AIPAC boasted of preparing 25,000 hot dogs for those attending.

During the conference, President Trump signed a proclamation recognising the Golan Heights as part of the state of Israel; AIPAC's crowning achievement in 2019. In Israel, however, political chaos prevented widespread joy about AIPAC's achievement or Trump's presence. Twice, in April and September, Israel went to the polls with no clear result and Netanyahu ruled for most of the year as an interim prime minister. By December it was clear that in 2020 there would be another election campaign. It seems once more the lobby, and in particular AIPAC, had their own concerns and were not involved in the dramatic debate about the future of the state they had been advocating for since its inception.

Once more Trump did not appear at the 2020 annual conference and sent his vice president Pence, but issued strong condemnation of the Democratic candidates who refused to attend, calling them anti-Jewish.

The 2020 conference was a charged affair: Netanyahu appeared alongside his rival, who began to challenge him seriously. Benny Gantz of the Blue and White Party (whose Hebrew name literally means 'the State Camp', although in the media it is referred to as the National Unity Party). To make sure that guests would not be interrupted at this event, in addition to the recorded requests at the outset of plenary sessions, two top board members took to the stage and pleaded for comity. One was Amy Friedkin of San Francisco, a past president of AIPAC who was close to House Speaker Nancy Pelosi. The other, Alan Franco of New Orleans, was a major funder of the Republican campaigns. 'The best way to persuade us is with facts, not fire', Friedkin stated, and Franco urged activists to refrain from cheering those who attacked political rivals.[145]

There was little reason to worry about such interruptions when Pence appeared on the podium, once more in the name of the absentee president. To repeated standing ovations, he listed Trump's Israel-related moves – moving the US embassy to Jerusalem, cutting funding for Palestinians (both to the Palestinian Authority and the UNRWA, the UN agency supporting Palestinian refugees) and leaving the Iran nuclear deal – and drew even louder applause when he attacked Bernie Sanders, misquoting the senator, but that did not matter to anyone. Pence culminated his speech with a call to re-elect Trump:

> The most pro-Israel president in history must not be replaced by one who would be the most anti-Israel president in the history of this nation, that's why you need four more years of President Trump in the White House.[146]

This rhetoric made the twin red and blue Stars of David lighting up the conference hall into a token gesture. But in 2020, AIPAC could still boast some Democratic support. Chuck Schumer and Mike Bloomberg attended the 2020 conference in person, while Joe Biden made an appearance via video link. The Democrats were only too happy to win the hearts of the AIPAC conference attendees.

The participating Democrats proved that bipartisanship within AIPAC could only be claimed against the backdrop of unwavering support for Israel and obedience to AIPAC's official line. Senator Cory Booker, a New Jersey Democrat who dropped out of the presidential race in 2018, got what was until that point the longest round of applause for a barnstorming speech upholding US–Israel ties:

> I see it as my duty to protect the bipartisan nature of this relationship of Israel with the United States ... as long as the people of Israel have to live under the threat of indiscriminate violence ... we must always as a matter of human values stand for Israel's security and defence.[147]

AIPAC made a nominal effort to represent the more progressive views of the American Jewish community, such as those of J Street. Attendees could go to an AIPAC-sponsored off-site session for 'peace builders', backing the two-state solution, which was well attended and included appearances by AIPAC's CEO, Howard Kohr, and president, Betsy Berns Korn – but was closed to the press. From Korn's opening speech it was clear that this was peace *à la* Trump, whom Korn warmly thanked for 'releasing a peace proposal that was developed in consultation with the leaders of Israel's two major political parties' – a known formula for building a Palestinian Bantustan in the West Bank's area A (comprising sixteen per cent of the West Bank).

A fringe session called 'Promoting Palestinian Prosperity' included four panellists who were American or Israeli. When someone from the floor asked why there were no Palestinians on the panel, one of the panellists – Brad Gordon, a top retired official of the lobby – agreed that it would have been a good idea to invite one. And there you are, as they say.

The unmistakeable American-accented baritone of Israeli prime minister Benjamin Netanyahu boomed on the last day of the convention, as he addressed a crowd of up to 18,000 participants. He was then in the final throes of his bid for re-election. He did not make it to the convention in person, so the crowd watched him through a patchy satellite feed on gigantic blue screens; although Netanyahu had met with President Donald Trump in Washington that week, he cut short his trip after yet another round of Israeli assaults on the Gaza Strip unfolded. It was difficult to hear what Netanyahu was saying at times, but the audience didn't care: the staunch supporters of Israel who filled the room gave him standing ovations. The only other speaker who won nearly as much applause that Tuesday morning was David Friedman, the US ambassador to Israel. He brought greetings from Trump, 'Israel's greatest ally ever to reside in the White House', as he put it. But his lauding of Trump paled in comparison to Netanyahu's praise for the president during his meeting with him at the White House the day before. Again, Netanyahu compared Trump to King Cyrus, and to Harry Truman, the US president who first recognised the state of Israel.[148]

At the end of the day, the 2020 conference was a cheerleading display for Netanyahu and Trump. Netanyahu needed this conference much more than Trump did. All the usual audio-visual histrionics turned the conference into a rally championing his premiership in the coming Israeli elections.

For all that AIPAC fêted Trump, it was not enough to push him over the line in the 2020 elections, where he lost to Joe Biden. Of course, Biden had been the one Democratic candidate who did not boycott the 2019 conference, and also appeared at the 2020 convention via video link, promising to fight anti-Semitism and champion a secure Israel.[149] AIPAC had no reason to fear the newcomer at the White House.

EARLY BIDENISM: MUCH OF THE SAME?

The pro-Trump riot on Capitol Hill on 6 January 2021 presented a conundrum for AIPAC. The man they had previously celebrated as a true friend of Israel had now become politically toxic. AIPAC broke with its convention of not commenting on domestic conflicts in the US and tweeted:

> We share the anger of our fellow Americans over the attack at the Capitol and condemn the assault on our democratic values and process … This violence, and President Trump's incitement of it, is outrageous and must end.[150]

The Anti-Defamation League followed suit with its own tweet:

> The violence at the US Capitol is the result of disinformation from
> our highest office ... Extremists are among the rioters in DC support-
> ing President Trump's reckless rhetoric on America's democratic
> institutions.[151]

Other member groups of the pro-Israel lobby decided not to go too far
in blaming the former president directly, keeping their powder dry in
the eventuality that he made a comeback. The American Jewish
Committee demanded that Trump 'call for an immediate end to the
riots and respect the certification process currently underway', conveniently overlooking the fact that Trump instigated the riot with his inflam-
matory speech. A similar stance was adopted by the Conference of
Presidents of Major American Jewish Organizations, who were also
careful not to name Trump at all:

> We are disgusted by the violence at the US Capitol and urge the riot-
> ers to disperse immediately ... Law and order must be restored, and
> the peaceful transition of administrations must continue.[152]

Once the embers of the January insurrection had turned to ash, AIPAC
swiftly embraced Trump again, along with all those who questioned the
results of the 2020 elections.[153] It remains an open question as to what
extent AIPAC still enjoys the support of the Jewish community, or even
if it needs it at all. It's quite possible that AIPAC could become the
domain of affluent Jews alone, but still be a formidable lobbying force.

Aaron David Miller, former adviser to six secretaries of state and
Middle East programme director at the Wilson Center, predicted that
under Biden, AIPAC, while persisting as 'a powerful voice', unlike in the
past would not be able to veto US Middle East policy. Neither AIPAC
nor the Israeli government was able to prevent the return of the
Americans to the negotiating table with Iran.[154]

But reviving the Iran deal didn't require much courage on Biden's
part. It was a reaffirmation of a tacit understanding between AIPAC and

the White House, which had existed since Gerald Ford's time, that AIPAC could and should influence policy on the Palestine issue, but it could not wield decisive power over America's policy towards the Middle East region. AIPAC's histrionics over the US's relations with other Arab states were the deviation from the norm, not America's willingness to negotiate with Iran.

The battle in the US today is staged between progressive Americans, including Jews, and the administration's policies, be they Democrat or Republican, towards apartheid inside Israel; the occupation of the West Bank; the ethnic cleansing in Jerusalem, south Hebron, the Jordan Valley and the Naqab; as well as the siege on Gaza. Under Biden's tenure, the administration continues to supply Israel with total international immunity.

This concludes the historical survey of AIPAC's and the wider lobby's relationship with the executive and legislative powers in the USA. Notwithstanding the fluctuations in the relationship between the lobby and various administrations, its basic aims since its inception have been fully achieved. However critical any particular administration was towards Israel, it did not undermine the huge financial and military aid to Israel, nor did it stop the continuous automatic American support for Israel in the international arena in general and in the UN in particular. Moreover, at the time of writing, AIPAC, within the wider lobby, still dominates the Capitol and can make or break any legislation that concerns Israel.

In fact, as Grant Smith has illustrated in his incisive book, *The Israeli Lobby Enters State Government: Rise of the Virginia Israel Advisory Board*, the lobby's presence in the past and in the present stretches way beyond the federal powerbases into the states themselves. He shows how a local lobby in Virginia was able to procure concrete financial support for Israel through influencing the state's government. He revealed the activities of a pro-Israel agency within the local government in Virginia, using businesses such as tobacco and gambling, and an intricate network meant to avoid tax issues and legal restrictions on advocacy, in order to influence American policy towards Israel. Exclusive contracts with Israel in the state of Virginia, in Smith's view, come at the expense of the local economy and local taxpayers pay the price. These agencies in state government also provide a powerful base for influencing the foreign policy of the USA, through their own lobbies on Capitol Hill. [155]

Moving successfully through the financial, economic and political corridors of power did not necessarily mean that public opinion at large, and sections of civil society in particular, were also swaying in AIPAC's direction. Ever since the beginning of this century, winning over society, as distinct from its political elites and even the mainstream media, was far more challenging for AIPAC, since money and political influence counted less here. In fact, since 2001 AIPAC has found itself at war with many sections of American civil society. This was a battle already being waged during the time of the Bush Jr, Obama, Trump and Biden administrations. The 'battle cry', so to speak, came from Israel, which recruited not only AIPAC but also a host of American Jewish organisations into a campaign meant to silence criticism against Israel in civil society and suppress any attempt to go beyond verbal condemnation into proactive operations such as boycott and divestment. So, allow me to go back to the moment the campaign was born and follow its progression to the present day.

10

The War Against American Civil Society

From 2001, Israeli policy makers noted a systemic change in attitudes towards Israel on both sides of the Atlantic. The traditional tools of advocacy and lobbying that were very effective in dealing with political elites and mainstream media or academia seemed less effective here.

The project of changing people's hearts and minds about Israel was assessed as an issue pertaining directly to Israel's national security, too important to be left in the hands of the pro-Israel lobby in the US. This would be directed from Israel.

The strategy was twofold. The first strategy was to rebrand Israel as the only progressive democracy in the twenty-first-century Middle East. The second was to respond to more assertive criticism of Israel in civil society with the traditional methods of intimidation: smearing and character assassination. Any strong words of criticism would be decried as 'delegitimisation of the Jewish state'. Of course, the second prong of the strategy made it harder for keen-eyed observers to believe in the narrative of the first one. But Israeli policy makers embraced this rebranding exercise in spectacular fashion.

A poster of an almost naked Miss Israel, the famous Superwoman Gal Gadot, and a poster of four fit young men, equally underdressed, were the face of Israel in 2007 in a campaign named Brand Israel commissioned by the Prime Minister's Office, the Foreign and Tourist Ministries and the Jewish Agency. This former Miss Israel was meant to convince young heterosexual American men of the rebranding of the Jewish state as a haven for young people, while the attractive men represented the Israeli LGBT community, advertising Tel Aviv as the gay capital of Israel. One wonders how Theodor Herzl or even David Ben-Gurion and Menachem Begin would have regarded this representation of Zionism as a soft pornographic dream. But everything in the struggle to dispel the negative image of Israel was deemed appropriate in what the policy makers saw as an existential matter. The local team working for the Israelis explained that such posters:

> allowed us to gear our message to the younger generation, especially males, and towards a demographic that did not see Israel as relevant or identify particularly with Israel.[1]

But in fact, the campaign targeted all walks of life with images and texts tailored to each group and its inclinations and preferences. Israel's image abroad was now commodified as a consumer product.

It began in the summer of 2005 when the Israeli Foreign Ministry, the Prime Minister's Office and the Finance Ministry concluded three years of consultation with American marketing executives and launched Brand Israel: a campaign to 'rebrand' the country's image to appear 'relevant and modern' instead of militaristic and religious. Huge sums of money were allocated for marketing the new image abroad in order to combat what the political and academic elite in Israel considered a global campaign to delegitimise the Jewish state. This was to be a gigantic effort and the team appointed to see it through was accordingly dubbed BIG (the Brand Israel Group).[2]

Freshly created front organisations were asked to disseminate this new version of Israel as a dream come true, emphasising beauty, fun and technological achievements. One such outfit was the David Project in America, which became very active in speaking for the campaign. One of its many actions was to try and counter the constant characterisation of Israel as one of the most hated states in the world (together with Iran and North Korea).[3] The David Project found that Israel was not among the first twenty-five states where people liked to belong. The project's purpose was to convince everyone that Israel was one of the happiest places on earth due to its technological achievements and supposedly high standards of living.

It was felt by the Brand Israel team that the country's history was also an asset that would help to sell Israel in the twenty-first century:

> In terms of heritage benchmarks, Israel is home to fundamental religious and historical landmarks, including the Western Wall, Church of the Holy Sepulchre, Al Aqsa Mosque, and the Baha'i Temple in Haifa. Israelis boast a high quality of life, and the country's democratic values focus on inclusion and political representation of all its citizens, including women and religious and racial minorities.[4]

The David Project came up with its own explanation for the discrepancy between what the state had to offer and its negative global image:

> We know misperceptions of Israel are rampant in the media; ordinary citizens across the globe see Israel cast as yet another violent nation in a region steeped in unrest and war. Conversations taking place in print, on television, and in the blogosphere often regard the Arab-Israeli conflict as both all-consuming and myopic; the diversity and excitement of Israeli society is often subsumed by twenty-second sound bites focusing on only one aspect of the Israeli story.[5]

And it identified the following challenges for the Brand Israel team:

> How do we change perceptions? How do we introduce nuance into global conversations surrounding Israel? How do we discuss the highlights and achievements of Israeli society, while also recognizing its weaknesses and shortcomings? What needs to happen to remove Israel from the bright spotlight of a violent conflict?[6]

The answer to these challenges was provided on the official website of the Israeli Foreign Ministry. The recommendation was to abandon aiming to win the argument with facts, information or moral points of view. These were dispensed with for the sake of a new idea that captivated the imagination of the Foreign Ministry: the need to brand Israel and market it like a product. Gideon Meir of Israel's Foreign Ministry told *Haaretz* that he would 'rather have a Style section item on Israel than a front-page story'.[7]

What this meant in practice was that any PR campaign for Israel had to try and avoid any association with the conflict or the Palestinian issue. This was the spirit of the guidelines given to yet another front organisation that was founded to cater particularly to the younger Jewish generation in the USA. It was called ISRAEL21c, and had been founded in 2001 with the mission of redefining 'the conversation about Israel [in the USA]' by showing 'how Israeli efforts have contributed incalculably to the advancement of healthcare, the environment, technology, culture, and global democratic values worldwide'.[8]

We can assume that the idea was to move the conversation away from the elephant in the room: the Israeli occupation. Like *Fawlty Towers*' most famous episode where the hotel owner is trying not to mention the Second World War whenever he has German guests, the message to activists was that mentioning the war (that is, the Palestinians) was not a good idea. This was articulated more explicitly by a PR expert recruited by Brand Israel who explained to the *Jewish Week* that it would be quite futile to argue about the Palestine issue:

> Proving that Israel is right, and the Palestinians are wrong may be emotionally satisfying for advocates, but not necessarily effective in changing people's way of thinking about Israel.[9]

And he added:

> You have a narrow bandwidth, where Israel can only win some of the argument. We are trying to broaden the bandwidth to include Israel's accomplishments.

Soon after, the work of the various organisations and individuals was put under one roof. This was an operative decision taken by the Foreign Ministry's first ever Brand Israel Conference, convened in Tel Aviv, which marked the official adoption of the campaign. Foreign Minister Tzipi Livni appointed Ido Aharoni to head Israel's first brand management office and awarded him a $4 million budget, in addition to the already established $3 million annual expenditure on *Hasbara* and $11 million for the Israeli Tourism Ministry in North America. Smaller budgets, but by no means insignificant, were distributed for work in Europe. The impact of American public opinion is indicated by Israeli politicians' focus on the US – they sensed that 'delegitimisation' had been particularly successful there. One would have thought, given how much money had been poured into it, that the US would serve as a safe bastion of pro-Israel bias for many decades to come. But the US was not the sole target; academics would try and convince Israeli politicians that the plague of 'delegitimisation' was rampant in the United Kingdom as well, as we shall see later.[10]

Aharoni recruited top people from the world of marketing and advertising. These included the Saatchi brothers (reported to be doing the job for free) and PR experts such as David Saranga, who told *PR Week* that the two groups Israel was targeting were 'liberals', and people aged sixteen to thirty (hence Miss Israel and the men in swimwear on the posters). In 2005 Aharoni's office hired TNS, a market research firm, to test new brand concepts for Israel in thirteen different countries. They also funded a pilot programme called 'Israel: Innovation for Life'.[11]

At the centre of the team were people who run the Brand Asset Valuator (BAV), the world's largest brand database, working alongside top publicists and marketing people. BAV specialises in exposing the target community's emotional attachments to brands. Fern Oppenheim, an advertising and marketing consultant and member of the Brand Israel Group, said the BAV data would serve a long-term, co-ordinated strategy that included ongoing research and evaluation: 'We want to be a resource everyone can benefit from', she said, 'the way a corporate management team would manage a brand'.[12]

The experts told the diplomats that Israel had failed to be liked in the past because:

> Americans know a lot about Israel, just not the right things. They
> think of Israel as a grim, war-torn country, not one booming with
> high-tech and busy outdoor cafes.[13]

Hence, in 2005 the mission was to sell Israel as a quasi-American society. This task was handed to Young & Rubicam, leading market experts
in the US. One of their managers, David Sable, explained that they were
about to assist in refashioning Israel as the reincarnation of a new USA,
because 'Americans don't see Israel as being like the US.'[14] Israel, as a
brand, was already strong in America, he conceded, but the trouble was
that 'it is better known than liked, and constrained by lack of relevance'.
Sable elaborated:

> Americans find Israel to be totally irrelevant to their lives and they
> are tuning out ... particularly 18–34-year-old males, the most signif-
> icant target.[15]

Brand Israel intended to change this by selecting aspects of Israeli
society to highlight that would bring Americans directly to them.
They started off by offering free trips for architectural writers, and
then for food and wine writers. The goal of these efforts 'was to
convey an image of Israel as a productive, vibrant and cutting-edge
culture'.[16]

By 2010, the charm offensive was preparing blueprints for the future.
One of these was succinctly summarised by Gary Rosenblatt from the
Jewish Week:

> Think of Israel as a product undergoing an overhaul to make it more
> competitive in the marketplace. What's called for are fewer stories
> explaining the rationale for the security fence, and more attention to
> scientists doing stem-cell research on the cutting edge or the young
> computer experts who gave the world Instant Messaging.[17]

A few years into the programme, the Israeli consul general in New York
proudly reported a 'paradigm shift' in America. Before Brand Israel, the

American public, for some unfathomable reason, had been unaware that Israel was a democratic, moral and successful state. Now they knew.

It was not only American PR and branding wizards that were recruited. The Israeli government also asked for the public to be more deeply involved. In a show of total mistrust in its professional diplomats, it recruited commercial television in Israel to seek alternative messengers for the rebranded Israel through a reality show called *The Ambassadors*. The winner of a thirteen-week elimination contest won a job with a Zionist advocacy group called Israel at Heart to supplement its diplomats with the best of Israel's youth. One such group were Ethiopian Jews from Israel, brought by Israel at Heart to speak in African American churches. Imagine bringing African Americans from Harlem to tell people in Brixton about the American dream and you may understand the absurdity of such a move.[18] They were replaced later by more professional selections of high school student cadres for the mission.

Moreover, the Foreign Ministry asked every Israeli performing artist to include a component of Brand Israel in their shows. A typical example of such a show was the tour undertaken in 2012 in the US and the UK by the dance company Batsheva; the tour was openly described by the Israeli Foreign Ministry as part of a new Brand Israel campaign. They were 'the best global ambassadors of Israel', the Ministry said.[19]

By 2010, the Israeli economic weekly, *Globes*, reported that the Foreign Ministry had allocated one hundred million shekels (over $26,260,000) to branding for the coming years. This money was mainly destined to help fight the growing 'delegitimisation' on online social networks. The Foreign Ministry was very optimistic about the chances of such a campaign. Its research unit 'found out' that social media users 'show sympathy and identity with content that interests them, regardless of the identity or the political affiliation of the publisher.'[20]

An early success had already been reported that year. Scott Piro, a gay Jewish public relations/social media professional, announced in a press release that Israel's Ministry of Tourism, the Tel Aviv Tourism Board and Israel's largest LGBT organisation, the Agudah, were joining together to launch Tel Aviv 'Gay Vibe', an online tourism campaign to promote Tel Aviv as a travel destination for LGBT Europeans. Critical observers called this initiative 'pinkwashing', comparing the invocation of women's rights in the nineteenth century to justify colonisation with the cynical deployment of gay rights as a tool to legitimise the continued oppression of Palestinians. [21]

Nevertheless, even the publicists didn't believe in their own reports of success. A new body was asked to join to find out why success was still elusive and what else could be done. This was the Jewish Agency's Reut Institute (*reut* meaning 'visibility' as well as 'friendship' in Hebrew). The institute claimed in 2010 that the threat to the state of Israel in the diplomatic and international area was increasing. They had good cause for concern. The UN was ready to publish a ground-breaking report about the Israeli occupation – and no amount of charm could salvage Brand Israel from its conclusions.[22]

Israel changed tack and went on the offensive. The report was analysed by the Reut Institute as a document that 'questions the right of Israel to exist', connecting it to the international outcry directed at Israel after its second attack on Lebanon in 2006. The international furore, according to this institute, was the product of a radical Islamist ideology originating in Iran, from which a web of 'delegitimisation' was spun with the help of Hezbollah and Hamas.

The problem, the Reut Institute suggested, was a 'conceptual inferiority' on the part of the ideological forces in Israel. Israel failed in marketing itself as a Jewish and democratic state and hence the vicious delegitimisation campaign was so successful.

If this campaign continued, the Reut Institute warned that Israel would become a pariah state and there would be no solution for the Palestinian question, hence necessitating a one-state solution. When Zionist bodies warn against the danger of a one-state solution, they are not thinking of a state in which every citizen, be they Jewish or Palestinian, has equal rights. As Prime Minister Ehud Olmert articulated it in 2007:

> If the day comes when the two-state solution collapses, and we face a South African-style struggle for equal voting rights (with Palestinians) … then, as soon as that happens, the state of Israel is finished.[23]

The Reut Institute report reaffirmed this perspective: 'A formative event in such an eventuality [the making of an apartheid state] is the collapse of the two-state solution.' But it seems that even the two-state solution wouldn't satisfy them – unless Israel was spared from any criticism at all:

> However, even in the event of an acceptable two-state solution, the de-legitimisation will continue, and would be focused probably on Israel's treatment of the Palestinian minority in its midst.[24]

So, what was to be done? 'It takes a network to fight a network', concluded the report, asking the government to gather the necessary forces to win the battle against delegitimisation through the internet. This would be assisted by the founding of new NGOs, but more importantly than anything else, the report declared that it was necessary 'to re-brand Israel. Currently Israel is branded as a violent and serial violator of international law'.[25]

So, at least according to the Reut Institute, all the money and experts in the world had not yet helped to rebrand Israel as a peaceful and attractive nation. The obvious solution of being less violent towards the Palestinians seems to have passed them by entirely. Instead, the Jewish Agency wanted the government to seek ways of pressuring the Western elites to broadcast a different image of Israel, and still hoped that Jewish communities abroad could deliver the goods.

Another outfit of the Jewish Agency was the Jewish People Policy Institute. It declared in 2010 that it was tasked with facing one of the greatest threats to Israel's national security and ergo to Jews as a whole: 'de-legitimization has to be understood not only as a threat to Israel but to particular Jewish existence everywhere'.[26] Although it consisted of demographers, historians, sociologists and propagandists, it behaved like a military unit in this context. In a similar way, its annual 'State of the Nation' conference at the Interdisciplinary Center Herzliya called Israel's marketing campaign 'a war', but not just a war – it was 'asymmetric warfare in the battle of ideas'. Since Israel could not be defeated militarily and economically, its enemies were trying to destroy it through ideas. It was an imbalanced conflict, because the enemy was all over the world, and very powerful, at least according to Israel.[27]

The Reut Institute saw the assimilation of young Jewish people into Gentile communities as part and parcel of delegitimisation – young Jews were 'distancing themselves from Israel'. This was reaffirmed by a famous article by Peter Beinart in the *New York Review of Books* in 2010, but Beinart suggested that the growing gulf between young Jews and the American Jewish establishment emerged from the desire not to be identified with the occupation and the criminal policies of the state.[28]

The Jewish Agency obviously did not accept such a perspective. In their eyes, the disaffection stemmed from the popularity of Reform Judaism in the US – a branch of the faith that was accorded little respect in Israel and whose conversion of newcomers to the Jewish faith was not recognised by the Rabbinical institutions in Israel. Consequently, in 2011, while the Reut Institute was asking for more aggressive lobbying, it wanted to put forward a vision of a more religiously pluralist Israel, to win round young, liberally minded American Jews.

But more forces were needed to recover from the 'conceptual inferiority' the Reut Institute had identified – they wanted to invent a scholarly scaffolding to justify Israel's behaviour. The ivory tower had to be put to work.

Until 2010, Zionist scholars had been busy struggling against post-Zionist criticism from within Israeli academia, which had once been prominent in the 1990s. But now scholarly knowledge was to be enlisted not only against the enemies from within, but also against those in the USA and Britain. The new campaign was led by the national religious university of Bar-Ilan and was soon joined by the University of Tel Aviv.

The main role of Israeli academia was to explain why Israel was still being delegitimised in 2010. Answers varied according to the academics' fields of expertise. One key group was those specialising in the history of anti-Semitism and Jewish Studies. They crafted a narrative that was intended to provide a diagnosis of the problem and a prescription to treat it.

This concentrated scholarly effort was meant to provide an intellectual framework connecting contemporary anti-Israel opinion with historical European anti-Semitism. This narrative was first articulated in response to the September 2001 World Conference against Racism in Durban, South Africa. This UN-sponsored NGO meeting was convened to discuss racism throughout the world, including Palestine. It was depicted by the Israeli government as the formal launch of the sinister delegitimisation campaign against Israel, as Arab delegates sought to pass a declaration describing Israel as a racist apartheid state. The fact that proceedings concluded three days before 9/11 did not escape the Brand Israel team and the two events were directly linked as two aspects of the same assault against the free world.

This connection between 9/11 and the 'delegitimisation campaign' was made very openly by Benjamin Netanyahu on various occasions. During a speech in the Knesset on 23 June 2011, he talked about an unholy alliance between radical Islam and the radical Left in the West, joining forces against the free democratic world, which Israel symbolised more than any other place on the globe. From that moment onwards, any international rulings against Israel (such the one issued by the International Court of Justice in The Hague against the apartheid wall) and any actions by civil and human rights organisations (such as the international flotilla that attempted to reach the besieged Gaza) were all stages in the well-structured plan devised in Durban.

A different perspective was provided by a group of ex-generals and previous heads of security services working in academia or in semi-academic institutes that served both the universities and the intelligence community. One such outfit was the Meir Amit Intelligence and Terrorism Information Center in Tel Aviv, which identified the same web of enemies as everyone before and after it: radical Islam working together with leftist anti-Zionists and right-wing anti-Semites.

The Israeli deputy foreign minister, Dani Ayalon, affirmed this interpretation of the problem in a speech he gave to the Jewish Agency in October 2010: 'Our enemies recruit agents who work under the pretence of human rights activism to delegitimise Israel.'[29] This was broadcast as an official Israeli declaration worldwide. In a speech in front of 150 legal experts who were invited to the Israeli Foreign Ministry, he echoed the Jewish Agency's position: 'Terrorists and their emissaries are distorting the international law in order to rob democracies [such as Israel] the right to defend itself.' And he added, 'This is a threat to peace for the whole world'.[30] In the Knesset he called for:

> A counter web made of Jewish and non-Jewish NGOs and academic institutions that would join forces in the front against the delegitimisation and describe the reality in the world as it really is.[31]

By 2011, the government had already invested millions in creating centres for Israeli Studies in various universities around the world, sending high school graduates – selecting the most handsome and articulate among them – to market a youthful, Western Israel. Special teams of tweeters, Facebookers and bloggers began to work 24/7, responding to anything that sounded remotely anti-Israel, while lobbies, modelled on AIPAC in the USA, were founded in Europe as well.

The whole campaign was conducted with military precision. General Dangot, the co-ordinator of Israeli policy in the occupied territories, spelled this out when he said, in specific reference to Hamas:

> The war on legitimisation and public opinion is not easier than that fought in the battlefield ... there is a culture of lies, distortion and fabrication.[32]

It was the Harold Hartog School of Government and Policy at Tel Aviv University that commissioned the most comprehensive analysis of the issue at hand. In 2010, it produced a ninety-page policy paper on this topic. The policy paper, and luminaries such as Alan Dershowitz, a frequent visitor to Tel Aviv University, were somewhat at a loss as to what countermeasures to offer that not already been tried before. The policy paper's author, Rommey Hassman, proposed an interdisciplinary tool that integrated strategic management, marketing and branding approaches with diplomatic and ideological doctrines and, added to the mix, an old Jewish notion called *tikkun olam* which posited the ethical and moral responsibility of the Jewish people to the world.[33] It assumed that the state of Israel could improve its image by emphasising the work it was doing in the field of humanitarian assistance and development, while, at the same time, strengthening its contribution to the developing world. He concluded: 'It is my hope that this publication will be helpful to academics and policymakers alike'.[34]

This paper recommended that the government of Israel market the nation through the following three steps:

1. Establish a national communications council: this council would be established in the framework of the Prime Minister's Office, and would be headed by the government's chief spokesperson. It would administer and oversee a network of government spokespersons, co-ordinating their stand on policy, security, and economic and social issues.

2. Market the nation: To do this, the Ministry of Foreign Affairs would function as the international marketing arm of the State of Israel. In this capacity, it would co-ordinate the marketing of Israel, supervising international press secretaries and spokespersons, contact with foreign journalists and media, and monitoring the international media. The Ministry would also be responsible for all of Israel's embassies, consulates, missions and representatives throughout the world.

3. Establish a Communications Division within the Israel Defence Forces (IDF): This unit would co-ordinate an expanded IDF Spokesperson's Bureau, any units in the military dealing with research and consciousness design, the network of soldier spokespersons, and Israel Army Radio (*Galei Zahal*). In working with the foreign media, the IDF Spokesperson's Bureau would function as an implementing body, acting on the recommendations of the Ministry of Foreign Affairs and under the guidance of the national communications council.

Since it was not possible to address all target markets simultaneously, priorities would have to be set. This paper prioritised marketing by country, based on a measure of the strength of the relationship between each country and the state of Israel.[35]

As is typical for Israel, structured strategic thinking was overtaken by domestic politics. Parts of the document quoted above were implemented, not as part of a clear strategy, but more as a makeshift policy here and there. A more structural and strategic effort in the 'war for legitimisation' was decided upon as a result of negotiations in the process of forming a coalition government. This is how the Israeli Ministry for Strategic Affairs was born and entrusted with the mission of forcing world public opinion to become unambiguously pro-Israel again.

The Ministry for Strategic Affairs grew out of various Israeli coalition governments' domestic considerations. Many ministries are invented to provide a ministry to heads of parties as an inducement to join a coalition government, and this ministry's origin story is no different.

In 2006, Avigdor Lieberman, the head of the hard-right party Yisrael Beiteinu, was courted by Ehud Olmert. Lieberman wanted the Home Security office, but he was ineligible on account of being under investigation for corruption, so they created a new ministry for him, the Ministry for Strategic Affairs. The office was disbanded in 2008. In 2009, the second Netanyahu government (2009–2013) resurrected the ministry and appointed Moshe Ya'alon, the former Chief of the General Staff. He declared that the office would be focusing on countering 'Palestinian incitement'. In 2014, the ministry was merged with the intelligence ministry, only to reappear once more as an independent ministry in 2015. By this point it had a real job on its hands.

In 2015, the ministry was instructed by the government to focus on what was seen as the spearhead of the global campaign to delegitimise Israel, that is, the BDS movement, which by that time could boast impressive achievements in recruiting academic, cultural and trade union institutions to its campaign. These successes meant that BDS began to attract the attention of the Israeli government and the lobby in the US in 2015, when a decade of its activity had started to affect public opinion in the US and in Britain.

In response, the budget of the Ministry of Strategic Affairs was increased, the extra funding coming from a special budget determined by Benjamin Netanyahu; the source of the money remains opaque. A task force called Ha-Maracha ('the campaign') was set up to undertake the battle, and to provide assistance to the lobby abroad in turning the tide.[36]

THE LOBBY AGAINST *THE LOBBY*: UNCOVERING THE ADVOCACY NETWORK FROM WITHIN

In this particular campaign, AIPAC was entrusted with targeting media outlets that Israel typically neglected; for instance, Al Jazeera. More specifically, the lobby was called to the battlefield after the network aired an investigative documentary called *The Lobby*. Although the first instalment was successfully broadcast in Britain, the second series, relating to the actions of the US lobby, could not be aired at all.

AIPAC successfully censored it, and it can now only be watched on YouTube.[37] In its actions, AIPAC revealed how much it could control the right to freedom of speech in the US. What was AIPAC so keen to cover up? Al Jazeera's reporter, James Anthony Kleinfeld, succeeded in posing as an enthusiastic supporter of Israel and was embraced by several pro-Israel advocacy organisations during the Obama and Trump eras. He was invited by outfits such as StandWithUs, the Brandeis Center, the Israel Project, the Foundation for Defense of Democracies, Israel on Campus Coalition, the Zionist Organization of America, Fuel for Truth and the Canary Mission.

Let's take a look at what these organisations are up to – all of them are still active today – beginning with StandWithUs (SWU), also known as Israel Emergency Alliance. Roz Rothstein, a family therapist from Los Angeles, founded it in 2001. It gained visibility around the time of Trump's election in 2016, with eighteen full-time officers in the US and branches elsewhere. According to recent research on the group, SWU regards the West Bank as part of Israel and supports the legitimisation of the illegal Israeli settlements in the West Bank. On their website they devote much space to the West Bank and call it the West Bank/Judea and Samaria. They suggest that the argument that the West Bank belongs to Israel and should be called Judea and Samaria is as morally and legally valid as the other point of view (i.e. that it is illegally occupied territory). We might see this as akin to stating that both opposition to apartheid in South Africa and support for the regime were morally and legally valid.[38]

SWU works in various areas. They are active on American campuses, where they imitate the work of an NGO in Israel called Im Tirtzu, a government-backed outfit whose main role is to monitor lecturers in Israeli universities in case they are conveying anti-Zionist messages in their lectures and classes. SWU has a similar army of foot soldiers carrying out similar missions. They are more systematic than their Israeli counterpart, and you can graduate with a diploma as a 'fellow' or 'ambassador' in many of its induction programmes for pro-Israel activism.[39] On campuses across the US, SWU tried to prevent students and faculty members from supporting the BDS movement. The various Netanyahu governments were very fond of Roz Rothstein, and the Israeli Ministry of Foreign Affairs helped fund SWU operations in the USA. Rothstein was lauded by the right-wing *Jerusalem Post* as one of the fifty most influential Jewish women in the world in 2016. In 2008, with the help of the *Jerusalem Post*, SWU started to publish the *Campus Post*, a monthly newspaper that included articles by *Jerusalem Post* writers on the topics of Israeli news, society and culture, while students and others in North America contributed articles about pro-Israel activism. However, this particular publication was short-lived.

SWU is also highly litigious: it has a legal section employing eighty lawyers, who weaponise legal procedures against BDS resolutions and pro-Palestinian activists on campus. It often wins – but on occasion it can be defeated. One of its most high-profile losses in the courts was its campaign against the Olympia Food Co-op in the state of Washington. This showdown, alongside two others involving Fordham University and the company Caterpillar, is useful in illustrating the extent of the lobby's legal capacity, and how unrelentingly it seeks to shut down any attempts to express solidarity with Palestine.

The Olympia Food Co-op began as a small store in downtown Olympia, Washington, in 1977. It was part of a network of food buying clubs that began to spring up in the area, and it focused on recycled materials when building its first shop and future branches. The Co-op is run by a board of directors. In 2010, they decided to institute a boycott of Israeli goods. Five of the Co-op members, aided by SWU, sued their colleagues, alleging that the board had acted beyond the scope of its authority and had breached its fiduciary duties. SWU initially took credit for filing the case, stating that it was a by-product of the partnership between SWU and the Israeli Ministry of Foreign Affairs. In various decisions by a local court and an appeal court in a process that lasted for eight years, the lawsuit was ruled as illegal. SWU ended up being ambiguous about its involvement in the case, and withdrew from the campaign, perhaps as it was uncomfortable with failure.[40]

On the face of it, the Fordham University case was no different – but this time SWU managed to win. In 2016, Fordham University, in New York City, declined an application from the group Students for Justice in Palestine (SJP) to be recognised as an official student group, claiming that its goals ran 'contrary to the mission and values of the university'. The SJP students filed a lawsuit which was successful in a lower New York court, arguing that Fordham was in breach of their own policies and regulations, which is forbidden in New York civil law under Article 78. The university filed an appeal in the Supreme Court of New York Appellate Division. In 2020, SWU filed an amicus brief in support of Fordham University's position. SWU founder Roz Rothstein said that Fordham is one of the first universities to 'recognise SJP's bigotry for what it is'. In the brief, SWU argued that the courts had limited jurisdiction in terms of dictating the decisions of private universities. Additionally, SWU argued that the university's decision was consistent with Title VI of the Civil Rights Act, which legislates that no person may be subject to discrimination on basis of race, colour or national origin under programmes receiving federal financial assistance. The New York State Appellate Division ruled in Fordham's favour and overturned the earlier ruling. By May 2021, the New York Court of Appeals denied the students' motion to appeal, ending the four-year-old legal case.[41]

Between the failure in Olympia and the success in Fordham, there were some inconclusive cases, such as the struggle to 'save' Caterpillar

– the world's largest construction equipment manufacturer – from the 'claws' of the BDS movement. Its flagship yellow bulldozer, the D9, has become the symbol of one of the most horrifying methods used by the Israeli occupation – the demolition of Palestinian homes. The Dubbi, or Teddy Bear (D9R), was the new and improved iteration, now protected from stones thrown by desperate victims. A Caterpillar D9R driver killed the American activist Rachel Corrie in Gaza in March 2003.

In 2005, the pro-Palestinian group Jewish Voice for Peace (JVP) introduced a resolution at a Caterpillar shareholder meeting. Among the Jewish activists, this group stands out as a grassroots organisation endorsing the BDS movement and lending its support to representatives such as Ilhan Omar, who, as we saw, have faced allegations of anti-Semitism from AIPAC.[42] It partnered in this action with four Roman Catholic orders of nuns. They called upon the company to investigate whether Israel used bulldozers to destroy Palestinian homes. JVP claimed that such usage violated the company's code of business conduct. SWU reacted by urging its members to buy Caterpillar stocks and to write letters of support to the company. It sent its representatives to shareholders, trying to persuade them that Caterpillar had been unfairly singled out. Ever since that meeting, members of the Palestine solidarity movement demonstrate, and attend the shareholders' meeting to introduce the topic again and again, while the D9s continue to demolish Palestinian houses to this day (as this book was being written, we saw these being used in the Jenin refugee camps in July 2023).[43]

The SWU also produced information kits that played fast and loose with factual accuracy. As Ian Lustick has shown, they rehashed some of the false claims and statistics of age-old Israeli propaganda, the most important of which was the claim that a substantial Jewish majority could be sustained even if Israel annexed the West Bank.[44]

Like many of these lobbying organisations, SWU had an office in Israel. We might wonder why – it had no operational purpose in Israel. The reason was financial; this office provided a legal basis for the Israeli funding for SWU. Another purpose was recruitment. In 2009, nearly fifteen per cent of the group's budget went to the Israeli office, which trains 150 Israeli students each year, in conjunction with the Ministry of

Foreign Affairs, to develop their advocacy skills. In January 2015, the investigative Israeli website the *Seventh Eye* reported that SWU would receive $254,000 from the Prime Minister's Office to set up a 'Social Media Ambassadors' programme to educate young people on how to use social media to promote Israel. However, according to SWU, the project did not materialise (SWU did not disclose where the money went instead).[45]

SWU is only the tip of the iceberg when it comes to modern lobbying fronts. Another outfit investigated by *The Lobby* was the Brandeis Center for Human Rights Under Law. This establishment was made necessary by obvious and blatant Israeli violations of international law that no charm offensive could reframe. To foil further undermining of Israel's legitimacy from this angle, the lobby needed to perform a discursive sleight of hand. A centre called the 'centre for human rights law' would be a disaster, as Israel violates these laws daily. But the untrained eye would not see the difference between human rights under law, i.e. domestic Israeli law, and international human rights law.

The purpose of this centre, established in 2012, was to portray Israel as a victim of human rights abuses. The trick was to frame any action against Israel as one against the Jewish people as whole, and hence anti-Semitic. In practice, their brief was to recruit Jewish law students to do more or less what the StandWithUs students were asked to do. 'Chapters' were created in many universities, seeking to detect BDS initiatives and generally what would be deemed as anti-Israel activity on campus.[46] Like StandWithUs, students were not just activists, but rather part of initiative with the catchy name of JIGSAW – JIGSAW stands for 'Justice Initiative Guiding Student Activists Worldwide'. The 'world' here means the US, like the World Series in American baseball.[47]

Its principal nemesis was the Middle East Studies Association (MESA). MESA was founded in 1965 and is a scholarly association of academics teaching and studying the Middle East. Most of the Middle Eastern departments of the world's universities are associated with MESA. In 2014, the Brandeis Center produced a report called *The Morass of Middle East Studies* that accused federally funded Middle East Studies departments at various colleges and universities of being biased against Israel. The organisation claimed that federal funds, provided to

129 international studies and foreign language centres at universities by Title VI of the Higher Education Act of 1965, had been abused and misused.[48]

The report was accompanied by a statement signed by ten pro-Israel groups, expressing concern over alleged misuse of taxpayer money, and arguing that the programmes 'disseminate anti-American and anti-Israel falsehoods'. The statement also called for changes to Title VI which should 'require recipients of Title VI funds to establish grievance procedures to address complaints that programs are not reflecting diverse perspectives and a wide range of views' and 'require the US Department of Education to establish a formal complaint-resolution process similar to that in use to enforce Title VI of the Civil Rights Act of 1964.'[49]

Highly professional and internationally acclaimed work on the Middle East by American scholars exposed the origins, mechanisms and targets of Israel's systematic abuse of civil rights. This academic work, which unearthed human rights violations, was accused by the Brandeis Center of being the real breach of civil rights. In this campaign, the Center worked together with another outfit called AMCHA ('Your People' in Hebrew); its full name is the AMCHA Initiative. It is a campus group that sees itself as an anti-Semitism watchdog, but in practice it only contends with BDS initiatives on campuses. It was founded in 2012 by a lecturer from UC Santa Cruz, Tammi Rossman-Benjamin, and an emeritus professor from UCLA, Leila Beckwith. It is a small outfit compared to others in terms of its finances. But it doesn't need much. Like the Canary Mission, of which more will be said later, it is busy identifying the 'anti-Israeli' lecturers on campuses. It is a very local enterprise, mainly targeting the pro-Palestine and Palestinian groups on the US West Coast by equating anti-Semitism with anti-Zionism or even mild criticism of Israel. Its main claim to fame was the cancellation of a Zoom meeting with Leila Khaled in 2020, after it placed Zoom under intense pressure. Leila Khaled became famous as a member of a team that hijacked a Trans World Airlines flight in 1969 between Rome and Tel Aviv and landed it in Damascus. A photo of her holding an AK-47 became as iconic as that of Che Guevara smoking a cigar.[50]

Liberal Zionists seemed to be quite appalled by AMCHA's activities. In October 2014, a group of Jewish professors wrote to the *Forward*:

> [AMCHA's] technique of monitoring lectures, symposia and conferences strains the basic principle of academic freedom on which the American university is built ... Moreover, its definition of anti-Semitism is so undiscriminating as to be meaningless. Instead of encouraging openness through its efforts, AMCHA's approach closes off all but the most narrow intellectual directions and has a chilling effect on research and teaching. AMCHA's methods lend little support to Israel, whose very survival depends on free, open, and vigorous debate about its future ... AMCHA's tactics are designed to stifle debate on issues debated in Israel and around the world, and the presumption that students must be protected from their own universities is misguided and destructive. Efforts such as these do not promote academic integrity, but rather serve to deaden the kind of spirited academic exchange that is the lifeblood of the university.[51]

The Brandeis Center mirrored the methods outlined above, but on a grander scale. As part of its activity, it targeted a student organisation at Harvard University that protested against the presence of SodaStream water machines on the campus. SodaStream is one of the biggest producers of soda worldwide, and has been owned by PepsiCo since 2018. Before 2015, its principal manufacturing site was in the occupied West Bank – but after a long BDS campaign, it agreed to move inside Israeli borders.

The Brandeis Center had their hands full as BDS gained momentum. One professional scholarly association after the other seriously considered boycotting Israeli academia. Brandeis was involved in trying to stop such initiatives by the Modern Language Association and the American Studies Association. Their most recent campaign was against Ben & Jerry's. In 2022, the company announced that it would not sell its ice cream in the occupied West Bank. It was difficult to find any substantial counterargument made by the Brandeis Center to the very carefully worded Ben & Jerry's announcement that also affirmed its commitment

Lobbying for Zionism on Both Sides of the Atlantic

to continuing to sell in Israel proper. It shows how disconnected the current pro-Israel bodies in the USA are from the reality on the ground when they attack companies that abide by international law:

> We believe it is inconsistent with our values for Ben & Jerry's ice cream to be sold in the Occupied Palestinian Territory (OPT). We also hear and recognize the concerns shared with us by our fans and trusted partners.
>
> We have a longstanding partnership with our licensee, who manufactures Ben & Jerry's ice cream in Israel and distributes it in the region. We have been working to change this, and so we have informed our licensee that we will not renew the license agreement when it expires at the end of next year.
>
> Although Ben & Jerry's will no longer be sold in the OPT, we will stay in Israel through a different arrangement. We will share an update on this as soon as we're ready.[52]

And on the Hill, the Brandeis Center joined other organisations in trying to promote legislation that aimed to equate anti-Semitism with criticism of Israel, as the best means of arresting changes in American civil society's attitude towards Israel. It supported the Anti-Semitism Awareness Act, a controversial piece of legislation introduced to the US Congress in 2016 which required the Department of Education to use its definition of anti-Semitism when 'reviewing, investigating, or deciding whether there has been a violation of title VI of the Civil Rights Act of 1964'. The definition stated that anti-Semitism is 'a certain perception of Jews, which may be expressed as hatred towards the Jews'. As Joe Cohn commented at the time on the Fire website, this is 'a description so broad that it allows for the investigation and punishment of core political speech, such as criticism on Israeli policy'.[53]

Less clandestine are the lobby's efforts on American campuses. Donations are deployed to build centres for Israel Studies to provide a veneer of scholarly legitimacy to Israel's nation-building project. At the same time, the lobby uses litigation in an attempt to defund programmes for Middle East Studies which are insufficiently pro-Israel.[54]

Other US lobbying organisations did not seek simply to change the mood of America-based corporations and campuses but to create a global shift in opinion in favour of Israel. One such outfit is the Foundation for Defense of Democracies. Its establishment was a knee-jerk neo-con reaction to 9/11, but one that from the very beginning worked in tandem with Israel's Ministry of Foreign Affairs. It began with advocating, in keeping with its tough neo-con image, sanctions and aggressive policies against North Korea, Iran, Russia and Afghanistan, but ended up focusing mainly on advocating for Israel. It waited, however, until 2019 to be properly registered as a lobby. It is coy about the sources of its funding, but interestingly one source claims its funder is the UAE, through a reported $2.5 million gift granted in 2017.[55]

The plethora of such outfits led to various attempts to create an umbrella organisation. One such endeavour was the Israel on Campus Coalition, founded in 2002 by Schusterman Family Foundation together with the veteran Jewish societies on American campuses. What this co-ordination effort intended to achieve was joint action against BDS and pro-Palestinian activism in colleges across America. They came to light when their mother organisation, Hillel House, was challenged by an internal group called Open Hillel, which was critical of Israel and open to dialogue with campus Palestinian societies, at least temporarily.[56] 'The enemy from within' was now the main target for monitoring. This went far enough to worry even the Jewish newspaper *Forward*, which wrote that they had built a 'sophisticated political intelligence operation on US campuses'.[57]

The internet is now a critical battlefield. Leading the way is the website Canary Mission, established in 2014, and several others like Campus Monitor are spearheading the lobby's campaigns in that domain. Canary Mission works like a secret service organisation, compiling files on student activists in universities, threatening to send their names to prospective employers. The Israeli government uses these lists to prevent pro-BDS American citizens from entering Israel. No one has sued Canary Mission for illegal activity, but it was severely criticised, not only by pro-Palestinian organisations but also by pro-Israel ones, as a racist project.[58] Jewish academics in Europe and in America have compared Canary Mission's activities to those employed by authoritarian regimes and during McCarthyism in the USA.[59]

The last outfit we should mention with regard to suppressing pro-Palestine activism is the Israel Project. It was founded by Jennifer Laszlo Mizrahi and friends of hers in 2003. Mizrahi also served as the president of the project until 2012. It was somewhat unique, as at first it targeted global cyberspace and tried to cater for the Arab world as well. It used to have an extensive Arabic media section but that was dropped in 2014 (this tried to operate independently as a different organisation called Al-Masdar ('the source') but that also closed, in 2019). In many ways both ambitions, of being global and serving the Arab world, were dropped by the time Al Jazeera looked into this particular NGO. By 2019, it had disappeared to all intents and purposes, due to funding problems. But while it existed, it had offices in Israel and the USA, its own publication called *The Tower*, and a student programme, and organised rather unique helicopter trips in Israel – the sheer cost of these possibly contributed to its downfall.

All these activities are comprehensively exposed in the Al Jazeera documentary *The Lobby – USA*.

Al Jazeera's undercover investigation revealed further evidence of surveillance and smear campaigns conducted by the Israel on Campus Coalition. An executive of this body outlined for the undercover journalist the organisation's intelligence-gathering and surveillance capabilities which the organisation claimed were directed towards pro-Palestine and BDS advocates. Other executives describe the organisation's surveillance efforts as a method of 'psychological warfare'. The film ultimately reveals that Israel on Campus Coalition co-ordinated closely with Canary Mission and the Israeli Ministry of Strategic Affairs.

These revelations could have shocked and appalled the American public. Unsurprisingly, the lobby, led by AIPAC, did all it could to stop its screening in the US. The network announced its intention to broadcast the programme in October 2017. Jewish American organisations began pressuring the Qatari government, which is responsible for funding Al Jazeera, and were able to obtain a promise that the instalment on the US would not be screened by the network in February 2018.

Clayton Swisher, the director of the outlet's investigative journalism wing, accused the network of capitulation to outside pressure and justified his use of undercover investigators as:

> used by many international broadcasters, including BBC and CNN, and is carefully managed, through multiple layers of legal and editorial review, to ensure it is performed consistently with local laws, industry regulations, and our own Code of Ethics.

Swisher suspended himself from working with the network as an act of protest against its decision on this issue.[60]

As typical of the lobby, on the one hand it prided itself on its ability to exert pressure on the Qatari government, while on the other hand, it demonstrated its total lack of gratitude by trying to undermine Al Jazeera's presence in the USA. In March 2018, a bipartisan group of US lawmakers, including Democratic Congressman Josh Gottheimer, Republican Congressman Lee Zeldin and Senator Ted Cruz, urged attorney general Jeff Sessions to investigate whether Al Jazeera should register as a foreign agent, further alleging that the network had infiltrated non-profit organisations, as well as accusing it of broadcasting anti-Semitic, anti-Israeli and anti-American content.[61]

But by then civil society had its own way of coping with such pressure and censorship. In late August and early September 2018, leaked portions of the documentary series were aired by several outlets including the *Electronic Intifada* (an act condemned by Al Jazeera).

To sum up, all these fronts and all these campaigns were doomed to fail as brutal Israeli actions continued on the ground, fully exposed to the world by brave journalists such as Shireen Abu Akleh, who was murdered by Israeli soldiers in May 2022, and by alternative media outlets and human rights organisations, especially those active in Palestine itself. So AIPAC failed to hold back the tidal wave of pro-Palestinian activism in civil society. It continues to promote legislation against BDS on a federal basis, or in specific states, but this tactic – which worked for a while, but not everywhere – often hardened the attitudes of pro-Palestinian activists.

Looking at AIPAC's website in 2023 and following its main activities since November 2022, when an extreme right-wing coalition won the Israeli national elections, one gets the impression that it still believes that what matters are politics from above and not from below. Its main project is now called AIPAC-PAC (Public Affairs Committee), which focuses on recruiting funds for pro-Israel candidates on Capitol Hill. It boasts of having 365 politicians on both sides of the aisle on its roster, and it has spent more than $17 million on them. Most of them, it claims, were elected in 2022. But the new government was not welcomed by the Biden administration, and time will tell how significant this will be for the overall ability of the lobby to influence American policy. As this book is being written, the American–Israeli relationship is at an unprecedented nadir because of what President Biden called the most extreme government Israel has had since he became a politician, back in the late 1960s. However, this book is not about predictions, but about detecting trends and structures. And this parallel movement of losing the sympathy of the public on the one hand, while still having clout with the political elite on the other, is not going to change any time soon. A similar parallel trajectory can be seen in Britain in the twenty-first century.

11

Lobbying for Israel in Twenty-First-Century Britain

A LITTLE DINNER AT MEIR'S

The building on 2 Palace Green in the southern section of Kensington Palace Gardens was designed by the architect Frederick Hering to house the author William Makepeace Thackeray – constructed with the striking red bricks in what became known as the 'Queen Anne revival' style in Thackeray's time. It's no accident that Thackeray himself was a Queen Anne enthusiast. Today it hosts the Israeli embassy.

In one of his more amusing novellas, *A Little Dinner at Timmins's*, Thackeray tells the story of a young couple intent on social climbing, living on 'neat little' Lilliput Street, who organised a dinner somewhat beyond their means, in order to advance what they believed was their rightful place in society, no matter what insults they incurred and how much money they lost in preparing this ill-fated feast. The little dinner soon snowballed into a disaster and put an end to the couple's ambitions of climbing the social ladder.

Over a century later, another little dinner took place in Thackeray's former home, in another attempt to climb a ladder – this time a conduit for political aspirations. This particular dinner in March 1994 cemented a personal friendship that affected the history of lobbying for Israel during the New Labour era. Unlike its fictional counterpart, this meal was a staggering success, converting Tony Blair into a fervid devotee of Israel and its policies, at a time when the wider British public was developing sincere doubts about the wisdom and morality of such an approach.

Tony Blair was then shadow home secretary under the Labour leader John Smith. Now Israel, at this embassy dinner, intended to do Blair an extraordinary favour in introducing him to Michael Levy, a former pop promoter turned fundraiser.

Levy was involved in many causes, most of them Jewish and Israeli ones. For instance, he raised £60 million for the charity Jewish Care, over which he later presided. A former colleague of him said, 'there's no one better in the country' when it came to fundraising. It is estimated that he raised hundreds of millions of pounds for various causes.[1]

As early as the time of John Smith, Levy stood out as a liaison between the Labour Party and some of its wealthier North London donors, who were involved in charity work in the Anglo-Jewish community and whose donations, at least according to one observer, 'crucially influenced' the party's strong pro-Israel stance under both Smith and Blair.[2] These included Sir Emmanuel Kaye of Kaye Enterprises, Sir Trevor Chinn of Lex Garages, Maurice Hatter of IMO Precision Controls and David Goldman of the Sage Software Group.[3] For the Labour Friends of Israel (LFI) of the mid-1990s, feeling somewhat dejected about pro-Palestinian tendencies among grassroots members, this was a crucial turning point. Nick Cosgrave, the director of LFI, said that Blair:

> brought back Labour Friends of Israel into the Labour Party, in a sense ... before the majority of supporters of Labour Friends felt uncomfortable with the Labour Party.[4]

In his memoirs, Levy recalled the dinner:

> The atmosphere was pleasantly relaxed and informal and Blair was very laid back. I wish I could say he immediately struck me as a future party leader and prime minister. In fact, as the lamb and red wine were served, my first impression of Blair – and of his wife, Cherie – was that they were bright, articulate, personable. They also struck me as extraordinarily young and unworldly.[5]

But he was nonetheless persuaded to give his backing to Blair in his future political endeavours. The dinner proved to be a very fruitful event. After John Smith's death in May, Levy donated around £7 million for the campaign and other needs of the aspiring new Labour leader.[6] Once elected, private donations continued to be important for the new leader of the Opposition, and with these he could hire spin doctors and PR experts such as Alastair Campbell, who became his press secretary, and Jonathan Powell, who became his chief of staff. This was the biggest Opposition leader's office in British history, employing some twenty full-time staff on appreciable salaries.[7] Blair's financial independence from the trade unions, Labour's traditional core funders, gave him the freedom he needed to transform Labour in his image.

Levy collected donations to a blind trust, known as the Labour Leader's Office Fund, raising nearly £2 million, a sum 'previously un-imaginable for a Labour leader' (he also invested his own money in this fund).[8] Blair maintained that he was unaware of the sources of these donations despite being in almost constant contact with Levy and even meeting some of the donors.[9]

We now know that the secret donors included funders of pro-Israel groups such as Trevor Chinn and Emmanuel Kaye. Levy had played a crucial role in persuading donors that Labour had changed. Blair told Levy, 'I am absolutely determined that we must not go into the next election financially dependent on the trade unions.' Instead, Blair became financially dependent on large donors, some of whom had very strong views on Israel.[10] According to Levy, the subject of Israel was second only to fundraising in his conversations with Tony Blair.

In effect, Levy made New Labour possible. Levy has subsequently described himself as 'a leading international Zionist' and he has since praised Blair for his 'solid and committed support of the State of Israel'.[11] If Blair needed consistent funding from very wealthy individuals to circumvent the need to liaise with unions, he also didn't want to invite too many questions about the money's sources. One of the better-known figures at Labour Friends of Israel was David Abrahams, a Jewish prop-erty developer. Under an arrangement made between a solicitor acting for Abrahams and two Labour Party officials, Abrahams donated £650,000 to the party by covenanting the money to his close associates, and thereby concealing his identity. The prime minister Gordon Brown claimed these actions broke the law, although this remained disputed.[12]

This was a relationship that only grew more intimate after the watershed election of May 1997, when Blair's New Labour finally swept into power. The Blairs, three years after meeting Michael and Gilda Levy, were accustomed to spending many weekends at Levy's manor, swimming and playing tennis. After Blair's official appointment as prime minister, Levy urged the Blairs to 'come over as usual'; as he recalled:

> When Tony and I finally made our way down to the tennis court, he suddenly stopped dead. He looked around, checking to make sure his security guards were not close enough to overhear him. And then he did something truly astonishing.
>
> He literally jumped up and down, like a small kid who had been let out of school for the day, and shouted, laughing out loud: 'I really did it!! Can you believe it? I'm prime minister! I'm prime minister! I'm prime minister!'[13]

In the summer of 1997, Blair put Levy on his first peerages list, nominating him as Baron Levy of Mill Hill. Three years later, working out of the Foreign Office building, Levy formally became the prime minister's personal envoy to the Middle East.

Blair's interest in the Middle East, Levy recounted, really began in 1995 when the Conservative prime minister, John Major, invited him and Liberal Democrat leader Paddy Ashdown to be part of Britain's official delegation to Yitzhak Rabin's funeral. The event in Jerusalem had, at least according to Levy, turned Blair into a great believer in Israel and no less in his ability to play a leading role in obtaining peace and stability in the future. Levy recalled that during the trip Blair:

> kept asking me questions, whenever I'd go to Israel, when I came back from Israel, what I thought of leaders, and that continued when he became Prime Minister.[14]

Levy praised Blair for entrusting him with the sensitive job of being the Middle East envoy. Blair credited him with having a professional and unbiased approach to the issue of Palestine. In fact, Levy was so trusted that his Jewish identity 'was never mentioned, by either of us. Not at all.'[15]

Ultimately Levy was estimated to have raised over £15 million for Blair before the 'cash for peerages' scandal brought Levy's fundraising to an end in the summer of 2006. In a dramatic twist, Scotland Yard even arrested Levy to investigate whether he had violated the 1925 Honours (Prevention of Abuses) Act.[16] However, no further legal action was taken against Levy.

The embroilment of the Levy–Blair connection in the 'cash for honours' affair was not primarily about influencing British policy towards Israel. Blair mainly wanted to free himself from being finan-cially dependent on the trade unions, especially necessary given Blair's refusal to repeal Thatcher's anti-union laws. But since Levy was part of the pro-Israel lobby before and after Blair, part of the quid pro quo was support for Israel, even if Blair was likely to have supported Israel even without donations from the lobby.

Although Levy attributes Blair's pro-Israel stance to his influence, he played a more significant role in forging the link between financial independence and the pursual of pro-Israel policies in the prime minis-ter's mind. Of course, Blair was already pro-Israel before visiting Israel or meeting Levy. At the start of his career as an MP in 1983, he joined LFI. He remained close to the group throughout his time in politics, regularly appearing at their events. Jon Mendelsohn, a former chairman of LFI, and later Gordon Brown's chief election fundraiser, described Tony Blair's achievement in transforming the Labour Party's position on Israel:

> Blair attacked the anti-Israelism that had existed in the Labour Party. Old Labour was cowboys-and-Indians politics, picking underdogs to support, but the milieu has changed. Zionism is pervasive in New Labour. It is automatic that Blair will come to Labour Friends of Israel meetings.[17]

Pro-Palestinian groups, whether on the Left or on the Right, were still far away from the corridors of power and the decision-making centres in Britain. And yet when Blair talked about 'anti-Israelism', he was tackling the continued shift towards solidarity with the Palestinian struggle that began in earnest in 1982, following the Israeli invasion of Lebanon. Its manifestation was the establishment in 2004 of the Palestine Solidarity Campaign, which still exists. It was very loyal to the PLO's positions and found this even easier after the Oslo Accords were signed in 1993; it thus galvanised public support for the two-state solution, the return of the Palestinian refugees and the end of the Israeli occupation of the West Bank and the Gaza Strip.

Looking back on his pro-Israel policy, Blair had only one regret. He felt he went too far in his support of Israel, as he told Donald Macintyre in 2017. It seems he felt contrite over siding with Israel and George W. Bush regarding the sanctions imposed on the Palestinian Authority after Hamas decisively won the Palestinian Legislative Council elections in 2006. Blair's government was part of a coalition that demanded the removal of Hamas and the imposition of Palestinian Authority rule in the West Bank and Gaza, although Hamas had won the democratic elections. The international community supported the Palestinian Authority president, Mahmoud Abbas, in his refusal to co-operate with the Hamas government. When Hamas took over governance of Gaza in 2007, Britain participated in the blockade of the Strip. The siege, and consequent boycott, supported by Blair, was a punitive action against the people of Gaza for electing Hamas – actions that were opposed by the Palestinian Authority. These actions allowed Israel to continue to this day with the inhuman land siege and naval blockade of the Strip, making life there almost impossible, according to the UN. In his 2017 interview, Blair pointed to the obvious and more decent alternative that Israel had rejected out of hand:

> In retrospect I think we should have, right at the very beginning, tried to pull [Hamas] into a dialogue and shifted their positions. I think that's where I would be in retrospect. But obviously it was very difficult, the Israelis were very opposed to it. But you know we could

have probably worked out a way whereby we did – which in fact we
ended up doing anyway, informally.[18]

This declaration irritated the Israeli policy makers. It came at a time
when the Hamas movement was receiving support for its efforts to
reconcile with the Palestinian Authority in talks hosted by the
Egyptian president, Abdel Fattah el-Sisi, which were welcomed by the
Trump administration. But by now, Blair was not in any position to
influence British policy and he was not the first policy maker in the
West who would become more critical towards Israel once they were
out of office.

Until that moment, Blair was, in the words of the former Israeli
prime minister, Ehud Olmert 'a true friend of the State of Israel'. Tzipi
Livni, who was Olmert's foreign minister, said: 'Tony Blair is a very
well-appreciated figure in Israel'.[19]

They had good reason to be thankful. Regardless of whatever
remorse Blair expressed after the fact, while he was in office, the lobby
didn't have a great deal to do. Blair's identification with American policy
and his buying into the 'clash of civilisations' fable of Samuel Huntington
'between a supposedly enlightened West and a backward Islamic world'
made him the best ally Israel could hope for.[20]

It would not be an exaggeration to say that Blair worked in tandem
with the pro-Israel lobby and that LFI was his port of call whenever he
sought counsel on the Palestine issue. In his speech to LFI's annual
reception at the Labour Party conference in September 2006, Blair said:
'I have never actually found it hard to be a friend of Israel, I am proud
to be a friend of Israel.'[21]

Despite this, Blair was not really an ideologically committed Zionist.
His pro-Americanism was the decisive factor in his foreign policy, and
he followed very closely George Bush's line of thinking concerning
Israel and the Middle East. When Israeli forces invaded Nablus, Jenin
and other Palestinian towns and villages during Israel's Operation
Defensive Shield in April 2002, Blair visited his closest ally Bush in
Crawford, Texas, and kept nodding his head in approval when Bush
declared that:

> We agree that the Palestinian leadership must order an immediate
> and effective cease-fire and crackdown on terrorist networks. And
> we agree that Israel should halt incursions in the Palestinian-
> controlled areas and begin to withdraw without delay from those
> cities it has recently occupied.[22]

In response to questions from journalists, wondering why the two states
did not pressure Israel to end its brutal attack, Blair suggested that he
relied on President Bush who had promised to put an end to the operations: 'I believe that Israel will heed the words of President Bush,' Blair
said, 'and will do so knowing that he speaks as a friend to Israel.'[23]

The united Bush–Blair front continued during the Second Lebanon
War in the summer of 2006. During the first week of August, just before
he met Bush in Washington, Cabinet ministers were pressing Blair to
break with the policy of the American administration and publicly criticise Israel over the scale of death and destruction in Lebanon. In the
party, Jack Straw, who had been dismissed from his position as foreign
secretary in May, led the critique of Blair's passivity in the face of the
destruction Israel wreaked in Lebanon. He explained that while he
'grieved for the innocent Israelis killed', he also grieved for 'ten times as
many innocent Lebanese men, women and children killed by Israeli
fire'.[24] The lobby didn't need to be mobilised to rebut Straw's concerns, as
remorse for the loss of Lebanese lives was only a minority position in
the British government.

Whenever Tony Blair appeared on Sky News for an interview, initially
he was not challenged on his Middle East policy, even when he was
loyally following the American line of action. But apparently when it
came to Western involvement in trying to end the Second Lebanon War,
his lack of independence and total obedience to the American policy
surprised his Sky interviewer, who wished to know why Britain accepted
the American decision to intervene only after it transpired that Israel
had clearly failed to achieve its goals in the campaign. Blair answered, 'I
will never apologise for Britain being a strong ally of the US.'[25]

This meant that, in collusion with the USA, the Israeli bombardment of Lebanon continued, as did the rocket attacks in the north of

Israel. The UN could not impose a ceasefire without American involvement. The former US ambassador to the UN, John Bolton, told the BBC that the US deliberately resisted calls for an immediate ceasefire during the Lebanon war. He said the US decided to join efforts to end the conflict only when it was clear Israel's campaign wasn't working.[26]

Towards the end of his term in office, Blair pursued a policy that reflected the old principles of the 'peace process', a course of action that led to his leadership of the Quartet and an appointment as its envoy for peace in the Middle East after his resignation as prime minister, dwelling in a luxurious annexe of the American Colony Hotel in Jerusalem on his many visits to the area. His main goal was to open a direct and permanent line of communication with the Palestinian Authority, and to play a role in an abortive attempt to overturn the election results in the Gaza Strip that saw the ascent of Hamas. He won the confidence of the Palestinian Authority for a while and they were willing to join him in a new peace conference, but Israel and the USA refused to play along, and the initiative dissipated.

Like Blair, his successor Gordon Brown was pro-Israel to the bone and did not cause any dramatic shift in the policy towards Israel. When it comes to British policies towards Israel and Palestine from above, there are mainly patterns of continuity and only very few moments of deviation from previous policies, which explains why the pro-Israel lobby has been relatively hands-off in terms of elite-level politics in twenty-first-century Britain. None of the British governments of this century have exerted any real pressure on Israel yet to retract its brutal policy towards the Palestinians – this only underscores the courage of George Brown and Alec Douglas-Home in the previous century. In this century, British governments all adhered to the same tropes when talking about Israel: an emotional identification with the Jewish people, occasionally genuine but often feigned; the invocation of the Holocaust; admiration for the achievements of Israel. Added to that they included the standard lines trotted out by the US State Department: a commitment to the two-state solution, questioning the unification of Jerusalem and asking for the problem of Palestinian refugees to be addressed. In principle, the Israeli state objected to these demands in the twenty-first century, but in practice it did not care much. The lobby's job was to express unhappiness with these positions and make sure that they remained empty words. Confrontations with the government occurred when these unpleasant statements were made a little too forcefully or too persistently, and especially when they were followed by sympathetic gestures towards the Palestinians. But the British and Israeli governments got along grandly in the meantime.

A good example of this mixture of emotional commitment to Zionism and Israel, while 'courageously' demanding Israeli 'concessions', can be seen in Gordon Brown's historic speech in July 2008 in front of the Knesset. He was the first prime minister ever to address the Knesset.

First comes the commitment – in his case probably quite genuine, at least in part, given his upbringing. His father was a minister in the Church of Scotland who was involved in pro-Israel activity during Brown's early childhood and influenced him to follow suit. That part of the speech was written with the help of Martin Gilbert, an acclaimed historian of the Holocaust. Gilbert was born into the Goldberg family who emigrated from Eastern Europe to Britain, and in 2019 he told an interviewer that he was involved from a very early age in Zionist activity that even got him in trouble at school.[27] Here is how Brown described his gratitude to Martin Gilbert for helping him with the speech:

Martin and Esther were my guides and advisers when as Prime Minister I travelled to Israel, and he helped me write the first speech given by a Prime Minister to the Israel Parliament, about the long struggle of Israel, both for survival and then to create a lasting peace. And when the then Prime Minister Ehud Olmert and I exchanged presents, it is a reflection of Martin's pre-eminence and our shared admiration for him that without either of us knowing it, I had chosen to give Olmert, a copy of Martin's *The Righteous* and he had chosen to give me a copy of Martin's *Story of Israel*.[28]

Here is part of Brown's speech in front of the Knesset:

My hometown – where I grew up not long after your independence in 1948 – is the small industrial town of Kirkcaldy on the eastern

coast of Scotland. Kirkcaldy is two thousand miles from Jerusalem
– but for me they are closely linked. Not in their landscapes and
certainly not their weather, but in the profound impact of your early
statehood years on my childhood.

My father was a Minister of the Church who learned Hebrew
and had a deep and lifelong affection for Israel. For three decades he
was a member of – and again and again Chairman of – the Church
of Scotland's Israel Committee. And he travelled back and forth to
Israel twice every year, often more.

After each trip, he would roll out the old film projector, plug it in
and load the film. More often than not, the projector would break
down – but he would always get it back up and running. And I will
never forget those early images of your home in my home and the
stories my father would tell.

He promised the Knesset that the next generation of his family would
continue in the same vein:

> My sons are still young children – they are just two and four. They
> have not yet made that journey to Jerusalem made by their grand-
> father and then his sons. But one day soon I look forward to bringing
> them here to see what their grandfather first came to see in the early
> years of statehood.[29]

At the same time, he was heckled by right-wing members of the Knesset
when he said 'candidly as a friend' that Israel should have to compromise with the Palestinians, end the settlements, and find a just solution
for Jerusalem (they should share the city with the Palestinians) and the
refugee problem. He called the settlements a 'blockade to peace', a position he reiterated in a press conference later, in December that year,
when he met the Palestinian prime minister, Salam Fayyad.

Liberal Zionists such as Jonathan Freedland tried to persuade the
Anglo-Jewish community that Brown was Israel's best friend ever,
regardless of the objections of the Israeli right. He wrote in the *Jewish
Chronicle*, in an article called 'The PM who understood Jews':

I defy JC readers to find a more pro-Israel, a more unequivocally
Zionist, statement by any serving British politician than the speech
Brown gave when he became the first UK Prime Minister to
address the Knesset, in July 2008. Marking the 60th anniversary of
the birth of the state, Brown ditched the technocratic language
and robotic delivery and waxed poetic, speaking of 'the centuries
of exile ended, the age-long dream realised, the ancient promise
redeemed – the promise that even amidst suffering, you will find
your way home to the fields and shorelines where your ancestors
walked.'[30]

Crucially, Brown didn't have to be the best possible friend of Israel to be
a reliable ally – he just had to do nothing. Perhaps the most perceptive
listeners who understood that his Knesset speech was, as the Palestinians
called it, *kalam fadi* ('hollow words') were a group of schoolchildren
who, as one eagle-eyed British journalist noticed, fell asleep very early
on during the prime minister's speech.[31]

All in all, Brown's short term in office was everything the pro-Israel
lobby hoped for. Britain stood aside when Israel carried out a callous
attack on the Gaza Strip in December 2008, with weapons made in
Britain. The British government had licensed £24 million of British
arms exports to Israel in the first half of 2006 – a £6 million increase on
exports licensed during the whole of 2007. Exports included components for combat aircraft, surface-to-air missiles, naval radars, electronic warfare equipment, weapon sights and military communications
technology.[32] British engines were installed in the Israeli 'drones' that
bombarded the Gaza Strip. This at least was what Amnesty International
and the UN agency in the Strip claimed at the time.[33]

If these top-down policies did result in any blunders, they involved
corruption, rather than any change of heart about Israel and Palestine.
During Brown's term in office the major scandal was the June 2007 'cash
for honours' affair. This scandal had several names: 'cash for peerages',
'loans for honours' or 'loans for peerages', and exposed an unethical,
maybe even illegal, connection between donations to the Labour Party
and the granting of peerages.

Brown's own chief fundraiser, Jon Mendelsohn, admitted, 'I knew about the scandal for weeks.' Mendelsohn also confessed that he was aware that David Abrahams was a 'controversial donor' and that he was channelling hundreds of thousands of pounds to Labour through a chain of middlemen.[34]

This was an unpleasant moment for the lobby and for the Anglo-Jewish community as a whole, especially when the Crown Prosecution Service asked the police to make further inquiries concerning what they dubbed 'donor-gate'. The prominence of Jewish donors prompted anxiety that the scandal would lead to a fresh outbreak of anti-Semitism. Not only were Mendelsohn and Abrahams Jewish; their common political platform was LFI, which is also how they were connected to Lord Levy.

But in their reporting of the issue, the mainstream Jewish media resolutely kept LFI out of it and honed in on the donors as Jews. In an interview Abrahams gave to the *Jewish Chronicle*, he expressed his fear that 'donor-gate' would be seen by the British public as a Jewish conspiracy (this fear was also expressed by Jon Benjamin, the executive director of the Board of Deputies interviewed by Nathan Jeffay for both *Forward* and *Haaretz* in its English edition).[35]

As an Israeli Jew, I probably cannot fully understand, or empathise with, the fear of anti-Semitism embedded in a community that has suffered from sporadic outbursts of anti-Semitism, while facing little systematic prejudice, in this century; although I acknowledge that the threat felt is real. Yet I think, knowingly or not, the Israeli and Zionist aspects of scandals such as the 'cash for honours' one are not addressed as distinct issues, but are lumped together with anti-Semitism. It is much easier to cry out 'anti-Semitism', where Jews have the moral high ground, rather than dig deeper and see that a scandal that involves support for Israel in the twenty-first century is not just about Jews, but rather about the suffering of the Palestinians from Israel's brutal policies. You didn't need to be an anti-Semite to raise your eyebrows at the revelation that the men in question, Abrahams and Mendelsohn, were highly involved with Labour Friends of Israel. It inevitably strengthened suspicions that pro-Israel Jews donated money to the Labour Party in order to benefit Israel.

This connection to Israel was highlighted by a number of British media outlets. The *Daily Telegraph* led with an explicit commentary on the link between Abrahams, LFI and attempts to influence policy towards Israel. To make this point even more obvious, it published a photograph of Abrahams shaking hands with the former Israeli ambassador to Britain, Zvi Heifetz, with the question beneath it: 'Who is the real donor?' Abrahams claimed all along that he gave money to Labour simply because he supported Labour, but it seems it also had to do with his wish to help the cause of LFI. Charitably speaking, he missed the point. The issue at stake wasn't his motivation, but the somewhat bizarre clandestine methods he employed in fundraising for Labour, while holding a prominent position in LFI. As Yasmin Alibhai-Brown put it at time in her column in the *Independent*, it was impossible to exclude LFI from the discussion about these scandals. Its *raison d'être* was to champion official Israeli policy; consequently, she alleged that Tony Blair's unconditional support for the 2006 Israel assault on Lebanon was partly the result of its influence. Alibhai-Brown argued that the scandal could only convince Islamist fanatics that there really was a worldwide Zionist conspiracy. Of course, they didn't need a scandal to think that. But to the wider public, the presumed association between policies favourable to Israel and donations to the Labour Party, going through LFI, could increase anti-Semitism.[36]

LFI survived as a lobby, despite alleged involvement in the 'cash for honours' affair. Neither Israel nor its lobby were too concerned with British public opinion on this – and in any case, the ire was mainly targeted at the politicians who granted peerages. They cared about the political elites, even as public trust in them was on the decline. The damage here was minor and short-lived – in 2014, Labour happily received £630,000 from a Labour Friends of Israel grandee, Sir David Garrard, who made a loan of £1 million to the party prior to the 2005 general election.[37] But the lobby *was* concerned about how the British electorate was responding to Israel's attacks on Gaza and the West Bank in this period. Politicians, chasing after votes, might forget their commitments to Israel. In particular, the lobby worried about constituencies with a high Muslim population.

DISCIPLINING THE MEDIA

The massive concrete building on 119 Farringdon Road in London hosted the *Guardian* from the 1960s, when it moved from Manchester, up until its later move to Kings Place in 2008. In April 2006, two visitors entered the then editor Alan Rusbridger's office uninvited; in fact, they barged angrily into his room. The first gentleman was Henry Grunwald, the president of the Board of Deputies, and his colleague was Gerald Maurice Ronson, a business tycoon and philanthropist.

The two did not even take off their coats. Ronson addressed Rusbridger immediately, skipping the formalities, and said: 'I've always said opinions are like arseholes, everyone's got one', and then added, 'I am in favour of free speech but there is a line which can't be crossed and, as far as I am concerned, you've crossed it, and you must stop this!'[38] The 'This' referred to by the two gentlemen was an article by Chris McGreal, a veteran journalist who wrote a piece in which he compared Israel to apartheid South Africa.

The affiliations of both gentlemen, who had no official connection to Israel, acting in a way that even Israeli diplomats would not have dared to, tell us how far some Anglo-Jewish organisations and leading figures have gone in deserting the interests of the Anglo-Jewish community at large and focusing almost entirely on partaking in Israel's war against its critics.

At the time, Grunwald represented a Board of Deputies that was uncannily akin to AIPAC in being more a front group for Israel rather than a representation of Anglo-Jews. This was evident as early as 2003. In that year, it reproduced an extract from a US State Department report claiming that the Palestinian Relief and Development Fund (Interpal) was funding terrorist organisations, but when Interpal threatened to sue for libel the Board retracted it and apologised.[39] Interpal is a London-based charity that raises money for Palestinian causes and is one of the largest Muslim-led charities in Europe.

The Board under Grunwald also failed to silence one of Israel's main critics in the UK, Ken Livingstone. In 2005, Livingstone compared a Jewish *Evening Standard* reporter, Oliver Finegold, to a concentration camp guard. The Board filed a complaint to the Standards Board of England, calling on Livingstone to apologise. Livingstone, who had a twenty-five-year running battle with the paper's owners, responded, 'There is no law against "unnecessary insensitivity" or even "offensiveness" to journalists harassing you as you try to go home.' The complaint against Livingstone was unsuccessful.[40]

By the time he burst into the editor's office, Grunwald also presided over another organisation, the Jewish Leadership Council (previously known as the Jewish Community Leadership Council), founded in 2003. The council acted as an umbrella group for various Jewish community organisations, charities, and Zionist and pro-Israel advocacy groups. It included important figures such as Lord Levy, Lord Janner and, by 2013, the treasurers of the Conservative Party, Howard Leigh and Stanley Fink.

In December 2006, the Leadership Council and the Board of Deputies joined forces and formed the Fair Play Campaign Group, in reality a pro-Israel advocacy organisation that co-ordinated activity against anti-Israel boycotts and other anti-Zionist campaigns.

Grunwald's colleague that day, Gerald Maurice Ronson, was a very affluent businessman. He inherited his father's furniture and real estate businesses and, famously, the company Heron. Ronson became notorious as one of the Guinness Four: four people convicted of fraud involving the trading of Heron company shares in the 1980s. For his role he was convicted in August 1990 and was charged with the crimes of conspiracy, false accounting and theft. He was fined and spent six months in jail. His criminal record did not stop him from receiving a CBE for his wide-ranging philanthropic work in 2012.[41]

They were at the *Guardian*'s office on behalf of LFI, which had decided to take it upon themselves to organise a well-co-ordinated attack against McGreal's 'dangerous' article. To this end, it sought the help of a new outfit, called BICOM (Britain Israel Communications and Research Centre).

BICOM was founded in 2001 by Poju Zabludowicz, inspired by the model of AIPAC in the USA. In fact, it sent representatives to participate in AIPAC's annual conferences. Zabludowicz was a Finnish-born

British billionaire, art collector, arms dealer and philanthropist. He was born into money: his father's fortune came from a strong connection to Soltam Systems, the Israeli manufacturer that is still a core part of the state's military industry.[42] He also spent considerable time in Israel and divided his life between Israel and the UK, having settled in the UK through marriage. By all the common criteria, he was at the time one of the richest people in the UK (he owned, according to one report, forty per cent of downtown Las Vegas). He also owned property in illegal Jewish settlements in the West Bank and had stakes in the shopping centre of the illegal settlement Ma'aleh Adumim, east of Jerusalem.

Zabludowicz contributed £1.4 million in two years to BICOM.[43] He also donated generously to the United Jewish Appeal, which collected money for Israel from local Jews. He was also a funder of the Conservative Party. In 2005, Zabludowicz was joined at the helm of BICOM by Ruth Smeeth, who would later become a Labour MP. BICOM worked very closely with Conservative Friends of Israel (CFI), and the benefactors of BICOM also helped to fund David Cameron's election campaign in 2005. BICOM used similar methods to those of LFI and CFI – including organising visits to Israel. The difference was that BICOM focused on sending journalists, and paid for their trips in the hope of getting favourable coverage. One typical trip occurred during the days of Operation Cast Lead (the Israeli assault on Gaza in 2008/2009); the journalists were introduced to military experts in Israel. One study claimed that this trip produced widespread analysis of Hamas as an Iranian proxy in newspapers such as the *Sunday Times* and the *News of the World*.[44]

In May 2011, BICOM organised the 'We Believe in Israel' conference, attended by 1,500 delegates, to try to counteract the horror in British society in response to the ongoing Israeli siege of the Gaza Strip, which had led the Co-operative Group to boycott particular Israeli goods. An even bigger event under the same banner was convened in March 2015 to fend off growing criticism of Israel in the wake of the 2014 assault on the Gaza Strip, the worst attack to date.

The coalition against McGreal's article was even wider than that. The campaign against him was joined by two additional outfits that were part of the lobby in the UK. The first was the Community Security

Trust (CST), which had split from the Board of Deputies in 1986 and included various Anglo-Jewish associations, such as the Association of Jewish Ex-Servicemen and Women. The CST was registered as a charity in 1994 and professed to provide safety, security and advice to the Jewish community in the UK.[45] At the end of 2021, several Muslim organisations in Britain demanded that the Charity Commission review the CST's status on account of its alleged Islamophobic activity.[46] Gerald Ronson, who joined Grunwald that day in the *Guardian* office, was the chairman of that body too.

Another relatively new organisation joined in from overseas: the Committee for Accuracy in Middle East Reporting in America (CAMERA), a pro-Israel media watchdog. It complained unsuccessfully against McGreal to the Press Complaints Commission, alleging that his article was 'based on materially false accusations'.[47]

When they faced the editor of the *Guardian*, the two envoys of this ad hoc coalition of the lobby were not content with just fuming about McGreal's piece. They also accused the *Guardian* of fanning the flames of anti-Semitism. Alan Rusbridger rejected these accusations, made mainly by Ronson:

> I mean I didn't want to get in a great row with Gerald Ronson, I just said I'd be interested in the evidence, I'm not sure how you make that causal connection between someone reading an article that is critical of the foreign policy of Israel and then thinking why don't I go out and mug Jews on the streets of London. I just can't believe that happens.[48]

Rusbridger recollected how effective this browbeating campaign was in 2006. He told a news outlet that:

> There are a lot of newspaper and broadcasting editors who have told me that they just don't think it's worth the hassle to challenge the Israeli line. They've had enough.[49]

The ferocity of these attacks can best be explained by the fact that it was getting increasingly difficult for the pro-Israel lobby to justify some of

Israel's actions at the beginning of the twenty-first century. Until 2010, as long as Labour was in government, this task fell on the shoulders of LFI. The difficulty was not only how Israel conducted itself but a growing grassroots antipathy among Labour and the Conservatives towards the Israeli state. LFI felt under such pressure that it co-operated with CFI, sharing the same contacts with the Israeli embassy and the same supporters, such as the businessmen Victor Blank and Trevor Chinn. Of course, their operations within their respective parties remained independent.

Blank was a well-known banker and for a time the director of the Royal Bank of Scotland; later on he was the chairman of Great Universal Stores, which owned Argos and other iconic companies. He was deeply entangled in the banking crisis of 2008 and 2009. Later, he became vice president of the Jewish Leadership Council, founded by Grunwald.

Trevor Chinn was a magnate who made his fortune from garages and services such as the RAC, and was heavily involved in charity work. He chaired the Joint Israel Appeal and was also part of the Jewish Leadership Council executive. He helped to fund Keir Starmer's bid for leadership of the Labour Party in 2020.[50]

With such backing until Labour left office in 2010, LFI was leading a new phase in lobbying for Zionism in Britain more than a century after it began. They were now supporting an Israel that had moved dramatically to the Right and had no regard for either Palestinian rights or their aspirations.

The transition from representing an Israel willing to negotiate to providing carte blanche for its new, more extreme face and policies was not smooth. Ehud Barak's Israeli Labor Party defeat in 2001, the subsequent governments of Ariel Sharon and Ehud Olmert and the re-election of Netanyahu in 2009 generated some unease among the general Anglo-Jewish community, and known figures in it were losing some of their confidence when it came to supporting Israel unconditionally.

Every now and then, leading Jewish figures would criticise one Israeli policy or another. The most frequent criticism was directed against the expansion of Jewish colonisation in the West Bank. In 2005, Simon Schama and Sir Malcolm Rifkind led an impressive list of people condemning such plans in a letter to the Israeli ambassador to the UK.[51] Several liberal Anglo-Jewish organisations also reacted to the ongoing siege of Gaza and wanted the Board of Deputies to be less supportive of Israel's policies there. One organisation, Yachad, presented a letter signed by 500 British Jews castigating the Board of Deputies for failing to criticise Israel's violence and singling out Hamas.[52]

In the first decade of the twenty-first century, the LFI and similar bodies were worried about what they deemed as the growing anti-Israel orientation of the mainstream media. This is why, from 2000, they targeted the *Guardian* and accused the paper of being anti-Zionist and even anti-Semitic. While the lobby in the UK itself was not entirely sure this was a successful campaign – and at times tried to engage in dialogue with the paper rather than attacking it instinctively – Israel's Government Press Office deemed it very effective and satisfactory. Its director, Danny Seaman, boasted that he had forced the *Guardian* to transfer correspondent Suzanne Goldenberg, whom Israel disliked, to Washington. 'We simply boycotted them,' claimed Seaman, 'the editorial boards got the message and replaced their people.'[53]

This quotation and the next ten or so references in the coming paragraphs are based on the excellent analysis provided by the former chief political editor of the *Spectator*, Peter Oborne, of this particular formative moment when the lobby was mainly clashing with the BBC and the *Guardian*. It appeared on *openDemocracy* and was written together with James Jones.[54]

Seaman was vindictive towards journalists he deemed anti-Israel, denying them entry to Israel or delaying their arrival. He was described by some of those targeted as a 'bully' who was 'at the forefront of the general harassment'. His language was quite often condescending and self-righteous, as can be seen from his reply to Alan Rusbridger, who had asked Seaman to withdraw his comments about Goldenberg's alleged anti-Semitism, reminding Seaman that he was targeting a very able journalist who had received numerous awards:

I will happily withdraw my comments about Ms. Goldenberg when your newspaper withdraws the biased, sometimes malicious and often incorrect reports which were filed by her during her unpleasant stay here.[55]

Rusbridger could not resist pointing out to Seaman that his 'success' in causing her relocation was not a punishment: 'only the Israelis would see a move to Washington as a demotion.' These accusations directed at Goldenberg were one of the early instances in this century of anti-Semitism being weaponised in order to castigate what was regarded as hostile reportage.

Throughout the 2000s, other media outlets and journalists were targeted as well. Antony Lerman, one of the leading Jewish historians and journalists, was labelled 'a nasty anti-Semite' on a website designed to expose anti-Semitism on the *Guardian*'s website, for an incisive critical article on the lobby and its carte blanche endorsement of Israeli policies. Lerman responded: 'I think there are people who are deliberately manipulating the use of the term anti-Semitism because they do see that it's useful in defending Israel.'[56]

In 2002, the *New Statesman* felt the wrath of the pro-Israel lobby in Britain. The lobby alleged that Peter Wilby, then the *New Statesman*'s editor, was complicit in anti-Semitism for allowing two articles criticising Israel to be included in one of its issues, which had a front cover emblazoned with the headline 'A Kosher Conspiracy'. It showed the Jewish Star of David piercing a Union Jack; an admittedly provocative image that accompanied two insightful and well-founded critical articles on Israel. One article was by Dennis Sewell, exploring the belief that pro-Zionists have undue influence on the media's coverage of the Middle East, and the other by John Pilger, who investigated the pro-Israel lobby in his usual erudite and perceptive style.

The lobby organised a demonstration near the journal's offices, under the name Action Against Anti-Semitism, demanding what they called 'an apology in writing'. Wilby apologised for the front cover but, to his credit, he did not cave in on the two articles that were targeted. The apology came through an editorial in which he wrote that the *New Statesman* 'opposes ... the policies of the present Israeli government' and that he would continue to 'highlight those policies and, where appropriate, to discuss the activities of lobbies in Britain and America that support them.[57] As for the image, Wilby conceded that the journal:

> used images and words in such a way as to create unwittingly the impression that the *New Statesman* was following an anti-Semitic tradition that sees the Jews as a conspiracy piercing the heart of the nation.

A year later, in 2003, it was the BBC's turn. At that time, Israel joined a small band of countries, including North Korea, Zimbabwe and Turkmenistan, that refused the BBC free access. The Israeli government imposed visa restrictions on BBC journalists and refused access to Israeli government figures after a documentary about its nuclear weapons, entitled *Israel's Secret Weapon*, was shown on the BBC World Service. Seaman was again orchestrating the campaign. He compared the BBC film to 'the worst of Nazi propaganda'.[58] When Ariel Sharon visited London in July 2003, the Israeli press officer banned BBC journalists from attending his press conferences.

Israel's nuclear capacities may not have been a secret any longer, but it did have another weapon in its arsenal: the allegation of anti-Semitism. This was targeted at the BBC's Orla Guerin. The Israeli government repeatedly complained to the BBC that she was 'anti-Semitic' and showed 'total identification with the goals and methods of Palestinian terror groups.' She was even blamed for fomenting anti-Semitic incidents in Britain.

When Guerin was based in the Middle East in 2004, she filed a report about a sixteen-year-old Palestinian would-be suicide bomber. Guerin said in the report that 'this is a picture that Israel wants the world to see', implying the Israelis were exploiting the boy for propaganda purposes. One of Israel's ministers, Natan Sharansky, joined the campaign and complained to the BBC about Guerin, accusing her of 'such a gross double standard to the Jewish state, it is difficult to see Ms Guerin's report as anything but anti-Semitic.' He continued to follow her career, so to speak, and when he learned that Guerin was being awarded an MBE, he declared:

It is very sad that something as important as anti-Semitism is not taken into consideration when issuing this award, especially in Britain where the incidents of anti-Semitism are on the rise.[59]

In 2004, the pressure on the BBC from pro-Israel groups and the Israeli government was so great that the head of BBC News, Richard Sambrook, felt obliged to act. He commissioned Malcolm Balen, a former head of ITV News and senior BBC executive, to prepare a report on the BBC's Middle East coverage from 2000 to 2004. It was 20,000 words long and the British taxpayer paid an undisclosed sum of money, rumoured to be quite handsome, for its composition. Through a Freedom of Information request, *openDemocracy*, on whose report we rely in this section, discovered that the BBC had spent over a quarter of a million pounds on legal fees relating to the case. We do not know what was written in the report; appeals to the courts in the name of the Freedom of Information Act were turned down. In October 2004, the High Court finally ruled that the BBC did not have to publish the report. Anyone associated with the lobby, directly or indirectly, was convinced that it was not published because it proved the anti-Israel bias of the BBC. Although the report was never released, the bits and pieces that both *openDemocracy* and the *Jewish Chronicle* were able to gather indicate that probably all the report did was to point out several occasions where it deemed reports were in need of more context; ironically because, at the time, according to the report, the dominant view was pro-Israel.[60]

The BBC turned into what one journalist called a 'hate figure' for pro-Israel groups, who resented what they saw as an anti-Israel bias. Ex-BBC journalists recalled that rarely a week went by without having to deal with complaints about their coverage of the Middle East.

In 2007, the pro-Israel lobby turned their ire towards the BBC's Middle East editor, Jeremy Bowen, then one of the most senior journalists in the UK. The BBC Trust (the BBC's governing body at the time) accused him of twenty-four cases of inaccuracy and breaching the code of impartiality in an article he wrote commemorating the fortieth anniversary of the June 1967 war. The 'inaccuracies' were a challenge to the lobby's narrative. As I have tried to show from the beginning of this book, Zionist lobbying and later Israeli lobbying, are, among other things, an attempt to control the narrative. Bowen used the narrative most scholars at the time were employing when writing about 1967; for instance, referring to the war as a chance to 'finish the unfinished business of Israel's independence war of 1948'. He also shared the common scholarly assessment of Zionism as a project of territorial expansionism, writing of Zionism's 'innate instinct to push out the frontier', and finally he repeated the well-known fact that the Jewish settlements were a breach of international law.

The Trust's accusations did not come out of the blue. It was once more a case of the Trust caving in to pressure from the pro-Israel lobby, which demanded Bowen's dismissal due to his 'anti-Israeli' coverage.[61] It was hardly explosive stuff – while it described Israel as a second 'Goliath', it blamed Nasser for stoking the fears of Israeli civilians. It simply did not conform to Israel's self-image as a plucky underdog fighting for its very life. Instead of Grunwald and Ronson, this time the mission was entrusted to Jonathan Turner and Gilead Ini. Turner would later chair an outfit called UK Lawyers for Israel. At the time he was working for the Zionist Federation, the obsolete outfit from the early days of lobbying for Zionism, now lacking a clear purpose. Gilead Ini was a recruit from the other side of the Atlantic; people like him increasingly took up the mantle of helping the pro-Israel lobby in Britain. He was a senior research analyst at CAMERA. CAMERA produced a new methodology – a line-by-line examination of every piece, highlighting mistakes ranging from straightforward typos to conflicting interpretations, to cast doubt on the professionalism of those who criticise Israel. Bowen's article was subjected to this intensive method of discrediting an author. Enumerating twenty-four 'biases' in the article and another four in another publication by Bowen, they initially failed to convince the BBC's editorial complaints unit. As two journalists who looked at the inaccuracies remarked: the 'corrections' were 'at best matters of opinion. In a majority of the cases, the complaints were found to have no merit, and where changes were made, they changed the meaning very little.'[62]

However, they then took their complaints to the BBC Trust, whose chair was either persuaded or perhaps even intimidated into ceding they had merit. I say intimidated, based on what Charlie Beckett, a former BBC news editor, wrote:

> The BBC investigated Jeremy Bowen because they were under such extraordinary pressure ... it struck a chill through the actual BBC newsroom because it signalled to them that they were under assault.[63]

Be that as it may, the Trust convened a special meeting chaired by David Liddiment, who had worked in TV entertainment for the BBC and ITV over the years. He was described by Jonathan Dimbleby as someone who:

> is admired as a TV entertainment wizard and former director of programmes at ITV but whose experience of the dilemmas posed by news and current affairs, especially in relation to the bitterly contested complexities of the Middle East is, perforce, limited.[64]

The charade of inaccuracies seemed to fascinate the fairly clueless. Liddiment and his colleagues found that Bowen had breached three accuracy guidelines and an impartiality one in his online report, and one accuracy guideline in his radio piece. The Zionist Federation and CAMERA at once called for Bowen to be sacked, calling his position 'untenable', while adding that what they called his 'biased coverage of Israel' had been a 'significant contributor to the recent rise in anti-Semitic incidents in the UK to record levels'.

This was a pattern the lobby now followed time and again, extending its remit to academics whose arguments were insufficiently sympathetic to Israel. The targeted writer or journalist was accused of intentional inaccuracies in the service of Israel's enemies that had inadvertently led to an increase in anti-Semitism. Nobody in the BBC Trust even attempted to unpack this completely implausible chain of causality. This was a pro-Israel interpretation that had to be accepted as the truth.

Accordingly, it interested precisely no one that Bowen had published a similar article in the *Jewish Chronicle* only a few days earlier that included the same 'contentious' sentences, such as 'Israel still bears a disastrous legacy' and 'Zionism's innate instinct to push out the frontier', as well as 'The Israeli generals, mainly hugely self-confident sabras in their late 30s and early 40s, had been training to finish the unfinished business of 1948 for most of their careers'.[65] These 'inaccuracies' apparently did not matter then. The *Jewish Chronicle* subsequently took the article down.

Jonathan Dimbleby was outraged and wrote an incisive article on the whole affair in the *Index on Censorship*. Unsurprisingly, this didn't go down well with the lobby. Turner employed the same method in trying to censor Dimbleby, demanding that he should no longer host the BBC's flagship radio programme *Any Questions?* Dimbleby became a victim of a process he so ably described:

> You don't have to search far on the web to find Zionist publications, lobby groups and bloggers all over the world using distorted versions of the report to justify their ill-founded prejudice that the BBC has a deep-seated and long-standing bias against the state of Israel. Conversely, millions of Palestinians, other Arabs and Muslims will by now have been confirmed in their – equally false – belief that the BBC is yet again running scared of Israeli propaganda.

The irony was that large sections of the public and the whole network of pro-Palestinian organisations were outraged by the BBC coverage in general, especially after the Israeli assaults on the Gaza Strip began in 2008. The worst manifestation of this biased coverage was the BBC's refusal to screen an aid appeal from Britain's top charities for the children of Gaza. The BBC has a long tradition of showing humanitarian appeals, including those that were seen as politically sensitive, such as the Lebanon appeal in 1982, and helped raise tens of millions of pounds for people in need around the world. But in January 2009, Mark Thompson, director general of the BBC, took the unprecedented decision of breaking away from other broadcasters and refusing to broadcast the Disasters Emergency Committee's appeal for Gaza, claiming it would compromise the BBC's impartiality. ITV and

Channel 4 screened the Gaza appeal, but Sky joined the BBC in refusing.

The BBC's decision undermined the humanitarian effort and probably resulted in the loss of millions of pounds that could have been raised. It had an undeniable impact. Brendan Gormley, chief executive of the Disasters Emergency Committee, was confident that the appeal for Gaza raised only about half of the expected total: £7.5 million. In the first forty-eight hours of the appeal, phone calls were down by 17,000 compared to the average.[66]

For some, this particular episode unambiguously proved how far the pro-Israel lobby's influence had reached. Ben Bradshaw, the secretary for culture at the time and a former BBC reporter, remarked, 'I'm afraid the BBC has to stand up to the Israeli authorities occasionally. Israel has a long reputation of bullying the BBC.' He added, 'I'm afraid the BBC has been cowed by this relentless and persistent pressure from the Israeli government and they should stand up against it.'[67]

Michael Mates, a member of the Intelligence and Security Committee and former Northern Ireland minister, said: 'the pro-Israel lobby in our body politic is the most powerful political lobby. There's nothing to touch them.' He also commented: 'I think their lobbying is done very discreetly, in very high places, which may be why it is so effective.[68]

The diligent Peter Oborne asked Charlie Beckett, the former BBC news editor, why he thought the corporation behaved in such a way, and he replied:

> If there was no pro-Israeli lobby in this country then I don't think [screening the appeal] would have been seen as politically problematic. I don't think it would be a serious political issue and concern for them if they didn't have that pressure from an extraordinarily active, sophisticated, and persuasive lobby sticking up for the Israeli viewpoint.[69]

Many years later, when Labour was in opposition, the British public had evidence of the pro-Israel lobby's influence put before it again, in an instalment of Channel 4's acclaimed programme, *Dispatches*. It was the third time the channel had dared to challenge the loyalty of mainstream TV media in Britain to the government's policy on the Israel/Palestine question. The first occasion was in 2003, when John Pilger's *Palestine is Still the Issue* was screened; this was a documentary graphically exposing Israeli abuses of Palestinians' basic civil and human rights in the occupied territories.[70] The second bold foray into challenging the pro-Israel narrative was Peter Kosminsky's *The Promise*, which provided a compelling fictional portrayal of the Nakba in 1948 as ethnic cleansing.[71]

The two earlier productions were only aired outside prime time. *Dispatches* marked the first time such a challenge to the lobby was broadcast on prime-time television. It was presented by Peter Oborne, who shone a light on 'one of the few remaining taboos in British politics *and* British political journalism'. The press commended the channel for taking the 'bold if unpopular move'.[72] Aside from exposing the operations of Labour Friends of Israel and Conservative Friends of Israel, it unveiled BICOM's tenacious work to suppress criticism of Israel. As it turned out, Oborne and the show's producers had performed a greater public service than they realised. The Conservatives would win power one year after the documentary aired, and without it, the covert role of CFI might have slipped under the radar.

UNDER THE SHADOW OF CFI

In 2009, the ballroom of the iconic Park Plaza Westminster Bridge Hotel in London, which overlooks the Houses of Parliament, hosted the annual convention of the Conservative Friends of Israel. The keynote speaker at the annual lunch on 18 June was the leader of the party, soon to become prime minister, David Cameron.

Until David Cameron addressed their conference, hardly anyone in the British media, let alone the wider public, knew what CFI was. This may have been a conscious decision on CFI's part – a low profile could only have done them favours in 2009. Six months before the meeting, Israel began a twenty-three-day assault on Gaza that ended with the death of about 1,400 Palestinians, including hundreds of children, in

Operation Cast Lead. Even ardent supporters of Israel found it difficult to justify this assault and its human cost. So, conveniently, CFI left it in the hands of its counterpart LFI to carry out the unpleasant task.

CFI was easy to underestimate. But even before its unexpected lurch into public consciousness, mainly as a result of the *Dispatches* programme, it had been a powerful actor on the political scene since 1995. Back then Conservative politician Robert Rhodes James lauded it as 'the largest organisation in Western Europe dedicated to the cause of the people of Israel'.[73] By 2009, according to *Dispatches*, around eighty per cent of Conservative MPs were members of CFI, leading Peter Oborne to call it 'by far Britain's most powerful pro-Israel lobbying group' in 2013.[74]

The *Dispatches* documentary claimed members of the group and their companies had donated over £10 million to the Conservative Party between 2001 and 2009. The group called this figure 'deeply flawed', saying that they have only donated £30,000 between 2004 and 2009, but that members of the group have undoubtedly made individual donations to the party. *Dispatches* described CFI as 'beyond doubt the most well-connected and probably the best-funded of all Westminster lobbying groups'.

In the Plaza's sparkling ballroom, David Cameron appeared in front of CFI and was very warmly received. To the great relief of the attendees, Cameron did not mention Cast Lead and its destruction of the Gaza Strip, aside from justifying Israel's right to defend itself and noting the contrast, to the great delight of the attendees, between the Jewish state and Hamas: 'Israel strives to protect innocent life – Hamas targets innocent life'.[75] He talked very differently when he became prime minister a year later, but he pleased the audience when he said:

> For the Palestinians themselves, their obligations are clear: Prove you are a reliable negotiating partner. Bring order to your own society. And renounce violence completely.[76]

The conclusion was clear: Israel and its lobby could count on David Cameron. When the Conservatives went into a coalition government, CFI was happy to flex its muscles again. CFI earned this influence as a result of the generous support it lent to Tory candidates in the elections. Among the names supported, according to a pamphlet published by James Jones and Peter Oborne, entitled *The Pro-Israel Lobby in Britain*, were Ed Vaizey, Greg Hands, Michael Gove, Brooks Newmark, Shailesh Vara, Grant Shapps, Adam Holloway, Joanne Cash and William Hague – almost all of them would serve in the Cabinet. Some were even taken on trips to Israel to solidify their connection to CFI. At the time, the organisation was chaired by MP Stephen Crabb, a devout evangelical Christian who alternated with a Jewish MP in this position, and Lord Eric Pickles.[77] In the pamphlet, Jones and Oborne also argue that:

> There is also a suggestion that some members of the CFI target MPs who are critical of Israel. For instance Karen Buck, the Labour MP for Regent's Park and Kensington North, has been an outspoken critic. Her Conservative opponent Joanne Cash, who works for the think tank Policy Exchange, has received cheques cumulatively worth at least £20,000.[78]

CFI reacted angrily to the allegations made in the *Dispatches* documentary:

> The documentary was deeply flawed in its crucial failure to draw any distinction between donations to the Conservative Party from individuals who may well broadly support the aims and objectives of CFI, and donations from the CFI itself. The allegation that CFI and its supporters have contributed £10 million to the Conservative Party in the last eight years has absolutely no basis in fact.[79]

However, CFI's focus was not on that documentary but rather on Cameron. The *Jewish Chronicle* gave its readers a quick assessment of Cameron and his government from the perspective of the pro-Israel lobby. Stuart Polak, director of CFI, said:

> We are delighted to see David Cameron as Prime Minister in Downing Street and William Hague as Foreign Secretary. Israel and

the Jewish community can feel assured that their issues and concerns will be addressed and taken seriously by the government. I have every confidence that pledges the Conservatives made before the election on important foreign and domestic issues will be implemented.[80]

The lack of any distinction between Jewish interests in Britain and Israeli interests had never been put forward so unashamedly. After decades of cautious navigation around Jews as British citizens and Jews as potential citizens of Israel, all caution was thrown to the wind. Jews in Britain were now conflated with Israel. And if there were doubts about certain personalities, all you needed to do was to read the *Jewish Chronicle* for clarification, and thus the paper assured its readers that Defence Secretary Liam Fox 'is known to be hawkish on the Middle East and will champion Israel's cause in Cabinet'.

The main task of the government, according to the *Jewish Chronicle*, was defined in the following way:

> On the touchstone issue of universal jurisdiction, the Tories are committed to legislative change to stop magistrates issuing warrants for visiting Israeli politicians. There is concern in some circles about the commitment of Attorney General Dominic Grieve. However, the new Justice Secretary, Ken Clarke, who would be responsible for pushing through the law change, is a recent visitor to Israel with CFI and considered a safe pair of hands.[81]

The lobby hence had nothing to worry about with regard to David Cameron and his coalition government. Unfortunately, it did have a bigger problem: Israel's own brutality.

Before the election, CFI could be both sanguine and complacent about the incoming government's support. But it soon transpired that even politicians who were helped by CFI or supported it found it difficult to toe the line when faced with the humanitarian catastrophe in Gaza and, to a lesser extent, with the overall systematic abuse of Palestinian rights in the West Bank. The Israeli siege of the Gaza Strip created shortages of food supplies, medicines and materials for infra-structure, and at the same time locked in nearly two million people – increasing the mental pressure on a population of whom many were 1948 refugees. And thus, the lobby no longer aimed to galvanise support for Israel – it directed its energies to suppressing critics. The lobby had to work hard to keep everyone in line, regardless of the developments on the ground, even after the Tories were in power.

By 2009, the Jewish lobby for Israel was resigned to the fact that there was no more liberal Zionism of any significance in Israel. Support for Israel now amounted to advocacy for the right-wing governments of Sharon, Olmert and Netanyahu. This process of reorientation began when Netanyahu was elected for the first time after Yitzhak Rabin's assassination in 1995 by a far-right extremist who opposed the Oslo Accords. The murder shocked the Anglo-Jewish community as a whole, but did not prompt any soul-searching about what the purpose of lobby-ing for Israel was.

No less challenging was the publication of the Goldstone Report in 2010, accusing Israel of targeting civilians intentionally. CFI's role was to ensure that the government did not endorse a UN resolution based on the report. Andrew Feldman, a fashion tycoon, a friend of Cameron from their shared time at Oxford and a senior member of CFI, was, according to some sources, present at a meeting between Cameron and William Hague, his foreign secretary, and influenced the drafting of a reassuring letter to CFI:

> Unless the draft resolution is redrafted to reflect the role that Hamas played in starting the conflict, we would recommend that the British Government vote to reject the resolution.[82]

Britain stayed true to its word in this instance and rejected the resolu-tion – the pressure had paid off.

The next challenge was to confront the desperate move in 2011 by the Palestinian Authority to appeal to the international community to avert the total demise of the two-state solution by unilaterally declaring the establishment of a Palestinian state. Effectively the Palestinian

Authority had no real sovereignty or power anywhere in historical Palestine. From 2011, CFI and the Board of Deputies were mobilised by Israel to pressure the government not to heed the Palestinian Authority's request, and largely succeeded.

In response to Palestinian civil society's frantic struggle to win over the international community, the main method used by both LFI and CFI was to intensify the frequency of politicians' trips to Israel. The MPs' trips were funded by Israel. As journalists have shown, over the years, more MPs went to Israel on LFI and CFI trips than to countries in Europe, America and Africa combined.[83] A trip to Israel, as well as joining either LFI or CFI, was a ticket for the young and ambitious to higher positions within Britain's major parties. This holds especially true for the Labour Party; chairs or vice chairs of LFI who later obtained ministerial positions include Jim Murphy, James Purnell and Ivan Lewis.[84]

As before, targeting the official political elites was a successful gambit. This tendency to criticise policy in the West Bank and the Gaza Strip here and there, while still being very loyal to Israel, tallied with overall British policy towards Israel. Cameron tried to stick to that policy on his first official visit to Israel as prime minister in March 2014, when he addressed the Knesset and declared that he was a British prime minister whose 'belief in Israel is unbreakable, and whose commitment to Israel's security will always be rock solid'. He made a point of referring to the 1917 Balfour Declaration, and to 'the proud and vital role' that Britain had played in 'helping to secure Israel as a homeland for the Jewish people'.[85]

At the same time, liberal Jews and the wider public found it hard to stomach total indifference towards the conditions of the Palestinians. For a while, some nominal sympathy with Palestinians was tolerated by the lobby's leaders, but only if it did not influence what they saw as the crucial organisations, such as the Board of Deputies. In 2014, the Board of Deputies had a spasm of 'liberal Zionism' and sought to counteract the growing anger about Israeli policies by putting out a joint statement with the Muslim Council of Britain calling for peace, following a particularly aggressive Israeli military operation in Gaza. This was Operation Protective Edge, which took place during June and July 2014, triggered by the abduction and killing of three young settlers in the West Bank, but caused more by Israel's desire to undermine a reconciliation unfolding between Hamas and the Palestinian Authority and Israel's annoyance at the continued building of Hamas's military capacity during a two-year ceasefire that had concluded in 2012. As a result of Israeli attacks, nearly a quarter of a million Palestinians were displaced in the Strip and hundreds of thousands of children (according to the UN 373,000) needed mental health support as a result of the traumatic events they experienced. A quarter of the houses in Gaza City were damaged. As we saw earlier, although there are debates about the number of Palestinians killed, all the sources, including the Israeli one, put them at over 2,000, which included nearly 500 children. The Israeli army lost sixty-six soldiers and six civilians died in the rocket attacks from Gaza.[86]

Although three-quarters of the Board approved the joint initiative, the angry backlash from the more influential right-wing members of the Board was intimidating enough to persuade the Board to distance itself from the Muslim Council of Britain.[87]

CFI didn't care too much about what the public thought – it focused on making sure the coalition government suffered no inconvenient pangs of conscience when they thought about Gaza. However, other lobbying groups decided to try and stop the decline of Israel's public image. They aimed to discipline the mainstream media, which was increasingly critical of the siege of Gaza and Israel's continued assaults on it.

In general, the mainstream media maintained the *omertà* concerning Israel's activities in the region, and didn't cause the lobby too much trouble. But this was the age of alternative media, alongside a civil society that became more hostile to Israel with every passing day. The main challenge came from networks such as Al Jazeera.

THE LOBBY BY AL JAZEERA

We have seen how the American lobby suppressed the screening of *The Lobby* in the US. Its British counterpart was not quite so successful, and hence in 2017 Al Jazeera broadcast an investigation of a large array of organisations that informally comprised the pro-Israel lobby in Britain.

This included the Jewish Labour Movement (formerly the British branch of Poale Zion), the Union of Jewish Students, CFI and LFI.

The programme deployed undercover journalists to expose the activities of the lobby groups. The main 'hero' of the piece was an employee of the Israeli embassy, Shai Masot, who conversed with every group involved about targeting pro-Palestinian politicians in Britain. He talked in the film about his desire to 'take down' politicians such as Alan Duncan, then minister of state in the Foreign Office (his crime was criticising Israeli settlements in the occupied West Bank), and Crispin Blunt, a civil servant whom Masot described as being too pro-Arab.

Other telling episodes showed attempts to dislodge the first Black Muslim woman to be elected as president of the National Union of Students, Malia Bouattia. Masot is heard in the film trying to solidify the lobby by guiding sympathetic students into launching a youth wing of LFI, claiming he has £1 million to Joan Ryan, the chair of LFI, for trips and visits. Although Labour and the Scottish National Party demanded an inquiry into the allegation that a foreign state interfered in the politics of a local party, Boris Johnson, then foreign secretary, rejected all these appeals.

Needless to say, the pro-Israel lobby in Britain condemned *The Lobby* as anti-Semitic. LFI published a panicked Twitter thread, in which the documentary was accused of 'typical anti-Semitic tropes' and a 'series of falsehoods'.[88] However, Ofcom – the communications regulator – dismissed complaints and ruled that Al Jazeera had not been anti-Semitic nor had it breached impartiality rules.

The fact that it didn't get its way in this instance did not cause the lobby to reconsider its campaign to suppress criticism of Israel. On the contrary, it intensified its efforts.

WEAPONISING ANTI-SEMITISM AND ISLAMOPHOBIA

We've seen how the dual strategy Israel employed in its attempt to stop the constant deterioration of its international image worked in the US. Its nicer, public-facing side focused on charming the targeted audience: the Israeli Ministry of Tourism presented an image of the most relaxed, tolerant and fun country in the world. In this fantasy, Israel was a state that had airbrushed those inconvenient Palestinians out of its land and was awarded the Golan Heights as a gift from Syria. Posters showing the Ministry's map of Greater Israel, which appeared on billboards on the London Underground, had no Golan Heights or Palestinian areas. Even the *Guardian* reproduced this cartographical fabrication in May 2009 and took several months to correct it on 15 July.[89]

But around 2010, the Netanyahu government reached the conclusion that the charm offensive wasn't enough to salvage Israel's reputation. He recruited teams of experts to find a solution to the problem – and many pointed the finger squarely at Britain. The proof for this was the emergence of Palestinian solidarity among broad sections of the British public, which Netanyahu accused of 'delegitimising' Israel.

In 2011, at the annual 'State of the Nation' conference at the Interdisciplinary Center Herzliya, delegitimisation was chosen as the major theme. One speaker after another portrayed this assault as part of the ills of 'Left wing post-modernism', which wants to 'conquer the sources of cultural production to control the truth'. As they put it, 'an op-ed in *The Guardian* or *Le Monde* will not make them Zionists'. In addition, they complained 'that Israel will also be blamed, no matter what it does', and finally, that Israelis should 'not wash their dirty laundry outside and present a united Israel'.[90]

The academics working for the Jewish Agency blamed the UN, Western legal systems and Western academia for the ongoing assault. It singled out Britain as the centre of the campaign to tarnish Israel's international image. One explanation provided by this team of experts for the shift in British public opinion was the increase in Britain's Muslim population. On the flipside of things, according to this report, there were still forces to reckon with that were on Israel's side, such as Tesco. I have no idea why Tesco was mentioned by these experts as an antidote to anti-Israel advocacy. The overall assessment was as follows:

> Britain is the capital of communication of the world. It is the centre of the world's principal NGOs but it is also a country with a fragile Jewish community. Amnesty and Oxfam are preoccupied with delegitimizing Israel. The government is more sympathetic so what

should be done? Whoever is the delegitimizer, including Israeli professors [supporting the BDS campaign], should be fought like in a war. They should be targeted and fought, not engaged intellectually; all the means not used before should be employed – this is the battlefield on the Israeli right to function, defend itself …[91]

The debate about Israel's conduct in the occupied territories was now a 'war' about the legitimacy of Israel itself. Israel's weapon of choice was equating criticism of Israel with anti-Semitism and 'Islamic terrorism'. It had been used throughout the history of the lobby in Britain, but was needed more than ever in 2014, when the disturbing images from Operation Protective Edge, the largest ever Israeli assault on the Gaza Strip, reached Britain. The Israeli assault triggered unprecedented protests and demonstrations in Britain against Israeli policy: tens of thousands demonstrated in London and other cities. This time many in the Muslim community in Britain joined forces with the various solidarity movements in the country. There were also demonstrations in front of supermarkets selling Israeli products. Even Nick Clegg, leader of the Liberal Democrats and deputy prime minister in Cameron's coalition government, added his voice to the general condemnation, accusing Israel of 'a deliberately disproportionate form of collective punishment.'[92] According to YouGov, across the population as a whole, sympathy for the Palestinians reached thirty per cent, the highest since YouGov tracking began in 2003.[93] Petitions across the country called upon municipalities to fly the Palestinian flag in solidarity with the people of Gaza.

The lobby reacted by launching the Campaign Against Anti-Semitism in 2014 while Operation Protective Edge was going on. From that moment onwards, any rebuke of Israel's actions in the Gaza Strip was immediately depicted as anti-Semitic. The campaign first targeted the Tricycle Theatre in London, which refused to host the Jewish Film Festival – an event funded by the Israeli embassy. The artistic director of the theatre stated:

The festival receives funding from the Israeli embassy and, given the current conflict in Israel and Gaza, we feel it is inappropriate to accept financial support from any government agency involved.

Stephen Pollard, the editor of the *Jewish Chronicle* at the time, tweeted a strident objection would come to characterise the *Jewish Chronicle* response to any acts of solidarity with the Palestinians in Britain: 'Be clear on this. Tricycle Theatre is now officially anti-Semitic. It is singling out the Jewish state for boycott.' The intimidating rebuke was effective; the theatre did a U-turn and invited the festival, without any preconditions, to take place there in years to come.[94]

Similar accusations were directed at the late Anglo-Jewish MP, Sir Gerald Kaufman, for comparing Israeli actions in 2015 to those of the Nazis and referring to 'Jewish money' that influenced Conservative policies on Israel. 'Jewish money' was immediately seized upon as an anti-Semitic trope, although the phrase was hardly controversial beforehand. As Tony Greenstein points out:

> The term 'Jewish money' is regularly used within the Jewish community. It simply means money belonging to Jews. I counted over 600 instances of its use in the *Jewish Chronicle* alone by searching their archives![95]

The Board of Deputies called on the Labour Party to discipline Kaufman and the pressure led Jeremy Corbyn to castigate him publicly for making 'completely unacceptable' remarks about the Jewish community.[96] It did not help Corbyn, who then in 2015 began to be systematically accused first of not doing enough about anti-Semitism and then of being an anti-Semite himself. Kaufman's condemnation continued even after his death in 2017 and ended with quite vicious obituaries written about him in the *Jewish Chronicle* and elsewhere.[97]

Another victim of this campaign was a Bristol University professor, Rebecca Gould. Gould, herself Jewish, wrote an article called 'Defining Anti-Semitism' in 2011, describing how the Holocaust intimidates people into self-censoring their views on Israel and suggested that Jewish people should stop 'privileging' the Holocaust.[98] It did include sentences that pro-Israel readers found hard to digest, but were legitimate under any principle of freedom of opinion: 'Israel must find a way of not passing on the crimes the Nazis introduced into the world onto the next generation of its citizens.'

The Campaign Against Anti-Semitism called on the university to fire her unless she retracted her article. At the time, this was a practically unprecedented move, and one that many liberal Jews felt was unwarranted. Even people like Kenneth Stern, an American academic who was the main author of the International Holocaust Remembrance Alliance's definition of anti-Semitism, later made infamous by disputes in Labour about its adoption, declared in testimony in the US Congress that the Campaign's behaviour was 'egregious' and that 'the exercise itself was chilling and McCarthy-like'. This widespread sympathy was not extended to David Miller, another Bristol University professor, whose 'crime' was linking Zionism with Islamophobia, ten years later. But in both cases the University of Bristol opened up an investigation. Gould quit while she was ahead and moved to Birmingham University. Miller was not so lucky – he was sacked.[99]

Before the election of Jeremy Corbyn, quite a few liberal Jews at the time felt uneasy with the way the Campaign worked. Anshel Pfeffer, the *Haaretz* London correspondent, wrote in 2015:

> The fact is too many Jews, both political leaders in public appearances and ordinary Jews on social media, are often too quick to bring up the Holocaust in order to make a point. The sad truth is that many Jews have cheapened the memory of the Holocaust by using it in an inappropriate fashion. Holding that opinion doesn't necessarily make you an anti-Semite.[100]

He further accused the Campaign of an 'eagerness to see the anti-Semitism in Britain, which inarguably exists, as much more widespread than it really is'.

While liberals on both sides of the Atlantic thought the Campaign's histrionics were disconnected from reality, one member of the informal pro-Israel lobby we met earlier in the chapter, BICOM, didn't see any issue with them. In seeking to equate criticism of Israel with anti-Semitism, it allied itself with some dubious bedfellows, some of whom were present at its annual convention in 2015. The Middle East Forum took part, an America-based NGO that, according to Hilary Aked, provided financial support to prominent European Islamophobes such as the Dutch politician Geert Wilders and Peder Jensen, aka 'Fjordman', a blogger who inspired Norway's far-right mass-murderer Anders Breivik.[101] This kind of spectacle could only discredit the lobby's case in the eyes of liberals and broader civil society.

Yet if many liberal Jews were sceptical about the legitimacy of BICOM and the Campaign's methods before 2015, that was soon to change. On 12 September 2015, Jeremy Corbyn was elected as leader of the Labour Party. The lobby, in both its formal and informal iterations, suddenly realised that it could no longer rely on inertia to keep the wheels of the party turning on pro-Israel tracks. Corbyn was a threat to everything the lobby had built within the party – and they needed to neutralise him. They set their sights on bringing down a politician at the very top.

FACING THE 'DANGER' OF CORBYNISM, 2015–2020

Jeremy Corbyn was the dark horse candidate in the 2015 leadership race – barely scraping enough MP nominations to get on the ballot paper. Corbynmania was a bolt out of the blue in a party that was close to moribund after a long rightward drift and two election defeats.

His election antagonised not only the pro-Israel lobby, but also the Blairite wing of the party. They saw the aged socialist as the return of the 'old' Labour they despised and tried to depose him from day one. Their criticisms were primarily ideological; they thought nationalisation was outdated and found him insufficiently pro-European. After the Leave campaign won out in the Brexit referendum in 2016, 172 Labour MPs supported a vote of no confidence in Corbyn, prompting a leadership challenge. Humiliatingly for his parliamentary opponents, Corbyn won again, with an even larger majority. A new tack had to be tried – and MPs were only too happy to co-operate with the lobby in turning the faint murmurs about anti-Semitism into an uproar.

The methodology is familiar to those of us who have been targeted by the lobby. A team was assembled to review Corbyn's past actions and words on behalf of the Palestinians and reframe them as instances of either indirectly fomenting anti-Semitism or directly contributing to its spread. As Corbyn was a long-time supporter of the Palestine Solidarity Campaign, and frequently spoke at its events, they found plenty of material they could manipulate and work with. The *Jewish Chronicle* lost all its inhibitions and claimed that Corbyn associated with 'Holocaust deniers, terrorists and some outright antisemites'.[102]

The campaign against Corbyn peaked when the former Chief Rabbi, Jonathan Sacks, defined several instances in Corbyn's political career as indicative of a chronicle of anti-Semitism. The most ridiculous among them was pointing to an event Corbyn hosted featuring the late Hajo Meyer, a survivor of Auschwitz, who volunteered as an ambulance driver in the occupied West Bank after retiring from a very successful business career in the Netherlands. Hajo Meyer considered Israeli abuse of Palestinians as abuse of the memory of the Holocaust – and said so at a Holocaust Memorial Day event, which Corbyn was hosting in 2010. This hit the headlines in 2018, and several Labour MPs were quick to condemn the entire event as totally unacceptable. Alarmed by the outcry, Corbyn apologised, saying he had appeared on platforms with people whose views he rejected completely. In my view this was a tactical error and exposed his vulnerability to these kinds of attacks by the lobby, who persisted with 'guilt by association' tactics in relation to many more incidents in Corbyn's political career.[103]

You wouldn't have guessed it from the media coverage, but Corbyn's views on Palestine were virtually identical to those expressed by most British diplomats and senior politicians ever since 1967: like them he supported a two-state solution and recognised the Palestinian Authority. At the time of his election, this position made him an outlier among the Palestine Solidarity Campaign, and the wider anti-Zionist movement, who endorsed a one-state solution. So why did the lobby see him as such a threat, especially as a potential future prime minister? Because they suspected, correctly, that he sincerely believed in a just two-state solution and wouldn't swallow Israel's excuses for obstructing it. In other words, he followed the lead of previous British statesmen who had the courage to stand up to the lobby's pressure.

Christopher Mayhew, George Brown and Jeremy Corbyn had much in common. They were in positions of power that could affect British policy towards Israel. They were all totally loyal to the official British policy supporting a two-state solution to the 'conflict'. None of them denied the right of Israel to exist, none of them had made any anti-Semitic remark in their lifetime and they were not anti-Semitic in any sense of the word. They were all targeted as if they dramatically deviated from British policy, denied the right of Israel to exist and were motivated by good old-fashioned anti-Semitism.

The 'risk' posed by Corbyn led the new president of the Board of Deputies, Marie Sarah van der Zyl, to intensify the attack on Corbyn in 2018, once it was clear he could not be removed through a leadership election. By profession Van der Zyl is a lawyer specialising in employment law. Her loyalty to Israel, she explained in an interview with the *Jewish Chronicle*, had to do with her past – she came to Britain in the famous Kindertransport and spent some time in Israel. She was determined to 'defend Israel's legitimacy and its centrality to Jewish identity'. Her presidency overlapped with the Trump era and she fully endorsed Trump's policies in the region, including moving the American embassy to Jerusalem.[104]

Van der Zyl chose i24NEWS, founded by a Jewish businessman from France (a former director of *France 24*) and another from Israel in 2013, to indict Corbyn of supposed anti-Semitism. In an interview in August 2018, Van der Zyl claimed repeatedly that Jeremy Corbyn had been 'spending more and more time with terrorists and extremists' and 'with people who threaten the security of Britain'. She seconded one of the presenter's outbursts that supporters of Jeremy Corbyn are 'a cult' and said that 'Jeremy Corbyn had declared war on the Jews at home'. According to Van der Zyl, Jeremy Corbyn's 'hatred of Israel and Zionism runs so deep' and 'he cannot separate that from anti-Semitism'. Van der Zyl praised the Tory party, claiming that 'The Tories have always shown themselves to be friends to the Jewish community.'[105]

This homage to the Conservatives was wildly incongruous with their actual record on anti-Semitism and Islamophobia, which was far worse than Labour's. A proper inquiry into their institutional anti-Semitism might have begun with Boris Johnson's 2004 novel

Seventy-Two Virgins, which depicted Jews as controlling the media and fixing elections, and then moved on to a leading Conservative like Jacob Rees-Mogg, who harangued fellow Jewish members of his party, Sir Oliver Letwin and the then Speaker John Bercow, calling them 'Illuminati who are taking the powers to themselves.'[106]

Michael Berkowitz, Professor of Modern Jewish History at University College London, explained:

> With his nod to 'Illuminati' – pointed at Letwin and Bercow – Rees-Mogg is knowingly trafficking in the portrayal of Jews as underhanded and sinister ... while studiously avoiding the word 'Jew'.[107]

Rees-Mogg also retweeted the comments of Alice Weidel, leader of the neo-Nazi German party, Alternative for Germany, but the Board of Deputies was in no hurry to decry his apparent anti-Semitism.[108]

When we grasp the gulf between Van der Zyl's hysterical reaction to Corbyn and his real position, we are getting very close to solving the conundrum posed at the beginning of this book. Defenders of Israel are constantly beset by self-doubt about the state's legitimacy, and this fuels the campaign to justify a project and later a state that could only be founded and sustained by the constant oppression of another nation. They react strongly to Israel's critics because they know they have a point – and they can't deny it.

Van der Zyl was not alone in her extreme diatribe against Corbyn. In the same year, Britain's three main Jewish newspapers jointly called a Corbyn-led government an 'existential threat to Jewish life' in Britain, which actually meant an existential threat to the pro-Israel lobby in Britain. It was – and not because Corbyn didn't affirm the existence of Israel; he did so repeatedly. It was because he believed in a just peace and stood with Palestinians to enable it.

The lobby scraped the very bottom of the barrel in order to damn Corbyn as an anti-Semite. One such piece of evidence was an offhand remark made by Corbyn on social media in 2012 relating to a mural he had seen (but later regretted not 'looking more closely'), Corbyn objected to its removal on a point of principle, as a violation of freedom of speech. The mural had been created by an American street artist and depicted Jewish bankers playing Monopoly on a table made of naked, exploited workers. While its content was obviously problematic, Corbyn's comment was one of many mountains made from molehills.

In 2016, already aware of the rumblings of discontent and shaken in the wake of an anti-Semitism scandal at the biggest student Labour Club in the country, Corbyn agreed to assemble a commission to inquire into alleged institutional anti-Semitism in the Labour Party. Moreover, two prominent Labour figures, the MP Naz Shah and the former mayor of London Ken Livingstone, had been suspended for alleged anti-Semitism. It was on the eve of the May 2016 local elections, and it was believed that the setting up of this commission would appease Corbyn's detractors in the media and within the party. In hindsight, we now know that nothing would have appeased them, short of Corbyn vacating the position of Labour leader.

During the brutal Israeli assault on Gaza in 2014, Naz Shah had retweeted a provocative remark that Israel should be relocated to the USA. In the ensuing controversy, Livingstone defended her, adding unnecessarily:

> When Hitler won his election in 1932 his policy then was that Jews should be moved to Israel. He was supporting Zionism before he went mad and ended up killing six million Jews.[109]

Hitler was not a Zionist by any stretch, but it is not a lie to point to the secret connections between Zionists, who saw his rise to power as an opportunity to increase Jewish emigration to Palestine, and Nazis, who, in 1933 at least, only aimed to remove the Jewish presence from Germany.[110] Both Shah's retweet and Livingstone's remark were not worthy of suspension by any stretch of the imagination, even if they were provocative. The problem was that these incidents kicked off a chain reaction that the pro-Israel lobby used to pursue its own interests. Any attempt to stop the dramatic escalation in events was itself seen as anti-Semitic.

The inquiry was led by the human rights lawyer and former head of Liberty, Shami Chakrabarti. Even before the committee began its investigation, several Labour Party members were suspended and some later expelled for alleged anti-Semitism.

In 2018, the lobby went back to the archive and found a clip from 2013 which they then construed as further damning evidence of Corbyn's anti-Semitism. It was from a speech he gave at the Palestinian Return Centre in London, in which he recalled a dispute between the Palestinian ambassador and a group of people who approached him after a speech the ambassador gave in Parliament. These people disliked what the ambassador said – although strikingly none of the media reportage around the controversy seems to have recorded what the ambassador said. It was clearly immaterial for the furore the lobby wanted to create. Corbyn said the 'Zionists' who berated the ambassador had two problems: 'they don't want to study history and secondly … they don't understand English irony', and that is despite living in Britain all their lives. Although he was intending to describe the group of activists who approached the ambassador after his speech, the lobby quickly leapt up to assert that 'Zionists' was a codeword for Jews in general.[111] The BBC reported that:

> Richard Millett, who believes he is one of the people Mr Corbyn was referring to, said the Labour leader's comments were racist and 'deeply anti-Semitic'.[112]

Even more absurd were reproaches of Corbyn for writing a new introduction to a reissued edition of the classic 1902 text *Imperialism: A Study* by John A. Hobson, an invaluable source in scholarly research. The book undoubtedly contains anti-Semitic statements, but it has been a core text in understanding turn-of-the-century imperialism for decades. Corbyn was right in referring to it in the new introduction as a brilliant book.[113]

The principle on which the Campaign Against Anti-Semitism operated was: throw enough mud and something will stick. One of their officers, Joe Glasman, boasted in a video that they had 'slaughtered' Corbyn.[114]

Corbyn articulated the concerns of many progressive people in Britain when he expressed anxiety about the way the new European initiative to confront Holocaust denial in Europe conflated it with criticism of Israel in the famous International Holocaust Remembrance Alliance (IHRA) definition that the British government tried to push every university to adopt. The IHRA is an association of thirty-one countries, which began as a Swedish initiative to combat ignorance about the Holocaust in the European education system; a noble project that totally failed in Sweden itself, where far-right parties with Nazi backgrounds have done extremely well in the September 2022 elections.

As Antony Lerman tells us, the IHRA text is not new. It is a reworking of an earlier 'working definition' of anti-Semitism produced under the auspices of the European Union Monitoring Centre on Racism and Xenophobia (EUMC) in 2005. The American Jewish Committee's international affairs director, Rabbi Andrew Baker, persuaded the EUMC director to adopt a definition that the American Jewish Committee had in mind and the EUMC duly did so. Lerman writes that 'the draft definition was never subjected to proper scrutiny' and was prepared exclusively by people chosen by the American Jewish Committee.[115]

The project was hijacked by Israel around 2013, to be used as a new means of defining anti-Semitism to include anti-Zionism and even moderate anti-Israel stances. The Israeli government lobbied both in the EU and in the UN for a detailed list of examples that would exemplify what anti-Semitism means, so that any criticism against Israel could be silenced through the weaponisation of these examples. The method was simple: a new interpretation of what Holocaust denial constituted was given through a list of examples that featured criticism of Zionism and the state of Israel. This definition, with its list of examples, was formally adopted by the IHRA in May 2016, and adopted by the UK government in December 2016. Importantly, it was not legally binding and was not intended to be used in legal cases or to enforce breaches of organisational rules. Corbyn, like many other human rights activists in Britain, had been happy to endorse a campaign against Holocaust denial, and the Labour National Executive Committee did, prior to the ensuing scandal, adopt the definition, excluding the examples relating to criticism of Israel. Even though these amendments were largely intended to make it easier to conduct disciplinary hearings, they were exploited by Margaret Hodge, an LFI member and MP, to condemn Corbyn as an anti-Semite and call for him to step down as a leader.[116]

You could only go wrong when this was the trajectory. Chakrabarti joined the Labour Party to gain members' trust, as she put it. As she attempted to find a middle ground, she was instantly subject to accusations of prejudice by the lobby, regardless of what the report's conclusions were. The report in fact went much further in its attempts to compromise with the pro-Israel wing of the party and the outside lobby than Labour's grassroots members would necessarily have wanted. By this point, Labour members were largely pro-Palestine and concerned about how criticism of Israel was being handled.

The report offered little guidance on how to navigate controversies like this. Among the report's recommendations was that: 'Labour members should resist the use of Hitler, Nazi and Holocaust metaphors, distortions and comparisons in debates about Israel–Palestine in particular'.[117] This was a step backwards from the pioneering work of Israeli scholars in the 1990s, who wrote extensively about how the memory of the Holocaust was being abused to demonise Palestinians and justify oppressive policies towards them. Distortion and falsification should obviously be impermissible, but examining the relationship between the Holocaust and the Nakba is a very important subject in current scholarship on Israel and Palestine in many parts of the world, including in Israel itself, and should not be used as evidence of anti-Semitism.[118]

The report chose not to look at racism as a whole as a threat to the legitimacy of the party, and consequently some of its guidance verged on the absurd. It stated that 'The party should increase the ethnic diversity of its staff' in reference to Anglo-Jews, since in British law the Jews are an ethnic and religious minority (that may be the text of the law, but ethnic diversity as an issue in Britain is far more concerned with colour and non-white minorities). Despite all the concessions made to the party's pro-Israel wing, the report nonetheless concluded that the party 'is not overrun by anti-Semitism, Islamophobia, or other forms of racism', i.e. that it was not institutionally anti-Semitic.

A month after the publication of the report in June 2016, Corbyn appointed Chakrabarti to the House of Lords and made her shadow attorney general. The lobby saw this as a signal to start discrediting the report. The pro-Israel and Blairite members seized upon this development. Senior party members Tom Watson and Wes Streeting, and others, questioned the credibility of the inquiry's findings.[119]

The next stage was unavoidable, as Chakrabarti's report was not enough for the lobby. A cross-party Home Affairs Select Committee initiated its own inquiry and used Watson and Streeting's criticism to conclude that the Chakrabarti Inquiry was 'ultimately compromised' by Chakrabarti's later acceptance of a peerage and position in the Shadow Cabinet. Corbyn's protestations against these allegations were disregarded, although he was absolutely right when he accused the Select Committee of 'political framing'.[120]

And then came the Equality and Human Rights Commission's (EHRC) inquiry into anti-Semitism in Labour. In a more reasonable world, or maybe years from now, if people were asked about what a leading institution for human rights would investigate in relation to Israel and Palestine, they would give the abuse of Palestinians' human rights as the answer. These reasonable people would be bewildered to learn that this respectable body saw their main job as analysing emails, Facebook posts and tweets to see if Labour members who were known supporters of Palestinian rights should be expelled from the party. It further devoted its precious time and energy to re-examining the Chakrabarti Report. Everyone and their dog seemed to be setting up their own inquiry committees to draw damning conclusions about Labour and anti-Semitism. We can only dream of what Britain would look like today if only such fervour could have been found for making homes safe after the Grenfell fire, averting the disastrous consequences of a bad Brexit deal or investing in healthcare provision.

Running to 130 pages, the EHRC report investigated seventy complaint files in order to determine whether Labour had breached the Equality Act with regard to its treatment of Jewish members. Needless to say, there was no serious discussion of what constitutes anti-Semitism, nor did it make any attempt to differentiate between anti-Semitism and anti-Zionism and criticism of Israel. In my humble view, this is one of the most shameful reports ever produced by a Commission that has practically abandoned representing the interests of the many people in Britain today whose human rights are not respected, including refugees, disabled people and those in poverty.

The main conclusion was that Labour needed to do more to 'regain the trust of the Jewish community'. There were of course Jews whose trust had to be regained, namely those who were influenced by the campaign against Corbyn, but it is important to remember there are many Jews who live in Britain who are not associated with the pro-Israel lobby and did not feel alienated by Corbyn's moral stance on Palestine. The report suggested that 'the Party needs to instil a culture that encourages members to challenge inappropriate behaviour and to report anti-Semitism complaints'. This provided carte blanche for a witch-hunt that unfolded after that, and it claimed Corbyn as its main victim – a real coup for his right-wing opponents within the party. By the time the EHRC report was published, in October 2020, long after Corbyn had resigned as Labour leader, Corbyn had at last understood the rabbit hole into which he had been pushed. He refused to accept the report's conclusions – and was promptly suspended by the new Labour leader Keir Starmer.[121]

What followed was inevitable: a relentless smear campaign against a principled politician who had stood alongside Jews in the 1970s to physically block neo-Nazis from marching into Wood Green. The Conservative John Bercow, a former Speaker for the House of Commons and an Anglo-Jew, categorically rejected any allegation of Corbyn being anti-Semitic.

This report was treated as definitive, despite its issues. Any attempt to raise the findings of an earlier report by Jennie Formby, who served as the party's general secretary, entitled 'The work of the Labour Party's Governance and Legal Unit in relation to anti-Semitism, 2014–2019', was dismissed. This report exonerated Corbyn from charges of being complacent on anti-Semitism and rather indicted most of his opponents within the party staff who, according to the report, did not act on the majority of complaints until Formby became general secretary.[122]

Keir Starmer, the new leader, refused to submit it to the EHRC as evidence for their investigation. It was leaked to the press in April 2020, shortly after Starmer's victory in the leadership election. None of the copious evidence presented stopped the Labour Right and much of the mainstream media from labelling Corbyn an anti-Semite in the months that followed.[123]

It should be said that Corbyn still enjoyed support at a grassroots level. A telling case of grassroots reaction to all allegations against Corbyn can be gleaned from the case of Pete Willsman. At a National Executive Committee meeting, he defended his support for Corbyn and suggested that a number of those in the Jewish community alleging severe and widespread anti-Semitism in the party were 'Trump fanatics' who were making claims 'without any evidence at all'. In 2018, even questioning the scale of anti-Semitism was taken to be anti-Semitic. Thus, he apologised 'for any offence caused to those present and those to whom my remarks were reported', as well as referring himself to equalities training. Willsman was treated as a liability – Tom Watson, the deputy leader of the party, denounced him as a 'loud-mouthed bully'. Momentum, now the premier organisation of the party's Left, condemned his comments as 'deeply insensitive and inappropriate' and dropped their support of his candidacy in the forthcoming Labour National Executive Committee elections. Contrary to the lobby's expectations, Willsman still won a seat. Labour Friends of Israel nonetheless demanded that he not take his seat – calling upon Jeremy Corbyn and Momentum to disavow him. Momentum did not endorse voting for him in the elections, causing a divide among the party Left. Its only official comment on the National Executive Committee elections came from the national co-ordinator Laura Parker: 'These results are a fantastic victory for ordinary grassroots members and another step forward in building a reinvigorated, democratic Labour party that is capable of winning the next election'. In any case Willsman had long since walked away from Momentum, believing it was not run properly.[124] But he had clearly been put on notice, and in 2019 he was suspended from the party, following a further controversy.

FROM CORBYN TO STARMER: THE LOBBY CELEBRATES

The defeat of Jeremy Corbyn in the 2019 elections and his subsequent resignation were celebrated by the lobby. 'The beast is slain', cried Joe Glasman, head of Political and Government Investigations within the Campaign Against Anti-Semitism.[125] Glasman stated this in a rather bloodthirsty Hannukah video, in which he compared Jeremy Corbyn to Antiochus IV, the Hellenistic king whom the Maccabees revolted against. 'Maccabees, we did it', he congratulated his followers – 'by word, and deed, by protest and tweet, by our spies and intel…'[126]

As for the new leader of Labour Party, Sir Keir Starmer, the lobby could not hide its satisfaction. 'After Corbyn, UK Labour elects Keir Starmer, Zionist with a Jewish wife, as Leader' proclaimed the headline of the *Israel Times*. And the piece began with: 'New opposition chief immediately apologises to Jews for anti-Semitism in ranks, vows to "tear out this poison".'[127]

Prior to his election as Labour leader, and at the time Starmer sold himself as belonging to the party Left in order to get the vote of the Corbyn voters, the pro-Israel papers ran into some problems when trying to find out more from Starmer about his views on Zionism. But he was clear about Israel – he had to be. His wife, Starmer reported, Victoria Alexander, came from a Jewish background and, through her, he had extended family living in Tel Aviv.[128]

'My wife's family is Jewish. Her dad is Jewish, their family came over from Poland. The extended family live in Israel', he told *Jewish News* in February. He had never been to Israel, but 'we're in regular contact with them and we've got various visits planned, basically to take our kids for the first time.'[129]

I hope the absurdity of these statements does not escape the reader. A position on foreign policy is being assumed from the religious or ethnic background of senior British politicians. Just imagine if politicians in Britain started framing their attitude to other conflicts, say in Eastern Europe or sub-Saharan Africa, with reference to their personal identities.

During a campaign event organised by LFI, other party leadership candidates said they were 'Zionists', while Starmer was hesitant. 'I do support Zionism', he later told *Jewish News*:

> I absolutely support the right of Israel to exist as a homeland. My only concern is that Zionism can mean slightly different things to different people, and ... to some extent it has been weaponized. I wouldn't read too much into that. I said it loud and clear – and meant it – that I support Zionism without qualification.[130]

He also told the *Jewish Chronicle*: 'If the definition of "Zionist" is someone who believes in the state of Israel, in that sense I'm a Zionist.'[131]

After his victory, outlets such as the *Israel Times* also examined Starmer's team, and expressed great satisfaction, although there were a few more questionable choices, such as Lisa Nandy, then chair of the Labour Friends of Palestine and the Middle East, as his shadow foreign secretary.

Angela Rayner was another mixed bag, criticising Israeli killings of Palestinians in the Great March of Return in 2018. She also praised Norman Finkelstein's book, *The Holocaust Industry*, which she called 'a seminal work'; which of course it is. However, under pressure she retracted her recommendation.[132]

But pro-Israel organisations had a lot to be happy about. A particular cause for celebration was Starmer's chief of staff, Morgan McSweeney, who was described by We Believe in Israel director Luke Akehurst as someone who 'will be a pivotal figure for dealing with Labour's anti-Semitism crisis'. Akehurst describes McSweeney as a 'solid supporter of Israel'. The pro-Israel lobby has always held this view: a good person is the one who understands that supporting Israel is the best way to tackle anti-Semitism.[133] As for We Believe in Israel, this was yet another lobby group, shadowing already existing outfits, and offering nothing new in lending a hand to the Israeli *Hasbara* effort.

Other appointees were suspected to be closet Zionists, such as the new shadow international trade secretary, Emily Thornberry:

Nevertheless, Thornberry is privately believed to be a staunch supporter of Israel, has also referred to herself as a 'Zionist', and is an ardent opponent of the BDS movement, calling campaigners 'bigots'.[134]

As for the Conservative Party, the lobby realised that the landslide 2019 victory had brought a new group of Conservative MPs to Parliament. CFI lost no time in enlisting them in its ranks. They were offered visits to Israel and meetings with top officials there. But there is a new face to these visits since 2019: they include visits to the areas controlled by the Palestinian Authority as well as Israel. In 2019, all those who were elected for the first time were taken on such a tour. But a year later the lobby parroted the Israeli right-wing condemnation of the Palestinian Authority as an enemy of Israel. Here is how CFI summarised its activities on Facebook, two years into the Conservative term of office:

> Throughout 2021, CFI and Conservative parliamentarians in both houses have continued to reflect the agenda Israel preferred to be at the centre of public concern away from the plight of the Palestinians. This agenda included including messages such as standing up for Israel's right to self-defence, condemning Iran's nuclear programme and accusing the Palestinian Authority of producing textbooks which incite hatred against Israel, while calling for funding peaceful coexistence, and deepening UK–Israel trade. 103 Conservative MPs and Lords made contributions in Parliament in support of CFI's campaign issues, including 45 from the 2019 intake.[135]

THE TEN PLEDGES

In their ultimately very successful campaign against Corbyn and Corbynism, the lobby had won a bigger victory: they had forged a seemingly ineradicable connection between anti-Israel sentiment and anti-Semitism in the public consciousness. The jewel in the crown of this victory was a document of ten pledges that the Board of Deputies insisted every future candidate for the Labour leadership must adopt (needless to say, Conservatives were exempt). They were published on the eve of the elections that brought Starmer to the post. Here are the ten pledges the Board was lobbying candidates to adopt, as they were published in the *Jewish Chronicle*. Among them was the promise to resolve outstanding cases of alleged anti-Semitism, to devolve the disciplinary process to an independent agent and to ensure transparency in the complaints process.

The paper summarised the remaining pledges as follows:

- Prevent re-admittance of prominent offenders.
- Provide no platform for those who have been suspended or expelled for anti-Semitism.
- The full adoption of the IHRA definition of anti-Semitism 'with all its examples and clauses and without any caveats'.
- To deliver anti-racism education programmes that have been approved by the Jewish Labour Movement, which would lead the training.
- To engage with the Jewish community via its 'main representative groups and not through fringe organisations' such as Jewish Voice for Labour.
- To replace 'bland, generic statements' on anti-Jewish racism with 'condemnation of specific harmful behaviours'.
- For the Labour leader to take personal responsibility for ending the 'anti-Semitism crisis'.[136]

The IHRA definition with all of its examples was drafted by those with a vested interest in the 'new anti-Semitism' that consisted of 'delegitimising Israel'. An institution originally intending to combat Holocaust denial in Europe now equated criticism of Israel with Holocaust denial.

But most importantly the pledges made a clear distinction between Jewish groups that were part of the pro-Israel lobby, including the Jewish Labour Movement, which were entrusted with educating the party about anti-Semitism, and anti-Zionist Jewish groups such as Jewish Voice for Labour, which the pledges claimed did not represent Jewish communities. Of course, the former groups are larger in size. But that doesn't mean engagement with minority groups within the Jewish community is somehow problematic. This blatant intervention by the Board in the affairs of a political party in Britain has the dangerous potential to increase anti-Semitism in the future, not fight against it.

Virtually all the candidates for party leadership embraced the pledges within hours, as one critic put it, 'swallowing them hook, line and sinker'.[137] The Labour Party was no longer merely co-operating with the lobby; it was its captive.

Labour was not the only target or challenge facing the pro-Israel lobby in Britain at that time. The lobby had to digest the continued shift within British public opinion on the question of Palestine. It was not just a question of widespread support for Palestinian rights within British civil society; now the lobby faced sectors of society that were prepared to be pro-active in actions against Israel such as boycotting its goods and its official representatives.

THE FIGHT AGAINST BDS

The UK Jewish community is dismayed by the decision of the Church of England's General Synod to pass a motion endorsing the Ecumenical Accompaniment Programme in Palestine and Israel (EAPPI).[138]

The Board of Deputies made this pronouncement in 2012 – the calm phrasing understating the real extent of their disappointment. The early 2010s were when the pro-Israel lobby noticed that the BDS movement was not just a whimsical and marginal expression of pro-Palestinian protest, but a powerful social movement that mobilised public opinion and offered engaged citizens a way to show their solidarity with Palestinians.

The decision of the General Synod, the highest legislative body of the Church of England to support the 'vital work' of the Ecumenical Accompaniment Programme in Palestine and Israel (EAPPI) woke the lobby up to the real threat posed by BDS to their own work. The scheme brings international church members to the West Bank to 'experience life under occupation' for three to four months, and expects them to campaign on their return for:

A just and peaceful resolution to the Israeli/Palestinian conflict through an end to the occupation, respect for international law and implementation of UN resolutions.[139]

The group members spend limited time – up to one week – inside the Green Line, the armistice line agreed after the Arab–Israeli War in 1948.

The initial campaign, which aimed to prevent the Synod from passing this decision, was not successful. The lobby's zeal backfired on them. As the BDS website put it:

'A few people said that all the lobbying from the Jewish side led us to vote the other way,' said the Rt. Revd. Nigel McCulloch, who is chair of the Council of Christians and Jews (CCJ), the UK's oldest Jewish-Christian interfaith group. 'There was over-lobbying by some members of the Jewish community.'[140]

The Board accused the CCJ of creating 'a cohort of very partisan but very motivated anti-Israel advocates who have almost no grasp of the suffering of normal Israelis'. It encouraged members of the Jewish community to express their concern before the vote in a letter campaign to senior members of the Church and to the *Church Times*, while other Jewish groups, as well as Chief Rabbi Lord Sacks and Anglican Friends of Israel, all called for the motion to be rejected.

The vote was taken despite the Archbishop of Canterbury at the time, Rowan Williams, stating during the debate that he did not want the Church to be associated with the delegitimisation of Israel and supporting the amendment removing the reference to EAPPI (which nevertheless remained in place).

The Synod passed the motion, and the Church was asked to encourage parishioners to volunteer for the programme and ask churches and synods to make use of the experience of returning participants.

The Board, realising the campaign of the entire lobby had failed, accused the Synod of showing a complete disregard for the importance of Anglican–Jewish relations. They were especially offended by the Church collaborating with 'marginal' groups in Israel, by which the Board meant human rights organisations that unmasked the reality of the occupation.

In their speeches, a number of Synod members had referred to the power of the lobby and the manipulation of Holocaust memory in its actions. The Board described these kinds of arguments as 'deeply offensive' and rais[ing] serious questions about the motivation of those behind this motion.'[141]

The BDS movement was now officially enemy number one of the lobby in Britain. Now we reach a true historical irony: the birthplace of the modern Zionist lobby became, a century later, the cradle of a global Palestine solidarity movement. Britain was one of the first countries in the world in which the BDS movement gained a foothold. Its civil society responded enthusiastically to the call for BDS made by 170 Palestinian NGOs on 9 July 2005. The signatories to this call represented the three major components of the Palestinian people: the refugees in exile, Palestinians under occupation in the West Bank and Gaza Strip and the second-class Palestinian citizens of the Israeli state.

Two years later, the first Palestinian BDS Conference was held in Ramallah in November 2007. The BDS National Committee (BNC) emerged out of this conference as the Palestinian co-ordinating body for the BDS campaign worldwide. The BNC has members from different Palestinian organisations and unions and is still active today.

Britain immediately became one of the BDS's major areas of activity where it has had a largely successful campaign in building solidarity and support for the Palestinian struggle. It was unable to reach the corridors of power or to influence mainstream politics and media; but it built a solid infrastructure within civil society and solidified the work of previous Palestinian activism. As such, BDS UK offers a basis for further and even more effective action in the future. Its main achievements offer us an insight into the role it could play in the years ahead.

Globally, BDS constitutes the most important advocacy movement for the rights of the Palestinians inside and outside Palestine. While

Zionist lobbying always, from the very inception of the movement until today, targeted the corridors of power – governments, mainstream media and academia – the Palestinian solidarity movement was unable to pressure the various governments to hold Israel accountable for its abuse of the Palestinians' civil and human rights over the years. In the UK, as elsewhere in the West, governments were largely indifferent to addressing the Palestinian plight after the 1948 war. The realisation that Western governments are either passive or intimidated by Israel emboldened activism in civil society even before BDS was formalised as a campaign. After it was announced, the actions from below intensified, as citizens understood the need to take action when their governments failed to represent their views on the international stage.

Conscientious citizens in Britain expected their various governments to accept Britain's historical responsibility for the Palestinian plight. After all, it was the British Empire that allowed the Zionist movement to gain a foothold in Palestine, colonise the country and eventually take it over by ethnically cleansing the indigenous people of Palestine. Without such protection, the Zionist project of settler colonialism, which was contingent on the mass displacement of the Palestinians, could not have materialised or been maintained. Throughout its thirty-year rule (1918–1948), Britain also permitted the Zionist movement to build a state within a state and prepare militarily for the ethnic cleansing of Palestine in 1948. And when the Zionist forces, which later became the IDF, began their ethnic cleansing operations in April 1948, mainly targeting the urban centres of Palestine, British officers stood by and in some cases (for instance, in Jaffa and Haifa) helped to facilitate the collective expulsion of more than one hundred thousand Palestinians.[142]

Successive British governments refused to acknowledge Britain's responsibility for the Palestinian catastrophe. This lack of historical accountability was manifested most clearly when Britain, in collaboration with the Israeli government, celebrated the centenary of the Balfour Declaration on 2 November 2017. To this day, the British government has never apologised for its role in creating over five million Palestinian refugees. Palestine activists attempted to raise awareness of the true consequences of the Balfour Declaration, to little avail in the corridors of power.[143]

This history explains the particular intensity of BDS activity in the UK. The widespread British response to the appeal for BDS helped to resolve some of the issues that had in the past troubled the global solidarity movement with the Palestinians. Previously, disunity in the Palestinian national movement, divided between Hamas and Fatah, and the lack of a cohesive ideology and strategy hampered global efforts to show solidarity. BDS offered a course of action which any Palestine activist could organise around.

BDS enabled supporters to mobilise collectively, without being embroiled in internal Palestinian disputes. The democratic nature of the movement and its flexibility in allowing local activists to decide how best to implement the BDS campaign contributed immensely to its popularity and effectiveness in the UK.[144]

The greatest success of the BDS movement in the UK has been how it has won ground in civil society. Among the sections of British civil society heeding the call from Palestine were trade unions representing thousands of workers, student unions, faith groups and local councils. BDS demands rights enshrined in international law. On this basis, targeting companies that work with Israel or universities that have institutional connections to Israeli academia is a legitimate protest against the complicity of these establishments in Israel's repeated violations of international law in its policies against Palestinians.

The BDS movement in the UK not only influenced public discussion about Israel/Palestine, but also affected the policies of businesses that had trading links with Israel. This was the result of well-chosen targets, with a particular focus on businesses that operated in the occupied territories.

The precursor to BDS, and the first successful response to Palestinian civil society's call for support, came from a union called the Association of University Teachers (AUT), which overwhelmingly passed a motion in favour of an academic boycott on Israel in 2005. A year later, NATFHE, then the largest union for teachers in further and higher education, voted in favour of a motion recommending that its members boycott Israeli academics and institutions that did not publicly declare their opposition to the occupation and Israel's racist policies.[145] This was an important step because the earlier support of the AUT was retracted under pressure from Israel and the pro-Zionist lobby in the UK. The same campaign was directed at NATFHE, but its general secretary explained why his union did not budge under such pressure:

> Many emails berate threats to deny academic freedom for Israeli professors but fail to mention that academic freedom in Palestine is a hollow joke. Even where staff and students are allowed freedom of movement to attend university, the material basis for a functioning academic life barely exists ... Actually it is not possible to be 'even handed' in the face of such injustice. The Palestinian people and Palestinian civil society including the universities need support and solidarity as never before and I will not be bullied into silence.[146]

The early courage of these forerunners paved the way for the National Union of Teachers (NUT), the largest teachers' union in Europe, passing a resolution backing the BDS movement in 2014, in the wake of the Israeli assault on Gaza.[147]

This was one of the first major milestones following the Palestinian call to action in Britain. What it did was introduce new concepts into the public debate about Palestine. This was also helped by the early events organised by students in the UK in solidarity with BDS. The students called their actions 'Israeli Apartheid Week', and the first unions that supported BDS utilised similar language, referring to the settler-colonial nature of Israel by using concepts such as apartheid, colonialism and later on even colonisation. The mainstream media continued to talk about a 'conflict', implying the existence of two equal sides, and 'peace', as if all you needed were two 'peace camps' on both sides lobbying for a just solution based on the partition of the country into two states (one stretching over more than eighty per cent of historical Palestine with full sovereignty, the other divided into two Bantustans with very restricted sovereignty).[148] The new language described more accurately the situation on the ground: a continued project of settler colonialism that had begun in the late nineteenth century and contin-ues to this very day. Reconciliation is achieved not through empty talk about peace but by demanding decolonisation.

By 2014 the NUT was not alone in expressing support for BDS. More trade unions had joined in the first years of that decade. The BDS campaign in the UK really took off when many of Britain's trade unions threw their weight behind it. Various trade unions voted unanimously for supporting BDS, such as the Transport Salaried Staffs' Association (TSSA), UNISON, the GMB, the PCS and the FBU (Fire Brigades' Union). Also worth mentioning in this context is the Royal Institute of British Architects, which at first backed the BDS movement but a few weeks later retracted their support after pressure from the lobby, while a group of British doctors called for a boycott of the Israeli Medical Association.

These exceptional demonstrations of solidarity reflected the princi-pled support of the British trade unions for the Palestinian cause, but they also were intended as moral condemnations of Israel's actions on the ground. This particular wave of endorsement came in the wake of an Israeli assault on a peaceful flotilla that tried to break through the inhuman siege Israeli imposed on the Gaza Strip in 2010 (the *Mavi Marmara* affair). Social movements are often reinvigorated in response to shocking events – and the death of ten activists at the hands of Israeli commandos incited widespread horror.

Parallel to advocacy within trade unions, from 2011 onwards several companies were targeted by the BDS movement. These were mainly corporations that operated in the occupied territories, including East Jerusalem.

The first effective action was directed at the Adidas sponsorship of the Jerusalem Marathon, which passed through occupied East Jerusalem. Their superstore at Covent Garden in London was the venue of a big protest, where a letter was submitted to be forwarded to the management in Europe.[149] The protestors attracted attention from shop staff, customers and the general public, and distributed flyers to custom-ers both inside the shop and outside on Oxford Street explaining that the Jerusalem Marathon was yet another attempt by Israel to whitewash its atrocious human rights record, and urging Adidas not to sponsor the 2012 Jerusalem Marathon which was to be held on 16 March. The store was evacuated and was forced to close for a time. Adidas, however, did not withdraw from the marathon.

The second was Ahava, a company that makes cosmetics products using mud and minerals from the Dead Sea, some of them produced from stolen Palestinian natural resources in the occupied West Bank territory and made in the illegal settlement of Mitzpe Shalem. In 2010, fortnightly demonstrations took place outside their central London flagship store, following a specific call to action from the Bil'in Popular Committee. Bil'in was one of the first villages affected by the construction of the segregation wall and became a focal point for demonstrations against it, led by the Popular Committee. Ahava's London store was forced to move following the sustained campaign from BDS activists. The campaign also convinced the major high street retailer John Lewis to stop stocking their products.[150]

BDS could also boast other major successes. The focused campaign against the French multinational firm Veolia meant that it sold off its stakes in its Israeli projects. In that same year, 2012, Tower Hamlets Council in London excluded Veolia from local procurement contracts because of its suspected activity in the occupied territories.[151]

Swansea Council also passed a motion to exclude Veolia from public contracts, and this was followed by other local councils in Edinburgh, Portsmouth, Richmond and West Midlands; all of them excluded Veolia from public procurement processes following pressure from campaigners for Palestinian rights.

In 2013, the University of Sheffield decided not to renew its waste collection contract with Veolia following a campaign initiated by the campus's Palestine Society and supported by the student union.[152] The campaign called on the university to cut its ties with the company over its contracts with the Israeli state to provide waste and transport services for illegal Israeli settlements in the occupied West Bank. Eventually, Veolia ended its role in illegal Israeli settlements after local councils in the UK and beyond dropped it from contracts worth more than £10 billion.[153]

Another target was G4S, the British private security giant, which provided equipment and services to the Israeli prison system, Israeli police and military checkpoints. G4S has come under considerable pressure from BDS campaigners since 2011. The first tangible success was to persuade the Bill and Melinda Gates Foundation to sell off its shares in the company.[154] But the campaign continued in other areas as well and achieved impressive results.

The campaign against G4S was not just taken up by the BDS movement. Almost all the Palestine solidarity groups participated. Led by the Palestine Solidarity Campaign and supported by the Scottish Trades Union Congress, this was a high-profile action.

Two brave activists occupied the roof of the G4S headquarters in London and when brought to justice, both defendants pleaded 'not guilty' on the basis that the activity they were accused of obstructing was unlawful. They were referring to G4S's contract with the Israeli Prison Service, its services to Israeli settlements and military checkpoints, and the use of unlawful restraint techniques in immigration detention centres. They were acquitted on the grounds that they had not caused enough disruption to be charged with aggravated trespass.[155]

A by-product of the campaign was pressure on a gas company, Good Energy, which had contracted a G4S company to conduct door-to-door energy meter readings from 2008. The campaign persuaded it to announce that it would end its business relationship with G4S due to its collaboration with the occupation. The company itself attributed its decision to G4S's role in the death of Jimmy Mubenga, an Angolan who died on a deportation flight while being 'restrained' by G4S guards, which sparked public outrage.[156] In the eyes of social activists, its role in Israel's oppression of Palestine and its part in abusing refugees in Britain were two sides of the same coin.

As in the US, Eden Springs and SodaStream were also targeted. Eden Springs produces mineral water from the occupied Golan Heights and SodaStream used to have a factory in an industrial zone in the occupied West Bank. Pressure from students at the London School of Economics led to the revocation of the university's contract with Eden Springs, and members of eight trade unions joined a long-running weekly picket of

SodaStream's only UK shop, EcoStream in Brighton, in 2014.[157] Although Eden tankers can still be seen in certain locations in the UK, SodaStream eventually moved its factory outside of the West Bank.

Some older causes were added to the campaign, such as the continued struggle against the Jewish National Fund (JNF) and its activities in the UK. As we've seen, the JNF was established in 1901 and was the principal tool for the Zionist colonisation of Palestine. It was an agency with which the Zionist movement bought land and profited from land purchase transactions. It was inaugurated by the fifth Zionist Congress and remained throughout the Mandatory years (1918–1948) the spearhead of the Zionisation of Palestine.

From the onset of its activities, it was destined to fulfil a role that was officially granted to it: becoming the custodian of the land in Palestine in the name of the Jewish people. It did not cease to fulfil this role after the creation of the state of Israel, but with time other missions were added to this primordial task.

It is crucial to review the history of the JNF if one wishes to understand its present role. This is particularly important due to the image of the JNF today as a 'green' and ecological organisation that safeguards Israel's natural landscape from being ruined by all the usual suspects – greedy contractors, government avarice and public indifference. In 1948, it oversaw a process which transformed hundreds of destroyed Palestinian villages into Jewish settlements and recreational parks. Today its 'enemies' are Palestinian farmers and Bedouins who try to keep the little piece of the land they still have. Their remaining land is ostensibly needed as 'nature reserves', but in practice will be given to Jewish settlers. From 1901 to 2023, the JNF did not change its tactics, nor did it deviate from its role as the principal Judaiser of Israel/Palestine. With the help of a front organisation called Himnuta, it now also targets the Palestinian residents of East Jerusalem as part of the expanding Judaisation in Greater Jerusalem. Through greenwashing, the JNF managed to present itself as an ecological organisation, rather than an arm of colonisation.

BDS and other organisations appealed to the Charity Commission to investigate whether the JNF racially discriminates on the ground in

Israel and Palestine, thus questioning its legality in Britain.[158] The Stop the JNF campaign made an application to the Charity Commission for the removal of JNF charities from the register of charities. The application gave evidence that the JNF is racist, and complicit in the ethnic cleansing of Palestinians. All UK charities are supposed to be for the public benefit. The Stop the JNF application demonstrated that the purpose of the JNF is contrary to the requirement of public benefit and does not qualify the organisation for charity status. Over five hundred people also wrote individual complaints to the Charity Commission. The issue is still pending, and no conclusion has been reached as yet.

On the ground, BDS activists joined other groups in shadowing JNF activity in the UK. The BDS groups in Scotland were, and still are, particularly active on this front. An event to be held at St Andrews Hotel in Edinburgh, aimed at raising funds for the Friends of the IDF and the JNF, was cancelled on police advice in the face of planned protests. So far, the JNF has not been severely affected by the BDS campaign. On the other hand, BDS's call for academic institutions to be part of the campaign was more successful.[159]

THE ACADEMIC BOYCOTT

The BDS campaign included a call for an academic boycott, focusing on institutions and not individuals. Even this institutional focus did not prevent it from being more controversial than the boycott of corporations. It was a much more elastic campaign, shaped by local interpretations of how best to implement it. Although it has largely failed to change the policies of university administrations, student unions and sympathetic academic staff have shown their support for it. Some chose not to participate in academic events in Israel, others rejected joint academic ventures with Israeli universities and some academic unions pressured their universities to freeze or cancel bilateral agreements with Israeli universities.

University management considered the academic boycott as a violation of freedom of expression, while academic communities saw it as a harsh, but necessary, dialogue with Israeli academia, which they blamed

for being complicit directly and indirectly in sustaining Israel's violations of Palestinians' human rights.

The ambivalence that accompanies the debate on the academic
boycott comes to light in an interview BDS activists conducted with
Jeremy Corbyn, when he was competing for the leadership of the Labour
Party. He said that the academic boycott was a 'very complicated' issue,
while endorsing the boycott of goods from settlements in the occupied
territories. He warned that the academic boycott 'was "very complicated" to implement without, for example, preventing Israeli dissidents
such as Ilan Pappe coming to speak in the UK'.[160] To this example,
PACBI, the committee overseeing the academic boycott in the UK,
responded:

> the guidelines published by PACBI – the Palestinian academic and
> cultural boycott campaign – do not in any way exclude someone like
> Pappe who does not represent a boycottable academic institution
> from speaking.[161]

But Corbyn did add that:

> If it is a university that is doing research into drones, taser weapons,
> or doing research into surveillance of the occupation in Gaza and
> elsewhere then they should be part of the boycott.[162]

By and large, the initiative within universities was carried forward by
students and the campuses became the main venue for BDS activities in
2011. One of the first student unions to take action was that of Sheffield
University. The union voted to support BDS campaigns by a large
majority in a referendum held in October 2011, with specific reference
to the campaign against Veolia:

> By passing it as official union policy it was possible to send a much
> stronger message to the university: that the student body as a whole
> does not want to incentivise companies, like Veolia, who suffer from
> such an abject lack of moral compass. Following the policy's success

in the October vote, we have worked with various groups to lobby and pressure the university into taking notice of the student voice. This has included an open letter signed by the Palestine Society and other campaigning groups, demonstrations on the concourse, letters from human rights groups in Palestine, Israel, and beyond, and direct lobbying from the sabbatical officers.[163]

Student actions spread all over the UK. In March 2011, Students for Justice in Palestine at Edinburgh University overwhelmingly passed (270 vs 20) a motion to boycott Israel. More specifically it decided to boycott Israeli goods in the university students' shops and supply chains. The meeting was ten people short of being quorate, but the point was clear. In these motions, the student unions called on their universities to 'do everything in its power to support the Boycott, Divestment and Sanctions campaign against the pariah state of Israel'.[164]

BDS activity in Edinburgh included disrupting official speakers on behalf of Israel, such as the adviser to the foreign minister, Avigdor Lieberman, and the Israeli ambassador, Ron Prosor.

Groups such as the UK's National Union of Students Black Students Campaign endorsed the Palestinian call for BDS at their national conference at the University of Warwick in 2014.[165] By 2017, at least seventeen British student unions had passed motions in support of BDS – and the number may still grow.

THE CAMPAIGN AGAINST ARMS SALES

Palestine solidarity activists also wanted to throw a spanner in the works of Israel's war machine by blocking British arms sales to Israel. It seemed at first to be quite fruitful when British arms sales to Israel faced High Court challenges in the wake of the Israeli assault on Gaza in the summer of 2014.[166] A leading UK law firm claimed that the government's failure to suspend existing export licences was illegal. The law firm Leigh Day, representing the Campaign Against Arms Trade (CAAT), wrote to the business secretary, Vince Cable, claiming that the failure by the British government to suspend licences for the export of military components to Israel was unlawful as there was a risk that they might have been used in Gaza. It said that it was instructed to seek a judicial review of the government's reluctance to suspend licences unless it agreed to stop the export of the components. It exposed the fact that the UK's controversial export policy was on a potential collision course with the EU. The move put the UK's multi-million-pound military export programme in the spotlight at a time when Israel's actions in Gaza were causing international concern and there was mounting disquiet about the role foreign states were playing in Israel's military-industrial complex. However, this campaign did not put a stop to arms sales to Israel.

One of the last actions of Jeremy Corbyn before he stepped down after the 2019 general election was to declare that a Labour government would impose a two-way arms embargo on Israel.[167] In an interview with *Electronic Intifada*, he reiterated his previous position, that Israeli universities involved in arms research should be boycotted. His views were echoed by the action of the trade unions. Both the Labour Party and the TUC voted in favour of ending the arms trade with Israel at their annual conferences.[168]

These actions were strongly opposed by Theresa May's Conservative government. It announced that it saw no reason to heed demands for conducting a review into arms licences granted to Israel two years after the 2014 assault on the Gaza Strip. As Corbyn put it, 'Certainly the trajectory of the Conservative government is to approve of continuous arms sales.'[169] The activists attempted to enlist the Foreign Office into the campaign as it includes Israel on a list of 'countries of concern' for human rights abuses. The UK's own export criteria, if implemented, would have banned military exports to countries which violate international humanitarian law, or when there is a 'clear risk' of the weapons being used 'to assert by force a territorial claim'. We can hardly think of a country that meets these conditions as perfectly as Israel does.[170]

The struggle over arms deals was taken to the streets and campaigners blockaded factories selling arms to Israel, calling for them to be shut down. One of them, UAV Engines Limited, makes drone engines for Elbit. The protests in summer 2014 proposed an embargo on arms sales to Israel as a key demand. It is a pity that Jeremy Corbyn was the only politician with the courage to suggest making it an actual policy, many years later.

Action also became more localised. In 2018, Glasgow City Council, for instance, promised supporters of Palestinian rights that it would no longer sponsor arms fairs featuring Israeli weapons manufacturers and would ensure that the city's guidelines for hosting events reflect that 'Glasgow is a human rights respecting city'.[171]

From the very beginning the pro-Israel lobby frames these challenges as a genuine threat to Israel's national security. The lobby knew how to convince their audience – the Conservative Party were proud supporters of the British arms trade and were resistant to anything that might put a dampener on sales. Accordingly, the lobby described the demands for a freeze on arms sales to Israel as a threat to local industry. In Conservative discourse, this kind of advocacy was entirely just: waging war against those who would not allow the British military industry to profit from war. Arms dealers used more chilling language, unwilling to let go of one of their most valuable clients. It is an industry that in 2014 alone licensed weapons to Israel worth over £40 million. Between 2008 and 2015, licences were granted for weapons exports to Israel to the value of £292 million.[172]

THE BACKLASH: WEAPONISING PREVENT AND HOLOCAUST DENIAL

The Conservative governments of David Cameron and Theresa May did all they could to intimidate local councils into discontinuing their support for BDS. In 2016, the May government banned any divestment action by local councils. Several local councils nonetheless withdrew their pension funds from companies associated with Israel.

The government's actions did not deter the BDS campaign. The activists took their case to the Supreme Court and had an impressive win there. The court disallowed the government ban on local government pension schemes that had decided to divest from Israeli companies as part of their support for the BDS campaign. The court ruled that these were ethical and legal positions.[173]

Failing to win on legal technicalities, the lobby attempted to portray BDS as an expression of anti-Semitism. The Boris Johnson government followed their lead – the 2019 Queen's speech included a commitment to banning BDS as a form of anti-Semitism.[174]

A parallel action was the inclusion of BDS as a security threat in the Prevent programme. This programme was calling upon universities to monitor and refer students deemed at risk of being 'radicalised'– in practice it mainly perpetuated Islamophobic assumptions about Muslim students. Although this could not be used to restrict BDS actions, by painting particular activists as promoting extremist activity, lobbying groups on campuses attempted to limit and cancel events. As far as I can tell, Prevent created an atmosphere of intimidation, rather than being an effective tool by itself for silencing freedom of speech on Palestine.

Prevent never identified clearly what 'extremism' means (while at least the police have a clearer definition for hate crimes). And thus, absurd events such as children's schools supporting the Palestinian struggle were referred under Prevent. Waving the Palestinian flag was considered extreme, and students were cautioned as being extremists under Prevent for displaying the flag or wearing the Palestinian keffiyeh.[175]

A telling example occurred in 2015, the year the Counter-Terrorism and Security Act came into force. A conference at the University of Southampton, with the title of 'International Law and the State of Israel: Legitimacy, Responsibility and Exceptionalism', was cancelled by the university under the pretext of 'health and safety issues', evidently prompted by pressure from the lobby. The organisers reacted to this by stating:

> The university claims that it does not have enough resources to miti-
> gate the risks, despite a clear statement from the police confirming
> that they are able to deal with the protest and ensure the security of
> the event.[176]

As *Middle East Eye* reported in 2019, and as I witnessed in several cases when I was invited to give a lecture on Palestine in British universities,

Prevent was used to force an 'independent' chair to be present at any event where the speaker, including myself, was suspected of being biased against Israel.[177]

The lobby knew it couldn't quell committed activists, even with these aggressive measures. But it could still build a public consensus against BDS as a threat to Israel and ergo Jews. Established Anglo-Jewish organisations, such as the Board of Deputies, and the community's main newspaper, the *Jewish Chronicle*, propagandised against BDS as intrinsically anti-Semitic. They tried to cause support for BDS to be treated as a violation of the guidance included in the IHRA definition of anti-Semitism, a definition that had been adopted by Labour in 2018.[178] In October 2020, Education Secretary Gavin Williamson threatened British universities with financial sanctions if they failed to adopt the IHRA definition, despite it being doubtful if such a move was even legal. This definition has now been adopted by over two hundred institutions to date. Some students have already reported disciplinary actions being started on the basis of this definition.[179]

I doubt whether any of these or similar measures will be able to stop support for the BDS movement and other activism for Palestine. The ongoing Israeli colonisation of the West Bank and the incremental ethnic cleansing that accompanies it, the continued inhuman siege on the Gaza Strip and the daily violations of the rights of the Palestinians in Israel will fuel the campaign for years to come. These realities on the ground serve as a rejoinder to Israel's relentless endeavour to sanitise its image abroad, through lobbying in the halls of power and through trying to silence grassroots activists.

On 3 July 2023, Michael Gove, the Secretary of State for Housing, Levelling Up and Communities, and old member of the CFI, brought Parliament a Bill declaring BDS activity illegal, for its second reading.[180] He unjustifiably attacked BDS as an anti-Semitic, terrorist organisation that needed to be outlawed in Britain. Any public institutions supporting it would be sanctioned by the government. His rhetoric could have been copied and pasted from Israeli *Hasbara*. He condemned descriptors of Israel that are widely accepted among academics and human rights organisations. The most absurd part of his speech was stating that local councils cannot pursue foreign policies that are not accepted by the government. The most severe gag on freedom of speech presented as legislation in the British Parliament since the Second World War received 278 ayes; BDS is well on its way to becoming illegal.

As alarming as this sounds – and there will be ramifications for brave academics, students and councillors, who are loyal to human rights and commonsensical justice – the BDS movement will exist as long as Israel continues to deny Palestine justice. The critical question is whether this movement will be able to bring about the imposition of government sanctions – as happened in South Africa. We should not be discouraged by the slow progress. It took decades for discussions within activist circles to translate into widespread international sanctions to end apartheid. Time will tell whether the widespread support for a proactive and just British position on Palestine eventually prompts the government to take action. Only one thing is clear: the energy poured into legitimising Israel by the lobby will be met with protests at every turn, by citizens who know the truth about Israel's conduct in Palestine.

Conclusion

We started with a conundrum: why does such a powerful state as Israel still struggle, in its own eyes, to be regarded as legitimate by people around the world, while governments embrace it happily? We've seen that the state's legitimacy from its inception was rarely questioned, and yet whoever questioned the state's policy on any issue, even very cautiously, was treated as if they were delegitimising the state as a whole.

This book arrives at three conclusions from its search for answers. The first is that the lobby's effort, from its beginnings in the mid-nineteenth century, and in all its forms and shapes, was not primarily about challenging the Palestinian narrative. There is such an effort, and I covered it in my book, *The Idea of Israel*, where I attempted to explain how both academia and the cinema in Israel were recruited for that particular mission. It is an endeavour that still continues today, to control the production of knowledge on Israel and Palestine. But all in all, the lobby, like the ideological movement it represented and later the state it advocated for, did not see Palestinians as an obstacle to the project of colonising and Zionising Palestine.

From the very start of the Zionist movement, Palestinians were at first ignored, and then in 1948 ethnically cleansed. They subsequently lost their homeland to Israel in 1967. You do not need to advocate against a group that was treated, like so many other victims of settler colonialism in the world, according to the logic of the elimination of the native. Australians and Canadians do not lobby against First Nations or Native populations. The Palestinians were not the challenge: the challenge was how to justify what was done to them. This might change if and when the Palestinian struggle liberates Palestine; but we are not there yet. It also does not mean that Israel and its advocates are right in ignoring the Palestinians or underestimating their power in the future, as we will discuss later. But Israel *does* see the question of Palestine itself as a 'solved' problem, a position they can maintain by brute force if nothing else. The trouble is getting other people to accept Israel's conclusions.

Israel needs to persuade the world, and itself, of the moral validity of the Zionist project and consequently the state of Israel. I would go as far as to say that up to this day the foremost groups the lobby wants to win over are those among the Jews and the Zionists who find it difficult to be fully convinced that Judaism is not a religion but a national identity, and more importantly, that this redefinition of Jewish identity justifies the settler-colonial project of establishing Israel in historical Palestine.

Historically, for those in the Jewish community who rejected Zionism, the moral issue was paramount. Even when Zionism was deemed as the only alternative when Nazism took over Germany in the early 1930s and its occupation of much of Europe was imminent, the moral dilemma was not solved for people such as Bertolt Brecht. In 1933 he reacted to the idea of proclaiming a Jewish state in Palestine by reflecting: 'Hitler has thus fascized [*faschisieren* in German] not only the Germans, but also the Jews'.[1] The writer Victor Klemperer wrote that 'Zionists are just as offensive as Nazis' in a diary entry from 1934, while experiencing at first hand the Nazi inferno.[2]

But while these wise voices urged caution, for many Jews, Zionism's cognitive dissonance had a certain appeal. Zionism promised not only national liberation, but the potential to become a secular European vanguard that would restore the Jews to the community of the most 'civilised nations' after Europe had expunged them. The religious idea of *Or Lagoyim*, 'Light unto the Nations', meaning bringing the Torah to the rest of the world, was replaced with bringing progress to the world. But Zionists themselves were doubtful they could achieve such a task.

WANTING TO BE IN A CLUB THAT DOES
NOT WANT TO HAVE YOU

Paraphrasing the famous Groucho Marx's letter of resignation to the Friars' club, 'I do not want to belong to any club that would accept me as one of its members', I would say that the lobby wanted to belong to a club that would not accept it. That club consisted of people who had problems with endorsing Zionism as a moral project and who gradually realised the price Palestinians paid for a European project of colonisation that was meant to solve the problem of anti-Semitism and satisfy a neo-crusader evangelical Christian desire to fulfil the prophecy of the 'Holy Land'.

The lobby, throughout the years of its existence, tried to galvanise people who were the most unlikely to overlook the shaky moral foundations on which the Zionist project was built; nor could they ignore the inherent problems of justice associated with the Palestinian catastrophe caused by the establishment of Israel in 1948, and even more so after Israel incorporated the West Bank and besieged the Gaza Strip. These were people from all over the world, whose religion, ethical worldview, life experience and many other factors made them supporters of oppressed and victimised people. Among them were quite a large number of Jews, and they were found in huge numbers in the anti-colonial movements of the Global South, in the minorities of the Global North and among people who refused to be indifferent to injustices, not just close to home but also abroad. They came from all walks of life, and generally political sociologists tended to define them as representing civil society or the conscientious sections of civil society or public opinion. They were activists with different levels of commitment. Occasionally, they could even be found in top-level politics.

The Zionists and later large sections of Israeli Jews wanted this diverse group of people to regard Zionism and Israel as a noble cause; in fact, as the Israeli historian Yosef Gorny put it, they should have recognised that Israel was one of the few successful projects of enlightenment and modernisation.[3] In this narrative, Jews not only 'returned' to their ancient homeland and 'redeemed' it, they also built the paragon of a democratic and socialist, or liberal, state and society. From our vantage point today, we realise that over the years an important part of Israeli Jewish society dispensed with these ambitions and instead wished to be a paragon of Jewish theocracy and messianism, a model dreamed up by Jewish fundamentalists in the past and embraced warmly by Christian fundamentalists, who, as I've shown, were the first Zionists in the modern era.

This is a structural anxiety accompanying the Zionist project from the outset. It became a genuinely realisable project, not a pipe dream, once it was deemed the best, and later the only, remedy for insurmountable nationalist and religious anti-Semitism in Europe. However, what was the remedy? To build a national-religious Jewish state in Palestine. Such a panacea for secular and progressive religious Jews, who were and are the majority of Zionist Jews in Israel and abroad, could have been morally problematic, unless they believed that Palestine was really given to them by God, even if they were atheists. Or they needed to believe that the land was empty, or perhaps that the Palestinians weren't victims at all but just another group of anti-Semites, necessitating a bitter struggle for survival. They may have thought they had no other option, and probably most of them felt and still do feel that today, but that does not brush aside the troubling conflation of the disease and the cure.

I do believe that the very fierce and at times vicious lobbying is because those directing and operating it know that the whole project they are protecting stands on very questionable moral ground for many people, including those they themselves see as decent and upstanding. That does not mean that they share this moral point of view; it just tells us that they understand they do not have the facts or moral arguments to rebut this basic human stance on rights and justice. It is easy to find allies, and Israel is good at it, among the extreme rights of the Global North and authoritarian and dictatorial regimes in the Global South. More importantly, the lobby learned on both sides of the Atlantic how little a role moral considerations play in governmental politics, even in democracies. The lobby worked on the assumption that staying in power and having a prosperous political career can surpass any other consideration in elite-level politics. You can either have ideological allies (Christian Zionists and Jewish communities) or buy them (by rewards or through intimidation). And then of course there are those who benefited economically from supporting the state of Israel, regardless of its policies on the ground.

But until recently there had been an obsession with receiving validation from those most reluctant to give it. I say until recently, as, while there are patterns of continuity in lobbying to date, there are also some dramatic challenges that are beyond the power of the lobby to control.

LOBBYING THE POLITICIANS AND IGNORING THEIR ELECTORATES

And here I come to the second conclusion. After the Second World War, the lobby quickly understood that the colonialist vocabulary used freely by the early Zionist movement and the employment of colonialist practices on the ground contravened the emerging consensus approach to the new ethics of a decolonised world, one recovering from the dark days of fascism and Nazism. Therefore, the lobby opted to focus on elites (cultural, economic and political), whose commitment to this new value system was only in word and not in deed. It was easier to obtain from them both legitimisation and the necessary material aid to implement the Zionist project and later sustain the state of Israel.

Elites can be bought, tempted and intimidated. From 1900 onwards, on both sides of the Atlantic, the lobby targeted literati, businessmen and politicians. This book focused on the latter group. Their method here was twofold: nurturing politicians from very early on as supporters of the cause, and undermining those who expressed moral qualms that could have led them to oppose Zionism or later criticise Israel.

Until this century their main efforts, on both sides of the Atlantic, were directed toward the political elites of the West and the Global North, who, in the nature of politics, cared less about issues of justice or history when it came the Global South and its future. Money, political influence and a well-oiled propaganda machine were needed here – ethical validation was irrelevant.

The lobby is a huge network of both paid staff and volunteers who work 24/7 for this project, while not actually having a lot to do when it comes to top-level politics. They have good reason to be satisfied as far as their influence on governments over the years is concerned. Both in the USA and in Britain, presidents and prime ministers know what Israel expects and tolerates. Ever since 1948, this self-censorship and subordination to Israel's wishes has triumphed over principled dissent. Parliament and Congress behave in a similar way, as do the mainstream media and academia. But in the age of the internet and alternative media, civil society cannot be controlled any more. The lobby feels compelled to nip any burgeoning sympathy for Palestine in the bud, whether that be in the form of a call for boycotts or in the form of humanitarian flotillas to Gaza. Knowledge production that supports the demands of Palestinians must also be suppressed. This is how advocacy for Israel will proceed, until local, regional and international actors have the courage to withstand these barrages of suppression through civil and legal action. It is already happening.

By the 1980s, both in Britain and in the USA, the lobby's aims became much more ambitious. The target now was to control the narrative wherever and whenever the Zionist one was challenged. The lobby is obsessed with controlling the conversation on Israel and Palestine and deems any failure in such an enterprise as an existential threat to Israel.

But despite its obvious failure to influence public opinion and politics from below, the lobby seems to appear in full force in places where it has already lost the battle, such as churches, community centres, city councils and universities, because it hates to lose power. And this is my third conclusion: the lobby's main target in many cases was securing its own survival, rather than that of Israel. As we reach the second half of the previous century and arrive in the twenty-first century, it seems that the lobby is seeking power for the sake of power.

POWER FOR THE SAKE OF POWER

Because the lobby, on both sides of the Atlantic, needed power to influence elites whose policies were detrimental to the future of Zionism and Israel, it accumulated such political muscle that preserving it became as precious as the cause it was supposed to protect. Thirst for power is a topic usually associated with the world of business and cynical politics. I

am not talking about it here in absolute terms, but when you are powerful, and members of Congress are rebuked in your offices like naughty
children for not fully following the guidelines given to them, fearing that
their careers might be targeted, then you want to maintain that power for
the sake of power, not just for the cause you need the power for. As
George Orwell's O'Brien, the party leader, says in *1984*, 'The Party seeks
power entirely for its own sake ... We are interested solely in power'; he
tells the novel's protagonist, Winston, that this is the first time in humanity that such people, who existed in the past, have been fully aware of
what they are doing, and they are not ashamed of it. This bleak Orwellian
view echoes that of Lord Acton, who warned that 'power tends to corrupt
and absolute power corrupts absolutely'. Of course the lobby is not an
authoritarian regime, but it acts decisively to preserve the power it does
have, regardless of whether it's really in the interest of the greater cause.

As we've seen, there have been multiple instances in which Israel
did not ask the lobby to go after a challenger to the Zionist narrative,
and yet all the might and the wrath of the lobby were employed more
often than not to tame or silence solidarity with the Palestinians.

LOOKING TOWARDS THE FUTURE

Israel's viability, indeed its very existence, is based on two pillars: a material and a moral one. The former is very solid, and Israel's exemplary
economic performance during the 2008 financial crisis was a testament
to this solidity. It is a high-tech nation, with prolific export-orientated
military and civil industries. For over ten years, it has been a member of
the OECD, a signifier of both its development and its general affluence.

The moral pillar, on the other hand, has been constantly eroded
over the years, a process that began in earnest after the first Intifada in
1987 and intensified in the wake of the Israeli assaults on the Gaza Strip
since 2006. Most of the critique was directed at the state's policies and
not against its existence. However, the Israeli government viewed this
criticism as an attempt to delegitimise the Jewish state. Therefore,
twenty-first-century lobbying has not been centred on defending Israel's
current policies in historical Palestine, but rather directed against any

imagined or real indication that the state and its ideology face international rebuke. The Israelis call it the struggle against delegitimisation.

THE QUESTION OF LEGALITY VERSUS LEGITIMACY

In this century, the battle for international legitimacy is focused on advocacy and argument. It can be best manifested in the question of whether Israel is an apartheid state, as claimed by Amnesty International, or a liberal democracy. The ability of the Palestinians and those who support them to persuade societies and governments alike of the validity of the apartheid argument will affect international policy towards Palestine and the Palestinians in the future. Similarly, if the pro-Israel lobby succeeds in persuading the same governments in particular that there is no basis for this argument, Israel will continue to enjoy international immunity for its policies on the ground in historical Palestine.

What still preserves Israel's international legitimacy, in particular in the West, is its Judeo-Christian religious endorsement, now that the secular one cannot easily be obtained. This religious legitimacy, as I have tried to show in this book, has deep historical roots dating back to the eighteenth century, when anti-Semitic non-Jews as well as philo-semitic non-Jews supported the Zionist project mainly for religious reasons. And it turned out that the unequivocal religious faith in Zionism had been blind from the beginning to the negative impact Zionism could have on the indigenous people of Palestine.

The quest for legitimacy has not ended, but the mission is frustrated by the lobby's inability to confront global civil society's moral indignation, engendered by Israel's ongoing oppression of the Palestinians. The lobby's methods have varied throughout the ages, but there are some common hallmarks – a huge and expansive effort directed at courting politicians and decision makers, with scant attention paid to building consensus in civil society. As we have seen in the book, this effort is silencing anti-Israel sections of society rather than winning them over. This focus explains the achievements of the lobbying effort as much as it exposes its weaknesses. What induces political elites to support Israel is much less effective when it comes to influencing public opinion.

Nowadays, lobbying for Zionism in the UK and the USA sets the lobby-ists against civil society in both countries, which needs to be convinced by moral arguments and cannot be easily cowed or seduced. This explains the shift by the lobby to weaponising anti-Semitism to procure public support for Israel.

But this quest is not the only thread that connects the past to the present in Zionist lobbying in the UK and the USA. Zionism began as a Christian project and thus the early lobbyists were what we would call Christian Zionists today. In the USA in particular, the Christian Zionist lobby has become as important as the Jewish lobby and has become by far the more vociferous during the years of the Trump administration (2016–2020), with its Christian Zionist vice president, Mike Pence, and the secretary of state, Mike Pompeo, being part of the lobbying infra-structure. It might lose some of its support now that Trump's term in office has come to an end; but he, or Republicans like him, can regain power. The vacillation in the fortunes of the Christian lobby should send a warning to scholars trying to assess the power of that particular lobby. In their seminal work *The Israel Lobby*, John Mearsheimer and Stephen Walt described this Christian lobby as a junior partner in the overall lobbying effort in the USA.[4] This appeared to be the case in 2007 – but the picture was very different nearly a decade later during the Trump era.

Power in the end made Israel a reality and lost Palestine. But power needs to be obtained, sustained and defended. People who hold power may be influenced by their societies, by moral considerations, political ambitions, economic interests, prejudices of their own and other factors. The project of building a state in the twilight of colonialism through colonisation needed affluent, well-oiled and committed advocacy. The Zionist movement provided such an enterprise from its very beginning: defeating Palestinian national aspirations, denying its demands, and controlling the historical narrative in the international arena. It secured a state, while being absolved of the ethnic cleansing it committed in 1948 and the ongoing occupation that dates back to the 1967 war. Under that occupation, and the siege on the Gaza Strip, the state of Israel violates international law daily, and yet still belongs to the community of 'civilised nations'.

But in the twenty-first century, cracks are beginning to appear in this solid edifice. Public opinion, conscientious politicians and above all a reawakened Palestinian liberation movement are demanding an end to these violations. What has become clear only recently to most of Israel's critics *and* advocates is that the violations will not stop as long as Israel remains committed to basic Zionist ideology that justifies an oxymoronic regime: a democratic Jewish ethno-state. After seventy-five years of statehood, the nature of an ethnic Jewish state has unfolded clearly, and it has been framed by critical scholars and by human rights organisations such as Amnesty International, among others, as an apartheid state – a term that used to be unsayable.

LEGITIMACY CAN ONLY COME FROM THE PALESTINIANS

The gradual erosion of Israel's international legitimacy owes much to Palestinian resistance and resilience. But more important than attributing the cracks in the wall to the Palestinian struggle is the fact that, however successful or unsuccessful that struggle is, only Palestinians can solve the issue of Israel's legitimacy.

Ironically, after all the efforts of the lobby, it still disregards the only group of people who really matter, if indeed legitimacy is what Israeli Jews and those who support them seek in the future: the Palestinians. Even a very feeble and in many ways defeated Palestinian leadership refuses to recognise Israel as a Jewish state or sign documents in which it pledges not to have any future demands, even if an agreement between the two sides is concluded. There are two reasons for the refusal of the Palestinian leadership to declare the conflict over.

The first is that the leadership does not recognise Israel as a Jewish state, because the Palestinians may accept Israel as a fait accompli, but it does not mean that they will justify morally and publicly the takeover of nearly eighty per cent of their homeland by this state, the exile of millions of Palestinians or the discrimination against Palestinian citizens of Israel. The current leadership in the West Bank and inside Israel have declared their willingness not to use any violence or armed struggle against these injustices but refuse to view them as bygones. In their mind, these humiliations were inflicted because Israel sees itself as a Jewish state.

The second reason for refusing to declare the conflict over has to do with the reality that unfolded after the Oslo Accords, which the Palestinian leadership realises would be the basis for any future two-state solution. It means that Israel would still control more than half of the West Bank, would monitor any bridge or road between the Gaza Strip and the West Bank, and would not allow repatriation of refugees, nor would it agree to a Palestinian capital in Jerusalem proper, and it would insist on economic and security domination over the Palestinian state.

In the final desperate attempt to salvage the 'peace process' born in Oslo in 1993, Israel and the US demanded that the Palestinian Authority recognise Israel as a Jewish state. In addition to that recognition, the Palestinian Authority was promised autonomous control over more than half of the West Bank and the Gaza Strip (should it be able to remove Hamas from there), if it gave up the right of return of Palestinian refugees and was content with a capital outside Jerusalem and a Judaised West Bank next to the Palestinian one. This was supposed to be the map of the future, sending a message to the world that the Palestinians accept this new set-up as final and just. This of course will never happen. Palestinians will never lend legitimacy to this state of affairs even as it unfolds right in front of our eyes.

The Israeli state might give up this attempt to seek legitimisation and become indifferent to its image as a pariah and rogue state in many sections of global civil society. After all, Western governments and their arbiters are only too happy to provide Israel with immunity, and the mainstream media and academia in the West whitewash Israel's conduct. So why do they care?

Among some Israelis, including those in leading positions, and among those who support Israel from abroad, there is a genuine belief that it is crucial for the state's existence that it enjoys international legitimacy. For many others inside Israel, it is a bonus, but not a crucial condition for the survival of the state. After all, rogue states in the world in the twenty-first century, as long as they are allies of NATO and the West or are too strong to confront, enjoy a free ride in international politics regardless of whether they commit war crimes or have a dismal human rights record. And thus, so far, Israel enjoys the privileges that come with being within the Western orbit of influence and freely uses the power of its army and its security services to quell the Palestinian resistance.

Israel's worry should therefore be less about a shift in Western attitudes towards Israel *per se*, but rather about a change in the way international politics are carried out in an age when a younger generation of constituencies all over the world are seeking, so far unsuccessfully, a way of injecting morality and justice into foreign policy. A growing mistrust in the political system stops many of these young visionaries from participating in the electoral process. In the case of the attempted revolution in the Arab world, many young people shunned hierarchies and organisations as means of changing political realities. It could be the case that one day attitudes towards Israel will serve as a political litmus test for identifying who belongs to this strong undercurrent in world politics. The die has already been cast in the world of human rights organisations, and, in this century, they condemn Israel, without hesitation, as a systematic violator of basic Palestinian civil and human rights.

THE 2022 ELECTION AND ITS IMPACT

In November 2022, a majority of the Israeli electorate voted in a right-wing, extreme and messianic government. It included the Likud, orthodox parties and extreme right parties, with a strong base in the West Bank settlements advocating transfer of Arabs, expansion of settlements and further legislation meant to make Israel more theocratic and less democratic.

Masses of people opposing these policies took to the streets on a weekly basis, once it was declared by the new government that some of these ideologies would form part of what a new minister of justice called the 'legal reform' – in essence a set of laws meant to give the government total control over the judicial system.

The demonstrators included many people who serve as reserves in the Israeli army and many who are part of the high-tech industry, who threatened not to serve in the first case, and in the second case to re-locate, if not themselves, then their fortunes outside of Israel.

It was not clear if this protest would succeed, as it was disrupted by a new war that broke out on 7 October 2023. I will not dwell on that war in this book; a historian's perspective can only be given after the passage of time. I will only say that I do not think it is a game changer and thus what I describe in these conclusions, I believe, will still be relevant in the future.

Even before that war, it was clear that Israel in 2023 was very far from seeking legitimacy from the Palestinians. On the contrary, since 2018 it has sought to delegitimise the Palestinian claim to Palestine (even to a small part of Palestine). Moreover, it seems to be led by a government that does not care about their state's delegitimisation. The Jewish electorate who voted and prevailed in the 2022 elections does not seem to care or worry about what its governments used to call the new anti-Semitism, namely the condemnation of Israel as an apartheid state, and they are led to believe that they are located in the best place in the world to face such a threat. Leading activists who had offered an alternative view have left the country, and the battle, as we have seen during the protests in Israel following the election of a right-wing government in Israel in November 2022, rages within Zionist ideology, without challenging it. It is a rivalry, some say even a civil war, between Zionists who wish to retain the status quo in Israel and those who want to make Israel more religious and more nationalistic. I call it the battle between *Fantasy Israel*, a state that is a binational apartheid state, which provides democratic, liberal and pluralistic life to one national group, and denies them to the other national group and hence is hailed by its citizens and its supporters as 'the only democracy in the Middle East', and the *State of Judea*, the settlers' state, now taking over Israel as a whole, wishing to build a racist and theocratic state, whose enemies are not just the Palestinians but also the secular Jews, and which is moved by impulses very similar to the ones motivating political Islamic move-ments in the Middle East.[5]

This comes back to the first conclusion of the book. From the moment the first Jewish settler set foot in the country, the Zionist self-image did not tally with the reality on the ground in historical Palestine.

In 2023 we learned that the dissonance between the Israeli Jewish self-image and reality in Israel was not caused by the oppression of the Palestinians, as it should have been. This is why the demonstrators rebut any suggestion that they should also protest against the occupation or the oppression of the Palestinians. This is not their fight. For them, the election of a messianic and theocratic Jewish government in November 2022 trashed the fantasy of at least half of the Israeli Jews that they were living in a modern secular democracy. They took to the streets in large numbers trying to restore the *Fantasy Israel* they imagined but which never really existed.

If the State of Judea triumphs over the State of Israel, future governments chosen by the remaining electorate will substitute the more subtle lobbying with aggressive attempts to suppress any criticism with the help of local advocacy groups, using legal action and intimidation, all backed by vast amounts of funding to ensure a chasm remains between the sentiments of civil society and the attitudes of government. According to an *Haaretz* editorial from 18 August 2023, AIPAC decided categorically to side with the legal reform offered by the government.

The problem is that such a political culture produces even more callous policies towards the Palestinians. This only intensifies the resolve of the Palestinian liberation movement to challenge Israel on the ground. This inevitable clash will erode Israel's international image even further and will strengthen the case of civil society when it brings its pressure to bear on governments to change course on the Israel/Palestine question.

In this respect, the lobbying has failed, but the project it was meant to sustain is still there. It can of course change and become a legitimate state by ending the policies that discriminate against the indigenous people of Palestine. Seismic changes have already occurred in the traditional powerbase of the lobby in the world: a large number of young American Jews are turning away from Israel, and if the trend continues, it might affect American policy in the future.

So far, despite the events in late 2023, Parliament and Congress still treat Israel as a loyal democratic ally, defending itself against common enemies. Congress gave a standing ovation to Israel's president in July

2023 and Parliament voted for legislation against BDS in the same month. But does it still have the support of the American Jewish community? Who would have thought that two former senior employees of AIPAC, Martin Indyk and Dan Kurtzer, who also were ambassadors to Israel at one point, would call on their government to cut military aid to Israel? Half of their political life was devoted to securing such aid![6]

But does Israel need its former allies? Those who brought the 2022 government to power do not wish to live in a democratic secular state. A more theocratic and nationalist state is their 'fantasy Israel'. Their rabbis and political leaders do not care about Israel's image, nor do they believe that delegitimisation is a problem in a world in which America's Trump, Hungary's Orbán and India's Modi exist. God is with them, as is a huge network of right-wing nationalist governments and fascist movements throughout the world. This means they do not need a lobby. Time will tell if without it, Zionism can prevail. It might well signal the end of Zionism.

The 2023 crisis may or may not transform Israel, but it has exposed something the lobbies could not have been aware of before our century. Even in our cynical world, the moral issues can suddenly become tied to material ones. Israel's high-tech industry derived much of its wealth from outside of Israel in 2023, as did many financial institutions. Wealth like this in a very politicised society relies on the protection of a strong and independent judicial system. The possible image of the Israeli judicial system as being under the thumb of the politicians, and not an independent power, paved the way for international and foreign courts to try soldiers and officers as potential war criminals. Suddenly, it appeared that any dent in Israel's image as a democracy could mean losing its economic growth and its legal immunity in the world. We might regret that the oppression of Palestinians has never triggered such processes, but nonetheless this is situation worth watching in the future.

This is the hopeful and positive scenario, so it is only right I close the book with it. The desperate and disastrous scenario is playing out in front of our eyes – we don't need any power of imagination to see Israel slide into a far-right, authoritarian regime. We need to believe in humanity and the power of justice to carve a different way forward, however tough the odds are.

Afterword: 7 October and the Future

As this book reached its final stages, Operation Al-Aqsa Flood by Hamas shook the world. Early on 7 October 2023, Hamas and other Palestinian resistance groups breached the apartheid wall separating Israel from Gaza. For Hamas, it was initially a shock success – they captured eleven military bases. But it swiftly degenerated into a series of war crimes and atrocities carried out by Hamas and others in Jewish settlements near the border, including a horrifying massacre at Re'im music festival, with over 300 dead. Among the 1,200 killed that day, the majority were civilians.

For a moment, and understandably so, Israel was the recipient of almost universal sympathy and support from governments worldwide. The Palace of Westminster was lit up in the colours of the Israeli flag in solidarity with the victims.

According to British law, Hamas is a terrorist organisation. The pro-Israel lobby hoped that the government's solidarity would result in carte blanche for Israel's retaliation.

As a means of enacting collective retribution for Hamas's action, Israel carpet bombed the Gaza Strip, including densely populated civilian areas, for weeks on end, and deprived Gaza of water, electricity, fuel and humanitarian aid. At the time of writing, the number of dead exceeds 16,000, with tens of thousands injured and more than a million internal refugees, after Israel ordered those living in the north of Gaza to vacate their homes and move to the south.

But while Western governments, in particular the UK, the US and Germany, refused to call for a ceasefire, emboldening Israel to strike out more violently than it otherwise might have, global civil society began protesting en masse, with turnout at demonstrations hitting hundreds of thousands. These people were not only calling for an end to Israeli operations in Gaza, but also criticising settler violence towards Palestinians in the West Bank and the laws passed by the Israeli government against Palestinian citizens of Israel.

In terms of the history of the lobby, it seems to me that the responses in the world to these events were clearly divided into two orientations. I refer to the first response as one put forward by 'global Israel' and the second as that of 'global Palestine'. By 'global Israel', I refer to a coalition that includes most governments, mainstream media and some parts of academia in the Global North, with the US and the UK at the forefront, and some governments in the Global South, with the tacit support of large multinational corporations and the military and security industries. Politically, the Right and the neo-Right are the most vocal members of this alliance, but it enjoys the support of most of the established social democratic parties in Europe and many members of the American Democratic Party.

'Global Israel' propagated the Israeli narrative of the events. According to this narrative, the 7 October attack is yet another chapter in the history of modern anti-Semitism, this time accomplished with brutality comparable to or even worse than the Nazis and ISIS. And it was all planned out in Tehran by the evil Iranian regime. The fact that Iran distanced itself from the Hamas operation almost immediately, concerned about being dragged into an unwanted regional war, did not trouble those who bought into this narrative wholesale.

This narrative does not serve Jewish interests. Comparing the killings, as horrific as they are, of 1,200 people to the industrial genocide of six million people by a modern nation state is the worst abuse of Holocaust memory one can think of, and one that would delight Holocaust deniers around the world. Hamas is undoubtedly responsible for war crimes against civilians, but to draw an equivalence between Hamas and Nazism minimises the unparalleled horror of the Holocaust.

'Global Palestine' took a different attitude. This is a coalition of civil society movements around the world, working in tandem with oppressed minorities, some governments in the Global South, and many human rights organisations, all showing solidarity with the Palestine struggle for liberation. It includes people of all faiths and none and from all walks of life. It is a movement that has achieved unprecedented popularity and support in recent years. Broadly, although not without contention, this coalition supports BDS, the one-state solution and the right of return for refugees.

The position of 'global Palestine' puts it at odds with the liberal Left within Israel. In the month following 7 October, the leading left-wing newspaper in Israel, *Haaretz*, regularly attacked the 'hypocrisy' of the global Left for supposedly downplaying Hamas's atrocities, while rushing to criticise Israel for its blanket attacks on Gaza. In its pages, liberal Zionists objected to the characterisation of Zionism as settler colonialism, arguing that this amounted to describing all Israelis as 'colonialists who deserve to die'. They also reproached the global Left for comparing Operation Al-Aqsa Flood to violence committed in twentieth-century national liberation struggles and maintaining that the justice of the Palestinian cause remained legitimate, regardless of the actions of Hamas. The liberal Left in Israel hence struggles to make common cause with those active in global Palestine.

The relative balance of power between these two global coalitions will help shape the future of Israel and Palestine. As harrowing as the end of 2023 has been in the history of Israel and Palestine, it is not likely to change anything fundamental on the ground. Palestinian refugees will continue to be denied their internationally recognised right of return; the West Bank will continue to be occupied and colonised; and whatever unfolds in Gaza, it will remain at the mercy of Israel. The Palestinian citizens in Israel, who have faced violent assaults following 7 October, will continue to live in an apartheid-like Jewish state.

'Global Israel' is still the one with all the cards to decide policies on the ground. 'Global Palestine' has been unable to alter international policies in the Global North so far, so Israel continues to be able to act with impunity.

But global support for Palestine now is much larger, and much more organised, than it used to be. In Britain, activists are picketing arms factories, organising school walkouts and protesting cultural institutions' complicity with Israel's attacks on Palestine. The lobby, as I have shown, successfully brought together separate interest groups to form a shield that could protect Israel from being held accountable for its violations of justice and humanitarian law. Now, however, there are cracks in this international shield, and they might grow in the years to come. At the end of the day, many people in the twenty-first century cannot continue to accept a colonisation project requiring military occupation and discriminatory laws to sustain itself. There is a point at which the lobby cannot endorse this brutal reality and continue to be seen as moral in the eyes of the rest of the world. I believe and hope this point will be reached within our lifetimes.

Acknowledgements

Although none of my colleagues were asked to read the manuscript, they had to bear with me, and offered thoughtful feedback on large sections that were presented as lectures or in more informal conversations. The list is too long to mention all of them, so this is a big collective thank you.

A special thanks to Rida Vaquas for patient and careful editing, as well as her vital corrections and commitment to bringing this manuscript to publication, and to Kathleen McCully.

I also want to thank Novin Doostdar, Juliet Mabey and the whole team at Oneworld with whom I have worked for over fifteen years. Their faith in me motivated me to complete projects, even when I was on the verge of giving up.

Finally, as always, I want to thank my family, Revital, Ido and Yonatan, for being there for me, tolerating my impossible absences and enduring the challenges and hardships that my moral and scholarly choices have exposed them to at times.

Select Bibliography

Aked, Hilary, *Friends of Israel: The Backlash against Palestine Solidarity*, London and New York: Verso, 2023.

Amoruso, Francesco, Ilan Pappe and Sophie Dichter-Devore, 'Introduction: Knowledge, Power, and the "Settler Colonial Turn" in Palestine Studies', *Interventions: A Journal of Post-Colonial Studies*, 21/4 (2019), pp. 451–463.

Aridan, Natan, *Advocating for Israel: Diplomats and Lobbyists from Truman to Nixon*, Lanham, MD: Lexington Books, 2017.

Aruri, Naseer, *Dishonest Broker: The US Role in Israel and Palestine*, New York: South End, 2003.

Ashton, Nigel, '"A Local Terrorist Made Good": The Callaghan Government and the Arab-Israeli Peace Process, 1977–79', *Contemporary British History*, 31/1 (2017), pp. 114–135.

Bar-Gal, Yoram, *Propaganda and Zionist Education: The Jewish National Fund, 1924–1927*, Rochester, NY: University of Rochester Press, 2003.

Beit-Hallahmi, Benjamin, *The Israeli Connection: Whom Israel Arms and Why*, London and New York, Pantheon Books, 1987.

Bermant, Azriel, *Margaret Thatcher and the Middle East*, Cambridge: Cambridge University Press, 2016.

Bierbrier, Doreen, 'The American Zionist Emergency Council: An Analysis of a Pressure Group', *American Jewish Historical Quarterly*, 60/1 (September 1970), pp. 82–105.

Bishop, Tim, 'The Question of Palestine in Harold Wilson's Labour Party, 1970–1976', *Webster Review of International History*, 1/1 (2021), pp. 41–70.

Borg, David, *Standing with Israel: Why Christians Support the Jewish State*, New York: Charisma Media, 2016.

Carter, Jimmy, *Palestine: Peace Not Apartheid*, New York: Simon & Schuster, 2007.

Christison, Kathleen, 'Splitting the Difference: The Palestinian-Israeli Policy of James Baker', *Journal of Palestine Studies*, 24/1 (Autumn 1994), pp. 39–50.

Davidson, Lawrence, *America's Palestine: Popular and Official Perceptions from Balfour to Israel's Statehood*, Gainesville: University Press of Florida, 2001.

Findley, Paul, *They Dare to Speak Out: People and Institutions Confront Israel's Lobby*, Washington: A Capella Books, 2003.

Fleshler, Dan, *Transforming America's Israel Lobby: The Limits of Its Power and the Potential for Change*, Washington: Potomac Books, 2009.

Fraser, Ronnie, 'The TUC and the Histadrut, 1945–1982: A Problematic Relationship', Doctor of Philosophy Thesis submitted to Royal Holloway, 1982.

Gat, Moshe, 'Britain and Israel Before and After the Six Day War, June 1967: From Support to Hostility', *Contemporary British History*, 18/1 (2004), pp. 54–77.

Halbwachs, Maurice, *The Collective Memory*, Chicago: University of Chicago Press, 1992.

Hixson, Walter, *Architects of Repression: How Israel and Its Lobby Put Racism, Violence and Injustice at the Center of US Middle East Policy*, Washington: Institute for Research: Middle Eastern Policy, 2021.

Jefferies, J.M.N., *Palestine: The Reality: The Inside Story of the Balfour Declaration*, London: Olive Branch, 2016.

Jensehaugen, Jorgen, *Arab-Israeli Diplomacy under Carter: The US, Israel and the Palestinians*, London: Bloomsbury Books, 2020.

Kaplan, Amy, *Our American Israel: The Story of an Entangled Alliance*, Cambridge: Harvard University Press, 2018.

Khalidi, Rashid, *Brokers of Deceit: How the US Has Undermined Peace in the Middle East*, Boston: Beacon Press, 2013.

Lewis, Geoffrey, *Balfour and Weizmann: The Zionist, the Zealot, and the Emergence of Israel*, London: Bloomsbury, 2009.

Lipstadt, Deborah E., 'America and the Holocaust', *Modern Judaism*, 10/3 (October 1990), pp. 283–296.

London, Louis, *Whitehall, and the Jews 1933–1948: British Immigration Policy, Jewish Refugees and the Holocaust*, Cambridge: Cambridge University Press, 2000.

Manuel, Frank E., *The Realities of American-Palestine Relations*, Washington: Public Affairs Press, 1949.

Mart, Michelle, *Eye on Israel: How America Came to View the Jewish State as an Ally*, Albany: State University of New York Press, 2006.

Mathew, William M., 'The Balfour Declaration and the Palestine Mandate, 1917–1923: British Imperialist Imperatives', *British Journal of Middle Eastern Studies*, 40/3 (2013), pp. 231–250.

Mearsheimer, John J., and Stephen M. Walt, *The Israel Lobby and US Foreign Policy*, London: Penguin, 2008.

Merkley, Paul Charles, *American Presidents, Religion, and Israel: The Heirs of Cyrus*, Westport, CT, and London: Praeger, 2004.

Obama, Barack, *The Audacity of Hope: Thoughts of Reclaiming the American Dream*, New York: Crown Publishing Group, 2006.

Oborne, Peter, and James Jones, 'The Pro-Israel Lobby in Britain: Full Text', *Open Democracy*, 13 November 2009.

Pappe, Ilan, *The Making of the Arab–Israeli Conflict, 1947–1951*, London and New York: I.B. Tauris, 2001.

Pappe, Ilan, *The Biggest Prison on Earth: A History of the Occupied Territories*, London and New York, Oneworld, 2018.

Philpot, Robert, *Margaret Thatcher: The Honorary Jew: How Britain's Jews Helped Shape the Iron Lady and Her Beliefs*, London: Biteback Publishing, 2017.

Rabi, Muhammed Abd al-Aziz, *US–PLO Dialogue: Secret Diplomacy and Conflict Resolution*, Miami: University of Florida Press, 1995.

Rausch, David A., 'Protofundamentalism's Attitudes towards Zionism, 1878–1918', *Jewish Social Studies*, 43/2 (Spring 1981), pp. 137–152.

Renton, James, *The Zionist Masquerade: The Birth of the Anglo-Zionist Alliance, 1914–1918*, London and New York: Palgrave Macmillan, 2007.

Rubenberg, Cheryl, *Israel and the American National Interest: A Critical Examination*, Chicago: University of Illinois Press, 1989.

Rose, Norman, *The Gentile Zionists: A Study in Anglo-Zionist Diplomacy, 1929–1939*, London: Frank Cass, 1973.

Rostinow, Doug, '"The Edge of the Abyss": The Origins of the Israeli Lobby, 1949–1954', *Modern American History*, 1/23–24, (2018), pp. 23–43.

Rovner, Adam, *In the Shadow of Zion: Promised Lands Before Israel*, New York: New York University Press, 2014.

Said, Edward W., *Orientalism*, London: Penguin Books, 2003.

Sasson, Theodore, *The New American Zionism*, New York and London: New York University Press, 2013.

Segev, Tom, *The Seventh Million: The Israelis and the Holocaust*, New York: Picador, 2000.

Shambrook, Peter, *Policy of Deceit: Britain and Palestine, 1914–1939*, London and New York: Oneworld Academic, 2023.

Sharif, Regina, 'Christians for Zion, 1600–1919', *Journal of Palestine Studies*, 5, 3/3 (Spring 1976), pp. 123–141.

Sizer, Stephen, *Christian Zionism: Roadmap to Armageddon?*, London: Inter-Varsity Press, 2004.

Smith, Grant F., *Big Israel: How Israel's Lobby Moves America*, Washington: Institute for Research: Middle Eastern Policy, 2016.

Snetsinger, John, *Truman, the Jewish Vote, and the Creation of Israel*, Washington: Hoover Institute, 1974.

Spector, Stephen, *Evangelicals and Israel: The Story of American Christian Zionism*, New York: Oxford University Press, 2009.

Terry, Janice J., 'The Carter Administration and the Palestinians', *Arab Studies Quarterly*, 12/1–2 (Winter/Spring 1990), pp. 153–165.

Vaughan, James, '"Keep Left for Israel": Tribune, Zionism and the Middle East, 1937–1967', *Contemporary British History*, 27/1 (March 2013), pp. 1–21.

Zakariah, Muhamad Hasrul, 'British Foreign Policy on the Palestinian Question in the Middle East Peace Negotiations: From Conservative to Labour (1970–1979)', *International Journal of Academic Research in Business and Social Sciences*, 8/11 (2018), pp. 1062–1092.

Zertal, Idit, *Israel's Holocaust and the Politics of Nationhood*, Cambridge: Cambridge University Press, 2005.

Zoughbie, Daniel D., *Indecision Points: George W. Bush and the Israeli-Palestinian Conflict*, Cambridge, MA: MIT Press, 2014.

Notes

All website links were accessed on 5 January 2024.

Preface

1. 'Board Concerned over Exeter University Conference on Israeli "Colonialism"', *Jewish Chronicle*, 11 August 2015.
2. *Interventions: Journal of Postcolonial Studies*, special issue, 'Settler Colonialism in Palestine', 21/4 (2019).
3. Bertrand Russell, *The Autobiography of Bertrand Russell*, London and New York: Taylor & Francis, 2014, p. 465.
4. Grant F. Smith, *Big Israel: How Israel's Lobby Moves America*, Washington: Institute for Research: Middle Eastern Policy, 2016, p. 2.
5. Walter L. Hixson, *Architects of Repression: How Israel and Its Lobby Put Racism, Violence and Injustice at the Center of US Middle East Policy*, Washington: Institute for Research: Middle Eastern Policy, p. 4.
6. John J. Mearsheimer and Stephen M. Walt, *The Israel Lobby and US Foreign Policy*, London: Penguin, 2008, p. xiii.

1   The Christian Harbingers of Zionism

1. Patrick Hutton, 'Collective Memory and Collective Mentalities: The Halbwachs–Ariés Connection', *Historical Reflections/Réflexions Historiques*, 15/2 (Summer 1988), pp. 315–316.
2. Maurice Halbwachs, *The Collective Memory*, Chicago: University of Chicago Press, 1992, p. 215.
3. Don Peretz, 'Origins of American Support for Israel', *Palestine-Israel Journal*, special issue, 'The USA and the Conflict', 4/3–4 (1997–1998), p. 41.
4. William Canton, *A History of the British and Foreign Bible Society*, London: John Murray, 1910, pp. 4–5.
5. Edward Said, *Orientalism*, London: Penguin Books, 2003.
6. Alexander Keith, *The Land of Israel According to the Covenant with Abraham, with Isaac, and with Jacob*, Edinburgh: William Whyte and Co., 1843, p. 43.
7. Victoria Clark, *Allies for Armageddon: The Rise of Christian Zionism*, New Haven: Yale University Press, 2007, p. 67.

8. *The Times*, 4 November 1840.
9. Donald M. Lewis, *The Origins of Christian Zionism: Lord Shaftesbury and Evangelical Support for the Jewish Homeland*, Cambridge: Cambridge University Press, 2010, p. 185.
10. Edwin Hodder, *The Life and Work of the Seventh Earl of Shaftesbury, K.G.*, volume 2, London: Cassel and Company, p. 478.
11. As cited in Adam M. Garfinkle, 'On the Origin, Meaning, Use and Abuse of a Phrase', *Middle Eastern Studies*, 27/4 (October 1991), pp. 542–543.
12. Bonnie Goodman, 'Colonel Charles Henry Churchill's Letter to Sir Moses Montefiore, a First in Supporting a Jewish State in Palestine', *Jerusalem Post*, 26 June 2018.
13. See, for more details, Jonathan Frankel, '"Ritual Murder" in the Modern Era: The Damascus Affair 1840', *Jewish Social Sciences*, 3/2 (Winter 1997), pp. 1–16.
14. Goodman, 'Colonel'.
15. Ibid.
16. Gabriel Polley, *Victorian Britain*, London and New York: Bloomsbury, 2022.
17. He made this comment after he toured Palestine with Montefiore. See Abigail Green, *Moses Montefiore: Jewish Liberator, Imperial Hero*, Cambridge, MA: Harvard University Press, 2010, pp. 214–215.
18. *Jewish Chronicle*, 10 November 1876, p. 501, column B.
19. Jo Glanville, 'A Gentile Touch', *Prospects*, 20 May 1988, summarizes the research on this point.
20. See 'The Restoration and Conversion of the Jews', Spurgeon Library, www.spurgeon.or/resource-library/sermons/the-restoration-and-concession-of-the-Jews
21. Peretz, *Origins*, p. 42.
22. Norman Rose, *The Gentile Zionists: A Study in Anglo-Zionist Diplomacy, 1929–1939*, London: Frank Cass, 1973.
23. Laurence Oliphant, *The Land of Gilead, with Excursions in the Lebanon*, Edinburgh and London: Blackwood and Sons, 1880.
24. David Cesarani, 'Israel and Jewish Christian Dialogue', *European Judaism*, 25/1 (Spring 1992), pp. 40–47.
25. *The Complete Diaries of Theodor Herzl*, New York: Yosselof, 1960, volume 1, book 2, p. 310 (10 March 1896).
26. Theodor Herzl to Rev. William Hechler, 16 March 1896, *The Diaries of Theodor Herzl*, edited by Marvin Lowenthal, Gloucester: Smith Publications, 1978, p. 105.
27. *The Complete Diaries*, p. 311 (16 March 1896).
28. Ibid., p. 330 (23 April 1896).

29. Ibid.
30. Ibid.
31. Ibid.
32. *Daily Mail*, 10 July 1896.

2   Lobbying for the Balfour Declaration

1. *Haboker*, 19 May 1940, 'among the Rothschilds in London'.
2. *Jewish Chronicle*, 17 January 1896.
3. Maja Gildin Zuckerman, 'The Maccabean Pilgrimage to Palestine and the Divergent Process of Zionist Meaning Making', *Jewish Culture and History*, 22/3 (2021), pp. 189–208.
4. No author, 'Theodor Herzl Had Many Opponents in His Struggle to Found a Jewish State', *Jewish Chronicle*, 28 April 2010.
5. Ari Shavit, *My Promised Land: The Triumph and Tragedy of Israel*, New York: Spiegel & Grau, 2013.
6. *Jewish Chronicle*, 22 January 1897.
7. Zuckerman, 'Maccabean Pilgrimage'.
8. Tom Segev, *State at Any Cost: The Life of David Ben-Gurion*, New York: Farrar, Straus & Giroux, 2019.
9. The *Jewish Chronicle* followed all his appearances in London in 1896, which also included a debate on his idea of the Jewish state in the Sons of Lodz Synagogue in London: *Jewish Chronicle*, 10–18 July 1896.
10. *Daily Graphic*, 26 November 1891.
11. Quoted in Colin Schindler, 'Zionism's Hated Hero', *Jewish Chronicle*, 28 April 2010.
12. Isaiah Friedman, 'Theodor Herzl: Political Activity and Achievements', *Israel Studies*, 9/3 (Autumn 2004), p. 62.
13. See www.towerhamletsmission.org/Tower_Hamlets_Mission/History.html
14. Schindler, 'Zionism's Hated Hero'.
15. See the background for this in Stuart A. Cohen, *The Communal Politics of Anglo Jewry, 1896–1920*, Princeton: Princeton University Press, 2014, pp. 47–78.
16. I gathered this information from several documents put up for sale; see www.invaluable.com/auction-lot/the-fourth-zionist-congress-in-london-designed-in-1-c-3184dd4a9f
17. This story appears in the blog of the National Library of Israel; see https://blog.nli.org.il/en/lbh_herzls_doctor/
18. Theodor Herzl, *Gesammelte Zionistische Werke*, Tel-Aviv: Hozaha Ivrit, 1934, volume 5, pp. 484–486.
19. Ibid.

20. *Manchester Courier*, 14 August 1900, quoted in Benjamin Jaffe, 'The British Press and Zionism in Herzl's Time (1894–1904), *The Jewish Historical Society of England*, 24 (1970–1973), pp. 89–100.

21. English Zionist Federation: *General Election, 1900: Opinions of Parliamentary Candidates on Zionism*, London: English Zionist Federation, 1901.

3   The Road to the Balfour Declaration

1. Taken from the Architects of Greater Manchester website; see https://manchestervictorianarchitects.org.uk/buildings/queens-hotel-portland-place-piccadilly-and-portland-street-manchester

2. Chaim Weizmann, *Trial and Error: The Autobiography of Chaim Weizmann*, London: Hamish Hamilton, 1949, p. 129.

3. See a good summary of this point of view in Gilbert Achcar, 'Zionism, Anti-Semitism and the Balfour Declaration', *Open Democracy*, 2 November 2017.

4. Sameh Habib and Pietro Stefanini, 'Introduction', in Habib and Stefanini (eds.), *Giving Away Other People's Land: The Making of the Balfour Declaration*, London: PRC, 2017, pp. 6–7.

5. Adam Rovner, *In the Shadow of Zion: Promised Lands Before Israel*, New York: New York University Press, 2014, pp. 50–51.

6. Weizmann's letter can be found in Meyer Weisgal (ed.), *The Letters and Papers of Chaim Weizmann*, volume VII, Oxford: Oxford University Press, 1968, p. 81.

7. Ibid.

8. The dialogue is recorded in Avi Shlaim, 'The Declaration that Changed History for Ever' (review of Geoffrey Lewis, *Balfour and Weizmann: The Zionist, the Zealot, and the Emergence of Israel*), (London: Bloomsbury 2009), *The Observer*, 28 June 2009.

9. University of Oxford, St Antony's College Middle East Centre, Samuel Collection GB165-0252, Samuel Collection, Breakup of the Ottoman Empire (Palestine) 14.2.15–20/7/20 DR 588.25, letter from Herbert Samuel dated 9 November 1914. See also Jonathan Schneer, *The Balfour Declaration, The Origins of the Arab Israeli Conflict*, London: Bloomsbury Books, 2011, pp. 107 and 155; and Adam Hogan, 'Zionism in the British Perspective: Settler Colonialism and Population Transfer in Palestine Mandate', PhD thesis submitted to the University of Exeter, 2021, p. 167.

10. Hogan, 'Zionism', p. 167.

11. John Bowle, *Viscount Samuel: A Biography*, London: Gollancz, 1957, p. 171. See the full correspondence in J.M.N Jefferies, *Palestine: The Reality: The Inside Story of the Balfour Declaration*, London: Olive Branch, 2016, p. 51.

12. Earl of Oxford and Asquith, *Memories and Reflections*, vol. II, Toronto: McClelland and Stewart, 1928, p. 65; see also Regina Sharif, 'Christians for Zion, 1600–1919', *Journal of Palestine Studies*, 5, 3/3 (Spring 1976), p. 129.

13. Ibid.

14. William M. Mathew, 'The Balfour Declaration and the Palestine Mandate, 1917–1923: British Imperialist Imperatives', *British Journal of Middle Eastern Studies*, 40/3 (2013), pp. 231–250.

15. www.haaretz.com/israel-news/2017-11-02/ty-article/.premium/the-love-triangle-that-changed-the-course-of-zionism/0000017f-e582-dea7-adff-f5fb9ed40000

16. The National Archives, London, 'The Future of Palestine', January 1915, memorandum by Herbert Samuel; see also Hogan, 'Zionism', p. 171.

17. Barnet Litvinoff (ed.), *The Letters and Papers of Chaim Weizmann*, volume 1, series B, August 1898–July 1931, Jerusalem: Transaction Books, 1983, pp. 122–124.

18. Peter Shambrook, *Policy of Deceit: Britain and Palestine, 1914–1939*, London and New York: Oneworld Academic, 2023.

19. Ibid.; Mayir Vereté, 'The Balfour Declaration and its Makers', *Middle Eastern Studies*, 6 (1970), pp. 48–76.

20. James Renton, *The Zionist Masquerade: The Birth of the Anglo-Zionist Alliance, 1914–1918*, London and New York: Palgrave Macmillan, 2007, pp. 4, 13.

21. Ibid., p. 15.

22. James Renton, 'Recognising Chaim Weizmann and Moses Gaster in the Founding Mythology of Zionism', in Michael Berkowitz (ed.), *Nationalism, Zionism and the Ethnic Mobilization of the Jews in 1900 and Beyond*, Leiden: Brill, 2004, pp. 129–151.

23. Ibid., p. 23.

24. Ibid., p. 38.

25. Ibid., p. 65.

26. University of Oxford, St Antony's College Middle East Centre, Samuel Collection, GB165-0252, Samuel Collection Break-up of the Ottoman Empire (Palestine) 14.2.15 – 20/7/20, DR 588.25, letter from Herbert Samuel dated 14 February 1915; see also Hogan, 'Zionism', p. 171.

27. The National Archives, London, CAB 42/6, G. 46; CAB 22/3 – December 1948 and War Committee debate on 16 December 1915.

28. Ibid.

29. Quoted in Allan Arkush, 'Max Nordau: The Post-Herzl Years', in Carsten Schapkow, Shmuel Schepkaru and Alan Levenson (eds), *The Festschrift Darkhei Noam*, Leiden: Brill, 2015, p. 236.

30. See   https:balfourproject.org/the-balfour-declaration-key-players-and-events-by-mary-grey/#https://balfourproject.org/427/

31. Mrs Edgar Dugdale, *The Balfour Declaration – Origins and Background*, London: Jewish Agency for Palestine, 1940, pp. 15–16; Weizmann, *Trial and Error*, p. 152.

32. Memorandum of Edwin Montagu on Anti-Semitism and the Present (British) Government – submitted to the British Cabinet, August 1917, www.jewishvirtuallibrary.org/montague-memo-on-british-government-s-anti-semitism

33. Ibid.

34. Ibid.

35. Ibid.

36. James Edward Renton, 'The Historiography of the Balfour Declaration: Toward a Multi-Causal Framework', *Journal of Israeli History*, 19/2 (1998), p. 111.

37. Neville Teller, 'The Balfour Declaration: Why Lord Balfour?', *Jerusalem Post*, 9 November 2017.

38. https://hansard.parliament.uk/Lords/1912-11-14/debates/5fe8924b-560b-47f8-8fea-00f48c8ce88f/ThePurchaseOfSilverForIndia

39. Read about the historiographical debate in Gizela C. Lebzelter, *Political Anti-Semitism in England*, New York: Holmes and Meyer, 1978, pp. 31–35, 108–162; and Bryan Cheyette, 'Hilaire Belloc and the "Marconi Scandal", 1900–1904: A Reassessment of the Interactionist Model of Racial Hatred', *Immigrants and Minorities*, 8/1–2 (1989), pp. 130–142. For more information on the line between economics and the Anglo-Jewish community, see Daniel Gutwein, *The Divided Elite: Economics, Politics and Anglo-Jewry*, Leiden: Brill, 1992.

40. Renton, *Zionist Masquerade*, pp. 73, 75–76.

41. Ibid., p. 96.

42. Albert Montefiore Hyamson, *Palestine: The Rebirth of an Ancient People*, London: Nabu Press, 1917.

43. Quoted in Schneer, *Balfour Declaration*, p. 209.

44. See more details in ibid., pp. 210–215.

45. Maryanne A. Rhett, *The Global History of the Balfour Declaration: Declared Nation*, London and New York: Routledge, 2015, p. 28.

4   Lobbying in Britain During the Mandate

1. www.jewishvirtuallibrary.org/quot-poalei-tziyon-our-platform-quot-ber-dov-borochov

2. See Sharett's archives, letter of Moshe Sharett to Berl Katznelson, 11 October 1923, www.sharett.org.il/cgi-webaxy/sal/sal.pl?lang=he&ID=880900_share tt_new&act=show&dbid=bookfiles&dataid=2596

3. Moshe Sharett, *London Days*, Tel Aviv: Moshe Sharett Heritage Society, volume 3, appendix 17; Poale Zion convention, Sharett's Report, 12/2/1921, *Contrass*, volume 78.

4. *Hansard*, https://hansard.parliament.uk/Lords/1912-11-14/debates/5fe8924b-560b-47f8-8fea-00f48c8ce88f/ThePurchaseOfSilverForIndia

5. Nur Masalha, *Expulsion of the Palestinians*, Washington DC: Institute of Palestinian Studies, 1992, p. 76, note 76; Jacques Kano, *The Problem of Land between Jews and Arabs*, Tel-Aviv: Sifriat Hapoelim, 1992, p. 46.

6. Carly Beckerman-Boys, 'The Reversal of the Passfield White Paper, 1930–31: A Reassessment', *Journal of Contemporary History*, 51/2 (2016), pp. 213–233.

7. See for instance Michael J. Cohen, 'The British Mandate in Palestine: The Strange Case of the 1930 White Paper', *European Journal of Jewish Studies*, 10/1 (2016), pp. 79–107.

8. Daily News Bulletin, Cables and News Dispatched by the *Jewish Telegraph*, volume 12, issue 82, 13 April 1931 (10 pages of speech).

9. Renton, *Zionist Masquerade*, p. 72.

10. Emphasis added.

11. Daily News Bulletin.

12. Ibid.

13. Winston Churchill, 'Zionism Versus Bolshevism: A Struggle for the Soul of the Jewish People', *Illustrated Sunday Herald*, 8 February 1920, p. 5.

14. Rosalyn D. Livshin, 'Nonconformity in the Manchester Jewish Community: The Case of Political Radicalism, 1889–1939', PhD thesis submitted to the University of Manchester, 2015, p. 91.

15. Ibid., p. 130.

16. Ibid., p. 6.

17. Masalha, *Expulsion of the Palestinians*, p. 76, note 76; Kano, *Problem of Land*, p. 46.

18. See Paul Kelemen, 'In the Name of Socialism: Zionism and the European Social Democracy in the Inter-war Years', *International Review of Social History*, 41/3 (1996), pp. 331–350.

19. Quoted in ibid, p. 338.

20. Ramsay MacDonald, *A Socialist in Palestine*, London: Jewish Socialist Labour Confederation Poale-Zion, 1922, p. 19.

21. Johan Franzén, 'Communism versus Zionism: The Comintern, Yishuvism, and the Palestine Communist Party', *Journal of Palestine Studies*, 36/2 (Winter 2007), pp. 6–24.

22. Andrew Sargent, 'The British Labour Party and Palestine 1917–1949', PhD thesis submitted to the University of Nottingham, 2003, pp. 15–16; Livshin, 'Nonconformity'.

23. *Hansard*, volume 135, columns 1438–1439, debate 2 December 1920.

24. Quoted in Harry Defries, *Conservative Party Attitudes to Jews, 1900–1950*, London and New York: Routledge, 2014, p. 126.

25. Bernard Porter, *The Lion's Share: A History of British Imperialism, 1850–2011*, London and New York: Routledge, 2014, pp. 223–224.

26. S.J. Goldsmith, 'Old "77" Leave London Scene', *The Jewish News* (New Jersey), 22 January 1965.

27. Ibid.

28. Yitzhak Elazari Volcani, 'Systematic Agricultural Colonization in Palestine', report presented at the 27th Zionist Congress, Prague 1933, published by the Zionist Central Bureau.

29. Quoted in Yoram Bar-Gal, *Propaganda and Zionist Education: The Jewish National Fund, 1924–1927*, Rochester, NY: University of Rochester Press, 2003, p. 12.

30. Daily News Bulletin.

31. An article by Berl Locker in the Hebrew daily *Davar*, 9 May 1958.

32. Nick Reynolds, *The War of the Zionist Giants: David Ben-Gurion and Chaim Weizmann*, New York: Lexington Books, 2019, p. 163.

33. Norman Rose, 'The Debate on Partition, 1937–38: The Anglo-Zionist Aspect: 1. The Proposal', *Middle Eastern Studies*, 6/3 (1970), pp. 297–318.

34. Litvinoff (ed.), *Weizmann*, volume 19, series A, January 1939–June 1940.

35. Dugdale, *Balfour*, p. 242; and see Michael Makovsky, *Churchill's Promised Land: Zionism and Statecraft*, New Haven: Yale University, 2007, p. 242.

36. The protocol was published in full by the newspaper *Yarden* (one of the few publications of the Revisionist movement in Palestine) on 10 June 1938.

37. Barry Kosmin, Antony Lerman and Jacqueline Goldberg, 'The Attachment of British Jews to Israel', *Institute for Jewish Policy Research Report*, 5 (November 1997), p. 3.

38. Goldsmith, 'Old "77" Leave London Scene'.

39. Kosmin et al., 'Attachment'.

40. Sharon Gewirtz, 'Anglo-Jewish Responses to Nazi Germany 1933–39: The Anti-Nazi Boycott and the Board of Deputies of British Jews', *Journal of Contemporary History*, 26/2 (April 1991), p. 263.

41. Richard Bolchover, *British Jewry and the Holocaust*, Cambridge: Cambridge University Press, 1993.

42. I discuss in full the debate between historians on this question in my book: Ilan Pappe, *The Idea of Israel: A History of Power and Knowledge*, London: Verso, 2016.

43. Tom Segev, *The Seventh Million: The Israelis and the Holocaust*, New York: Picador, 2000; Idith Zertal, *Israel's Holocaust and the Politics of Nationhood*, Cambridge: Cambridge University Press, 2005.

44. Attributed to Ben-Gurion (before the Second World War) by Martin Gilbert in 'Israel Was Everything', *New York Times*, 21 June 1987.

45. Antonio Espinoza, 'Allen Wells, *Tropical Zion: General Trujillo, FDR and the Jews of Sosua* (Review)', *Holocaust and Genocide Studies*, 24/3 (2010), pp. 488–491.

46. Louise London, *Whitehall and the Jews 1933–1948: British Immigration Policy, Jewish Refugees and the Holocaust*, Cambridge: Cambridge University Press, 2000.

47. Ibid.

48. All the quotations from this debate are from *Hansard*, volume 389, columns 1118–1204, debate 13 May 1943.

49. London, *Whitehall*.

50. This is taken from a website called Experiencing History: Holocaust Sources in Context; see https://perspectives.ushmm.org/item/letter-of-selig-brodetsky-and-leonard-stein-to-the-british-under-secretary-of-state-for-foreign-affairs

51. Paul Kelemen, *The British Left and Zionism: A History of Divorce*, Manchester: Manchester University Press, 2012, p. 35.

52. Ibid., p. 21.

53. Richard Crossman, *Palestine Mission: A Personal Record*, London: Hamish Hamilton, 1946, p. 61.

54. Ibid., p. 62.

55. Raphael Langham, 'The Bevin Enigma: What Motivated Ernest Bevin's Opposition to the Establishment of a Jewish State in Palestine', *Jewish Historical Studies*, 44 (2012), pp. 165–178.

56. Ibid., p. 165.

57. *The Times*, 14 November 1945.

58. James Vaughan, '"Keep Left for Israel": Tribune, Zionism and the Middle East, 1937–1967', *Contemporary British History*, 27/1 (March 2013), p. 3, note 16.

59. Ibid., p. 43.

60. Ibid., p. 3.

61. Norman Rose, 'Churchill and Zionism', in Robert Blake and Roger W. Louis (eds), *Churchill; A Major New Assessment of His Life in Peace and War*, Oxford: Oxford University Press, 1996, p. 160.

62. Quoted by John Newsinger, 'The Labour Party, Anti-Semitism and Zionism', *International Socialism*, 153 (3 January 2017).

63. Ibid.

64. Kelemen, *The British Left*, pp. 36–37.

65. Jane Power, 'Real Unions: Arab Labour Unions in British Palestine', Master's thesis submitted to Simon Fraser University, 1960, p. 77; see also on the 321

Ignition website an article, with no author name, on the topic: http://321ignition.free.fr/pag/en/ana/pag_003/pag.htm

5   Early Zionist Lobbying in the USA

1. Quoted in www.jewishvirtuallibrary.org/jsource/US-Israel/adams.html
2. Max Rodenbeck, 'Of Missionary Zeal and Its Consequences', *New York Times*, 23 August 2005.
3. See an article Stephen Sizer wrote for the Balfour Project website: 'The Road to Balfour: The History of Christian Zionism' (24 November 2012), https://balfourproject.org/the-road-to-balfour-the-history-of-christian-zionism-by-stephen-sizer-2/
4. David A. Rausch, 'Protofundamentalism's Attitudes towards Zionism, 1878–1918', *Jewish Social Studies*, 43/2 (Spring 1981), pp. 137–152.
5. Ibid., p. 143.
6. Yacov Ariel, *Evangelizing the Chosen People: Missions to the Jews in America*, Chapel Hill: University of North Carolina Press, pp. 14–19.
7. Norman W. Mathers, *Battle for Orthodoxy, American Religious Thought, 1870–1910*, Eugene: Wipf and Stock, 2018, pp. 78–79.
8. Quoted in David O. Beale, *In Pursuit of Purity; American Fundamentalism since 1950*, Greenville: Bob Jones University Press, 1986, p. 32.
9. Nicholas James Claxton, 'The Niagara Creed: Its History, Theology, and Relevance', paper submitted as part of PhD program to Bob Jones University, Greenville, 2019.
10. From Blackstone Library, Branford CT, CN 540, box 6, folder 9; see https://fromthevault.wheaton.edu/2020/07/01/to-show-kindness-to-israel-william-blackstones-memorial/
11. The text of the memorial is available at https://en.wikisource.org/wiki/Blackstone_Memorial
12. Ibid.
13. *Chicago Tribune*, 20 September 1867.
14. Ibid., 30 December 1868.
15. Ernst Ströter, 'The Second Coming of Christ in Relation to Israel', Addresses to the Second Coming of the Lord Delivered at the Prophetic Conference, Allegheny, PA, 3–6 December 1895, Pittsburgh, PA, n.d.
16. Quoted in David Borg, *Standing with Israel: Why Christians Support the Jewish State*, New York: Charisma Media, 2016, pp. 98, 107–109.
17. Ibid., p. 98.
18. Stephen Sizer, *Christian Zionism: Roadmap to Armageddon?*, London: Inter-Varsity Press, 2004, pp. 70–74.
19. Rausch, 'Protofundamentalism's Attitudes', p. 139.

20. Maidhc Ó Cathail, 'The Scofield Bible – The Book That Made Zionists of America's Evangelical Christians', *Washington Report on Middle East Affairs*, October 2015, pp. 45–46.
21. Ibid.
22. Walker Robins, 'Jacob Gartenhaus: The Southern Baptist Jew', *Journal of Southern Religion*, 19 (2017), https://jsreligion.org/vol19/robins/
23. Quoted in Lawrence Davidson, *America's Palestine: Popular and Official Perceptions from Balfour to Israel's Statehood*, Gainesville: University Press of Florida, 2001, p. 2.
24. George Antonius, *The Arab Awakening*, Beirut: Khayats, 1975.
25. See Ilan Pappe, 'Arab Nationalism', in Gerard Delanty and Krishan Kumar (eds), *The Sage Handbook of Nations and Nationalisms*, London: Sage, 2006, pp. 500–503.
26. Davidson, *America's Palestine*, p. 8, note 25.
27. Joseph M. Canfield, *The Incredible Scofield and His Book*, Vallecito: Ross House Books, 1988.
28. Quoted in Donald Neff, *Fallen Pillars: US Policy Towards Palestine and Israel since 1945*, Washington: Institute of Palestine Studies, 2002, p. 9.
29. Ibid.
30. Ibid., p. 10.
31. Quoted in Naomi Wiener Cohen, 'The Reaction of Reform Judaism to Political Zionism (1897–1922)', *Publications of the American Jewish Historical Society*, 40/4 (June 1951), p. 374, note 43.
32. www.jewishvirtuallibrary.org/louis-brandeis-on-dual-loyalty-libel-against-jews. This became such an iconic quote that it was used to decorate dinner plates; see www.brandeis.edu/library/archives/exhibits/ldb-100/zionism/dinner-plate.shtml
33. Another iconic quote of his, repeated on many occasions; see, for instance, David Wecht, 'Heed Brandeis' Call to be Better Jews', *Pittsburgh Jewish Chronicle*, 2 June 2016.
34. Yaakov Ariel, 'Eschatology, Evangelism, and Dialogue: The Presbyterian Mission to the Jews, 1920–1960', *Journal of Presbyterian History*, 75/1 (Spring 1997), p. 30.
35. See Weizmann to Louis Brandeis, 8 April 1917, in Leonard Stein (ed.), *The Letters and Papers of Chaim Weizmann*, series A, volume 7, London: Oxford University Press, 1968, pp. 505–506.
36. Zionist Archives, Jerusalem, Jacob de Haas Archives, Rothschild and Chaim Weizmann to Brandeis (cable), 21 April 1917 (received 25 April).
37. *New York Times*, 27 December 1917.
38. Davidson, *America's Palestine*, p. 15.

39. Ibid.
40. Quoted in Dan Fleshler, *Transforming America's Israel Lobby: The Limits of Its Power and the Potential for Change*, Washington: Potomac Books, 2009, p. 105, note 21.
41. American Jewish Congress, *Report on Proceedings of the American Jewish Congress*, Philadelphia, PA, 1918, p. 2.
42. Ibid., p. 3.
43. Ibid., p. 6.
44. Ibid., p. 28.
45. Ibid., p. 82.
46. Ibid., p. 54.
47. Ibid., p. 58.
48. Ibid.
49. Ibid.
50. Ibid.
51. Ibid., p. 21.
52. Quoted in James Loeffler, 'Nationalism without a Nation: On the Invisibility of American Jewish Politics', *Jewish Quarterly Review*, 105/3 (Summer 2015), p. 369.
53. Khaled Elgindy, *Blind Spot: America and the Palestinians, from Balfour to Trump*, Washington: Brookings Institution Press, 2019, pp. 5–6.
54. Donald M. Love, *Henry Churchill King of Oberlin*, New Haven: Yale University Press, 1956.
55. Davidson, *America's Palestine*, p. 6.
56. David Hapgood, *Charles R. Crane: The Man Who Bet on People*, New York: Xlibris, 2000, pp. 56–63.
57. Harry N. Howard, *The King Crane Commission: An American Inquiry into the Middle East*, Beirut: Khayats, 1963.
58. Andrew Patrick, *America's Forgotten Middle East Initiative: The King Crane Commission of 1919*, London and New York: I.B. Tauris, 2015, p. 237.
59. This is described in full throughout *America's Forgotten Middle East Initiative* (ibid.) and also appears in Lori Allen, *A History of False Hope: Investigative Commissions in Palestine*, Stanford: Stanford University Press, 2020, pp. 31–70.
60. Michael Reimer, 'The King-Crane Commission at the Juncture of Politics and Historiography', *Critique: Critical Middle Eastern Studies*, 15/2 (Summer 2006), p. 129.
61. https://balfourproject.org/the-king-crane-commission-and-palestine-1919/
62. Allen, *History of False Hope*.

63. Davidson, *America's Palestine*, p. 146, note 27.

64. Ibid., p. 4, note 13.

65. Quoted in Frank E. Manuel, *The Realities of American-Palestine Relations*, Washington: Public Affairs Press, 1949, p. 284.

66. Quoted in Charles Israel Goldblatt, 'The Impact of the Balfour Declaration in America', *American Jewish Historical Quarterly*, 57/4 (June 1968), p. 500.

6   American Zionists and the Holocaust

1. Department of State, USA, Office of the Historians, 'The Immigration Act of 1924', https://history.state.gov/milestones/1921-1936/immigration-act/

2. A statistic published in the *Holocaust Encyclopedia*; see https://encyclope-dia.ushmm.org/content/en/article/the-united-states-and-the-refugee-crisis-1938-41

3. Ibid.

4. Daniel A. Gross, 'The US Government Turned Away Thousands of Jewish Refugees, Fearing They Were Nazi Spies', *Smithsonian Magazine*, 18 November 2015.

5. Ibid.

6. Deborah E. Lipstadt, 'America and the Holocaust', *Modern Judaism*, 10/3 (October 1990), pp. 283–296.

7. See Patrick, *America's Forgotten Middle East Initiative*.

8. Neff, *Fallen Pillars*, p. 20.

9. Quoted in Samuel Halperin and Irwin Oder, 'The United States in a Search of a Policy: Franklin D. Roosevelt and Palestine', *Review of Politics*, 24/3 (1962), p. 322.

10. Ibid.

11. Nick Anderson, 'They Risked Their Lives to Rescue Scores of People from the Nazis. Few Knew Their Story Until Now', *Washington Post*, 19 September 2016.

12. Kathryn Perry Walters, '20,000 Fewer: The Wagner-Rogers Bill and the Jewish Refugee Crisis', MA thesis submitted to Virginia Polytechnic Institute and State University, 2019.

13. Aaron Berman, *Nazism, the Jews, and American Zionism, 1933–1948*, Detroit: Wayne State University Press, 1990.

14. See description at www.nypap.org/preservation-history/biltmore-hotel/

15. American Jewish Congress, 'Review of Year 5703', *American Jewish Year Book*, 45 (30 September 1943–17 September 1944), p. 207.

16. Hixson, *Architects*, p. 16.

17. Peter Novick, *The Holocaust and Collective Memory: The American Experience*, London: Bloomsbury, 2001, p. 43.

18. Ibid.
19. Neff, *Fallen Pillars*, p. 21.
20. Quoted in ibid.
21. Quoted in Hixson, *Architects*, p. 16.
22. Ibid.
23. Doreen Bierbrier, 'The American Zionist Emergency Council: An Analysis of a Pressure Group', *American Jewish Historical Quarterly*, 60/1 (September 1970), p. 83.
24. Daniel F. Rice, *Reinhold Niebuhr and John Dewey: An American Odyssey*, Albany: State University of New York Press, 1993.
25. Irwin Oder, 'The US and the Palestine Mandate 1920–1948', PhD thesis submitted to Columbia University, 1956, pp. 254–255.
26. Hixson, *Architects*, p. 18.
27. A very detailed scrutiny year by year of the allocations can be found in Marc Lee Raphael, *A History of the United Jewish Appeal*, Providence: Brown Judaic Studies, 2020, pp. 1–22.
28. Bierbrier, 'American Zionist', p. 84.
29. Raphael, *History*, p. 18.
30. Isaac Levitats, 'Pro-Palestine and Zionist Activities', *American Jewish Year Book*, 45 (30 September 1943–17 September 1944), p. 208.
31. Ibid.
32. Neff, *Fallen Pillars*, p. 21.
33. Bierbrier, 'American Zionist', p. 89, note 23.
34. Ibid., p. 89.
35. Leon I. Feuer, 'The Forgotten Year', *American Zionist*, LVIII (November–December 1967), p. 18.
36. Bierbrier, 'American Zionist', p. 90.
37. Ibid.
38. See www.bbc.co.uk/programmes/n3csw9gj
39. All this information is outlined in great detail in Bierbrier, 'American Zionist'.
40. Ibid., p. 91.
41. Quoted in ibid., p. 90, note 40.
42. Ibid.
43. Ibid., pp. 92–94.
44. Ibid.
45. Robert Skloot, '"We Will Never Die": The Success and Failure of a Holocaust Pageant', *Theatre Journal*, 37/2 (May 1985), pp. 167–180.
46. *Jewish Telegraphic Agency News Bulletin*, 12/223, 1 October 1945.
47. Ibid.

48. Ibid.

49. Ibid.

50. Ibid.

51. Samuel Halperin, *The Political World of American Zionism*, Detroit: Wayne University Press, 1961, pp. 183–185.

52. Hixson, *Architects*, p. 11.

53. Isaiah L. Kenen, *Israel's Defense Line: Her Friends and Foes in Washington*, Washington: Prometheus Books, 1981, p. 1.

54. Ibid.

55. Ibid.

56. Amikam Nachmani, *Great Power Discord in Palestine: The Anglo-American Committee of Inquiry into the Problems of European Jewry and Palestine, 1944–46*, New York and London: Routledge, 2005.

57. Leonard Dinnerstein, 'America, Britain, and Palestine: The Anglo-American Committee of Inquiry and the Displaced Persons, 1945–46', *Diplomatic History*, 4/3 (Summer 1980), pp. 283–301.

58. Hixson, *Architects*, p. 19.

59. Bierbrier, 'American Zionist', p. 100.

60. Halperin, *Political World*, p. 101.

7   Lobbying for Israel in Postwar Britain

1. Quoted in Ron Fuchs and Gilbert Herbert, 'Austen St. Barbe Harrison and the Representational Buildings of the British Mandate in Palestine, 1922–1937', *Architectural History*, 43 (2000), pp. 281–333.

2. Ibid.

3. Ibid.

4. Ibid.

5. Alan Cunningham, 'Palestine – The Last Days of the Mandate', *International Affairs* (Royal Institute of International Affairs), 24/4 (October 1948), p. 490.

6. See the description of these contacts in Avi Shlaim, *Collusion across the Jordan: King Abdullah, the Zionist Movement and the Partition of Palestine*, New York: Columbia University Press, 1988.

7. Ilan Pappe, *The Ethnic Cleansing of Palestine*, London and New York: Oneworld Publications, 2007.

8. Vaughan, 'Keep Left'; see also Cecil Brown, 'The British Labour Party and Palestine, 1917–1948', *Jewish Historical Studies*, 36 (1999–2001), p. 154; and Ian Mikardo, *Backbencher*, London: Weidenfeld & Nicolson, 1988, pp. 98–99.

9. Vaughan, 'Keep Left', p. 11.

10. Quoted in ibid., p. 13.

11. Ronnie Fraser, 'The TUC and the Histadrut, 1945–1982: A Problematic Relationship', DPhil thesis submitted to Royal Holloway, 1982, p. 71.
12. Ibid., pp. 236–237.
13. Ibid., p. 240.
14. Report from London in *Davar*, 13 November 1955.
15. See Avi Shlaim, 'Conflicting Approaches to Israel's Relations with the Arabs: Ben-Gurion and Sharett, 1953–1955', *Middle East Journal*, 37/2 (1983), pp. 180–201.
16. It was called Operation Black Arrow; see Benny Morris, *Righteous Victims: A History of Zionist-Arab Conflict, 1881–1999*, London: Vintage, 2001, p. 283.
17. Nigel John Ashton, *Eisenhower, Macmillan and the Problem of Nasser: Anglo-American Relations and Arab Nationalism, 1955–59*, London and New York: Palgrave Macmillan, 1996, p. 50.
18. *Observer*, 20 November 1955.
19. William Burns, *Economic Aid and American Policy towards Egypt, 1955–1981*, Albany: State University of New York Press, 1985, p. 45; Orna Almog, *Britain, Israel and the United States, 1955–1958: Beyond Suez*, London and New York: Routledge, 1985, p. 51.
20. See *Hansard*, debate 12 December 1955, https://hansard.parliament.uk/commons/1955-12-12/debates/1969970a-47b7-9a01-a79a73a01ec6/CommonsChamber
21. Ibid.
22. See Fraser, 'TUC', p. 34; Ronald Haym, *Britain's Declining Empire: The Road to Decolonisation, 1918–1968*, Cambridge: Cambridge University Press, 2006, p. 396; Stephen Howe, *Anticolonialism in British Politics*, Oxford: Clarendon Press, 1993, pp. 268–293.
23. Fraser, 'TUC', p. 38.
24. Ibid.
25. Quoted in June Edmunds, *The Left and Israel: Party-Policy Change and Internal Democracy*, London and New York: Macmillan Press, 2000, p. 56.
26. Ibid., pp. 42–46.
27. Todd M. Endelman, *The Jews of Britain, 1656–2000*, Berkeley: University of California Press, 2002, p. 235.
28. www.youtube.com/watch?v=69bNe_o7OIQ?__ref=vk.api
29. See the famous cartoon depicting the whole affair in https://socialistworker.co.uk/features/labour-in-cartoons-4-1957-aneurin-bevan-goes-nuclear/
30. For more on this, see Langham, 'Bevin Enigma'.
31. See the report in the Jewish Telegraphic Agency, www.jta.org/archive/bevan-urges-arabs-to-abandon-their-boycott-of-israel
32. Ibid.

33. Vaughan, 'Keep Left', p. 6.

34. Ibid., pp. 84–85.

35. Geoffrey Goodman, *The Awkward Warrior. Frank Cousins: His Life and Times*, London: Davis-Poynter, 1979, pp. 536–537.

36. I have explored this in detail in Ilan Pappe, *The Biggest Prison on Earth: A History of the Occupied Territories*, London and New York: Oneworld, 2017.

37. Liddell Hart Centre, London, Mayhew Papers, Volume 9/4, transcript of *Panorama*, recorded from transmission, 5 June 1967, also quoted in James Vaughan, 'Mayhew's Outcasts: Anti-Zionism and the Arab Lobby in Harold Wilson's Labour Party', *Israel Affairs*, 21/1 (2015), pp. 27–47.

38. Ibid.

39. Ibid., p. 30.

40. Ibid.

41. Ibid., p. 29.

42. See Omar J. Salamanca et al., 'Past is Present: Settler Colonialism in Palestine', *Settler Colonial Studies*, 2/1 (2012), special issue.

43. Vaughan, 'Mayhew's Outcasts', p. 29.

44. *Sunday Times* interview, 15 June 1969.

45. Philip Ziegler, *Wilson: The Authorised Life of Lord Wilson of Rievaulx*, London: Weidenfeld & Nicolson, 1993, pp. 340–341.

46. Vaughan, 'Mayhew's Outcasts', p. 39.

47. The National Archives, London, PREM 1, speech by George Brown, 21 June 1967.

48. A very thorough analysis of Brown's speech can be found in Arieh Kochavi, 'George Brown and British Policy towards Israel in the Aftermath of the Six Day War', *Israel Studies*, 22/1 (Spring 2017), pp. 1–23.

49. Moshe Gat, 'Britain and Israel Before and After the Six Day War, June 1967: From Support to Hostility', *Contemporary British History*, 18/1 (2004), p. 65.

50. Frank Brenchley, *Britain and the Middle East: Economic History*, London and New York: I.B. Tauris, 2001, p. 154.

51. *Maariv*, 2 November 1967.

52. See Pappe, *Biggest Prison on Earth*.

53. Gat, 'Britain', p. 67.

54. Ibid.

55. See Pappe, *Biggest Prison on Earth*.

56. Philip Rawstone, 'MPs Accuse Mr Brown of "Taking Sides"', *Guardian*, 23 June 1967.

57. Robert Philpot, 'When the UK's Left-Wing Prime Minister was One of Israel's Closest Friends', *Times of Israel*, 30 March 2019.

58. Ibid.
59. Ibid.
60. Ibid.
61. Ibid.
62. Ibid.
63. Quoted in Philpot, 'UK's Left-Wing Prime Minister'.
64. Harold Wilson, *The Chariot of Israel: Britain, America, and the State of Israel*, London: Weidenfeld & Nicolson, 1981, p. 2.
65. 'Wilson, True Friend of Israel', *Jewish Chronicle*, 7 October 2014.
66. All quotes are from Philpot, 'UK's Left-Wing Prime Minister'.
67. Wilson, *Chariot of Israel*, p. 123.
68. Kochavi, 'George Brown', p. 5.
69. Gat, 'Britain'.
70. Greer Fay Cashman, 'Selling Israel', *Jerusalem Post*, 26 November 1990.
71. Peter Niesewand, 'More Protests at PLO Visit', *Guardian*, 11 August 1975.
72. Vaughan, 'Mayhew's Outcasts', p. 31.
73. Ibid., p. 35.
74. Goodman, *Awkward Warrior*, pp. 536–537.
75. Based on Mayhew's papers at the Liddell Hart Centre, London, quoted by Vaughan, 'Mayhew's Outcasts', p. 36, note 101.
76. Ibid., p. 32.
77. Fraser, 'TUC', p. 646.
78. The National Archives, London, FCO 17/20, Foggon Minute, 5 January 1968.
79. Ibid.
80. Lord Home, *The Way the Wind Blows*, London: Collins, 1976, appendix B.
81. Ibid.
82. Ibid.
83. Parliamentary *Hansard*, 22 October 1973.
84. Lord Home, *Way*, p. 260.
85. Muhamad Hasrul Zakariah, 'British Foreign Policy on the Palestinian Question in the Middle East Peace Negotiations: From Conservative to Labour (1970–1979)', *International Journal of Academic Research in Business and Social Science*s, 8/11 (2018), p. 1080.
86. Ibid.; and see Lord Home, *Way*, and Zakariah, 'British Foreign Policy', p. 1074, quoting Parson on 24 October 1973.
87. Lord Home, *Way*, p. 258.
88. Paper prepared by Alastair Noble for the Foreign and Commonwealth office, n.d., www.diplomatie.gouv.fr/IMG/pdf/ONU_alastair_noble.pdf

89. See Rawstone, 'MPs Accuse Mr Brown'.

90. Eric Marsden, 'Anti-British Feeling Runs High in Jerusalem', *The Times*, 17 October 1973, p. 9; Eric Marsden, 'Bitter Attack on Britain by Mr Eban', *The Times*, 25 October 1973, p. 8.

91. The National Archives, London, CAB/128/53/14, cabinet meeting, 8 November 1973.

92. Ibid.

93. Zakariah, 'British Foreign Policy'.

94. Ibid., p. 1080.

95. Vaughan, 'Keep Left', p. 13.

96. Christopher Mayhew, 'Redressing the Balance', in *The Council for the Advancement of Arab–British Understanding: The First 25 Years 1967–1992*, London: CAABU, 1992.

97. *Yedioth Ahronoth*, 28 November 1976 (in Hebrew).

98. *Jewish Chronicle*, 29 March 1974.

99. Quoted in Vaughan, 'Keep Left', p. 17.

100. Uri Davis, *The JNF/KKL: A Charity Complicit with Ethnic Cleansing*, London: MEMO Publications, 2023.

101. Quoted in Philpot, *Margaret Thatcher*, p. 33.

102. https://api.parliament.uk/historic-hansard/commons/1974/oct/30/debate-on-the-address

103. James Callaghan, *Time and Change*, London: HarperCollins, 1987, p. 290.

104. Tim Bishop, 'The Question of Palestine in Harold Wilson's Labour Party, 1970–1976', *Webster Review of International History*, 1/1 (2021), p. 14.

105. Ibid.

106. Nigel Ashton, '"A Local Terrorist Made Good": The Callaghan Government and the Arab-Israeli Peace Process, 1977–79', *Contemporary British History*, 31/1 (2017), p. 116.

107. *Hansard*, 21 March 1979.

108. Joint declaration on 29 June 1977.

109. Ashton, 'Local Terrorist', p. 126.

110. *Issues and Answers*, 2 February 1975.

111. Parliamentary *Hansard*, 25 June 1975.

112. Quoted in Zakariah, 'British Foreign Policy', p. 1080.

113. Quoted in ibid.

114. Avi Shlaim, *Lion of Jordan: The Life of King Hussein in War and Peace*, London: Penguin, 2008.

115. Ashton, 'Local Terrorist', p. 123.

116. Zakhariah, 'British Foreign Policy', p. 1082.

117. Ashton, 'Local Terrorist', p. 123.
118. The National Archives, London, FCO 93/1562, letter from Owen to Moonman, 27 November 1978.
119. Telegram from Michael Tait in the British Embassy in Amman to London, quoted in *Jewish Chronicle*, 5 October 2012.
120. Philpot, *Margaret Thatcher*.
121. Azriel Bermant, *Margaret Thatcher and the Middle East*, Cambridge: Cambridge University Press, 2016.
122. Ibid., p. 44.
123. 'When Thatcher Turned against Israel', *Jewish Chronicle*, 5 October 2012.
124. Ibid.
125. Ashton, 'Local Terrorist', p. 126.
126. Ibid.
127. Ibid.
128. Bermant, *Margaret Thatcher*, p. 62.
129. Dana El Kurd, *Polarized and Demobilized: Legacies of Authoritarianism in Palestine*, London: C. Hurst and Co., 2019.
130. The National Archives, London, FCO 93/1562, G. Walden to the Minister and Defence, 23 September 1979.
131. *Guardian*, 27 May 1986.
132. This correspondence is covered in full in the excellent thesis by Fraser, 'TUC', pp. 195–202.
133. 'Israel Denies Torture of Arab Prisoners', *The Times*, 20 June 1977.
134. Amnesty International, *Amnesty International Report 2017/18 – Israel and the Occupied Territories*, 22 February 2018, pp. 207–211.
135. Colin Shindler, 'Media: New Moon's Guiding Light – Colin Shindler on a Magazine Aiming to Attract a Generation of Disaffected Jews', *Guardian*, 10 September 1990.
136. Jo Thomas, 'Britain Calls Off a Meeting with Jordan-Palestine Unit', *New York Times*, 15 October 1985.
137. Bermant, *Margaret Thatcher*, p. 132.
138. Quoted in ibid., p. 134.
139. Ibid.
140. Douglas Davis, 'Britain's BIPAC Israel Lobby Goes Bust', *Jerusalem Post*, 6 December 1999.
141. 'UK News in Brief: Prize for Article in Guardian/Lynne Reid Banks', *Guardian*, 18 June 1986.
142. Jay Bushinsky, 'Fatchett Meets PM Today, Arafat Tomorrow', *Jerusalem Post*, 14 January 1998.
143. Davis, 'Britain's BIPAC Israel Lobby'.

8   Lobbying for Israel in Twentieth-Century America

1. Charlene Mires, *Capital of the World: The Race to Host the United Nations*, New York: New York University Press, 2015, pp. 190–196.
2. 'The United Nations by the Waters of Flushing', *Time Magazine*, 12 May 1947.
3. See UN Archives, www.un.org/unispal/document/auto-insert-210902/
4. John Snetsinger, *Truman, the Jewish Vote, and the Creation of Israel*, Washington: Hoover Institute, 1974, p. 66.
5. David A. Friedman, 'Against the Experts: Harry S. Truman, David K. Niles, and the Birth of the State of Israel, 1945–1948', thesis, Whitman College, 2011.
6. Robert J. Donovan, *Conflict and Crisis: Presidency of Harry S. Truman, 1945–48*, Independence: University of Missouri Press, 1996, p. 330.
7. James Forrestal, *The Forrestal Diaries*, New York: Viking Press, 1951, pp. 330, 346.
8. Donovan, *Conflict and Crisis*, p. 331.
9. Ibid.
10. Ibid., p. 330.
11. See Simha Flapan, *The Birth of Israel: Myths and Realities*, New York: Pantheon Books, 1987, pp. 13–54.
12. For this part of the history, see Pappe, *Ethnic Cleansing of Palestine*, pp. 72–80.
13. See Ilan Pappe, *The Making of the Arab-Israeli Conflict, 1947–1951*, London and New York: I.B Tauris, 1994, p. 36.
14. You can watch the short speech at www.criticalpast.com/video/65675035917_US-Ambassador-Warren-Austin_UN-General-Assembly_Israel-Palestine-issue
15. Quoted in Hixson, *Architects*, p. 23.
16. Hixson, *Architects*, p. 23.
17. Harry S. Truman, *Memoirs: Years of Trial and Hope*, Garden City: Doubleday, 1955–1956, p. 158.
18. Hixson, *Architects*, p. 24, note 51.
19. Quoted in Peter L. Hahn, *Caught in the Middle East: The US Policy Toward the Arab-Israeli Conflict 1945–1961*, Chapel Hill: University of North Carolina Press, 2004, p. 50.
20. Hixson, *Architects*, p. 24; Irvine H. Anderson, *Biblical Interpretation and Middle East Policy*, Gainesville: University Press of Florida, 2005, p. 75.
21. Jeffrey Herf, *Israel's Moment: International Support for and Opposition to Establishing the Jewish State, 1945–1949*, Cambridge: Cambridge University Press, 2022.
22. See the full text of the telegram in Pappe, *Making*, p. 238.

23. See ibid., pp. 203–243.

24. Natan Aridan, *Advocating for Israel: Diplomats and Lobbyists from Truman to Nixon*, Lanham: Lexington Books, 2017, p. 37.

25. Hixson, *Architects*, p. 27.

26. Evan Wilson, *A Calculated Risk: The US Decision to Recognize Israel*, Cincinnati: Clerisy Press, 2008, p. 129.

27. Hixson, *Architects*, p. 29.

28. See Joseph Heller, *Superpower Rivalry, the United States, the Soviet Union, and the Arab-Israeli Conflict, 1948–67*, Sde Boker: Ben-Gurion Institute for the Study of Israel and Zionism, 2010, pp. 47–62.

29. Hixson, *Architects*, p. 30.

30. Ibid.

31. Doug Rossinow, "'The Edge of the Abyss": The Origins of the Israeli Lobby, 1949–1954', *Modern American History*, 1/23–24 (2018), p. 39 (there is a whole debate described in this article about who really founded the Congress, for those interested in such questions).

32. Hugh Wilford, *America's Great Game: The CIA's Secret Arabists and the Shaping of the Modern Middle East*, New York: Basic Books, 2013, p. 118.

33. Ibid.

34. Quoted in Paul Charles Merkley, *American Presidents, Religion, and Israel: The Heirs of Cyrus*, Westport and London: Praeger, 2004, p. 30.

35. Issac Alteras, *Eisenhower and Israel: US–Israel Relations, 1953–1960*, Gainesville: University of Florida Press, 1993, p. 258.

36. Hixson, *Architects*, p. 32.

37. H. Paul Jeffers, *The Napoleon of New York: Mayor Fiorello LaGuardia*, Toronto: John Wiley & Sons, 2002.

38. W. Brooke Graves, *Administration of the Lobby Registration Provision of the Legislation Reorganization Act of 1946: An Analysis of Experience During the 80th Congress*, Washington: US Government Printing Office, 1949.

39. Isaiah L. Kenen, *All My Causes: An 80 Years Life Span in Many Lands and for Many Causes, Some We Won Some We Lost, but We Never Gave Up*, Washington: Near East Research, 1985.

40. See Ilan Pappe, 'The Junior Partner: Israel's Role in the 1958 Crisis', in W. Roger Louis and Roger Owen (eds), *A Revolutionary Year: The Middle East in 1958*, London and New York: I.B. Tauris, 2002, pp. 221–244.

41. Cheryl Rubenberg, *Israel and the American National Interest: A Critical Examination*, Chicago: University of Illinois Press, 1989, pp. 329–377.

42. Hixson, *Architects*, p. 35.

43. Rubenberg, *Israel*.

44. Quoted by Hixson who mined Kenen's private papers; Hixson, *Architects*, p. 34.

45. Ibid.

46. Ibid., p. 36.

47. Amy Kaplan, *Our American Israel, The Story of an Entangled Alliance*, Cambridge, MA: Harvard University Press, 2018, p. 72; Michelle Mart, *Eye on Israel: How America Came to View the Jewish State as an Ally*, Albany: State University of New York Press, 2006, p. 176.

48. www.presidency.ucsb.edu/documents/speech-senator-john-f-kennedy-zionists-america-convention-statler-hilton-hotel-new-york-ny

49. See interview with Avner Cohen on the Wilson Center website, www.wilsoncenter.org/myer-feldman

50. Hixson, *Architects*, p. 38.

51. Memorandum for president, 'Your Meeting with Israel Prime Minister Ben-Gurion', 25 May 1961; State Department, 'Talking Outline for Subjects to be Raised by the President'; both in JFK Library, Boston MA, Papers of President Kennedy, President's Office Files, Israel, General, 1961–1963, Box 119A.

52. Shay Hazkani, 'Catastrophic Thinking: Did Ben-Gurion Try to Rewrite History?', *Haaretz*, 16 May 2013.

53. 'Myer Feldman, 92: Presidential Advisor and Special Olympics Official', *Los Angeles Times*, 5 March 2007.

54. See Alfred M. Lilienthal, 'J. William Fulbright: A Giant Passes', *Washington Report on Middle East Affairs*, April/May 1995, p. 50.

55. Ibid.

56. Ibid.

57. Ibid.

58. Hixson, *Architects*, p. 37.

59. Ibid., pp. 50, 92.

60. Grant F. Smith, *Foreign Agents*, Washington: Institute for Research: Middle East Policy, 2007, pp. 19–65.

61. Lilienthal, 'Fulbright', p. 93.

62. Josh Nathan-Kazis, 'Fledging Jewish News Service Rocks Boat with Strident Pro-Israeli Message', *Forward*, 28 June 2013.

63. Hixson, *Architects*, p. 37.

64. Lilienthal, 'Fulbright', p. 93.

65. Ibid.

66. Ibid.

67. Douglas Little, 'The Making of a Special Relationship, the United States and Israel, 1957–1968', *International Journal of Middle Eastern Studies*, 25/4 (November 1993), p. 111.

68. Quoted in Hixson, *Architects*, p. 44.

69. Ibid.

70. Ibid.
71. State Department, *Foreign Relations of the United States, 1964–1968*, vol. XVIII, document 333, memorandum from the president's special assistant (Rostow) to President Johnson, 15 November 1966.
72. Ibid.
73. 'Israel at 18: Partner in Progress', *Near East Report* (May 1966), p. B-4.
74. Shlomo Ben-Ami, *Scars of War, Wounds of Peace*, New York: Oxford University Press, 2006, pp. 125–127.
75. http://nationalhumanitiescenter.org/tserve/twenty/tkeyinfo/jewishexpb.htm
76. Quoted in Hixson, *Architects*, p. 50.
77. See the discussion in Pappe, *The Biggest Prison on Earth*, pp. 35–40.
78. Quoted in David Remnick, 'The Seventh Day: Why the Six Day War is Still Being Fought', *New Yorker*, 21 May 2007.
79. Martin Van Creveld, *The Sword and the Olive: A Critical History of the Israeli Defense Forces*, New York: PublicAffairs, 2002, p. 172.
80. Richard B. Parker, 'The June 1967 War: Some Mysteries Explored', *Middle East Journal*, 46/2 (Spring 1992), pp. 177–197.
81. The most recent analysis of the whole affair can be found in James Scott, *The Attack on the Liberty: The Untold Story of Israel's Deadly 1967 Assault on a US Spy Ship*, New York: Simon & Schuster, 2009.
82. See Philip Weiss, 'The Not-So-Secret Life of Mathilde Krim', *Mondoweiss*, 26 January 2018.
83. Rashid Khalidi, *Brokers of Deceit: How the US Has Undermined Peace in the Middle East*, Boston: Beacon Press, 2013; Naseer Aruri, *Dishonest Broker: The US Role in Israel and Palestine*, New York: South End, 2003.
84. Arno J. Mayer, *Ploughshares into Swords: From Zionism to Israel*, London and New York: Verso Books, 2008, p. x; and see Chomsky's interview with *Chronicles of Dissent* in 1992, https://chomsky.info/dissent01/
85. See https://jcpa.org/article/the-evolution-of-aipacs-political-operation-in-washington-over-50-years-an-eyewitness-perspective/
86. Walter L. Hixson, 'Dr Henry Kissinger: The Myth of the Great Statesman', *Washington Report on Middle Eastern Studies* (January–February 2022), pp. 33–45.
87. *New York Times*, 20 May 1972.
88. Naseer Aruri, 'The Nixon Doctrine and the Mideast', *New York Times*, 20 May 1972.
89. 'Voices for Peace', *Near East Report*, 12 (30 April 1969), pp. 34–35.
90. Peter Golden, *Quiet Diplomat: Biography of Max F. Fisher*, New York: Cornwall Books, 1992.

91. 'Statement by the President', *Near East Report*, 14 (4 February 1970), p. 54.

92. 'Convergence of US-Israel Interests', *Near East Report* (30 December 1970), p. 198.

93. Joseph Kraft, 'Those Arabists in the State Department', *New York Times*, 7 November 1971.

94. Ibid.

95. Mohamed Abdel Shakur, Sohair Mehanna and Nicholas S. Hopkins, 'War and Forced Migration in Egypt: The Experience of Evacuation from the Suez Canal Cities (1967–1976)', *Arab Studies Quarterly*, 27/3 (Summer 2005), p. 22.

96. Henry Kissinger, *White House Years*, New York: Simon & Schuster, 2011, pp. 431–432. See the in-depth analysis of the Kissinger and Nixon relationship on this matter in Gil Ribak, 'A Jew for all Seasons: Henry Kissinger, Jewish Expectations and the Yom Kippur War', *Israel Studies Forum*, 25/2 (Fall 2010), pp. 1–25.

97. Quoted in Hixson, *Architects*, p. 73.

98. Hixson, 'Dr. Henry Kissinger'.

99. Hixson, *Architects*, p. 44.

100. 'TheKissingerMemorandum',https://merip.org/1981/05/kissinger-memorandum-to-isolate-the-palestinians

101. Gerald Ford, *A Time to Heal: The Autobiography of Gerald R. Ford*, New York: Harper and Row, 1979, p. 240.

102. Yitzhak Rabin, *The Rabin Memoirs*, Berkeley: University of California Press, 1996, p. 256.

103. Ford, *Time to Heal*, p. 298.

104. Yitzhak Rabin, *The Rabin Memoirs*, New York: Little, Brown and Co., 1979, p. 261.

105. Arlene Lazarowitz, 'American Jewish Leaders and President Gerald R. Ford: Disagreements over the Middle East Reassessment Plan', *American Jewish History*, 98/3 (July 2014), p. 188.

106. Ibid., p. 189.

107. Ibid.

108. Laura Porter, 'Air Force One Lifts Off at 9:30 and He is Gone', *Telegram and Gazette*, 17 March 1977.

109. Ibid.

110. Ibid.

111. Janice J. Terry, 'The Carter Administration and the Palestinians', *Arab Studies Quarterly*, 12/1–2 (Winter/Spring 1990), p. 153; see also Arlene Lazarowitz, 'Ethnic Influence and American Foreign Policy: American

Jewish Leaders and President Jimmy Carter', *Shofar*, 29/1 (Fall 2010), pp. 112–114.

112. Jorgen Jensehaugen, *Arab-Israeli Diplomacy under Carter: The US, Israel and the Palestinians*, London: Bloomsbury Books, 2020, pp. 4–5.

113. Paul Findley, *They Dare to Speak Out: People and Institutions Confront Israel's Lobby*, Washington: A Capella Books, 2003; Paul Findley, 'Congress and the Pro-Israel Lobby', *Journal of Palestine Studies*, 15/1 (Autumn 1985), pp. 104–113.

114. A good summary can be found in David Samel, 'The Legacy of Joan Peters and 'From Time Immemorial', *Mondoweiss*, 17 January 2015.

115. Terry, 'Carter Administration', p. 154.

116. Farouk A. Sankari, 'The Effects of the American Media on Public Opinion and the Middle East Policy Choices', *American-Arab Affairs* (Spring 1987), p. 2.

117. Ibid.

118. Alan Hart, *Arafat: Terrorist or Peacemaker?*, London: Sidgwick & Jackson, 1984, pp. 440–441.

119. Lazarowitz, 'Ethnic Influence', p. 116.

120. Carter Presidential Library, Atlanta GA, Geographic File, box 12, Sanders to Carter, 6 March 1978.

121. State Department, *The Foreign Relations of the US, 1977–1980*, volume 1, document 14, editorial note, p. 572, quoting from Carter, *Public Papers*, volume 1, 1979, p. 314.

122. Jimmy Carter, *Palestine: Peace Not Apartheid*, New York: Simon & Schuster, 2007.

123. Ibid., p. 196.

124. Ibid., p. 44.

125. Ibid., p. 52.

126. Mearsheimer and Walt, *Israel Lobby*, pp. 130–158.

127. Quoted in the film *Kings of Capitol Hill*, director Mor Loushy, 2020; see www.docnyc.net/film/kings-of-capitol-hill/

128. Arnon Gutfeld, 'The 1981 AWACS Deal: AIPAC and Israel Challenge Reagan', *Mideast Security and Policy Studies*, 157, Ramat Gan: Begin-Sadat Center for Strategic Studies, Bar-Ilan University, 2018, p. 27.

129. Ibid.

130. 'The 1987 AIPAC Conference', *Journal of Palestine Studies*, 17/1 (Autumn 1987) pp. 107–113.

131. https://jcpa.org/article/the-evolution-of-aipacs-political-operation-in-washington-over-50-years-an-eyewitness-perspective/

132. Ibid.

133. Helena Cobban, 'The US-Israeli Relationship in the Reagan Era', *Conflict Quarterly* (Spring 1989), p. 25.

134. Ibid.

135. Findley, *They Dare*; Findley, 'Congress'.

136. Findley, 'Congress'.

137. Ibid.

138. Ibid.

139. Ibid.

140. Loushy, *Kings of Capitol Hill*.

141. Ibid.

142. Ibid.

143. Findley, 'Congress'.

144. Ibid.

145. Ibid.

146. Israel Lobby Archives, letter, 14 June 1982; see www.israellobby.org/reagan/

147. Israel Lobby Archives, letter, 14 March 1984; see ibid.

148. Cobban, 'US-Israeli Relationship', p. 13.

149. Israel Lobby Archives, Thomas A. Dine, 'The American-Israeli Alliance and the South African Problem', 4 October 1987.

150. Benjamin Beit-Hallahmi, *The Israeli Connection: Whom Israel Arms and Why*, London and New York: Pantheon Books, 1987, pp. 109–111.

151. Morris J. Amitay, 'A Field Day for Jewish PACs', *Congress Monthly* (June 1983), p. 11.

152. See the full documentation at www.israellobby.org/economy/

153. Ibid.

154. Ronald J. Olive, *Capturing Jonathan Pollard: How One of the Most Notorious Spies in American History Was Brought to Justice*, Annapolis: Naval Institute Press, 2006.

155. Amier Oren, 'Jonathan Pollard: The Spy Who Came in from the Street', *Haaretz*, 20 November 2015.

156. Charles R. Babcock, 'Dispute in Pro-Israeli Lobby Boils to the Surface', *Washington Post*, 21 December 1988.

157. Ibid.

158. Ibid.

159. Bernard Gwertzman, 'Reagan Administration Held 9-Month Talks with PLO', *New York Times*, 19 February 1984.

160. The law can be found at www.govinfo.gov/content/pkg/STATUTE-99/pdf/STATUTE-99-Pg190.pdf

161. Muhammed Abd al-Aziz Rabi, *US–PLO Dialogue: Secret Diplomacy and Conflict Resolution*, Miami: University of Florida Press, 1995.

162. See www.jewishvirtuallibrary.org/president-reagan-statement-agreeing-to-dialogue-with-the-plo-december-1988

163. See Babcock, 'Dispute'.

164. Cheryl A. Rubenberg, 'The US-PLO Dialogue: Continuity or Change in American Policy?', *Arab Studies Quarterly*, 11/4 (Fall 1989), p. 1.

165. 'PLO Observer Mission to the UN Remains Open', 100th Congress, second session, chapter 7, Foreign Policy; see https://library.cqpress.com/cqalmanac/document.php?id=cqal88-1142433

166. Douglass M. Bloomfield, 'Reagan Years Marked the Beginning of a Long, Roller-Coaster Ride for Israel!', *Jewish News of North California*, 11 June 2004.

167. See more recollections at www.youtube.com/watch?v=ZzkvXp4eihU

168. The book was published by Zondervan Publishing House in Grand Rapids, Michigan in 1970.

169. See the Pilgrimage Panorama website, www.itsgila.com/highlightsarmageddon.htm

170. Quoted in Nathan Krystall, 'The De-Arabization of West Jerusalem 1947–50', *Journal of Palestine Studies*, 27/2 (Winter 1998), pp. 11–12.

171. Erin Lauer, 'American Christian Zionism and US Policy on Settlements in the Palestinian Occupied Territories', Honours degree essay, American University, 2009.

172. Quoted in Jan Nederveen Pieterse, 'The History of a Metaphor: Christian Zionism and the Politics of Apocalypse', *Archives de sciences sociales des religions*, 36/75 (July–September 1991), p. 75.

173. See Jerry Falwell, 'Future-World: An Agenda for the Eighties', in Jerry Falwell, Ed Hobson and Ed Hindson (eds), *The Fundamentalist Phenomenon: The Resurgence of Conservative Christianity*, New York: Doubleday, 1981, pp. 186–223. For more on his role, see Merrill Simon, *Jerry Falwell and the Jews*, New York: Jonathan David Publishers, 1984; and Stephen Spector, *Evangelicals and Israel: The Story of American Christian Zionism*, New York: Oxford University Press, 2009.

174. See https://religionnews.com/1996/01/20/news-feature-palestinian-christian-cleric-asks-of-jerusalem-whose-land-is-i/

175. Mearsheimer and Walt, *Israel Lobby*.

176. See full report in William Rivers Pitt and Scott Ritter, *War on Iraq*, New York: Context Books, 2003.

177. Aruri, *Dishonest Broker*, pp. 127–148.

178. Mearsheimer and Walt, *Israel Lobby*, pp. 56, 58.

179. See John Judis, 'On the Home Front: The Gulf War's Strangest Bedfellows', *Washington Post*, 23 June 1991.

180. Lynn Teo Simarski, 'The Rhetoric of Reassurance at AIPAC's 31st Annual Policy Conference', *Journal of Palestine Studies*, 20/1 (Autumn 1990), pp. 92–100.

181. Ibid.

182. Ibid.

183. Ibid.

184. Kathleen Christison, 'Splitting the Difference: The Palestinian-Israeli Policy of James Baker', *Journal of Palestine Studies*, 24/1 (Autumn 1994), p. 42.

185. 'Baker's Ultimatum to Israel: "Call Us If You Really Want Peace"', *LA Times*, 13 June 1990.

186. Christison, 'Splitting the Difference', note 6.

187. Quoted in ibid., p. 45.

188. Quoted in Eric Cortellessa, 'How "Lonely, Little" George H.W. Bush Changed the US-Israel Relationship', *Times of Israel*, 2 December 2018.

189. Nathan Guttman, 'Mideast Mediator Martin Indyk Draws Ire from Both Sides of Israeli Spectrum', *Jewish Daily Forward*, 2 August 2013.

190. Christison, 'Splitting the Difference', pp. 39–50.

191. See a good report on the Association for Diplomatic and Studies and Training website: https://adst.org/2015/10/the-1991-madrid-peace-conference/

192. Jonathan Steele, 'James Baker: The Man Who Said No to Israel', *Middle East Eye*, 13 July 2021.

193. Noam Chomsky, 'The Responsibility of Intellectuals', *New York Review of Books*, 13 February 1967, www.chomsky.info/articles/19670223.htm. See also an updated version of this essay: Noam Chomsky, 'The Responsibility of Intellectuals, Redux: Using Privilege to Challenge the State', *Boston Review*, 1 September 2011.

194. David Ben-Gurion Archives, Sde Boker, David Ben-Gurion's diary, 27 October 1948.

195. Kenneth Waltz, *Theory of International Politics*, Berkeley: University of California Press, 1979.

196. Anne Thomas Sulton, *Inner-City Crime Control: Can Community Institutions Contribute?*, Washington: Police Foundation, 1991.

197. Jewish Virtual Library, www.jewishvirtuallibrary.org/president-clinton-speech-to-the-aipac-policy-conference-may-1995

198. Ibid.

199. Loushy, *Kings of Capitol Hill*.

200. See Institute for Advanced Strategic and Political Studies, 'A Clean Break: A New Strategy for Securing the Realm', 1996, https://web.archive.org/web/20140125123844/http://www.iasps.org/strat1.htm

201. 'Project for a New American Century (PNAC): A Complete List of PNAC Signatories and Contributing Writers', *A Think Tank Named PNAC (The*

Project for New American Century), FreePress.org, version placed on the website on 30 April 2004.

202. Quoted in Donald Neff, 'American Impatience Grows', *Middle East International*, 579 (17 July 1998), pp. 10–11.

203. Leon T. Hadar, 'Pax Americana's Four Pillars of Folly', *Journal of Palestine Studies*, 27/3 (Spring 1998), p. 56.

204. Ibid.

9   Lobbying for Israel in Twenty-First-Century America

1. See 'AIPAC, 18 Years Ago: Bush vs. Gore', *Jewish News of Northern California* (reproducing a Jewish Telegraphic Agency article from 26 May 2000), 7 March 2018.

2. Ibid.

3. Hixson, *Architects*, p. 96.

4. Ibid.

5. Daniel E. Zoughbie, *Indecision Points: Geroge W. Bush and the Israeli-Palestinian Conflict*, Cambridge, MA: MIT Press, 2014.

6. https://afsi.org/about-us/

7. James D. Besser, 'Washington Watch', *Jewish Journal*, 29 March 2001.

8. Peter Beaumont, 'Pull Back, Bush Orders Sharon', *Guardian*, 7 April 2002.

9. Mary McGrory, 'DeLay Diplomacy', *Washington Post*, 5 May 2002.

10. Mearsheimer and Walt, *Israel Lobby*, pp. 229–262.

11. Stephen M. Walt, 'On "Conspiracy Theories"', *Foreign Policy*, 26 March 2010, https://foreignpolicy.com/2010/03/26/on-conspiracy-theories/

12. *Haaretz*, 10 February 2002.

13. The text of the speech is at www.americanrhetoric.com/speeches/netan-yahu4-10-02.htm

14. His words are transcribed from C-SPAN; see www.theglobalist.com/before-iran-benjamin-netanyahu-to-congress-on-iraq/

15. https://edition.cnn.com/2002/WORLD/meast/08/15/peres.iraq/index.html

16. For sources, see Mearsheimer and Walt, *Israel Lobby*, pp. 233–238; see also Dov Waxman, 'From Jerusalem to Baghdad? Israel and War in Iraq', *International Studies Perspectives*, 10/1 (February 2009), pp. 1–17.

17. Quoted in Stephen M. Walt, 'I Don't Mean to Say I Told You So, But...', *Foreign Policy*, 8 February 2010, https://foreignpolicy.com/2010/02/08/i-dont-mean-to-say-i-told-you-so-but/

18. Eli Clifton, 'AIPAC's 2001–2004 "Briefing Book" Made Case for Regime Change in Iraq', *Lobelog*, 11 August 2015, https://lobelog.com/aipacs-2002-briefing-book-made-case-for-regime-change-in-iraq/

19. Quoted in ibid.

20. See Spencer S. Hsu, 'Moran Says Jews Are Pushing War', *Washington Post*, 11 March 2003.

21. Ibid.

22. Richard T. Cooper, 'Semantics Skirmish on 9/11 Report', *Los Angeles Times*, 26 June 2004.

23. Quoted in Martin Ortega, 'Iraq: A European Point of View', *Institute for Security Studies Occasional Papers*, 40 (December 2002), p. 9.

24. Mearsheimer and Walt, *Israel Lobby*, pp. 229–262.

25. John Prados and Christopher Ames, 'The Iraq War – Part II: Was There Even a Decision? US and British Documents Give No Indication Alternatives Were Seriously Considered', *National Security Archives Electronic Briefing*, 28 (1 October 2010).

26. Ibid.

27. Statement made on 19 March 2003.

28. Ibid.

29. David Singer and Lawrence Grossman (eds), *American Jewish Yearbook 2003*, New York: American Jewish Committee, 2003, p. 87.

30. 'War in Iraq Timing of AIPAC Conference Raises Concerns on How to Frame Message', *Jewish Telegraphic Agency*, 24 March 2003.

31. Ibid.

32. Ibid.

33. Ibid.

34. Dana Milbank, 'For Israel Lobby Group, War Is Topic A, Quietly', *Washington Post*, 1 April 2003.

35. Ibid.

36. Ibid.

37. Ibid.

38. Ibid.

39. 'War in Iraq Timing of AIPAC Conference'.

40. Milbank, 'For Israel Lobby Group'.

41. Ibid.

42. 'War in Iraq Timing of AIPAC Conference'.

43. Loushy, *Kings of Capitol Hill*.

44. 'War in Iraq Timing of AIPAC Conference'.

45. *New York Times*, 5 February 2004.

46. You can watch the speech on YouTube: www.youtube.com/watch?v=Jh PUvN4Z_Yg

47. Ibid.

48. Alternatively you can read the text at George W. Bush Administration: Address to AIPAC Policy Conference, *Jewish Telegraphic Agency*, 18 May

2004, www.jewishvirtuallibrary.org/president-bush-address-to-the-aipac-policy-conference-may-2004

49. The letter can be found at https://georgewbush-whitehouse.archives.gov/news/releases/2004/04/20040414-3.html

50. Theodore Sasson, *The New American Zionism*, New York and London: New York University Press, 2013, p. 41.

51. Dana Milbank, 'AIPAC's Big, Bigger, Biggest Moment', *Washington Post*, 24 May 2005, p. 14.

52. James Besser, 'AIPAC and Sharon Get What They Need', *Jewish Journal*, 26 May 2005.

53. Ibid.

54. Ibid.

55. Luke Mullins, 'AIPAC: Big but Not the Only Game in Town', *Roll Call*, 25 May 2005, https://rollcall.com/2005/05/25/aipac-big-but-not-the-only-game-in-town/

56. Milbank, 'AIPAC's Big, Bigger, Biggest Moment', p. 14.

57. Ibid.

58. Ibid.

59. Ibid.

60. AIPAC obtained most of the documents under the Act of Freedom of Information and they can be seen at www.israellobby.org/09092010/default.asp

61. Milbank, 'AIPAC's Big, Bigger, Biggest Moment', p. 14.

62. Ibid.

63. Mearsheimer and Walt, *Israel Lobby*, p. 24.

64. Aruri, *Dishonest Broker*, p. 37.

65. Barbara Ferguson, 'Hilliard Ousted in Alabama for Being Too Pro-Arab', *Arab News*, 27 June 2002.

66. I wish to thank my friend Iftah Shavit who brought this case to my attention and to Provost for granting me an interview on 25 August 2022.

67. Hixson, *Architects*, pp. 111–112.

68. Sizer, *Christian Zionism*.

69. Tim LaHaye, Jerry B. Jenkins and Sandi Swanson, *The Authorized Left Behind Handbook*, Carol Stream: Tyndale House Publishers, 2005.

70. Jeff McAllister, 'GameShark: Left Behind: Eternal Forces Review', *Gameshark.com*, 1 December 1007.

71. Stephen Jacobs, 'Simulating the Apocalypse: Theology and Structure of the Left Behind Games', *Online-Heidelberg Journal of Religions on the Internet*, 7 (2015), https://doi.org/10.11588/rel.2015.0.18509

72. www.washingtonpost.com/news/politics/wp/2018/05/14/half-of-evangelicals-support-israel-because-they-believe-it-is-important-for-fulfilling-end-times-prophecy/

73. www.daytopray.com/

74. 'Ninth Annual Prayer Day Unites Nations', *Miami Times*, 3 October 2010.

75. See its website: www.cac.org.il/

76. 'Israel Allies Foundation (IAF) – Washington DC', *Cause IQ*, 23 January 2020.

77. 'Knesset Christian Allies Caucus Celebrates Anniversary', *Y-NET*, 10 January 2008.

78. 'Sen. Ted Cruz Emerges as a Leading Defender of Israel, Wows Zionist Groups', *Fox News*, 2 December 2014.

79. You can now listen to the speech as well read its transcript at www.npr.org/templates/story/story.php?storyId=91150432&t=1657889817348

80. Hixson, *Architects*, pp. 111–112.

81. Chris McGreal, 'Goldstone Family Drawn into Row over Gaza Report', *Guardian*, 30 April 2010.

82. Richard Goldstone, 'Reconsidering the Goldstone Report on Israel and War Crimes', *Washington Post*, 1 April 2011; Hina Jilani, Christine Chinkin and Desmond Traver, 'Goldstone Report: Statement Issued by Members of the UN Mission on Gaza War', *Guardian*, 14 April 2011.

83. The speech can be watched on YouTube: www.youtube.com/watch?v=B_889oBKkNU

84. *Jerusalem Post*, 18 May 2010.

85. Barack Obama, *The Audacity of Hope: Thoughts on Reclaiming the American Dream*, New York: Crown Publishing Group, 2006.

86. Ibid.

87. Ibid., p. 334.

88. Ibid.

89. Ibid., p. 335.

90. Mark Landler, 'Comments on Israel by Top Contender for Defense Secretary Are Scrutinized', *New York Times*, 18 December 2012; Stephen Walt, 'The Art of Smear', *Foreign Policy*, December 2012, p. 2.

91. Ibid.

92. Ibid.

93. Ibid.

94. The text of the speech can be found at https://obamawhitehouse.archives.gov/the-press-office/2011/05/22/remarks-president-aipac-policy-conference-2011

95. Ibid.

96. Julian Borger, 'Eighteen Days in Vienna: How the Iran Nuclear Deal was Done', *Guardian*, 14 July 2015.

97. 'Iran Nuclear Talks: "Framework" Deal Agreed', *BBC Online*, 2 April 2015.

98. Julie Hirschfeld Davis, 'Pro-Israeli AIPAC Creates Group to Lobby against Iran Deal', *New York Times*, 17 July 2015.

99. M.J. Rosenberg, 'AIPAC Spent Millions of Dollars to Defeat the Iran Deal; Instead, It May Have Destroyed Itself', *Nation*, 12 October 2015.

100. Harriet Sherwood, 'Netanyahu's Bomb Diagram Succeeds – But Not in the Way the PM Wanted', *Guardian*, 27 September 2012.

101. James Fallows, 'A Headline Worth Studying in *The New York Times*; The Man Bites Dog/Dog Bites Man Conundrum Applied to Story Telling', *Atlantic*, 8 August 2015.

102. Eli Lake, 'Pro-Israeli Lobby Prepared to Battle Obama over Iran; AIPAC is Pushing Congress to Squash the Nuclear Deal, If There Is One', *Bloomberg*, 23 June 2015, www.bloomberg.com/view/articles/2015-06-23/pro-israel-lobby-prepares-to-battle-obama-over-iran

103. Borger, 'Eighteen Days'.

104. Rosenberg, 'AIPAC Spent Millions of Dollars'.

105. Paul Kane, 'Chris Coons and Bob Casey Back Iran Deal, Putting Obama One Vote from Major Diplomatic Victory', *Washington Post*, 1 September 2015.

106. In Karoun Demirjian and Carl Morelllo, 'How AIPAC Lost the Iran Deal fight', *Washington Post*, 3 September 2015.

107. Ibid.

108. Natasha Mozgovaya, 'J Street Opposes Palestinian Statehood Bid at UN', *Haaretz*, 8 September 2011.

109. See the Group's website: https://jstreet.org/about-us/myths-facts-about-j-street/our-support-for-israel/

110. Hilary Leila Krieger, 'J Street Goes on Offensive, Targets 2 US Candidates', *Jerusalem Post*, 13 July 2012.

111. Michael Abramovitz, 'Jewish Liberals to Launch a Counterpoint to AIPAC', *Washington Post*, 15 April 2008.

112. Hilary Leila Krieger, 'Muslims and Arabs Among J Street Donors', *Jerusalem Post*, 14 August 2009.

113. Bill Allison, 'How AIPAC May Win by Losing the Iran Deal', *Foreign Policy*, 11 September 2015.

114. Eli Lake, 'Soros Revealed as the Funder of Liberal Jewish-American Lobby', *Washington Times*, 24 September 2010; and see an extended discussion in Matthew Yglesias, 'The Controversy over Ilhan Omar and AIPAC Money, Explained', *Vox*, 6 March 2019.

115. *New York Times*, 26 September 2002.

116. 'Conservatives Launch Group to Attack Supporters of Obama's Israel Policies', *Jewish Telegraphic Agency*, 19 September 2009.

117. Adrienne Dunn, 'Fact Check', *USA Today*, 17 October 2020, https://eu.usatoday.com/story/news/factcheck/2020/10/17/fact-check-trump-quote-very-fine-people-charlottesville/5943239002/

118. Julia Ioffe, 'How Much Responsibility Does Trump Bear for the Synagogue Shooting in Pittsburgh?', *Washington Post*, 28 October 2018.

119. See their website's announcement: https://actionnetwork.org/petitions/call-on-aipac-to-withdraw-their-trump-invitation

120. Ibid.

121. See their website: www.ifnotnowmovement.org

122. www.facebook.com/events/188138268232957/

123. www.urj.org/press-room/reform-movement-response-news-donald-trump-will-speak-aipac-policy-conference#sthash.ZrYVW7wO.dpuf

124. https://facebook.com/fighttrump

125. This can be watched on YouTube: www.youtube.com/watch?v=2ZGgMJ3QDAQ

126. Rebecca Shimoni Stoil, 'Student Activists: AIPAC Won't Let Us Protest Trump', *Times of Israel*, 16 March 2016.

127. See the online article at www.politico.com/story/2016/03/aipac-trump-slams-obama-221081

128. Bess Levin, 'Trump: "A Lot of People Say" George Soros is Funding the Migrant Caravan', *Vanity Fair*, 31 October 2018.

129. See www.reuters.com/article/us-iran-nuclear-scientist-idUSKBN28710E

130. Tom O'Connor, 'Israel's Netanyahu Says on Video He Was Behind Trump's Decision to Leave Iran Deal', *Newsweek*, 18 July 2018.

131. See www.politico.com/story/2016/11/israel-donald-trump-bannon-231374

132. 'Steve Bannon Described US Jews as "Enablers of Jihad"', *Haaretz*, 5 February 2017.

133. 'Jewish Group Calls to "Reject Occupation" in Protest at AIPAC Conference', *Jerusalem Post*, 27 March 2017.

134. Ron Kampeas, 'In Search of Common Good: Snapshots from the AIPAC Conference', *Times of Israel*, 29 March 2017.

135. The speech can be watched on YouTube: www.c-span.org/video/?442121-1/aipac-conference-prime-minister-netanyahu-remarks

136. See www.972mag.com/chuck-schumer-thinks-theres-no-peace-because-palestinians-dont-believe-in-torah/

137. Ali Younes, 'Protesters Gather at the Start of 2018 AIPAC Conference', *Al Jazeera*, 4 March 2018, www.aljazeera.com/news/2018/3/4/protesters-gather-at-start-of-2018-aipac-conference

138. Reports and quotes from https://edition.cnn.com/2019/08/15/politics/aipac-ilhan-omar-rashida-tlaib-israel/index.html

139. Ibid.

140. Ibid.

141. www.brookings.edu/media-mentions/20190323-deutsche-welle-natan-sachs/

142. *Haaretz*, 17 March 2019.

143. www.politico.com/story/2019/03/20/moveon-2020-democrats-aipac-1229865

144. *Jerusalem Post*, 13 March 2019.

145. Ron Kampeas, 'Sanders and Trump Skip AIPAC, but Take Center Stage Anyway', *Times of Israel*, 3 March 2020, www.jta.org/2020/03/02/politics/sanders-and-trump-skip-aipac-but-take-center-stage-anyway

146. Ibid.

147. Ibid.

148. Andrew Silow-Carol, 'Who is King Cyrus, and Why did Netanyahu Compare Him to Trump', *Times of Israel*, 8 March 2018.

149. See https://twitter.com/AIPAC/status/1234239804734394368

150. Ron Kampeas, 'US Jewish Groups Express "Outrage", "Disgust" at DC Violence, Criticize Trump', *Times of Israel*, 7 January 2021.

151. www.adl.org/jan-6-insurrection-one-year-later

152. Kampeas, 'US Jewish Groups'.

153. Jacob Magid, 'AIPAC Defends Endorsement of Republicans who Questioned the 2020 Elections', *Times of Israel*, 18 March 2022.

154. Interestingly Miller said these words in defence of Chuck Hagel, the former American defense secretary, who said the same thing and was accused of being anti-Semitic. See Chris McGreal, 'Chuck Hagel "Not Antisemitic for Saying the Pro-Israel Lobby has a Powerful Voice"', *Guardian*, 7 January 2013.

155. Grant F. Smith, *The Israeli Lobby Enters State Government: Rise of the Virginia Israel Advisory Board*, Washington: Institute for Research, Middle East Policy, 2019.

10 The War Against American Civil Society

1. The quote is taken from Sarah Shulman, 'A Documentary Guide to "Brand Israel" and the Art of Pinkwashing', *Mondoweiss*, 30 November 2011.

2. Ibid.

3. The David Project, www.davidproject.co.uk

4. Ibid.

5. Ibid.

6. Ibid.
7. Quoted in Schulman, 'Documentary'.
8. Israel21c.org/about/
9. Schulman, 'Documentary'.
10. Ibid.
11. Reported in *Yedioth Ahronoth*, 27 July 2011.
12. Quoted in Gary Rosenblatt, 'Marketing a New Image', *Jewish Week*, 20 January 2005.
13. Ibid.
14. Ibid.
15. Ibid.
16. Ibid.
17. Ibid.
18. See their website: www.israelatheart.org
19. 'Calls to Boycott Batsheva in the Edinburgh Festival', *Haaretz*, 17 July 2012.
20. As reported in Schulman, 'Documentary'. *Globes* reported on 9 March 2011 that the Ministry of Education decided to invest 45 million shekels in furthering the campaign, and about $88 million dollars were invested in presenting Tel Aviv as the gay capital of Israel.
21. Schulman, 'Documentary'.
22. The report can also be found in English: Reut Institute, 'The Delegitimization Challenge: Creating a Political Firewall', www.reut-institute.org, 13 February 2010.
23. Interview with *Haaretz*, 28 November 2007.
24. Reut Institute, 'Delegitimization Challenge'.
25. Ibid.
26. This also exists in English: Jewish People Policy Institute, 'Annual Assessment 2010', Executive Report 7, p. 182.
27. Lea Landman, 'Winning the Battle of the Narrative', *Tenth Herzliya Annual Report*, 31 January–3 February 2010, pp. 56–60.
28. Peter Beinart, 'The Failure of the American Jewish Establishment', *New York Review of Books*, 10 June 2010.
29. Publicised by the Israeli Ministry of Foreign Affairs as a press report; see *Yedioth Ahronoth*, 22 October 2010.
30. www.inn.co.il/news/208624
31. https://machsomwatch.org/he/node/50455
32. Eitan Dangot, 'Strategies for Countering Delegitimization and for Shaping Public Perceptions', panel discussion, Countering Assaults on Israel's Legitimacy, S. Daniel Abraham Center for Strategic Dialogue, Netanya Academic College, 16 April 2012.

33. Rommey Hassman, *The Israel Brand: Nation Marketing under Constant Conflict*, Policy Paper, Hartog Harold School of Government, University of Tel Aviv, April 2008.

34. Ibid., p. 5. All quotations from this policy paper are my own translation.

35. Ibid., pp. 57–58.

36. B.Z. Itamar, 'This Is How the Truth Army of Israel Collapsed', *Seventh Eye*, 20 January 2021 (Hebrew); see www.the7eye.org.il/399982

37. www.youtube.com/watch?v=3lSjXhMUVKE

38. David Cronin, Sarah Marusek and David Miller, *The Israel Lobby and the European Union*, Glasgow: Public Interest Investigations, 2016.

39. Lauren Schmidt, 'Shagririm: Israel-American Ambassadors on Campus', *Jewish Press*, 5 May 2013.

40. Phan Nguyen, 'Who's Who Behind the Olympia Food Co-op Lawsuit', *Mondoweiss*, 22 February 2012; 'StandWithUs Invests Nearly Half a Million Dollars in Ongoing Anti-BDS Lawsuit against Olympia Food Co-op', *Mondoweiss*, 29 May 2015; 'Former Olympia Food Co-op Board Members Move to End Seven-Year Lawsuit over Boycott of Israeli Goods', Center for Constitutional Rights, 16 November 2017.

41. https://palestinelegal.org/case-studies/2017/3/9/fordham-bans-students-for-justice-in-palestine

42. #IStandWithIlhan.

43. Teresa Watanabe, 'Jews Target Caterpillar Shareholder Effort', *Los Angeles Times*, 13 April 2015.

44. Ian Lustick, 'What Counts Is the Counting: Statistical Manipulation as Solution to Israel's Demographic Problem', *Middle East Journal*, 67/2 (Spring 2013), pp. 189–190.

45. 'Prime Minister Office Hires Rightist Israel Advocacy Group for 1 Million Shekels', *Haaretz*, 13 January 2015; see also Nathan Guttman, 'StandWithUs Draws Line on Israel', *Forward*, 27 November 2011; 'Israel to Bankroll 1 Million NIS StandWithUS Venture', *Times of Israel*, 15 January 2015.

46. See its website: https://brandeiscenter.com/

47. https://thejewishnews.com/2018/11/06/brandeis-center-to-equip-law-students-to-fight-anti-semitism/; www.brandeis.edu/president/letters/2023-03-02-new-collaboration-to-combat-antisemitism.html

48. 'Pro-Israel Groups Question Federal Funds for Middle East Centers', *Inside Higher Education*, 18 September 2014.

49. Peter Schmidt, 'Supporters of Israel Say Programs in Middle East Studies Misuse US Funds', *Chronicle of Higher Education Blogs: The Ticker*, 17 September 2014.

50. Colleen Flaherty, 'Zoom Draws a Line', *Inside Higher Education*, 25 September 2020.

51. 'Statement by Jewish Studies Professors in North America Regarding the *Amcha* Initiative', *Forward*, 1 October 2014.

52. www.benjerry.com/about-us/media-center/opt-statement

53. www.thefire.org/news/anti-semitism-awareness-act-continues-threaten-free-speech-campus

54. 'Pro-Israel Groups Question Federal Funds for Middle East Centers', *Inside Higher Education*, 18 September 2014.

55. Desmond Butler, Tom LoBianco, Bradley Klapper, Chad Day and Richard Lardner, 'Witness in Mueller Probe Aided UAE Agenda in Congress', *Associated Press*, 26 March 2018.

56. www.thetower.org/article/open-hillel-is-a-much-bigger-problem-than-you-think/

57. 'Campus Pro-Israel Group "Monitored" Progressive Jewish Students', *Forward*, 25 September 2018.

58. John Nathan-Kazis, 'Canary Mission's Threat Grows, from the US Campuses to the Israeli Border', *Forward*, 3 August 2018.

59. 'US Website Using Hatred to Silence Criticism on Israel', *Arab News*, 23 October 2019.

60. Clayton Swisher, 'We Made a Documentary Exposing the "Israel Lobby", Why Hasn't It Run?', *Forward* 8 March 2018.

61. Bill Allison, 'Lawmakers Push for US Review of Al-Jazeera as Foreign Agent', *Bloomberg News*, 7 March 2018.

11   Lobbying for Israel in Twenty-First-Century Britain

1. Euan Ferguson, 'There Was Once a Jolly Man', *Observer*, 19 March 2006.

2. John Lloyd, editorial, *New Statesman*, 27 February 1998.

3. 'JC Power 100: Sacks Stays on Top, as New Names Emerge', *Jewish Chronicle*, 9 May 2008.

4. Lloyd, editorial.

5. Lord Levy, *A Question of Honour*, New York: Simon & Schuster, 2006, p. 123.

6. Robin Ramsay, 'Blair and Israel', *Lobster*, 43 (2002), www.lobster-magazine.co.uk/issue/43/. The £7million figure is also quoted in 'Blair Stands by Levy after £5,000 Tax Bill is Revealed', *Telegraph*, 26 June 2000.

7. 'JC Power 100'.

8. Levy, *A Question of Honour*, p. 103.

9. 'Lord Levy: Labour's Fundraiser', *BBC News*, 20 June 2000; Ramsay, 'Blair'.

10. Lloyd, editorial.

11. Quoted in Jonas E. Alexis, *Christianity and Rabbinic Judaism: Surprising Differences, Conflicting Visions, and Worldview Implications – From the Early Church to Our Modern Time*, New York: Westbow Press, 2012, p. 346.

12. Quotes from www.palestinechronicle.com/the-influence-of-israel-in-west minster/ and 'Labour Helped Abrahams Set Up Secret Cash Transfers', *Guardian*, 6 December 2007.

13. Ibid., p. 126.

14. Lord Levy, 'Honours Even', *Jewish Chronicle*, 16 May 2008.

15. Ibid.

16. Lloyd, 'Blair'.

17. www.opendemocracy.net/en/opendemocracyuk/pro-israel-lobby-in-britain-full-text/

18. Interview with Samuel Osborne in the *Observer*, 15 October 2017.

19. Quoted in Arjan El-Fassed, 'Tony Blair: A True Friend of Israel', *Electronic Intifada*, 29 June 2007, https://electronicintifada.net/content/tony-blair-true-friend-israel/7038

20. As phrased so accurately in ibid.

21. Ibid.

22. www.c-span.org/video/?c4765953/user-clip-bush-blair-crawford-texas

23. Ibid.

24. Rashmee Roshan Lall, 'Jack Straw Stands Up for Lebanon', *Times of India*, 31 July 2006.

25. El-Fassed, 'Tony Blair'.

26. 'Bolton Admits Lebanon Truce Block', *BBC News*, 22 March 2007.

27. http://kosharovsky.com/interview-with-martin-gilbert/

28. See www.martingilbert.com/gordon-brown/

29. 'Gordon Brown Promises to Back Israel Against Iran', *Guardian*, 28 July 2008.

30. Jonathan Freedland, 'The PM Who Understood Jews', *Jewish Chronicle*, 13 May 2010.

31. Ibid.

32. These figures were supplied by the Campaign Against Arms Trade; see https://socialistworker.co.uk/features/why-is-britain-supplying-arms-to-israel-s-war-machine/

33. https://socialistworker.co.uk/news/gordon-brown-gives-israel-a-licence-to-kill/

34. James Chapman, 'I Knew About the Scandal for Weeks, Admits Top Fundraiser', *Daily Mail*, 29 November 2007.

35. See *Jewish Chronicle*, 7 December 2007; and Nathan Jeffay, 'Magnate in UK Scandal: I Feared Charges of a "Jewish Conspiracy"', *Haaretz*, 7 December 2007.

36. Yasmin Alibhai-Brown, 'The Shadowy Role of Labour Friends of Israel', *Independent*, 3 December 2007.
37. 'Poll Cash Race Led to Secret Deals' *Guardian*, 14 March 2006.
38. http://news.bbc.co.uk/1/hi/uk/4564784.stm
39. Hugh Muir, 'Livingstone Faces Inquiry over Nazi Guard Jibe at Jewish Reporter', *Guardian*, 12 February 2005.
40. Adrian Milne and James Long, *Guinness Scandal: Biggest Story in the City's History*, London: M. Joseph, 1980; James Saunders, *Nightmare: Ernest Saunders and the Guinness Affair*, London: Arrow Books, 1988; Jonathan Guinness, *Requiem for a Family Business*, London and New York: Macmillan Press, 1979.
41. Quoted in Peter Oborne and James Jones, 'The Pro-Israel Lobby in Britain: Full Text', *Open Democracy*, 13 November 2009, www.opendemocracy.net/en/opendemocracyuk/pro-israel-lobby-in-britain-full-text; see also Stephen Bates, 'Sacks Accuses Synod of Bulldozer Ill-Judgment', *Guardian*, 17 February 2006.
42. Stella Korin-Lieber, 'Pujo Zabludowicz Mulls Risking Stake in El Al Parent', *Globes*, 4 February 2013 (in Hebrew).
43. www.theguardian.com/world/2009/jan/04/biscom-israel-lobby-poju-zabludowicz
44. See www.bicom.org.uk/wp-content/uploads/2016/01/BICOM-forecast-2016-FINAL.pdf
45. 'The Story of the CST: Jewish Community Protection in the UK', *Jewish News*, 7 April 2015; Geoffrey Alderman, 'Our Unrepresentative Security', *Jewish Chronicle*, 18 April 2011.
46. www.ihrc.org.uk/31838/
47. https://camera-uk.org/2015/09/09/the-guardians-chris-mcgreal-gets-it-wrong-on-israel-again/
48. Diane Langford, 'British TV Documentary Tackles Taboo of Israel's Lobby', *Electronic Intifada*, 18 November 2009, https://electronicintifada.net/content/british-tv-documentary-tackles-taboo-israels-lobby/8542
49. Quoted in Oborne and Jones, 'Pro-Israel Lobby'.
50. Lee Harpin, 'Hard-Left Attacks Labour Leader Sir Keir Starmer after Donation from Jewish Philanthropist', *Jewish Chronicle*, 20 April 2019.
51. Harriet Sherwood, 'Israel's West Bank Plans Condemned by Leading Jewish Leaders', *Guardian*, 5 June 2020.
52. Ibid.
53. Oborne and Jones, 'Pro-Israel Lobby'.
54. Ibid.
55. Ibid.

56. Ibid.

57. Jessica Hodgson, 'Editor Apologises for "Kosher Conspiracy" Furore', *Guardian*, 7 February 2002.

58. www.smh.com.au/world/middle-east/bbc-documentary-angers-israel-20030702-gdh0y2.html

59. Oborne and Jones, 'Pro-Israel Lobby'.

60. Ibid.; 'The BBC Spent £330,000 Suppressing Balen Report', *Jewish Chronicle*, 30 August 2012.

61. Oborne and Jones, 'Pro-Israel Lobby'.

62. Ibid.

63. The quotes are all from ibid.

64. Ibid.

65. Ibid.

66. Jenny Percival, 'BBC Refuses Airtime to Gaza Aid Appeal', *Guardian*, 23 January 2009.

67. Ibid.

68. Ibid.

69. Ibid.

70. johnpilger.com/videos/palestine-is-still-the-issue

71. This can now be watched on YouTube: www.youtube.com/watch?v=6BBjjJ0QHoY (this may not be viewable in your country).

72. Langford, 'British TV Documentary'.

73. Quoted in Peter Oborne, 'The Cowardice at the Heart of Our Relationship with Israel', *Daily Telegraph*, 12 December 2012.

74. Peter Oborne, 'Iran Nuclear Deal: Ill-informed Friends of Israel are Refusing to Face Facts', *Daily Telegraph*, 27 November 2013.

75. Speech by Conservative Party leader David Cameron to the Conservative Friends of Israel Annual Lunch held in London on 18 June 2009, https://thinkpress.files.wordpress.com/2009/06/200961914361_cameron-speech-18-june-2009.doc

76. Ibid.

77. Peter Osborne, 'Inside Britain's Israel Lobby', *Channel 4 Dispatches*, 16 November 2009

78. www.channel4.com/culture/microsites/D/dispatches/israel/proisraellobbypamphlet.pdf, p. 13

79. www.thejc.com/news/news/dispatches-israel-lobby-lm-the-reaction-1.12462

80. 'Jews and Muslims are Conservative Co-Chairs', *Jewish Chronicle*, 13 May 2010.

81. Ibid.

82. See Muir, 'Livingstone Faces Inquiry'.

83. See, for instance, 'Israel Is the Main Destination for MP Junkets, So Why Isn't Anyone Talking about It?', *Middle East Monitor*, 6 January 2017; Oborne and Jones, 'Pro-Israeli Lobby'; Ian Black, 'Pro-Israeli Lobby Group Bankrolling Tories, Film Claims', *Guardian*, 16 November 2019.

84. Ibid.

85. www.gov.uk/government/speeches/david-camerons-speech-to-the-knesset-in-israel

86. www.ochaopt.org/content/key-figures-2014-hostilities

87. www.jewishnews.co.uk/board-distances-itself-from-muslim-council-of-britain-over-muslim-brotherhood-links/

88. Asa Winstanley, 'Labour Friends of Israel Denies Funding for Israeli Spy', *Electronic Intifada*, 17 July 2019, https://electronicintifada.net/blogs/asa-winstanley/labour-friends-israel-denies-funding-israeli-spy

89. It was first reported in the *Guardian* on 22 May 2009 and removed on 15 July that year.

90. Summary of the Eleventh Herzliya Conference, *Haaretz*, 16, 17 and 18 September 2011.

91. www.runi.ac.il/media/ql4dtunc/legitimacy-brosh-2011.pdf

92. Reported in the *Huffington Post*, 17 July 2014, www.huffingtonpost.co.uk/2014/07/17/israel-gaza-nick-clegg-_n_5594357.html?1405607269

93. See https://yougov.co.uk/topics/politics/articles-reports/2014/08/05/sympathy-palestinians-more-common-britain-france-a

94. Hannah Ellis-Petersen, 'Tricycle Theatre Refuses to Host UK Jewish Film Festival While It Has Israeli Embassy Funding', *Guardian*, 6 August 2014.

95. Tony Greenstein, 'Gerald Kaufman – From Labour Zionist to Israel's Bitterest Critic', *Mondoweiss*, 17 March 2017, https://mondoweiss.net/2017/03/kaufman-zionist-bitterest/

96. Rowena Mason, 'Gerald Kaufman's "Jewish Money" Remark Condemned by Corbyn', *Guardian*, 3 November 2015.

97. Gloria Tessler, 'Obituary: Gerald Kaufman', *Jewish Chronicle*, 13 March 2017.

98. https://thetab.com/uk/bristol/2017/02/21/bristol-lecturer-investigated-university-anti-semitic-statements-28660

99. https://ms-my.facebook.com/StandWithUs/posts/10158886641672689

100. Anshel Pfeffer, 'UK Anti-Semitism Report Highlights Disturbing Trend – Among British Jews', *Haaretz*, 14 January 2014.

101. Hilary Aked, 'Critics Banned, Islamophobes Welcomed at "We Believe in Israel" UK Conference', *Electronic Intifada*, 17 March 2005, https://

electronicintifada.net/blogs/hilary-aked/critics-banned-islamophobes-welcomed-we-believe-israel-uk-conference. As this book was being written, Hilary Aked's excellent book on this phenomenon appeared: Hilary Aked, *Israel's Friends: The Backlash Against Palestine Solidarity*, London and New York: Verso, 2023.

102. Rowena Mason, '*Jewish Chronicle* Accuses Corbyn of Associating with Holocaust Deniers', *Guardian*, 13 August 2015.

103. Sarah Marsh, 'Corybn Apologises over Event Where Israel was Compared to Nazis', *Guardian*, 1 August 2018.

104. Lee Harpin, 'Board President: Corbyn has "Declared War on Jews"', *Jewish Chronicle*, 22 August 2018.

105. Ibid.

106. www.ucl.ac.uk/european-institute/news/2019/sep/jacob-rees-moggs-alarming-cry-illuminati

107. Ibid.

108. www.independent.co.uk/news/uk/politics/jacob-rees-mogg-afd-germany-far-right-twitter-brexit-alice-weidel-a8848826.html

109. www.bbc.co.uk/news/uk-politics-39443891

110. Klaus Polkehn, 'The Secret Contacts: Zionism and Nazi Germany, 1933–1941', *Journal of Palestine Studies*, 5/3–4 (Spring–Summer 1976), pp. 54–82; Joesph Massad, 'Zionism, Anti-Semitism and Colonialism', *Al Jazeera*, 24 December 2012.

111. Heather Stewart and Andrew Sparrow, 'Jeremy Corbyn: I Used the Term "Zionist" in Accurate Political Sense', *Guardian*, 24 August 2018.

112. www.bbc.co.uk/news/uk-politics-45301548

113. Heather Stewart and Sarah Marsh, 'Jewish Leaders Demand Explanation over Corbyn Book Foreword', *Guardian*, 1 May 2019.

114. Asa Winstanley, 'We "Slaughtered" Jeremy Corbyn, Says Israel's Lobbyist', *Electronic Intifada*, 10 January 2020.

115. www.opendemocracy.net/en/opendemocracyuk/labour-should-ditch-ihra-working-definition-of-antisemitism-altogether/

116. Dan Sabbagh, 'Hodge Urges Corbyn to Rebuild Trust after Labour Antisemitism Row', *Guardian*, 5 September 2018.

117. Chakrabarti Inquiry, 30 June 2016, https://labour.org.uk/wp-content/uploads/2017/10/Chakrabarti-Inquiry-Report-30June16.pdf

118. Ibid.

119. Marcus Dysch, 'Anger as Labour Leader Jeremy Corbyn Hands Shami Chakrabarti a Peerage', *Jewish Chronicle*, 4 August 2016.

120. Ibid.

121. Peter Walker and Jessica Elgot, 'Jeremy Corbyn Rejects Overall Findings of EHRC Report on Antisemitism in Labour', *Guardian*, 29 October 2020.

122. Asa Winstanley, 'Leaks Show How Labour Sabotaged Corbyn', *Electronic Intifada*, 17 April 2020, https://electronicintifada.net/blogs/asa-winstanley/leaks-show-how-labour-sabotaged-corbyn

123. www.bbc.co.uk/news/uk-politics-54742096

124. www.politicshome.com/news/article/jeremy-corbyn-ally-who-dismissed-antisemitism-allegations-is-reelected-onto-labours-ruling-body

125. https://electronicintifada.net/blogs/asa-winstanley/we-slaughtered-jeremy-corbyn-says-israel-lobbyist

126. www.jewishvoiceforlabour.org.uk/article/corbynism-and-chanukah-a-response-to-joe-glasman/

127. 'After Corbyn, UK Labour Elects Keir Starmer, Zionist with Jewish Wife, as Leader', *Times of Israel*, 4 April 2020.

128. Ibid.

129. www.jewishnews.co.uk/labour-suspends-vice-chair-of-local-party-over-starmers-jewish-wife-remark/

130. Ibid.

131. Jack Wallis Simons, 'Israel Is Not an Apartheid State, Says Keir Starmer as He Apologises for Corbyn Years', *Jewish Chronicle*, 7 April 2022.

132. Lee Harpin, 'Angela Rayner Apologises for Praising Controversial Holocaust Book', *Jewish Chronicle*, 28 November 2018.

133. Zaher Birawi and Robert Andrews, 'Keir Starmer as Labour Party Leader: What This Means for Palestine', *Middle East Monitor*, 14 April 2020.

134. Ibid.

135. https://cfoi.co.uk/informed-year-in-review-2021/

136. Ben Weich, 'Board Demands Labour Candidates Sign Up to "Pledges"', *Jewish Chronicle*, 10 January 2020.

137. Birawi and Andrews, 'Keir Starmer'.

138. https://jewishmanchester.org/tag/general-synod/

139. https://bdsmovement.net/news/church-england-'backfires'

140. Ibid.

141. https://nj.com/opinion/2020/01/bds-is-anti-zionist-not-anti-semitic-opinion.html

142. See Pappe, *Ethnic Cleansing of Palestine*.

143. The Balfour Project reports on these activities: https://balfourproject.org/

144. Bill Mullen and Ashley Dawson, *Against Apartheid: The Case of Boycotting Israeli Universities,* London: Haymarket Books, 2015, p. 32; Jens Hanssen and Amal N. Ghazal, *The Oxford Handbook of Contemporary Middle*

Eastern and North African History, New York: Oxford University Press, 2020, p. 693.

145. See PACBI Statement: NATFHE Leads the Way in Moral Responsibility: British Academics Vote for Boycotting Israeli Apartheid, 29 May 2006.

146. Ibid.

147. NUT's annual conference decision; see https://web.archive.org/web/20140723190455/http://www.teachers.org.uk/files/nut-final-agenda.pdf

148. On the new language and its implications see Noam Chomsky and Ilan Pappe, *On Palestine*, London: Penguin Books, 2010.

149. In a similar way the firm Puma was targeted. By 2018, the pressure bore fruit with regard to Adidas; see https://bdsmovement.net/news/team-justice-scores-adidas-no-longer-sponsoring-israel-football-association

150. Harriet Sherwood, 'Israel Accused of Pillaging Dead Sea Resources in Occupied Territory', *Guardian*, 3 September 2012.

151. 'Boycott Movement Claims Victory as Veolia Ends All Investment in Israel', *Newsweek*, 9 January 2015.

152. Michael Deas, 'Sheffield University Dumps Veolia, Capping Successful Year for UK Student Palestine Movement', *Electronic Intifada*, 3 May 2013.

153. Ibid.

154. Paul Di Stefano and Mostafa Henaway, 'Boycotting Apartheid from South Africa to Palestine', *Peace Review*, 26/1 (2014), p. 23.

155. See report by the Palestine BDS National Committee/UK, 2 December 2016, https://bdsmovement.net/news/2016-bds-impact-round-up

156. See G4S timeline on the BDS UK website: https://bdsmovement.net/g4s-timeline

157. On the LSE boycott, see https://bdsmovement.net/news/london-school-economics-joins-boycott-eden-springs; and on the Ecostream boycott, see https://corporatewatch.org/ecostream-campaign-victorious/

158. See Stop the JNF Media Release, 20 May 2013, www.stopthejnf.org/charity-commission-to-investigate-whether-jnf-racial-discrimination-is-lawful/

159. Scottish Palestine Solidarity Campaign announcement, 26 April 2013, https://bdsmovement.net/tags/uk?page=3

160. 'Jeremy Corbyn Backs Boycott of Israeli Universities Involved in Arms Research', *Electronic Intifada*, 2 August 2015, https://electronicintifada.net/blogs/asa-winstanley/jeremy-corbyn-backs-boycott-israeli-universities-involved-arms-research

161. Ibid.

162. Ibid.

163. Deas, 'Sheffield University'.

164. Press release by Students for Justice in Palestine (Edinburgh University), 'Edinburgh University Students Vote Overwhelmingly for Boycott of Israeli Goods', 16 March 2011.

165. Report by Ben White, https://bdsmovement.net/news/black-students-conference-uk-national-union-students-endorses-bds

166. Jamie Doward, 'British Arms Sales to Israel Face High Court Challenge', *Observer*, 16 August 2014.

167. 'UK Labour Party Votes to Stop Arms Trade with Israel, Apply International Law to Trade, and Support Refugee Return', *Electronic Intifada*, 23 September 2019, see on the BDS website: https://bdsmovement.net/news/uk-labour-party-votes-stop-arms-trade-israel-apply-international-law-trade-and-support-refugee

168. Ibid.

169. Ibid.

170. See the full BDS report and reasoning at https://bdsmovement.net/military-embargo

171. Palestine BDS National Committee (BNC) and Scottish Palestine Solidarity Campaign (SPSC), 'Glasgow City Council Concedes to Supporters of Palestinian Rights, Vows to Refrain from Sponsoring Future Arms Fairs', 27 July 2018, https://bdsmovement.net/news/glasgow-city-council-concedes-supporters-palestinian-rights-vows-refrain-sponsoring-future-arms#:~:text=Glasgow%20City%20Council%20promises%20supporters,a%20human%20rights%20respecting%20city.%E2%80%9D

172. An even more accurate assessment can be found in the updated reports at https://caat.org.uk/resources/countries/israel/

173. The whole affair is described in detail in 'UK High Court Rules in Favour of Local Councils who Support Boycott of Israeli Occupation', *Middle East Eye*, 29 July 2016, www.middleeasteye.net/news/uk-court-dismisses-call-ban-council-boycotts-israeli-settlement-goods

174. Benjamin Kentish, 'Boris Johnson Government to Ban Boycotting Israel and Other Countries, in Crackdown on BDS Movement', *Independent*, 19 December 2019.

175. https://blogs.soas.ac.uk/cop/wp-content/uploads/2021/06/Pro-Palestine-Activism-and-Prevent-2.pdf

176. Ali Abunimah, 'University of Southampton Cancels Conference after Government, Israel Lobby Pressure', *Electronic Intifada*, 31 March 2015, https://electronicintifada.net/blogs/ali-abunimah/univ-southampton-cancels-conference-after-government-israel-lobby-pressure

177. Areeb Ullah, 'Revealed: UK Universities Accused of Closing Down Free Speech on Palestine', *Middle East Eye*, 25 November 2017, www.middleeast-

eye.net/news/revealed-uk-universities-accused-closing-down-free-speech-palestine

178. 'Labour Adopts IHRA Anti-Semitism Definition in Full', *Guardian*, 4 September 2018.
179. https://gal-dem.com/universities-ihra-guidelines-palestine/
180. See Bill at https://bills.parliament.uk/bills/3475

Conclusion

1. A letter to Helli shown to me by Finn Lunker; I am very grateful to him. The full quote is: 'In Paris, Döblin horrified me by proclaiming a Jewish state, with its own soil, bought from Wall Street. Concerned about their sons, everyone (including Zweig here) is now clinging to land speculation. Hitler has thus fascized [i.e. turned into fascists – FL] not only the Germans but also the Jews'.
2. Victor Klemperer, *I Will Bear Witness 1933–41, A Diary of the Nazi Years*, New York: Modern Library, 1999, pp. 291–292.
3. Yosef Gorny, 'Thoughts on Zionism as a Utopian Ideology', *Modern Judaism*, 18/3 (October 1998), pp. 241–251.
4. Mearsheimer and Walt, *Israel Lobby*, p. 130.
5. www.maariv.co.il/news/israel/Article-964744
6. Ben Samuels, 'Former US Ambassadors: Time to Reconsider Military Assistance to Israel', *Haaretz*, 22 July 2023.

Index

Abbas, Mahmoud 342, 436
Abd al-Hamid II, Sultan 18, 29
Abdullah I of Jordan, King 159, 161, 204
Aberdeen, Lord 55
Abourezk, James 283
Abraham Accords (2020) 252
Abrahams, David 433–4, 443, 444
Abrams, Elliot 335
Abu Akleh, Shireen 429
Abu Iyad 301
Abu Jihad 301
Abu-Lughod, Ibrahim 321
Abu Lutuf 197
academia vii–ix, 145–6, 323–4, 414–17
    and BDS 495–7
    and peace process 325–6
Acheson, Dean 225
Adams, John 94
Adams, Michael 185
Adidas 491–2
Adler, Chief Rabbi Dr Hermann 17–18, 22, 26
AET (American Educational Trust) 386
Afghanistan 346, 427
AFME (American Friends of the Middle East) 235
Africa 168; see also Egypt; South Africa
African Americans 356, 362, 393–4
African National Congress (ANC) 213, 395
AFSI (Americans for a Safe Israel) 340–1
Aharoni, Ido 409

Ahava 492
Ainley, Ben 67
AIPAC (American Israel Public Affairs Committee) xvi, 29, 237–43, 386, 429–30
    and African Americans 393–4
    and anti-Israel targeting 362
    and AZEC 137, 141
and Baker 322
    and Biden 402–3
    and Bush Sr 312–13
    and Carter 276–7, 278, 279, 280–4
    and Clinton 332–7
    and conferences 315–22, 359–61
    and Congress 261–2, 263–4
    and espionage 297–9
    and Ford 272–3
    and Fulbright 247–8, 249–51
    and Greater Israel 258–61
    and Iran nuclear deal 380–3
    and Iraq War 343–5, 346–8, 348–53
    and Israel loyalty 290–2
    and Johnson 252
    and Lebanon 294
    and Likud 322–3
    and The Lobby 419, 428–9
    and local government 403–4
    and 1967 war 254–7
    and Obama 370–1, 372–3, 374–8
    and Palestine 319–20
    and peace process 324
    and PLO 300–5, 314–15
    and Reagan 286–90, 295–6
    and resignations 299–300
    and Rogers Plan 264–5
    and Sharon 357–9
    and trade unions 142
    and Trump 388, 390–3, 394–401

    and 2000 election 338–9
AJA (Anglo-Jewish Association) 49
Akehurst, Luke 482
Akzin, Benjamin 154
Al Jazeera 419, 428–9, 464–5
Albright, Madeleine 323
Alexander II of Russia, Tsar 15
Alexander, David Lindo 49, 53
Algeria 187
Ali, Muhammad 7, 8, 9
Alibhai-Brown, Yasmin 444
Aliens Act (1905) 32
Allen, Lori 123
Alpha project 164–5, 233
Ambassadors, The (TV show) 411
AMCHA 424–5
American civil society 261, 301–2, 350, 356, 363–4
American Council for Judaism 154–5, 235
American Jewish Committee 106–7, 113, 119, 154, 272, 402
American Jewish Conference 140
American Jewish Congress 112–20, 123, 136, 139–40
American Palestine Committee 127, 138, 144–5, 229
American Zionist Federation 110–11, 123, 130–1
Amery, Leopold Charles Maurice Stennett 71
Amitay, Morris 281, 289, 297, 349
Amnesty International 214, 442, 510
Amran, David Werner 115
Andover Seminary (MA) 104–5

Andrews, Eamonn 189
Anglo-Jewish community
    44–52, 66, 79–82, 449–50
Anglo-Palestine Bank 76
Anti-Defamation League
    257–8, 281, 291, 350, 402
anti-Semitism vii, ix, xvii, 1, 3
    and AIPAC 290–1
    and Anti-Defamation League
        257–8
    and Balfour 33, 34
    and BDS 500, 501–2
    and Bevin 160
    and Britain 49–50, 86–7
    and Communism 66–7
    and Conservative Party
        472–3
    and Corbyn 470–2, 473–5,
        478–80
    and critics of Israel 209
    and donors 443
    and Eastern Europe 119
    and Kristol 386
    and media 450–8
    and Norris 103
    and ten pledges 484–5
    and Trump 388–9,
        391–3
    and USA 129–30
    and weaponisation 465–70
    see also pogroms
Anti-Semitism Awareness Act
    (2016) 426
anti-Zionist Committee for
    Justice and Peace in the
    Holy Land 153
Antonius, George: *The Arab
    Awakening* 105
apartheid 183, 203, 213, 285,
    286
Arab-American community
    283, 304
Arab League 159, 184–5, 241,
    277
Arab Revolt 72–4
'Arabists' 124, 225, 232, 263,
    385–6
    and Kissinger 265–6
    and Lebanon 295
Arabs 2, 42, 69, 105
    and Britain 78–9, 90, 180,
        192–3

and British Mandate 59–60
and democracy 152
and King-Crane legacy
    121–4
and USA 119–20, 153
see also 1967 Arab–Israeli
    War
Arad, Eyal 352
Arafat, Yasser 185, 296, 301,
    302, 342, 360
    and Clinton 336, 338
    and Oslo Accords 330–1
architecture 156–7
Argov, Shlomo 208–9, 211,
    293–4
Al-Arish 33
aristocracy 44–52
arms, *see* military aid
Aruri, Naseer 260, 361
Ashdown, Paddy 434
Asher, Robert 299
Ashrawi, Hanan 321
Ashton, Nigel 165, 205, 208
Asia 28
Asquith, Herbert, Lord 36–7,
    42
Attlee, Clement 88–92, 162
Austin, David 94–5
Austin, Warren 225
AUT (Association of University
    Teachers) 489–90
AWACS (Airborne Warning
    and Control System)
    287–8, 289–90
Ayalon, Dani 415–16
AZEC (American Zionist
    Emergency Council)
    136–7, 138, 139–50, 155
    and Alpha plan 233
    and expansion 235
    and funds 248
    and partition 226

Baghdad Pact 165
Baker, Rabbi Andrew 476
Baker, James 295, 304, 314,
    317–18, 319, 322
Balen, Malcolm 453
Balfour, Arthur, Lord 31–4, 42,
    43–4, 77
Balfour Declaration 10, 37, 51,
    64, 71

and beginnings 30, 31–4, 38–9
    and centenary 488–9
    and final draft 52–4
    and 1939 White Paper 74
    and Palestinian resistance
        60–2
    and Rothschild 45, 46
    and USA 109–12, 114, 115,
        126–7
Ball, George 283
Bank, Uri 369
banking 26, 45, 46, 50
Banks, Lynne Reid 216
Bannon, Steve 392
Bantustans 202, 210
Barak, Ehud 338, 343
Barkat, Reuven 161
Baruch, Bernard 222
BAV (Brand Asset Valuator)
    409–10
BBC 143, 174, 197, 452–8
BDS (Boycott, Divestment and
    Sanctions) movement
    395–6, 418, 420, 422,
    425–6, 499–500, 501–2
    and academia 495–7
    and fight against 485–95
Beck, Glenn 373–4
Beckerman-Boys, Carly 62
Beckett, Charlie 455, 457
Beckwith, Leila 424
Begin, Menachem 139, 155,
    202, 203, 213, 292
    and Camp David 279, 282
    and Christian Zionists 308,
        310
    and Lebanon 294
    and Thatcher 207–8, 217
Beinart, Peter 414
Ben-Ami, Jeremy 383
Ben-David, Lenny 261
Ben-Gurion, David 57, 58, 75,
    133, 240, 243
    and Alpha project 165, 233
    and Egypt 166
    and Holocaust 83
    and Jewish Agency 77
    and Morgenthau 324
    and Peel Commission 78
    and refugees 230–1, 245
Ben & Jerry's 425–6
Ben-Yehuda, Eliezer 12

Benedict XV, Pope 52
Benisch, Abraham 49
Benn, Tony 91
Bennett, Naftali 385
Bentwich, Herbert 20, 21–2
Bercow, John 473, 479
Bergson, Peter 155
Berkowitz, Michael 473
Berman, Aaron 132
Bermuda 131–2
Bernadotte, Count Folke 228
Bevan, Aneurin 'Nye' 170–1
Bevin, Ernest 65–6, 90–2, 158, 159, 160–1, 175–6
Beydoun, Naseer 384
Bible, the 6–7, 63, 96–8, 102, 394
Bible Society (London) 3–6, 6
BICOM (Britain Israel Communications and Research Centre) 446–7, 458, 469–70
Biden, Joe 373, 387, 399, 402–3, 430
Bierbrier, Doreen 143–4, 153
Biltmore Conference 132–7
Biola University (CA) 98
BIPAC (British-Israel Public Affairs Committee) 214–17
Black Lives Matter 393, 394
Black Panthers 394
Blackstone, William Eugene 98–100, 101–2, 105
Blackstone Memorial 99
Blair, Tony 182, 217, 347, 431–9
Blank, Victor 449
Bloom, Sol 222
Bloomberg, Mike 399
Bloomfield, Douglas M. 288–9, 299, 303–5, 352
Blum, Leon 57
Blunt, Crispin 465
B'nai B'rith 140, 226, 281
Board of Deputies vii, xvi–xvii, 8, 49, 213
    and Balfour Declaration 53
    and BDS 485–7
    and Gaza 450
    and Grunwald 445–6
    and Protective Edge 463–4

    and Rothschild 46
    and World Jewish Congress 82
Bolling, Landrum 283
Bolshevism 48, 67
Bolton, John 439
Booker, Cory 400
Borg, David 101
Borochov, Dov Ber: *Our Platform* 55–6
Boschwitz, Rudy 288
Bouattia, Malia 465
Boucher, Richard 348–9
Bowen, Jeremy 453–6
Bradshaw, Ben 457
Brand Israel 405–12
Brandeis, Louis Dembitz 108–9, 110, 114, 127
Brandeis Center for Human Rights Under Law 419, 423–6
Brando, Marlon 147
Brecht, Bertolt 504
Breivik, Anders 470
Britain, *see* Great Britain
British Mandate x, 151–2, 157–9
Brockway, Fenner 92
Brodetsky, Selig 82
Brookes, James H. 97
Brown, George 178–81, 183–4, 439, 472
Brown, Gordon 182, 217, 434, 439–43
Brown, William Andreas 321
Brun, Nathan 37
Brzezinski, Zbigniew 277–8, 282
Bumpers, Dale 250, 287–8
Burns, Arthur 266
Bush, George H.W., Sr 295, 299, 312, 314–15
    and Palestine 318, 319
    and peace process 325, 326
    and PLO 302
Bush, George W., Jr 339, 340–2, 345–6, 348–9, 353–5
    and 'Arabists' 385–6
    and Palestine 357, 436, 437–8
Buttigieg, Pete 397

Byroade, Henry 235–6

CAABU (Council for the Advancement of Arab-British Understanding) 185
Cable, Vince 497
Cabot Lodge, Henry 127
Callaghan, James 182–3, 198, 199–200, 201, 203, 205
CAMERA (Committee for Accuracy in Middle East Reporting in America) 448, 454, 455
Cameron, David 458, 459, 460–1, 462, 463, 499
Camp David Accords (1978) 201, 202, 279–80
Campaign Against Anti-Semitism 467–8, 469–70
Campbell, Alastair 433
Canada 57, 96–8
Canary Mission 419, 427–8
Cantor, Eddie 146
Capitol Hill riot 401–2
Carlucci, Frank 289
Carrington, Lord 175–6
Carter, Jimmy 201, 202–3, 210, 259, 273–9, 279–84
    Palestine: Peace Not Apartheid 285–6
Cash, Joanne 460
Castro, Julian 397
Caterpillar 420, 421–2
Cattan, Henry 220
Cazalet, Edward 13, 70
Cazalet, Victor 13, 70–1
CCJ (Council of Christians and Jews) 486
Cesarani, David 13
CFI (Conservative Friends of Israel) 196, 447, 449, 458–64, 483
Chakrabarti, Shami 474–5, 477, 478
Chamberlain, Joseph 33
Charrington, Frederick 25
Cheney, Dick 317, 335, 345, 346, 347
China 268, 379
Chinn, Sir Trevor 432, 433, 449
Chomsky, Noam 261, 323

Christian Allies Caucus 368
Christian Council on Palestine
    127, 138, 144
Christian fundamentalism 97,
    98, 310, 369–70
Christian Zionist movement
    94–6, 94–100, 124–6, 127,
    511
    and Andoverians 104–5
    and AZEC 144–5
    and Balfour Declaration
        109–10
    and Bush Jr 340–1, 353
    and Israel solidarity 306–12
    and Lebanon 310–11
    and Left Behind Project
        365–7
    and 1940s 137–9
    and Obama 373, 386
    and pilgrimage 367–8
    and Prophecy Conferences
        100–3
    and Wilson 182
Christianity x, xvii, 1–2, 3–4,
    485–7
and Maccabean pilgrimage
    21–2
    and millennialists 4–5
    and missions 10–11
    and Palestine 63
    and Shaftesbury 6–8
    and USA 2–3
    and Zionism 14
Christians United for Israel
    364
Christopher, Warren 333
Church, *see* Christianity
Churchill, Col Charles Henry
    8, 9–10
Churchill, Winston 31, 67, 70,
    79, 92, 140–1
CIA (Central Intelligence
    Agency) 244, 252, 295
civil society 212–14, 510–11;
    see also American civil
    society
Clark Street Methodist Church
    (Chicago) 98–9
class 56, 68
*Clean Break: A New Strategy for
    Securing the Realm, A*
    334–5

Clegg, Nick 467
Cliff, Tony 67
Clifford, Clark 227
Clinton, Bill 274, 322–4, 326,
    328, 329–30, 331
    and AIPAC 332–7, 338–9
Clinton, Hillary 373, 389, 390
Cobban, Helena 289–90
Cocks, Valerie 199
Coffin, Henry Sloane 153
Cohen, Steve 382
Cold War 158, 252
colonialism xi–xii; *see also*
    decolonisation; settler
    colonialism
Committee for a Jewish Army
    147
Committee for Intellectual
    Mobilization 145
Communism 48, 66–7, 69, 90
Connelly, Matt 222–3
Conservative Party 30, 32, 65,
    70–1, 173
    and anti-Semitism 472–3
    and arms sales 498, 499
    and Eden 163, 164–7
    see also Cameron, David;
        CFI Douglas-Home, Sir
        Alec; Thatcher, Margaret
Coons, Chris 382
COP (Conference of Presidents
    of Major American Jewish
    Organizations) xvi–xvii,
    231–2, 235, 353, 402
    and AIPAC 241, 264
Corbyn, Jeremy 198, 468,
    470–81, 496, 498, 499
Corrie, Rachel 422
Cotten, Joseph 146
Coughlin, Father Charles 129
Cousins, Frank 172, 173, 188
Cowen, Joseph 29–30
Crabb, Stephen 460
Crane, Charles 121–2, 123, 124
Cripps, Stafford 91
Cromer, Lord 33, 192
Crosland, Anthony 191
Crossman, Richard 89–90, 91
Cruz, Ted 369–70, 389, 429
CST (Community Security
    Trust) 447–8
Cunningham, Sir Alan 157–8

Curtatone, Joe 363
Cutler, Col Harry 115
Czech Republic 233, 345

Darby, John Nelson 95–6, 104
David, King 5
David Project 406–7
Davies, John 193–4
Davis, Arthur 362
Davis, Uri 199
Day, Sir Robin 174–5
Dayan, Moshe 165, 205, 268
De Gaulle, Charles 244
De Haas, Jacob 108
decolonisation 168, 203, 270,
    491
Defense Policy Board 345–6
DeLay, Tom 342
Dermer, Ron 382, 396
Dershowitz, Alan 416
Deutch, Ted 396
Deutsche Gewerkschaftsbund
    188
Dimbleby, Jonathan 455, 456
Dine, Tom 289, 291, 305, 316,
    317
Disasters Emergency
    Committee 456–7
Dispatches (documentary)
    457–8, 459
Dispensationalism 95, 102, 365
Disraeli, Benjamin 11–12, 35
Dollis Hill (London) 55, 57–8
Douglas-Home, Sir Alec
    189–96, 200, 202, 439
Drell, Sidney 381
Dreyfus, Charles 33
Druze 8
dual loyalty problem 108–9
Dugdale, Blanche Elizabeth
    Campbell ('Baffy') 43–4,
    77–9
Dulles, Allen W. 126, 235, 236,
    237, 239
Dulles, John Foster 233, 236
Duncan, Alan 465
Dyson, Freeman 381

EAPPI (Ecumenical
    Accompaniment
    Programme in Palestine
    and Israel) 485–7

Earle, Edward: *Foreign Affairs* 125
East Jerusalem 178–9, 184, 260
Eban, Abba 76, 174, 231–2, 237, 241, 255
  and Brown 184
  and Douglas-Home 193
  and Wilson 182
ECs (Emergency Committees) 141–3, 144
Eden, Anthony 164–7, 196
Eden Springs 493–4
Edmunds, June 168–9
Edward VII of Great Britain, King (Prince of Wales) 3
EEC (European Economic Community) 195, 202–3, 207–8
Egypt 6, 7, 33, 60, 247
  and Britain 196
  and Camp David 279–80
  and Lloyd George 42
  and 1967 war 255–6
  and peace negotiations 201, 202
  and Sinai Peninsula 270–1
  see also Nasser, Gamal Abdel; Sadat, Anwar; Suez Canal
EHRC (Equality and Human Rights Commission) 478–80
Eisenhower, Dwight 232–3, 234, 236–7, 239, 257
Eitan, Rafael 298
El Kurd, Dana 210
Eliot, George: *Daniel Deronda* 12
Elkus, Abram I. 111
Elliot, Walter 77–8, 79
Elon, Benny 369
employment 56
Engel, Eliot 396
English Zionist Federation 28–9, 42–3, 62–5, 75, 169, 172
Enlightenment 15
Eshkol, Levi 176, 179
espionage 256–7, 297–8, 361
ethnic cleansing x, xiii, 63, 153, 159, 188, 488
Ethridge, Mark 229, 230

EUMC (European Union Monitoring Centre on Racism and Xenophobia) 476
European Union (EU) 270, 273, 353, 379, 476, 498
Exeter University ix, vii–viii
Exodus (film) 242
Exodus 1947 (ship) 90
Eytan, Walter 168, 230–1

Fabian Society 58
Factor, John 248
FAFO 326
Fakhrizadeh, Mohsen 392
Falkender, Marcia 182
Falwell, Jerry 310, 341, 368
far right 368–9
Farwell Hall (Chicago) 100–1
Fascism 67, 90, 128
Fatah 185, 283
Faulds, Andrew 197, 198, 204
FBI (Federal Bureau of Investigation) 129, 248, 297, 361
Fedayeen 168
Federation of American Zionists 107–8
Feinberg, Abraham 231, 243, 245–6
Feldman, Andrew 462
Feldman, Myer 243–4, 245, 249, 251, 252
Fidler, Michael 196
Findley, Paul 280, 283, 290–2
Fink, Stanley 446
Finkelstein, Norman: *The Holocaust Industry* 482
Finn, James 6
Firestone, Harvey 223
First World War 34–6, 40, 43, 52, 71
  and TUC promises 92–3
  and USA 119–20
Fish, Hamilton 127
Fisher, Max 264–5
Flushing Meadows, *see* United Nations
Foggon, George 188
Ford, Gerald 270–3, 277
Ford, Henry 130

Fordham University (NYC) 421
Formby, Jennie 479
Fortas, Abe 154, 258–9
Foundation for Defense of Democracies 419, 427
Fox, Liam 461
Foxman, Abraham 350, 361
France 35–6, 38, 39–40, 42, 54
  and Balfour Declaration 52
  and Egypt 167
  and King-Crane legacy 122–3
  and nuclear weapons 244
  and Poale Zion 57
  and Suez Crisis 158, 239
Francis, Ron 363
Franco, Alan 399
Frank, Leo 257–8
Franklin, Larry 361
Fraser, Ronnie 167–8
Frederick I, Grand Duke of Baden 16, 17
Freedland, Jonathan 441–2
Freedom Watch 347
French Revolution 15
Friedkin, Amy 349, 350, 351, 399
Friedman, David 401
Friedman, Isaiah 24
Friendly Societies 20
Frist, Bill 359–60
Fuel for Truth 419
Fuerth, Leon S. 352
Fulbright, James William 246–51
fundamentalism, *see* Christian fundamentalism
fundraising 138–9, 240–2, 248–9, 384–5
  and Iraq War 352–3
  and New Labour 432, 433–4, 435, 443–4
Future of Palestine, The (memorandum) 37

G4S 493
Gadot, Gal 405
Gaitskell, Hugh 167, 168
Galloway, George 212
Gantz, Benny 399
Garment, Leon 266

Garrard, Sir David 444
Gartenhaus, Jacob 102–3
Garwin, Richard 381
Gaster, Chief Rabbi Moses 20, 40
Gat, Moshe 179
Gawler, Sir George 11
Gaza Strip 104, 174, 201, 239–40
    and aid appeal 456–7
    and Al-Aqsa Flood 518–21
    and autonomous rule 202
    and Baker 318
    and Carter 279, 282
    and Cast Lead 371–2, 458–9, 461–2
    and disengagement 355–9
    and Hamas 436–7
    and Jordan 204
    and Protective Edge 377, 463–4
    and UN 256
Geddes, Charles 167–8
General Jewish Labour Bund 56
Germany 16–18, 41, 219; *see also* Nazi Germany
Gewirtz. Sharon 82
Gideon, Clarence Earl 258–9
Gilbert, Martin 440
Gildersleeve, Virginia 153
Gilmour, Ian 185
Gingrich, Newt 335
Gladstone, William Ewart 55
Glasman, Joe 475, 481
Glaspie, April 314
Glazebrook, Rev Otis 111
Gobat, Samuel 104
Goebbels, Joseph 67
Golan Heights 174, 269, 282, 398
Golden, Jonathan 255
Goldenberg, Suzanne 450–1
Goldman, David 432
Goldmann, Nahum 135, 136, 235
Goldsmid, Osmond D'Avigdor 80–1
Goldstone, Richard 372
Goldwater, Barry 245, 252
Gore, Al 338–9, 352
Gormley, Brendan 457

Gorny, Yosef 505
Gorst, John 204
Gottheil, Richard 107–8, 130
Gottheimer, Josh 429
Gould, Rebecca 468–9
Gove, Michael 460, 501–2
Grady, Henry 152
Graham, Billy 368
Great Alie Street (London) 22–4
Great Assembly Hall (London) 24–6
Great Britain 6–16, 212–14
    and anti-Semitism 466–70
    and anti-Zionism 41–2
    and Arab alliances 78–9
    and Arab Revolt 72–4
    and architecture 156–7
    and arms sales 497–9
    and AZEC 148–9
    and Bible Society 3–6
    and Dugdale 77–9
    and fourth Zionist Congress 26–30
    and French negotiations 39–40
    and Holocaust 82–3, 84
    and King-Crane legacy 122–3
    and Lloyd George 42–3
    and lobbying xiv–xv, xvi–xvii
    and London venues 22–6, 75–7
    and Maccabean Club 19–22
    and Manchester 31–3
    and media 445–6, 450–8
    and Palestine 35–6, 37–8, 60, 61–2, 71–2, 520–1
    and Parliament 85–8
    and refugees 84
    and Suez 239
    and USA 94
    and Weizmann 43–4
    see also Anglo-Jewish community; Balfour Declaration; BIPAC (British-Israel Public Affairs Committee); British Mandate; Conservative Party; English Zionist

    Federation; Labour Party; Poale Zion
Great Russell Street (London) 75–7, 78, 79–80, 81–2
Greater Israel 104, 174, 181, 254, 257–61
Greenwood, Anthony 91, 171, 172
Grey, Edward 36
Gromyko, Andrei 220
Gross, Daniel 129
Grunwald, Henry 445–6
Guardian (newspaper) 445, 448, 450–1
Guerin, Orla 452–3
guerrilla warfare 72–3
Gulf War 318–19

Habib, Philip 293
Hadar, Leon 337
Hadassah 136
Hagee, John 102, 364
Hagel, Chuck 375
Hague, William 460, 462
Haig, Alexander 301
Hain, Peter 197
Halbwachs, Maurice 1–2
Haley, Nikki 394
Hall, Glenvil 172
Hamas 336, 372, 376–7, 436–7, 515, 518–21
Hammami, Said 191
Hammerstein, Oscar 113
Hands, Greg 460
Haram al-Sharif (Jerusalem) 339
Harding, Warren G. 127
Harman, Avraham 244, 255
Harman, Jane 360
Harris, David 396
Harris, Kamala 393, 397
Harris, Zelda 215
Harrison, Austen St Barbe 156
Harrison, Benjamin 105
Hart, Parker Thompson 266
Hashemites 38, 42, 71, 74
Hassman, Rommey 416–17
Hastert, Dennis 359–60
Hatikvah (anthem) 147–8, 359
Hatter, Maurice 432
Hawke, Bob 368

Hayday, Fred 173
Hayford, Jack W. 368
Healy, Denis 166
Heath, Edward 190, 193, 195, 198
Hebrew Committee 155
Hechler, William 16–18, 96
Hecht, Ben 147
Hecker, Siegfried 381
Heifetz, Zvi 444
Heikal, Mohamed Hassanein 185
Helms, Richard 244, 252
Henderson, Arthur 58, 91
Henderson, Loy 220, 225
Herf, Jeffrey 228
Hersch, Seymour 298
Herut 139
Herzl, Theodor 15, 16–18, 96, 101, 102, 107–8
    Altneuland ('Old New Land') 29
    and aristocracy 44
    Der Judenstaat 99
    and Eastern Europeans 32
    and London 19–20, 21, 22, 23–4, 25–8
    and Rothschilds 45
    and Uganda 33
    and Wise 130
Herzog, Chaim 182
Hezbollah 294
High Commissioner's Palace (Palestine) 156–7
hijackings 187–8
Hilliard, Earl 290, 362
Hirsch, Baron Maurice de 80
Histadrut 92, 93, 161–3, 167, 187–8, 212–13
Hitler, Adolf 67, 150–1, 246, 474
Hixson, Walter L. xv–xvi, 227–8, 240, 242, 259
Hobson, John A.: *Imperialism: A Study* 475
Hodge, Margaret 477
Holloway, Adam 460
Holocaust ix, x, 150–1, 468–9, 475–7
    and USA 131–2, 138–9
    and *We Will Never Die* 147–8

and Zionism 82–4
Hoover, Herbert 128–9, 273
Hope, John 31
Hope-Simpson committee 61–2
Hopkins, Garland Evan 153
Hoz, Dov 65–6, 77
human rights 423, 478
Huntington, Samuel 369, 437
al-Husayni, Hajj Amin 71–2
Hussein of Jordan, King 204–5, 213, 240, 258, 336
Hussein of Mecca, Sharif 38, 71
Husseini, Faisal 321
Hutton, Patrick 1–2
Hyamson, Albert Montefiore 51–2

IAF (Israel Allies Foundation) 368–9
Ibn Saud of Saudi Arabia, King 154
IDF (Israel Defence Forces) 417, 488
IfNotNow 388–9, 393
IHRA (International Holocaust Remembrance Alliance) 476–8, 484, 501
Im Tirtzu 420
immigrants 32, 84, 85–6, 316
    and London 23, 24
    and Russia 97
    and USA 90–1, 128–9, 391
    see also refugees
Indyk, Martin 320, 332–3, 337, 517
Ini, Gilead 454
Institute of Arab American Affairs 153
intelligence 297–8
Intifadas:
    First 300–1, 302
    Second 331, 338, 339
Iran 153, 313, 343, 347, 402–3
    and Clinton 333–4
    and Jewish spies trial 339
    and nuclear deal 360, 378–83, 387
    and sanctions 427
    and Trump 389–90, 392
Iraq 38, 240, 313–15, 342–8
    and Baghdad Pact 165

and Hashemites 335
and Israel 295, 348–56
and Liberation Act (1998) 335
and Osirak bombing 210
Irgun 175, 259
Irving, Edward 104
Isaacs, Gerald 45
Isaacs, Godfrey 50
Islam 2, 38, 59–61, 125, 365
    and Britain 466, 467
    and Cruz 369–70
    and radical 415
Islamophobia xvii, 448, 465–70
Israel 57
    and academic narrative 414–17
    and AIPAC 242
    and Al-Aqsa Flood 518–21
    and Alpha project 164–5
    and Anglo-Jewish community 449–50
    and arms 244–5
    and Blackstone 99
    and Blair 431–9
    and Britain 158, 161, 193–4
    and Brown (George) 178–80
    and Brown (Gordon) 439–43
    and Camp David 279–80
    and Christian Zionists 365–7
    and delegitimisation ix, xii, 12, 413–15, 405, 409, 411–16, 466–7, 509–10
    and Eden 165–6
    and Egypt 167, 239–40, 267–8
    and Elliot 79
    and Fulbright 247
    and funds 248–9, 250
    and Gaza siege 371–2
    and Iraq 318–19
    and Iraq War 342–3, 348–56
    and Johnson 251–4
    and Jordan 204–5
    and Kenen 150–1
    and Lebanon 211–12, 292–5
    and LFI 443–4
    and marketing 417–18
    and Mayhew 176–7
    and Nixon 262–3

and Oslo Accords 334–5
and Palestine 512–14
and peace negotiations 201, 202
and PLO 314–15
and rebranding 405–12
and Sinai Peninsula 270–1
and South Africa 296–7
and state declaration 155
and Thatcher 206–8, 209–10
and 2022 election 514–17
and tourism 465–6
and Truman recognition 100
and Trump 389–90
and TUC 161–3, 167–8
and UN 177–8, 219
and USA 227–8, 271–3
and Wilson 181–5, 198–9
see also BIPAC; Greater Israel; Jerusalem; Netanyahu, Benjamin; 1967 Arab–Israeli War; pro-Israel lobby; Zionism
Israel on Campus Coalition 419, 427, 428
Israel Project 393–4, 419, 428
Italy 52, 54

J Street 362, 383–6, 400
Jabotinsky, Vladimir Ze'ev 41, 51, 71
Jackson, Colin 185
Jackson, Henry 289
Jacobson, Edward 227
Jakobovits, Immanuel 177
James, Robert Rhodes 459
Janner, Barnett 91, 169–70, 172, 446
Jarring, Gunnar 264
JCA (Jewish Colonization Association) 80–1
Jenkins, Roy 182
Jensen, Peder 'Fjordman' 470
Jerusalem 60–1, 224, 310
    and capital status 316
    and Gobat School 103–4
    and internationalisation 228, 229, 231
    and Marathon 491–2
    and Qatamon 308–9
    and US embassy 339, 371, 394

and Western Wall 60–1
    see also East Jerusalem
Jesus Christ 2, 5, 95; *see also* Messiah
Jesus is Coming (Blackstone) 98
Jewish Agency 66, 75, 77, 80, 89
    and Britain 159
    and funds 248–9
    and Jordan 204
    and Peel Commission 78
    and Suez 169–70
    and UN 219–20
    and Washington office 136
Jewish Colonial Trust 29
Jewish Labour Movement, *see* Poale Zion
Jewish Leadership Council 446
Jewish People Policy Institute 413–14
Jewish Socialist Labour Party 59
Jewish Working Men's Club and Lads' Institute (London) 22–4
Jews x, xvi–xvii, 8–9, 56, 58
    and American youth 414
    and Britain 177
    and chosen people status 95
    and Communism 66–7
    and London 22–4, 25–6
    and national status 97, 112–14, 119
    and Sykes 39
    see also anti-Semitism; Holocaust; immigrants; refugees; 'return of the Jews'; Zionism
Jews Against Trump 388
Jezreel Valley 63
JNF (Jewish National Fund) 75, 76–7, 199, 494–5
Johnson, Boris 465, 500
Seventy-Two Virgins 472–3
Johnson, Lyndon B. 249, 251–4, 258, 259, 273–4
    and 1967 war 255, 256–7
Johnson-Reed Act (1924) 128
Jones, James 460
Jordan 161, 164, 174, 240, 325–6
    and arms 252

and BIPAC 217
and Britain 201
and Israel 204–5
and refugee camps 176
    see also Hashemites; Transjordan
Jordan River 174, 234, 244–5
JTA (Jewish Telegraphic Agency) 249
Judd, Frank 204
JVP (Jewish Voice for Peace) 422

Kahn, Zadoc 28
Kaplan, Amy 242
Karmi, Ghada 188, 197
Kasich, John 389
Kaufman, Sir Gerald 468
Kaye, Sir Emmanuel 432, 433
Keith, Alexander: *The Evidence of Prophecy* 6
Kenen, Isaiah Leo 'Si' 150–3, 226, 232, 234–5, 251
    and AIPAC 238–9, 240–1, 248, 261–2
    and Greater Israel 257, 258
Kennedy, John F. 232, 243–6, 249, 251, 259
Kennedy, Ted 289
Kerry, John 354, 377, 378
Khaled, Leila 424
Khalidi, Rashid 260
al-Khalidi, Yusuf Dia 28
Khalilzad, Zalmay 335
kibbutzim 63, 171, 183
Kindertransport 84
King, Henry 120–2, 123, 124
King, William 138
King-Crane report 120–6
Kings of Capitol Hill (film) 352–3
Kirkpatrick, Jeane 295
Kissinger, Henry 187, 262–3, 264, 267, 268, 269, 336–7
    and Arabists 265–6
    and PLO 270
Klein, Morton 340, 341
Kleinfeld, James Anthony 419
Klemperer, Victor 504
Klinghoffer, Leon 354
Knox, Philander 106
Knox Helm, Sir Alexander 162

Koch, Ed 322
Kohr, Howard 400
Kollek, Teddy 182
Korn, Betsy Berns 400
Kosminsky, Peter: *The Promise* 458
Krim, Mathilde 259
Kristol, William 335, 386
Kurtzer, Daniel C. 340–1, 517
Kuwait 314, 315, 318–19

La Guardia, Fiorello H. 237–8
Labor Party (Israeli) 269, 328–9
Labour Party 88–92, 159–60, 185–9
  and Eden speech 166–7
  and Egypt 167–8
  and 1975–79 government 199–206
  and Poale Zion 57, 58, 59, 65–6, 168–9
  and ten pledges 483–5
  and TUC 161–3
  see also Blair, Tony; Brown, George; Brown, Gordon; Corbyn, Jeremy; LFI; Mayhew, Christopher; Starmer, Sir Keir; Wilson, Harold
Lake Success, *see* United Nations
'Land for Peace' plan 263–4, 268–9
Lansing, Robert 111–12, 120
Laski, Harold 170
Lasky, Neville 82
LATAM 298
Late Great Planet Earth, The (film) 306–7
Latry, François 62
Lavon, Pinhas 165
Lawrence, T.E. 71
Lazarowitz, Arlene 272
Lazzaron, Rabbi Morris 153
League of British Jews 48
League of Nations 54, 59, 123
Lebanon 60, 121, 193, 240
  and Christian fundamentalism 310–11
  and Israeli invasion 210, 211–12

and 1982 war 292–5, 300
and 2006 war 362, 364, 438–9
Lee, Jennie 171
Left Behind Project 365–7
legality 510–12
legitimacy 510–14
Leigh, Howard 446
Lerman, Antony 451, 476
letters 143–4, 149
Letwin, Sir Oliver 473
Levenberg, Schneier 161–2
Levinthal, Rabbi B.L. 115
Levy, David 321
Levy, Edward, Jr 299
Levy, Michael 432–3, 434–5, 446
LFI (Labour Friends of Israel) 170–3, 175, 205, 449, 480
  and Blair 432, 433–4, 435, 437
  and Israel 443–4
  and trips 463
  and Wilson 183, 199
LGBT community 406, 411–12
Libby, Lewis 335
Liberty (ship) 256–7
Liddiment, David 455
Lieberman, Avigdor 368, 418
Likud Party 41, 213, 269, 308, 322–3
Lilienthal, Alfred 249, 250
Lindsey, Hal: *The Late Great Planet Earth* 306–7
Lipsky, Louis 136, 231
Lipstadt, Deborah 129
Livingstone, Ken 445–6, 474
Livni, Tzipi 409, 437
Lloyd George, David 36, 42–3, 44, 50, 62–5
  and Zionism 51, 52
LMEC (Labour Middle East Council) 185–7, 196–7
Lobby, The (documentary) 419, 428–9, 464–5
lobbying xiv–xvii, 238; *see also* pro-Israel lobby
Locker, Berl 77
Loeffler, James 119
London, Louise: *Whitehall and the Jews* 84, 87

London Society for Promoting Christianity Amongst the Jews 6
Lord Mayor's Banquet (London) 163–4
Lott, Trent 335
Loushy, Mor 352
Lovers of Zion 20
Lovett, Robert 222, 223
Lowther, Col Claude 70
Löwy, Albert 49
Lustick, Ian 422

McAteer, Edward E. 341
Maccabean Club (London) 19–22
McCormack, John W. 148
McDonald, James 230
MacDonald, Malcolm 74
MacDonald, Ramsay 61–2, 69
McGrath, J. Howard 149
McGreal, Chris 445, 446, 448
Mack, John 85–6, 87–8
McKinney, Cynthia 290, 362
McMahon, Sir Henry 38
Macmillan, Harold 166
McSweeney, Morgan 482
Madison Square Garden (NYC) 146–8
Madrid peace conference (1991) 319–21, 329
Magnus, Sir Philip 48
Major, John 217, 434
Mandela, Nelson 183
Mapai party 57, 172, 174
Mapam party 162, 172
Marconi affair 35, 49–50
Marks, Simon 75
Marmor, Kalman 67–8
Maronites 212
Marshall, George 220
Mart, Michelle 242
Marxism 48, 67
Masot, Shai 465
Mates, Michael 457
May, Theresa 498, 499
Mayer, Arno 261
Mayhew, Christopher 92, 160, 174–7, 188–9, 472
  and LMEC 185, 186
Mazar, Dan 367–8
Mead, James M. 148

Meir, Gideon 408
Meir, Golda 168, 176, 179, 243, 268
Melchett, Lady Eva Violet 45
Melville, Herman 94
Mendelsohn, Jon 435, 443
Merrill, Selah 105, 106, 225
MESA (Middle East Studies Association) 423–4
Messiah 4, 5, 103, 104, 138, 307, 311
Meyer, Hajo 471
Middle East Quartet 353
Mikardo, Ian 159–60, 172, 181–2
military aid xii, 236–7, 244, 271–2, 361
    and AIPAC 260
    and Britain 442, 497–9
    and Bush Sr 312
    and Carter 280
    and embargos 226–7
    and Jordan 252
    and Lebanon 293
    and Obama 387
    and Reagan 287–8, 289–90
    and South Africa 296–7
millennialists 4–5, 14
Miller, Aaron David 402
Miller, David 469
Miller, David Hunter 120
Ministry for Strategic Affairs 418–19, 421
missionaries 104–5, 125–6
Mitchell, Mayer 'Bubba' 316
Mizrahi, Jennifer Laszlo 428
MNF (multi-national UN peace-keeping force) 294
Moberly, Sir John 173
Momentum 480
Mond, Alfred 45
Mondale, Walter 282
Monsky, Henry 140
Montagu, Edwin Samuel 35, 37, 46–8
Montagu, Sir Samuel 19, 22, 23
Montefiore, Claude 20, 49
Montefiore, Sir Moses 8–9, 20
Moody, Dwight 98, 102
Moonman, Eric 181, 184–5, 205, 214

Moran, James 344–5
Morgan, J.P. 99
Morgenthau, Hans 324, 325
Morrison, Herbert 152, 171
Mosaddegh, Mohammad 153
Moskowitz, Irving 368–9
Mosley, Oswald 90
Mossad 298
Mroz, John Edwin 301
Mubarak, Hosni 330
Muhammad, Prophet 60–1
Muni, Paul 147
Munich Olympics 201
Murray, Lord Alexander 50
Muslim-Christian Associations 116
Muslim Council of Britain 463, 464
Muslims, *see* Arabs; Islam

Nakba, *see* 1948 Arab–Israeli War
Nakhleh, Issa 221
Namier, Lewis 81
Nandy, Lisa 482
Nasser, Gamal Abdel 163, 164–5, 196, 233
    and 1967 war 174, 175, 180, 254–5
    and Suez Canal 166, 167, 239
NATFHE 489–90
nationalism 14–15
Native Americans 356, 394
Nazi Germany x, 67, 76, 128, 504; *see also* Holocaust
Near East Report (journal) 240–1, 248, 250, 265
Neff, Donald 141
neo-conservatives 137, 262, 286, 299, 334, 335
    and Christian fundamentalism 370
    and Iraq War 345–6
Netanyahu, Benjamin 151, 321, 335, 399, 400–1
    and Britain 466
    and Bush Jr 353
    and Christian Zionists 308, 309–10, 311, 334
    and Clinton 336, 338
    and elections 398

and Iran nuclear deal 380–1, 383
    and Iraq War 343
    and Ministry of Strategic Affairs 419
    and 9/11 attacks 415
    and Obama 372, 373, 374, 377
    and Thatcher 217
    and Trump 392, 393, 394
Netanyahu, Benzion 151
Neumann, Emanuel 149
New Labour, *see* Blair, Tony; Brown, Gordon
New Statesman (magazine) 451–2
New Witness, The (journal) 50
Newmark, Brooks 460
Newsinger, John 93
Niagara Bible Conference 96–8
Niebuhr. Reinhold 137
Niles, David 222, 231
9/11 attacks 328, 331, 337, 339–40, 344, 415
1948 Arab–Israeli War 157–8, 159, 204
1967 Arab–Israeli War 146, 155, 173–6, 180–1, 254–7
Nixon, Richard 243, 245, 261, 262–3, 264, 265
    and Egypt 267–8
    and impeachment 270
    and peace process 325
Norris, Frank 103
North Korea 406, 427
nuclear weapons 244, 253, 452; *see also* Iran
NUT (National Union of Teachers) 490, 491
Nutting, Sir Anthony 185

Obama, Barack 274, 298, 327, 370–8, 387–8
    and Iran 378–83
    and Trump 390
Oberlin College (OH) 120–1
Oborne, Peter 450, 457, 458, 459, 460
Ocasio-Cortez, Alexandria 395, 397
October war (1973) 195, 268–9

oil 153–4, 193, 195, 312–14
Oliphant, Laurence: *The Land
   of Gilead* 13
Olmert, Ehud 327, 331, 355,
   412, 418, 437
Olympia Food Co-op (WA)
   420–1
Omar, Ilhan 395, 396–7, 422
one-state solution viii, 396,
   412, 471, 520
Operations:
   Al-Aqsa Flood (2023)
      518–21
   Cast Lead (2008–9) 371–2,
      447, 458–9, 461–2
   Defensive Shield (2002) 341,
      437–8
   Desert Fox (1998) 335
   Protective Edge (2014) 377,
      463–4, 467
   Shock and Awe (2003) 365
Orbán, Viktor 388
Orientalism 5–6, 21, 125
Ormsby-Gore, William 81
O'Rourke, Beto 397
Orwell, George: *1984* 509
Oslo Accords (1993) 322, 326,
   328–31, 332, 334–5
Ottoman Empire 4, 14, 54, 99,
   106
   and Britain 6, 7, 10, 11
   and First World War 35–6
Our Hope (journal) 102
Owen, David 200, 202, 205

Packwood, Bob 317
Palais Coburg (Vienna) 378–9
Palestine vii–viii, x, xiii, 503–4
   and academic study viii–ix
   and AIPAC 316–17
   and American Jewish
      Congress 115–17
   and Anglo-French negotia-
      tions 39–40
   and architecture 156–7
   and BDS 395–6
   and Bevin 90
   and biblical allusions 63
   and Blair 436–7
   and Brand Israel 408
   and British Zionism 6–16,
      41–2

and Bush Jr 340–2, 349,
   353–5
and Callaghan 199–200
and Carter 276–7, 278–86
and Christianity 1–2
and civil war 224–5
and Clinton 323
and Corbyn 471
and Douglas-Home 189–92,
   194–6
and East Jerusalem 260
and Eisenhower 232–3
and first Zionist settlers
   15–16
and Fulbright 247
and 'global' 519–21
and Israeli legitimacy
   512–14, 515
and J Street 384
and JCA 80
and King-Crane legacy 121,
   122
and Labour Party 185–9,
   196–8
and Maccabean Club 20–2
and Madrid conference 319,
   320–1
and Mayhew 175–6
and media 457–8
and military rule 162, 171
and missionaries 125–6
and national movement
   266–7
and Obama 372–4, 376–7
and Palestinians 27–8
and Park Britannia 198–9
and partition 159
and Poale Zion 56, 57, 57–8
and Prevent programme
   500–1
and Qibya 234–5
and resistance 60–2, 71–5
and 'return of the Jews' 4–5
and solidarity movement
   386–7, 394, 395, 422,
   487–8
and Somerville 363–4
and South Africa 183
and terrorism 201–2
and Thatcher 210–11
and trade unions 93, 212–13
and trusteeship 225–7

and UN 218–24
and USA 2–3, 104–6
and Venice Declaration
   207–8
see also Arabs; Balfour
   Declaration; BDS; British
   Mandate; Fedayeen; Gaza
   Strip; Intifadas PCC;
   PLO; refugees; 'return of
   the Jews'; settler colonial-
   ism; two-state solution;
   West Bank
Palestine Speaks (radio show)
   146
Palestinian Islamic Jihad 336
Palmerston, Henry John
   Temple, Lord 7–8
Panorama (TV programme)
   174–5
Patrick, Andrew 123
PCC (Palestine Conciliation
   Commission) 228–31
peace process 323–4, 325–31,
   383–6
Pearl, Daniel 354
Peel, Robert 73–4
Peel Commission 78
Pelosi, Nancy 360, 399
Pence, Michael 393, 394, 398,
   399, 511
Percy, Charles 290, 291
Peres, Shimon 182, 217, 343
Peretz, Don 3
Perle, Richard 289, 335, 346,
   360
Peters, Joan 281
petitions 143–4
Pfeffer, Anshel 469
Phalangists 212
Philistines 63
PICA (Palestine Jewish
   Colonization Association)
   80–1
Pickles, Eric, Lord 460
Pilger, John 451, 458
Pinkus, Lillian 391, 393
Pinsker, Leon: *Auto-
   Emancipation* 16
Piro, Scott 411
PLO (Palestine Liberation
   Organization) 184–5,
   186, 187, 188, 270

and BIPAC 215, 216
and Black Panthers 394
and Britain 193, 195, 203–4,
    209
and Bush Sr 314
and Carter 279, 283, 285–6
and Hammami 191
and Lebanon 211–12, 293–4
and legitimacy 205–6
and Oslo Accords 329,
    330–1
and USA 300–5, 328
    see also Arafat, Yasser
PNAC (Project for the New
    American Century) 335
Poale Zion 55–9, 65–6, 67–9,
    168–9, 172, 186
pogroms 14, 15, 16, 27, 32, 83
Polak, Stuart 460–1
Poland 57, 119
Pollard, Jonathan Jay 297–9
Pollard, Stephen 468
Pomeranz, Jacob 59
Pompeo, Mike 511
Powell, Colin 346, 351
Powell, Jonathan 433
power 508–9, 511
premillennialism 102–3, 104–5
Prevent programme 500–1
pro-Israel lobby vii–viii, x–xii,
    xv–xvii, 507–9
    and Christian fundamental-
        ism 310
    and Palestine Studies viii–ix
    and Somerville 363–4
    see also AIPAC; Board of
        Deputies; CFI; Christian
        Zionist movement; LFI
Prophecy Conferences 100–3
Provost, Denise 363, 364
Public Committee Against
    Torture in Israel 214
'Purchase of Silver for India'
    scandal 49, 50
Puritans 94

Qaddumi, Farouk, *see* Abu
    Lutuf
Al-Qaeda 328, 345, 346
al-Qassam, Izz ad-Din 72–3
Qatar 428–9
Qibya Massacre 234–5

Quandt, William B. 277–8, 302
Quayle, Dan 317
Queen's Hotel (Manchester)
    31–2
Queen's Royal Hotel (Niagara-
    on-the-Lake) 96–8

Raab, Max 288
Rabi, Muhammed 302
Rabin, Yitzhak 210–11, 270,
    321, 322, 333
    and assassination 334, 462
    and Ford 271, 273
    and funeral 434–5
race 2, 5–6, 129, 373; *see also*
    anti-Semitism; Arabs;
    Jews
rallies 146–7, 148, 149–50, 171
Rausch, David 97
Rayner, Angela 482
Reading, Rufus Daniel Isaacs,
    Lord 44–5, 50, 80
Reagan, Ronald 286–92, 293,
    295–6, 310, 368
    and Lebanon 294–5
    and PLO 302, 303, 305
Reddaway, John 185, 197
Rees-Mogg, Jacob 473
Reform Judaism 101, 130, 389,
    414
refugees x, 164, 245, 281
    and Britain 86–8
    and Evian Conference 76
    and Lebanon massacres 212
    and Nazi Germany 83–4
    and right of return 163, 193,
        197, 229–31, 233–4
    and USA 128–9, 131–2
Reid, Harry 359–60
Reimer, Michael 122
Religious Roundtable 341
Renton, James 39
restorationism 94–6, 97–8, 101
'return of the Jews' 1, 2,
    4–5
    and Blackstone 98–100
    and Britain 9–12
    and Niagara 97–8
    and Prophecy Conferences
        100–3
    and Shaftesbury 6–7
    and USA 94, 95

Reut Institute 412–13, 414
Revisionist Zionist movement
    41, 139, 155
Revivi, Oded 398
Reynolds, Nick 78
Rhodes, Cecil 46
Ribicoff, Abraham 289
Rice, Condoleezza 359, 360
Richard, Lord Ivor 200
Ridley, George 85
Rifkind, Sir Malcolm 449–50
Riley, William B. 102
riots 60–1
Robertson, Pat 310, 368
Robinson, Edward G.
    146, 147
Rockefeller, John D. 99
Rogers, Edith Nourse 131
Rogers, William 263, 264–5,
    267
Romania 27, 119
Romney, Mitt 374
Ronson, Gerald Maurice 445,
    446, 448
Roosevelt, Eleanor 147, 227
Roosevelt, Franklin D. 124,
    129, 130, 273
Roosevelt, Kermit 153
Rose, Billy 147
Rosen, Steven 289, 299, 352,
    361
Rosenblatt, Gary 343–4, 410
Rosenthal, Benjamin S. 288
Ross, Dennis 328, 331, 337
Rossman-Benjamin, Tammi
    424
Rostow, Walt 253
Rothschild, Baron Abraham
    Edmond Benjamin James
    de 45, 80
    and Brandeis 110
Rothschild, Lionel Nathan de
    48
Rothschild, Lionel Walter, Lord
    44, 45, 46, 53
Rothschild, Lord 19, 23
Rothstein, Roz 419, 420, 421
Rouhani, Hassan 379
Rubenberg, Cheryl 304
Rubio, Marco 396
Rumsfeld, Donald 335, 345,
    346

Rusbridger, Alan 445, 448, 450–1
Rusk, Dean 244, 252
Russell, Bertrand xiv
Russia 333, 353, 379, 427; *see also* Russian Empire; Soviet Union
Russian Empire 7, 15, 36, 41
and Poale Zion 57
and USA 97, 98, 99
and workers' movements 56
Ryan, Joan 465

Saatchi brothers 409
Sable, David 410
Sacher, Harry 75
Sacher, Michael 216
Sachs, Natan 397
Sacks, Chief Rabbi Jonathan 471
Sadat, Anwar 202, 267, 268, 273, 279, 282
Saddam Hussein 313–14, 315, 318–19, 335, 349, 354–5
and Iraq War 343, 345
and WMDs 347
Said, Edward 5–6, 321
Orientalism 125
St Louis (ship) 129
Salisbury, Lord 18
Sambrook, Richard 453
Samuel, Sir Herbert 32, 35–6, 37, 42, 44, 46
and Balfour Declaration 53
and British Mandate 54
and Hyamson 51
and Lloyd George 64
and Marconi scandal 50
Sanders, Bernie 397, 399
Sanders, Edward 284
Sandys, Duncan 175
Saranga, David 409
Sarna, Jonathan D. 255
Sartawi, Issam 283
Saudi Arabia 153–4, 215–16, 313, 341
and AWACS 287–8, 289–90
Saunders, Harold 278
Savoy Hotel (London) 62–5, 77, v
Schama, Simon 449–50
Schumer, Chuck 394, 399

Scofield, Cyrus 102
Scotland 197
Seaman, Danny 450–1
Second Coming of the Messiah, *see* Messiah
Second Lebanon War 362, 364, 438–9
Second World War 78–9; *see also* Holocaust; Nazi Germany
secularisation 14–15
Segev, Tom 83
self-determination 60, 68, 120
Sella, Aviem 298
Sessions, Jeff 429
settler colonialism vii, x, xiii, 15–16
and IAF 368–9
and Mayhew 176
and Obama 373, 376, 387–8
and restorationists 101
and socialism 68, 69–70
and USA 2–3, 98
and West Bank 449–50
7 October 2023 515, 518–21
'77', *see* Great Russell Street (London)
Sewell, Dennis 451
Shafi, Haidar Abdel 320–1
Shaftesbury, Anthony Ashley-Cooper, Earl of 4, 5, 6–8, 24
Shah, Naz 474
Shalit, Gilad 377
Shalom, Silvan 351
Shamir, Yitzhak 217, 304–5, 317, 321
Shanghai International Settlement 84
Shapps, Grant 460
Sharansky, Natan 452–3
Sharett, Moshe 59, 66, 136, 164–6
Sharon, Ariel 211–12, 213, 339, 452
and Bush Jr 341–2, 353
and Gaza Strip 355, 356–9
and Iraq War 342–3
and Lebanon 294
and peace process 327, 331
and Qibya 234

Sharp, Martha 131
Sharp, Waitstill 131
Shavit, Ari: *My Promised Land* 20
Shavit, Iftah 363
Shaw, George Bernard: *Arthur and the Acetone* 43
Shaw, Lord 61
Shuckburgh, Sir Evelyn 164, 165
al-Shukeiri, Ahmad 185
Shultz, George 288, 292, 301, 302, 304, 312
Sieff, Israel 75
Silberman, Morton 293
Silver, Abba Hillel 134–6, 140, 141–2, 146, 149, 155
and alliances 151
and Truman 227
and UN 220
Simon, Paul 291
Sinai Peninsula 174, 239–40, 256, 257, 282
and withdrawal 267, 268, 270–1
Sisco, Joseph J. 266, 336
el-Sisi, Abdel Fattah 437
Six Day War, *see* 1967 Arab–Israeli War
Sizer, Stephen 365
SJP (Students for Justice in Palestine) 421
Smeeth, Ruth 447
Smith, Gerald 129
Smith, Grant F. xv
The Israeli Lobby Enters State Government: Rise of the Virginia Israel Advisory Board 403–4
Smith, John 432, 433
Smith, Martin A. 123
socialism 55–6, 57, 67–70, 89–90
and Israel 172
and USA 117–18
and Zionism 197–8
see also Labour Party
SodaStream 425, 493–4
Sokolow, Nahum 40, 52
Somerville Divestment Project 363–5
Soros, George 385, 388, 391–2

South Africa 183, 202, 210, 286, 296–7
Soviet Union 137, 252, 268, 328
  and Carter 282–3
  and immigrants 316
  and Reagan 295–6
  and Syria 174
  and UN 219, 220
Spurgeon, Charles Haddon 12
Starmer, Sir Keir 480, 481–3
State Department, *see* United States of America
Stearns, Robert 368
Steel, David 189
Stein, Leonard 80
Steinberg, Rabbi Milton 145
Stern, Kenneth 469
Straw, Jack 438
Streeting, Wes 478
Ströter, Ernst 101
students, *see* academia
Suez Canal 12, 40, 46, 267
  and 1956 crisis 158, 166–70, 196
Swisher, Clayton 429
SWU (StandWithUs) 419–23
Sykes, Mark 39–41, 52
Sykes–Picot Agreement (1916) 40, 121
Syria 6, 7–9, 60, 72, 174
  and King-Crane legacy 121, 122–3
  and Lebanon 212, 294

Taft, William Howard 106
terrorism 168, 201–2, 341, 354, 500–1; *see also* 9/11 attacks
TGWU (Transport and General Workers' Union) 65–6
Thackeray, William Makepeace 431
Thatcher, Margaret 196, 206–11, 213, 215–16, 310
Thomas, James Henry 59
Thompson, Mark 456
Thornberry, Emily 482–3
Thorpe, Jeremy 175
Tiran Straits 174
Tlaib, Rashida 395, 396–7

Toward Peace in the Middle East (report) 278
trade unions 65–6, 142, 433, 435, 489–91; *see also* TUC (Trades Union Council)
Transjordan 38, 73, 74, 159
Tricycle Theatre 467–8
Trujillo, Rafael 83
Truman, Harry 100, 103, 138, 226, 230
  and financial aid 232
  and Israel recognition 227–8
  and partition 220, 225
Trump, Donald 276, 327, 370, 388–402
Truth, The (journal) 97
TUC (Trades Union Congress) 89, 92–3, 167–8, 186
  and Histradut 187–8
  and Israel 161–3, 172–3
  and Palestine 212–13
Turkey 35, 36, 121, 165, 217; *see also* Ottoman Empire
Turner, Jonathan 454, 456
two-state solution 322, 341, 353, 412–13, 462–3
  and Corbyn 471–2
  and Obama 373, 377

Uganda 33, 34, 43, 56, 57, 101
UJA (United Jewish Appeal) 138–9
Ukraine 57
Union for Reform Judaism 389
Union of American Hebrew Congregations 107
United Israel Appeal 139
United Nations (UN) x, 152, 191–2, 201, 256
  and Israel membership 177–8
  and partition 158–9, 160, 218–24
  and two-state solution 352
  see also UNSCOP
United States of America (USA) xv–xvii, 516–17
  and anti-Semitism 129–30
  and AZEC 141–50
  and Baghdad Pact 165

and Balfour Declaration 109–12, 115, 126–7
and Biltmore Conference 132–7
and Blackstone 98–100
and Britain 187, 195
and Christian Zionism 94–6, 124–6, 137–9
and colonisation xiii, 2–3
and Congress 233–4
and EEC 202–3
and immigration 90–1
and Israel reassessment 271–3
and Jewish Congress 112–20
and Jewish refugees 83, 84
and Kenen 150–3
and King-Crane legacy 120–6
and Lebanon 293–4
and Near East Division 105–6
and oil companies 153–4, 312–13
and Palestine 104–5, 192
and PLO 300–5
and Poale Zion 57
and Prophecy Conferences 100–3
and Reading 45
and refugees x, 128–9, 229–30
and Sykes 40–1
and trade unions 163
and trusteeship 225–7
and UN 218–24
and Zionism 130–2, 139–40
see also AIPAC (American Israel Public Affairs Committee); American Jewish community; Bush, George H.W.; Bush, George W.; Carter, Jimmy; Clinton, Bill; Eisenhower, Dwight; Ford, Gerald; Johnson, Lyndon B.; Nixon, Richard; Obama, Barack; Reagan, Ronald; Truman, Harry; Trump, Donald; Wilson, Woodrow

universities, *see* academia
UNSCOP 89, 159, 219–20
Uris, Leon 242
US Army 294–5
USSR, *see* Soviet Union

Vaizey, Ed 460
Vámbéry, Arminius 18
Van der Zyl, Marie Sarah 472, 473
Vance, Cyrus 278, 282
Vara, Shailesh 460
Vatican 52
Vaughan, James 175, 176, 185
Veliotes, Nicholas 301
Venice Declaration 207–8
Veolia 492, 496–7
Vereté, Mayir 39
Versailles Peace Conference 121, 122
Victoria of Great Britain, Queen 3
Videla, Gonzáles 145
Vietnam War 246–7, 255

Wagner, Cosima 33–4
Wagner, Robert 131, 144
Wallace, Edwin Sherman 13
Wallace, Henry A. 145
Waltz, Kenneth 325
war crimes 372
Ward, Col Sir Lambert 86–7
Warren, Elizabeth 397
Watkins, David 197
Watson, Tom 478, 480
We Believe in Israel 482
We Will Never Die (musical) 147–8
weapons of mass destruction (WMDs) 347, 351
Webb, Beatrice 91
Webb, Sidney (later Lord Passfield) 58, 61, 62, 64
Weidel, Alice 473
Weill, Kurt 147
Weinberger, Caspar 295, 312
Weisberg, Aaron 248
Weissman, Keith 334, 361
Weizmann, Chaim 13, 15, 30, 40, 45

and Balfour 32–4, 43–4, 52
and Balfour Declaration 49, 53, 62
and Bevan 170
and Biltmore Conference 133, 134
and Brandeis 110
and Dugdale 77
and Jewish brigade 79
and Lloyd George 42–3, 65
and London 57–8, 72
and 1939 White Paper 74–5
and Roosevelt 130
and Samuel 35, 37
and settlements 69–70
and socialism 67–8
and Truman 226, 227
and UN 222
Welles, Orson 306
West Bank 104, 174, 201, 202, 253–4
and Baker 318
and Carter 279, 282
and companies 425–6
and ethnic cleansing 188
and Greater Israel 258, 357
and Jordan 204
and settler expansion 449–50
and SWU 419–20
Wexler, Robert 383
White Paper (1939) 74–5, 78, 140–1, 146
Wilby, Peter 451, 452
Wilder, Douglas 317
Wilders, Geert 470
William of Prussia, Prince 3
Williams, Rowan, Archbishop of Canterbury 486
Williamson, Gavin 501
Willkie, Wendell 138
Willsman, Peter 480
Wilson, Evan 232
Wilson, Harold 91, 169, 176–7, 181–5, 196–9, 203
Wilson, Woodrow 109, 110, 111–12, 115, 119–20, 121
Wise, Stephen S. 107, 108, 130, 136, 149
Wolfowitz, Paul 335, 346

Woodhead Commission 74, 81
workers, *see* employment; socialism; trade unions
Workers' Circle 388
Workers of Zion, *see* Poale Zion
World Jewish Congress 45, 82, 223
World Zionist Congress 75, 109
World Zionist Organization 66, 77, 80
Wye River Memorandum (1998) 336

Ya'alon, Moshe 418
Yagol, Yonah 212–13
Yedioth Ahronoth (newspaper) 197
Yellen, Janet 388
Yisrael Beiteinu party 368
Yom Kippur War, *see* October war (1973)
Young, Andrew 283

Zabludowicz, Poju 446–7
Zangwill, Israel 19, 29
Zeldin, Lee 429
Zertal, Idith 83
Zion Square bombing 201
Zionism x, xi–xiii, xv, 5–6, 504–7
and American Jewish community 106–9
and American Jewish Congress 113–20
and Anglo-Jewish community 44–52, 79–81
and Arab Revolt 73–4
and Attlee government 88–92
and AZEC 141–50
and Biltmore Conference 132–7
and Britain 6–16, 41–4
and Carter 277
and Christianity 1–2, 3
and civil society 510–11
and colonialism 69–70
and Conservative Party 70–1
and Dugdale 77–9

and Great Russell Street
  75–7
and Hechler 16–18
and Herzl 24, 25–6
and Hitler 474
and the Holocaust 82–4
and Irgun 175, 259
and Kenen 150–3
and King-Crane legacy 122,
  123
and locations 33
and Maccabean Club 20–2
and Mandate termination
  157–8
and Mikardo 159–60
and nationalism 14–15

and Palestinian attacks 225
and Palestinian resistance
  60–1
and Parliament 85–8
and peace process 327–8
and Samuel 35–6, 37
and socialism 67–8, 197–8
and Starmer 482–3
and trade unions 92–3
and Truman 226, 227
and UN 218–24
and US Christianity 94–100
and USA 40–1, 130–2,
  139–41
see also Balfour Declaration;
  Christian Zionist

movement; English
  Zionist Federation; Poale
  Zion
Zionist Congress 26–30, 107
Zionist Federation of Great
  Britain and Ireland 34–5,
  213–14
Zionist Literary Society 106
Zionist Organization of
  America 419
Zoughbie, Daniel: *Indecision
  Points* 340
Zuckerman, Maja Gildin 20–1
Zuckerman, Mortimer 343